Seventh Edition

The Standard Handbook of Modern United States Paper Money

By Chuck O'Donnell

P.O. Drawer A, Williamstown, NJ 08094
(609) 629-5160

700 E. State St., Iola, WI 54990

Copyright MCMLXXXII by Krause Publications, Inc.

Library of Congress Catalog Card Number: 81-86466
International Standard Book Number: 0-87341-068-8

INDEX

SUBJECT	PAGE
Bibliography	31
Changeover pairs	330
Classes of small size notes	15
Credits	7
Dating our currency	28
Dedication	6
Design of our currency	20, 25
Emergency currency	
North Africa	25
Hawaii	25
Experimental notes	22
Federal Reserve System	23
Foreword	5
Grading currency	28
How to collect	26
In God We Trust on currency	21
Low Serial number prices	334
Motto on our currency	21
Mules (see under denomination)	21
Narrow margin notes	29
Novel Serial Numbers	333
Numbering our currency	28
Numbering System (O'Donnell)	9
Portraits on U.S. Currency	20, 25
Potential new discoveries	335
Preface	8
Production of our currency	17
Sheet layouts	11
Signatures on our currency	16
Star notes	19
Terms describing notes	10
Test notes	22
Trial notes	22
Uncut sheets	324
Wide margin notes	29
ONE DOLLAR NOTES	
Federal Reserve Notes	44
Legal Tender	33
Silver Certificates	43
United States Notes	33
TWO DOLLAR NOTES	
Legal Tender	101
United States Notes	101
Federal Reserve Notes	104

SUBJECT	PAGE
FIVE DOLLAR NOTES	
Federal Reserve Notes	113
Legal Tender	110
Silver Certificates	107
United States Notes	110
TEN DOLLAR NOTES	
Federal Reserve Notes	168
Federal Reserve Bank Notes	163
Gold Certificates	164
Legal Tender Notes	164
Silver Certificates	164
United States Notes	164
TWENTY DOLLAR NOTES	
Federal Reserve Notes	214
Federal Reserve Bank Notes	213
Gold Certificates	213
Legal Tender Notes	213
United States Notes	213
FIFTY DOLLAR NOTES	
Federal Reserve Notes	265
Federal Reserve Bank Notes	264
Gold Certificates	264
ONE HUNDRED DOLLAR NOTES	
Federal Reserve Notes	293
Federal Reserve Bank Notes	292
Gold Certificates	292
Legal Tender Notes	291
FIVE HUNDRED DOLLAR NOTES	
Federal Reserve Notes	315
Gold Certificates	314
ONE THOUSAND DOLLAR NOTES	
Federal Reserve Notes	317
Gold Certificates	317
FIVE THOUSAND DOLLAR NOTES	
Federal Reserve Notes	319
Gold Certificates	319
TEN THOUSAND DOLLAR NOTES	
Federal Reserve Notes	322
Gold Certificates	321
ONE HUNDRED THOUSAND DOLLAR NOTES	
Gold Certificates	323

Here is the most comprehensive catalog on U.S. paper money ever published!

The

Standard Catalog of

UNITED STATES PAPER MONEY

First Edition

by Chester L. Krause and Robert F. Lemke

Documenting 120 years of paper money circulated by the Federal Government!

The **Standard Catalog of U.S. Paper Money** meets the diverse needs of collectors and dealers who are involved — or will soon be involved — in the fascinating field of United States paper money. Check *all* its important features!

- Over **3500 currency items** listed
- More than **10,000 valuations** in 3 grades of preservation
- **Full documentation** of federally-issued notes from the Civil War to $1 notes now in production

$14.50

- Comprehensive sections on **fractional currency, encased postage stamps and postage stamp envelopes** used as Civil War emergency currency
- Over **13,000 note-issuing banks** — alphabetically by state and city with charter numbers
- **National Bank Note valuations** given by type and signature combinations, denomination and state of issue
- Krause-Lemke numbering system **cross-reference** to established Friedberg, Hessler and Donlon systems
- 204 pages, **big 8½x11 format**

For your copy, see your local hobby dealer or order directly from **Krause Publications, Dept. ARL, 700 E. State St., Iola, WI 54990.**

FOREWORD

Hello-and welcome to the wonderful world of paper money collecting. However you decide to collect — and there are dozens of ways detailed in the introduction — the days ahead should hold much pleasure and much challenge as you pursue your hobby. Surely, if horse racing is the "sport of kings" - then "ragpicking" is the sport of Angels!

We'd like first of all to admit to our own very limited knowledge in the field covered by this catalog. And yet within the pages of this book there are literally thousands of previously unpublished facts about the paper currency passing through our hands, much of which will surely become the sought-after rarities of tomorrow.

This book is written by a collector for collectors. All that is currently known about our present "Philippine size" currency is contained herein. It is the sincere hope of the author that this effort will be only the foundation that will spark the interest of all paper money collectors everywhere to contribute to the building of an edifice that will ultimately represent all that "can" be known to supercede all that "is" known.

While there is a great deal of pride of authorship, we humbly admit we "don't know it all" — and welcome your comments as well as your contributions of any facts including serial numbers higher and lower than shown. We assure you not only of our gratitude for any contribution of information but a place on the credit page of future editions. We earnestly solicit your help and interest in helping us add to the facts presented.

Whether the author is right or wrong in information presented is not important. What IS IMPORTANT is the knowledge and facts that can be added so that all who pursue this pleasureable hobby can have a complete and factual account of the money of our times!

chuck o'donnell

DEDICATION

Lest history forget, the author dedicates this documentation of the present knowledge of paper money to all the officials, collectors and dealers whose combined efforts are certain to preserve historic examples of the art and culture of the currency of our times.

At the risk of missing some who should be listed, we especially dedicate this volume to:

The entire staff, past and present, of the Bureau of Engraving and Printing, Washington, D.C., whose cooperation with and help to me have been so kind and so complete.

Jim Alston	Dorothy Gerschenson	Phil Lampkin	John J. and Gehring C. Pittman
Tom Bain	Nathan Goldstein II	Julian Leidman	Ed Rochette
Ruth Bauer	Ralph Goldstone	Art and Betty Leister	Margo Russell
Aubrey and Adeline Bebee	Dave Gorlin	Bob Lemke	Tom and Eleanor Settle
Walter Breen	Ted Gozanski	Leon Lindheim	Jim Seville
Dan Brown	Leon Hendrickson	Lee Martin	Neil Shafer
Amon Carter Jr.	Gene Hessler	Bob and Betty Medlar	David J. Shapiro
Robert and Lee Condo	John Hickman	Lester Merkin	Sam Sloat
Grover Criswell	Bob Hohn	John and Opal Morris	Sidney Smith
Tom DeLorey	Dick Hoober	Sheldon and Bernice Moses	Edwin B. Strauss
Bill Donlon	Eve Jubanyik	Barbara Mueller	Jas W. Thompson
Mill and Edie Dutkin	Art and Paul Kagin	Dr. John A. Muscalus	Graeme Ton Jr.
Jerry and Jane Finnell	Sol Kaplan	Ed Nuece	Ted Uhl
Ed Fleischmann	Ted Kemm	Frank A. Nowak	Louis Van Belkum
John J. Ford Jr.	Abe Kosoff	Dean Oakes	Tom Werner
Dennis Forgue	Chet Krause	Vernon and Helen Oswald	Ralph and Harriet E. Werve
Harry J. Forman	Ed Kuszmar	M. Perlmutter	Neil Wimmer

CREDITS

The author wishes to especially acknowledge the outstanding assistance and helpful suggestions from the following:

Leon Goodman	Rev. Frank Hilliard Hutchins	Betty Russell
Janice Hagerty	Harry Jones	Fred Schwan
Pete Huntoon	Seymour Kashin	John Schwartz

and for the following individuals whose contributions are gratefully acknowledged:

Paul Abrahams
Wm. R. Acker
Dick Alexander
Richard B. Anderson
Paul Angenend
William Anton Jr.
Don Apte
William R. Armstrong
Nelson Page Aspen
Johnny O. Baas
Jim Bakel
Harold E. Baker
Steve Balaze
Richard J. Balbaton
Americus Bandes
Robert E. Barnes
Biggs Bates
Dudley L. Bauerlein
Frank Bennett
Leonard Berger
Henry Bergos
William C. Blaisdell
Dave Boeshaar
John W. Bottger
George R. Bowers
W. L. Brady
Roy Broome
Stanley Brown
David Caciola
Fred Cady
Hugh M. Caraher
Barry Carson
Mike Carter
Joel Cohen
John Coleman
Tom Conklin
Robert H. Cornell
Mike Crabb Jr.
Michael Cure
Guy Dahlke
William A. Daub
James F. Dayton
A. E. Dell Aira
J. P. DeLong
James N. DeMoss
Elgie Dillman
Joseph H. Donovan
William Doovas
George Duda
W. Cecil Dunbar Jr.
Allen S. Edwards III

Jim Eggert
David Esperson
Steven Ewald
Mike Farren
E. J. Fellows
Clarence Finger
George A. Flanagan
Ed Fleischmann
Thomas J. Foster
Wise Friedman
Meyer Fulda
Mrs V. Furer
Roger J. Gartner
Greg Gaskill
Sig Goldstein
Jim Greene
George Greenberg
Hal Greimann
Gil Gustavus
David Hakes
Col. Jerry A. Harns
Alvin Hackard
Marc D. Harrison
John A. Henderson
William Hershkowitz
Lorn Hillier
Ralph Hinkle
R. J. Hodges
Leonard Holden
J. T. Holleman
Richard Hood
Glen Howard
Don Huetson
Lauren Iseki
Robert Jackson
Louis W. Jamme
R. D. Johnson
F. W. Jones
Glen I. Jorde
Jack Keller
Marty Kendra
Robert King Jr.
John W. Kinney
Harold R. Klein Jr.
Jerry Kleindolph
Charles Kollo
Ed Konstanty
Dr. Jules Korman
Marlin Kravitz
Stanton Kreider
F. L. Kretschmar

Ed Kuethe
J. A. Lange
Ernst O. Leffler
Ed Lehr
Fred V. Lester
D. O. Levy
Charles P. Link
Robert H. Lloyd
James E. Lund
C. Dale Lyon
W.J. Macomber
Phil A. MacKay
E.A. Mann
James Martin
John T. Martin
Robert Mason
Alan Matre
Jim McAdow
William McClaren
Robert C. McCurdy
George T. McDuffie
William McLaughlin
Steve Michaels
W.G. Miller
J.W. Mills
Tom Morrissey
Wayne W. Moser
Thomas H. Mulligan
Dick Murcott
Doug Murray
John F. Nelson
Ray L. Newburn Jr.
George Obeslo
Bill Ogline
Wm. B. O'Kelly, MD
Raymond E. Olson
J. Monroe Osborne
J. Roy Pennell Jr.
George Perz
Orin Peterson
H.H. Pinkerton
George Pollock Jr
Don Potts
J. Kenneth Purcell
T. Talcott Purnell
A.F. Quilio Jr.
Brian P. Reback
Fred Reed
William F. Reulbach
Charles C. Riley
Thos. P. Rockwell

Dorothy Robson
H.A. Russell
Joe Sande
Al Sanders
Bernard Schaaf, MD
William A. Saub
Dave Schlingman
Howard Scheir
Walt Schilling
George M. Shubert
Don L. Schumann
Chuck Schwab
Leon Silverman
Wheeler Sloman
Harold Slotta
Russell Snyder
William S. Snyder
J.T. Sobeck
Michael Spack
Frank A. Stacey
Melvin D. Stark
Helen P. Steve
James Still
E.T. Strobridge Jr.
Jake Sureck
Diane Schwartz
Mike Tauber
Patti Van Hoogen
William Vasko
Marty Vink
Fred Voecks
R.W. Volkers
A.R. Walters
Owen Warms
Ed Warren
Richard Waszkiewicz
William F. Watts
S.W. Weston
Thomas W. Wheat
James L. Wiese
Eric Wilkerson
N.E. Williams
Tommy Wills
Ross L. Woodman
Thomas A. Woodworth
Rev. Edmund J. Yahn
Allen M. Young
Virgil Young
Ed Zegers

PREFACE TO SEVENTH EDITION

This edition has been enlarged to include all classes of modern size U.S. Currency through the $10,000.00 denomination. For the first time, accurate totals printed are published for the $10.00 through $10,000.00 notes. These totals were obtained by laborious research from the original plate record cards at the Bureau, which is the initial record of the number of impressions (sheets) taken from each plate. While allowance for a difference between "total printed" and "total issued" must be made we know that the rate of spoilage (star note replacements) was extremely low and hence feel that the best available figures are total notes printed. We also know that during certain periods, several different Series were being run concurrently and intermingled when sent to the Third printing (serial numbering). For this reason serial numbers previously published anywhere are invalid and inaccurate. We must rely on observation and reports from collectors of "high" or "low" serial numbers observed as most accurate. In this regards, a report of high and low serial numbers DOES NOT indicate a consecutive run of serial numbers because of the intermingling of different series as explained above. This also explains why we have higher serial numbers in earlier series than the "high" given for particular series. The intermingling of series also explains the relatively high number of changeover or so-called changeover pairs in some series.

Much information has been added to the section on uncut sheets.

Extensive changes have been made in format which should increase the ease and joy of reading.

We hope these changes will please you. Your suggestions, ideas, information and comments are most cordially welcomed.

chuck o'donnell

THE O'DONNELL NUMBERING SYSTEM
for current size United States paper currency

This system has been devised to facilitate the quick, easy, accurate identification of every piece of current United States paper money. The flexibility of the system will afford every collector and dealer a positive identification of each note for inventory, advertising, sale or description for any purpose.

The basic number is divided into three parts:

Part 1 — one or two digit Roman numeral indicating the DENOMINATION of the note.
I one
II two
V five
X ten
XX twenty
L fifty
C one hundred
D five hundred
M one thousand
$\overline{V}$ (V under a line) five thousand
$\overline{X}$ (X under a line) ten thousand

Part 2 — A single letter for the CLASS of the note.
F Federal Reserve Note, green seal
G Gold Certificate, gold seal
L Legal Tender (United States Note), red seal
N National Currency, brown seal
S Silver Certificate, blue seal

Part 3 — Series year abbreviated to two digits PLUS a single letter year suffix as appropriate.
28 Series of 1928
28A Series of 1928A etc. for B,C,D, etc.
34 Series of 1934
35 Series of 1935
35A Series of 1935A etc. for B,C,D, etc.

Complete amplification of identification is easily made by adding any necessary details such as:
ISS34 Block AB would be $1.00 silver certificate, Series of 1934, Block AB.
IIL28C mule CA would be $2.00 legal tender, Series of 1928C mule, Block CA.
IS35A trial K 20 895 155 C would be the $1.00 silver certificate, Series of 1935A, trial note, with specific serial number.

We believe this system is so simple that a single reading of the explanation will suffice. No memory work is required.

This system has been devised and copyrighted by Chuck O'Donnell, P.O. Drawer A, Williamstown, N.J. 08094. Permission for its use will be granted on request.

TERMS USED IN DESCRIBING A NOTE

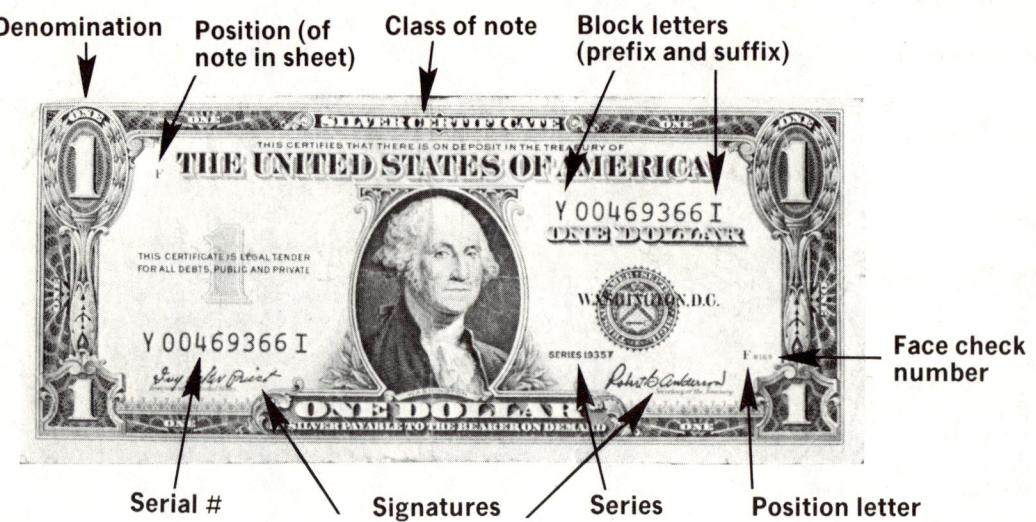

SHEET LAYOUT FOR 12 SUBJECT SHEET

Note: Check letters A through L were used in upper left corner of 12 subject sheets. Left side of sheet had check letters A through F. Right side had check letters G through L.

11

SHEET LAYOUT FOR 18 SUBJECT SHEET

Note: Check letters A through R were used in upper left corner of 18 subject sheets. Left third of sheet had check letters A through F, center section had G through L and right third of sheet had M through R.

12

SHEET LAYOUT FOR 32 SUBJECT SHEET

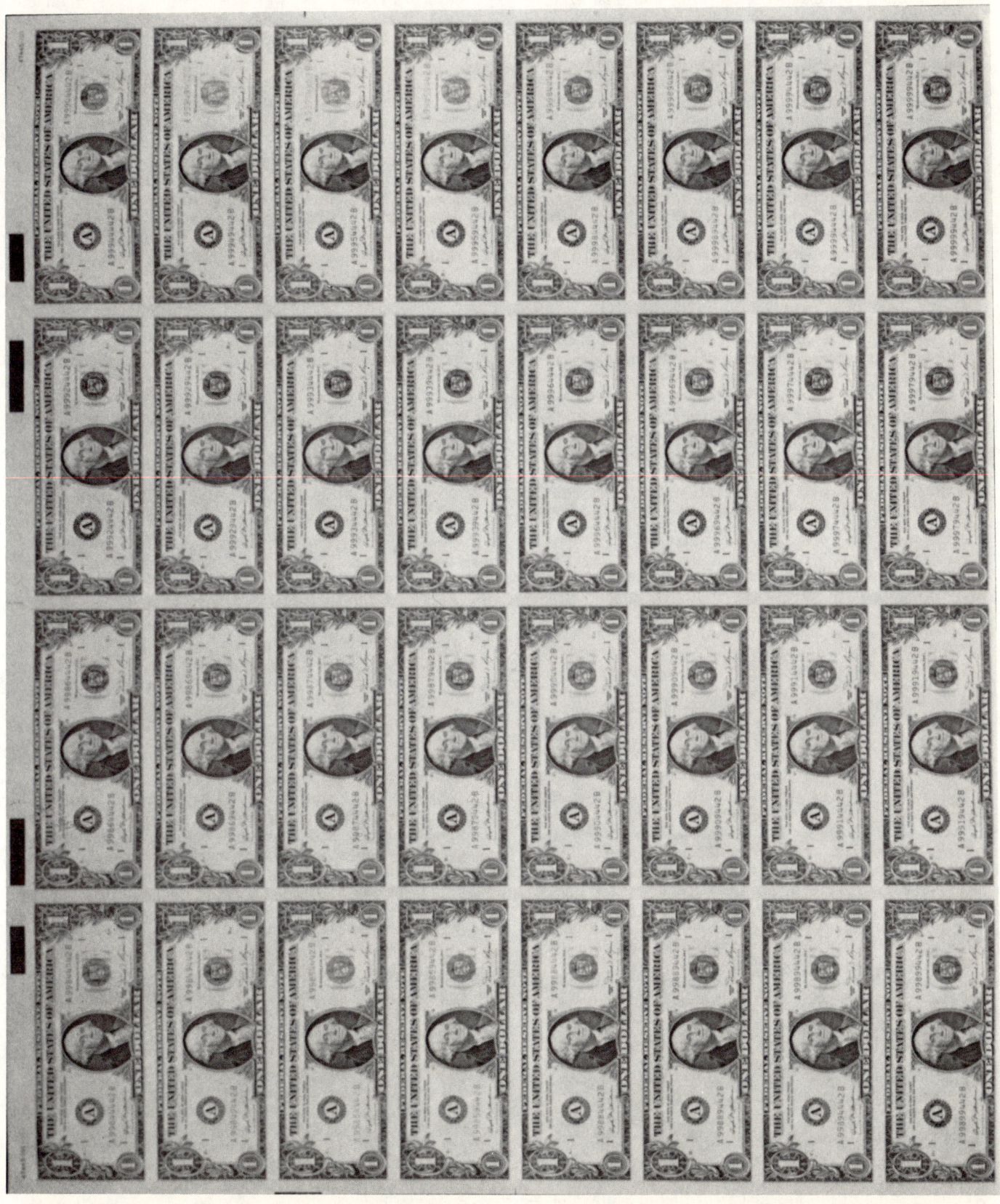

13

INTRODUCTION

A complete bibliography of detailed and authentic general information is included after this intoduction, hence the author has decided to limit this portion of the book to an overview background on U.S. currency and deal exclusively with points of interest for the current size currency.

Historically, Continental Currency was issued by authority of the Continental Congress to help finance the Revolutionary War. This currency very quickly became worthless — and prompted the phrase "not worth a continental". From the time of the establishment of a coinage system in 1793 until 1861 the government issued only Treasury Notes which were not paper money as we know it, but rather were actual promissory notes which bore interest and were callable at the Treasurer's desire. Only the Series of 1815 served briefly as "actual money" and these were non-interest bearing bills of $5.00, $10.00, $20.00 and $50.00.

The various states and territories, in order to meet the needs of commerce, authorized certain banks and corporations to issue paper notes. Under extremely lax controls these banks were permitted to print and issue currency to the amount of money on deposit with the bank. If times became hard, and this was a frequent occurrence, borrowers defaulted on their loans, depositors demanded their deposits which could not be met — and the bank failed. This gave rise to our present references to "broken" bank notes. Even though worthless, many collectors enjoy the color and beauty of these notes, most of which can be obtained even today at relatively low prices.

The terms "Red Dog" and "Yellow Dog" arose during the period of State authorized issues. "Red Dog" originated in reference to banknotes issued by a Michigan bank about 1845 which bore an endorsement stamped in red ink by an Ohio firm that afterwards went bankrupt. A similar issue was circulated in New York. The term "wildcat" was derived from the figure of a wildcat imprinted on banknotes by a bank whose issues were worthless.

Many colorful terms have been applied to our paper money, perhaps the best known of all being "greenbacks" which comes from the almost exclusive use of green ink on the back of U.S. currency. The most frequently asked question at the Bureau of Engraving and Printing in Washington is "why did the government select green for our currency?" The bureau says that it has no factual answer for this question. When the present size currency was first approved, it is known that substantial quantities of green pigment were on hand. The green was also known to be relatively high in resistance to chemical and physical change, and green was psychologically identified with "good money". Since there appeared to be no valid reason for a change, it is assumed that the green was a continuation of custom. It is known that color tints were used early in the 1800's as a deterrent to counterfeiting. As photography advanced during the 1800's, counterfeiters learned that they could remove the colored tints, make any number of copies, then restore an imitation of the colored parts. The solution was a development of an ink that could not be erased without destroying the paper. This was accomplished and patent rights obtained by one of the founders of the American Banknote Co., the firm that produced some of the first issues of United States currency. Other interesting appellations are "Jackass" notes — a series of $10.00 legal tender notes, Series of 1869, 1875, 1878, and 1880 showing Daniel Webster. When the bill is held upside down, the "stock" eagle of the BEP, which is in the lower center of the face of the bill, resembles the head of a donkey. The "lazy deuce" is named from the $2.00 National Bank Note, Series of 1875 because the "2" is horizontal or laying down across the face of the bill. The "watermelon" note takes it's name from the shape of the large zeroes on the back of the $100.00 Treasury Note, Series of 1890.

THE ACTUAL BEGINNING

of U.S. currency as we know it began with the Act of Congress, July 17, 1861 which authorized the issuance of Demand Notes followed on August 5, 1861 and other Acts in 1862 authorizing the issue of Legal Tender Notes (also called United States Notes), then Compound Interest Treasury Notes, Interest Bearing Notes, Refunding Certificates, Gold Certificates, Silver Certificates, Treasury or Coin Notes, National Bank Notes, Federal Reserve Bank Notes and Federal Reserve Notes.

FRACTIONAL CURRENCY

Issues of 3, 5, 10, 15, 25, and 50 cent denominations in paper and so-called Postage Currency were necessitated by the extreme shortage of "metal" coinage during the Civil War.

PHILIPPINE CURRENCY

Although the first "reduced" size notes appeared on Jan. 10, 1929 their "beginning" is directly traceable to a committee recommendation under Secretary of the Treasury MacVeagh, who served under President Taft. This committee, after exhaustive study, reported favorably on the advantages and savings from adoption of smaller size notes, identical in size to the

"PHILIPPINE SIZE CURRENCY"

which had proven highly successful. Thus we might very well consider referring to our present day currency as Philippine size to distinguish it from small (fractional) or large (horse blanket) monies. World War I and the intervening situations (MacVeagh left office one week after accepting the committee recommendations) apparently prevented adoption of the idea. On August 20, 1925, Secretary of the Treasury Andrew W. Mellon appointed a committee to study the whole Question of "currency design, printing operations, issuance, and related interests associated with replacing the large size currency with smaller notes". Practically every element in government was represented on the committee, broken down into eight sub-committees, each assigned a prime facet of the study. In May of 1927, Secretary Mellon accepted the recommendations of his committee and directed the Bureau of Engraving and Printing to translate the plan into reality. The new notes were standardized as far as the face portraits and backs were concerned. Washington was chosen for the $1.00 note because his portrait was familiar to everyone and this note had the greatest circulation. Because of the sentiment for martyred Presidents, and because of the contrast of his flowing beard, to the clean-shaven Washington, Garfield was selected for the $2.00 note. (No explanation is available for the switch from Garfield to Jefferson for the $2.00 bill actually issued). Lincoln was selected for the $5.00 note because he stood next to Washington in the ranks of American heroes. Alexander Hamilton was chosen for the $10.00 note, Andrew Jackson for the $20.00, Ulysses S. Grant for the $50.00, Benjamin Franklin for the $100.00, William McKinley for the $500.00, Grover Cleveland for the $1,000.00, James Madison for the $5,000.00 and Salmon P. Chase for the $10,000.00

CLASSES OF SMALL SIZE ISSUES

UNITED STATES NOTES-also called Legal Tender notes are the longest lived of U.S. currency. First authorized in the Act of Congress May 3, 1878, Legal Tender notes are still current today. The May 3, 1878, act required that an outstanding amount of $346,681,016.00 be maintained. These notes have been issued in $1.00, $2.00, $5.00 and $100.00. Printed but not issued were the $10.00 and $20.00 denominations. Only one issue of the $1.00 was printed, the Series of 1928. On Aug. 10, 1966, the Treasury announced no more $2.00 notes would be printed and later discontinued the printing of $5.00 United States notes. The $100.00 U.S. note was printed in Series 1966 and 1966A with star notes printed for only the 1966 series. All small size U.S. notes have red seals.

SILVER CERTIFICATES were authorized by Acts of Congress of Feb. 28, 1878, and Aug. 4, 1886. The blue seal distinguishes this class of currency printed in denominations of $1.00, $5.00, and $10.00 in the small size. The silver law of 1963, which was designed to free the Treasury stockpile of silver bullion (security backing up Silver Certificates) paved the way for obsolescence of this class of currency. The Treasury stopped the redemption of Silver Certificates in silver dollars in 1964 and discontinued bullion redemption on June 24, 1968, based on $1.29 per ounce.

GOLD CERTIFICATES — first authorized by the Currency Act of Mar. 3, 1863, have beautiful seals of yellow and in small size are much scarcer than the large size Gold Certificates. Gold Certificates were issued in denominations of $10.00, $20.00, $50.00, $100.00, $500.00, $1,000.00, $5,000.00 and $10,000.00 for general circulation and in the $100,000.00 for inter-bank use. The $100,000.00 denomination with portrait of Woodrow Wilson was Series of 1934. All other issued denominations were Series of 1928. Gold Certificates were printed for Series 1928A and Series 1934 but were never released and have since been destroyed. On Dec 28, 1933, the Secretary of the Treasury issued an order forbidding the holding of Gold Certificates, and unlike gold coin, made no provision for collectors to hold them. Banks were ordered to turn in all stocks of Gold Certificates. On April 24, 1964, Secretary Dillon removed restrictions against the holding of Gold Certificates, applicable to Series 1928 only, in small size notes.

FEDERAL RESERVE BANK NOTES — first authorized under Act of Dec. 23, 1913, bore an obligation by the issuing bank rather than the United States. The notes were secured by U.S. Bonds deposited by the issuing bank with the Treasurer of the United States. The bonds were called in by President Roosevelt and the outstanding amount became obligations of the United States. All small size are Series of 1929 and have a brown seal. These notes were also titled "National Currency". These notes are already quite scarce, especially the "star" notes and are avidly collected. According to the Treasury records, a little less than two million dollars is still outstanding for this series.

FEDERAL RESERVE NOTES — first authorized by Act of Congress, Dec. 23, 1913, and bearing the familiar green seal — were reduced in size along with other notes in 1928. These notes are the mainstay of our contemporary currency and with the issue of the $1.00 note in 1963 have created a whole new field for collectors of paper money. Prior to the appearance of the $1.00 Federal Reserve Notes most collectors collected only the "type" or a single piece of each series. Dealers were quick to "package" sets (one note from each of the twelve Federal Reserve Districts) both in "plain" (alphabetic suffix) and in "star" (asterisk) suffix. This practice is rapidly spreading to the higher denominations and nearly all collectors now seek ALL twelve districts of each series both in plain and star suffix. With the introduction of the new equipment in BEP first used on the 1969B series and called COPE of Currency Overprinting and Processing Equipment, many collectors try to obtain a specimen of each group printed on both COPE and CONVENTIONAL (the old equipment). In addition we have recently discovered the "star" notes are not always consecutively numbered as was reported by BEP for many years but frequently have a "skip" of 160,000 within or at the beginning of the star runs. This in turn has created groups of star serials, and again, many collectors try to obtain a specimen from every group.

NATIONAL BANK NOTES — Thousands of collectors enjoy National Bank Notes. Some try to form a collection with one note from each state (or territory) or with a note from the capital city of each state. Some try to obtain a note from each issuing bank in their home state or home town. Collectors are also fond of notes with interesting place names such as Painted Post (N.Y.) or Intercourse (Pa.). Some collect by charter number — the bank number that appears on the face of the note.

PAPER CURRENCY IN GENERAL CIRCULATION

Only two kinds (classes) of paper currency are now being printed.

Federal Reserve Notes are issued and retired with the varying requirements of the country for currency. These notes constitute over 99 percent of the total paper currency in circulation. They are issued by the Federal Reserve Banks under Government auspices in denominations of $1.00, $2.00, $5.00, $10.00, $20.00, $50.00 and $100.00. On July 14, 1969, The Department of the Treasury announced that the issuance of currency in the $500.00, $1,000.00, $5,000.00 and $10,000.00 would be discontinued immediately because of the lack of demand for them. Federal Reserve Notes are obligations of the United States and are a first lien on the assets of the issuing Federal Reserve Bank. In addition they are secured by a pledge of collateral equal to the face value of the notes. The collateral must consist of the following assets, alone or in any combination: [1] gold certificates, [2] Special Drawing Right Certificates, [3] United States Government Securities, and [4] "eligible paper" as described by statute.

United States Notes, which make up less than one percent of the circulating currency, are now being printed only in the $100.00 denomination. On Aug. 10, 1966, the Treasury Department announced that no further $2.00 United States notes would be printed. The last $5.00 United States notes were checked out of the vault of the Treasurer of the United States on April 1, 1969. As required by the Act of May 31, 1878, the amount of United States notes outstanding is maintained at $322,539,016.00.

Relatively small amounts of several discontinued classes of currency notes are still outstanding. It is assumed that most of these notes are in the possession of collectors. These types are as follows: Demand Notes, Fractional Currency, Gold Certificates, National Bank Notes, Treasury Notes of 1890, Federal Reserve Bank Notes and Silver Certificates.

SIGNATURE COMBINATIONS

From the beginning of small size currency, there have been only twenty different signature combinations on our currency. All signature combinations are obtainable at very reasonable prices if one does not limit his collection to a single "class" or "denomination".

All signatures on small currency appear on the face of the note. All United States Notes, silver and gold certificates, and Federal Reserve Notes carry two signatures — the signature of the Treasurer of the United States at the lower left and the signature of the Secretary of the Treasury at the lower right. The National Currency and Federal Reserve Bank Notes have four signatures — all have E. E. Jones, Register of the Treasury at the upper left and W. O. Woods, Treasurer, at the top right. In the lower left appears the signature of the Cashier of the individual bank, and in the lower right, the signature of the President of the individual bank. The Federal Reserve Bank Note have the signature of the bank Cashier in the lower left and the signature of the Governor of the Bank in the lower right, with the following exceptions: New York notes have the signature of the Deputy Governor in the lower left instead of the Cashier; Chicago has the Assistant Deputy Governor replacing the Cashier's signature; and St. Louis has the signature of the Controller replacing that of the Cashier.

TERMS OF OFFICE AND NOTES BEARING THEIR SIGNATURES

TREASURER   SECRETARY   STARTED   ENDED

H.T. Tate   A.W. Mellon   4-30-28   1-17-29
Series 1928: $1 silver certificate; $2 Legal Tender; $5, $10, $20 FRN

Walter O. Woods A. W. Mellon   1-18-29   2-12-32
Series 1928: $5 Legal Tender; $50, $100, $500, $5,000, $10,000 FRN; $10, $20, $50, $100, $500, $1,000, $5,000, $10,000 Gold certificates
Series 1928A: $2 Legal Tender; $1 silver certificate; $5, $10, $20, $50 and $100 FRN.
Series 1928B: $5, $10, $20 FRN.

Walter O. Woods Ogden L. Mills   2-13-32   3-3-33
Series 1928A: $5 Legal Tender; $10, $20, $100 gold certificates (Not released)
Series 1928B: $1 silver certificate; $2 Legal Tender
Series 1928C: $5, $10, $20 FRN.

Walter O. Woods W.H. Woodin   3-4-33   5-31-33
Series 1928: $1 Legal Tender
Series 1928C: $1 silver certificate
Series 1928D: $5 FRN.

W.A. Julian   W. H. Woodin   6-1-33   12-31-33
Series 1928D: $1 silver certificate
Series 1933: $10 Silver certificate

W.A. Julian   Henry Morgenthau, Jr.   1-1-34   7-22-45
Series 1928B: $5 Legal Tender
Series 1928C: $2, $5 Legal Tender
Series 1928D: $2 Legal Tender
Series 1928E: $1 silver certificate
Series 1933A: $10 silver certificate
Series 1935: $1 silver certificate
Series 1935A: $1 silver certificate, $1 Africa, $1 Hawaii and the $1 R and S experimentals.

TREASURER   SECRETARY   STARTED   ENDED

Series 1934: $1, $5, $10 silver certificate; $5, $10 Africa silver certificate; $5, $10, $20, $50, $100, $500, $1,000, $5,000, $10,000 FRN; $5, $20 Hawaii FRN overprint.
Series 1934A: $5, $10 silver certificate; $5, $10 Africa silver certificate; $5, $10, $20, $100, $1,000 FRN; $5, $10, $20 FRN with Hawaii overprint.

W.A. Julian   Fred M. Vinson   7-23-45   7-23-46
Series 1928D: $5 Legal Tender
Series 1928E: $2 Legal Tender
Series 1934B: $5, $10 silver certificate; $5, $10, $20, $50, $100 FRN
Series 1935B: $1 silver certificate

W.A. Julian   John W. Snyder   7-25-46   5-29-49
Series 1928E: $5 Legal Tender
Series 1928F: $2 Legal Tender
Series 1934C: $5, $10 silver certificate; $5, $10, $20, $50, $100 FRN
Series 1935C: $1 silver certificate

Georgia Neese Clark   John W. Snyder   6-21-49   1-20-53
Series 1928F: $5 Legal Tender
Series 1928G: $2 Legal Tender
Series 1934D: $5, $10 silver certificate; $5, $10, $20, $50, $100 FRN
Series 1935D: $1 silver certificate
Series 1950: $5, $10, $20, $50, $100 FRN

Ivy Baker Priest George M. Humphrey   1-28-53   7-28-57
Series 1935E: $1 silver certificate
Series 1950A: $5, $10, $20, $50, $100 FRN
Series 1953: $2, $5 Legal Tender; $5, $10 silver certificate

Ivy Baker Priest Robert B. Anderson   7-29-57   1-20-61
Series 1935F: $1 silver certificate
Series 1950B: $5, $10, $20, $50, $100 FRN
Series 1953A: $2, $5 Legal Tender; $5, $10 silver certificate
Series 1957: $1 silver certificate

Elizabeth Rudel Smith   C. Douglas Dillon   1-30-61   4-13-62
Series 1935G: $1.00 silver certificate
Series 1935B: $2.00, $5.00 legal tender; $5.00, $10.00 silver certificate
Series 1950C: $5.00, $10.00, $20.00, $50.00, $100.00 FRN
Series 1957A: $1.00 silver certificate

Kathryn O'Hay Granahan   C. Douglas Dillon   1-3-63   3-31-65
Series 1935H: $1.00 silver certificate
Series 1950D: $5.00, $10.00, $20.00, $50.00, $100.00 FRN
Series 1950E: $50.00, $100.00 FRN
Series 1953C: $2.00, $5.00, legal tender; $1.00, $5.00 silver certificates. (The $5.00 silver certificate was NOT released).
Series 1963: $1.00, $5.00, $10.00, $20.00 FRN; $2.00, $5.00 legal tender
Series 1957B: $1.00 silver certificate

TREASURER	SECRETARY	STARTED	ENDED

Kathryn O'Hay
 Granahan   Henry H. Fowler 4-1-65   10-13-66
Series 1950E: $5.00, $10.00, $20.00, $50.00, $100.00 FRN
Series 1963A: $1.00, $5.00, $10.00, $20.00, $50.00, $100.00 FRN
Series 1963A: $2.00 legal tender
Series 1966: $100.00 legal tender

Kathryn O'Hay
 Granahan   Joseph W. Barr   12-21-68   1-20-69
Series 1963B: $1.00 FRN

Dorothy Andrews
 Elston   David. M. Kennedy   5-8-69   9-16-70
Series 1969: $1.00, $5.00, $10.00, $20.00, $50.00, $100.00 FRN
Series 1966A: $100.00 Legal Tender

Dorothy Andrews
 Kabis   David M. Kennedy   9-17-70   2-1-71
Series 1969A: $1.00 FRN

Dorothy Andrews
 Kabis   John B. Connally, Jr.   2-18-71   7-3-71
Series 1969A: $5.00, $10.00, $20.00, $50.00, $100.00 FRN
Series 1969B: $1.00 FRN

Romana Acosta
 Banuelos   John B. Connally, Jr.   12-17-71   6-12-72
Series 1969B: $5.00, $10.00, $20.00, $50.00, $100.00 FRN
Series 1969C: $1.00 FRN

Romana Acosta
 Banuelos   George P. Shultz 6-12-72   5-8-74
Series 1969C: $5.00, $10.00, $20.00, $50.00, $100.00 FRN
Series 1969D: $1.00 FRN

Francine I. Neff   William E. Simon 6-12-74   1-19-76
Series 1974: $1.00, $5.00, $10.00, $20.00, $50.00, $100.00 FRN
Series 1976 $2.00 FRN

Azie Taylor
 Morton   W. Michael Blumenthal   9-12-77   8-1-79
Series 1977: $1.00, $5.00, $10.00, $20.00, $50.00, $100.00 FRN

Azie Taylor
 Morton   J. William Miller 8-6-79   1-4-81
Series 1977A: $1.00, $5.00, $10.00 FRN

Angela M.
 Buchanan   Donald T. Regan 3-17-81   —
Series 1981 $1.00 FRN

PRINTING PAPER CURRENCY

From ancient times, man has used cut or scratched lines to decorate his most prized possessions. By the end of the Roman Empire — and on up through the middle ages, man had learned to fill these little cut lines, with a dark, gummy substance, smoke the surface, then wipe off the plate, and by pressing wet paper against the smoke-covered gum, transfer the image to the paper.

By mid-15th century, this art had been most highly developed in both Italy and Germany — and one of the first to actually engrave in ferrous metal for printing was the German, Albrecht Durer. Durer's finest work was done on copper plates, first by hand rollers, then later, on the copper plate printing press, which was invented about 1545. The production of book illustrations and title pages over a long period most certainly developed the disciplines and skills for engraving plates first used in printing security papers.

Paper money of the finest quality was printed by copper plates in mid-17th century England. The first official paper money in America was issued by the Massachusetts Bay Colony in 1690 to pay soldiers returning from unsuccessful campaigns in Canada. The crudely engraved copper plates used for this issue invited the skills of many counterfeiters who had fled Europe to escape the consequences of their art in that area. By mid-18th century, several of the colonies were issuing very attractive notes, but because no transfer process was available and all plates had to be recut or newly engraved by hand, it was impossible to make printing plates bearing two identical designs. All of this, despite the very severe penalties for counterfeiting, made counterfeiting fairly easy and greatly practiced.

The end of the 18th century seems to be the beginning of the American banknote printing industry. One Jacob Perkins of Massachusetts invented a method of punching lettering and designs into the walls of steel cylinders and crossing them with engraved intersecting lines. These were then rolled into copper plates, and multiple intaglio impressions of exact fidelity were produced. In 1812, Asa Spencer of Connecticut patented an engine-turning device to ornament watches. A stationary point traced or cut an endless design of perfect regularity, and this means was quickly recognized as an effective deterrent for foiling the work of the counterfeiter. Perkins purchased the patent rights to this machine in 1815 and introduced it to the banknote business.

From it's beginning until 1861, the goverment found no need to issue paper money except for the issue of 1815 — which in reality was a "loan" issue — but which did actually circulate as "money" for a short time.

By Act of Congress July 17, 1861, the first paper money issued by the U.S. Government came into being. Actually, the Bureau was established on August 29, 1862 and was the result of the need for financing the Civil War — a plan proposed by Secretary of the Treasury Salmon P. Chase [under Lincoln] as both a system of taxation and one of floating loans. From it's inception until recently, currency was produced from "wet" method printing on intaglio plates. To explain these two terms — "wet" printing simply means that the paper is "wet" when printed. This "wetting" is required because of the extreme pressures necessary to force the paper down into the incised lines of the plates in order to pick up the ink deposited therein. "Intaglio" — as opposed to cameo — means that the design is "cut" or "incised" into the flat plate as compared to the "raised" letters on the more familiar type of printing. Experiments as early as 1938 in methods of "dry" printing were conducted and with the development of nonoffset ink perfected to the degree that the "dry" method was used starting in 1952.

Through the years the Bureau has been in operation, plate sizes have increased from 2-subject, to 4-subject, to 8-subject, and finally in 1929, with the introduction of the small size currency, all plates were standardized at 12-subject size. This 12-subject plate was considered "maximum" size under the "wet" method of printing because of the shrinkage and size variation of the sheets during the alternate wetting and drying of the paper between the printing of the back and the printing of the face of the notes. It was also necessary during this period to "tissue" each sheet of printed paper to prevent the "offset" of the ink prior to drying.

With the development of nonoffset green ink in 1950 and a black ink in 1952, the door was opened for increasing the size of the plates. In August, 1952 18-subject plates were first used, and by September 1953 all plates had been converted to 18-subjects. With the introduction of the "dry" method for the printing operation, plate size again became subject to change, and the 32-subject plate currently used was adopted. Illustrations showing the numbering of the various plate layouts follow this narrative.

Flatbed hand presses used by the Bureau since 1862 gave way to the steam press in 1878 and to an electric "motorized" press in 1898. Flatbed presses have continued to be used but are now being phased out in the modernization plans of the Bureau. In 1953 the Bureau purchased a sheet fed rotary press to be used in the development of ink, materials, and methods for expanding production. A second press obtained in 1954 expedited this work of development. Back in 1949 a method of automatically "polishing" the plates [to wipe the ink from the surface of the plate] supplanted the "hand-polishing" method, and a semi-automatic sheet feed attachment had been installed on the presses. In 1951 an automatic "take-off" device of the currency, and in 1952 the automatic "take-off" device was installed on the presses printing the faces. Fully automatic "feed" devices were installed on all presses during 1953 and 1954.

Standards employed by the Bureau of Engraving and Printing for the manufacture of the United States paper money are very rigid. The intaglio process of printing is used to print the basic back and face designs. This process provides maximum security against counterfeiting.

There is currently an effort by the Bureau to permit surface printing for the back of our currency. An intaglio is an incised design which is cut or engraved below the surface and which produces an impression in relief. This third-dimensional effect is most difficult to produce and requires the combined handiwork of highly skilled artists, steel engravers, and plate printers.

When a new currency note is to be issued, designs are discussed with interested Government officials and then submitted to the designers of the Bureau of Engraving and Printing, who prepare a final model. The final model must be approved by the Secretary of the Treasury. Photographic copies of the approved model are furnished to the engravers.

The engravers reproduce the currency designs in pieces of soft steel, known as "dies" by working with steel cutting instruments, called gravers, and powerful magnifying glasses. Each separate design, such as the portrait, the vignette, the ornaments, and the lettering, is hand cut by an engraver who has been specially trained in that particular style. A geometric lathe is used to cut the intricate lacy ornaments and borders and a ruling machine is used to cut the fine cross-hatched lines in the portraits. It is practically impossible for an engraver to exactly reproduce his own work or that of another engraver.

When the hand-engraved pieces of soft steel, or dies, have been completed, they are cleaned, and then hardened by being heated in sodium cyanide and quickly dipped into brine. The design of each die is then transferred to a roll or cylinder of soft steel by placing the die on the bed of a transfer press and, under tremendous pressure, forcing the face of the soft roll into the intaglio engraving on the hard die. The result is an exact duplicate of the original design standing out in relief on the face of the roll. To make a master die by the transfer process, the rolls from these several dies are passed separately over the soft die steel under great pressure. Different portions of the engraving are thereby united on the die in their proper positions. The master die is then finished and hardened and a master roll is made bearing one subject, or all the designs necessary to make up one currency note. An engraved steel master plate can then be made from the master roll on the transfer press.

The electrolytic process is used for making plates for the printing of paper currency. The engraved steel master plate is placed in a nickel plating bath and by means of electro-deposition another plate is built thereon to a required thickness. This plate is referred to as an alto, and when it is removed from the master plate the design stands out in relief on a flat surface. A duplicate plate of the original steel master is then reproduced in the nickel plating bath from this relief design. These duplicate plates, with the design in the intaglio or cut-in impression as on the original master, are then electrolytically plated with chromium and made ready for printing.

All denominations of United States paper currency are now being printed on modern high-speed sheet-fed rotary presses by the dry intaglio process, which provides for a relatively high degree of dimensional stability in the paper. Specially manufactured distinctive paper, procured from private contractors under strict Government control, is used for printing of all notes.

Each plate on the rotary presses prints a sheet of 32 subjects (notes). The most recently acquired presses are the two-plate monocolor presses formerly referred to as the Magna Press.

The "Two-Plate Monocolor Intaligo Press" [Press #303], formerly referred to as the Magna Press, is a high speed, sheet-fed currency press. As the name implies, it operates with two 32-subject currency plates at speeds in excess of 8,000 sheets per hour.

Press #303 was accepted by the Bureau on Feb. 11, 1976, after the successful completion of its acceptance trial. It was the first of four such presses ordered by the Bureau to be delivered during 1976. The presses are operated in tandem, that is, two presses being paired together — one to print backs, the other faces — as is the Bureau practice for currency press operations.

Press #303 is equipped with a high speed feeder that can accommodate 10,000 sheets of currency paper. A continuous feed system allows the printers to stack 10,000 sheets in the feeder reserve as a 10,000 sheet load of paper is being printed. As the first load of 10,000 sheets nears completion, the second load is moved upward in the feeder until the first load is setting on top of the second load. When the feeder feeds the last sheet of the first load, the first sheet of the second load is in position to be fed as if it were part of the first load. This system can be continued load after load indefinitely. However, Bureau accountability procedures require the press to be stopped after each 20,000 increment of production to verify the count.

The press is equipped with two delivery sheet receivers. Design considerations include the capability to stack all sheets printed from one plate in one delivery pile and the sheets from the other to be stacked in the second delivery. This system provides a favorable advantage for currency examiners in their quality control function.

The wiping system uses three paper wipers. The wipers reciprocate in a fixed position. After the engraved plates are charged with ink, the plate cylinder continues to rotate, making contact with each of the three wipers which remove the surface ink from the plates, but do not disturb the ink in the engraved lines. Here again, engineering anticipated a reluctance to stop the press to replace clean wiper rolls or remove used ones, therefore design considerations allow these operations to be performed safely while the press continues to print at operational speed.

The engraved plate format will not be changed to accommodate the new presses. Therefore, the currency notes printed from the Two-Plate Monocolor Intaglio presses are indistinguishable from those printed on other currency presses.

Each plate on the rotary presses prints a sheet of 32 subjects, or notes. The most recently acquired rotary presses accomodate four plates and print 8,000 sheets per hour, an increase of over 200 percent as compared to the amount printed on the first rotary presses purchased by the Bureau.

Upon completion of the basic back and face printings by the intaglio method, the 32-subject sheets are trimmed to a uniform dimension and the serial numbers, the Treasury seal, and the case of Federal Reserve Notes, the Federal Reserve Bank designations are simultaneously overprinted on the face of each note by the typographic process on two-color rotary presses. The full size sheets are cut in half and a detailed examination made to identify imperfect notes for later removal. The 16-subject sheets are then further cut, by guilotine paper cutting machines, into individual notes. After a final note examination for removal of imperfect notes and their replacement with "star" notes, the currency is securely banded and wrapped for delivery. Each currency package contains 40 bands of 100 notes each, or 4,000 notes, and weighs about 8½ pounds.

Newly designed currency numbering and processing equipment was put into use during processing of Series 1969B $1.00 notes. To facilitate maximum utilization of this equipment a significant portion of the daily currency production is examined in half sheet, 16 subjects, and only perfect sheets are used for simultaneous printing of serial numbers, seals, and bank designations with this equipment. The numbers are electronically checked for accuracy, the sheets cut to notes, and the notes counted in units of 100, banded, and delivered from the machine for packaging prior to delivery to the banks.

Despite spiraling costs of material and labor, the progressive improvements in presses and processing methods have reduced the cost of producing United States currency from $9.00 per thousand notes in 1957 to $8.02 per thousand notes in 1970. Full utilization of the newer presses and the overprinting and processing equipment will result in further significant savings.

Recently a change was made in the method of printing the series designation and the signatures of the Secretary of the Treasury and the Treasurer of the United States on currency notes. Since 1953, these signatures had been overprinted typographically, following the printing of the face design. Upon conversion in April 1968, to the dry-printing method on high-speed, sheet-fed, rotary presses, it was found to be more efficient and economical to incorporate the signatures and the series date as integral parts of the face intaglio design. The engraved signature technique for dry-printing currency was first used in the production of a new $100.00 United States note, Series 1966, which was first issued in 1968. This technique was also used in the printing of $1.00 Federal Reserve notes, Series 1963B and was continued in all currency production beginning with the Series 1969 notes.

STAR NOTES

On April 14, 1910, Director of the Bureau of Engraving and Printing wrote to Lee McClung, the Treasurer, suggesting "that the Bureau be authorized to prepare a stock of notes numbered in sequence, distinguished from all other notes by a special letter or character printed before/after the serial number... that these notes be substituted for defective specimens... with notation on the package indicating the package contained such substitutes." On April 18, 1910, Director Ralph received the green light to proceed. Ralph must have anticipated approval because on April 17, 1910 Ralph sent a rush order to the American Numbering Company in Brooklyn, N.Y., specifying eight "stars" for use on automatic numbering blocks. Evidently the star blocks arrived promptly for the Bureau finished the first package with stars on June 20, 1910, and delivered them to Treasurer McClung on July 12, 1910. Thus the earliest possible star notes are those of 1910 with the Vernon-McClung signature. The first pack of stars was numbered 75612001A thru 75612100A and were Series 1899 Silver Certificates.

During production [printing] of our currency, it is inevitable that some misprints, smudged notes, or otherwise imperfect notes will be made. At the time of examination, these imperfect notes are replaced by new, perfect notes that have an "asterisk" or "star" on one end of the serial number. One has no problem believing that the percentage of spoiled notes is very small, and hence the number of star notes is rather limited. In the early series of our small size notes, the spoilage percentage has been accurately estimated at less than 1% of total notes.

Star notes are used as replacements for damaged or defective, improperly printed, smudged, over-inked or otherwise unsatisfactory notes printed during the production run. They are generally printed prior to the production run, though if an insufficient quantity is originally printed they may be printed during the production run. The star notes are serially numbered from a separate serial register, cut and packed 100 to the "pad" and turned over to the Inspection Section of the Bureau. During the production run examination process, notes found to be defective are pulled out and replaced by a star note. NO attempt is made to replace any defective note with the same serial numbr star note, in fact the serial number of the star note may be several million numbers away from the note being replaced. The star note is recognized because of the asterisk [or star] at the end of the serial number on Federal Reserve Notes and at the beginning of the serial number on all other classes of notes.

When a note is spoiled in the course of manufacture it has to be replaced. To replace it with a note of exactly the same serial number as that on the imperfect note would require special machinery and would be costly and delaying. In consequence "star" notes are substituted. Except that they have their own special serial number and a star, these notes are the same as others. On United States Notes, a red star is substituted for the prefix letter; On Federal Reserve Notes, a green star is substituted for the suffix letter.

Formerly a star note was used to eplace the 100,00,000th note instead of a note with serial 00 000 000 as printed. We know of at least one instance where, through error the note with serial A 00 000 000 A escaped replacement in the Bureau and was shown at the ANA convention in Boston, Mass., in 1973 by John Morrissey. This is the only known case were such a serial number reached the public in the current size notes. Several such notes are known in the large size notes.

PAPER CURRENCY DESIGNS

The selection of designs used on our paper currency, including the selection of portraits, is a responsibility of the Secretary of the Treasury, who acts with the advice of responsible Bureau heads, such as the Director of the Bureau of Engraving and Printing and the Treasurer of the United States.

None of the letters, numbers, or symbols on any of the currency issued under the authority of the United States has any sectarian significance whatsoever.

Those design features that have historical or idealistic significance, as distinct from purely ornamental or security implications are:

The Great Seal of the United States. Both obverse and reverse of the Great Seal of the United States are reproduced on the backs of $1.00 notes. The Great Seal was adopted in 1782. Its obverse depicts an American eagle breasted by a shield with our national colors. The eagle holds in his right talon an olive branch, symbolic of peace, of 13 leaves and 13 berries. In his left talon he holds 13 arrows signifying the original colonies' fight for liberty. A ribbon flying from the beak of the eagle is inscribed with the Latin motto, "E Pluribus Unum," which is translated "One out of many", in reference to the unity of the 13 colonies as one government. Over the eagle's head is a constellation of 13 five-pointed stars surrounded by a wreath of clouds.

The reverse of the seal depicts a pyramid, with the Roman numerals "MDCCLXXVI" on its base (1776), the year of the Declaration of Independence. The pyramid represents permanence and strength. Its unfinished condition symbolizes that there is still work to be done to form a more perfect government and signifies the expectation that new states would be admitted to the Union. The eye in the triangular glory represents an all-seeing Deity. The words "Annuit Coeptis," translates as "He (God) has favored our undertakings", refer to the many interpositions of Divine Providence in the forming of our government. "Novus Ordo Seclorum", translates as "A new order of the ages", signifying a new American era.

Portraits of Great Americans. The law specifies that "No portrait shall be placed upon any of the bonds, securities, notes, fractional or postal currency of the United States while the original of such portrait is living." [31 U.S.C. 413] By tradition, the portraits on the faces of our paper money are those of deceased statesmen whose places in history are well known to the American people.

Pictures of famous buildings or monuments. Along with the introduction of small-sized currency notes in 1929, uniform back designs were adopted, many of them incuding vignettes of buildings or monuments closely associated with the persons pictured on the faces of the notes. The portraits and back designs on United States currency notes now being printed are:

$1.00	Federal Reserve Note	Washington	Great Seal of the U.S.
$5.00	Federal Reserve Note	Lincoln	Lincoln Memorial
$10.00	Federal Reserve Note	Hamilton	U.S. Treasury Bldg.
$20.00	Federal Reserve Note	Jackson	White House
$50.00	Federal Reserve Note	Grant	U.S. Capitol
$100.00	Federal Reserve Note	Franklin	Independence Hall
$100.00	United States Note	Franklin	Independence Hall

Though not now being printed, the $2.00 Series 1976 (so-called Bicentennial issue) Federal Reserve Note, had Jefferson on the face and "Signing of the Declaration of Independence" on the back.

Portraits on notes no longer being printed were: McKinley on the $500.00 note; Cleveland on the $1,000.00 note; Madison on the $5,000.00 note; and Chase on the $10,000.00 note.

The largest denomination of currency ever printed was the $100,000.00 Gold Certificate of 1934 which featured the potrait of President Wilson. This note was designed for official transactions only and none of these notes ever circulated outside the Federal Reserve system.

PLATE POSITION NUMBERS

The small capital letter and number which appear in the upper left-hand corner just below the denomination numeral on the face of the bill are referred to as the plate position number. This item designates the position of the note on the 32-subject face plate from which a particular bill was printed.

Plate position number (frequently called the check letter) is the letter that appears in the upper left corner of the face of the note on the 12-subject and 18-subject sheets and the letter and number that appears in the upper left corner of the face of the 32-subject sheets. Check letters A through L were used on 12-subject sheets, A through R were used on the 18-subject sheet and A through H with the number 1, 2, 3 or 4 is used on the 32-subject sheet. Imagine that the 32-subject sheet is divided into four sections of eight notes each. A section would consist of two rows of notes, two notes wide (horizontally) and four notes vertical. The top left section (or quandrant) is known as the first quadrant, hence each check letter in that quadrant will be followed by the figure 1, e.g. A1, B1, C1, D1 for notes in the left vertical row and E1, F1, G1, H1 in the right vertical row. The lower left quadrant is similarly arranged with the figure 2 following the check letters. Top right quadrant is the third quadrant and has the figure 3 following the check letters while the fourth quadrant is the lower right fourth of the sheet. During the inspection of the printed sheet, it is possible to determine exactly what portion of the plate produced defective notes.

PLATE SERIAL NUMBER

The plate serial number appears in the MARGIN of the 32-subject sheet (similar to the plate number on a sheet of postage stamps) and is trimmed off during the cutting operation.

CHECK NUMBERS

The tiny number in the lower right of both face and back — sometimes erroneously called the "plate" number. Actually the plate number is printed in the margin of the sheet, exactly as on a sheet of postage stamps, and is trimmed off during the cutting of the notes. The official terminology at the Bureau is "check" number for the cross-reference to the plate number. Many collectors find great enjoyment in trying to establish a consecutive run of these check numbers, however one must recognize that the Bureau does not use ALL numbers in a series. The face and back check numbers are not related to each other. While some series start out with "1" for both face and back, they soon expand to wide difference typified by the $1.00 silver certificate starting in 1957. Series 1957 started with both face and back check number 1. By the end of the 1957B series, the back check number went only to 447 while the front check number was approaching 800. the $1.00 Federal Reserve note Series of 1963 started with face check number 1, but continued with back check numbers in the 400 series, it being fairly easy to find a 1963 note with back check lower than those on the 1957B notes.

LABEL SETS

Regardless of denomination, notes produced at BEP are packaged in 40 "straps" of 100 notes each. This package, commonly called a "brick", has wooden blocks placed at each end of the stack, a "label" denoting contents and are tied together with two steel straps. It is then wrapped in heavy kraft paper and a duplicate label denoting contents affixed to one end of the brick with a label of the Treasury seal affixed to the other end. Until Series 1974 the label showed the number of notes (4,000), the Series year, the denomination of the notes inside, and the serial number of the FIRST AND LAST NOTE. With the Series 1974, the label remained the same EXCEPT that it showed ONLY the serial number of the FIRST note in the brick. In recent years many collectors attempted obtain these labels, with the first and last note in the brick and the term "label set" was applied. Although it appeared to be a novel approach to collecting, interest waned and today there seems to be very little interest in this area.

SERIES DATE

Prior to Series 1974, the series date on the face of each bill indicated the year in which the face design of the note wa adopted. The capital letter following the series year indicates that a minor change was authorized in a particular series. Such a change occurred with a new Secretary of the Treasury of Treasurer of the United States was appointed, and accordingly a change in the signature on the face was made for one or both officials. This policy was changed when William E. Simon became Secretary of the Treasury. He directed that the series year would be changed whenever there was a change in the Office of the Secretary of the Treasury.

IN GOD WE TRUST

"In God We Trust" owes its presence on United States coins and notes largely to the increased religious sentiment existing during the Civil War. Salmon P. Chase, then Secretary of the Treasury, received a number of appeals from devout persons throughout the country, urging that Deity be recognized suitably on our coins in a manner similar to that commonly found on the coins of other nations. Accordingly, on Nov. 20, 1861, Secretary Chase instructed the Director of the Mint at Philadelphia to prepare a motto "expressing — this national recognition". The Secretary wrote "No nation can be strong except in the strength of God, or safe except in His defence". The approved form of the motto first made its appearance on the two-cent coin, authorized by Act of Congress dated April 22, 1864. First appearance of the motto on our paper money was on the silver dollars shown on the back of the $5.00 1886.

A law passed by the 84th Congress and approved by the President on July 11, 1955, provides that "In God We Trust" shall appear on all United States paper currency and coins. One-dollar bills bearing the inscription were first made available to the public at most of the country's banks on Oct. 1, 1957. As the Bureau of Engraving and printing converted to the dry intaglio process of printing, the motto "In God We Trust" was included in the back design of all classes and denominations of paper currency.

Matthew H. Rothert, past President of the American Numismatic Association, presented the suggestion to Secretary of the Treasury George W. Humphrey in November, 1953, and is credited with the ultimate adoption of the idea.

THE $ SIGN

The origin of the $ sign has been variously accounted for, with perhaps the most widely accepted explanation being that it is the result of evolution, independently in different places, of the Mexican or Spanish "P's" for pesos, or piastres, or pieces of eight. The theory, derived from a study of old manuscripts, is that the "S" gradually came to be written over the "P" developing a close equivalent of the $ mark, which eventually evolved. It was widely used before the adoption of the United States dollar in 1785.

MULES

It is understood that during the printing of the Series 1935 silver certificates, the authorities received many complaints from the currency inspectors over the size [.020 mm] of the check numbers. Remedial action resulted in an enlargement of the check numbers to .040 mm.

The Bureau considered this change sufficiently important to designate it as a new series [such designation being normal for design or signature changes only]. We feel that such a change by the Bureau warrants placing the notes that bear the small size check number on one side and the large size check number on the other side in the MAJOR variety category.

The $1.00 silver certificate Series 1935A, the $2.00 U.S. note series 1928D, the $5.00 silver certificate Series 1934A, $10.00 silver certificate Series 1934A, the $5.00, $10.00, $20.00 $50.00 and $100.00 Federal Reserve Notes Series 1934A were designed for use of the large size check numbers. Therefore when we find a note whose face bears one size check number and whose back bears a DIFFERENT size check number, we know that we are looking at a "hybrid" or "muled" note.

Without regard to the "cutoff" numbers for the small size check numbers which are given in the text, MULE notes are easily distinguished by comparing the face check with the back check. This can be done without harming the note by rolling half of the face so that the face and back check numbers are adjacent to each other.

TRIAL NOTES

It has long been known the experimentation with the paper stock in our currency was being conducted. The very popular red R and S notes are perhaps the widest known specimens of the experiments. Not so well known until the First Edition of Standard Handbook are the experimental issues of 1928A and 1928B $1.00 silver certificates and the experimental issue of 1935 $1.00 silver certificates. Since the word EXPERIMENTAL has become an accepted designation in syngraphic circles for any formula change in the paper stock, the authors were confronted with a need for a different term to describe experiments going on in OTHER than paper formulae.

The term TRIAL note was selected since it most accurately described what was taking place. Actually a change in type size or arrangement of data on the note to determine how it would fit, or how it would look was a "trial" for whatever new design was being considered. Trial notes are distinguishable ONLY by the specific number of the face and back check numbers used for "trial" purposes. These face and back check numbers were discovered only after persistent research in old Bureau records. All known face and back check numbers are given in the main text of this catalog.

EXPERIMENTAL NOTES

Every paper money collector knows the experimental "Red R and S" notes — $1.00 silver certificates, Series 1935-A. Not so familiar however, are the experimental notes of $1.00 silver certificates, Series of 1928-A and the experimental notes of the $1.00 silver certificates, Series of 1928-B. Unfortunately, even the Bureau of Engraving and Printing seems to have lost trace of these experimentals since they are recorded as being Series 1928E. Again, an experimental issue of the $1.00 silver certificate, Series 1935 was made and, like it's predecessors — and the succeeding 1935A "R and S" — no results seem to be available. Details of these experimental issues are given in the text under the denomination and series year. For the red R and S notes, approximately one million of each were placed in circulation in June 1944. It was intended to compile statistics as the notes were returned for redemption as to the "wear" characteristics — however the returns were so small that the volume never reached sufficient proportions for a valid analysis. The 1928A and 1928B experimentals, as well as the 1935 issue of experimentals were much better disguised and reasons for the Bureau's failure to record results have never been properly explained.

New experiments conducted in 1981 on so-called Natick test paper resulted in the printing of $1.00 notes for Series 1977A (Richmond) serials E 76 800 001 H through E 80 640 000 H, a total of 3,840,000 notes and for $1.00 Series 1977A (Philadelphia) serials C 07 052 001* through C 07 060 000*, a total of 256,000 notes with a gap of 12,000 serial numbers between positions. BEP also printed $10.00 Series 1977A notes for Richmond in August 1981 with serials E 05 772 001* through E 05 780 000*. A total of 256,000 notes with 12,000 serial number gap between positions.

SERIAL NUMBERS

The two identical numbers, one in the lower left and one in the upper right face of the note is called the serial number. The prefix will always be that of the issuing bank while the suffix letter will be "A" for the first 100 million notes, "B" for the second one hundred million notes, etc. for Federal Reserve notes. On the $100.00 United States notes, the prefix letter will be "A" with suffix letter "A" for the first 100 million notes. The PREFIX letter would then change to "B" for the second 100 million notes. The suffix letter would remain "A" until the prefix letter reached "Z" [the letter O is not used because of its similarity to the figure O] at which time the prefix letter would revert to "A" and the suffix letter would become "B" etc.

THE TREASURY SEAL

Except for freaks or errors, every piece of paper money of small size carries an imprint of the Treasury seal. It is the distinguishing mark which "validates" our currency, and in a manner of speaking is the "authority", coupled with the expression of obligation and the two signatures that make a valid contract between the United States government and the holders of its currency. The seal takes a different shape, sometimes small, sometimes large - a spiked circle plain or scalloped or perhaps a circle of rays. It may be different colors to indicate the "class" of currency it adorns. In mentioning seal color it behooves the collector to beware of and alert to - OFF-COLOR seals particularly the orange seals on legal tender notes. These have invariably been "bleached". There are of course color gradations - notably the light (yellow green) and dark (green) seals on the Federal Reserve Notes of Series 192B, 1934 and 1934A due to a variation in ink formulation. The light and dark seals create a variety for the collector. It is believed that Governor Morris designed the seal shortly before the Continental Congress (probably about 1778) and the design was approved by the Continental Congress for use by the Treasury. When the constitution was adopted the Treasury adopted the same seal with only slight changes. "The Seal of the Treasury of North America" is inscribed in Latin (Theasur. Amer. Septent Sigil) around the seal. A square for rectitude, a key for safety, and a set of scales for equality are distinguishable features on the seal. A modern version with inscription in English and removal of some of the heraldry was approved and first appeared on the $100.00 U.S. Note Series in 1966.

THE NEW TREASURY SEAL

After nearly two centuries of doing business with a seal whose Latin wording translates as "Seal of the Treasury of North America", the Treasury Department has a new one reading, in plain English, "The Department of the Treasury".

Colored lithographs of the redesigned seal, which also now bears the date "1789" to record the year of the department's creation, can be bought from its Bureau of Engraving and Printing.

Aside from the new wording and the added date, the Treasury Seal remains relatively unchanged, its arms depicting balance scales, a key and a chevron with 13 stars. Since it was used by the Board of Treasury under the Articles of Confederation, the basic design antedates the Federal Government itself.

OLD SEAL   **NEW SEAL**

In 1778 the Continental Congress named John Witherspoon, Gouverneur Morris and Richard Henry Lee to design seals for the Treasury and the Navy. The committee reported on a design for the Navy the following year but there is no recrod of a report about one for the Treasury.

The Treasury considers that the actual creator of its seal probably was Francis Hopkinson, who is known to have submitted bills to the Congress in 1780 authorizing design of departmental seals, including the Board of Treasury. Although it is not certain that Hopkinson was the designer, the seal is similar to others by Him. Also obscured by the absence of historical proof is the reason for original wording that embraced all North America.

Treasury Order No. 212 dated January 29, 1968 and signed by Henry H. Fowler officially approved the new Treasury seal.

The design, described in heraldic terms follows:

Arms: Or, a chevron azure between in chief a pair of balanced scales and in base key ward downward to dexter, both azure, with 13 mullets argent on the chevon. The arms displayed upon a circular background of American blue. Within a legend ring surrounding the arms and circumscribed by two concentric white rings appears the inscription The Department of the Treasury in white capital letters of Cheltenham Bold font. Also, within the legend ring, directly below the base of the shield appears the date 1789 in white numerals of Cheltenham Bold font.

THE GREAT SEAL OF THE UNITED STATES

Series 1935 $1.00 silver certificates are the first to carry both the obverse and reverse of the Great Seal. The positioning of the two sides of the seal as incorporated in the original design was the opposite to that actually adopted. The Great Seal was adopted in 1782 - even before the adoption of our Constitution. On the front is depicted an American eagle breasted by a shield with our national colors. The bird holds in his right talon an olive branch, symbolic of peace, of 13 leaves and 13 berries. In the left talon is a bundle of 13 arrows signifying the original colonies fight for freedom. A ribbon flying from the beak carries the motto "E Pluribus Unum" which is translated "One out of many", a reference to the unity of the 13 colonies.

Over the eagle's head is a constellation of 13 five-point stars surrounded by a wreath of clouds. The reverse of the seal is also rich in symbolism. The pyramid is representative of permanence and strength. At its base in Roman numerals appears "1776," the year of the Declaration of Independence. The structure's unfinished condition denotes that there was still work to be done to form a more perfect government and signifies the expectation that new States would be added to the Union. The eye in the triangular glory represents an all-seeing Deity and with the motto "Anuit Coeptis" alludes to the many signal interpositions of Divine Providence in the forming of our Government. The motto is translated "He (God) has favored our undertakings." "Novus Ordo Seclorum" is translated as "A new order of the ages" and in the words of the designers of the seal, signifies "the beginning of the New American Era."

THE FEDERAL RESERVE SYSTEM

President Woodrow Wilson signed the Federal Reserve Act establishing the Federal Reserve System on December 23, 1913. The original purposes were to give the country an elastic currency, provide facilities for discounting commercial paper and to improve the supervision of banking.

The Federal Reserve System combines public and private participation to serve the public welfare efficiently. Functions of the Federal Reserve are carried on through twelve Reserve Banks and their twenty-four branches and through central coordination by the Board of Governors in Washington, D.C. This unique banking mechanism brings together a wide diversity of knowledge and experience.

In order that the Federal Reserve might effectively serve the large area and diverse resources of the country, the Federal Reserve Act divided the country into twelve districts. Boundaries of the Federal Reserve Districts do not follow state lines — in many instances part of a state is in one district and the other part of the state in a different district.

Each District has a Federal Reserve Bank, and most of the Banks have branches. Districts and branches are:

District	Symbol	Bank
BOSTON	A	600 Atlantic Avenue, Boston, Massachusetts 02106 — (617) 973-3800
NEW YORK	B	33 Liberty Street (Federal Reserve P.O. Station), New York, New York 10045 (212) 791-5823 (Telephone 24 hours a day, including Saturday & Sunday)
Buffalo Branch		160 Delaware Avenue (P.O. Box 961), Buffalo, New York 14240 — (716) 849-5046
PHILADELPHIA	C	100 North Sixth Street (P.O. Box 90), Philadelphia, Pennsylvania 19105 (215) 574-6580

District	Symbol	Bank
CLEVELAND	D	1455 East Sixth Street (P.O. Box 6387), Cleveland, Ohio 44101 — (216) 241-2800
Cincinnati Branch		150 East Fourth Street (P.O. Box 999), Cincinnati, Ohio 45201 — (513) 721-4787 ext. 333
Pittsburgh Branch		717 Grant Street (P.O. Box 867), Pittsburgh, Pennsylvania 15230 — (412) 261-7864
RICHMOND	E	701 East Byrd Street (P.O. Box 27622), Richmond, Virginia 23261 — (804) 643-1250
Baltimore Branch		114-120 East Lexington Street (P.O. Box 1378), Baltimore, Maryland 21203 — (301) 539-6552
Charlotte Branch		401 South Tryon Street (P.O. Box 30248), Charlotte, North Carolina 28230 — (704) 373-0200
ATLANTA	F	104 Marietta Street, N.W. Atlanta, Georgia 30303 — (404) 586-8657
Birmingham Branch		1801 Fifth Avenue, North (P.O. Box 10447), Birmingham, Alabama 35202 (205) 252-3141 ext. 215
Jacksonville Branch		515 Julia Street, Jacksonville, Florida 32231 — (904) 354-8211 ext. 211
Miami Branch		3770 S.W. 8th Street, Coral Gables, Florida 33134 (P.O. Box 847, Miami, Florida 33152) (305) 448-5732
Nashville Branch		301 Eighth Avenue, North Nashville, Tennessee 37203 — (615) 259-4006
New Orleans Branch		525 St. Charles Avenue (P.O. Box 61630), New Orleans, Louisiana 70161 (504) 586-1505 ext. 230, 240, 242
CHICAGO	G	230 South LaSalle Street (P.O. Box 834), Chicago, Illinois 60690 — (312) 786-1110 (Telephone 24 hours a day, including Saturday & Sunday)
Detroit Branch		160 Fort Street, West (P.O. Box 1059), Detroit, Michigan 48231 (313) 961-6880 ext. 372, 373
ST. LOUIS	H	411 Locust Street (P.O. Box 442), St. Louis, Missouri 63166 — (314) 444-8444
Little Rock Branch		325 West Capitol Avenue (P.O. Box 1261), Little Rock, Arkansas 72203 (501) 372-5451 ext. 270
Louisville Branch		410 South Fifth Street (P.O. Box 899), Louisville, Kentucky 40201 (502) 587-7351 ext. 237, 301
Memphis Branch		200 North Main Street (P.O. Box 407), Memphis, Tennessee 38101 — (800) 238-5293 ext. 225
MINNEAPOLIS	I	250 Marquette Avenue, Minneapolis, Minnesota 55480 — (612) 340-2051
Helena Branch		400 North Park Avenue, Helena, Montana 59601 — (406) 442-3860
KANSAS CITY	J	925 Grand Avenue (Federal Reserve Station), Kansas City, Missouri 64198 — (816) 881-2783
Denver Branch		1020 16th Street (P.O. Box 5228, Terminal Annex), Denver, Colorado 80217 (303) 292-4020
Oklahoma City Branch		226 Northwest Third Street (P.O. Box 25129), Oklahoma City, Oklahoma 73125 (405) 235-1721 ext. 182
Omaha Branch		102 South Seventeenth Street, Omaha, Nebraska 68102 (402) 341-3610 ext. 242
DALLAS	K	400 South Akard Street (Station K), Dallas, Texas 75222 (214) 651-6177
El Paso Branch		301 East Main Street (P.O. Box 100), El Paso, Texas 79999 (915) 544-4730 ext. 57
Houston Branch		1701 San Jacinto Street (P.O. Box 2578), Houston, Texas 77001 (713) 659-4433 ext 19, 74, 75, 76
San Antonio Branch		126 East Nueva Street (P.O. Box 1471), San Antonio, Texas 78295 (512) 224-2141 ext. 61, 66
SAN FRANCISCO	L	400 Sansome Street (P.O. Box 7702), San Francisco, California 94120 (415) 392-6639
Los Angeles Branch		409 West Olympic Boulevard (P.O. Box 2077, Terminal Annex), Los Angeles, California 90051 (213) 683-8563
Portland Branch		915 S.W. Stark Street (P.O. Box 3436), Portland, Oregon 97208 — (503) 228-7584
Salt Lake City Branch		120 South State Street (P.O. Box 30780), Salt Lake City, Utah 84127 — (801) 355-3131 ext. 251, 270
Seattle Branch		1015 Second Avenue (P.O. Box 3567), Seattle, Washington 98124 — (206) 442-1650

Board of Governors - (of the Federal Reserve System) 20th St. & Constitution Ave., Washington, D.C. 20551.

Each of the twelve Federal Reserve Banks is a corporation organized and operated for public service. The Federal Reserve Banks differ from privately managed banks in that profits are not the object of their operations and in that their shareholders - the members of the Federal Reserve System - do not have proprietorship rights, power, and privileges that customarily belong to the stockholders of privately managed corporations.

The provisions of the law for the selection of Reserve Bank Directors and the management of the Reserve Banks indicate the public nature of these Banks. Each Federal Reserve Bank has nine directors. Three of them are known as Class A directors, three as Class B directors, and three as Class C directors. Directors in Class A and Class B are elected by member banks, one Class A and one Class B director are elected by small banks, one Class A and one Class B director are elected by the banks of medium size, and one Class A and one Class B director by large banks. The three Class A directors must be bankers, the three Class B directors must be actively engaged in the district in commerce, agriculture or some other industrial pursuit and must not be officers, directors, or employees of any bank. The three Class C directors are designated by the Board of Governors of the Federal Reserve System. They must not be officers, directors, employees, or stockholders of any bank. One of them is designated by the Board of Governors as chairman of the Reserve Bank's board of directors and one as deputy chairman. The Chairman, by law, is designated Federal Reserve Agent and has special responsibilities on behalf of the Board of Governors in Washington. Thus, a majority of each Federal Reserve Bank's directors are not bankers. The directors are responsible for the conduct of the business of the Reserve Bank in the public interest, subject to the Board of Governors. The directors appoint the Reserve Bank officers, but the law requires that their choice of president and first vice president, whose terms are for five years, be approved by the Board of Governors. Each branch also has its own board of directors, a majority are selected by the Reserve Bank; the remainder by the Board of Governors.

Board of Governors - consists of seven Presidential appointees who must be confirmed by the Senate. Their terms are for fourteen years and their terms are so arranged that one expires every two years. No two members of the Board may come from the same District. The Board supervises the operations of the Federal Reserve System, issues regulations that interpret and apply the provisions of law relating to Reserve Bank operations and directs Reserve Bank operations and Reserve Bank activities in examination and supervision of banks. The Board approves the budget for the Reserve Banks, approves the salaries of all officers and employees of the Reserve Banks and Branches, and approves such expenditures as those of construction or major alteration of bank buildings.

Each Federal Reserve Bank and branch is examined at least once a year by the Board's field examiners, who determine the financial condition of the Bank and compliance with the laws and regulations. The examination includes a comprehensive review of the expenditures to insure that they are properly controlled and appropriate for a Reserve Bank. It is customary to have representatives of a public accounting firm observe the examination to provide an outside evaluation of the adequacy and effectiveness of the examination procedures.

Operations of each Reserve Bank are audited on a year-round basis by the Bank's internal audit staff under the direction of a resident General Auditor. He is responsible to the Bank's board of directors through its chairman and its audit committee. Each year the Board's examiners review the internal audit programs at all of the Banks to insure that the coverage is adequate and the procedures effective. The Board represents the Federal Reserve System in most of its relations with the executive departments of the Government and with congressional committees. It is required to exercise special supervision over foreign contacts and international operations of Reserve Banks. The Board submits an annual report to Congress and publishes a weekly statement of the assets and liabilities of the Federal Reserve Banks. Expenses incurred by the Board in carrying out its duties are paid out of assessments upon the Reserve Banks, and the Boards accounts are audited each year by certified public accountants.

DESIGNS FOR FEDERAL RESERVE NOTES

Face and back designs for $5.00 through $10,000.00 Federal Reserve Notes are standard for each denomination. All series 1928 have large black letter of issuing district in black Federal Reserve seal to left of portrait, with green Treasury seal at right imposed over the denomination spelled out i.e. FIVE, TEN, TWENTY, etc. The letter in the seal changed to the number of the issuing district for series 1928B for the $5.00, $10.00 and $20.00 and for series 1928A for the $50.00 and $100.00. All other denominations continued the letter in the seal.

DENOMINATION	PORTRAIT	BACK DESIGN
1.00	Washington	Reverse and obverse of Great Seal
2.00	Jefferson	Signing of the Declaration of Independence
5.00	Lincoln	Lincoln Memorial
10.00	Hamilton	U.S. Treasury Building
20.00	Jackson	White House
50.00	Grant	U.S. Capitol
100.00	Franklin	Inependence Hall
500.00	McKinley	500 above FIVE HUNDRED DOLLARS
1,000.00	Cleveland	ONE THOUSAND DOLLARS
5,000.00	Madison	5000 above FIVE THOUSAND
10,000.00	Chase	TEN THOUSAND DOLLARS imposed on 10,000

Series 1934 through Series 1934D is similar to the 1928 series except that $5.00 through $100.00 have issuing bank number in the seal. Face and back check numbers were doubled in size for series 1934A and later issues. The word "THE" was dropped from the Federal Reserve seal for all denominations printed for series 1934B and later. A new design, adding a balcony to the White House and enlarging the shrubbery was adopted for the $20.00 note series 1934C, both old and new designs appear on series 1934C.

The series 1934 and 1934A $1,000.00 note has the series date in lower left and upper right corners.

Series 1950 through 1950E has smaller Federal Reserve and Treasury seals. Series date removed from upper left and the word "of" omitted in series date at lower right.

Series 1963 to date similar to the 1950 series, the motto IN GOD WE TRUST was added to the back design on the $5.00, $10.00 and $20.00 for series 1963 and to the $50.00 and $100.00 notes for series 1963A.

The new Treasury seal was used on all Federal Reserve Notes series 1969 and later.

AFRICA AND HAWAII SERIES

United States Silver Certificates printed with the Treasury seal in yellow, rather than the usual blue, were used in the initial stages of America's World War II military operations in North Africa and Sicily. The distinctive seal was adopted to facilitate isolation of the currency in event that military reverses caused any substantial amounts to fall into enemy hands. Denominations issued were $1, 5, and $10. Circulation of the yellow seal currency was confined for some time to the military zones of operation, but subsequently restrictions against its circulation in the United States were removed. Except for the yellow seal it is identical with other United States money of the same type.

On Dec. 7, 1941 a Japanese task force built around six aircraft carriers launched a surprise attack against the United States Pacific Fleet at Pearl Harbor, Hawaii, that virtually paralyzed the United States military forces in that area. A specially marked U.S. currency was introduced into Hawaii in July, 1942, as an economic defense against a possible Japanese occupation. The notes were overprinted HAWAII horizontally on the back and vertically at each end on the face to facilitate their demonetization in the event they fell into enemy hands. Only the overprinted notes were allowable in Hawaii after Aug. 15, 1942, except in rare instances approved by the Governor of Hawaii. Notes utilized for this purpose were the $1.00 Silver Certificate Series 1935A and the San Francisco Federal Reserve notes of $5.00 Series 1934 and 1934A, the $10.00 Series 1934A and the $20.00 Series 1934 and 1934A. All of the Hawaii overprinted currency carried brown seals and serial numbers and the Julian-Morgenthau signatures. The prohibition of unmarked currency in Hawaii remained in effect until Oct. 21, 1944.

FANCY FACTS AND FICTION

Facts: Notes are 2.61 by 6.14 long. Laid end to end there would be approximately 11,900 notes per mile. Notes are .0043 inches thick, stacked there would be 233 notes per inch. 490 notes would weigh one pound, one million notes would be about a ton and would occupy about 42 cubic feet. The Bureau uses about 3,500 tons of paper and about 1,000 tons of ink each year.

Fiction: The government is considering using different colored notes — false. The government is considering Braille notes — false. The government is considering "flat" printing for the backs of our currency — true. There are no "branch" printing plants — true. The government is secretly printing new (designs) notes and will recall all current notes in order to trap tax dodgers and criminals — false. The government is considering discontinuance of notes higher than $100.00 — true, this has already been accomplished.

HOW PAPER MONEY ENTERS CIRCULATION

The distribution of paper currency is made through the Federal Reserve banks and their branches.

Member banks of the Federal Reserve System carry their reserve accounts with the Federal Reserve bank of their district. When member banks need additional currency, they authorize the Federal Reserve bank to charge their reserve account and ship the currency. The Federal Reserve banks will ship on such requests such currency as is required. Usually, nonmember banks procure their currency through a correspondent member bank located in the same city with the Fderal Reserve Bank, or by arrangement whereby the currency is shipped direct to the nonmember bank with reserve account of the correspondent bank being charged for the shipment.

DESTRUCTION OF UNFIT CURRENCY

When paper currency becomes worn and no longer fit for general use, it is withdrawn from circulation, destroyed, and replaced by new notes. The worn out notes are destroyed by incineration or pulverization. The destruction process is not complete until the notes have been reduced to an unidentifiable residue so that no recovery is possible of the notes or of the distinctive paper on which they are printed. There is a reliable report that a test was conducted to utilize the pulverized paper in the manufacture of wall board, however no results of this test have been announced. Before being destroyed the currency is verified as to genuineness, kind, value, and number of pieces. One dollar bills make up the bulk of the currency which is retired because of unfitness. One dollar bills normally last about 18 months and almost 2 billion of them are in circulation. Higher-denomination bills last much longer.

Currencies in all denominations below $500 that are no longer fit for use are verified and destroyed at Federal Reserve banks and branches throughout the country, and by the United States Treasurer's Office, under procedures prescribed by the Department of the Treasury. Federal Reserve notes in denominations of $500 and above are canceled with distinctive perforations and cut in half lengthwise. The lower halves are shipped to the Department of the Treasury in Washington, D.C. where they are verified and destroyed. The upper halves are retained by the Federal Reserve banks and destroyed after the banks are notified by the Treasury that the lower halves have been verified.

EXCHANGE OF MUTILATED PAPER CURRENCY

Lawfully held paper money of the United States which has been mutilated will be exchanged at its face value if clearly more than one half of the original note remains. Fragments of such mutilated currency which are not clearly more than one half of the original note will be exchanged at face value only if the Treasurer of the United States is satisfied that the missing portions have been totally destroyed. His (Her) judgment shall be based on such evidence of total destruction as he deems necessary and shall be final. No relief will be granted on account of paper currency of the United States which has been totally destroyed. The public should address all correspondence regarding mutilated currency to the Office of the Treasurer of the United States, Room 1123, Main Treasury Bldg, Washington, D.C. 20220.

PREMIUMS ON CURRENCY

The Department of the Treasury NEVER pays a premium for old or rare paper money. Information regarding the current numismatic value of paper money can best be obtained from private coin and paper money dealers.

Notes issued by the Confederate States during the Civil War and the various states or state banks are not redeemable by the United States. Foreign currency is neither receivable nor redeemable by the United States.

LEGAL TENDER

Public Law 89-81, the Coinage Act of July 23, 1965, defines Legal Tender as follows:

"All coins and currencies of the United States (including Federal Reserve notes and circulating notes of Federal Reserve banks and national banking associations), regardless of when coined or issued, shall be legal tender for all debts, public and private, public charges, taxes, duties, and dues".

REGULATIONS COVERING REPRODUCTIONS OF CURRENCY AND OTHER INSTRUCTIONS

Printed reproductions of paper currency, checks, bonds, revenue stamps and securities of the United States and foreign governments are permissible for numismatic, educational, historical and newsworthy purposes.

HOW TO COLLECT

A fascinatingly beautiful and representative collection of small size currency in crisp, uncirculated condition can be formed for a very nominal investment. This collection would include six notes — one for each class described above. It might additionally include both Type 1 and Type 2 notes of National Currency. Difference between the two types is explained in the text. While all of the classes except Federal Reserve notes and United States notes are now obsolete, they are still easily obtainable from any paper money dealer for a very nominal sum. Specimens of the Federal Reserve note can be obtained from any bank at face.

No doubt by the time the novice completed his collection of the classes, he will want to obtain a specimen of the "emergency" issues (of World War II). The Hawaii overprint and the yellow seal African notes. While prices for these notes are escalating rapidly they can still be obtained at fairly nominal prices. By now the novice is surely a victim and his numismatic fever will send him scurrying after the trial and experimental issues. Most widely known (though by no means the scarcest) of the experimental issues are the red R and S pair. See main text for details.

Then, like an aerial bomb, the collector can go in a thousand different directions or have a choice of colors! He can collect by becoming a specialist in one denomination or he can collect types only. He may collect only one class — trying to obtain all the different issues of a single color seal, or he can collect signature combinations. He can collect error notes — or he can take the BIG plunge by attempting to collect Federal Reserve notes by district, either of one or of all denominations. Whatever his choice and pocketbook — he can go on and on and on.

It is quite certain the NO COMPLETE collection of small size notes exists. This is not necessarily due to a lack of finances — but to the almost incredible number of different small size notes that have been issued. In 1929, when small-sized notes were first issued, there were more than 7,700 different chartered national banks, each with it's own distinctive notes. With possibly five denominations per bank average it can readily be seen that this class alone comprises over 35,000 different notes. Another important factor, rapidly being overcome, is the complete lack of research applied to small-size notes. Such important notes as the experimentals of the $1.00 series 1928A and 1928B were unknown (mistakenly thought to be Series 1928E) prior to the publication of the first edition of this work. Varieties and "mules" were completely unpublished — and largely unknown — again — until our first edition. Many varieties and mules still undiscovered await the energetic and persevering collector who is willing to seek out the unknown.

Somewhere between the six note collection — and perfection — you are sure to find something that will appeal to and stimulate you. It is almost certain that if one exercises some discretion and patience, purchasing only nice notes at reasonable prices — he will — in a fairly short time be amazed at the price his collection will bring in a readily available market.

TYPE COLLECTION

A single note of each DESIGN with one demonination forms a type collection. Of course type collecting can be extended to other denominations. A prize-winning collection might be formed by obtaining all types of $1.00 silver certificates for example — or possibly the $5.00 Federal Reserve notes — both of which now have perhaps less than 10 types for either issue. Varieties and mules may be added for completeness.

FANCY NUMBERS

Palindromes — or radar — notes are notes on which the serial number reads the same backwards or forwards, without regard to prefix or suffix letters. In addition to these, many collectors like "sequence" notes — with serial numbers like 01 234 567 or inverse sequence such as 98 765 432 etc. Repeaters, such as 12 12 12 12 or 2222 3333 are very popular. Perhaps the most outstanding of the fancy numbers are those which have all eight digits the same, such as 11 111 111 or 44 444 444 etc.

LOW NUMBERS

Serial numbers under 9999 are generally considered low numbers — with serial number 00 000 001 of course being perfection. Today, most collectors are quite happy to find a note starting wth four zeroes, and delighted to find one with 5, 6 or 7 zeroes. Naturally the notes rise in price with the number of zeroes at the beginning.

SPECIAL NUMBERS

One collector has spent years searching for a note with serial number 07 231 938 — which happens to represent his birth date — July 23, 1938! Another collector is looking for his army serial number — while others seek their membership number in various organizations or societies. This type of collection is NOT recommended unless you are very YOUNG or very PATIENT — or both.

BLOCK COLLECTING

The DADDY of them all! And by far the most challenging [and seemingly impossible] of all. The "term" BLOCK applies to the prefix and suffix letters of serial number. ONE note is One block — and each different combination of either prefix or suffix denotes a different block. In some cases, either the prefix or suffix is replaced by an asterisk — but this only adds another block to the series. A note with serial number A 00 000 100 A would be called block AA — while a note with serial number G 00 000 100 B would be called block GB. There are well over 700 block letters known and the issue of the $1.00 Federal Reserve Note is rapidly increasing this number. Actually the exact number of "blocks" is not known since early Bureau records are known to be inaccurate and there is every reason to believe that several blocks are as yet undiscovered. See text for potential new discoveries.

VARIETY COLLECTORS

And there are many — enjoy the constant search of variations in scroll, plate length, height, size of type on check numbers or position letters, marginal differences of the printed portions, and similar varieties. Most widely known of the varieties are the wide and narrow margin notes and the mules.

GROUP COLLECTING

With the introduction of new, automatic equipment in the Bureau for doing the THIRD PRINTING (overprint of district bank seals and serial numbers) — called COPE — which stands for Currency Overprinting and Processing Equipment — a vast new expansion has intrigued the collector. First of the COPE notes were issued in Series 1969B — with serial numbers between B 31 360 001 B and B 37 760 000 B. Because many collectors DID NOT realize the importance of the notes printed on CONVENTIONAL equipment — with serial numbers BEFORE AND AFTER (and later in between) the COPE groups — the notes came and went through the banks — and today are as scarce as that proverbial "hen's tooth"! In addition — even those who realized the importance of the various groups have found it impossible to locate even circulated specimens of all groups. Several groups in particular seem almost impossible. In the use of the COPE equipment it is customary to run UP to production unit 156 (each unit represents 20,000 sheets of 32 subjects) which takes the serial number up to 99 840 000. Because the 157th production unit prints one quarter of the sheet with regular (alphabetic suffix) notes and three quarters with star suffix, it can readily be seen that the 157th production unit which until now has been done on conventional equipment, will produce only 160,000 notes. Searching for even one specimen of this group (serial number 99 840 001 thru 99 999 999) has so far proven almost hopeless. Even the most particular collectors are delighted to find even ONE CIRCULATED piece in this group. The result is that prices for NEW, current notes in certain groups is

FANTASTIC! For a real shock, consult the main body of the text for price estimates of the $1.00 Federal Reserve Notes, Series of 1969C and 1969D. Prices promise to get higher!

DATING AND NUMBERING OUR CURRENCY

Unlike coins, which are dated the year in which they are struck (with exceptions), our paper money was dated the year in which the face design of the note was approved. On taking office, Secretary of the Treasury William E. Simon changed this long standing practice (first established by Secretary Morgenthau) and directed that a NEW SERIES would be produced when a change in the Office of the Secretary of the Treasury occurred. The date is expressed as Series of (date). As an example, under the old policy, the first current size $1.00 Federal Reserve note had design approval in 1963 and hence is known as Series of 1963. When a change occurred, such as in one of the signatures, a small alphabetic was added to the date. Secretary Dillon was succeeded by Secretary Fowler, the series became Series of 1963A, Barr succeeded Fowler and the series became Series of 1963B. Under the new policy, when Simon became Secretary, all series became Series of 1974. Again, a policy change, and when the $2.00 was approved, it became Series of 1976. The policy, at least as of now, is the original policy of dating when face design is approved.

Numbering the small size notes has followed two patterns. Federal Reserve notes of all denominations have always carried the designated letter of the district as a prefix. Suffix starts a new series with A, changes to B after 100,000,000 notes (a star replaces the 100,000,000th note), changes to C after another 100,000,000 and so on down to L. For Federal Reserve notes the suffix letter goes not further in the alphabet than L, then reverts to A. The suffix letter also reverts to A on a new Series date. All other notes (and only the U.S. notes are being printed now) had a prefix letter of A and a suffix letter of A. After 100,000,000 notes the suffix letter became B, another 100,000,000 and the suffix changed to C, etc, etc down to the letter Z. (the letter O was never used because of its similarity to the number 0) After the suffix Z was completed with 100,000,000 notes, the prefix letter changed to B with suffix A, another 100,000,000 notes and suffix B mated with prefix B. This continued with prefix B through Z suffix, then prefix C through Z suffix etc.

In the 12-subject sheets the serial numbering was consecutive that is Position A would be 00 000 001, Position B would be 00 000 002, Position C would be 00 000 003 etc to Position L which bore 00 000 012.

Starting with the 18-subject sheets in 1952, notes were numbered with "skips" equal to the number of sheets in the production unit. At that time the unit was eight thousand, hence Position A would be serial 00 000 001, Position B would be 00 008 001, Position C would be 00 016 001 and so on through Position R which would be 00 144 001.

The 32-subject notes are printed in four quadrants of eight notes. The upper left quadrant sheet position letters are A1 thru H1, the lower left quadrant A2 thru H2, the upper right quadrant is A3 thru H3 and the lower right quadrant is A4 thru H4. The numbering advances 20,000 numbers per position starting with position A1 thru H1, then A2 thru H2, A3 thru H3 and finally A4 thru H4. In 1981 the production unit was changed to 40,000 sheets so that now the numbering advances 40,000 numbers between positions.

GRADING

As in coins, grading is probably the most controversial area in paper money. For some strange reason the note in question is always better in the eyes of the seller than in the eyes of the buyer. Even scrupulously honest folks, will disagree, though seldom more than one grade. I'm sure you get just as much as a laugh from the ad that reads — such-and-such a note CRISP UNCIRCULATED except has a few wrinkles or maybe a "minor tear" — or one corner missing — etc. I would also hope that when you finish laughing — you avoid doing business with such advertisers. What he is really saying is that he had a "dog" — and he'd like to sell it at an unbelievable price. I'd suggest you avoid such advertisers!

We believe the following criteria will enable you to properly and accurately grade any note:

Crisp Uncirculated — A new bill, never used, clean and crisp. Keep in mind that some notes in certain series were NOT clean and crisp when printed. The 1935A $1.00 silver certificate is a good example of this — many of the 1935 have a dirty look to the paper, some are quite "limp" — and were so when originally issued. (CU)

Extremely Fine-About Uncirculated — Note is still crisp but may show minor wrinkles or few dirt specks. NO heavy folds or creases. No stains or severe dirty spots. (EF-AU)

Very Fine — Shows some use, but still has some crispness. May have a few heavy folds but no creases that break the paper. Must have a uniformly nice appearance. (VF)

Very Good-Fine — Shows circulation, may have heavy folds or possibly few creases that break the paper. May have minor stains. (VG-F)

Good — Entire note is there but may have minor tear. No crispness, may be dirty, stained, or have ink marking in field. Generally described as "average circulated". (G)

Below these grades are fair and poor. Generally considered uncollectible except in the rarest notes.

VALUATIONS

Man has not yet devised a way to overcome the basic law of supply and demand. In addition to this basic law, there are many other factors that govern the value of collectible notes, so many in fact that the accurate pricing of some notes is nearly impossible. The rarity of certain blocks is still questionable. The future will almost certainly bring to light other copies of some notes now considered unique [only one specimen known]. It is hoped that with the publication of this catalog, many collectors will note a "prize" in their own collections which might otherwise go unknown. It is sincerely hoped that a finder will also report such notes so that they may be included in future editions of this work. There is no question that if quantities of any presently scarce or rare notes appear, the price will drop. You will observe many price drops herein as well as many price increases consistent with the continued lack of supply and market conditions. We have attempted to price the various block letters in each series by what has been learned of their rarity or scarcity, determined over a period of 40 years, examination and analysis of auction and conventional sales and the kind assistance of dealers and collectors throughout the world.

COUNTERFEIT DETECTION

In 1977-1978 secret experiments were conducted with the intent to put an "identifier" — possibly a magnetic fiber — into the currency paper. Although the tests proved successful, approval for its use was not forthcoming and the process was not put into practice.

In testimony before the Appropriations Committee of the House in 1978, Bureau Director Seymour Berry had this conversation with Rep. Steed:

Mr. Berry: This committee is aware, I believe, that we are planning to put an identifier in our currency. We call it a signature. This will be invisible to the naked eye; it will be machine readable, at very, very high speeds, and it will be compatible with the currency handling systems that are being installed in the various Federal Reserve banks. I have been given to understand that recently the Board of Governors of the Federal Reserve System has approved the procurement of the equipment that will be required to implant that signature. The acquisition of the equipment will be funded by the Federal Reserve System.

Mr. Steed: What is the situation about the signature? Is the signature that is being put into the currency going to be kept a secret process?

Mr. Berry: Yes. I might elaborate on that a bit.

We implanted this signature into a dollar bill and sent it to the Bureau of Standards for analysis. It took them four months before they could define an ingredient, and defining an ingredient in itself means nothing, because you must have the technology to reproduce it. We were favorably impressed with the amount of time it took them to, so to speak, break the code, which was rather a simple one since we used only one ingredient and not a combination.

Mr. Steed: Will this signature also lend itself to be identifiable in the cash registers of the merchants of the country?

Mr. Berry: It could be.

I have seen a little device about the size of a calculator with all sorts of white buttons, and if you put a treated note on that, it lights up while an untreated note does not. There are many capabilities for this type of system.

Mr. Steed: It wouldn't necessarily mean that every bill would have to be treated that way, but anytime a bank or any place handling a lot of currency had any question, the cashier, whoever, could make this test right easy and quickly then?

Mr. Berry: Yes, eventually it would get to that. I can foresee, if I were marketing this equipment, where it even could be incorporated into a cash register. As you well know, when you give a cashier a $20 bill, as a matter of practice they lay the bill on the top of the register to make sure they are making change for the right denomination. It would be just as simple to lay the bill on the device and see whether the light goes on.

Mr. Steed: You ought to patent that idea.

Mr. Berry: I think someone else already has that in mind, Mr. Chairman.

The last subject I would like to touch on, in my informal remarks, is our continuing constructive —

Mr. Steed: Pardon me, one further thing: When you start this, how long do you think it will be before the existing currency will have been replaced by the signature-type currency?

Mr. Berry: It is very difficult to chart the flow of low denomination currency, and the higher denominations have circulation lives of up to 22 years for $100 bills. I am not certain at this point whether all denominations will be treated this way at the outset. We are planning, in conjunction with this treatment, to identify the currency being treated by a new series, perhaps a different colored seal, or something of that nature. Beyond that, I cannot respond specifically to your question, Mr. Chairman.

Mr. Steed: You see no insurmountable obstacles on the transfer?

Mr. Berry: No. I think we will be the only nation in the world doing this.

Mr. Steed: Well, I think we are close to a time when counterfeiters ought to start thinking of another way of making a living.

Mr. Berry: Hopefully.

WIDE AND NARROW MARGINS

Many collectors, and some dealers as well, have never been able to understand the term "wide" or "narrow" margin when applied to the 1935D $1.00 silver certificate. The difference is quite limited and difficult to understand unless both notes are available for comparison. The "green" border below the large printed words ONE DOLLAR at the bottom of the back of the note is the identifying area. If this strip is thin, it is referred to as a "narrow" margin. If it is thick, it is called a "wide" margin. We believe the photograph below will give a clear picture of the difference.

The wide and narrow backs on the $5.00 1928F U.S. Notes and the $5.00 1934D silver certificates can be distinguished by the small circle on the lower right corner of the back of the bill. A careful examination of the illustration shown on next page will show three double lines in the right half of the circle of the wide back. The narrow back has only two double lines.

The wide and narrow backs on the $10.00 1934D silver certificates are distinguished by the ribbon through figure 10 in the bottom right corner of the back of the note. If there is an area of green between the end of the ribbon and the white margin at the edge of the note, it is a wide back. If this ribbon extends completely to the printed edge of the note, it is a narrow back. The illustration on the next page shows the difference.

$1.00 Narrow and Wide

Tom DeLorey and Ed Neuce first reported the difference in number of "chevrons" on the $1.00 1935D wide and narrow backs.

Wide

Narrow

$5.00 Wide, Narrow, Wide II

$10.00 Wide

$10.00 Narrow

BIBLIOGRAPHY

AUTHOR	TITLE
Affleck, C.J. and Douglas, B.M.	Confederate Bonds and Certificates
A.N.A. Numismatist June 1926	Signers of the Continental Currency
Blake, George H.	United States Paper Money
Babin, Gregory and Leonard L.	Presidential Candidates
Butler, George B.	Suppression of small bills
Bradbeer, W.W.	Confederate and South States Currency
Breck, Samuel	Historical Sketch, Continental Paper Money
Bieciuk, H and Corbin, H.G.	Texas Confederate County Notes and Private Sript
Bowen, Harold L.	State Bank Notes of Michigan
Boggs, Winthrop S.	Ten Decades Ago (1840-1850)
Courtney, W.A.	How it Was Done (Story of Clearing House Script)
Carothers, Neil	Fractional Currency
Chase, P.H.	Confederate Treasury Notes
Cornely, R.W. and Murphy, Claude Jr.	Georgia Obsolete Currency
Criswell, Grover C. Jr.	North American Currency
Criswell, Grover C. Jr.	Southern States Currency
Criswell, Grover C. Jr. and Clarence L.	Criswell's Currency Series
Crofoot, Herman K.	Francis E. Spinner
Curto, James J.	Michigan Depression Script of the 1930's
Davis, R.E.	Early Illinois Paper Money
Dillistin, William H.	Historical Directory of the Banks of the State of New York
Dillistin, William H.	Bank Note Reporters and Counterfeit Detectors
Dillistin, William H.	A Descriptive History of National Bank Notes
Dillistin, William H.	National Bank Notes in the Early Years
Donlon, William P.	United States Small Size Paper Money
Friedberg, Robert	Paper Money of the United States
Fuller, Claud E.	Confederate Currency and Stamps
Gettys, Loyd	Portraits on the Two Dollar Issues of the United States Paper Money, Demand Notes
Grant, Bushnell & Co.	The National Counterfeit Detector
Gresham, Otto	The Greenbacks That Won the Civil and World Wars
Grinnell, Albert A.	U.S. Paper Money from a Collector's Viewpoint
Hammer, T.R.	Notes on the Fractional Currency Shield
Hammer, T.R.	Paper Money Oddities
Hammer, T.R.	First Gold Notes of America
Harper's Magazine 1863	Continental Paper Money
Hessler, Gene	The Comprehensive Catalog of U.S. Paper Money
Hoober, Richard T.	Snapshots of Colonial Notes Signers
Kemm, Ted	Official Guide U.S. Paper Money
Klander, Charles	Illustrated Price List of Paper Money
Knox, J.J.	United States Notes
Kosoff, A.	72nd Auction Sale U.S. Currency and Talmadge Quarter Eagles
Kosoff, A.	Postage Currency and Fractional Currency of the U.S.
Krause, Chester L.	Standard Catalog of United States Paper Money
Lemke, Robert F.	Standard Catalog of United States Paper Money
Life Magazine (1944)	Invasion Money of Axis and Allies
Limpert, Dr. Frank A.	U.S. Postage and Fractional Currency
Limpert, Dr. Frank A.	United States Paper Money
Lloyd, Robert H.	Cataloging Your Invasion Notes
Lloyd, Robert H.	National Bank Notes, Federal Reserve Bank Notes and Federal Reserve Notes — 1928 to 1950
Marckoff, Fred P.	Collecting U.S. Currency by Signatures.
McKay, George L.	Early American Currency
Marckoff, Fred P.	A Summary Listing of Know Illinois Obsolete Notes
Mehl, B. Max	Priced Catalog of the B.W. Smith Sales
Muscalus, Dr. John A.	The Use of Banking Enterprises in the Financing of Public Education
Muscalus, Dr. John A.	Dictionary of Paper Money
Muscalus, Dr. John A.	Index of State Bank Notes that Illustrate Presidents
Muscalus, Dr. John A.	Views of Towns, Cities, Falls, and Buildings Illustrated on 1800 to 1866 Bank Paper Money
Muscalus, Dr. John A.	Index of State Bank Notes that Illustrate Characters and Events
Muscalus, Dr. John A.	Famous Paintings Introduced on Paper Money of State Banks
Muscalus, Dr. John A.	Early Business College Bank Notes
Muscalus, Dr. John A.	Bibliography of Histories of Specific Banks
Muscalus, Dr. John A.	County Script Issued in the U.S.
Muscalus, Dr. John A.	Paper Money of Early Educational Institutions and Organizations
Moore, Waldo C.	The Buffalo Hunt
Morgenthau, Henry Jr.	The Background of our Invasion Currency
Musser, Dwight L.	World Paper Money Collectors Guide
Musser, Dwight L.	Foreign Paper Money Journal
Musser, D. L. and Sten, G.J.	World Coin and Currency Handbook
Phillips, Henry Jr.	Historical Account of the Paper Currency of the American Colonies
Philpot, Wm. A. Jr.	Star Notes, The Numismatist, Sept. 1967
Raymond, Wayte	U.S. Notes, 1861 to 1923
Raymond, Wayte	Standard Paper Money Catalog
Scoot, Stamp & Coin Co.	Paper Money
Schultz, Walter F.	Checklist of Fractional Currency
Shafer, Neil	Guidebook of Modern U.S. Currency
Sheheen, Austin M.	South Carolina Obsolete Notes
Slabaugh, Arlie D.	Confederate States Paper Money
Smith, L.D.	But Don't Send Ashes
Sprinkle, Frank F.	Uncut Sheets of Obsolete Bills and Old Bank Checks
Sumner, William C.	History of American Currency
Thobe, Urban	A Study of the Fractional Currency Shield
Thomas A.O.	Money of the Republic of Texas
Valentine, D.W.	Fractional Currency of the United States
Werlich, Robert	United States, Canadian, and Confederate Paper Money
Wismer, D.C.	Descriptive List of Obsolete Paper Money of N.J.
Wismer, D.C.	Descriptive List of N.Y. Obsolete Paper Money
Wismer, D.C.	Descriptive List of Old Paper Money Issued in Ohio
Wismer, D.C.	Descriptive List of Penna. Obsolete Bank Notes.
Zerbe, Farran	Bryan Money

and

The History of the Bureau of Engraving and Printing, for sale by the Superintendent of Documents, U.S. Government Printing Office, Washington, D.C. 20402, at $7.00.

Attention
PAPER MONEY COLLECTORS

Subscribe to the Bank Note Reporter, the only monthly newspaper serving the specialized needs of the paper money collector.

Your subscription will bring you special reports on auction sales, new discoveries, new issues, upcoming events and collector organizations.

You'll enjoy articles on military currency, bonds, Confederate notes, Fractional currency, state bank notes and, of course, U.S. large and small size currency.

Historical features, plenty of photos and lots of trustworthy advertising — plus an accurate value guide — will also be at your fingertips in each 36-page issue.

Join a select group of paper money collectors who use the Bank Note Reporter for enjoyment, research and as an excellent place to buy and sell notes!

Your no-risk guarantee
If for any reason you decide to cancel your subscription, simply drop us a note before you receive your second issue and we'll refund your entire payment. After the second issue we'll refund on all undelivered issues. Try Bank Note Reporter — your risk is virtually nothing!

Bank Note Reporter is offered by Krause Publications, publishers of this Standard Handbook of Modern U.S. Paper Money, along with Numismatic News, World Coin News, Coins magazine and the popular Standard Catalog of World Paper Money.

Bank Note Reporter
Iola, WI 54990

Bank Note Reporter AM8
700 E. State St., Iola, Wisconsin 54990

Please enter my subscription as follows:

name _____

address _____

city _____

state _____ zip _____

Addresses outside the U.S., including Canada and Mexico please add $4 per year for postage and handling. Payment in U.S. funds.

( ) 1 year (12 issues) .... $ 9   ☐ New
( ) 2 years (24 issues) .... $16   ☐ Renewal
( ) 3 years (36 issues) .... $24   ☐ Extension
( ) Check enclosed ( ) MasterCard/Visa

account no. _____

expiration date mo. _____ yr. _____

signature _____

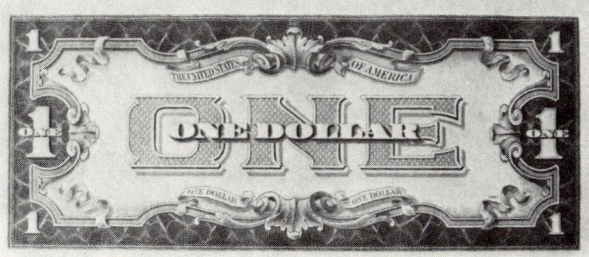

CAT. NO IL28
$1.00 UNITED STATES NOTE - LEGAL TENDER (RED SEAL) (12 subject)
SERIES 1928

SERIAL NUMBERS:
(Official Range)   A 00 000 001 A through A 01 872 012 A
Star Notes:
(Low Official)   * 00 000 001 A through * 00 007 892 A High observed)

PLATE SERIALS: Face check # 1 through #36 (exceptions #12, #31 and #33-35). NOTE: Check #12 has been seen despite Bureau records that it was not used.

SIGNATURES: Walter O. Woods, Treasurer of the United States
W.H. Woodin, Secretary of the Treasury

This series was printed in April and May 1933 but the majority were not released until the recession of 1948-49. These were then issued in Puerto Rico as an economy measure as follows:

| Nov. 1948 | 400,000 | Jan. 1949 | 500,000 | Feb. 1949 | 400,000 |
| Mar. 1949 | 420,000 | Apr. 1949 | 144,000 | | |

Puerto Rico was chosen to keep the "odd one-time" issue from causing sorting problems in the Federal Reserve Banks on the Mainland.

DESIGN: This is the only $1.00 small size note with red seal. Treasury seal is to left of portrait of Washington with large ONE in grey at right.

ESTIMATED VALUES   VG/F   CU
                        A--A   22.50   100.00
                        *--A   1000.00   3000.00

TOTAL BLOCKS KNOWN: Two

$1 SILVER CERTIFICATE, SERIES OF 1928

Obverse or face of note-
Color-Black
Title, in upper border-"SILVER CERTIFICATE"
Obligation-"This certifies that there has been deposited in the Treasury of the United States of America One Silver dollar payable to the bearer on demand".
Legend, left of portrait-On series 1928, 1928 A, 1928 B, 1928 C and 1928 D, it is, "This certificate is receivable for all public dues and when so received may be reissued".
On series 1928 E it is, "This certificate is legal tender for all debts public and private".
Portrait-Washington, with name "Washington" beneath.
Color of seal and serial number-Blue
Location of portrait-Center
Locations of serial number-Two; one near right and one near lower left corner.
Location of seal-Left of portrait, imprinted over legend.
Location of large "ONE" in Roman letters-Right of portrait
Changes in this series-

Series	Signatures	Legend
1928	H.T. Tate and A.W. Mellon	"This certificate is receivable for all public dues and when so received may be reissued".
1928 A	W.O. Woods and A.W. Mellon	"
1928 B	W.O. Woods and Ogden L. Mills	"
1928 C	W.O. Woods and W.H. Woodin	"
1928 D	W.A. Julian and W.H. Woodin	"
1928 E	W.A. Julian and Henry Morgenthau, Jr.	"This certificate is legal tender for all debts public and private".

Ornamental border with elliptical counters in the upper right and left corners each containing a figure "1", and "ONE" is in the upper part of the counter. In the lower right and left corners are pentagonal counters each containing the figure "1". At each end of the note, the upper and lower counters are joined by fancy scroll work and "ONE" is between the scroll work and the margin of the note, "ONE" appears twice in upper and lower borders. Directly below the title, "SILVER CERTIFICATE", is "THIS CERTIFIES THAT THERE HAS BEEN DEPOSITED IN THE TREASURY OF", in small lettering, with "THE UNITED STATES OF AMERICA", in large lettering, below it. This wording is a part of the obligation. In the lower border is the remainder of the obligation, "ONE SILVER DOLLAR", in large lettering, over "PAYABLE TO THE BEARER ON DEMAND", in smaller lettering. Series designation appears between the upper left corner and the portrait. Series designation with "WASHINGTON, D.C." above it, appears between the lower right corner and the portrait.

Reverse or back of note-
Color-Green
Main embellishment-Ornate "ONE"
Lathe work border. In each corner is a small figure "1" and in the center of each end of the note is a larger figure "1" with "ONE" across its face. In the center is an ornamental "ONE" with "ONE DOLLAR" across its face. "THE UNITED STATES OF AMERICA" is on a ribbon running through scroll work below the upper border, and "ONE DOLLAR" is in two places on a ribbon through scroll work above the lower border. A scroll is in the center of the border at each end.
Portrait: George Washington from a painting by Gilbert Charles Stuart. Stuart was born in Middletown, R.I. in 1755. After moving to London he lived and worked with Benjamin West (1778-1782) and soon became a fashionable portrait painter. In 1792 he returned to America and painted portraits of George Washington, Thomas Jefferson, John Adams, James Madison and many of the distinguished men of the period. The Stuart portraits of Washington, representing the subject in his later years are the most famous of both artist and sitter. One of the best is the well-known "Gibbs-Channing" portrait now in the Metropolitan Museum, New York. The portrait used on the $1.00 note was engraved by G. F. C. Smillie from the athenaeum portrait. Engraving started according to the engravers diary on 11/9/1917 and was completed on

May 8, 1918. It was first used on the $1.00 FRN Series 1918. George Frederick Cummings Smillie, portrait and picture engraver was born in New York City, Nov. 22, 1854. He was a pupil of the National Academy of Design in New York in 1871, studied under his Uncle James Smillie (of the N.A.D.) and worked as an engraver for the American Bank Note Co from 1871 to 1887. He was named manager of the Canadian Bank Note Co in 1887 remaining with that firm until 1888. He became the manager of the Homer Lee Bank Note Co. and held that position until 1894 when he was appointed principal engraver of the Bureau of Engraving and Printing. He was appointed superintendent of the Bureau's Picture engraving department in 1918. He remained with the Burea until retirement on March 31, 1922. He died in Washington, D.C. Jan. 21, 1924.

CAT. NO. IS28
$1.00 SILVER CERTIFICATE (BLUE SEAL) (12 subject)
SERIES 1928

In March 1964, Secretary of the Treasury Dillon halted the redemption of Silver Certificates in silver dollars and on June 24, 1968, redemption in silver bullion was discontinued.

SERIAL NUMBERS:
  (Low Official) A00 000 001A through L52 708 065A (High Observed)

Star Notes:
  (Low Official) *00 000 001A through *12 444 406A (High Observed)

PLATE SERIALS: Face check #2 through #1022
  Back check numbers begin with #1.

SIGNATURES: H.T. Tate, Treasurer of the United States
  A.W. Mellon, Secretary of the Treasury

DESIGN: Face design for series 1928 through 1928E has blue Treasury seal to left of portrait of Washington with ONE in grey letters to right. Back design has large ONE with ONE DOLLAR imposed.

TOTAL QUANTITY PRINTED: 638,296,908 Notes

ESTIMATED VALUES:

	VG/F	CU
A--A through G--A	6.00	15.00
H--A	10.00	25.00
I--A	75.00	150.00
J--A	100.00	150.00

	VG/F	CU
K--A	125.00	200.00
L--A	175.00	250.00
*--A	17.50	50.00

TOTAL BLOCKS KNOWN: Thirteen.

CAT. NO. IS28A
$1.00 SILVER CERTIFICATE (BLUE SEAL) (12 subject)
SERIES 1928A

SERIAL NUMBERS:
  (Low Observed) E 10 344 253 A through J 52 968 559 B (High Observed)

Star Notes:
  (Low Observed) * 08 885 503 A through * 35 790 882 A (High Observed)

PLATE SERIALS: Face check #5 through #1814

SIGNATURES: Walter O. Woods, Treasurer of the United States
  A.W. Mellon, Secretary of the Treasury

TOTAL QUANTITY PRINTED: 2,267,809,500 Notes

ESTIMATED VALUES:

	VG/F	CU
E--A	15.00	50.00
F--A	10.00	35.00
G--A through A--B	3.50	10.00
G--A through G--B	5.00	12.00
H--B	15.00	35.00
I--B	100.00	200.00
J--B	50.00	100.00
*--A	10.00	25.00

EXPERIMENTALS: X--B, Y--B, and Z--B.
TOTAL BLOCK KNOWN: Thirty-five (including experimentals).

CAT. NO IS28A and IS28B
$1.00 SILVER CERTIFICATE (BLUE SEAL) (12 subject)
SERIES 1928A and 1928B

EXPERIMENTAL ISSUE

The first major experimental group of small notes was printed in November 1932 and delivered to the Treasury for release into circulation in January and February of 1933, during the period of the $1.00 Series 1928A and 1928B. The experimental set was to determine the effect of changing the relative amounts of linen and cottem paper fibers. The X--B and Y--B groups were each printed on paper of different proportions of the rag content with the Z--B group as the control, using the distinctive paper in regular use. The special numbers assigned to this experiment are given below.

The experimentals are randomly mixed between both series 1928A and 1928B because they were serially numbered from a single number register. An estimate of quantities printed within each is not yet possible.

SERIAL NUMBERS:
  (Official Ranges) X00 000 001B through X10 728 000B
  Y00 000 001B through Y10 248 000B
  Z00 000 001B through Z10 248 000B

TOTAL QUANTITIES PRINTED:
  X--B (both series) 10,728,000 notes
  Y--B (both series) 10,248,000 notes
  Z--B (both series) 10,248,000 notes

ESTIMATED VALUES

		VG/F	CU
1928 A	X--B	$35.00	$250.00
1928 A	Y--B	35.00	150.00
1928 A	Z--B	35.00	175.00
1928 B	X--B	35.00	150.00
1928 B	Y--B	35.00	175.00
1928 B	Z--B	35.00	150.00

TOTAL BLOCKS KNOWN: Six (Three in each series)

CAT. NO IS28B
$1.00 SILVER CERTIFICATE (BLUE SEAL) (12 Subject)
SERIES 1928B

SERIAL NUMBERS:
(Low Official) V51 000 001A through J53 889 926B (High Observed)
Star Notes:
(Low Observed) *27 276 950A through *37 548 972A (High Observed)

Experimental notes were also printed in this series, and are identifiable by block letter X--B, Y--B, and Z--B as in series 1928A.

PLATE SERIALS:
Face check #2 through #567.

SIGNATURES:
Walter O. Woods, Treasurer of the United States
Ogden I. Mills, Secretary of the Treasury

TOTAL QUANTITY PRINTED:
674,597,808 Notes.

ESTIMATED VALUES:

		VG/F	CU
	V--A	$75.00	$200.00
	W--A	100.00	250.00
	X--A	50.00	100.00
	Y--A	10.00	17.50
	Z--A	7.50	15.00
A--B through	J--B	6.00	12.50
	*--A	17.50	50.00

EXPERIMENTALS:
X--B, Y--B, and Z--B
TOTAL BLOCKS KNOWN:
Nineteen (including experimentals).

CAT. NO. IS28C
$1.00 SILVER CERTIFICATE (BLUE SEAL) (12 SUBJECT)
SERIES 1928C

SERIAL NUMBERS:
(Low Official) B29 448 001B through J43 315 356B (High Observed)
Star Notes:
(Low Observed) *33 390 295A through *36 697 318A (High Observed)

PLATE SERIALS: Face check #1 through #9 (check numbers #5 and #10 were master plates and were not used.)
SIGNATURES: Walter O. Woods, Treasurer of the United States
W.H. Woodin, Secretary of the Treasury

TOTAL QUANTITY PRINTED: 5,364,348 notes.

ESTIMATED VALUES:

		VG/F	CU
	B--B	$150.00	$400.00
	C--B	250.00	750.00
D--B through	I--B	150.00	400.00
	J--B	500.00	1000.00
	*--A	500.00	1000.00

TOTAL BLOCKS KNOWN: Ten

CAT. NO IS28D
$1.00 SILVER CERTIFICATE (BLUE SEAL) (12 Subject)
SERIES 1928D

SERIAL NUMBERS:
(Low Official) D82 596 001B through J54 890 954B (High Observed)
Star Notes:

(Low Observed) *35 006 672A through *36 738 857A (High Observed)

PLATE SERIALS: Face check #1 through #49.

SIGNATURES: W.A. Julian, Treasurer of the United States
W.H. Woodin, Secretary of the Treasury

TOTAL QUANTITY PRINTED: 14,451,372 notes.

ESTIMATED VALUES:

		VG/F	CU
D--B through	J--B	$75.00	$200.00
	*--A	500.00	1000.00

TOTAL BLOCKS KNOWN: Eight

CAT. NO. IS28E
$1.00 SILVER CERTIFICATE (BLUE SEAL) (12 Subject)
SERIES 1928E

SERIAL NUMBERS:
(Official Range) F72 000 001B through J55 796 000B
Star Notes:
(Low Observed) *35 821 073A through *37 560 000A (High Official)
* 36 525 762 A (High Observed)

PLATE SERIALS: Face checks #1 through #12. Check #5 and #6 were masters.

SIGNATURES: W.A. Julian, Treasurer of the United States
Henry Morgenthau, Jr., Secretary of the Treasury

TOTAL QUANTITY PRINTED: 3,519,324 notes.

ESTIMATED VALUES:

		VG/F	CU
F--B through	J--B	$300.00	$1000.00
	*--A	2500.00	5000.00

TOTAL BLOCKS KNOWN: Six

This is the last certificate of the old type to read "This certifies that there has been deposited in the Treasury of the United States of America ONE SILVER DOLLAR payable to the bearer on demand." It is the last issue that could be definitely exchanged for a silver dollar, representing such a deposit.

CAT. NO. IS34
$1.00 SILVER CERTIFICATE (BLUE SEAL) (12 Subject)
SERIES 1934

SERIAL NUMBERS:
(Official Range) A00 000 001A through G82 176 000A
Star Notes:
(Low Official) *00 000 001A through *07 660 451A (High Observed)

PLATE SERIALS: Face check #1 through #838. Back check numbers end at #3096

SIGNATURES: W.A. Julian, Treasurer of the United States
Henry Morgenthau, Jr., Secretary of the Treasury

DESIGN: Face design for series 1934 has large blue skeletal 1 to left of portrait of Washington with blue Treasury seal at right. Back design same as 1928.

ESTIMATED VALUES:

		VG/F	CU
A--A through	G--A	$5.00	15.00
	*--A	50.00	250.00

TOTAL BLOCKS KNOWN: Eight

TREASURY DEPARTMENT
Washington

FOR IMMEDIATE RELEASE   **Press Service**
Thursday, August 15, 1935   No. 5-59

Secretary Mongenthau today announced that production of a new $1 Silver Certificate is under way at the Bureau of Engraving and Printing.

The new certificate is of the same size as currency now in circulation, but represents changes both in the method of printing signatures and in design.

The new certificate is not yet ready for issue and ample notice will be given before it is put into circulation.

The important change in the face of the new certificate deals with the method of printing signatures on the notes. The signatures of the Secretary of the Treasury and of the Treasurer of the United States, instead of being printed with the rest of the design, will be typographically overprinted later, from steel dies, when the bills are numbered and sealed. There are a number of minor changes in the design of the face.

The design of the back of the note presents for the first time, on any money issued by the United States, a representation of both the obverse and reverse of the Great Seal of the United States, first adopted in 1782, prior to the adoption of the Constitution.

The obverse of the Great Seal is the familiar American eagle with a shield, grasping an olive branch in one talon and arrows in the other talon, surmounted by thirteen stars and the Latin motto "E Pluribus Unum."

The reverse of the Great Seal, used for the first time on money, shows an unfinished pyramid, surmounted by an eye in a triangular glory. The pyramid bears in Roman numberals the year of the Declaration of Independence, 1776. Above the eye is the Latin motto, "Annuit Coeptis", rendered as "He (God) favored our undertakings." The motto at the bottom is "Novus Ordo Seclorum" and is translated as "A new order of the ages." The eye and triangular glory symbolize an all-seeing Deity. The pyramid is the symbol of strength and its unfinished condition denotes the belief of the designers of the Great Seal that there was still work to be done. Both the mottoes on the reverse of the seal are condensations of excerpts from Virgil's Aeneid.

The first committee on the Great Seal was formed on the afternoon of July 4, 1776, and consisted of Benjamin Franklin, Thomas Jefferson, and John Adams. The Great Seal as finally adopted was largely the work of Charles Thompson, Secretary of Congress, and William Barton, a private citizen of Philadelphia. The design was officially adopted on June 20, 1782, by Fundamental Law. The Great Seal was again ratified after the Constitution was adopted in 1789.

The only previous use of the reverse of the Great Seal, according to Treasury Records, was in 1882, when a centennial medal was issued by the United States mint to celebrate the 100th anniversary of the Great Seal's adoption.

The Fundamental Law which established the Great Seal includes the following inscription of the reverse:
"A Pyramid unfinished. In the zenith an Eye in a Triangle, surrounded with a Glory, proper: over the Eye these words, 'Annuit Coeptis'.
On the base of the Pyramid the numerical letters, MDCCLXXVI, and underneath, the following motto, 'Novus Ordo Seclorum'."

The explanation of the reverse design written at the time by Mr. Barton, one of the designers, is: "The pyramid on the reverse signifies strength and duration. The eye over it, with the motto 'Annuit Coeptis' (Prosper our Endeavors), alludes to the many signal interpositions of Providence in favor of the American Cause, the date underneath is that of the Declaration of Independence and the words under it signify the beginning of the new American Era, which commenced from that date."

Following is a more detailed description of the face and back designs: FACE- The face of the series 1935, $1 Silver Certificate, printed in black, is similar to the present series 1934 design, now in circulation with the following changes:

The large ruled face "One" has been removed from the note and is replaced with the words "One Dollar" in Roman lettering having a graduated ruled face with a ruled shadow approximately 1" below the top edge of the note. Below this, in black Roman lettering, is the wording "Washington, D.C." On the left of the portrait across the Gothic lettering, a shaded figure "1" is engraved, taking the place of the blue surface-printed figure "1" on the present issue. Space is provided below on either side of the portrait to permit of the printing of the signatures of both the Secretary of the Treasury and the Treasurer of the United States from steel engraved dies at the time the notes are being numbered and sealed. The Treasury Seal is reduced to ⅝" in diameter, and printed in blue above the words "Washington, D.C.", on the right side of the note. The serial numbers have been reduced in size and are printed in blue in the same positions as on the series 1934 note. The words "Series of 1935" appear farther to the left in the upper left-hand corner, and farther to the right in the lower right portion of the note.
BACK-The back is printed in green. The design comprises the obverse and reverse sides of the Great Seal of the United States as adopted by the Congress in 1782. The reverse of the Great Seal is on the left center and carries the Latin Words "Annuit Coeptis" and "Novus Ordo Seclorum". The obverser of the Great Seal in on the right center. The impressions of the obverse and reverse of the Great Seal are enclosed by a circular cycloid line pattern and ornamental acanthus leaf scroll work. Below the reverse side are the words "The Great Seal", and below the obverse are the words "of the United States". The outer portion of the note consists of the usual conventional geometrical lathe design, with the title "The United States of America" in white-face Roman letters across the top of the note in the lathe work. The words "One Dollar" in similar lettering appear in the lower panel of lathe work, having a ruled tint on their face. In each corner is a large white-faced numeral "1", and extended across this figure is the word "One" in white Roman lettering. Between the reverse and obverse of the Great Seal is the word "One" in a ruled face Roman letter having a ruled shadow. This word is approximately 1⅞" long and 11/16" in height. A small cycloid pattern is used to furnish a lacelike edging in the inner edges of the lathe work.

CAT. NO. IS35
$1.00 SILVER CERTIFICATE (BLUE SEAL) (12 Subject)
SERIES 1935

SERIAL NUMBERS:
  (Official Range) A 00 000 001 A through R 81 552 000 A. (1)
  Star Notes:
  (Low Official) * 00 000 001 A through *21 824 212 A (High Observed)
Experimental notes were printed in this series which are identifiable by block letters A--B, B--B, and C--B.

PLATE SERIALS: Face check #1 through #1391
              Back check #1 through #929

SIGNATURES: W.A. Julian, Treasurer of the United States
             Henry Morgenthau, Jr., Secretary of the Treasury

DESIGN: Face design for series 1935 through 1957B has smaller 1 in grey to left of portrait of Washington, smaller blue Treasury seal at right. Back design has large ONE shadowed in center, reverse of the Great Seal of the United States to the left, obverse of the Great Seal to right. IN GOD WE TRUST on portion of 1935G, and all 1935H, 1957, and 1957A and 1957B notes. Face and back check numbers doubled in size for series 1935A and later.

ESTIMATED VALUES:

		VG/F	CU
A--A through	M--A	$ 5.00	$ 12.50
	N--A	7.50	15.00
	P--A	15.00	40.00
Q--A and	R--A	50.00	125.00
	*--A	25.00	100.00

EXPERIMENTALS: A--B, B--B, and C--B.

TOTAL BLOCKS KNOWN: Twenty One (including experimentals).

(1) includes MULES

CAT. NO. IS35
$1.00 SILVER CERTIFICATE (BLUE SEAL) (12 Subject)
SERIES 1935 MULE

These are Series 1935 notes with the larger back check numbers (#930 or higher) and are actually Series 1935 faces on Series 1935A backs.

SERIAL NUMBERS:
  (Low Observed)
  M 81 121 635 A through R 78 692 602 A (High Observed)
  Star Notes:
  (Low Observed)
  * 21 825 275 A through * 22 243 949 A (High Observed)
ALL SERIES 1935 MULES ARE SCARCE.

ESTIMATED VALUES:

		VG/F	CU
	N--A	$100.00	$300.00
	M--A	50.00	100.00
	P--A	35.00	75.00
Q--A and	R--A	50.00	150.00
	*--A	100.00	300.00

TOTAL BLOCKS KNOWN: Six

CAT. NO. IS35
$1.00 SILVER CERTIFICATE (BLUE SEAL) (12 Subject)
SERIES 1935 EXPERIMENTALS

A paper experiment patterned after the $1.00 Series 1928A and 1928B set was again tried during the $1.00 Series 1935. In this case the printing began on March 16, 1937 on the A--B block, utilizing the distinctive paper with a special finish. The printing of this group ended April 28, 1937. Printing started again on November 26, 1937 with the B--B block using special paper. On December 1, 1937, the C--B block was begun on regular paper as the control, and both terminated together on December 10th. These were all delivered within the year 1937. The special numbers assigned to this experiment are given below.

SERIAL NUMBERS:
  (Official Ranges)
  A 00 000 001 B through A 06 180 000 B
  B 00 000 001 B through B 03 300 000 B
  C 00 000 001 B through C 03 300 000 B

TOTAL QUANTITIES PRINTED:
  A--B 6,180,000 notes
  B--B 3,300,000 notes
  C--B 3,300,000 notes

ESTIMATED VALUES:

	VG/F	CU
A--B	$15.00	$40.00
B--B	125.00	250.00
C--B	125.00	250.00

TOTAL BLOCKS KNOWN: Three

ILLUSTRATION: On Following page

CAT. NO. IS35A
$1.00 SILVER CERTIFICATE (BLUE SEAL) (12 Subject)
SERIES 1935A

SERIAL NUMBERS:
  (Official Range)
  M 07 668 001 A through D 45 624 000 D

(Low Observed)
M 82 936 477 A
Star Notes:
(Low Observed)
* 17 599 387 A through * 02 651 672 B (High Observed)

PLATE SERIALS: Face check numbers begin at #1
Back check numbers begin at #930

SIGNATURES: W.A. Julian, Treasurer of the United States
Henry Morgenthau, Jr., Secretary of the Treasury

ESTIMATED VALUES:

	VG/F	CU
M--A	$150.00	$350.00
N--A	10.00	20.00
P--A	5.00	10.00
Q--A through C--D (1)	3.00	4.50
D--D	5.00	10.00
*--A	5.00	15.00
*--B	75.00	150.00

TOTAL BLOCKS KNOWN: Sixty Nine

(1) Serial numbers 70 884 001 through 72 068 000 and 73 884 001 through 75 068 000 for block S--C were used on 1935A experimental notes.

CAT. NO. IS35A
$1.00 SILVER CERTIFICATE (BLUE SEAL) (12 Subject)
SERIES 1935A MULE

These are Series 1935A notes with the micro back check numbers (#929 or lower) and are actually Series 1935A faces on series 1935 backs.

SERIAL NUMBERS:
(Low Observed)
M 07 777 770 A through E 96 998 982 B (High Observed)
Star Notes:
(Low Observed)
* 17 140 096 A through * 37 095 331 A (High Observed)

ESTIMATED VALUES:

	VG/F	CU
M--A	$5.00	$30.00
N--A through U--A	6.00	25.00
V--A and W--A	8.00	35.00
X--A through Z--A	15.00	75.00
A--B	25.00	100.00
B--B	35.00	150.00
C--B	25.00	50.00
D--B	100.00	200.00
E--B	300.00	500.00
*--A	50.00	150.00

TOTAL BLOCKS KNOWN: Nineteen

CAT. NO. IS35A
$1.00 SILVER CERTIFICATE (YELLOW SEAL) (12 Subject)
NORTH AFRICA
SERIES 1935A

SERIAL NUMBERS:
(Official Ranges)
B 30 000 001 C through B 31 000 000 C
B 51 624 001 C through B 52 624 000 C
B 99 000 001 C through B 99 999 999 C
C 60 000 001 C through C 62 000 000 C
C 78 000 001 C through C 79 904 000 C
F 41 952 001 C through F 41 964 000 C
I 30 000 001 C through I 40 000 000 C
R 90 000 001 C through R 99 999 999 C

Star Notes:
(Low Observed)
* 68 367 175 A * 79 627 768 A (High Observed)

SIGNATURES: Same as Series 1935A

ESTIMATED VALUES:

BLOCKS	VG/F	CU
B--C	$9.00	$35.00
C--C	8.00	50.00
F--C	15.00	100.00
I--C	8.00	50.00
R--C	8.00	50.00
*--A	100.00	500.00

TOTAL BLOCKS KNOWN: Six.

CAT. NO. IS35A
$1.00 SILVER CERTIFICATE (BROWN SEAL) (12 Subject)
HAWAII
SERIES 1935A

SERIAL NUMBERS:
(Official Ranges)
Y 68 628 001 B through Y 71 628 000 B
Z 99 000 001 B through Z 99 999 999 B
A 99 000 001 C through A 99 999 999 C
C 00 000 001 C through C 07 000 000 C
F 41 964 001 C through F 41 976 000 C
L 75 996 001 C through L 78 996 000 C
P 31 992 001 C through P 37 032 000 C
S 39 996 001 C through S 54 996 000 C

38

Star Notes:
(Low Observed)
* 64 818 233 A   * 91 137 451 A (High Observed)

SIGNATURES: Same as Series 1935A.

ESTIMATED VALUES:

BLOCKS	VG/F	CU
Y--B	$10.00	$100.00
Z--B	20.00	150.00
A--C	35.00	250.00
C--C	7.00	50.00
F--C	12.50	75.00
L--C, P--C, S--C	7.00	50.00
*--A	100.00	500.00

TOTAL BLOCKS KNOWN: Nine.

CAT. NO. IS35A
$1.00 SILVER CERTIFICATE (BLUE SEAL) (12 Subject)
SERIES 1935A
EXPERIMENTAL R AND S

The most recent and best known of the experimental printings were the "R" and "S" overprint issues onto a portion of the S-C block of Series 1935A. In this case, the red "R" was overprinted on the regular distinctive paper and the red "S" on a special paper. They were delivered June 20, 1944 and issued into circulation to test their comparative durabilities. No conclusive results were determined from the trial issue. (Bureau of Printing and Engraving records show that 12,000 star notes of each of "R" and "S" were printed).
The special numbers assigned to this experiment are given below.

SERIAL NUMBERS:
(Official Ranges)
"R" S 70 884 001 C through S 72 068 000 C
"S" S 73 884 001 C through S 75 068 000 C

Star Notes:
(Low Observed)
"R" * 91 177 120 A through * 91 186 006 A (High Observed)
"S" * 91 188 395 A through * 91 191 519 A (High Observed)

TOTAL QUANTITIES PRINTED:
"R" 1,184,000 notes
"S" 1,184,000 notes

ESTIMATED VALUES:

		VG/F	CU
"R" note:			
	S--C	$25.00	$250.00
	*--A	1,000	5,000.00
"S" note:			
	S--C	25.00	200.00
	*--A	1,000	5,000.00

TOTAL BLOCKS KNOWN: Four.

CAT. NO. IS35A
$1.00 SILVER CERTIFICATE (BLUE SEAL) (12 Subject)
SERIES 1935A TRIAL NOTE

SERIAL NUMBERS:
(Low observed) K20 895 155 C and K 20 895 156 C (High Observed)

PLATE SERIAL: Back check number 470.

TOTAL QUANTITY PRINTED: 2,402,700 notes.

ESTIMATED VALUE: K--C Rare (only three known. One of these is damaged)

TOTAL BLOCKS KNOWN: One

CAT. NO. IS35B
$1.00 SILVER CERTIFICATE (BLUE SEAL) (12 Subject)
SERIES 1935B

SERIAL NUMBERS:
(Official Range) C 93 384 001 D through M 00 648 000 D
Star notes:
(Low Observed) * 02 749 841 B through * 12 668 468 (High Observed)

SIGNATURES: W.A. Julian, Treasurer of the United States
Fred M. Vinson, Secretary of the Treasury

ESTIMATED VALUES:

	VG/F	CU
C--D	$35.00	$75.00
D--D thru K--D	5.00	10.00
L--D	7.50	15.00
M--D	250.00	500.00
*--B	12.50	50.00

TOTAL BLOCKS KNOWN: Twelve.

CAT. NO. IS35C
$1.00 SILVER CERTIFICATE (BLUE SEAL) (12 Subject)
SERIES 1935C

SERIAL NUMBERS:
(Low Official) K 99 996 001 D through U 86 153 076 E (High Observed)
Star Notes:
(Low Observed) * 12 972 850 B through * 49 474 913 B (High Observed)

SIGNATURES: W.A. Julian, Treasurer of the United States
John W. Snyder, Secretary of the Treasury

ESTIMATED VALUES:

	VG/F	CU
K--D	$25.00	$60.00
L--D through S--E	2.50	5.00
T--E	4.00	7.00
U--E	5.00	10.00
*--B	5.00	15.00

TOTAL BLOCKS KNOWN: Thirty six.

CAT. NO. IS35D
$1.00 SILVER CERTIFICATE (BLUE SEAL) (12 Subject)
SERIES 1935D WIDE

SERIAL NUMBERS:
(Official Ranges)   R 88 104 001 E through F 99 999 999 G
                    H 00 000 001 G M 74 613 868 G (High Observed)

Star Notes:
(Low Observed)   * 49 624 428 B * 06 038 641 C (High Observed)

PLATE SERIALS: Back check number: wide: #5015 or lower
SIGNATURES: Georgia Neese Clark, Treasurer of the United States
                    John W. Snyder, Secretary of the Treasury

ESTIMATED VALUES:
TYPE I WIDE:

	VG/F	CU
R--E	$35.00	$75.00
S--E through F--G	2.00	4.00
H--G and I--G	5.00	10.00
J--G	10.00	20.00
K--G	20.00	40.00
L--G	50.00	100.00
M--G	75.00	150.00
*--B	3.50	7.50
*--C	150.00	250.00

TOTAL BLOCKS KNOWN: Forty eight.

CAT. NO. IS35D
$1.00 SILVER CERTIFICATE (BLUE SEAL) (12 Subject)
SERIES 1935D NARROW

SERIAL NUMBERS:
(Low Observed)   U 54 722 558 E through M 98 128 000 G (High Official) (except G--G)

Star Notes:
(Low Observed)   *55 213 765 B * 07 044 000 C (High Official)

PLATE SERIALS: Back check numbers: Narrow #5017 or higher.

TYPE II NARROW:

	VG/F	CU
U--E	$750.00	$2500.00
V--E	25.00	60.00
W--E	20.00	40.00
X--E	10.00	20.00
Y--E and Z--E	5.00	10.00
A--F through M--G (except G--G)	2.00	4.00
*--B	3.50	7.50
*--C	7.50	20.00

TOTAL BLOCKS Known: Forty-five.

TREASURY DEPARTMENT

WASHINGTON, D.C.

IMMEDIATE RELEASE,
Thursday, April 2, 1953

The Treasury announced today that it is placing in circulation $1 silver certificates, Series 1935, which differ in a slight detail from silver certificates now in circulation.

The change made in the new notes is in the "check letters". These are small letters in the upper left-hand and lower right-hand areas on the face of the notes. The check letters heretofore used ranged from "A" through "L". The new notes have additional check letters which include "M" through "R". No change has been made in the design or size of the individual notes.

The addition of the six new check letters became necessary when the Bureau of Engraving and Printing began printing $1 bills with 18 notes to the sheet instead of 12 notes as heretofore. Each "check letter" indicates the particular position of the note on the sheet when it is printed.

The presses used in the Bureau of Engraving and Printing for printing currency are being converted as rapidly as possible to accommodate the larger size sheet. It is contemplated that before the end of this year all of the currency will be produced in 18-subject sheets. This will include not only silver certificates but also United States notes and Federal Reserve notes. There are substantial amounts of currency on hand printed in 12-subject sheets and considerable time will elapse before all of the 12-subject notes are put into circulation. In the meantime, notes from both the 12-subject sheets and the 18-subject sheets will be circulated.

The adoption of the new procedure for printing currency in 18-subject sheets makes it possible to increase the output of currency notes and to decrease the cost of printing.

CAT. NO. IS35D
$1.00 SILVER CERTIFICATE (BLUE SEAL) (18 Subject)
SERIES 1935D NARROW

SERIAL NUMBERS:
(Official Ranges) G 00 000 001 G through G 99 999 999 G
N 00 000 001 G through N 46 944 000 G

Star Notes:
(Low Official) ✽ 00 000 001 D ✽ 05 023 672 (High Observed)
PLATE SERIALS Face plate numbers 7463 or higher (with some alternating back to 12 subject sheets). Back plate numbers 5689 or higher (wih some alternating back to 12 subject sheets)

ESTIMATED VALUES:
	VG/F	CU
G--G and N--G	$4.00	$8.00
✽--D	20.00	50.00

TOTAL BLOCKS KNOWN: Three.

CAT. NO. IS35E
$1.00 SILVER CERTIFICATE (BLUE SEAL) (18 Subject)
SERIES 1935E

SERIAL NUMBERS:
(Official Range) N 46 944 001 G through P 81 000 000 I
Star Notes:
(Low Observed) ✽05 054 838 D through ✽ 56 708 222 F (High Observed)

SIGNATURES: Ivy Baker Priest, Treasurer of the United States
George M. Humphrey, Secretary of the Treasury

ESTIMATED VALUES:
	CU
N--G through P--I	$4.00
✽--D, ✽--E, ✽--F	7.50

TOTAL BLOCKS KNOWN: Fifty-five.

CAT. NO. IS35F
$1.00 SILVER CERTIFICATE (BLUE SEAL) (18 Subject)
SERIES 1935F

SERIAL NUMBERS:
(Official Range) P 81 000 01 I through B 54 000 000 J
and B 71 640 001 J through B 72 000 000 J
Star Notes:
(Low Observed) ✽ 57 373 438 F through ✽ 10 419 572 G (High Observed)

SIGNATURES: Ivy Baker Priest, Treasurer of the United States
Robert B. Anderson, Secretary of the Treasury.

ESTIMATED VALUES:
	VG/F	CU
P--I through B54--J		$6.00
B71--J	$150.00	750.00
✽--F ✽--G		7.50

TOTAL BLOCKS KNOWN: Sixteen.

CAT. NO. IS35G
$1.00 SILVER CERTIFICATE (BLUE SEAL) (18 Subject)
SERIES 1935G NO MOTTO

SERIAL NUMBERS:
(Official Range) B 54 000 001 J through B 71 640 000 J
B 72 000 001 J through D 48 960 000 J
Star Notes:
(Low Observed) ✽10 455 957 G ✽ 19 024 268 G (High Observed)
PLATE SERIALS: Back check #6786 or lower
SIGNATURES: Elizabeth Rudel Smith, Treasurer of the United States
C. Douglas Dillon, Secretary of the Treasury

ESTIMATED VALUES:
	CU
B--J through D--J	$4.00
(IncludesBoth B--J Groups)	
✽--G	6.00

TOTAL BLOCKS KNOWN: Five.

CAT. NO. IS35G
$1.00 SILVER CERTIFICATE (BLUE SEAL) (18 Subject)
SERIES 1935G MOTTO

SERIAL NUMBERS:
(Official Range) D48 960 001J through D80 280 000J
Star Notes:
(Low Observed) ✽19 088 056G
✽ 20 149 712 G (High Observed)
PLATE SERIALS: Back Check #6787 or higher
SIGNATURES: Same as 1935G without motto.

ESTIMATED VALUES:
	CU
D--J	$4.50
✽--G	15.00

TOTAL BLOCKS KNOWN: Two.

IMMEDIATE RELEASE
Thursday, July 25, 1957. H-1411

The Bureau of Engraving and Printing of the Treasury Department today began printing a new series of one dollar notes bearing the inscription "In

41

God We Trust". The notes will be placed in circulation beginning October 1.

An Act of Congress approved by the President on July 11, 1955, provided that the inscription — long shown on coins — should become a part of the design of United States currency. It was agreed that the changes should be made in connection with the installation in the Bureau of Engraving and Printing of new high-speed rotary intaglio presses, using the dry-print method and producing 32 notes to the sheet. Older presses have been limited to wet-process printing, in sheets of only 18 notes each.

Two of the new high-speed presses have now been installed and are in operation. Six more are to be added.

The inscription "In God We Trust" on the new one dollar notes appears just above the large word ONE on the reverse (green) side of the notes, which are silver certificates. It has not yet been determined when other denominations bearing the inscription will be produced.

The signature of Robert B. Anderson, who becomes Secretary of the Treasury on July 29, upon the resignation of Secretary Humphrey, will appear on the new notes. Treasury officials explained that placing of the notes in circulation would have to be delayed until October to permit the production of an adequate supply for all sections of the country.

Secretary Humprey and Secretary-designate Anderson visited the Bureau of Engraving and Printing, together, and watched the first sheets of the new currency come off the new presses.

Cost of the new presses will be $1,583,528. The first press is to be delivered in 120 days, and the remaining seven within one year. Their purchase results from more than two years of experimental operation of a sample press supplied by the DeLaRue Company. A German-built sample press also has been tried out experimentally, and is being purchased separately for further research in multicolor printing operations.

Bids for the new press equipment were invited by the Bureau of Engraving and Printing on January 4 from six domestic and two foreign manufacturers. The only bid submitted was that of the Hoe Company.

The Bureau endeavored several years ago to interest American printing press manufacturers in designing and developing new presses of the type now being acquired, but because of the limited market the domestic manufacturers did not feel warranted in doing the necessary research and developmental work at their own expense.

The Bureau of Engraving and Printing announced that acquisition of the new presses will not occasion any reduction in the presently-employed force of plate printers. A committee of technical experts which passed on the acceptability of the new presses and the quality of the currency printed on them approved the purchase unanimously, the committee including representatives of the plate printers.

The new high-speed press units will provide the Bureau with substantially increased flexibility of printing operations in meeting its currency production requirements.

The Bureau has determined that the spoilage rate in the operation of the new presses will be lower than for the older equipment now is use.

CAT. NO. IS35H
$1.00 SILVER CERTIFICATE (BLUE SEAL) (18 Subject)
SERIES 1935H

SERIAL NUMBERS:
  (Official Range) D80 280 001J through E10 800 000J
  Star Notes:
  (Low Observed) *20 160 854G *21 596 000G (High Official)
PLATE SERIALS: Face check #8648 or lower.
  Back check #6876 or lower. (Last plate used for 18 subject sheets)
SIGNATURES: Kathryn O'Hay Granahan, Treasurer of the United States
  C. Douglas Dillon, Secretary of the Treasury

ESTIMATED VALUES:		CU
D--J and E--J		$3.50
*--G		6.00

TOTAL BLOCKS KNOWN: Three.

TREASURY DEPARTMENT   **IMMEDIATE RELEASE,**
WASHINGTON, D.C.   Friday, February 1, 1957. H-1276

The Bureau of Engraving and Printing of the Treasury Department has signed a contract with R. Hoe & Co., Inc., of New York City under which eight new high-speed, rotary intaglio printing presses to be custom built by Thomas DeLaRue & Co., Ltd., of London will be supplied to the Bureau.

The presses will be used for dry-print production of paper currency, in sheets of 32 notes each. The presses now in use at the Bureau are limited to wet-process printing, in sheets of only 18 notes each.

CAT. NO IS37
$1.00 SILVER CERTIFICATE (BLUE SEAL) (32 Subject)
SERIES 1957

SERIAL NUMBERS:
  (Official Range) A00 000 001A through B09 600 000B
  Star Notes:
  (Official Range) *00 000 001A through *07 640 000D
PLATED SERIALS: Both face and back numbers begin at #1 with 32 subject sheets.
SIGNATURES: Ivy Baker Priest, Treasurer of the United States
  Robert B. Anderson, Secretary of the Treasury

ESTIMATED VALUES:	CU
A--A through H--A	$4.00
I--A	7.50
J--A	4.00
K--A	5.00
L--A	7.50
M--A	5.00
N--A	4.00
P--A	5.00
Q--A	7.50
R--A	7.50
S--A through A--B	4.00
B--B	15.00
*--A through *--C	5.00
*--D	10.00

TOTAL BLOCKS KNOWN: Thirty-one.

CAT. NO. IS57A
$1.00 SILVER CERTIFICATE (BLUE SEAL) (32 Subject)
SERIES 1957A

SERIAL NUMBERS:
   (Official Range) A00 000 001A through Q94 080 000A
   Star Notes:
   (Official Range) *00 000 001A through *94 720 000A
SIGNATURES: Elizabeth Rudel Smith. Treasurer of the United States
   C. Douglas Dillon, Secretary of the Treasury

ESTIMATED VALUES: **CU**
                          Q--A   5.00
        A--A through Q--A $3.00
                          *--A   4.00

TOTAL BLOCKS KNOWN: Seventeen.

CAT. NO. IS57B
$1.00 SILVER CERTIFICATE (BLUE SEAL) (32 Subject)
SERIES 1957B

SERIAL NUMBERS:
   (Official Range) Q94 080 001A through Y12 480 000A
   Star Notes:
   (Official Range) *94 880 001A through *44 160 000B

PLATE SERIALS: Face check #789 was the official high.
   Back check #447 is highest known.
SIGNATURES: Kathryn O'Hay Granahan, Treasurer of the United States
   C. Douglas Dillon, Secretary of the Treasury

ESTIMATED VALUES: **CU**
                          Q--A $5.00
        R--A through Y--A   2.00
                          *--A   7.50
                          *--B   3.00

TOTAL BLOCKS KNOWN: Twelve.

NOTES

FEDERAL RESERVE
press release

For immediate release   **November 26, 1963**

The Board of Governors of the Federal Reserve System and the Treasury Department announced today that more than 50 million new $1 Federal Reserve notes are going into circulation. Issuance of the new $1 notes, authorized by Congress last June, has already begun at all 12 Federal Reserve Banks and their 24 Branches to commercial banks in every part of the country. This will make more silver available for coinage purposes and help to meet the increased demand for currency in connection with pre-Christmas business.

To facilitate the widest possible distribution, the initial supply of the new notes is being distributed through normal commercial banking channels; none of the first 50 million notes will be available to the public at any of the Federal Reserve Banks or Branches.

The new $1 Federal Reserve notes clearly resemble the present $1 silver certificates, which ultimately they will replace completely. The back of the new notes and the portrait of George Washington on the face will be exactly the same as the silver certificates. The main difference will be the addition of a symbol, appearing to the left of the portrait, identifying the issuing Federal Reserve Bank, and the wording on the face of the bill. The notes bear the signatures of the Secretary of the Treasury and the Treasurer of the United States, as do Federal Reserve notes of other denominations.

The new notes will read (above the portrait): "The United States of America" and (below the portrait) "One Dollar". The legend stating that the bill "Is Legal Tender For All Debts, Public and Private", appearing on the silver certificates will also appear on the new Federal Reserve notes, but the new notes will not contain any reference to silver. Thus, they will not carry the language: "This Certifies That There Is On Deposit In The Treasury Of The United States of America" (above portrait) and "One Dollar in Silver Payable To The Bearer on Demand" (below the portrait).

Federal Reserve notes have been the basic circulating currency of the United States for many years, comprising over 85 per cent (more than $30 billion) of the face amount of all currency in circulation today. They are backed 100 per cent by collateral in the form of gold certificates, U.S. Government securities, or short-term paper discounted or purchased by the Federal Reserve Banks.

CAT. NO. IF63
$1.00 FEDERAL RESERVE NOTE (GREEN SEAL) (32 Subject)
SERIES 1963

PLATE SERIALS: Face check numbers begin at #1. Back check numbers continued from silver certificates.
SIGNATURES: Kathryn O'Hay Granahan, Treasurer of the United States.
   C. Douglas Dillon, Secretary of the Treasury.

	DISTRICT	TOTAL NOTES PRINTED	BLOCKS	ESTIMATED VALUE VG/F	CU	LOW OFFICIAL SERIAL NUMBER	HIGH OFFICIAL SERIAL NUMBER
1	A BOSTON		A--A		3.00	A00 000 001A	A87 680 000A
			A--*		4.00	A00 000 001*	A06 400 000*
2	B NEW YORK		B--A		3.00	B00 000 001A	B99 999 999A
			B--B		5.00	B00 000 001B	B99 999 999B
			B--C	25.00	100.00	B00 000 001C	B19 200 000C
			B--*		4.00	B00 000 001*	B06 400 000*
			B--*		4.00	B06 560 001*	B13 440 000*
			B--*		10.00	B13 600 001*	B15 360 000*
3	C PHILADELPHIA		C--A		3.00	C00 000 001A	C99 999 999A
			C--B		25.00	C00 000 001B	C23 680 000B
			C--*		4.00	C00 000 001*	C06 400 000*
			C--*		5.00	C06 560 001*	C10 880 000*
4	D CLEVELAND		D--A		3.00	D00 000 001A	D99 999 999A
			D--B	25.00	100.00	D00 000 001B	D08 320 000B
			D--*		4.00	D00 000 001*	D07 680 000*
			D--*		50.00	D07 840 001*	D08 320 000*
5	E RICHMOND		E--A		3.00	E00 000 001A	E99 999 999A
			E--B		5.00	E00 000 001B	E59 520 000B
			E--*		4.00	E00 000 001*	E06 400 000*
			E--*		5.00	E06 560 001*	E12 160 000*
6	F ATLANTA		F--A		3.00	F00 000 001A	F99 999 999A
			F--B		15.00	F00 000 001B	F99 999 999B
			F--C	10.00	35.00	F00 000 001C	F21 120 000C
			F--*		4.00	F00 000 001*	F07 680 000*
			F--*		4.00	F07 840 001*	F16 000 000*
			F--*		5.00	F16 160 001*	F19 200 000*
7	G CHICAGO		G--A		3.00	G00 000 001A	G99 999 999A
			G--B	5.00	15.00	G00 000 001B	G99 999 999B
			G--C		3.00	G00 000 001C	G79 360 000C
			G--*		4.00	G00 000 001*	G04 480 000*
			G--*		4.00	G04 640 001*	G12 160 000*
			G--*		4.00	G12 320 001*	G19 840 000*
8	H ST. LOUIS		H--A		3.00	H00 000 001A	H99 840 000A
			H--*		4.00	H00 000 001*	H09 600 000*
9	I MINNEAPOLIS		I--A		3.00	I00 000 001A	I44 800 000A
			I--*		4.00	I00 000 001*	I05 120 000*
10	J KANSAS CITY		J--A		3.00	J00 000 001A	J88 960 000A
			J--*		4.00	J00 000 001*	J08 960 000*
11	K DALLAS		K--A		3.00	K00 000 001A	K85 760 000A
			K--*		4.00	K00 000 001*	K08 960 000*
12	L SAN FRANCISCO		L--A		3.00	L00 000 001A	L99 999 999A
			L--B	5.00	15.00	L00 000 001B	L99 999 999B
			L--*		4.00	L00 000 001*	L07 040 000*
			L--*		4.00	L07 200 001*	L12 800 000*
			L--*		5.00	L12 960 001*	L14 720 000*

TOTAL BLOCKS: Thirty-four. TOTAL GROUPS: Forty-five.

CAT. NO. IF63A
$1.00 FEDERAL RESERVE NOTE (GREEN SEAL) (32 Subject)
SERIES 1963A

SERIAL NUMBERS: All districts started both regular and star notes with serial 00 000 001.
SIGNATURES: Kathryn O'Hay Granahan, Treasurer of the United States
   Henry H. Fowler, Secretary of the Treasury
ESTIMATED VALUES: All $2.00 CU except as noted.

	DISTRICT	TOTAL NOTES PRINTED	BLOCKS	ESTIMATED VALUE VG/F	CU	LOW OFFICIAL SERIAL NUMBER	HIGH OFFICIAL SERIAL NUMBER
1	A BOSTON		A--A		3.00	A00 000 001A	A99 999 999A
			A--B		3.00	A00 000 001B	A99 999 999B
			A--C		3.00	A00 000 001C	A99 999 999C
			A--D		3.00	A00 000 001D	A19 840 000D
			A--*		3.50	A00 000 001*	A08 960 000*
			A--*		4.00	A09 120 001*	A12 800 000*
			A--*		4.00	A12 960 001*	A18 560 000*
			A--*		10.00	A18 720 001*	A19 840 000*
2	B NEW YORK		B--A		3.00	B00 000 001A	B99 999 999A
			B--B		50.00	B00 000 001B	B99 999 999B
			B--C		15.00	B00 000 001C	B99 999 999C
			B--D		3.00	B00 000 001D	B99 999 999D
			B--E		10.00	B00 000 001E	B99 999 999E
			B--F		3.00	B00 000 001F	B99 999 999F
			B--G		3.00	B00 000 001G	B57 600 000G
			B--*		3.50	B00 000 001*	B14 080 000*
			B--*		3.50	B14 240 001*	B21 760 000*
			B--*		3.50	B21 920 001*	B25 600 000*
			B--*		3.50	B25 760 001*	B30 720 000*
			B--*		3.50	B30 880 001*	B39 040 000*
			B--*		3.50	B39 200 001*	B44 160 000*
			B--*		3.50	B44 320 001*	B48 640 000*
3	C PHILADELPHIA		C--A		3.00	C00 000 001A	C99 999 999A
			C--B		5.00	C00 000 001B	C99 999 999B
			C--C		3.00	C00 000 001C	C99 999 999C
			C--D		3.00	C00 000 001D	C75 520 000D
			C--*		3.50	C00 000 001*	C10 240 000*
			C--*		3.50	C10 400 001*	C14 720 000*
			C--*		3.50	C14 880 001*	C21 120 000*
			C--*		3.50	C21 280 001*	C26 240 000*
4	D CLEVELAND		D--A		3.00	D00 000 001A	D99 999 999A
			D--B		4.00	D00 000 001B	D99 999 999B
			D--C		3.00	D00 000 001C	D99 999 999C
			D--D		3.00	D00 000 001D	D37 120 000D
			D--*		3.50	D00 000 001*	D10 240 000*
			D--*		3.50	D10 400 001*	D12 800 000*
			D--*		3.50	D12 960 001*	D19 200 000*
			D--*		3.50	D19 360 001*	D21 120 000*
5	E RICHMOND		E--A		3.00	E00 000 001A	E99 999 999A
			E--B		4.00	E00 000 001B	E99 999 999B
			E--C		3.00	E00 000 001C	E99 999 999C
			E--D		3.00	E00 000 001D	E99 999 999D
			E--E		3.00	E00 000 001E	E99 999 999E
			E--F		3.00	E00 000 001F	E32 000 000F
			E--*		3.50	E00 000 001*	E12 800 000*
			E--*		3.50	E12 960 001*	E18 560 000*

DISTRICT	TOTAL NOTES PRINTED	BLOCKS	ESTIMATED VALUE VG/F	CU	LOW OFFICIAL SERIAL NUMBER	HIGH OFFICIAL SERIAL NUMBER
		E--*		3.50	E18 720 001*	E23 680 000*
		E--*		3.50	E23 840 001*	E30 080 000*
		E--*		3.50	E30 240 001*	E37 760 000*
		E--*		3.50	E37 920 001*	E41 600 000*
6	F ATLANTA	F--A		3.00	F00 000 001A	F99 999 999A
		F--B		4.00	F00 000 001B	F99 999 999B
		F--C		4.00	F00 000 001C	F99 999 999C
		F--D		4.00	F00 000 001D	F99 999 999D
		F--E		3.00	F00 000 001E	F99 999 999E
		F--F		3.00	F00 000 001F	F99 999 999F
		F--G		3.00	F00 000 001G	F36 480 000G
		F--*		3.50	F00 000 001*	F08 960 000*
		F--*		3.50	F09 120 001*	F16 640 000*
		F--*		3.50	F16 800 001*	F21 120 000*
		F--*		3.50	F21 280 001*	F25 600 000*
		F--*		3.50	F25 760 001*	F32 640 000*
		F--*		3.50	F32 800 001*	F38 400 000*
		F--*		5.00	F38 560 001*	F40 960 000*
7	G CHICAGO	G--A		3.00	G00 000 001A	G99 999 999A
		G--B		5.00	G00 000 001B	G99 999 999B
		G--C		5.00	G00 000 001C	G99 999 999C
		G--D		3.00	G00 000 001D	G99 999 999D
		G--E		3.00	G00 000 001E	G99 999 999E
		G--F		4.00	G00 000 001F	G99 999 999F
		G--G		3.00	G00 000 001G	G99 999 999G
		G--H		3.00	G00 000 001H	G84 480 000H
		G--*		3.50	G00 000 001*	G12 800 000*
		G--*		3.50	G12 960 001*	G20 480 000*
		G--*		3.50	G20 640 001*	G26 880 000*
		G--*		4.00	G27 040 001*	G30 080 000*
		G--*		4.00	G30 240 001*	G33 280 000*
		G--*		3.50	G33 440 001*	G40 960 000*
		G--*		3.50	G41 120 001*	G46 720 000*
		G--*		3.50	G46 880 001*	G52 480 000*
8	H ST. LOUIS	H--A		3.00	H00 000 001A	H99 999 999A
		H--B		3.00	H00 000 001B	H99 999 999B
		H-C		3.00	H00 000 001C	H17 920 000C
		H--*		3.50	H00 000 001*	H07 040 000*
		H--*		3.50	H07 200 001*	H13 440 000*
		H--*		3.50	H13 600 001*	H17 920 000*
9	I MINNEAPOLIS	I--A		3.00	I00 000 001A	I99 999 999A
		I--B		4.00	I00 000 001B	I12 160 000B
		I--*		3.50	I00 000 001*	I04 480 000*
		I--*		3.50	I04 640 001*	I07 040 000*
10	J KANSAS CITY	J--A		3.00	J00 000 001A	J99 999 999A
		J--B		3.00	J00 000 001B	J99 999 999B
		J--C		3.00	J00 000 001C	J19 200 000C
		J--*		3.50	J00 000 001*	J07 040 000*
		J--*		3.50	J07 200 001*	J12 160 000*
		J--*		4.00	J12 320 001*	J14 720 000*
11	K DALLAS	K--A		3.00	K00 000 001A	K99 999 999A
		K--B		3.00	K00 000 001B	K99 999 999B
		K--C		3.00	K00 000 001C	K88 960 000C
		K--*		3.50	K00 000 001*	K07 680 000*
		K--*		3.50	K07 840 001*	K12 800 000*
		K--*		3.50	K12 960 001*	K18 560 001*
		K--*		25.00	K18 560 001*	K18 564 000*
		K--*		25.00	K18 580 001*	K18 584 000*
		K--*		25.00	K18 600 001*	K18 604 000*
		K--*		25.00	K18 620 001*	K18 624 000*
		K--*		25.00	K18 640 001*	K18 644 000*
		K--*		25.00	K18 660 001*	K18 664 000*
		K--*		25.00	K18 680 001*	K18 684 000*
		K--*		25.00	K18 700 001*	K18 704 000*
		K--*		25.00	K18 720 001*	K18 724 000*
		K--*		25.00	K18 740 001*	K18 744 000*
		K--*		25.00	K18 760 001*	K18 764 000*
		K--*		25.00	K18 780 001*	K18 784 000*
		K--*		25.00	K18 800 001*	K18 804 000*

DISTRICT	TOTAL NOTES PRINTED	BLOCKS	ESTIMATED VALUE VG/F	CU	LOW OFFICIAL SERIAL NUMBER	HIGH OFFICIAL SERIAL NUMBER
		K--*		25.00	K18 820 001*	K18 824 000*
		K--*		25.00	K18 840 001*	K18 844 000*
		K--*		25.00	K18 860 001*	K18 864 000*
		K--*		25.00	K18 880 001*	K18 884 000*
		K--*		25.00	K18 900 001*	K18 904 000*
		K--*		25.00	K18 920 001*	K18 924 000*
		K--*		25.00	K18 940 001*	K18 944 000*
		K--*		25.00	K18 960 001*	K18 964 000*
		K--*		25.00	K18 980 001*	K18 984 000*
		K--*		25.00	K19 000 001*	K19 004 000*
		K--*		25.00	K19 020 001*	K19 024 000*
		K--*		25.00	K19 040 001*	K19 044 000*
		K--*		25.00	K19 060 001*	K19 064 000*
		K--*		25.00	K19 080 001*	K19 084 000*
		K--*		25.00	K19 100 001*	K19 104 000*
		K--*		25.00	K19 120 001*	K19 124 000*
		K--*		25.00	K19 140 001*	K19 144 000*
		K--*		25.00	K19 160 001*	K19 164 000*
		K--*		25.00	K19 180 001*	K19 184 000*
12 L SAN FRANCISCO		L--A		3.00	L00 000 001A	L99 999 999A
		L--B		25.00	L00 000 001B	L99 999 999B
		L--C		35.00	L00 000 001C	L99 999 999C
		L--D		10.00	L00 000 001D	L99 999 999D
		L--E		3.00	L00 000 001E	L99 999 999E
		L--F		3.00	L00 000 001F	L76 800 000F
		L--*		3.50	L00 000 001*	L10 880 000*
		L--*		3.50	L11 040 001*	L24 960 000*
		L--*		5.00	L25 120 001*	L26 880 000*
		L--*		3.50	L27 040 001*	L31 360 000*
		L--*		3.50	L31 520 001*	L39 680 000*
		L--*		3.50	L39 840 001*	L42 880 000*

TOTAL BLOCKS: Sixty-nine. TOTAL GROUPS: One Hundred-fourteen.

CAT. NO. IF63B
$1.00 FEDERAL RESERVE NOTE (GREEN SEAL) (32 Subject)
SERIES 1963B

SIGNATURES: Kathryn O'Hay Granahan, Treasurer of the United States
Joseph W. Barr, Secretary of the Treasury

DISTRICT	TOTAL NOTES PRINTED	BLOCKS	ESTIMATED VALUE VG/F	CU	LOW OFFICIAL SERIAL NUMBER	HIGH OFFICIAL SERIAL NUMBER
2 B NEW YORK		B--G		3.00	B57 600 001G	B99 999 999G
		B--H		3.00	B00 000 001H	B80 640 000H
		B--*		3.00	B48 800 001*	B52 480 000*
5 E. RICHMOND		E--F		3.50	E32 000 001F	E99 999 999F
		E--G		3.00	E00 000 001G	E25 600 000G
		E--*		5.00	E41 600 001*	E42 880 000*
		E--*		5.00	E43 040 001*	E44 800 000*
7 G CHICAGO		G--H		5.00	G84 480 001H	G99 999 999H
		G--I		3.00	G00 000 001I	G75 520 000I
		G--*		3.00	G52 640 001*	G55 040 000*
10 J KANSAS CITY		J--C		4.00	J19 200 001C	J64 000 000C
12 L SAN FRANCISCO		L--F		3.00	L76 800 001F	L99 999 999F
		L--G		3.00	L00 000 001G	L83 200 000G
		L--*		3.00	L43 040 001*	L46 080 000*

TOTAL BLOCKS: Thirteen. TOTAL GROUPS: Fourteen.

TREASURY DEPARTMENT
WASHINGTON, D.C.
June 4, 1969

**FOR RELEASE AFTER 11:00 A.M.
WEDNESDAY, JUNE 4, 1969**

TREASURY SECRETARY KENNEDY AND TREASURER OF
THE U.S. ELSTON WITNESS NUMBERING OF NEW CURRENCY

Treasury Secretary David M. Kennedy and Treasurer of the United States Dorothy Andrews Elston today witnessed the numbering of the first one dollar Federal Reserve Notes bearing their signatures in ceremonies at the Bureau of Engraving and Printing.

It was the first time that an issue of currency notes bearing signatures of both the new Secretary and the Treasurer had been prepared since 1961, when those of Secretary C. Douglas Dillon and Treasurer Elizabeth Rudel Smith appeared on the Series 1957A notes.

The new Kennedy-Elston notes will be designated Series 1969, replacing the present Series 1963B notes. The major Series-year change is based on the first use of the new Department of the Treasury Seal — adopted last year — on Federal Reserve Notes in addition to the change in signatures of the Secretary and the Treasurer.

The new series notes will be produced for each of the 12 Federal Reserve Banks. Because of the major Series-year change, the serial numbers for each of the 12 banks will revert to 00 000 001A preceded by the prefix letter associated with each of the banks.

Shipments to each of the Federal Reserve Banks will be made in near future as total conversion to the new notes is completed in the Bureau of Engraving and Printing. All denominations of United States currency will be converted to the Kennedy 1969 Series.

**CAT. NO. IF69
$1.00 FEDERAL RESERVE NOTE (GREEN SEAL) (32 Subject)
SERIES 1969**

SIGNATURES: Dorothy Andrews Elston, Treasurer of the United States
David M. Kennedy, Secretary of the Treasury

	DISTRICT	TOTAL NOTES PRINTED	BLOCKS	ESTIMATED VALUE VG/F	CU	LOW OFFICIAL SERIAL NUMBER	HIGH OFFICIAL SERIAL NUMBER
1	A BOSTON		A--A		3.00	A00 000 001A	A99 200 000A
			A--*		3.00	A00 000 001*	A05 120 000*
2	B NEW YORK		B--A		3.00	B00 000 001A	B99 999 999A
			B--B		3.00	B00 000 001B	B99 999 999B
			B--C		3.00	B00 000 001C	B69 120 000C
			B--*		3.00	B00 000 001*	B03 200 000*
			B--*		3.00	B03 360 001*	B08 320 000*
			B--*		3.00	B08 480 001*	B14 080 000*
3	C PHILADELPHIA		C--A		3.00	C00 000 001A	C68 480 000A
			C--*		3.00	C00 000 001*	C03 360 000*
			C--*		25.00	C05 120 001*	C05 133 000*
			C--*		25.00	C05 140 001*	C05 153 000*
			C--*		25.00	C05 160 001*	C05 173 000*
			C--*		25.00	C05 180 001*	C05 193 000*
			C--*		25.00	C05 200 001*	C05 213 000*
			C--*		25.00	C05 220 001*	C05 233 000*
			C--*		25.00	C05 240 001*	C05 253 000*
			C--*		25.00	C05 260 001*	C05 273 000*
			C--*		25.00	C05 280 001*	C05 293 000*
			C--*		25.00	C05 300 001*	C05 313 000*
			C--*		25.00	C05 320 001*	C05 333 000*
			C--*		25.00	C05 340 001*	C05 353 000*

DISTRICT	TOTAL NOTES PRINTED	BLOCKS	ESTIMATED VALUE VG/F CU	LOW OFFICIAL SERIAL NUMBER	HIGH OFFICIAL SERIAL NUMBER
		C--*	25.00	C05 360 001*	C05 373 000*
		C--*	25.00	C05 380 001*	C05 393 000*
		C--*	25.00	C05 400 001*	C05 413 000*
		C--*	25.00	C05 420 001*	C05 433 000*
		C--*	25.00	C05 440 001*	C05 453 000*
		C--*	25.00	C05 460 001*	C05 473 000*
		C--*	25.00	C05 480 001*	C05 493 000*
		C--*	25.00	C05 500 001*	C05 513 000*
		C--*	25.00	C05 520 001*	C05 533 000*
		C--*	25.00	C05 540 001*	C05 553 000*
		C--*	25.00	C05 560 001*	C05 573 000*
		C--*	25.00	C05 580 001*	C05 593 000*
		C--*	25.00	C05 600 001Z*	C05 613 000*
		C--*	25.00	C05 620 001*	C05 633 000*
		C--*	25.00	C05 640 001*	C05 653 000*
		C--*	25.00	C05 660 001*	C05 673 000*
		C--*	25.00	C05 680 001*	C05 693 000*
		C--*	25.00	C05 700 001*	C05 713 000*
		C--*	25.00	C05 720 001*	C05 733 000*
		C--*	25.00	C05 740 001*	C05 753 000*
4	D CLEVELAND	D--A	3.00	D00 000 001A	D99 999 999A
		D--B	3.00	D00 000 001B	D20 480 000B
		D--*	3.00	D00 000 001*	D05 120 000*
		D--*	5.00	D05 280 001*	D05 760 000*
5	E RICHMOND	E--A	3.00	E00 000 001A	E99 999 999A
		E--B	3.00	E00 000 001B	E99 999 999B
		E--C	3.00	E00 000 001C	E50 560 000C
		E--*	3.00	E00 000 001*	E03 840 000*
		E--*	3.00	E04 000 001*	E08 960 000*
		E--*	5.00	E09 120 001*	E10 880 000*
6	F ATLANTA	F--A	3.00	F00 000 001A	F99 999 999A
		F--B	3.00	F00 000 001B	F85 120 000B
		F--*	3.00	F00 000 001*	F05 120 000*
		F--*	4.00	F05 280 001*	F07 680 000*
7	G CHICAGO	G--A	3.00	G00 000 001A	G99 999 999A
		G--B	3.00	G00 000 001B	G99 999 999B
		G--C	3.00	G00 000 001C	G99 999 999C
		G--D	3.00	G00 000 001D	G59 520 000D
		G--*	5.00	G00 000 001*	G03 840 000*
		G--*	4.00	G04 000 001*	G08 960 000*
		G--*	5.00	G09 120 001*	G10 240 000*
		G--*	4.00	G10 400 001*	G12 160 000*
8	H ST. LOUIS	H--A	3.00	H00 000 001A	H74 880 000A
		H--*	3.00	H00 000 001*	H03 840 000*
9	I MINNEAPOLIS	I--A	3.00	I00 000 001A	I48 000 000A
		I--*	3.00	I00 000 001*	I01 920 000*
10	J KANSAS CITY	J--A	3.00	J00 000 001A	J95 360 000A
		J--A	3.00	J00 000 001*	J05 760 000*
11	K DALLAS	K--A	3.00	K00 000 001A	K99 999 999A
		K--B	3.00	K00 000 001B	K13 440 000B
		K--*	3.00	K00 000 001*	K03 840 000*
		K--*	5.00	K04 000 001*	K05 120 000*
12	L SAN FRANCISCO	L--A	3.00	L00 000 001A	L99 999 999A
		L--B	3.00	L00 000 001B	L99 999 999B
		L--C	3.00	L00 000 001C	L26 240 000C
		L--*	4.00	L00 000 001*	L03 840 000*
		L--*	4.00	L04 000 001*	L08 320 000*
		L--*	5.00	L08 480 001*	L09 600 000*

TOTAL BLOCKS: Thirty-six. TOTAL GROUPS: Eighty.
FOOTNOTE: After completion of the printing of Series 1969A 13,000 sheets of Series 1969 (remember the series and signatures were in the second printing for this series) without third printing were on hand. Rather than waste these sheets, the Bureau decided to overprint them as star notes. The production schedule called for star notes for Philadelphia, so the 13,000 sheets were scheduled for this district. Serial numbers up to 05 120 000 had already been used for 1969A Philadelphia star notes, so the first serial number assigned for this production was 05 120 001. In regular production, the production unit is 20,000 sheets, hence there are 20,000 serial numbers different between each position (see 32 subject sheet layout). With only 13,000 sheets to run, this meant a gap of 7,000 numbers between each position of this particular run. This was not discovered until 15 to 18 months AFTER the notes had gone through the banks, and recovery of the high numbered stars was extremely limited even in circulated condition.

THE DEPARTMENT OF THE TREASURY	U.S. CURRENCY WITH NEW	NEWS
TREASURER OF THE UNITED STATES	SIGNATURE RELEASED	WASHINGTON, D.C. 20220
SUNDAY, DECEMBER 13		(202) 964-2333

Christmas shoppers will soon be using a new issue of "green".

U.S. Currency bearing the new name of "Dorothy Andrews Kabis" in the lower left-hand corner was shipped to Federal Reserve banks and branches a few days ago. Commercial banks should be receiving the new 1969A series currency from the Federal Reserve shortly.

This is the first time in history there has been a name change for the Treasurer of the United States on the nation's currency while the Treasurer remained in office. The new currency bears the signatures of Secretary of the Treasury David M. Kennedy and Treasurer of the United States Dorothy Andrews Kabis.

Mrs. Kabis, formerly Dorothy Andrews Elston, assumed her new name this past September 17th when she married Walter L. Kabis of Odessa, Delaware. Kabis is Chairman of Delaware's Air and Water Resource Commission.

Just a year and a half ago on June 4, 1969 the Secretary and the Treasurer witnessed the numbering of the Elston-Kennedy 1969 series notes which replaced the 1963B series. That change was effected since the basic design of the bill changed — namely, the use of the new Treasury seal and of the signatures of both the new Secretary and Treasurer. The 1963B series bore the name of Joseph Barr, who was Secretary for the one month preceding the swearing in of Secretary Kennedy. There were 458,880,000 Barr bills printed. Last year was the first time since 1961 an issue of currency bore both a new Secretary's and a new Treasurer's signature.

The 1969A series will not revert numerically back to 00 000 001A, as did the 1969 series, but will continue the consecutive numbering where the 1969 series leaves off.

Approximately 3,597,536,000 Elston-Kennedy bills with a face value of $24,613,280,000 have been printed in the last 18 months. About $14 billion worth is of the one dollar denomination (60% of the nation's currency is of the one dollar denomination). The one dollar bill has a life of 18 months while other denominations last relatively longer.

The Bureau of Engraving and Printing is replacing old, worn-out 1969 series plates with those bearing the new Kabis signature, making the transition quite simple and economical. Hence, presses are producing Elston-Kennedy and Kabis-Kennedy bills simultaneously until all the old plates wear out and are replaced. Printing of the new Kabis-Kennedy bills began October 26th.

The plates used on the four high speed presses for one dollar bills bear 32 notes. A dry intaglio process is used to prevent shrinkage and distortion. It also provides greatest security against possible counterfeiting since intaglio is an incised design which produces an impression in relief and is highly difficult to copy.

The bills are first printed in green ink on the back and the next day in black ink on the face. It is the plates which print the face of the currency that contain the signatures of the Treasurer of the United States and the Secretary of the Department of the Treasury.

The stacks, 20,000 sheets deep of 32 bills each, are then trimmed in preparation for the "Overprinting" by two-color presses which print the Federal Reserve bank data in black ink and Treasury seal and serial number in green ink.

The sheets are then cut and examined for defects. Rejects are marked by examiners, lifted out, and replaced with "star" notes which have an independent series of serial numbers. A "star" note which is identified by a green star after the serial number is also used for the 100,000,000th note since the presses carry only eight digits. "Star" notes occur on an average of three times out of every one hundred notes.

CAT. NO. IF69A
$1.00 FEDERAL RESERVE NOTE (GREEN SEAL) (32 Subject)
SERIES 1969A

SIGNATURES: Dorothy Andrews Kabis, Treasurer of the United States
David M. Kennedy, Secretary of the Treasury

	DISTRICT	TOTAL NOTES PRINTED	BLOCKS	ESTIMATED VALUE VG/F	CU	LOW OFFICIAL SERIAL NUMBER	HIGH OFFICIAL SERIAL NUMBER
1	A BOSTON		A--A		5.00	A99 200 001A	A99 999 999A
			A--B		3.00	A00 000 001B	A39 680 000B
			A--*		3.00	A05 280 001*	A06 400 000*
2	B NEW YORK		B--C		3.00	B69 120 001C	B99 999 999C
			B--D		3.00	B00 000 001D	B91 520 000D
			B--*		3.00	B14 240 001*	B20 480 000*
3	C PHILADELPHIA		C--A		3.00	C68 480 001A	C99 999 999A
			C--B		10.00	C00 000 001B	C13 440 000B
			C--*		3.00	C03 360 001*	C05 120 000*
4	D CLEVELAND		D--B		3.00	D20 480 001B	D50 560 000B
			D--*		3.00	D05 760 001*	D07 040 000*

DISTRICT	TOTAL NOTES PRINTED	BLOCKS	ESTIMATED VALUE VG/F CU	LOW OFFICIAL SERIAL NUMBER	HIGH OFFICIAL SERIAL NUMBER
5 E RICHMOND		E--C	3.00	E50 560 001C	E99 999 999C
		E--D	15.00	E00 000 001D	E16 640 000D
		E--*	3.00	E10 880 001*	E12 160 000*
		E--*	3.00	E12 320 001*	E14 080 000*
6 F ATLANTA		F--B	3.00	F85 120 001B	F99 999 999B
		F--C	3.00	F00 000 001C	F55 680 000C
		F--*	3.00	F07 840 001*	F10 240 000*
7 G CHICAGO		G--D	3.00	G59 520 001D	G99 999 999D
		G--E	3.00	G00 000 001E	G35 200 000E
		G--*	4.00	G12 160 001*	G13 440 000*
		G--*	3.00	G13 600 001*	G16 640 000*
8 H ST. LOUIS		H--A	3.00	H74 880 001A	H99 999 999A
		H--B	3.00	H00 000 001B	H16 300 000B
		H--*	4.00	H03 840 001*	H04 480 000*
		H--*	4.00	H04 640 001*	H05 120 000*
9 I MINNEAPOLIS		I--A	3.00	I48 000 001A	I69 760 000A
		I--*	5.00	I01 920 001*	I02 560 000*
10 J KANSAS CITY		J--A	3.00	J95 360 001A	J99 999 999A
		J--B	3.00	J00 000 001B	J35 840 000B
		J--*	3.00	J05 920 001*	J07 040 000*
11 K DALLAS		K--B	3.00	K13 440 001B	K40 960 000B
		K--*		none printed	
12 L SAN FRANCISCO		L--C	3.00	L26 240 001C	L78 080 000C
		L--*	3.00	L09 600 001*	L13 440 000*

TOTAL BLOCKS: Thirty-one. TOTAL GROUPS: Thirty-four.

THE DEPARTMENT OF THE TREASURY
BUREAU OF ENGRAVING AND PRINTING

NEWS

FOR IMMEDIATE RELEASE

April 20, 1971

Nation's Currency Gets New Signature

   The nation's currency underwent a change today when the first bills were printed bearing the signature of Secretary of the Treasury John B. Connally. The Secretary witnessed the printing of the new 1969 B Series one-dollar bills for the Dallas Federal Reserve District at a ceremony today at the Bureau of Engraving and Printing.
   The 1969 Series bills bearing the signature of Secretary Connally and Treasurer of the United States Dorothy Andrews Kabis replace the 1969A Series bills which were cosigned by former Secretary of the Treasury David M. Kennedy and Mrs. Kabis. It is estimated that well over 550 million Kabis-Kennedy one-dollar bills were printed for all 12 Federal Reserve Districts. Previous to Mrs. Kabis' marriage her signature appeared along with former Secretary Kennedy's signature as Dorothy Andrews Elston on 3,597,536,000 pieces of currency.
   Delivery of the Kabis-Connally bills will begin next month according to the request of the Federal Reserve, and will become available to the public sometime thereafter, consistent with inventory and other issue considerations of the 12 Federal Reserve Districts. Higher denomination Kabis-Connally bills will be printed at a later time.
   Officials attending the ceremony were the Secretary and Mrs. Connally, Mrs. Kabis, Deputy Assistant Secretary William Dickey, and James Conlon, Director of Bureau of Engraving and Printing.

CAT. NO. 69B
$1.00 FEDERAL RESERVE NOTE (GREEN SEAL) (32 Subject)
SERIES 1969B

   Ultra modern overprinting equipment called COPE (Currency Overprinting and Processing Equipment) was first used for issues in this series. Despite the fact that the printing blocks were exactly identical, when the notes appeared there was a distinct difference in the appearance of the serial numbers between notes done on COPE and notes done on the old, conventional equipment. This afforded the collector the first variety in the $1.00 Federal Reserve Notes. The serial numbers from COPE appeared to be heavier in the body of the digits and thus appeared to be shorter in height than conventional notes. Also COPE serial numbers appeared to "lay" on top of the paper rather than being printed into the paper. Collectors were quick to note the difference, most collectors now seek to obtain specimens of the various groups. Many collectors have recognized the relatively short runs done on conventional equipment (in fact so short several groups have not yet been found) and are avidly seeking all groups of both conventional and COPE runs. The name "GROUP" collecting has become accepted for this endeavor.

SIGNATURES: Dorothy Andrews Kabis, Treasurer of the United States
  John B. Connally, Secretary of the Treasury.

	DISTRICT	TOTAL NOTES PRINTED	BLOCKS	ESTIMATED VALUE VG/F CU	LOW OFFICIAL SERIAL NUMBER	HIGH OFFICIAL SERIAL NUMBER	
1	A BOSTON		A--A	3.00	A00 000 001A	A94 720 000A	cv
			A--*	3.00	A00 000 001*	A01 920 000*	cv
2	B NEW YORK		B--A	3.00	B00 000 001A	B99 999 999A	cv
			B--B	3.50	B00 000 001B	B31 360 000B	cv
			B--B	5.00	B31 360 001B	B37 760 000B	cp
			B--B	5.00	B37 760 001B	B42 880 000B	cv
			B--B	3.00	B42 880 001B	B99 840 000B	cp
			B--B	10.00	B99 840 001B	B99 999 999B	cv
			B--C	3.00	B00 000 001C	B99 840 000C	cp
			B--C	10.00	B99 840 001C	B99 999 999C	cv
			B--D	3.00	B00 000 001D	B29 440 000D	cp
			B--*	3.00	B00 000 001*	B04 480 000*	cv
			B--*	5.00	B04 640 001*	B05 760 000*	cv
			B--*	5.00	B05 920 001*	B06 400 000*	cv
			B--*	5.00	B06 560 001*	B07 040 000*	cv
3	C PHILADELPHIA		C--A	3.00	C00 000 001A	C99 999 999A	cv
			C--B	3.00	C00 000 001B	C33 280 000B	cv
			C--*	5.00	C00 000 001*	C01 280 000*	cv
			C--*	4.00	C01 440 001*	C03 200 000*	cv
4	D CLEVELAND		D--A	3.00	D00 000 001A	D91 520 000A	cv
			D--*	3.00	D00 000 001*	D04 480 000*	cv
5	E RICHMOND		E--A	3.00	E00 000 001A	E99 999 999A	cv
			E--B	3.00	E00 000 001B	E57 600 000B	cv
			E--B	3.00	E57 600 001B	E77 440 000B	cp
			E--B	15.00	E77 440 001B	E80 000 000B	cv
			E--*	7.50	E00 000 001*	E00 640 000*	cv
			E--*	3.00	E00 800 001*	E03 840 000*	cv
6	F ATLANTA		F--A	3.00	F00 000 001A	F99 999 999A	cv
			F--B	3.00	F00 000 001B	F70 400 000B	cv
			F--*	7.50	F00 000 001*	F00 640 000*	cv
			F--*	3.00	F00 800 001*	F03 840 000*	cv
7	G CHICAGO		G--A	3.00	G00 000 001A	G99 999 999A	cv
			G--B	3.00	G00 000 001B	G99 999 999B	cv
			G--C	5.00	G00 000 001C	G01 280 000C	cv
			G--C	4.00	G01 280 001C	G04 480 000C	cp
			G--*	3.00	G00 160 001*	G03 200 000*	cv
			G--*	4.00	G03 360 001*	G04 480 000*	cv
8	H ST. LOUIS		H--A	3.00	H00 000 001A	H59 520 000A	cv
			H--*	3.00	H00 000 001*	H01 920 000*	cv
9	I MINNEAPOLIS		I--A	3.00	I00 000 001A	I33 920 000A	cv
			I--*	3.00	I02 560 001*	I03 200 000*	cv
10	J KANSAS CITY		J--A	3.00	J00 000 001A	J67 200 000A	cv
			J--*	3.00	J00 000 001*	J02 560 000*	cv
11	K DALLAS		K--A	3.00	K00 000 001A	K99 999 999A	cv
			K--B	3.00	K00 000 001B	K16 640 000B	cv
			K--*	3.00	K00 000 001*	K03 840 000*	cv
			K--*	4.00	K04 000 001*	K05 120 000*	cv
12	L SAN FRANCISCO		L--A	3.00	L00 000 001A	L92 160 000A	cv
			L--A	4.00	L92 160 001A	L99 840 000A	cp
			L--A	10.00	L99 840 001A	L99 999 999A	cv
			L--B	5.00	L00 000 001B	L08 960 000B	cp
			L--B	3.00	L08 960 001B	L99 999 999B	cv
			L--C	3.00	L00 000 001C	L08 960 000C	cv
			L--*	5.00	L00 000 001*	L00 640 000*	cv
			L--*	4.00	L00 800 001*	L03 840 000*	cv
			L--*	5.00	L04 000 001*	L05 760 000*	cv

TOTAL BLOCKS: Thirty-five.
TOTAL GROUPS: Fifty-six.

CAT. NO. IF69C
$1.00 FEDERAL RESERVE NOTE (GREEN SEAL) (32 Subject)
SERIES 1969C

SIGNATURES: Romana Acosta Banuelos, Treasurer of the United States
John B. Connally, Secretary of the Treasury.

	DISTRICT	TOTAL NOTES PRINTED	BLOCKS	ESTIMATED VALUE VG/F CU	LOW OFFICIAL SERIAL NUMBER	HIGH OFFICIAL SERIAL NUMBER	
1	A BOSTON				none printed		
2	B NEW YORK		B--D	3.00	B29 440 001D	B76 160 000D	cp
			B--D	25.00	B76 160 001D	B79 360 000D	cv
			B--*		none printed		
3	C PHILADELPHIA				none printed		
4	D CLEVELAND		D--A	3.00	D91 520 000A	D99 999 999A	cv
			D--B	3.00	D00 000 001B	D07 040 000B	cv
			D--*	5.00	D04 640 001*	D05 120 000*	cv
5	E RICHMOND		E--B	3.00	E80 000 001B	E99 999 999B	cv
			E--C	3.00	E00 000 001C	E09 600 000C	cv
			E--C	3.00	E09 600 001C	E41 600 000C	cp
			E--*	5.00	E04 000 001*	E04 480 000*	cv
6	F ATLANTA		F--B	3.00	F70 400 001B	F99 999 999B	cv
			F--C	3.00	F00 000 001C	F31 360 000C	cv
			F--*	3.00	F04 000 001*	F07 680 000*	cv
7	G CHICAGO		G--C	3.00	G04 480 001C	G95 360 000C	cp
			G--C	5.00	G95 360 001C	G99 999 999C	cv
			G--D	3.00	G00 000 001D	G41 600 000D	cv
			G--*	3.00	G04 640 001*	G05 768 000*	cv
			G--*	25.00	G05 780 001*	G05 788 000*	cv
			G--*	25.00	G05 800 001*	G05 808 000*	cv
			G--*	25.00	G05 820 001*	G05 828 000*	cv
			G--*	25.00	G05 840 001*	G05 848 000*	cv
			G--*	25.00	G05 860 001*	G05 868 000*	cv
			G--*	25.00	G05 880 001*	G05 888 000*	cv
			G--*	25.00	G05 900 001*	G05 908 000*	cv
			G--*	25.00	G05 920 001*	G05 928 000*	cv
			G--*	25.00	G05 940 001*	G05 948 000*	cv
			G--*	25.00	G05 960 001*	G05 968 000*	cv
			G--*	25.00	G05 980 001*	G05 988 000*	cv
			G--*	25.00	G06 000 001*	G06 008 000*	cv
			G--*	25.00	G06 020 001*	G06 028 000*	cv
			G--*	25.00	G06 040 001*	G06 048 000*	cv
			G--*	25.00	G06 060 001*	G06 068 000*	cv
			G--*	25.00	G06 080 001*	G06 088 000*	cv
			G--*	25.00	G06 100 001*	G06 108 000*	cv
			G--*	25.00	G06 120 001*	G06 128 000*	cv
			G--*	25.00	G06 140 001*	G06 148 000*	cv
			G--*	25.00	G06 160 001*	G06 168 000*	cv
			G--*	25.00	G06 180 001*	G06 188 000*	cv
			G--*	25.00	G06 200 001*	G06 208 000*	cv
			G--*	25.00	G06 220 001*	G06 228 000*	cv
			G--*	25.00	G06 240 001*	G06 248 000*	cv
			G--*	25.00	G06 260 001*	G06 268 000*	cv
			G--*	25.00	G06 280 001*	G06 288 000*	cv
			G--*	25.00	G06 300 001*	G06 308 000*	cv
			G--*	25.00	G06 320 001*	G06 328 000*	cv
			G--*	25.00	G06 340 001*	G06 348 000*	cv
			G--*	25.00	G06 360 001*	G06 368 000*	cv
			G--*	25.00	G06 380 001*	G06 388 000*	cv

	DISTRICT	TOTAL NOTES PRINTED	BLOCKS	ESTIMATED VALUE VG/F CU	LOW OFFICIAL SERIAL NUMBER	HIGH OFFICIAL SERIAL NUMBER	
8	H ST. LOUIS		H--A	3.00	H59 520 001A	H83 200 000A	cv
			H--*	5.00	H01 920 001*	H02 560 000*	cv
9	I MINNEAPOLIS		I--A	3.00	I33 920 001A	I59 520 000A	cv
			I--*	5.00	I03 200 001*	I03 840 000*	cv
10	J KANSAS CITY		J--A	3.00	J67 200 001A	J99 999 999A	cv
			J--B	3.00	J00 000 001B	J05 760 000B	cv
			J--*	3.00	J02 720 001*	J03 840 000*	cv
11	K DALLAS		K--B	3.00	K16 640 001B	K46 080 000B	cv
			K--*	5.00	K05 120 001*	K05 760 000*	cv
12	L SAN FRANCISCO		L--C	3.00	L08 960 001C	L99 999 999C	cv
			L--D	3.00	L00 000 001D	L10 240 000D	cv
			L--*	5.00	L05 760 001*	L07 040 000*	cv
			L--*	5.00	L07 200 001*	L08 320 000*	cv

TOTAL BLOCKS: Twenty-five.
TOTAL GROUPS: Sixty
FOOT NOTE: A situation similar to the 1969 high Philadelphia stars occurred in this series with Chicago stars. 8,000 sheets were run starting with G05 760 001* with a gap of serial numbers between each position.

CAT. NO. IF69D
$1.00 FEDERAL RESERVE NOTE (GREEN SEAL) (32 Subject)
SERIES 1969D

SIGNATURES: Romano Acosta Banuelos, Treasurer of the United States
George P. Shultz, Secretary of the Treasury

	DISTRICT	TOTAL NOTES PRINTED	BLOCKS	ESTIMATED VALUE VG/F CU	LOW OFFICIAL SERIAL NUMBER	HIGH OFFICIAL SERIAL NUMBER	
1	A BOSTON		A--A	2.00	A00 000 001A	A39 040 000A	cv
			A--A	2.00	A39 040 001A	A52 480 000A	cp
			A--A	2.00	A52 480 001A	A99 999 999A	cv
			A--B	2.00	A00 000 001B	A87 040 000B	cv
			A--*	3.50	A00 000 001*	A00 640 000*	cv
			A--*	3.50	A00 800 001*	A01 280 000*	cv
2	B NEW YORK		B--A	3.00	B00 000 001A	B03 840 000A	cv
			B--A	2.00	B03 840 001A	B26 240 000A	cp
			B--A	3.00	B26 240 001A	B32 640 000A	cv
			B--A	2.00	B32 640 001A	B56 320 000A	cp
			B--A	2.00	B56 320 001A	B75 520 000A	cv
			B--A	2.00	B75 520 001A	B99 840 000A	cp
			B--A	15.00	B99 840 001A	B99 999 999A	cv
			B--B	2.00	B00 000 001B	B11 520 000B	cp
			B--B	2.00	B11 520 001B	B34 560 000B	cv
			B--B	2.00	B34 560 001B	B53 120 000B	cp
			B--B	2.00	B53 120 001B	B60 800 000B	cv
			B--B	2.00	B60 800 001B	B99 840 000B	cp
			B--B	15.00	B99 840 001B	B99 999 999B	cv
			B--C	2.00	B00 000 001C	B99 200 000C	cp
			B--C	15.00	B99 200 001C	B99 999 999C	cv
			B--D	5.00	B00 000 001D	B01 920 000D	cv
			B--D	2.00	B01 920 001D	B99 840 000D	cp
			B--D	15.00	B99 840 001D	B99 999 999D	cv
			B--E	3.00	B00 000 001E	B02 560 000E	cp
			B--E	2.00	B02 560 001E	B11 520 000E	cv
			B--E	2.00	B11 520 001E	B68 480 000E	cp
			B--*	3.00	B00 160 001*	B01 280 000*	cv
			B--*	3.00	B01 440 001*	B01 920 000*	cv
			B--*	3.00	B02 080 001*	B03 200 000*	cv
			B--*	3.00	B03 360 001*	B05 120 000*	cv

DISTRICT	TOTAL NOTES PRINTED	BLOCKS	ESTIMATED VALUE VG/F CU	LOW OFFICIAL SERIAL NUMBER	HIGH OFFICIAL SERIAL NUMBER	
3 C PHILADELPHIA		C--A	2.00	C00 000 001A	C60 800 000A	cv
		C--A	2.00	C60 800 001A	C76 800 000A	cp
		C--A	2.00	C76 800 001A	C99 999 999A	cv
		C--B	2.00	C00 000 001B	C99 999 999B	cv
		C--C	2.00	C00 000 001C	C18 560 000C	cv
		C--*	3.00	C00 000 001*	C03 200 000*	cv
		C--*	3.00	C03 360 001*	C03 840 000*	cv
		C--*	3.50	C04 400 001*	C04 480 000*	cv
4 D CLEVELAND		D--A	2.00	D00 000 001A	D99 999 999A	cv
		D--B	2.00	D00 000 001B	D61 440 000B	cv
		D--*	3.00	D00 000 001*	D01 920 000*	cv
		D--*	3.00	D02 080 001*	D02 560 000*	cv
5 E RICHMOND		E--A	2.00	E00 000 001A	E17 280 000A	cv
		E--A	2.00	E17 280 001A	E63 360 000A	cp
		E--A	2.00	E63 360 001A	E84 480 000A	cv
		E--A	2.00	E84 480 001A	E99 840 000A	cp
		E--A	15.00	E99 840 001A	E99 999 999A	cv
		E--B	2.00	E00 000 001B	E33 280 000B	cp
		E--B	2.00	E33 280 001B	E99 999 999B	cv
		E--C	2.00	E00 000 001C	E14 720 000C	cv
		E--C	2.00	E14 720 001C	E46 720 000C	cp
		E--C	2.00	E46 720 001C	E99 999 999C	cv
		E--D	2.00	E00 000 001D	E27 520 000D	cv
		E--D	2.00	E27 520 001D	E48 640 000D	cp
		E--D	3.00	E48 640 001D	E51 840 000D	cv
		E--D	2.00	E51 840 001D	E74 240 000D	cp
		E--*	3.00	E00 160 001*	E05 120 000*	cv
		E--*	3.00	E05 280 001*	E08 320 000*	cv
		E--*	3.00	E08 480 001*	E08 960 000*	cv
6 F ATLANTA		F--A	2.00	F00 000 001A	F45 440 000A	cv
		F--A	2.00	F45 440 001A	F64 000 000A	cp
		F--A	2.00	F64 000 001A	F99 999 999A	cv
		F--B	2.00	F00 000 001B	F46 080 000B	cp
		F--B	2.00	F46 080 001B	F79 360 000B	cv
		F--B	2.00	F79 360 001B	F99 840 000B	cp
		F--B	15.00	F99 840 001B	F99 999 999B	cv
		F--C	2.00	F00 000 001C	F31 360 000C	cp
		F--C	2.00	F31 360 001C	F71 040 000C	cv
		F--C	2.00	F71 040 001C	F90 240 000C	cp
		F--C	2.00	F90 240 001C	F99 999 999C	cv
		F--D	2.00	F00 000 001D	F67 200 000D	cv
		F--D	2.00	F67 200 001D	F77 440 000D	cp
		F--*	3.00	F00 000 001*	F03 200 000*	cv
		F--*	3.00	F03 360 001*	F03 840 000*	cv
		F--*	3.00	F04 000 001*	F04 480 000*	cv
		F--*	3.00	F04 640 001*	F05 760 000*	cv
7 G CHICAGO		G--A	2.00	G00 000 001A	G37 120 000A	cv
		G--A	2.00	G37 120 001A	G66 560 000A	cp
		G--A	2.00	G66 560 001A	G99 999 999A	cv
		G--B	2.00	G00 000 001B	G53 760 000B	cv
		G--B	2.00	G53 760 001B	G99 840 000B	cp
		G--B	15.00	G99 840 001B	G99 999 999G	cv
		G--C	2.00	G00 000 001C	G15 360 000C	cv
		G--C	2.00	G15 360 001C	G99 840 000C	cp
		G--C	15.00	G99 840 001C	G99 999 999C	cv
		G--D	2.00	G00 000 001D	G39 680 000D	cp
		G--D	2.00	G39 680 001D	G46 080 000D	cv
		G--D	2.00	G46 080 001D	G78 080 000D	cp
		G--*	3.00	G00 000 001*	G03 200 000*	cv
			3.00	G03 360 001*	G03 840 000*	cv
			3.00	G04 400 001*	G04 480 000*	cv
			3.50	G04 640 001*	G05 120 000*	cv
			25.00	G05 120 001*	G05 130 000*	cv
			25.00	G05 140 001*	G05 150 000*	cv
			25.00	G05 160 001*	G05 170 000*	cv
			25.00	G05 180 001*	G05 190 000*	cv
			25.00	G05 200 001*	G05 210 000*	cv
			25.00	G05 220 001*	G05 230 000*	cv
			25.00	G05 240 001*	G05 250 000*	cv

DISTRICT	TOTAL NOTES PRINTED	BLOCKS	ESTIMATED VALUE VG/F CU	LOW OFFICIAL SERIAL NUMBER	HIGH OFFICIAL SERIAL NUMBER	
			25.00	G05 260 001*	G05 270 000*	cv
			25.00	G05 280 001*	G05 290 000*	cv
			25.00	G05 300 001*	G05 310 000*	cv
			25.00	G05 320 001*	G05 330 000*	cv
			25.00	G05 340 001*	G05 350 000*	cv
			25.00	G05 360 001*	G05 370 000*	cv
			25.00	G05 380 001*	G05 390 000*	cv
			25.00	G05 400 001*	G05 410 000*	cv
			25.00	G05 420 001*	G05 430 000*	cv
			25.00	G05 440 001*	G05 450 000*	cv
			25.00	G05 460 001*	G05 470 000*	cv
			25.00	G05 480 001*	G05 490 000*	cv
			25.00	G05 500 001*	G05 510 000*	cv
			25.00	G05 520 001*	G05 530 000*	cv
			25.00	G05 540 001*	G05 550 000*	cv
			25.00	G05 560 001*	G05 570 000*	cv
			25.00	G05 580 001*	G05 590 000*	cv
			25.00	G05 600 001*	G05 610 000*	cv
			25.00	G05 620 001*	G05 630 000*	cv
			25.00	G05 640 001*	G05 650 000*	cv
			25.00	G05 660 001*	G05 670 000*	cv
			25.00	G05 680 001*	G05 690 000*	cv
			25.00	G05 700 001*	G05 710 000*	cv
			25.00	G05 720 001*	G05 730 000*	cv
			25.00	G05 740 001*	G05 750 000*	cv
8 H ST. LOUIS		H--A	2.00	H00 000 001A	H29 440 000A	cv
		H--A	2.00	H29 440 001A	H42 240 000A	cp
		H--A	2.00	H42 240 001A	H99 999 999A	cv
		H--B	2.00	H00 000 001B	H68 480 000B	cv
		H--*	3.00	H00 000 001*	H01 280 000*	cv
		H--*	3.00	H01 440 001*	H01 920 000*	cv
9 I MINNEAPOLIS		I--A	2.00	I00 000 001A	I83 200 000A	cv
		I--*		none printed	none printed	
10 J KANSAS CITY		J--A	2.00	J00 000 001A	J99 999 999A	cv
		J--B	2.00	J00 000 001B	J85 760 000B	cv
		J--*	3.00	J00 000 001*	J00 640 000*	cv
		J--*	3.00	J00 800 001*	J03 200 000*	cv
11 K DALLAS		K--A	2.00	K00 000 001A	K99 999 999A	cv
		K--B	2.00	K00 000 001B	K29 440 000B	cv
		K--B	2.00	K29 440 001B	K42 240 000B	cp
		K--B	2.00	K42 240 001B	K58 240 000B	cv
		K--*	3.00	K00 000 001*	K05 760 000*	cv
		K--*	3.00	K05 920 001*	K06 400 000*	cv
12 L SAN FRANCISCO		L--A	2.00	L00 000 001A	L52 480 000A	cv
		L--A	2.00	L52 480 001A	L96 000 000A	cp
		L--A	2.00	L96 000 001A	L99 999 999A	cv
		L--B	2.00	L00 000 001B	L20 480 000B	cv
		L--B	2.00	L20 480 001B	L99 840 000B	cp
		L--B	15.00	L99 840 001B	L99 999 999B	cv
		L--C	3.00	L00 000 001C	L02 560 000C	cv
		L--C	2.00	L02 560 001C	L28 800 000C	cp
		L--C	2.00	L28 800 001C	L35 200 000C	cv
		L--C	2.00	L35 200 001C	L52 480 000C	cp
		L--C	2.00	L52 480 001C	L87 680 000C	cv
		L--C	2.00	L87 680 001C	L99 840 000C	cp
		L--C	15.00	L99 840 001C	L99 999 999C	cv
		L--D	2.00	L00 000 001D	L08 960 000D	cp
		L--D	2.00	L08 960 001D	L16 640 000D	cv
		L--D	2.00	L16 640 001D	L40 320 000D	cp
		L--D	2.00	L40 320 001D	L99 999 999D	cv
		L--E	5.00	L00 000 001E	L00 640 000E	cv
		L--*	3.00	L00 000 001*	L04 480 000*	cv
		L--*	3.00	L04 640 001*	L05 120 000*	cv
		L--*	3.00	L05 280 001*	L05 760 000*	cv
		L--*	3.00	L05 920 001*	L06 400 000*	cv
		L--*	3.00	L06 560 001*	L07 040 000*	cv

TOTAL BLOCKS: Forty-seven.
TOTAL GROUPS: One Hundred sixty-five.

CAT. NO. IF74
$1.00 FEDERAL RESERVE NOTE (GREEN SEAL) 32 Subject
SERIES 1974

SIGNATURES: Francine I. Neff, Treasurer of the United States.
William E. Simon, Secretary of the Treasury.
PLATE SERIALS: Face check begins with #1. Back check continues from previous series. Back check 1472 is lowest observed. Back check 905 is an error, should be 1905.

	DISTRICT	TOTAL NOTES PRINTED	BLOCKS	ESTIMATED VALUE VG/F	CU	LOW OFFICIAL SERIAL NUMBER	HIGH OFFICIAL SERIAL NUMBER	
1	A BOSTON	99,999,999	A--A		3.00	A00 000 001A	A99 999 999A	cv
		99,999,999	A--B		3.00	A00 000 001B	A34 560 000B	cv
					3.00	A34 560 001B	A99 840 001B	cp
					25.00	A99 840 001B	A99 999 999B	cv
		69,760,000	A--C		3.00	A00 000 001C	A69 760 000C	cp
		1,728,000	A--*		3.50	A00 160 001*	A01 280 000*	cv
					3.50	A01 440 001*	A01 920 000*	cv
					25.00	A01 936 001*	A01 940 000*	cv
					25.00	A01 956 001*	A01 960 000*	cv
					25.00	A01 976 001*	A01 980 000*	cv
					25.00	A01 996 001*	A02 000 000*	cv
					25.00	A02 016 001*	A02 020 000*	cv
					25.00	A02 036 001*	A02 040 000*	cv
					25.00	A02 056 001	A02 060 000*	cv
					25.00	A02 076 001	A02 080 000*	cv
					25.00	A02 096 001*	A02 100 000*	cv
					25.00	A02 116 001*	A02 120 000*	cv
					25.00	A02 136 001*	A02 140 000*	cv
					25.00	A02 156 001*	A02 160 000*	cv
					25.00	A02 176 001*	A02 180 000*	cv
					25.00	A02 196 001*	A02 200 000*	cv
					25.00	A02 216 001*	A02 220 000*	cv
					25.00	A02 236 001*	A02 240 000*	cv
					25.00	A02 256 001*	A02 260 000*	cv
					25.00	A02 276 001*	A02 280 000*	cv
					25.00	A02 296 001*	A02 300 000*	cv
					25.00	A02 316 001*	A02 320 000*	cv
					25.00	A02 336 000*	A02 340 000*	cv
					25.00	A02 356 001*	A02 360 000*	cv
					25.00	A02 376 001*	A02 380 000*	cv
					25.00	A02 396 001*	A02 400 000*	cv
					25.00	A02 416 001*	A02 420 000*	cv
					25.00	A02 436 001*	A02 440 000*	cv
					25.00	A02 456 001*	A02 460 000*	cv
					25.00	A02 476 001*	A02 480 000*	cv
					25.00	A02 496 001*	A02 500 000*	cv
					25.00	A02 516 001*	A02 520 000*	cv
					25.00	A02 536 001*	A02 540 000*	cv
					25.00	A02 556 001*	A02 560 000*	cv
2	B NEW YORK	99,999,999	B--A		3.00	B00 000 001A	B92 800 000A	cp
					5.00	B92 800 001A	B99 999 999A	cv
		99,999,999	B--B		3.00	B00 000 001B	B05 760 000B	cv
					3.00	B05 760 001B	B99 840 000B	cp
					25.00	B99 840 001B	B99 999 999B	cv
		99,999,999	B--C		3.00	B00 000 001C	B11 520 000C	cv
					3.00	B11 520 001C	B67 840 000C	cp
					10.00	B67 840 001C	B71 040 000C	cv
					5.00	B71 040 001C	B77 440 000C	cp
					3.00	B77 440 001C	B87 040 000C	cv
					3.00	B87 040 001C	B99 840 000C	cp
					25.00	B99 840 001C	B99 999 999C	cv
		99,999,999	B--D		3.00	B00 000 001D	B09 600 000D	cp
					3.00	B09 600 001D	B29 440 000D	cv
					3.00	B29 440 001D	B61 440 000D	cp
					3.00	B61 440 001D	B81 280 000D	cv
					3.00	B81 280 001D	B99 840 000D	cp
					25.00	B99 840 001D	B99 999 999D	cv
		99,999,999	B--E		5.00	B00 000 001E	B06 400 000E	cp
					3.00	B06 400 001E	B43 520 000E	cv
					3.00	B43 520 001E	B99 840 000E	cp
					25.00	B99 840 001E	B99 999 999E	cv

DISTRICT	TOTAL NOTES PRINTED	BLOCKS	ESTIMATED VALUE VG/F	CU	LOW OFFICIAL SERIAL NUMBER	HIGH OFFICIAL SERIAL NUMBER	
	99,999,999	B--F		3.00	B00 000 001F	B99 840 000F	cp
				25.00	B99 840 001F	B99 999 999F	cv
	99,840,000	B--G		3.00	B00 000 001G	B99 840 000G	cp
	40,320,000	B--H		3.00	B00 000 001H	B40 320 000H	cp
	5,808,000	B--*		3.50	B00 160 001*	B01 280 000*	cv
				3.50	B01 440 001*	B02 560 000*	cv
				3.50	B02 720 001*	B03 200 000*	cv
				3.50	B03 360 001*	B03 840 000*	cv
				3.50	B04 400 001*	B05 120 000*	cv
				3.50	B05 280 001*	B05 760 000*	cv
				25.00	B05 776 001*	B05 780 000*	cv
				25.00	B05 796 001*	B05 800 000*	cv
				25.00	B05 816 001*	B05 820 000*	cv
				25.00	B05 836 001*	B05 840 000*	cv
				25.00	B05 856 001*	B05 860 000*	cv
				25.00	B05 876 001*	B05 880 000*	cv
				25.00	B05 896 001*	B05 900 000*	cv
				25.00	B05 916 001*	B05 920 000*	cv
				25.00	B05 936 001*	B05 940 000*	cv
				25.00	B05 956 001*	B05 960 000*	cv
				25.00	B05 976 001*	B05 980 000*	cv
				25.00	B05 996 001*	B06 000 000*	cv
				25.00	B06 016 001*	B06 020 000*	cv
				25.00	B06 036 001*	B06 040 000*	cv
				25.00	B06 056 001*	B06 060 000*	cv
				25.00	B06 076 001*	B06 080 000*	cv
				25.00	B06 096 001*	B06 100 000*	cv
				25.00	B06 116 001*	B06 120 000*	cv
				25.00	B06 136 001*	B06 140 000*	cv
				25.00	B06 156 001*	B06 160 000*	cv
				25.00	B06 176 001*	B06 180 000*	cv
				25.00	B06 196 001*	B06 200 000*	cv
				25.00	B06 216 001*	B06 220 000*	cv
				25.00	B06 236 001*	B06 240 000*	cv
				25.00	B06 256 001*	B06 260 000*	cv
				25.00	B06 276 001*	B06 280 000*	cv
				25.00	B06 296 001*	B06 300 000*	cv
				25.00	B06 316 001*	B06 320 000*	cv
				25.00	B06 336 001*	B06 340 000*	cv
				25.00	B06 356 001*	B06 360 000*	cv
				25.00	B06 376 001*	B06 380 000*	cv
				25.00	B06 396 001*	B06 400 000*	cv
				25.00	B06 416 001*	B06 420 000*	cv
				25.00	B06 436 001*	B06 440 000*	cv
				25.00	B06 456 001*	B06 460 000*	cv
				25.00	B06 476 001*	B06 480 000*	cv
				25.00	B06 496 001*	B06 500 000*	cv
				25.00	B06 516 001*	B06 520 000*	cv
				25.00	B06 536 001*	B06 540 000*	cv
				25.00	B06 556 001*	B06 560 000*	cv
				25.00	B06 576 001*	B06 580 000*	cv
				25.00	B06 596 001*	B06 600 000*	cv
				25.00	B06 616 001*	B06 620 000*	cv
				25.00	B06 636 001*	B06 640 000*	cv
				25.00	B06 656 001*	B06 660 000*	cv
				25.00	B06 676 001*	B06 680 000*	cv
				25.00	B06 696 001*	B06 700 000*	cv
				25.00	B06 716 001*	B06 720 000*	cv
				25.00	B06 736 001*	B06 740 000*	cv
				25.00	B06 756 001*	B06 760 000*	cv
				25.00	B06 776 001*	B06 780 000*	cv
				25.00	B06 796 001*	B06 800 000*	cv
				25.00	B06 816 001*	B06 820 000*	cv
				25.00	B06 836 001*	B06 840 000*	cv
				25.00	B06 856 001*	B06 860 000*	cv
				25.00	B06 876 001*	B06 880 000*	cv
				25.00	B06 896 001*	B06 900 000*	cv
				25.00	B06 916 001*	B06 920 000*	cv
				25.00	B06 936 001*	B06 940 000*	cv

DISTRICT	TOTAL NOTES PRINTED	BLOCKS	ESTIMATED VALUE VG/F	CU	LOW OFFICIAL SERIAL NUMBER	HIGH OFFICIAL SERIAL NUMBER	
				25.00	B06 956 001*	B06 960 000*	CV
				25.00	B06 976 001*	B06 980 000*	CV
				25.00	B06 996 001*	B07 000 000*	CV
				25.00	B07 016 001*	B07 020 000*	CV
				25.00	B07 036 001*	B06 040 000*	CV
				3.50	B07 040 001*	B07 680 000*	CV
				25.00	B07 696 001*	B07 700 000*	CV
				25.00	B07 716 001*	B07 720 000*	CV
				25.00	B07 736 001*	B07 740 000*	CV
				25.00	B07 756 001*	B07 760 000*	CV
				25.00	B07 776 001*	B07 780 000*	CV
				25.00	B07 796 001*	B07 800 000*	CV
				25.00	B07 816 001*	B07 820 000*	CV
				25.00	B07 836 001*	B07 840 000*	CV
				25.00	B07 856 001*	B07 860 000*	CV
				25.00	B07 876 001*	B07 880 000*	CV
				25.00	B07 896 001*	B07 900 000*	CV
				25.00	B07 916 001*	B07 920 000*	CV
				25.00	B07 936 001*	B07 940 000*	CV
				25.00	B07 956 001*	B07 960 000*	CV
				25.00	B07 976 001*	B07 980 000*	CV
				25.00	B07 996 001*	B08 000 000*	CV
				25.00	B08 016 001*	B08 020 000*	CV
				25.00	B08 036 001*	B08 040 000*	CV
				25.00	B08 056 001*	B08 060 000*	CV
				25.00	B08 076 001*	B08 080 000*	CV
				25.00	B08 096 001*	B08 100 000*	CV
				25.00	B08 116 001*	B08 120 000*	CV
				25.00	B08 136 001*	B08 140 000*	CV
				25.00	B08 156 001*	B08 160 000*	CV
				25.00	B08 176 001*	B08 180 000*	CV
				25.00	B08 196 001*	B08 200 000*	CV
				25.00	B08 216 001*	B08 220 000*	CV
				25.00	B08 236 001*	B08 240 000*	CV
				25.00	B08 256 001*	B08 260 000*	CV
				25.00	B08 276 001*	B08 280 000*	CV
				25.00	B08 296 001*	B08 300 000*	CV
				25.00	B08 316 001*	B08 320 000*	CV
				25.00	B08 328 001*	B08 340 000*	CV
				25.00	B08 348 001*	B08 360 000*	CV
				25.00	B08 368 001*	B08 380 000*	CV
				25.00	B08 388 001*	B08 400 000*	CV
				25.00	B08 408 001*	B08 420 000*	CV
				25.00	B08 428 001*	B08 440 000*	CV
				25.00	B08 448 001*	B08 460 000*	CV
				25.00	B08 468 001*	B08 480 000*	CV
				25.00	B08 488 001*	B08 500 000*	CV
				25.00	B08 508 001*	B08 520 000*	CV
				25.00	B08 528 001*	B08 540 000*	CV
				25.00	B08 548 001*	B08 560 000*	CV
				25.00	B08 568 001*	B08 580 000*	CV
				25.00	B08 588 001*	B08 600 000*	CV
				25.00	B08 608 001*	B08 620 000*	CV
				25.00	B08 628 001*	B08 640 000*	CV
				25.00	B08 648 001*	B08 660 000*	CV
				25.00	B08 668 001*	B08 680 000*	CV
				25.00	B08 688 001*	B08 700 000*	CV
				25.00	B08 708 001*	B08 720 000*	CV
				25.00	B08 728 001*	B08 720 000*	CV
				25.00	B08 748 001*	B08 760 000*	CV
				25.00	B08 768 001*	B08 780 000*	CV
				25.00	B08 788 001*	B08 800 000*	CV
				25.00	B08 808 001*	B08 820 000*	CV
				25.00	B08 828 001*	B08 840 000*	CV
				25.00	B08 848 001*	B08 860 000*	CV
				25.00	B08 868 001*	B08 880 000*	CV
				25.00	B08 888 001*	B08 900 000*	CV
				25.00	B08 908 001*	B08 920 000*	CV
				25.00	B08 928 001*	B08 940 000*	CV

	DISTRICT	TOTAL NOTES PRINTED	BLOCKS	ESTIMATED VALUE VG/F	CU	LOW OFFICIAL SERIAL NUMBER	HIGH OFFICIAL SERIAL NUMBER	
					25.00	B08 948 001*	B08 960 000*	cv
3	C PHILADELPHIA	99,999,999	C--A		3.00	C00 000 001A	C99 999 999A	cv
		99,999,999	C--B		3.00	C00 000 001B	C46 080 000B	cv
					3.00	C46 080 001B	C99 840 000B	cp
					25.00	C99 840 001B	C99 999 999B	cv
		99,840,000	C--C		3.00	C00 000 001C	C99 840 000C	cp
		8,960,000	C--D		5.00	C00 000 001D	C08 960 000D	cp
		1,600,000	C--*		3.50	C00 160 001*	C01 280 000*	cv
					3.50	C01 440 001*	C01 920 000*	cv
4	D CLEVELAND	99,999,999	D--A		3.00	D00 000 001A	D99 999 999A	cv
		99,999,999	D--B		3.00	D00 000 001B	D26 880 000B	cv
					3.00	D26 880 001B	D99 840 000B	cp
					25.00	D99 840 001B	D99 999 999B	cv
		40,960,000	D--C		3.00	D00 000 001C	D40 960 000C	cp
		960,000	D--*		3.50	D00 160 001*	D00 640 000*	cv
					3.50	D00 800 001*	D01 280 000*	cv
5	E RICHMOND	99,999,999	E--A		25.00	E00 000 001A	E00 640 000A	cv
					25.00	E00 640 001A	E01 920 000A	cp
					3.00	E01 920 001A	E21 760 000A	cv
					3.00	E21 760 001A	E97 920 000A	cp
					15.00	E97 920 001A	E99 999 999A	cv
		99,999,999	E--B		3.00	E00 000 001B	E56 960 000B	cv
					3.00	E56 960 001B	E96 640 000B	cp
					10.00	E96 640 001B	E99 999 999B	cv
		99,999,999	E--C		15.00	E00 000 001C	E02 560 000C	cv
					3.00	E02 560 001C	E43 520 000C	cp
					5.00	E43 520 001C	E49 920 000C	cv
					3.00	E49 920 001C	E65 280 000C	cp
					3.00	E65 280 001C	E83 200 000C	cv
					3.00	E83 200 001C	E99 840 000C	cp
					25.00	E99 840 001C	E99 999 999C	cv
		99,999,999	E--D		3.00	E00 000 001D	E99 840 000D	cp
					25.00	E99 840 001D	E99 999 999D	cv
		99,999,999	E--E		3.00	E00 000 001E	E99 840 000E	cp
					25.00	E99 840 001E	E99 999 999E	cv
		99,840,000	E--F		3.00	E00 000 001F	E99 840 000F	cp
		44,160,000	E--G		3.00	E00 000 001G	E44 160 000G	cp
		4,960,000	E--*		3.50	E00 160 001*	E00 640 000*	cv
					3.50	E00 800 001*	E01 280 000*	cv
					3.50	E01 440 001*	E03 840 000*	cv
					3.50	E04 000 001*	E04 480 000*	cv
					3.50	E04 640 001*	E05 760 000*	cv
6	F ATLANTA	99,999,999	F--A		3.00	F00 000 001A	F99 840 000A	cp
					25.00	F99 840 001A	F99 999 999A	cv
		99,999,999	F--B		25.00	F00 000 001B	F01 920 000B	cv
					3.00	F01 920 001B	F12 160 000B	cp
					15.00	F12 160 001B	F15 360 000B	cv
					3.00	F15 360 001B	F61 440 000B	cp
					3.00	F61 440 001B	F93 440 000B	cv
					10.00	F93 440 001B	F99 840 000B	cp
					25.00	F99 840 001B	F99 999 999B	cv
		99,999,999	F--C		3.00	F00 000 001C	F99 840 000C	cp
					25.00	F99 840 001C	F99 999 999C	cv
		99,999,999	F--D		25.00	F00 000 001D	F00 640 000D	cv
					3.00	F00 640 001D	F30 080 000D	cp
					10.00	F30 080 001D	F37 120 000D	cv
					3.00	F37 120 01D	F62 720 000D	cp
					15.00	F62 720 001D	F65 280 000D	cv
					3.00	F65 280 001D	F99 840 000D	cp
					25.00	F99 840 001D	F99 999 999D	cv
		99,840,000	F--E		3.00	F00 000 001E	F99 840 000E	cp
		99,840,000	F--F		3.00	F00 000 001F	F99 840 000F	cp
		5,632,000	F--*		3.50	F00 160 001*	F00 640 000*	cv
					3.50	F00 800 001*	F02 560 000*	cv
					3.50	F02 720 001*	F03 840 000*	cv
					3.50	F04 000 001*	F04 480 000*	cv
					25.00	F04 496 001*	F04 500 000*	cv
					25.00	F04 516 001*	F04 520 000*	cv
					25.00	F04 536 001*	F04 540 000*	cv
					25.00	F04 556 001*	F04 560 000*	cv

DISTRICT	TOTAL NOTES PRINTED	BLOCKS	ESTIMATED VALUE VG/F	CU	LOW OFFICIAL SERIAL NUMBER	HIGH OFFICIAL SERIAL NUMBER	
				25.00	F04 576 001*	F04 580 000*	CV
				25.00	F04 596 001*	F04 600 000*	CV
				25.00	F04 616 001*	F04 620 000*	CV
				25.00	F04 636 001*	F04 640 000*	CV
				25.00	F04 656 001*	F04 660 000*	CV
				25.00	F04 676 001*	F04 680 000*	CV
				25.00	F04 696 001*	F04 700 000*	CV
				25.00	F04 716 001*	F04 720 000*	CV
				25.00	F04 736 001*	F04 740 000*	CV
				25.00	F04 756 001*	F04 760 000*	CV
				25.00	F04 776 001*	F04 780 000*	CV
				25.00	F04 796 001*	F04 800 000*	CV
				25.00	F04 816 001*	F04 820 000*	CV
				25.00	F04 836 001*	F04 840 000*	CV
				25.00	F04 856 001*	F04 860 000*	CV
				25.00	F04 876 001*	F04 880 000*	CV
				25.00	F04 896 001*	F04 900 000*	CV
				25.00	F04 916 001*	F04 920 000*	CV
				25.00	F04 936 001*	F04 940 000*	CV
				25.00	F04 956 001*	F04 960 000*	CV
				25.00	F04 976 001*	F04 980 000*	CV
				25.00	F04 996 001*	F05 000 000*	CV
				25.00	F05 016 001*	F05 020 000*	CV
				25.00	F05 036 001*	F05 040 000*	CV
				25.00	F05 056 001*	F05 060 000*	CV
				25.00	F05 076 001*	F05 080 000*	CV
				25.00	F05 096 001*	F05 100 000*	CV
				25.00	F05 116 001*	F05 120 000*	CV
				25.00	F05 136 001*	F05 140 000*	CV
				25.00	F05 156 001*	F05 160 000*	CV
				25.00	F05 176 001*	F05 180 000*	CV
				25.00	F05 196 001*	F05 200 000*	CV
				25.00	F05 216 001*	F05 220 000*	CV
				25.00	F05 236 001*	F05 240 000*	CV
				25.00	F05 256 001*	F05 260 000*	CV
				25.00	F05 276 001*	F05 280 000*	CV
				25.00	F05 296 001*	F05 300 000*	CV
				25.00	F05 316 001*	F05 320 000*	CV
				25.00	F05 336 001*	F05 340 000*	CV
				25.00	F05 356 001*	F05 360 000*	CV
				25.00	F05 376 001*	F05 380 000*	CV
				25.00	F05 396 001*	F05 400 000*	CV
				25.00	F05 416 001*	F05 420 000*	CV
				25.00	F05 436 001*	F05 440 000*	CV
				25.00	F05 456 001*	F05 460 000*	CV
				25.00	F05 476 001*	F05 480 000*	CV
				25.00	F05 496 001*	F05 500 000*	CV
				25.00	F05 516 001*	F05 520 000*	CV
				25.00	F05 536 001*	F05 540 000*	CV
				25.00	F05 556 001*	F05 560 000*	CV
				25.00	F05 576 001*	F05 580 000*	CV
				25.00	F05 596 001*	F05 600 000*	CV
				25.00	F05 616 001*	F05 620 000*	CV
				25.00	F05 636 001*	F05 640 000*	CV
				25.00	F05 656 001*	F05 660 000*	CV
				25.00	F05 676 001*	F05 680 000*	CV
				25.00	F05 696 001*	F05 700 000*	CV
				25.00	F05 716 001*	F05 720 000*	CV
				25.00	F05 736 001*	F05 740 000*	CV
				25.00	F05 756 001*	F05 760 000*	CV
				25.00	F05 772 001*	F05 780 000*	CV
				25.00	F05 792 001*	F05 800 000*	CV
				25.00	F05 812 001*	F05 820 000*	CV
				25.00	F05 832 001*	F05 840 000*	CV
				25.00	F05 852 001*	F05 860 000*	CV
				25.00	F05 872 001*	F05 880 000*	CV
				25.00	F05 892 001*	F05 900 000*	CV
				25.00	F05 912 001*	F05 920 000*	CV
				25.00	F05 932 001*	F05 940 000*	CV
				25.00	F05 952 001*	F05 960 000*	CV

DISTRICT	TOTAL NOTES PRINTED	BLOCKS	ESTIMATED VALUE VG/F	CU	LOW OFFICIAL SERIAL NUMBER	HIGH OFFICIAL SERIAL NUMBER	
				25.00	F05 972 001*	F05 980 000*	cv
				25.00	F05 992 001*	F06 000 000*	cv
				25.00	F06 012 001*	F06 020 000*	cv
				25.00	F06 032 001*	F06 040 000*	cv
				25.00	F06 052 001*	F06 060 000*	cv
				25.00	F06 072 001*	F06 080 000*	cv
				25.00	F06 092 001*	F06 100 000*	cv
				25.00	F06 112 001*	F06 120 000*	cv
				25.00	F06 132 001*	F06 140 000*	cv
				25.00	F06 152 001*	F06 160 000*	cv
				25.00	F06 172 001*	F06 180 000*	cv
				25.00	F06 192 001*	F06 200 000*	cv
				25.00	F06 212 001*	F06 220 000*	cv
				25.00	F06 232 001*	F06 240 000*	cv
				25.00	F06 252 001*	F06 260 000*	cv
				25.00	F06 272 001*	F06 280 000*	cv
				25.00	F06 292 001*	F06 300 000*	cv
				25.00	F06 312 001*	F06 320 000*	cv
				25.00	F06 332 001*	F06 340 000*	cv
				25.00	F06 352 001*	F06 360 000*	cv
				25.00	F06 372 001*	F06 380 000*	cv
				25.00	F06 392 001*	F06 400 000*	cv
				3.50	F06 400 001*	F07 680 000*	cv
7	G CHICAGO	99,999,999	G--A	3.00	G00 000 001A	G16 000 000A	cp
				3.00	G16 000 001A	G99 999 999A	cv
		99,999,999	G--B	3.00	G00 000 001B	G64 640 000B	cp
				3.00	G64 640 001B	B74 880 000B	cv
				3.00	G74 880 001B	G89 600 000B	cp
				3.00	G89 600 001B	G99 999 999B	cv
		99,999,999	G--C	3.00	G00 000 001C	G20 480 000C	cv
				3.00	G20 480 001C	G99 840 000C	cp
				25.00	G99 840 001C	G99 999 999C	cv
		99,999,999	G--D	3.00	G00 000 001D	G99 840 000D	cp
				25.00	G99 840 001D	G99 999 999D	cv
		73,600,000	G--E	3.00	G00 000 001E	G73 600 000E	cp
		4,992,000	G--*	3.50	G00 160 001*	G01 920 000*	cv
				3.50	G02 080 001*	G03 200 000*	cv
				3.50	G03 360 001*	G03 840 000*	cv
				3.50	G04 000 001*	G04 480 000*	cv
				25.00	G04 492 001*	G04 500 000*	cv
				25.00	G04 512 001*	G04 520 000*	cv
				25.00	G04 532 001*	G04 540 000*	cv
				25.00	G04 552 001*	G04 560 000*	cv
				25.00	G04 572 001*	G04 580 000*	cv
				25.00	G04 592 001*	G04 600 000*	cv
				25.00	G04 612 001*	G04 620 000*	cv
				25.00	G04 632 001*	G04 640 000*	cv
				25.00	G04 652 001*	G04 660 000*	cv
				25.00	G04 672 001*	G04 680 000*	cv
				25.00	G04 692 001*	G04 700 000*	cv
				25.00	G04 712 001*	G04 720 000*	cv
				25.00	G04 732 001*	G04 740 000*	cv
				25.00	G04 752 001*	G04 760 000*	cv
				25.00	G04 772 001*	G04 780 000*	cv
				25.00	G04 792 001*	G04 800 000*	cv
				25.00	G04 812 001*	G04 820 000*	cv
				25.00	G04 832 001*	G04 840 000*	cv
				25.00	G04 852 001*	G04 860 000*	cv
				25.00	G04 872 001*	G04 880 000*	cv
				25.00	G04 892 001*	G04 900 000*	cv
				25.00	G04 912 001*	G04 920 000*	cv
				25.00	G04 932 001*	G04 940 000*	cv
				25.00	G04 952 001*	G04 960 000*	cv
				25.00	G04 972 001*	G04 980 000*	cv
				25.00	G04 992 001*	G05 000 000*	cv
				25.00	G05 012 001*	G05 020 000*	cv
				25.00	G05 032 001*	G05 040 000*	cv
				25.00	G05 052 001*	G05 060 000*	cv
				25.00	G05 072 001*	G05 080 000*	cv
				25.00	G05 092 001*	G05 100 000*	cv

DISTRICT	TOTAL NOTES PRINTED	BLOCKS	ESTIMATED VALUE VG/F	CU	LOW OFFICIAL SERIAL NUMBER	HIGH OFFICIAL SERIAL NUMBER	
				25.00	G05 112 001*	G05 120 000*	CV
				25.00	G05 132 001*	G05 140 000*	CV
				25.00	G05 152 001*	G05 160 000*	CV
				25.00	G05 172 001*	G05 180 000*	CV
				25.00	G05 192 001*	G05 200 000*	CV
				25.00	G05 212 001*	G05 220 000*	CV
				25.00	G05 232 001*	G05 240 000*	CV
				25.00	G05 252 001*	G05 260 000*	CV
				25.00	G05 272 001*	G05 280 000*	CV
				25.00	G05 292 001*	G05 300 000*	CV
				25.00	G05 312 001*	G05 320 000*	CV
				25.00	G05 332 001*	G05 340 000*	CV
				25.00	G05 352 001*	G05 360 000*	CV
				25.00	G05 372 001*	G05 380 000*	CV
				25.00	G05 392 001*	G05 400 000*	CV
				25.00	G05 412 001*	G05 420 000*	CV
				25.00	G05 432 001*	G05 440 000*	CV
				25.00	G05 452 001*	G05 460 000*	CV
				25.00	G05 472 001*	G05 480 000*	CV
				25.00	G05 492 001*	G05 500 000*	CV
				25.00	G05 512 001*	G05 520 000*	CV
				25.00	G05 532 001*	G05 540 000*	CV
				25.00	G05 552 001*	G05 560 000*	CV
				25.00	G05 572 001*	G05 580 000*	CV
				25.00	G05 592 001*	G05 600 000*	CV
				25.00	G05 612 001*	G05 620 000*	CV
				25.00	G05 632 001*	G05 640 000*	CV
				25.00	G05 652 001*	G05 660 000*	CV
				25.00	G05 672 001*	G05 680 000*	CV
				25.00	G05 692 001*	G05 700 000*	CV
				25.00	G05 712 001*	G05 720 000*	CV
				25.00	G05 732 001*	G05 740 000*	CV
				25.00	G05 752 001*	G05 760 000*	CV
				25.00	G05 776 001*	G05 780 000*	CV
				25.00	G05 796 001*	G05 800 000*	CV
				25.00	G05 816 001*	G05 820 000*	CV
				25.00	G05 836 001*	G05 840 000*	CV
				25.00	G05 856 001*	G05 860 000*	CV
				25.00	G05 876 001*	G05 880 000*	CV
				25.00	G05 896 001*	G05 900 000*	CV
				25.00	G05 916 001*	G05 920 000*	CV
				25.00	G05 936 001*	G05 940 000*	CV
				25.00	G05 956 001*	G05 960 000*	CV
				25.00	G05 976 001*	G05 980 000*	CV
				25.00	G05 996 001*	G06 000 000*	CV
				25.00	G06 016 001*	G06 020 000*	CV
				25.00	G06 036 001*	G06 040 000*	CV
				25.00	G06 056 001*	G06 060 000*	CV
				25.00	G06 076 001*	G06 080 000*	CV
				25.00	G06 096 001*	G06 100 000*	CV
				25.00	G06 116 001*	G06 120 000*	CV
				25.00	G06 136 001*	G06 140 000*	CV
				25.00	G06 156 001*	G06 160 000*	CV
				25.00	G06 176 001*	G06 180 000*	CV
				25.00	G06 196 001*	G06 200 000*	CV
				25.00	G06 216 001*	G06 220 000*	CV
				25.00	G06 236 001*	G06 240 000*	CV
				25.00	G06 256 001*	G06 260 000*	CV
				25.00	G06 276 001*	G06 280 000*	CV
				25.00	G06 296 001*	G06 300 000*	CV
				25.00	G06 316 001*	G06 320 000*	CV
				25.00	G06 336 001*	G06 340 000*	CV
				25.00	G06 356 001*	G06 360 000*	CV
				25.00	G06 376 001*	G06 380 000*	CV
				25.00	G06 396 001*	G06 400 000*	CV
				25.00	G06 404 001*	G06 420 000*	CV
				25.00	G06 424 001*	G06 440 000*	CV
				25.00	G06 444 001*	G06 460 000*	CV
				25.00	G06 464 001*	G06 480 000*	CV
				25.00	G06 484 001*	G06 500 000*	CV

DISTRICT	TOTAL NOTES PRINTED	BLOCKS	ESTIMATED VALUE VG/F	CU	LOW OFFICIAL SERIAL NUMBER	HIGH OFFICIAL SERIAL NUMBER	
				25.00	G06 504 001*	G06 520 000*	cv
				25.00	G06 524 001*	G06 540 000*	cv
				25.00	G06 544 001*	G06 560 000*	cv
				25.00	G06 564 001*	G06 580 000*	cv
				25.00	G06 584 001*	G06 600 000*	cv
				25.00	G06 604 001*	G06 620 000*	cv
				25.00	G06 624 001*	G06 640 000*	cv
				25.00	G06 644 001*	G06 660 000*	cv
				25.00	G06 664 001*	G06 680 000*	cv
				25.00	G06 684 001*	G06 700 000*	cv
				25.00	G06 704 001*	G06 720 000*	cv
				25.00	G06 724 001*	G06 740 000*	cv
				25.00	G06 744 001*	G06 760 000*	cv
				25.00	G06 764 001*	G06 780 000*	cv
				25.00	G06 784 001*	G06 800 000*	cv
				25.00	G06 804 001*	G06 820 000*	cv
				25.00	G06 824 001*	G06 840 000*	cv
				25.00	G06 844 001*	G06 860 000*	cv
				25.00	G06 864 001*	G06 880 000*	cv
				25.00	G06 884 001*	G06 900 000*	cv
				25.00	G06 904 001*	G06 920 000*	cv
				25.00	G06 924 001*	G06 940 000*	cv
				25.00	G06 944 001*	G06 960 000*	cv
				25.00	G06 964 001*	G06 980 000*	cv
				25.00	G06 984 001*	G07 000 000*	cv
				25.00	G07 004 001*	G07 020 000*	cv
				25.00	G07 024 001*	G07 040 000*	cv
8 H ST. LOUIS	99,999,999	H--A		3.00	H00 000 001A	H99 999 999A	cv
	99,999,999	H--B		3.00	H00 000 001B	H33 280 000B	cv
				3.00	H33 280 001B	H99 840 000B	cp
				25.00	H99 840 001B	H99 999 999B	cv
	91,520,000	H--C		3.00	H00 000 001C	H91 520 000C	cp
	2,880,000	H--*		3.50	H00 160 001*	H02 560 000*	cv
				3.50	H02 720 001*	H03 200 000*	cv
9 I MINNEAPOLIS	99,999,999	I--A		3.00	I00 000 001A	I74 880 000A	cv
				3.00	I74 880 001A	I99 840 000A	cp
				25.00	I99 840 001A	I99 999 999A	cv
	44,160,000	I--B		3.00	I00 000 001B	I44 160 000B	cp
	480,000	I--*		5.00	I00 160 001*	I00 640 000*	cv
10 J KANSAS CITY	99,999,999	J--A		3.00	J00 000 001A	J79 360 000A	cv
				3.00	J79 360 001A	J99 840 000A	cp
				25.00	J99 840 001A	J99 999 999A	cv
	99,840,000	J--B		3.00	J00 000 001B	J99 840 000B	cp
	23,680,000	J--C		3.00	J00 000 001C	J23 680 000C	cp
	2,144,000	J--*		3.50	J00 000 001*	J01 280 000*	cv
				3.50	J01 440 001*	J01 920 000*	cv
				25.00	J01 932 001*	J01 940 000*	cv
				25.00	J01 952 001*	J01 960 000*	cv
				25.00	J01 972 001*	J01 980 000*	cv
				25.00	J01 992 001*	J02 000 000*	cv
				25.00	J02 012 001*	J02 020 000*	cv
				25.00	J02 032 001*	J02 040 000*	cv
				25.00	J02 052 001*	J02 060 000*	cv
				25.00	J02 072 001*	J02 080 000*	cv
				25.00	J02 092 001*	J02 100 000*	cv
				25.00	J02 112 001*	J02 120 000*	cv
				25.00	J02 132 001*	J02 140 000*	cv
				25.00	J02 152 001*	J02 160 000*	cv
				25.00	J02 172 001*	J02 180 000*	cv
				25.00	J02 192 001*	J02 200 000*	cv
				25.00	J02 212 001*	J02 220 000*	cv
				25.00	J02 232 001*	J02 240 000*	cv
				25.00	J02 252 001*	J02 260 000*	cv
				25.00	J02 272 001*	J02 280 000*	cv
				25.00	J02 292 001*	J02 300 000*	cv
				25.00	J02 312 001*	J02 320 000*	cv
				25.00	J02 332 001*	J02 340 000*	cv
				25.00	J02 352 001*	J02 360 000*	cv
				25.00	J02 372 001*	J02 380 000*	cv
				25.00	J02 392 001*	J02 400 000*	cv

DISTRICT	TOTAL NOTES PRINTED	BLOCKS	ESTIMATED VALUE VG/F CU	LOW OFFICIAL SERIAL NUMBER	HIGH OFFICIAL SERIAL NUMBER	
			25.00	J02 412 001*	J02 420 000*	cv
			25.00	J02 432 001*	J02 440 000*	cv
			25.00	J02 452 001*	J02 460 000*	cv
			25.00	J02 472 001*	J02 480 000*	cv
			25.00	J02 492 001*	J02 500 000*	cv
			25.00	J02 512 001*	J02 520 000*	cv
			25.00	J02 532 001*	J02 540 000*	cv
			25.00	J02 552 001*	J02 560 000*	cv
			25.00	J02 576 001*	J02 580 000*	cv
			25.00	J02 596 001*	J02 600 000*	cv
			25.00	J02 616 001*	J02 620 000*	cv
			25.00	J02 636 001*	J02 640 000*	cv
			25.00	J02 656 001*	J02 660 000*	cv
			25.00	J02 676 001*	J02 680 000*	cv
			25.00	J02 696 001*	J02 700 000*	cv
			25.00	J02 716 001*	J02 720 000*	cv
			25.00	J02 736 001*	J02 740 000*	cv
			25.00	J02 756 001*	J02 760 000*	cv
			25.00	J02 776 001*	J02 780 000*	cv
			25.00	J02 796 001*	J02 800 000*	cv
			25.00	J02 816 001*	J02 820 000*	cv
			25.00	J02 836 001*	J02 840 000*	cv
			25.00	J02 856 001*	J02 860 000*	cv
			25.00	J02 876 001*	J02 880 000*	cv
			25.00	J02 896 001*	J02 900 000*	cv
			25.00	J02 916 001*	J02 920 000*	cv
			25.00	J02 936 001*	J02 940 000*	cv
			25.00	J02 956 001*	J02 960 000*	cv
			25.00	J02 976 001*	J02 980 000*	cv
			25.00	J02 996 001*	J03 000 000*	cv
			25.00	J03 016 001*	J03 020 000*	cv
			25.00	J03 036 001*	J03 040 000*	cv
			25.00	J03 056 001*	J03 060 000*	cv
			25.00	J03 076 001*	J03 080 000*	cv
			25.00	J03 096 001*	J03 100 000*	cv
			25.00	J03 116 001*	J03 120 000*	cv
			25.00	J03 136 001*	J03 140 000*	cv
			25.00	J03 156 001*	J03 160 000*	cv
			25.00	J03 176 001*	J03 180 000*	cv
			25.00	J03 196 001*	J03 200 000*	cv
11 K DALLAS	99,999,999	K--A	3.00	K00 000 001A	K37 120 000A	cv
			3.00	K37 120 001A	K82 560 000A	cp
			3.00	K82 560 001A	K99 999 999A	cv
	99,999,999	K--B	3.00	K00 000 001B	K11 520 000B	cv
			3.00	K11 520 001B	K26 240 000B	cp
			3.00	K26 240 001B	K57 600 000B	cv
			3.00	K57 600 001B	K99 840 000B	cp
			25.00	K99 840 001B	K99 999 999B	cv
	99,840,000	K--C	3.00	K00 000 001C	K99 840 000C	cp
	30,720,000	K--D	3.00	K00 000 001D	K30 720 000D	cp
	1,216,000	K--*	3.50	K00 160 001*	K00 640 000*	cv
			3.50	K00 800 001*	K01 280 000*	cv
			25.00	K01 292 001*	K01 300 000*	cv
			25.00	K01 312 001*	K01 320 000*	cv
			25.00	K01 332 001*	K01 340 000*	cv
			25.00	K01 352 001*	K01 360 000*	cv
			25.00	K01 372 001*	K01 380 000*	cv
			25.00	K01 392 001*	K01 400 000*	cv
			25.00	K01 412 001*	K01 420 000*	cv
			25.00	K01 432 001*	K01 440 000*	cv
			25.00	K01 452 001*	K01 460 000*	cv
			25.00	K01 472 001*	K01 480 000*	cv
			25.00	K01 492 001*	K01 500 000*	cv
			25.00	K01 512 001*	K01 520 000*	cv
			25.00	K01 532 001*	K01 540 000*	cv
			25.00	K01 552 001*	K01 560 000*	cv
			25.00	K01 572 001*	K01 580 000*	cv
			25.00	K01 592 001*	K01 600 000*	cv
			25.00	K01 612 001*	K01 620 000*	cv
			25.00	K01 632 001*	K01 640 000*	cv

DISTRICT	TOTAL NOTES PRINTED	BLOCKS	ESTIMATED VALUE VG/F	CU	LOW OFFICIAL SERIAL NUMBER	HIGH OFFICIAL SERIAL NUMBER	
				25.00	K01 652 001*	K01 660 000*	cv
				25.00	K01 672 001*	K01 680 000*	cv
				25.00	K01 692 001*	K01 700 000*	cv
				25.00	K01 712 001*	K01 720 000*	cv
				25.00	K01 732 001*	K01 740 000*	cv
				25.00	K01 752 001*	K01 760 000*	cv
				25.00	K01 772 001*	K01 780 000*	cv
				25.00	K01 792 001*	K01 800 000*	cv
				25.00	K01 812 001*	K01 820 000*	cv
				25.00	K01 832 001*	K01 840 000*	cv
				25.00	K01 852 001*	K01 860 000*	cv
				25.00	K01 872 001*	K01 880 000*	cv
				25.00	K01 892 001*	K01 900 000*	cv
				25.00	K01 912 001*	K01 920 000*	cv
12 L SAN FRANCISCO	99,999,999	L--A		3.00	L00 000 001A	L99 999 999A	cv
	99,999,999	L--B		3.00	L00 000 001B	L27 520 000B	cv
				3.00	L27 520 001B	L65 280 000B	cp
				3.00	L65 280 001B	L97 280 000B	cv
				15.00	L97 280 001B	L99 840 000B	cp
				25.00	L99 840 001B	L99 999 999B	cv
	99,999,999	L--C		3.00	L00 000 001C	L21 760 000C	cp
				5.00	L21 760 001C	L30 080 000C	cv
				3.00	L30 080 001C	L53 760 000C	cp
				3.00	L53 760 001C	L75 520 000C	cv
				7.50	L75 520 001C	L81 920 000C	cp
				3.00	L81 920 001C	L99 999 999C	cv
	99,999,999	L--D		3.00	L00 000 001D	L99 840 000D	cp
				25.00	L99 840 001D	L99 999 999D	cv
	99,999,999	L--E		3.00	L00 000 001E	L99 840 000D	cp
				25.00	L99 840 001E	L99 999 999E	cv
	99,999,999	L--F		3.00	L00 000 001F	L99 840 000F	cp
				25.00	L99 840 001F	L99 999 999F	cv
	99,840,000	L--G		3.00	L00 000 001G	L99 840 000G	cp
	37,120,000	L--H		3.00	L00 000 001H	L37 120 000H	cp
	3,520,000	L--*		3.50	L00 160 001*	L00 640 000*	cv
				3.50	L00 800 001*	L01 280 000*	cv
				3.50	L01 440 001*	L02 560 000*	cv
				3.50	L02 720 001*	L03 200 000*	cv
				3.50	L03 360 001*	L03 840 000*	cv
				3.50	L04 000 001*	L04 480 000*	cv

TOTAL BLOCKS: Sixty eight.
TOTAL GROUPS: Six hundred sixty seven.

IF77
$1.00 FEDERAL RESERVE NOTE (GREEN SEAL) 32 Subject
Series 1977

SIGNATURES: Azie Taylor Morton, Treasurer of the United States.
  W. Michael Blumenthal, Secretary of the Treasury.
PLATE SERIALS: Face and back check numbers continued from previous series.

DISTRICT	TOTAL NOTES PRINTED	BLOCKS	ESTIMATED VALUE VG/F	CU	LOW OFFICIAL SERIAL NUMBER	HIGH OFFICIAL SERIAL NUMBER	
1 A BOSTON	99,840,000	A--A		3.00	A00 00 001A	A99 840 00A	cp
	88,320,000	A--B		3.00	A00 000 001B	A88 320 000B	cp
	2,048,000	A-*		25.00	A00 016 001*	A00 020 000*	cv
				25.00	A00 056 001*	A00 060 000*	cv
				25.00	A00 076 001*	A00 080 000*	cv
				25.00	A00 096 001*	A00 100 000*	cv
				25.00	A00 116 001*	A00 120 000*	cv
				25.00	A00 136 001*	A00 140 000*	cv
				25.00	A00 156 001*	A00 160 000*	cv
				25.00	A00 176 001*	A00 180 000*	cv
				25.00	A00 196 001*	A00 200 000*	cv
				25.00	A00 216 001*	A00 220 000*	cv
				25.00	A00 236 001*	A00 240 000*	cv
				25.00	A00 256 001*	A00 260 000*	cv
				25.00	A00 276 001*	A00 280 000*	cv
				25.00	A00 296 001*	A00 300 000*	cv
				25.00	A00 316 001*	A00 320 000*	cv

DISTRICT	TOTAL NOTES PRINTED	BLOCKS	ESTIMATED VALUE VG/F	CU	LOW OFFICIAL SERIAL NUMBER	HIGH OFFICIAL SERIAL NUMBER	
				25.00	A00 336 001*	A00 340 000*	cv
				25.00	A00 356 001*	A00 360 000*	cv
				25.00	A00 376 001*	A00 380 000*	cv
				25.00	A00 396 001*	A00 400 000*	cv
				25.00	A00 416 001*	A00 420 000*	cv
				25.00	A00 436 001*	A00 440 000*	cv
				25.00	A00 456 001*	A00 460 000*	cv
				25.00	A00 476 001*	A00 480 000*	cv
				25.00	A00 496 001*	A00 500 000*	cv
				25.00	A00 516 001*	A00 520 000*	cv
				25.00	A00 536 001*	A00 540 000*	cv
				25.00	A00 556 001*	A00 560 000*	cv
				25.00	A00 576 001*	A00 580 000*	cv
				25.00	A00 596 001*	A00 600 000*	cv
				25.00	A00 616 001*	A00 620 000*	cv
				25.00	A00 636 001*	A00 640 000*	cv
				3.50	A00 640 001*	A02 560 000*	cv
				25.00	A02 576 001*	A02 580 000*	cv
				25.00	A02 596 001*	A02 600 000*	cv
				25.00	A02 616 001*	A02 620 000*	cv
				25.00	A02 636 001*	A02 640 000*	cv
				25.00	A02 656 001*	A02 660 000*	cv
				25.00	A02 676 001*	A02 680 000*	cv
				25.00	A02 696 001*	A02 700 000*	cv
				25.00	A02 716 001*	A02 720 000*	cv
				25.00	A02 736 001*	A02 740 000*	cv
				25.00	A02 756 001*	A02 760 000*	cv
				25.00	A02 776 001*	A02 780 000*	cv
				25.00	A02 796 000*	A02 800 000*	cv
				25.00	A02 816 001*	A02 820 000*	cv
				25.00	A02 836 001*	A02 840 000*	cv
				25.00	A02 856 001*	A02 860 000*	cv
				25.00	A02 876 001*	A02 880 000*	cv
				25.00	A02 896 001*	A02 900 000*	cv
				25.00	A02 916 001*	A02 920 000*	cv
				25.00	A02 936 001*	A02 940 000*	cv
				25.00	A02 956 001*	A02 960 000*	cv
				25.00	A02 976 001*	A02 980 000*	cv
				25.00	A02 996 001*	A03 000 000*	cv
				25.00	A03 016 001*	A03 020 000*	cv
				25.00	A03 036 001*	A03 040 000*	cv
				25.00	A03 056 001*	A03 060 000*	cv
				25.00	A03 076 001*	A03 080 000*	cv
				25.00	A03 096 001*	A03 100 000*	cv
				25.00	A03 116 001*	A03 120 000*	cv
				25.00	A03 136 001*	A03 140 000*	cv
				25.00	A03 156 001*	A03 160 000*	cv
				25.00	A03 176 001*	A03 180 000*	cv
				25.00	A03 196 001*	A03 200 000*	cv
				25.00	A03 212 001*	A03 220 000*	cp
				25.00	A03 232 001*	A03 240 000*	cp
				25.00	A03 252 001*	A03 260 000*	cp
				25.00	A03 272 001*	A03 280 000*	cp
				25.00	A03 292 001*	A03 300 000*	cp
				25.00	A03 312 001*	A03 320 000*	cp
				25.00	A03 332 001*	A03 340 000*	cp
				25.00	A03 352 001*	A03 360 000*	cp
				25.00	A03 372 001*	A03 380 000*	cp
				25.00	A03 392 001*	A03 400 000*	cp
				25.00	A03 412 001*	A03 420 000*	cp
				25.00	A03 432 001*	A03 440 000*	cp
				25.00	A03 452 001*	A03 460 000*	cp
				25.00	A03 472 001*	A03 480 000*	cp
				25.00	A03 492 001*	A03 500 000*	cp
				25.00	A03 512 001*	A03 520 000*	cp
				25.00	A03 532 001*	A03 540 000*	cp
				25.00	A03 552 001*	A03 560 000*	cp
				25.00	A03 572 001*	A03 580 000*	cp
				25.00	A03 592 001*	A03 600 000*	cp
				25.00	A03 612 001*	A03 620 000*	cp

DISTRICT	TOTAL NOTES PRINTED	BLOCKS	ESTIMATED VALUE VG/F	CU	LOW OFFICIAL SERIAL NUMBER	HIGH OFFICIAL SERIAL NUMBER	
				25.00	A03 632 001*	A03 640 000*	cp
				25.00	A03 652 001*	A03 660 000*	cp
				25.00	A03 672 001*	A03 680 000*	cp
				25.00	A03 692 001*	A03 700 000*	cp
				25.00	A03 712 001*	A03 720 000*	cp
				25.00	A03 732 001*	A03 740 000*	cp
				25.00	A03 752 001*	A03 760 000*	cp
				25.00	A03 772 001*	A03 780 000*	cp
				25.00	A03 792 001*	A03 800 000*	cp
				25.00	A03 812 001*	A03 820 000*	cp
				25.00	A03 832 001*	A03 840 000*	cp
				3.50	A03 840 001*	A04 480 000*	cp
2	B NEW YORK	99,840,000	B--A	3.00	B00 000 001A	B99 840 000A	cp
		99,840,000	B--B	3.00	B00 000 001B	B99 840 000B	cp
		99,840,000	B--C	3.00	B00 000 001C	B99 840 000C	cp
		99,840,000	B--D	3.00	B00 000 001D	B99 840 000D	cp
		99,840,000	B--E	3.00	B00 000 001E	B99 840 000E	cp
		99,840,000	B--F	3.00	B00 000 001F	B99 840 000F	cp
		36,480,000	B--G	3.00	B00 000 001G	B36 480 000G	cp
		10,112,000	B--*	25.00	B00 012 001*	B00 020 000*	cv
				25.00	B00 032 001*	B00 040 000*	cv
				25.00	B00 052 001*	B00 060 000*	cv
				25.00	B00 072 001*	B00 080 000*	cv
				25.00	B00 091 001*	B00 100 000*	cv
				25.00	B00 112 001*	B00 120 000*	cv
				25.00	B00 132 001*	B00 140 000*	cv
				25.00	B00 152 001*	B00 160 000*	cv
				25.00	B00 172 001*	B00 180 000*	cv
				25.00	B00 192 001*	B00 200 000*	cv
				25.00	B00 212 001*	B00 220 000*	cv
				25.00	B00 232 001*	B00 240 000*	cv
				25.00	B00 252 001*	B00 260 000*	cv
				25.00	B00 272 001*	B00 280 000*	cv
				25.00	B00 292 001*	B00 300 000*	cv
				25.00	B00 312 001*	B00 320 000*	cv
				25.00	B00 332 001*	B00 340 000*	cv
				25.00	B00 352 001*	B00 360 000*	cv
				25.00	B00 372 001*	B00 380 000*	cv
				25.00	B00 392 001*	B00 400 000*	cv
				25.00	B00 412 001*	B00 420 000*	cv
				25.00	B00 432 001*	B00 440 000*	cv
				25.00	B00 452 001*	B00 460 000*	cv
				25.00	B00 472 001*	B00 480 000*	cv
				25.00	B00 492 001*	b00 500 000*	cv
				25.00	B00 512 001*	B00 520 000*	cv
				25.00	B00 532 001*	B00 540 000*	cv
				25.00	B00 552 001*	B00 560 000*	cv
				25.00	B00 572 001*	B00 580 000*	cv
				25.00	B00 592 001*	B00 600 000*	cv
				25.00	B00 612 001*	B00 620 000*	cv
				25.00	B00 632 001*	B00 640 000*	cv
				3.50	B00 640 001*	B04 480 000*	cv
				25.00	B04 496 001*	B04 500 000*	cv
				25.00	B04 516 001*	B04 520 000*	cv
				25.00	B04 536 001*	B04 540 000*	cv
				25.00	B04 556 001*	B04 560 000*	cv
				25.00	B04 576 001*	B04 580 000B	cv
				25.00	B04 596 001*	B04 600 000C	cv
				25.00	B04 616 001*	B04 620 000*	cv
				25.00	B04 636 001*	B04 640 000*	cv
				25.00	B04 656 001*	B04 660 000*	cv
				25.00	B04 676 001*	B04 680 000*	cv
				25.00	B04 696 001*	B04 700 000*	cv
				25.00	B04 716 001*	B04 720 000*	cv
				25.00	B04 736 001*	B04 740 000*	cv
				25.00	B04 756 001*	B04 760 000*	cv
				25.00	B04 776 001*	B04 780 000*	cv
				25.00	B04 796 001*	B04 800 000*	cv
				25.00	B04 816 001*	B04 820 000*	cv
				25.00	B04 836 001*	B04 840 000*	cv

DISTRICT	TOTAL NOTES PRINTED	BLOCKS	ESTIMATED VALUE VG/F	CU	LOW OFFICIAL SERIAL NUMBER	HIGH OFFICIAL SERIAL NUMBER	
				25.00	B04 856 001*	B04 860 000*	cv
				25.00	B04 876 001*	B04 880 000*	cv
				25.00	B04 896 001*	B04 900 000*	cv
				25.00	B04 916 001*	B04 920 000*	cv
				25.00	B04 936 001*	B04 940 000*	cv
				25.00	B04 956 001*	B04 960 000*	cv
				25.00	B04 976 001*	B04 980 000*	cv
				25.00	B04 996 001*	B05 000 000*	cv
				25.00	B05 016 001*	B05 020 000*	cv
				25.00	B05 036 001*	B05 040 000*	cv
				25.00	B05 056 001*	B05 060 000*	cv
				25.00	B05 076 001*	B05 080 000*	cv
				25.00	B05 096 001*	B05 100 000*	cv
				25.00	B05 116 001*	B05 120 000*	cv
				3.50	B05 120 001*	B08 320 000*	cv
				3.50	B08 320 001*	B10 880 000*	cp
				25.00	B10 896 001*	B10 900 000*	cv
				25.00	B10 916 001*	B10 920 000*	cv
				25.00	B10 936 001*	B10 940 000*	cv
				25.00	B10 956 001*	B10 960 000*	cv
				25.00	B10 976 001*	B10 980 000*	cv
				25.00	B10 996 001*	B11 000 000*	cv
				25.00	B11 016 001*	B11 020 000*	cv
				25.00	B11 036 001*	B11 040 000*	cv
				25.00	B11 056 001*	B11 060 000*	cv
				25.00	B11 076 001*	B11 080 000*	cv
				25.00	B11 096 001*	B11 100 000*	cv
				25.00	B11 116 001*	B11 120 000*	cv
				25.00	B11 136 001*	B11 140 000*	cv
				25.00	B11 156 001*	B11 160 000*	cv
				25.00	B11 176 001*	B11 180 000*	cv
				25.00	B11 196 001*	B11 200 000*	cv
				25.00	B11 216 001*	B11 220 000*	cv
				25.00	B11 236 001*	B11 240 000*	cv
				25.00	B11 256 001*	B11 260 000*	cv
				25.00	B11 276 001*	B11 280 000*	cv
				25.00	B11 296 001*	B11 300 000*	cv
				25.00	B11 316 001*	B11 320 000*	cv
				25.00	B11 336 001*	B11 340 000*	cv
				25.00	B11 356 001*	B11 360 000*	cv
				25.00	B11 376 001*	B11 380 000*	cv
				25.00	B11 396 001*	B11 400 000*	cv
				25.00	B11 416 001*	B11 420 000*	cv
				25.00	B11 436 001*	B11 440 000*	cv
				25.00	B11 456 001*	B11 460 000*	cv
				25.00	B11 476 001*	B11 480 000*	cv
				25.00	B11 496 001*	B11 500 000*	cv
				25.00	B11 516 001*	B11 520 000*	cv
3	C PHILADELPHIA	99,840,000	C--A	3.00	C00 000 001A	C99 840 000A	cp
		99,840,000	C--B	3.00	C00 000 001B	C99 840 000B	cp
		17,280,000	C--C	3.00	C00 000 001C	C17 280 000C	cp
		3,840,000	C--*	25.00	C00 016 001*	C00 020 000*	cv
				25.00	C00 036 001*	C00 040 000*	cv
				25.00	C00 056 001*	C00 060 000*	cv
				25.00	C00 076 001*	C00 080 000*	cv
				25.00	C00 096 001*	C00 100 000*	cv
				25.00	C00 116 001*	C00 120 000*	cv
				25.00	C00 136 001*	C00 140 000*	cv
				25.00	C00 156 001*	C00 160 000*	cv
				25.00	C00 176 001*	C00 180 000*	cv
				25.00	C00 196 001*	C00 200 000*	cv
				25.00	C00 216 001*	C00 220 000*	cv
				25.00	C00 236 001*	C00 240 000*	cv
				25.00	C00 256 001*	C00 260 000*	cv
				25.00	C00 276 001*	C00 280 000*	cv
				25.00	C00 296 001*	C00 300 000*	cv
				25.00	C00 316 001*	C00 320 000*	cv
				25.00	C00 336 001*	C00 340 000*	cv
				25.00	C00 356 001*	C00 360 000*	cv
				25.00	C00 376 001*	C00 380 000*	cv

DISTRICT	TOTAL NOTES PRINTED	BLOCKS	ESTIMATED VALUE VG/F	CU	LOW OFFICIAL SERIAL NUMBER	HIGH OFFICIAL SERIAL NUMBER	
				25.00	C00 396 001*	C00 400 000*	cv
				25.00	C00 416 001*	C00 420 000*	cv
				25.00	C00 436 001*	C00 440 000*	cv
				25.00	C00 456 001*	C00 460 000*	cv
				25.00	C00 476 001*	C00 480 000*	cv
				25.00	C00 496 001*	C00 500 000*	cv
				25.00	C00 516 001*	C00 520 000*	cv
				25.00	C00 536 001*	C00 540 000*	cv
				25.00	C00 556 001*	C00 560 000*	cv
				25.00	C00 576 001*	C00 580 000*	cv
				25.00	C00 596 001*	C00 600 000*	cv
				25.00	C00 616 001*	C00 620 000*	cv
				25.00	C00 636 001*	C00 640 000*	cv
				3.50	C00 640 001*	C01 280 000*	cv
				25.00	C01 288 001*	C01 300 000*	cv
				25.00	C01 308 001*	C01 320 000*	cv
				25.00	C01 328 001*	C01 340 000*	cv
				25.00	C01 348 001*	C01 360 000*	cv
				25.00	C01 368 001*	C01 380 000*	cv
				25.00	C01 388 001*	C01 400 000*	cv
				25.00	C01 408 001*	C01 420 000*	cv
				25.00	C01 428 001*	C01 440 000*	cv
				25.00	C01 448 001*	C01 460 000*	cv
				25.00	C01 468 001*	C01 480 000*	cv
				25.00	C01 488 001*	C01 500 000*	cv
				25.00	C01 508 001*	C01 520 000*	cv
				25.00	C01 528 001*	C01 540 000*	cv
				25.00	C01 548 001*	C01 560 000*	cv
				25.00	C01 568 001*	C01 580 000*	cv
				25.00	C01 588 001*	C01 600 000*	cv
				25.00	C01 608 001*	C01 620 000*	cv
				25.00	C01 628 001*	C01 640 000*	cv
				25.00	C01 648 001*	C01 660 000*	cv
				25.00	C01 668 001*	C01 680 000*	cv
				25.00	C01 688 001*	C01 700 000*	cv
				25.00	C01 708 001*	C01 720 000*	cv
				25.00	C01 728 001*	C01 740 000*	cv
				25.00	C01 748 001*	C01 760 000*	cv
				25.00	C01 768 001*	C01 780 000*	cv
				25.00	C01 788 001*	C01 800 000*	cv
				25.00	C01 808 001*	C01 820 000*	cv
				25.00	C01 828 001*	C01 840 000*	cv
				25.00	C01 848 001*	C01 860 000*	cv
				25.00	C01 868 001*	C01 880 000*	cv
				25.00	C01 888 001*	C01 900 000*	cv
				25.00	C01 908 001*	C01 920 000*	cv
				3.00	C01 920 001*	C02 560 000*	cv
				3.00	C02 560 001*	C03 200 000*	cp
				3.00	C03 200 001*	C03 840 000*	cp
				25.00	C03 856 001*	C03 860 000*	cp
				25.00	C03 876 001*	C03 880 000*	cp
				25.00	C03 896 001*	C03 900 000*	cp
				25.00	C03 916 001*	C03 920 000*	cp
				25.00	C03 936 001*	C03 940 000*	cp
				25.00	C03 956 001*	C03 960 000*	cp
				25.00	C03 976 001*	C03 980 000*	cp
				25.00	C03 996 001*	C04 000 000*	cp
				25.00	C04 016 001*	C04 020 000*	cp
				25.00	C04 036 001*	C04 040 000*	cp
				25.00	C04 056 001*	C04 060 000*	cp
				25.00	C04 076 001*	C04 080 000*	cp
				25.00	C04 096 001*	C04 100 000*	cp
				25.00	C04 116 001*	C04 120 000*	cp
				25.00	C04 136 001*	C04 140 000*	cp
				25.00	C04 156 001*	C04 160 000*	cp
				25.00	C04 176 001*	C04 180 000*	cp
				25.00	C04 196 001*	C04 200 000*	cp
				25.00	C04 216 001*	C04 220 000*	cp
				25.00	C04 236 001*	C04 240 000*	cp
				25.00	C04 256 001*	C04 260 000*	cp

	DISTRICT	TOTAL NOTES PRINTED	BLOCKS	ESTIMATED VALUE VG/F	CU	LOW OFFICIAL SERIAL NUMBER	HIGH OFFICIAL SERIAL NUMBER	
					25.00	C04 276 001*	C04 280 000*	cp
					25.00	C04 296 001*	C04 300 000*	cp
					25.00	C04 316 001*	C04 320 000*	cp
					25.00	C04 336 001*	C04 340 000*	cp
					25.00	C04 356 001*	C04 360 000*	cp
					25.00	C04 376 001*	C04 380 000*	cp
					25.00	C04 396 001*	C04 400 000*	cp
					25.00	C04 416 001*	C04 420 000*	cp
					25.00	C04 436 001*	C04 440 000*	cp
					25.00	C04 456 001*	C04 460 000*	cp
					25.00	C04 476 001*	C04 480 000*	cp
4	D CLEVELAND	99,840,000	D--A		3.00	C04 480 001*	C05 760 000*	cp
		99,840,000	D--B		3.00	D00 000 001A	D99 840 000A	cp
		13,440,000	D--C		3.00	D00 000 001B	D99 840 000B	cp
		2,048,000	D--*		3.00	D00 000 001C	D13 440 000C	cp
					25.00	D00 012 001*	D00 020 000*	cv
					25.00	D00 032 001*	D00 040 000*	cv
					25.00	D00 052 001*	D00 060 000*	cv
					25.00	D00 072 001*	D00 080 000*	cv
					25.00	D00 092 001*	D00 100 000*	cv
					25.00	D00 112 001*	D00 120 000*	cv
					25.00	D00 132 001*	D00 140 000*	cv
					25.00	D00 152 001*	D00 160 000*	cv
					25.00	D00 172 001*	D00 180 000*	cv
					25.00	D00 192 001*	D00 200 000*	cv
					25.00	D00 212 001*	D00 220 000*	cv
					25.00	D00 232 001*	D00 240 000*	cv
					25.00	D00 252 001*	D00 260 000*	cv
					25.00	D00 272 001*	D00 280 000*	cv
					25.00	D00 292 001*	D00 300 000*	cv
					25.00	D00 312 001*	D00 320 000*	cv
					25.00	D00 332 001*	D00 340 000*	cv
					25.00	D00 352 001*	D00 360 000*	cv
					25.00	D00 372 001*	D00 380 000*	cv
					25.00	D00 392 001*	D00 400 000*	cv
					25.00	D00 412 001*	D00 420 000*	cv
					25.00	D00 432 001*	D00 440 000*	cv
					25.00	D00 452 001*	D00 460 000*	cv
					25.00	D00 472 001*	D00 480 000*	cv
					25.00	D00 492 001*	D00 500 000*	cv
					25.00	D00 512 001*	D00 520 000*	cv
					25.00	D00 532 001*	D00 540 000*	cv
					25.00	D00 552 001*	D00 560 000*	cv
					25.00	D00 572 001*	D00 580 000*	cv
					25.00	D00 592 001*	D00 600 000*	cv
					25.00	D00 612 001*	D00 620 000*	cv
					25.00	D00 632 001*	D00 640 000*	cv
					25.00	D00 656 001*	D00 660 000*	cv
					25.00	D00 676 001*	D00 680 000*	cv
					25.00	D00 696 001*	D00 700 000*	cv
					25.00	D00 716 001*	D00 720 000*	cv
					25.00	D00 736 001*	D00 740 000*	cv
					25.00	D00 756 001*	D00 760 000*	cv
					25.00	D00 776 001*	D00 780 000*	cv
					25.00	D00 796 001*	D00 800 000*	cv
					25.00	D00 816 001*	D00 820 000*	cv
					25.00	D00 836 001*	D00 840 000*	cv
					25.00	D00 856 001*	D00 860 000*	cv
					25.00	D00 876 001*	D00 880 000*	cv
					25.00	D00 896 001*	D00 900 000*	cv
					25.00	D00 916 001*	D00 920 000*	cv
					25.00	D00 936 001*	D00 940 000*	cv
					25.00	D00 956 001*	D00 960 000*	cv
					25.00	D00 976 001*	D00 980 000*	cv
					25.00	D00 996 001*	D01 000 000*	cv
					25.00	D01 016 001*	D01 020 000*	cv
					25.00	D01 036 001*	D01 040 000*	cv
					25.00	D01 056 001*	D01 060 000*	cv
					25.00	D01 076 001*	D01 080 000*	cv
					25.00	D01 096 001*	D01 100 000*	cv

DISTRICT	TOTAL NOTES PRINTED	BLOCKS	ESTIMATED VALUE VG/F	CU	LOW OFFICIAL SERIAL NUMBER	HIGH OFFICIAL SERIAL NUMBER	
				25.00	D01 116 001*	D01 120 000*	CV
				25.00	D01 136 001*	D01 140 000*	CV
				25.00	D01 156 001*	D01 160 000*	CV
				25.00	D01 176 001*	D01 180 000*	CV
				25.00	D01 196 001*	D01 200 000*	CV
				25.00	D01 216 001*	D01 220 000*	CV
				25.00	D01 236 001*	D01 240 000*	CV
				25.00	D01 256 001*	D01 260 000*	CV
				25.00	D01 276 001*	D01 280 000*	CV
				25.00	D01 292 001*	D01 300 000*	CV
				25.00	D01 312 001*	D01 320 000*	CV
				25.00	D01 332 001*	D01 340 000*	CV
				25.00	D01 352 001*	D01 360 000*	CV
				25.00	D01 372 001*	D01 380 000*	CV
				25.00	D01 392 001*	D01 400 000*	CV
				25.00	D01 412 001*	D01 420 000*	CV
				25.00	D01 432 001*	D01 440 000*	CV
				25.00	D01 452 001*	D01 460 000*	CV
				25.00	D01 472 001*	D01 480 000*	CV
				25.00	D01 492 001*	D01 500 000*	CV
				25.00	D01 512 001*	D01 520 000*	CV
				25.00	D01 532 001*	D01 540 000*	CV
				25.00	D01 552 001*	D01 560 000*	CV
				25.00	D01 572 001*	D01 580 000*	CV
				25.00	D01 592 001*	D01 600 000*	CV
				25.00	D01 612 001*	D01 620 000*	CV
				25.00	D01 632 001*	D01 640 000*	CV
				25.00	D01 652 001*	D01 660 000*	CV
				25.00	D01 672 001*	D01 680 000*	CV
				25.00	D01 692 001*	D01 700 000*	CV
				25.00	D01 712 001*	D01 720 000*	CV
				25.00	D01 732 001*	D01 740 000*	CV
				25.00	D01 752 001*	D01 760 000*	CV
				25.00	D01 772 001*	D01 780 000*	CV
				25.00	D01 792 001*	D01 800 000*	CV
				25.00	D01 812 001*	D01 820 000*	CV
				25.00	D01 832 001*	D01 840 000*	CV
				25.00	D01 852 001*	D01 860 000*	CV
				25.00	D01 872 001*	D01 880 000*	CV
				25.00	D01 892 001*	D01 900 000*	CV
				25.00	D01 912 001*	D01 920 000*	CV
				3.50	D01 920 001*	D02 560 000*	CV
				25.00	D02 576 001*	D02 580 000*	CV
				25.00	D02 596 001*	D02 600 000*	CV
				25.00	D02 616 001*	D02 620 000*	CV
				25.00	D02 636 001*	D02 640 000*	CV
				25.00	D02 656 001*	D02 660 000*	CV
				25.00	D02 676 001*	D02 680 000*	CV
				25.00	D02 696 001*	D02 700 000*	CV
				25.00	D02 716 001*	D02 720 000*	CV
				25.00	D02 736 001*	D02 740 000*	CV
				25.00	D02 756 001*	D02 760 000*	CV
				25.00	D02 776 001*	D02 780 000*	CV
				25.00	D02 796 001*	D02 800 000*	CV
				25.00	D02 816 001*	D02 820 000*	CV
				25.00	D02 836 001*	D02 840 000*	CV
				25.00	D02 856 001*	D02 860 000*	CV
				25.00	D02 876 001*	D02 880 000*	CV
				25.00	D02 896 001*	D02 900 000*	CV
				25.00	D02 916 001*	D02 920 000*	CV
				25.00	D02 936 001*	D02 940 000*	CV
				25.00	D02 956 001*	D02 960 000*	CV
				25.00	D02 976 001*	D02 980 000*	CV
				25.00	D02 996 001*	D03 000 000*	CV
				25.00	D03 016 001*	D03 020 000*	CV
				25.00	D03 036 001*	D03 040 000*	CV
				25.00	D03 056 001*	D03 060 000*	CV
				25.00	D03 076 001*	D03 080 000*	CV
				25.00	D03 096 001*	D03 100 000*	CV
				25.00	D03 116 001*	D03 120 000*	CV

DISTRICT	TOTAL NOTES PRINTED	BLOCKS	ESTIMATED VALUE VG/F CU	LOW OFFICIAL SERIAL NUMBER	HIGH OFFICIAL SERIAL NUMBER	
			25.00	D03 136 001*	D03 140 000*	cv
			25.00	D03 156 001*	D03 160 000*	cv
			25.00	D03 176 001*	D03 180 000*	cv
			25.00	D03 196 001*	D03 200 000*	cv
			3.50	D03 200 001*	D03 840 000*	cv
			25.00	D03 852 001*	D03 860 000*	cp
			25.00	D03 872 001*	D03 880 000*	cp
			25.00	D03 892 001*	D03 900 000*	cp
			25.00	D03 912 001*	D03 920 000*	cp
			25.00	D03 932 001*	D03 940 000*	cp
			25.00	D03 952 001*	D03 960 000*	cp
			25.00	D03 972 001*	D03 980 000*	cp
			25.00	D03 992 001*	D04 000 000*	cp
			25.00	D04 012 001*	D04 020 000*	cp
			25.00	D04 032 001*	D04 040 000*	cp
			25.00	D04 052 001*	D04 060 000*	cp
			25.00	D04 072 001*	D04 050 000*	cp
			25.00	D04 092 001*	D04 100 000*	cp
			25.00	D04 112 001*	D04 120 000*	cp
			25.00	D04 132 001*	D04 140 000*	cp
			25.00	D04 152 001*	D04 160 000*	cp
			25.00	D04 172 001*	D04 180 000*	cp
			25.00	D04 192 001*	D04 200 000*	cp
			25.00	D04 212 001*	D04 220 000*	cp
			25.00	D04 232 001*	D04 240 000*	cp
			25.00	D04 252 001*	D04 260 000*	cp
			25.00	D04 272 001*	D04 280 000*	cp
			25.00	D04 292 001*	D04 300 000*	cp
			25.00	D04 312 001*	D04 320 000*	cp
			25.00	D04 332 001*	D04 340 000*	cp
			25.00	D04 352 001*	D04 360 000*	cp
			25.00	D04 372 001*	D04 380 000*	cp
			25.00	D04 392 001*	D04 400 000*	cp
			25.00	D04 412 001*	D04 420 000*	cp
			25.00	D04 432 001*	D04 440 000*	cp
			25.00	D04 452 000*	D04 460 000*	cp
			25.00	D04 472 001*	D04 480 000*	cp
			25.00	D04 488 001*	D04 500 000*	cp
			25.00	D04 508 001*	D04 520 000*	cp
			25.00	D04 528 001*	D04 540 000*	cp
			25.00	D04 548 001*	D04 560 000*	cp
			25.00	D04 568 001*	D04 580 000*	cp
			25.00	D04 588 001*	D04 600 000*	cp
			25.00	D04 608 001*	D04 620 000*	cp
			25.00	D04 628 001*	D04 640 000*	cp
			25.00	D04 648 001*	D04 660 000*	cp
			25.00	D04 668 001*	D04 680 000*	cp
			25.00	D04 688 001*	D04 700 000*	cp
			25.00	D04 708 001*	D04 720 000*	cp
			25.00	D04 728 001*	D04 740 000*	cp
			25.00	D04 748 001*	D04 760 000*	cp
			25.00	D04 768 001*	D04 780 000*	cp
			25.00	D04 788 001*	D04 800 000*	cp
			25.00	D04 808 001*	D04 820 000*	cp
			25.00	D04 828 001*	D04 840 000*	cp
			25.00	D04 848 001*	D04 860 000*	cp
			25.00	D04 868 001*	D04 880 000*	cp
			25.00	D04 888 001*	D04 900 000*	cp
			25.00	D04 908 001*	D04 920 000*	cp
			25.00	D04 928 001*	D04 940 000*	cp
			25.00	D04 948 001*	D04 960 000*	cp
			25.00	D04 968 001*	D04 980 000*	cp
			25.00	D04 988 001*	D05 000 000*	cp
			25.00	D05 008 001*	D05 020 000*	cp
			25.00	D05 028 001*	D05 040 000*	cp
			25.00	D05 048 001*	D05 060 000*	cp
			25.00	D05 068 001*	D05 080 000*	cp
			25.00	D05 088 001*	D05 100 000*	cp
			25.00	D05 108 001*	D05 120 000*	cp
			3.50	D05 120 001*	D05 760 000*	cp

DISTRICT	TOTAL NOTES PRINTED	BLOCKS	ESTIMATED VALUE VG/F CU	LOW OFFICIAL SERIAL NUMBER	HIGH OFFICIAL SERIAL NUMBER	
5 E RICHMOND	99,840,000	E--A	3.00	E00 000 001A	E99 840 000A	cp
	99,840,000	E--B	3.00	E00 000 001B	E99 840 000B	cp
	99,840,000	E--C	3.00	E00 000 001C	E99 840 000C	cp
	99,840,000	E--D	3.00	E00 000 001D	E99 840 000D	cp
	19,200,000	E--E	3.00	E00 000 001E	E19 200 000E	cp
	000	E--*	25.00	E00 016 001*	E00 020 000*	cv
			25.00	E00 036 001*	E00 040 000*	cv
			25.00	E00 056 001*	E00 060 000*	cv
			25.00	E00 076 001*	E00 080 000*	cv
			25.00	E00 096 001*	E00 100 000*	cv
			25.00	E00 116 001*	E00 120 000*	cv
			25.00	E00 136 001*	E00 140 000*	cv
			25.00	E00 156 001*	E00 160 000*	cv
			25.00	E00 176 001*	E00 180 000*	cv
			25.00	E00 196 001*	E00 200 000*	cv
			25.00	E00 216 001*	E00 220 000*	cv
			25.00	E00 236 001*	E00 240 000*	cv
			25.00	E00 256 001*	E00 260 000*	cv
			25.00	E00 276 001*	E00 280 000*	cv
			25.00	E00 296 001*	E00 300 000*	cv
			25.00	E00 316 001*	E00 320 000*	cv
			25.00	E00 336 001*	E00 340 000*	cv
			25.00	E00 356 001*	E00 360 000*	cv
			25.00	E00 376 001*	E00 380 000*	cv
			25.00	E00 396 001*	E00 400 000*	cv
			25.00	E00 416 001*	E00 420 000*	cv
			25.00	E00 436 001*	E00 440 000*	cv
			25.00	E00 456 001*	E00 460 000*	cv
			25.00	E00 476 001*	E00 480 000*	cv
			25.00	E00 496 001*	E00 500 000*	cv
			25.00	E00 516 001*	E00 520 000*	cv
			25.00	E00 536 001*	E00 540 000*	cv
			25.00	E00 556 001	E00 560 000*	cv
			25.00	E00 576 001*	E00 580 000*	cv
			25.00	E00 596 001*	E00 600 000*	cv
			25.00	E00 616 001*	E00 620 000*	cv
			25.00	E00 636 001*	E00 640 000*	cv
			3.50	E00 640 001*	E01 920 000*	cv
			25.00	E01 928 001*	E01 940 000*	cv
			25.00	E01 948 001*	E01 960 000*	cv
			25.00	E01 968 001*	E01 980 000*	cv
			25.00	E01 988 001*	E02 000 000*	cv
			25.00	E02 008 001*	E02 020 000*	cv
			25.00	E02 028 001*	E02 040 000*	cv
			25.00	E02 048 001*	E02 060 000*	cv
			25.00	E02 068 001*	E02 080 000*	cv
			25.00	E02 088 001*	E02 100 000*	cv
			25.00	E02 108 001*	E02 120 000*	cv
			25.00	E02 128 001*	E02 140 000*	cv
			25.00	E02 148 001*	E02 160 000*	cv
			25.00	E02 168 001*	E02 180 000*	cv
			25.00	E02 188 001*	E02 200 000*	cv
			25.00	E02 208 001*	E02 220 000*	cv
			25.00	E02 228 001*	E02 240 000*	cv
			25.00	E02 248 001*	E02 260 000*	cv
			25.00	E02 268 001*	E02 280 000*	cv
			25.00	E02 288 001*	E02 300 000*	cv
			25.00	E02 308 001*	E02 320 000*	cv
			25.00	E02 328 001*	E02 340 000*	cv
			25.00	E02 348 001*	E02 360 000*	cv
			25.00	E02 368 001*	E02 380 000*	cv
			25.00	E02 388 001*	E02 400 000*	cv
			25.00	E02 408 001*	E02 420 000*	cv
			25.00	E02 428 001*	E02 440 000*	cv
			25.00	E02 448 001*	E02 460 000*	cv
			25.00	E02 468 001*	E02 480 000*	cv
			25.00	E02 488 001*	E02 500 000*	cv
			25.00	E02 508 001*	E02 520 000*	cv
			25.00	E02 528 001*	E02 540 000*	cv
			25.00	E02 548 001*	E02 560 000*	cv

DISTRICT	TOTAL NOTES PRINTED	BLOCKS	ESTIMATED VALUE VG/F CU	LOW OFFICIAL SERIAL NUMBER	HIGH OFFICIAL SERIAL NUMBER	
			3.50	E02 560 001*	E03 840 000*	cp
			3.50	E03 840 001*	E05 120 000*	cv
			3.50	E05 120 001*	E07 040 000*	cp
			25.00	E07 056 001*	E07 060 000*	cp
			25.00	E07 076 001*	E07 080 000*	cp
			25.00	E07 096 001*	E07 100 000*	cp
			25.00	E07 116 001*	E07 120 000*	cp
			25.00	E07 136 001*	E07 140 000*	cp
			25.00	E07 156 001*	E07 160 000*	cp
			25.00	E07 176 001*	E07 180 000*	cp
			25.00	E07 196 001*	E07 200 000*	cp
			25.00	E07 216 001*	E07 220 000*	cp
			25.00	E07 236 001*	E07 240 000*	cp
			25.00	E07 256 001*	E07 260 000*	cp
			25.00	E07 276 001*	E07 280 000*	cp
			25.00	E07 296 001*	E07 300 000*	cp
			25.00	E07 316 001*	E07 320 000*	cp
			25.00	E07 336 001*	E07 340 000*	cp
			25.00	E07 356 001*	E07 360 000*	cp
			25.00	E07 376 001*	E07 380 000*	cp
			25.00	E07 396 001*	E07 400 000*	cp
			25.00	E07 416 001*	E07 420 000*	cp
			25.00	E07 436 001*	E07 440 000*	cp
			25.00	E07 456 001*	E07 460 000*	cp
			25.00	E07 476 001*	E07 480 000*	cp
			25.00	E07 496 001*	E07 500 000*	cp
			25.00	E07 516 001*	E07 520 000*	cp
			25.00	E07 536 001*	E07 540 000*	cp
			25.00	E07 556 001*	E07 560 000*	cp
			25.00	E07 576 001*	E07 580 000*	cp
			25.00	E07 596 001*	E07 600 000*	cp
			25.00	E07 616 001*	E07 620 000*	cp
			25.00	E07 736 001*	E07 640 000*	cp
			25.00	E07 756 001*	E07 660 000*	cp
			25.00	E07 776 001*	E07 680 000*	cp
6 F ATLANTA	99,840,000	F--A	3.00	F00 000 001A	F99 840 000A	cp
	99,840,000	F--B	3.00	F00 000 001B	F99 840 000B	cp
	99,840,000	F--C	3.00	F00 000 001C	F99 840 000C	cp
	99,840,000	F--D	3.00	F00 000 001D	F99 840 000D	cp
	99,840,000	F--E	3.00	F00 000 001E	F99 840 000E	cp
	65,920,000	F--F	3.00	F00 000 001F	F65 920 000F	cp
	8,960,000	F--*	25.00	F00 012 001*	F00 020 000*	cv
			25.00	F00 032 001*	F00 040 000*	cv
			25.00	F00 052 001*	F00 060 000*	cv
			25.00	F00 072 001*	F00 080 000*	cv
			25.00	F00 092 001*	F00 100 000*	cv
			25.00	F00 112 001*	F00 120 000*	cv
			25.00	F00 132 001*	F00 140 000*	cv
			25.00	F00 152 001*	F00 160 000*	cv
			25.00	F00 172 001*	F00 180 000*	cv
			25.00	F00 192 001*	F00 200 000*	cv
			25.00	F00 212 001*	F00 220 000*	cv
			25.00	F00 232 001*	F00 240 000*	cv
			25.00	F00 252 001*	F00 260 000*	cv
			25.00	F00 272 001*	F00 280 000*	cv
			25.00	F00 292 001*	F00 300 000*	cv
			25.00	F00 312 001*	F00 320 000*	cv
			25.00	F00 332 001*	F00 340 000*	cv
			25.00	F00 352 001*	F00 360 000*	cv
			25.00	F00 372 001*	F00 380 000*	cv
			25.00	F00 392 001*	F00 400 000*	cv
			25.00	F00 412 001*	F00 420 000*	cv
			25.00	F00 432 001*	F00 440 000*	cv
			25.00	F00 452 001*	F00 460 000*	cv
			25.00	F00 472 001*	F00 480 000*	cv
			25.00	F00 492 001*	F00 500 000*	cv
			25.00	F00 512 001*	F00 520 000*	cv
			25.00	F00 532 001*	F00 540 000*	cv
			25.00	F00 552 001*	F00 560 000*	cv
			25.00	F00 572 001*	F00 580 000*	cv

DISTRICT	TOTAL NOTES PRINTED	BLOCKS	ESTIMATED VALUE VG/F	CU	LOW OFFICIAL SERIAL NUMBER	HIGH OFFICIAL SERIAL NUMBER	
				25.00	F00 592 001*	F00 600 000*	cv
				25.00	F00 612 001*	F00 620 000*	cv
				25.00	F00 632 001*	F00 640 000*	cv
				25.00	F00 648 001*	F00 660 000*	cv
				25.00	F00 668 001*	F00 680 000*	cv
				25.00	F00 688 001*	F00 700 000*	cv
				25.00	F00 708 001*	F00 720 000*	cv
				25.00	F00 728 001*	F00 740 000*	cv
				25.00	F00 748 001*	F00 760 000*	cv
				25.00	F00 768 001*	F00 780 000*	cv
				25.00	F00 788 001*	F00 800 000*	cv
				25.00	F00 808 001*	F00 820 000*	cv
				25.00	F00 828 001*	F00 840 000*	cv
				25.00	F00 848 001*	F00 860 000*	cv
				25.00	F00 868 001*	F00 880 000*	cv
				25.00	F00 888 001*	F00 900 000*	cv
				25.00	F00 908 001*	F00 920 000*	cv
				25.00	F00 928 001*	F00 940 000*	cv
				25.00	F00 948 001*	F00 960 000*	cv
				25.00	F00 968 001*	F00 980 000*	cv
				25.00	F00 988 001*	F01 000 000*	cv
				25.00	F01 008 001*	F01 020 000*	cv
				25.00	F01 028 001*	F01 040 000*	cv
				25.00	F01 048 001*	F01 060 000*	cv
				25.00	F01 068 001*	F01 080 000*	cv
				25.00	F01 088 001*	F01 100 000*	cv
				25.00	F01 108 001*	F01 120 000*	cv
				25.00	F01 128 001*	F01 140 000*	cv
				25.00	F01 148 001*	F01 160 000*	cv
				25.00	F01 168 001*	F01 180 000*	cv
				25.00	F01 188 001*	F01 200 000*	cv
				25.00	F01 208 001*	F01 220 000*	cv
				25.00	F01 228 001*	F01 240 000*	cv
				25.00	F01 248 001*	F01 260 000*	cv
				25.00	F01 268 001*	F01 280 000*	cv
				3.50	F01 280 001*	F03 840 000*	cv
				3.50	F03 840 001*	F04 480 000*	cp
				3.50	F04 480 001*	F07 040 000*	cv
				3.50	F07 040 001*	F07 680 000*	cp
				3.50	F07 680 001*	F09 600 000*	cv
7	G CHICAGO	99,840,000	G--A	3.00	G00 000 001A	G99 840 000A	cp
		99,840,000	G--B	3.00	G00 000 001B	G99 840 000B	cp
		99,840,000	G--C	3.00	G00 000 001C	G99 840 000C	cp
		99,840,000	G--D	3.00	G00 000 001D	G99 840 000D	cp
		99,840,000	G--E	3.00	G00 000 001E	G99 840 000E	cp
		99,840,000	G--F	3.00	G00 000 001F	G99 840 000F	cp
		16,640,000	G--G	3.00	G00 000 001G	G16 640 000G	cp
		9,472,000	G--*	25.00	G00 016 001*	G00 020 000*	cv
				25.00	G00 036 001*	G00 040 000*	cv
				25.00	G00 056 001*	G00 060 000*	cv
				25.00	G00 076 001*	G00 080 000*	cv
				25.00	G00 096 001*	G00 100 000*	cv
				25.00	G00 116 001*	G00 120 000*	cv
				25.00	G00 136 001*	G00 140 000*	cv
				25.00	G00 156 001*	G00 160 000*	cv
				25.00	G00 176 001*	G00 180 000*	cv
				25.00	G00 196 001*	G00 200 000*	cv
				25.00	G00 216 001*	G00 220 000*	cv
				25.00	G00 236 001*	G00 240 000*	cv
				25.00	G00 256 001*	G00 260 000*	cv
				25.00	G00 276 001*	G00 280 000*	cv
				25.00	G00 296 001*	G00 300 000*	cv
				25.00	G00 316 001*	G00 320 000*	cv
				25.00	G00 336 001*	G00 340 000*	cv
				25.00	G00 356 001*	G00 360 000*	cv
				25.00	G00 376 001*	G00 380 000*	cv
				25.00	G00 396 001*	G00 400 000*	cv
				25.00	G00 416 001*	G00 420 000*	cv
				25.00	G00 436 001*	G00 440 000*	cv
				25.00	G00 456 001*	G00 460 000*	cv

DISTRICT	TOTAL NOTES PRINTED	BLOCKS	ESTIMATED VALUE VG/F	CU	LOW OFFICIAL SERIAL NUMBER	HIGH OFFICIAL SERIAL NUMBER	
				25.00	G00 476 001*	G00 480 000*	cv
				25.00	G00 496 001*	G00 500 000*	cv
				25.00	G00 516 001*	G00 520 000*	cv
				25.00	G00 536 001*	G00 540 000*	cv
				25.00	G 00 556 001*	G00 560 000*	cv
				25.00	G00 576 001*	G00 580 000*	cv
				25.00	G00 596 001*	G00 600 000*	cv
				25.00	G00 616 001*	G00 620 000*	cv
				25.00	G00 636 001*	G00 640 000*	cv
				25.00	G00 648 001*	G00 660 000*	cv
				25.00	G00 668 001*	G00 680 000*	cv
				25.00	G00 688 001*	G00 700 000*	cv
				25.00	G00 708 001*	G00 720 000*	cv
				25.00	G00 728 001*	G00 740 000*	cv
				25.00	G00 748 001*	G00 760 000*	cv
				25.00	G00 768 001*	G00 780 000*	cv
				25.00	G00 788 001*	G00 800 000*	cv
				25.00	G00 808 001*	G00 820 000*	cv
				25.00	G00 828 001*	G00 840 000*	cv
				25.00	G00 848 001*	G00 860 000*	cv
				25.00	G00 868 001*	G00 880 000*	cv
				25.00	G00 888 001*	G00 900 000*	cv
				25.00	G00 908 001*	G00 920 000*	cv
				25.00	G00 928 001*	G00 940 000*	cv
				25.00	G00 948 001*	G00 960 000*	cv
				25.00	G00 968 001*	G00 980 000*	cv
				25.00	G00 988 001*	G01 000 000*	cv
				25.00	G01 008 001*	G01 020 000*	cv
				25.00	G01 028 001*	G01 040 000*	cv
				25.00	G01 048 001*	G01 060 000*	cv
				25.00	G01 068 001*	G01 080 000*	cv
				25.00	G01 088 001*	G01 100 000*	cv
				25.00	G01 108 001*	G01 120 000*	cv
				25.00	G01 128 001*	G01 140 000*	cv
				25.00	G01 148 001*	G01 160 000*	cv
				25.00	G01 168 001*	G01 180 000*	cv
				25.00	G01 188 001*	G01 200 000*	cv
				25.00	G01 208 001*	G01 220 000*	cv
				25.00	G01 228 001*	G01 240 000*	cv
				25.00	G01 248 001*	G01 260 000*	cv
				25.00	G01 268 001*	G01 280 000*	cv
				3.50	G01 280 001*	G07 040 000*	cv
				3.50	G07 040 001*	G10 240 000*	cp
8	H ST. LOUIS	99,840,000	H--A	3.00	H00 000 001A	H99 840 000A	cp
		99,840,000	H--B	3.00	H00 000 001B	H99 840 000B	cp
		2,048,000	H--*	3.50	H00 000 001*	H00 640 000*	cv
				3.50	H00 640 001*	H01 280 000*	cp
				3.50	H01 280 001*	H01 920 000*	cv
				25.00	H01 936 001*	H01 940 000*	cp
				25.00	H01 956 001*	H01 960 000*	cp
				25.00	H01 976 001*	H01 980 000*	cp
				25.00	H01 996 001*	H02 000 000*	cp
				25.00	H02 016 001*	H02 020 000*	cp
				25.00	H02 036 001*	H02 040 000*	cp
				25.00	H02 056 001*	H02 060 000*	cp
				25.00	H02 076 001*	H02 080 000*	cp
				25.00	H02 096 001*	H02 100 000*	cp
				25.00	H02 116 001*	H02 120 000*	cp
				25.00	H02 136 001*	H02 140 000*	cp
				25.00	H02 156 001*	H02 160 000*	cp
				25.00	H02 176 001*	H02 180 000*	cp
				25.00	H02 196 001*	H02 200 000*	cp
				25.00	H02 216 001*	H02 220 000*	cp
				25.00	H02 236 001*	H02 240 000*	cp
				25.00	H02 256 001*	H02 260 000*	cp
				25.00	H02 276 001*	H02 280 000*	cp
				25.00	H02 296 001*	H02 300 000*	cp
				25.00	H02 316 001*	H02 320 000*	cp
				25.00	H02 336 001*	H02 340 000*	cp
				25.00	H02 356 001*	H02 360 000*	cp
				25.00	H02 376 001*	H02 380 000*	cp

DISTRICT	TOTAL NOTES PRINTED	BLOCKS	ESTIMATED VALUE VG/F	CU	LOW OFFICIAL SERIAL NUMBER	HIGH OFFICIAL SERIAL NUMBER	
				25.00	H02 396 001*	H02 400 000*	cp
				25.00	H02 416 001*	H02 420 000*	cp
				25.00	H02 436 001*	H02 440 000*	cp
				25.00	H02 456 001*	H02 460 000*	cp
				25.00	H02 476 001*	H02 480 000*	cp
				25.00	H02 496 001*	H02 500 000*	cp
				25.00	H02 516 001*	H02 520 000*	cp
				25.00	H02 536 001*	H02 540 000*	cp
				25.00	H02 556 001*	H02 560 000*	cp
9 I MINNEAPOLIS	99,840,000	I--A		3.00	I00 000 001A	I99 840 000A	cp
	15,360,000	I--B		3.00	I00 000 001B	I15 360 000B	cp
	2,560,000	I--*		3.50	I00 000 001*	I01 920 000*	cv
				3.50	I01 920 001*	I02 560 000*	cp
10 J KANSAS CITY	99,840,000	J--A		3.00	J00 000 001A	J99 840 000A	cp
	99,840,000	J--B		3.00	J00 000 001B	J99 840 000B	cp
	23,680,000	J--C		3.00	J00 000 001C	J23 680 000C	cp
	3,840,000	J--*		25.00	J00 012 001*	J00 020 000*	cv
				25.00	J00 032 001*	J00 040 000*	cv
				25.00	J00 052 001*	J00 060 000*	cv
				25.00	J00 072 001*	J00 080 000*	cv
				25.00	J00 192 001*	J00 100 000*	cv
				25.00	J00 112 001*	J00 120 000*	cv
				25.00	J00 132 001*	J00 140 000*	cv
				25.00	J00 152 001*	J00 160 000*	cv
				25.00	J00 172 001*	J00 180 000*	cv
				25.00	J00 192 001*	J00 200 000*	cv
				25.00	J00 212 001*	J00 220 000*	cv
				25.00	J00 232 001*	J00 240 000*	cv
				25.00	J00 252 001*	J00 260 000*	cv
				25.00	J00 272 001*	J00 280 000*	cv
				25.00	J00 292 001*	J00 300 000	cv
				25.00	J00 312 001*	J00 320 000*	cv
				25.00	J00 332 001*	J00 340 000*	cv
				25.00	J00 352 001*	J00 360 000*	cv
				25.00	J00 372 001*	J00 380 000*	cv
				25.00	J00 392 001*	J00 400 000*	cv
				25.00	J00 412 001*	J00 420 000*	cv
				25.00	J00 432 001*	J00 440 000*	cv
				25.00	J00 452 001*	J00 460 000*	cv
				25.00	J00 472 001*	J00 480 000*	cv
				25.00	J00 492 001*	J00 500 000*	cv
				25.00	J00 512 001*	J00 520 000*	cv
				25.00	J00 523 001*	J00 540 000*	cv
				25.00	J00 552 001*	J00 560 000*	cv
				25.00	J00 572 001*	J00 580 000*	cv
				25.00	J00 592 001*	J00 600 000*	cv
				25.00	J00 612 001*	J00 620 000*	cv
				25.00	J00 632 001*	J00 640 000*	cv
				25.00	J00 656 001*	J00 660 000*	cv
				25.00	J00 676 001*	J00 680 000*	cv
				25.00	J00 696 001	J00 700 000*	cv
				25.00	J00 716 001*	J00 720 000*	cv
				25.00	J00 736 001*	J00 740 000*	cv
				25.00	J00 756 001*	J00 760 000*	cv
				25.00	J00 776 001*	J00 780 000*	cv
				25.00	J00 796 001*	J00 800 000*	cv
				25.00	J00 816 001*	J00 820 000*	cv
				25.00	J00 836 001*	J00 840 000*	cv
				25.00	J00 856 001*	J00 860 000*	cv
				25.00	J00 876 001*	J00 880 000*	cv
				25.00	J00 896 001*	J00 900 000*	cv
				25.00	J00 916 001*	J00 920 000*	cv
				25.00	J00 936 001*	J00 940 000*	cv
				25.00	J00 956 001*	J00 960 000*	cv
				25.00	J00 976 001*	J00 980 000*	cv
				25.00	J00 996 001*	J01 000 000*	cv
				25.00	J01 016 001*	J01 020 000*	cv
				25.00	J01 036 001*	J01 040 000*	cv
				25.00	J01 056 001*	J01 060 000*	cv
				25.00	J01 076 001*	J01 080 000*	cv
				25.00	J01 096 001*	J01 100 000*	cv

DISTRICT	TOTAL NOTES PRINTED	BLOCKS	ESTIMATED VALUE VG/F	CU	LOW OFFICIAL SERIAL NUMBER	HIGH OFFICIAL SERIAL NUMBER	
				25.00	J01 116 001*	J01 120 000*	cv
				25.00	J01 136 001*	J01 140 000*	cv
				25.00	J01 156 001*	J01 160 000*	cv
				25.00	J01 176 001*	J01 180 000*	cv
				25.00	J01 196 001*	J01 200 000*	cv
				25.00	J01 216 001*	J01 220 000*	cv
				25.00	J01 236 001*	J01 240 000*	cv
				25.00	J01 256 001*	J01 260 000*	cv
				25.00	J01 276 001*	J01 280 000*	cv
				25.00	J01 292 001*	J01 300 000*	cv
				25.00	J01 312 001*	J01 320 000*	cv
				25.00	J01 332 001*	J01 340 000*	cv
				25.00	J01 352 001*	J01 360 000*	cv
				25.00	J01 372 001*	J01 380 000*	cv
				25.00	J01 392 001*	J01 400 000*	cv
				25.00	J01 412 001*	J01 420 000*	cv
				25.00	J01 432 001*	J01 440 000*	cv
				25.00	J01 452 001*	J01 460 000*	cv
				25.00	J01 472 001*	J01 480 000*	cv
				25.00	J01 492 001*	J01 500 000*	cv
				25.00	J01 512 001*	J01 520 000*	cv
				25.00	J01 532 001*	J01 540 000*	cv
				25.00	J01 552 001*	J01 560 000*	cv
				25.00	J01 572 001*	J01 580 000*	cv
				25.00	J01 592 001*	J01 600 000*	cv
				25.00	J01 612 001*	J01 620 000*	cv
				25.00	J01 632 001*	J01 640 000*	cv
				25.00	J01 652 001*	J01 660 000*	cv
				25.00	J01 672 001*	J01 680 000*	cv
				25.00	J01 692 001*	J01 700 000*	cv
				25.00	J01 712 001*	J01 720 000*	cv
				25.00	J01 732 001*	J01 740 000*	cv
				25.00	J01 752 001*	J01 760 000*	cv
				25.00	J01 772 001*	J01 780 000*	cv
				25.00	J01 792 001*	J01 800 000*	cv
				25.00	J01 812 001*	J01 820 000*	cv
				25.00	J01 832 001*	J01 840 000	cv
				25.00	J01 852 001*	J01 860 000*	cv
				25.00	J01 872 001*	J01 880 000*	cv
				25.00	J01 892 001*	J01 900 000*	cv
				25.00	J01 912 001*	J01 920 000*	cv
				3.50	J01 920 001*	J04 480 000*	cv
				3.50	J04 480 001*	J05 120 000*	cp
10 K DALLAS	99,840,000	K--A		3.00	K00 000 001A	K99 840 000A	cp
	99,840,000	K--B		3.00	K00 000 001B	K99 840 000B	cp
	89,600,000	K--C		3.00	K00 000 001C	K89 600 000C	cp
	4,608,000	K--*		25.00	K00 012 001*	K00 020 000*	cv
				25.00	K00 032 001*	K00 040 000*	cv
				25.00	K00 052 001*	K00 060 000*	cv
				25.00	K00 072 001*	K00 080 000*	cv
				25.00	K00 092 001*	K00 100 000*	cv
				25.00	K00 112 001*	K00 120 000*	cv
				25.00	K00 132 001*	K00 140 000*	cv
				25.00	K00 152 001*	K00 160 000*	cv
				25.00	K00 172 001*	K00 180 000*	cv
				25.00	K00 192 001*	K00 200 000*	cv
				25.00	K00 121 001*	K00 220 000*	cv
				25.00	K00 232 001*	K00 240 000*	cv
				25.00	K00 252 001*	K00 260 000*	cv
				25.00	K00 272 001*	K00 280 000*	cv
				25.00	K00 292 001*	K00 300 000*	cv
				25.00	K00 312 001*	K00 320 000*	cv
				25.00	K00 332 001*	K00 340 000*	cv
				25.00	K00 352 001*	K00 360 000*	cv
				25.00	K00 372 001*	K00 380 000*	cv
				25.00	K00 392 001*	K00 400 000*	cv
				25.00	K00 412 001*	K00 420 000*	cv
				25.00	K00 432 001*	K00 440 000*	cv
				25.00	K00 452 001*	K00 460 000*	cv
				25.00	K00 472 001*	K00 480 000*	cv
				25.00	K00 492 001*	K00 500 000*	cv

DISTRICT	TOTAL NOTES PRINTED	BLOCKS	ESTIMATED VALUE VG/F	CU	LOW OFFICIAL SERIAL NUMBER	HIGH OFFICIAL SERIAL NUMBER	
				25.00	K00 512 001*	K00 520 000*	CV
				25.00	K00 532 001*	K00 540 000*	CV
				25.00	K00 552 001*	K00 560 000*	CV
				25.00	K00 572 001*	K00 580 000*	CV
				25.00	K00 592 001*	K00 600 000*	CV
				25.00	K00 612 001*	K00 620 000*	CV
				25.00	K00 632 001*	K00 640 000*	CV
				25.00	K00 652 001*	K00 660 000*	CV
				25.00	K00 672 001*	K00 680 000*	CV
				25.00	K00 692 001*	K00 700 000*	CV
				25.00	K00 712 001*	K00 720 000*	CV
				25.00	K00 732 001*	K00 740 000*	CV
				25.00	K00 752 001*	K00 760 000*	CV
				25.00	K00 772 001*	K00 780 000*	CV
				25.00	K00 792 001*	K00 800 000*	CV
				25.00	K00 812 001*	K00 820 000*	CV
				25.00	K00 832 001*	K00 840 000*	CV
				25.00	K00 852 001*	K00 860 000*	CV
				25.00	K00 872 001*	K00 880 000*	CV
				25.00	K00 892 001*	K00 900 000*	CV
				25.00	K00 912 001*	K00 920 000*	CV
				25.00	K00 932 001*	K00 940 000*	CV
				25.00	K00 952 001*	K00 960 000*	CV
				25.00	K00 972 001*	K00 980 000*	CV
				25.00	K00 992 001*	K01 000 000*	CV
				25.00	K01 012 001*	K01 020 000*	CV
				25.00	K01 032 001*	K01 040 000*	CV
				25.00	K01 052 001*	K01 060 000*	CV
				25.00	K01 072 001*	K01 080 000*	CV
				25.00	K01 092 001*	K01 100 000*	CV
				25.00	K01 112 001*	K01 120 000*	CV
				25.00	K01 132 001*	K01 140 000*	CV
				25.00	K01 152 001*	K01 160 000*	CV
				25.00	K01 172 001*	K01 180 000*	CV
				25.00	K01 192 001*	K01 200 000*	CV
				25.00	K01 212 001*	K01 220 000*	CV
				25.00	K01 232 001*	K01 240 000*	CV
				25.00	K01 252 001*	K01 260 000*	CV
				25.00	K01 272 001*	K01 280 000*	CV
				25.00	K01 292 001*	K01 300 000*	CV
				25.00	K01 312 001*	K01 320 000*	CV
				25.00	K01 332 001*	K01 340 000*	CV
				25.00	K01 352 001*	K01 360 000*	CV
				25.00	K01 372 001*	K01 380 000*	CV
				25.00	K01 392 001*	K01 400 000*	CV
				25.00	K01 412 001*	K01 420 000*	CV
				25.00	K01 432 001*	K01 440 000*	CV
				25.00	K01 452 001*	K01 460 000*	CV
				25.00	K01 472 001*	K01 480 000*	CV
				25.00	K01 492 001*	K01 500 000*	CV
				25.00	K01 512 001*	K01 520 000*	CV
				25.00	K01 532 001*	K01 540 000*	CV
				25.00	K01 552 001*	K01 560 000*	CV
				25.00	K01 572 001*	K01 580 000*	CV
				25.00	K01 592 001*	K01 600 000*	CV
				25.00	K01 612 001*	K01 620 000*	CV
				25.00	K01 632 001*	K01 640 000*	CV
				25.00	K01 652 001*	K01 660 000*	CV
				25.00	K01 672 001*	K01 680 000*	CV
				25.00	K01 692 001*	K01 700 000*	CV
				25.00	K01 712 001*	K01 720 000*	CV
				25.00	K01 732 001*	K01 740 000*	CV
				25.00	K01 752 001*	K01 760 000*	CV
				25.00	K01 772 001*	K01 780 000*	CV
				25.00	K01 792 001*	K01 800 000*	CV
				25.00	K01 812 001*	K01 820 000*	CV
				25.00	K01 832 001*	K01 840 000*	CV
				25.00	K01 852 001*	K01 860 000*	CV
				25.00	K01 872 001*	K01 880 000*	CV
				25.00	K01 892 001*	K01 900 000*	CV
				25.00	K01 912 001*	K01 920 000*	CV

DISTRICT	TOTAL NOTES PRINTED	BLOCKS	ESTIMATED VALUE VG/F	CU	LOW OFFICIAL SERIAL NUMBER	HIGH OFFICIAL SERIAL NUMBER	
				25.00	K01 932 001*	K01 940 000*	cv
				25.00	K01 952 001*	K01 960 000*	cv
				25.00	K01 972 001*	K01 980 000*	cv
				25.00	K01 992 001*	K02 000 000*	cv
				25.00	K02 012 001*	K02 020 000*	cv
				25.00	K02 032 001*	K02 040 000*	cv
				25.00	K02 052 001*	K02 060 000*	cv
				25.00	K02 072 001*	K02 080 000*	cv
				25.00	K02 092 001*	K02 100 000*	cv
				25.00	K02 112 001*	K02 120 000*	cv
				25.00	K02 132 001*	K02 140 000*	cv
				25.00	K02 152 001*	K02 160 000*	cv
				25.00	K02 172 001*	K02 180 000*	cv
				25.00	K02 192 001*	K02 200 000*	cv
				25.00	K02 212 001*	K02 220 000*	cv
				25.00	K02 232 001*	K02 240 000*	cv
				25.00	K02 252 001*	K02 260 000*	cv
				25.00	K02 272 001*	K02 280 000*	cv
				25.00	K02 292 001*	K02 300 000*	cv
				25.00	K02 312 001*	K02 320 000*	cv
				25.00	K02 332 001*	K02 340 000*	cv
				25.00	K02 352 001*	K02 360 000*	cv
				25.00	K02 372 001*	K02 380 000*	cv
				25.00	K02 392 001*	K02 400 000*	cv
				25.00	K02 412 001*	K02 420 000*	cv
				25.00	K02 432 001*	K02 440 000*	cv
				25.00	K02 452 001*	K02 460 000*	cv
				25.00	K02 472 001*	K02 480 000*	cv
				25.00	K02 492 001*	K02 500 000*	cv
				25.00	K02 512 001*	K02 520 000*	cv
				25.00	K02 532 001*	K02 540 000*	cv
				25.00	K02 552 001*	K02 560 000*	cv
				25.00	K02 568 001*	K02 580 000*	cv
				25.00	K02 588 001*	K02 600 000*	cv
				25.00	K02 608 001*	K02 620 000*	cv
				25.00	K02 628 001*	K02 640 000*	cv
				25.00	K02 648 001*	K02 660 000*	cv
				25.00	K02 668 001*	K02 680 000*	cv
				25.00	K02 688 001*	K02 700 000*	cv
				25.00	K02 708 001*	K02 720 000*	cv
				25.00	K02 728 001*	K02 740 000*	cv
				25.00	K02 748 001*	K02 760 000*	cv
				25.00	K02 768 001*	K02 780 000*	cv
				25.00	K02 788 001*	K02 800 000*	cv
				25.00	K02 808 001*	K02 820 000*	cv
				25.00	K02 828 001*	K02 840 000*	cv
				25.00	K02 848 001*	K02 860 000*	cv
				25.00	K02 868 001*	K02 880 000*	cv
				25.00	K02 888 001*	K02 900 000*	cv
				25.00	K02 908 001*	K02 920 000*	cv
				25.00	K02 928 001*	K02 940 000*	cv
				25.00	K02 948 001*	K02 960 000*	cv
				25.00	K02 968 001*	K02 980 000*	cv
				25.00	K02 988 001*	K03 000 000*	cv
				25.00	K03 008 001*	K03 020 000*	cv
				25.00	K03 028 001*	K03 040 000*	cv
				25.00	K03 048 001*	K03 060 000*	cv
				25.00	K03 068 001*	K03 080 000*	cv
				25.00	K03 088 001*	K03 100 000*	cv
				25.00	K03 108 001*	K03 120 000*	cv
				25.00	K03 128 001*	K03 140 000*	cv
				25.00	K03 148 001*	K03 160 000*	cv
				25.00	K03 168 001*	K03 180 000*	cv
				25.00	K03 188 001*	K03 200 000*	cv
				3.50	K03 200 001*	K05 760 000*	cv
				3.50	K05 760 001*	K06 400 000*	cp
12 L SAN FRANCISCO	99,840,000	L--A		3.00	L00 000 001A	L99 840 000A	cp
	99,840,000	L--B		3.00	L00 000 001B	L99 840 000B	cp
	99,840,000	L--C		3.00	L00 000 001C	L99 840 000C	cp
	99,840,000	L--D		3.00	L00 000 001D	L99 840 000D	cp

DISTRICT	TOTAL NOTES PRINTED	BLOCKS	ESTIMATED VALUE VG/F	CU	LOW OFFICIAL SERIAL NUMBER	HIGH OFFICIAL SERIAL NUMBER	
	99,840,000	L--E		3.00	L00 000 001E	L99 840 000E	cp
	17,280,000	L--F		3.00	L00 000 001F	L17 280 000F	cp
	8,320,000	L--*		25.00	L00 012 001*	L00 020 000*	cv
				25.00	L00 032 001*	L00 040 000*	cv
				25.00	L00 052 001*	L00 060 000*	cv
				25.00	L00 072 001*	L00 080 000*	cv
				25.00	L00 092 001*	L00 100 000*	cv
				25.00	L00 112 001*	L00 120 000*	cv
				25.00	L00 132 001*	L00 140 000*	cv
				25.00	L00 152 001*	L00 160 000*	cv
				25.00	L00 172 001*	L00 180 000*	cv
				25.00	L00 192 001*	L00 200 000*	cv
				25.00	L00 212 001*	L00 220 000*	cv
				25.00	L00 232 001*	L00 240 000*	cv
				25.00	L00 252 001*	L00 260 000*	cv
				25.00	L00 272 001*	L00 280 000*	cv
				25.00	L00 292 991*	L00 300 000*	cv
				25.00	L00 312 001*	L00 320 000*	cv
				25.00	L00 332 001*	L00 340 000*	cv
				25.00	L00 352 001*	L00 360 000*	cv
				25.00	L00 372 001*	L00 380 000*	cv
				25.00	L00 392 001*	L00 400 000*	cv
				25.00	L00 412 001*	L00 420 000*	cv
				25.00	L00 432 001*	L00 440 000*	cv
				25.00	L00 452 001*	L00 460 000*	cv
				25.00	L00 472 001*	L00 480 000*	cv
				25.00	L00 492 001*	L00 500 000*	cv
				25.00	L00 512 001*	L00 520 000*	cv
				25.00	L00 532 001*	L00 540 000*	cv
				25.00	L00 552 001*	L00 560 000*	cv
				25.00	L00 572 001*	L00 580 000*	cv
				25.00	L00 592 001*	L00 600 000*	cv
				25.00	L00 612 001*	L00 620 000*	cv
				25.00	L00 632 001*	L00 640 000*	cv
				25.00	L00 648 001*	L00 660 000*	cv
				25.00	L00 668 001*	L00 680 000*	cv
				25.00	L00 688 001*	L00 700 000*	cv
				25.00	L00 708 001*	L00 720 000*	cv
				25.00	L00 728 001*	L00 740 000*	cv
				25.00	L00 748 001*	L00 760 000*	cv
				25.00	L00 768 001*	L00 780 000*	cv
				25.00	L00 788 001*	L00 800 000*	cv
				25.00	L00 808 001*	L00 820 000*	cv
				25.00	L00 828 001*	L00 840 000*	cp
				25.00	L00 848 001*	L00 860 000*	cv
				25.00	L00 868 001*	L00 880 000*	cv
				25.00	L00 888 001*	L00 900 000*	cv
				25.00	L00 908 001*	L00 920 000*	cv
				25.00	L00 928 001*	L00 940 000*	cv
				25.00	L00 948 001*	L00 960 000*	cv
				25.00	L00 968 001*	L00 980 000*	cv
				25.00	L00 988 001*	L01 000 000*	cv
				25.00	L01 008 001*	L01 020 000*	cv
				25.00	L01 028 001*	L01 040 000*	cv
				25.00	L01 048 001*	L01 060 000*	cv
				25.00	L01 068 001*	L01 080 000*	cv
				25.00	L01 088 001*	L01 100 000*	cv
				25.00	L01 108 001*	L01 120 000*	cv
				25.00	L01 128 001*	L01 140 000*	cv
				25.00	L01 148 001*	L01 160 000*	cv
				25.00	L01 168 001*	L01 180 000*	cv
				25.00	L01 188 001*	L01 200 000*	cv
				25.00	L01 208 001*	L01 220 000*	cv
				25.00	L01 228 001*	L01 240 000*	cv
				25.00	L01 248 001*	L01 260 000*	cv
				25.00	L01 268 001*	L01 280 000*	cv
				3.50	L01 280 001*	L03 840 000*	cv
				3.50	L03 840 001*	L05 120 000*	cp
				3.50	L05 120 001*	L06 400 000*	cv
				3.50	L06 400 001*	L08 960 000*	cp

IF77A
$1.00 FEDERAL RESERVE NOTE (GREEN SEAL) 32 Subject
SERIES 1977A

SIGNATURES: Azie Taylor Morton, Treasurer of the United States
   J. William Miller, Secretary of the Treasury
PLATE SERIALS: Highest face check #3297. Highest back check #2185.
EQUIPMENT: All printings are cope except as noted.

	DISTRICT	TOTAL NOTES PRINTED	BLOCKS	ESTIMATED VALUE VG/F	CU	LOW OFFICIAL SERIAL NUMBER	HIGH OFFICIAL SERIAL NUMBER
1	A BOSTON	11,520,000	A--B		3.00	A88 320 001B	A99 840 000B
		99,840,000	A--C		3.00	A00 000 001C	A99 840 000C
		93,440,000	A--D		3.00	A00 000 001D	A93 440 000D
		2,432,000	A--*		25.00	A04 496 001*	A04 500 000*
					25.00	A04 516 001*	A04 520 000*
					25.00	A04 536 001*	A04 540 000*
					25.00	A04 556 001*	A04 560 000*
					25.00	A04 576 001*	A04 580 000*
					25.00	A04 596 001*	A04 600 000*
					25.00	A04 616 001*	A04 620 000*
					25.00	A04 636 001*	A04 640 000*
					25.00	A04 656 001*	A04 660 000*
					25.00	A04 676 001*	A04 680 000*
					25.00	A04 696 001*	A04 700 000*
					25.00	A04 716 001*	A04 720 000*
					25.00	A04 736 001*	A04 740 000*
					25.00	A04 756 001*	A04 760 000*
					25.00	A04 776 001*	A04 780 000*
					25.00	A04 796 001*	A04 800 000*
					25.00	A04 816 001*	A04 820 000*
					25.00	A04 836 001*	A04 840 000*
					25.00	A04 856 001*	A04 860 000*
					25.00	A04 876 001*	A04 880 000*
					25.00	A04 896 001*	A04 900 000*
					25.00	A04 916 001*	A04 920 000*
					25.00	A04 936 001*	A04 940 000*
					25.00	A04 956 001*	A04 960 000*
					25.00	A04 976 001*	A04 980 000*
					25.00	A04 996 001*	A05 000 000*
					25.00	A05 016 001*	A05 020 000*
					25.00	A05 036 001*	A05 040 000*
					25.00	A05 056 001*	A05 060 000*
					25.00	A05 076 001*	A05 080 000*
					25.00	A05 096 000*	A05 100 000*
					25.00	A05 116 001*	A05 120 000*
					25.00	A05 136 001*	A05 140 000*
					25.00	A05 156 001*	A05 160 000*
					25.00	A05 176 001*	A05 180 000*
					25.00	A05 196 001*	A05 200 000*
					25.00	A05 216 001*	A05 220 000*
					25.00	A05 236 001*	A05 240 000*
					25.00	A05 256 001*	A05 260 000*
					25.00	A05 276 001*	A05 280 000*
					25.00	A05 296 001*	A05 300 000*
					25.00	A05 316 001*	A05 320 000*
					25.00	A05 336 001*	A05 340 000*
					25.00	A05 356 001*	A05 360 000*
					25.00	A05 376 001*	A05 380 000*
					25.00	A05 396 001*	A05 400 000*
					25.00	A05 416 001*	A05 420 000*
					25.00	A05 436 001*	A05 440 000*
					25.00	A05 456 001*	A05 460 000*
					25.00	A05 476 001*	A05 480 000*
					25.00	A05 496 001*	A05 500 000*
					25.00	A05 516 001*	A05 520 000*
					25.00	A05 536 001*	A05 540 000*
					25.00	A05 556 001*	A05 560 000*
					25.00	A05 576 001*	A05 580 000*
					25.00	A05 596 001*	A05 600 000*
					25.00	A05 616 001*	A05 620 000*
					25.00	A05 636 001*	A05 640 000*

DISTRICT	TOTAL NOTES PRINTED	BLOCKS	ESTIMATED VALUE VG/F	VALUE CU	LOW OFFICIAL SERIAL NUMBER	HIGH OFFICIAL SERIAL NUMBER
				25.00	A05 656 001*	A05 660 000*
				25.00	A05 676 001*	A05 680 000*
				25.00	A05 696 001*	A05 700 000*
				25.00	A05 716 001*	A05 720 000*
				25.00	A05 736 001*	A05 740 000*
				25.00	A05 756 001*	A05 760 000*
				25.00	A05 764 001*	A05 780 000*
				25.00	A05 784 001*	A05 800 000*
				25.00	A05 804 001*	A05 820 000*
				25.00	A05 824 001*	A05 840 000*
				25.00	A05 844 001*	A05 860 000*
				25.00	A05 864 001*	A05 880 000*
				25.00	A05 884 001*	A05 900 000*
				25.00	A05 904 001*	A05 920 000*
				25.00	A05 924 001*	A05 940 000*
				25.00	A05 944 001*	A05 960 000*
				25.00	A05 964 001*	A05 980 000*
				25.00	A05 984 001*	A06 000 000*
				25.00	A06 004 001*	A06 020 000*
				25.00	A06 024 001*	A06 040 000*
				25.00	A06 044 001*	A06 060 000*
				25.00	A06 064 001*	A06 080 000*
				25.00	A06 084 001*	A06 100 000*
				25.00	A06 104 001*	A06 120 000*
				25.00	A06 124 001*	A06 140 000*
				25.00	A06 144 001*	A06 160 000*
				25.00	A06 164 001*	A06 180 000*
				25.00	A06 184 001*	A06 200 000*
				25.00	A06 204 001*	A06 220 000*
				25.00	A06 224 001*	A06 240 000*
				25.00	A06 244 001*	A06 260 000*
				25.00	A06 264 001*	A06 280 000*
				25.00	A06 284 001*	A06 300 000*
				25.00	A06 304 001*	A06 320 000*
				25.00	A06 324 001*	A06 340 000*
				25.00	A06 344 001*	A06 360 000*
				25.00	A06 364 001*	A06 380 000*
				25.00	A06 384 001*	A06 400 000*
				25.00	A06 416 001*	A06 420 000*
				25.00	A06 436 001*	A06 440 000*
				25.00	A06 456 001*	A06 460 000*
				25.00	A06 476 001*	A06 480 000*
				25.00	A06 496 001*	A06 500 000*
				25.00	A06 516 001*	A06 520 000*
				25.00	A06 536 001*	A06 540 000*
				25.00	A06 556 001*	A06 560 000*
				25.00	A06 576 001*	A06 580 000*
				25.00	A06 596 001*	A06 600 000*
				25.00	A06 616 001*	A06 620 000*
				25.00	A06 636 001*	A06 640 000*
				25.00	A06 656 001*	A06 660 000*
				25.00	A06 676 001*	A06 680 000*
				25.00	A06 696 001*	A06 700 000*
				25.00	A06 716 001*	A06 720 000*
				25.00	A06 736 001*	A06 740 000*
				25.00	A06 756 001*	A06 760 000*
				25.00	A06 776 001*	A06 780 000*
				25.00	A06 796 001*	A06 800 000*
				25.00	A06 816 001*	A06 820 000*
				25.00	A06 836 001*	A06 840 000*
				25.00	A06 856 001*	A06 860 000*
				25.00	A06 876 001*	A06 880 000*
				25.00	A06 896 001*	A06 900 000*
				25.00	A06 916 001*	A06 920 000*
				25.00	A06 936 001*	A06 940 000*
				25.00	A06 956 001*	A06 960 000*
				25.00	A06 976 001*	A06 980 000*
				25.00	A06 996 001*	A07 000 000*
				25.00	A07 016 001*	A07 020 000*

DISTRICT	TOTAL NOTES PRINTED	BLOCKS	ESTIMATED VALUE VG/F	CU	LOW OFFICIAL SERIAL NUMBER	HIGH OFFICIAL SERIAL NUMBER
				25.00	A07 036 001*	A07 040 000*
				25.00	A07 052 001*	A07 060 000*
				25.00	A07 072 001*	A07 080 000*
				25.00	A07 092 001*	A07 100 000*
				25.00	A07 112 001*	A07 120 000*
				25.00	A07 132 001*	A07 140 000*
				25.00	A07 152 001*	A07 160 000*
				25.00	A07 172 001*	A07 180 000*
				25.00	A07 192 001*	A07 200 000*
				25.00	A07 212 001*	A07 220 000*
				25.00	A07 232 001*	A07 240 000*
				25.00	A07 252 001*	A07 260 000*
				25.00	A07 272 001*	A07 280 000*
				25.00	A07 292 001*	A07 300 000*
				25.00	A07 312 001*	A07 320 000*
				25.00	A07 332 001*	A07 340 000*
				25.00	A07 352 001*	A07 360 000*
				25.00	A07 372 001*	A07 380 000*
				25.00	A07 392 001*	A07 400 000*
				25.00	A07 412 001*	A07 420 000*
				25.00	A07 432 001*	A07 440 000*
				25.00	A07 452 001*	A07 460 000*
				25.00	A07 472 001*	A07 480 000*
				25.00	A07 492 001*	A07 500 000*
				25.00	A07 512 001*	A07 520 000*
				25.00	A07 532 001*	A07 540 000*
				25.00	A07 552 001*	A07 560 000*
				25.00	A07 572 001*	A07 580 000*
				25.00	A07 592 001*	A07 600 000*
				25.00	A07 612 001*	A07 620 000*
				25.00	A07 632 001*	A07 640 000*
				25.00	A07 652 001*	A07 660 000*
				25.00	A07 672 001*	A07 680 000*
				3.50	A07 680 001*	A08 960 000*

(1) Currently in print. High serial printed through October 1981

DISTRICT	TOTAL NOTES PRINTED	BLOCKS		ESTIMATED VALUE VG/F CU	LOW OFFICIAL SERIAL NUMBER	HIGH OFFICIAL SERIAL NUMBER
2 B NEW YORK	63,360,000	B--G		3.00	B36 480 001G	B99 840 000G
	99,840,000	B--H		3.00	B00 000 001H	B99 840 000H
	99,840,000	B--I		3.00	B00 000 001I	B99 840 000I
	99,840,000	B--J		3.00	B00 000 001J	B99 840 000J
	99,840,000	B--K		3.00	B00 000 001K	B99 840 000K
	99,840,000	B--L		3.00	B00 000 001L	B99 840 000L
	29,440,000	B--A	(1)	3.00	B00 000 001A	B29 440 000A
	9,984,000	B--*		3.50	B11 520 001*	B14 720 000*
				25.00	B14 732 001*	B14 740 000*
				25.00	B14 752 001*	B14 760 000*
				25.00	B14 772 001*	B14 780 000*
				25.00	B14 792 001*	B14 800 000*
				25.00	B14 812 001*	B14 820 000*
				25.00	B14 832 001*	B14 840 000*
				25.00	B14 852 001*	B14 860 000*
				25.00	B14 872 001*	B14 880 000*
				25.00	B14 872 001*	B14 880 000*
				25.00	B14 912 001*	B14 920 000*
				25.00	B14 932 001*	B14 940 000*
				25.00	B14 952 001*	B14 960 000*
				25.00	B14 972 001*	B14 980 000*
				25.00	B14 992 001*	B15 000 000*
				25.00	B15 012 001*	B15 020 000*
				25.00	B15 032 001*	B15 040 000*
				25.00	B15 052 001*	B15 060 000*
				25.00	B15 072 001*	B15 080 000*
				25.00	B15 092 001*	B15 100 000*
				25.00	B15 112 001*	B15 120 000*
				25.00	B15 132 001*	B15 140 000*
				25.00	B15 152 001*	B15 160 000*
				25.00	B15 172 001*	B15 180 000*
				25.00	B15 192 001*	B15 200 000*
				25.00	B15 212 001*	B15 220 000*
				25.00	B15 232 001*	B15 240 000*
				25.00	B15 252 001*	B15 260 000*

DISTRICT	TOTAL NOTES PRINTED	BLOCKS	ESTIMATED VALUE VG/F CU	LOW OFFICIAL SERIAL NUMBER	HIGH OFFICIAL SERIAL NUMBER
			25.00	B15 272 001*	B15 280 000*
			25.00	B15 292 001*	B15 300 000*
			25.00	B15 312 001*	B15 320 000*
			25.00	B15 332 001*	B15 340 000*
			25.00	B15 352 001*	B15 360 000*
			3.50	B15 360 001*	B16 000 000*
			25.00	B16 016 001*	B16 020 000*
			25.00	B16 036 001*	B16 040 000*
			25.00	B16 056 001*	B16 060 000*
			25.00	B16 076 001*	B16 080 000*
			25.00	B16 096 001*	B16 100 000*
			25.00	B16 116 001*	B16 120 000*
			25.00	B16 136 001*	B16 140 000*
			25.00	B16 156 001*	B16 160 000*
			25.00	B16 176 001*	B16 180 000*
			25.00	B16 196 001*	B16 200 000*
			25.00	B16 216 001*	B16 220 000*
			25.00	B16 236 001*	B16 240 000*
			25.00	B16 256 001*	B16 260 000*
			25.00	B16 276 001*	B16 280 000*
			25.00	B16 296 001*	B16 300 000*
			25.00	B16 316 001*	B16 320 000*
			25.00	B16 336 001*	B16 340 000*
			25.00	B16 356 001*	B16 360 000*
			25.00	B16 376 001*	B16 380 000*
			25.00	B16 396 001*	B16 400 000*
			25.00	B16 416 001*	B16 420 000*
			25.00	B16 436 001*	B16 440 000*
			25.00	B16 456 001*	B16 460 000*
			25.00	B16 476 001*	B16 480 000*
			25.00	B16 496 001*	B16 500 000*
			25.00	B16 516 001*	B16 520 000*
			25.00	B16 536 001*	B16 540 000*
			25.00	B16 556 001*	B16 560 000*
			25.00	B16 576 001*	B16 580 000*
			25.00	B16 596 001*	B16 600 000*
			25.00	B16 616 001*	B16 620 000*
			25.00	B16 636 001*	B16 640 000*
			25.00	B16 640 001*	B22 400 000*
3 C PHILADELPHIA	82,560,000	C--C	3.00	C17 280 001C	C99 840 000C
	99,840,000	C--D	3.00	C00 000 001D	C99 840 000D
	14,080,000	C--E	3.00	C00 000 001E	C14 080 000E
	2,688,000	C--*	3.50	C05 760 001*	C06 400 000*
			25.00	C06 416 001*	C06 420 000*
			25.00	C06 436 001*	C06 440 000*
			25.00	C06 456 001*	C06 460 000*
			25.00	C06 476 001*	C06 480 000*
			25.00	C06 496 001*	C06 500 000*
			25.00	C06 516 001*	C06 520 000*
			25.00	C06 536 001*	C06 540 000*
			25.00	C06 556 001*	C06 560 000*
			25.00	C06 576 001*	C06 580 000*
			25.00	C06 596 001*	C06 600 000*
			25.00	C06 616 001*	C06 620 000*
			25.00	C06 636 001*	C06 640 000*
			25.00	C06 656 001*	C06 660 000*
			25.00	C06 676 001*	C06 680 000*
			25.00	C06 696 001*	C06 700 000*
			25.00	C06 716 001*	C06 720 000*
			25.00	C06 736 001*	C06 740 000*
			25.00	C06 756 001*	C06 760 000*
			25.00	C06 776 001*	C06 780 000*
			25.00	C06 796 001*	C06 800 000*
			25.00	C06 816 001*	C06 820 000*
			25.00	C06 836 001*	C06 840 000*
			25.00	C06 856 001*	C06 860 000*
			25.00	C06 876 001*	C06 880 000*
			25.00	C06 896 001*	C06 900 000*
			25.00	C06 916 001*	C06 920 000*
			25.00	C06 936 001*	C06 940 000*

DISTRICT	TOTAL NOTES PRINTED	BLOCKS	ESTIMATED VALUE VG/F	CU	LOW OFFICIAL SERIAL NUMBER	HIGH OFFICIAL SERIAL NUMBER
				25.00	C06 956 001*	C06 960 000*
				25.00	C06 976 001*	C06 980 000*
				25.00	C06 996 001*	C07 000 000*
				25.00	C07 016 001*	C07 020 000*
				25.00	C07 036 001*	C07 040 000*
				3.50	C07 040 001*	C08 960 000*
4 D CLEVELAND	86,400,000	D--C		3.00	D13 440 001C	D99 840 000C
	88,320,000	D--D		3.00	D00 000 001D	D88 320 000D
		D--*		25.00	D05 772 001*	D05 780 000*
				25.00	D05 792 001*	D05 800 000*
				25.00	D05 812 001*	D05 820 000*
				25.00	D05 832 001*	D05 840 000*
				25.00	D05 852 001*	D05 860 000*
				25.00	D05 872 001*	D05 880 000*
				25.00	D05 892 001*	D05 900 000*
				25.00	D05 912 001*	D05 920 000*
				25.00	D05 932 001*	D05 940 000*
				25.00	D05 952 001*	D05 960 000*
				25.00	D05 972 001*	D05 980 000*
				25.00	D05 992 001*	D06 000 000*
				25.00	D06 012 001*	D06 020 000*
				25.00	D06 032 001*	D06 040 000*
				25.00	D06 052 001*	D06 060 000*
				25.00	D06 072 001*	D06 080 000*
				25.00	D06 092 001*	D06 100 000*
				25.00	D06 112 001*	D06 120 000*
				25.00	D06 132 001*	D06 140 000*
				25.00	D06 152 001*	D06 160 000*
				25.00	D06 172 001*	D06 180 000*
				25.00	D06 192 001*	D06 200 000*
				25.00	D06 212 001*	D06 220 000*
				25.00	D06 232 001*	D06 240 000*
				25.00	D06 252 001*	D06 260 000*
				25.00	D06 272 001*	D06 280 000*
				25.00	D06 292 001*	D06 300 000*
				25.00	D06 312 001*	D06 320 000*
				25.00	D06 332 001*	D06 340 000*
				25.00	D06 352 001*	D06 360 000*
				25.00	D06 372 001*	D06 380 000*
				25.00	D06 392 001*	D06 400 000*
				25.00	D06 416 001*	D06 420 000*
				25.00	D06 436 001*	D06 440 000*
				25.00	D06 456 001*	D06 460 000*
				25.00	D06 476 001*	D06 480 000*
				25.00	D06 496 001*	D06 500 000*
				25.00	D06 516 001*	D06 520 000*
				25.00	D06 536 001*	D06 540 000*
				25.00	D06 556 001*	D06 560 000*
				25.00	D06 576 001*	D06 580 000*
				25.00	D06 596 001C	D06 600 000*
				25.00	D06 616 001D	D06 620 000*
				25.00	D06 636 001*	D06 640 000*
				25.00	D06 656 001*	D06 660 000*
				25.00	D06 676 001*	D06 680 000*
				25.00	D06 696 001*	D06 700 000*
				25.00	D06 716 001*	D06 720 000*
				25.00	D06 736 001*	D06 740 000*
				25.00	D06 756 001*	D06 760 000*
				25.00	D06 776 001*	D06 780 000*
				25.00	D06 796 001*	D06 800 000*
				25.00	D06 816 001*	D06 820 000*
				25.00	D06 836 001*	D06 840 000*
				25.00	D06 856 001*	D06 860 000*
				25.00	D06 876 001*	D06 880 000*
				25.00	D06 896 001*	D06 900 000*
				25.00	D06 916 001*	D06 920 000*
				25.00	D06 936 001*	D06 940 000*
				25.00	D06 956 001*	D06 960 000*
				25.00	D06 976 001*	D06 980 000*
				25.00	D06 996 001*	D07 000 000*

DISTRICT	TOTAL NOTES PRINTED	BLOCKS	ESTIMATED VALUE VG/F	CU	LOW OFFICIAL SERIAL NUMBER	HIGH OFFICIAL SERIAL NUMBER
				25.00	D07 016 001*	D07 020 000*
				25.00	D07 036 001*	D07 040 000*
				3.50	D07 040 001*	D07 680 000*
				25.00	D07 692 001*	D07 700 000*
				25.00	D07 712 001*	D07 720 000*
				25.00	D07 732 001*	D07 740 000*
				25.00	D07 752 001*	D07 760 000*
				25.00	D07 772 001*	D07 780 000*
				25.00	D07 792 001*	D07 800 000*
				25.00	D07 812 001*	D07 820 000*
				25.00	D07 832 001*	D07 840 000*
				25.00	D07 852 001*	D07 860 000*
				25.00	D07 872 001*	D07 880 000*
				25.00	D07 892 001*	D07 900 000*
				25.00	D07 912 001*	D07 920 000*
				25.00	D07 932 001*	D07 940 000*
				25.00	D07 952 001*	D07 960 000*
				25.00	D07 972 001*	D07 980 000*
				25.00	D07 992 001*	D08 000 000*
				25.00	D08 012 001*	D08 020 000*
				25.00	D08 032 001*	D08 040 000*
				25.00	D08 052 001*	D08 060 000*
				25.00	D08 072 001*	D08 080 000*
				25.00	D08 092 001*	D08 100 000*
				25.00	D08 112 001*	D08 120 000*
				25.00	D08 132 001*	D08 140 000*
				25.00	D08 152 001*	D08 160 000*
				25.00	D08 172 001*	D08 180 000*
				25.00	D08 192 001*	D08 200 000*
				25.00	D08 212 001*	D08 220 000*
				25.00	D08 232 001*	D08 240 000*
				25.00	D08 252 001*	D08 260 000*
				25.00	D08 272 001*	D08 280 000*
				25.00	D08 292 001*	D08 300 000*
				25.00	D08 312 001*	D08 320 000*
				3.50	D08 320 001*	D09 600 000*
5 E RICHMOND	80,640,000	E--E		3.00	E19 200 001E	E99 840 000E
	99,840,000	E--F		3.00	E00 000 001E	E99 840 000F
	99,840,000	E--G		3.00	E00 000 001G	E99 840 000G
	97,280,000	E--H		3.00	E00 000 001H	E97 280 000H
	6,360,000	E--*	(1)	3.50	E00 000 001*	E00 640 000*
				25.00	E00 652 001*	E00 660 000*
				25.00	E00 672 001*	E00 680 000*
				25.00	E00 692 001*	E00 700 000*
				25.00	E00 712 001*	E00 720 000*
				25.00	E00 732 001*	E00 740 000*
				25.00	E00 752 001*	E00 760 000*
				25.00	E00 772 001*	E00 780 000*
				25.00	E00 792 001*	E00 800 000*
				25.00	E00 812 001*	E00 820 000*
				25.00	E00 832 001*	E00 840 000*
				25.00	E00 852 001*	E00 860 000*
				25.00	E00 872 001*	E00 880 000*
				25.00	E00 892 001*	E00 900 000*
				25.00	E00 912 001*	E00 920 000*
				25.00	E00 932 001*	E00 940 000*
				25.00	E00 952 001*	E00 960 000*
				25.00	E00 972 001*	E00 980 000*
				25.00	E00 992 001*	E01 000 000*
				25.00	E01 012 000*	E01 020 000*
				25.00	E01 032 001*	E01 040 000*
				25.00	E01 052 001*	E01 060 000*
				25.00	E01 072 001*	E01 080 000*
				25.00	E01 092 001*	E01 100 000*
				25.00	E01 112 001*	E01 120 000*
				25.00	E01 132 001*	E01 140 000*
				25.00	E01 152 001*	E01 160 000*
				25.00	E01 172 001*	E01 180 000*
				25.00	E01 192 001*	E01 200 000*
				25.00	E01 212 001*	E01 220 000*

DISTRICT	TOTAL NOTES PRINTED	BLOCKS	ESTIMATED VALUE VG/F	CU	LOW OFFICIAL SERIAL NUMBER	HIGH OFFICIAL SERIAL NUMBER
				25.00	E01 232 001*	E01 240 000*
				25.00	E01 252 001*	E01 260 000*
				25.00	E01 272 001*	E01 280 000*
				3.50	E01 280 001*	E04 480 000*
				25.00	E04 496 001*	E04 500 000*
				25.00	E04 516 001*	E04 520 000*
				25.00	E04 536 001*	E04 540 000*
				25.00	E04 556 001*	E04 560 000*
				25.00	E04 576 001*	E04 580 000*
				25.00	E04 596 001*	E04 600 000*
				25.00	E04 616 001*	E04 620 000*
				25.00	E04 636 001*	E04 640 000*
				25.00	E04 656 001*	E04 660 000*
				25.00	E04 676 001*	E04 680 000*
				25.00	E04 696 001*	E04 700 000*
				25.00	E04 716 001*	E04 720 000*
				25.00	E04 736 001*	E04 740 000*
				25.00	E04 756 001*	E04 760 000*
				25.00	E04 776 001*	E04 780 000*
				25.00	E04 796 001*	E04 800 000*
				25.00	E04 816 001*	E04 820 000*
				25.00	E04 836 001*	E04 840 000*
				25.00	E04 856 001*	E04 860 000*
				25.00	E04 876 001*	E04 880 000*
				25.00	E04 896 001*	E04 900 000*
				25.00	E04 916 001*	E04 920 000*
				25.00	E04 936 001*	E04 940 000*
				25.00	E04 956 001*	E04 960 000*
				25.00	E04 976 001*	E04 980 000*
				25.00	E04 996 001*	E05 000 000*
				25.00	E05 016 001*	E05 020 000*
				25.00	E05 036 001*	E05 040 000*
				25.00	E05 056 001*	E05 060 000*
				25.00	E05 076 001*	E05 080 000*
				25.00	E05 096 001*	E05 100 000*
				25.00	E05 116 001*	E05 120 000*
				3.50	E05 120 001*	E07 040 000*
				25.00	E07 052 001*	E07 060 000*
				25.00	E07 072 001*	E07 080 000*
				25.00	E07 092 001*	E07 100 000*
				25.00	E07 112 001*	E07 120 000*
				25.00	E07 132 001*	E07 140 000*
				25.00	E07 152 001*	E07 160 000*
				25.00	E07 172 001*	E07 180 000*
				25.00	E07 192 001*	E07 200 000*
				25.00	E07 212 001*	E07 220 000*
				25.00	E07 232 001*	E07 240 000*
				25.00	E07 252 001*	E07 260 000*
				25.00	E07 272 001*	E07 280 000*
				25.00	E07 292 001*	E07 300 000*
				25.00	E07 312 001*	E07 320 000*
				25.00	E07 332 001*	E07 340 000*
				25.00	E07 352 001*	E07 360 000*
				25.00	E07 372 001*	E07 380 000*
				25.00	E07 392 001*	E07 400 000*
				25.00	E07 412 001*	E07 420 000*
				25.00	E07 432 001*	E07 440 000*
				25.00	E07 452 001*	E07 460 000*
				25.00	E07 472 001*	E07 480 000*
				25.00	E07 492 001*	E07 500 000*
				25.00	E07 512 001*	E07 520 000*
				25.00	E07 532 001*	E07 540 000*
				25.00	E07 552 001*	E07 560 000*
				25.00	E07 572 001*	E07 580 000*
				25.00	E07 592 001*	E07 600 000*
				25.00	E07 612 001*	E07 620 000*
				25.00	E07 632 001*	E07 640 000*
				25.00	E07 652 001*	E07 660 000*
				25.00	E07 672 001*	E07 680 000*

DISTRICT	TOTAL NOTES PRINTED	BLOCKS	ESTIMATED VALUE VG/F	CU	LOW OFFICIAL SERIAL NUMBER	HIGH OFFICIAL SERIAL NUMBER
6 F ATLANTA	33,920,000	F--F		3.00	F65 920 001F	F99 840 000F
	99,840,000	F--G		3.00	F00 000 001G	F99 840 000G
	99,840,000	F--H		3.00	F00 000 001H	F99 840 000H
	99,840,000	F--I		3.00	F00 000 001I	G99 840 000I
	62,720,000	F--J		3.00	F00 000 001J	F62 720 000J
	5,376,000	F--*		25.00	F09 616 001*	F09 620 000*
				25.00	F09 636 001*	F09 640 000*
				25.00	F09 656 001*	F09 660 000*
				25.00	F09 676 001*	F09 680 000*
				25.00	F09 696 001*	F09 700 000*
				25.00	F09 716 001*	F09 720 000*
				25.00	F09 736 001*	F09 740 000*
				25.00	F09 756 001*	F09 760 000*
				25.00	F09 776 001*	F09 780 000*
				25.00	F09 796 001*	F09 800 000*
				25.00	F09 816 001*	F09 820 000*
				25.00	F09 836 001*	F09 840 000*
				25.00	F09 856 001*	F09 860 000*
				25.00	F09 876 001*	F09 880 000*
				25.00	F09 896 001*	F09 900 000*
				25.00	F09 916 001*	F09 920 000*
				25.00	F09 936 001*	F09 940 000*
				25.00	F09 956 001*	F09 960 000*
				25.00	F09 976 001*	F09 980 000*
				25.00	F09 996 001*	F10 000 000*
				25.00	F10 016 001*	F10 020 000*
				25.00	F10 036 001*	F10 040 000*
				25.00	F10 056 001*	F10 060 000*
				25.00	F10 076 001*	F10 080 000*
				25.00	F10 096 001*	F10 100 000*
				25.00	F10 116 001*	F10 120 000*
				25.00	F10 136 001*	F10 140 000*
				25.00	F10 156 001*	F10 160 000*
				25.00	F10 176 001*	F10 180 000*
				25.00	F10 196 001*	F10 200 000*
				25.00	F10 216 001*	F10 220 000*
				25.00	F10 236 001*	F10 240 000*
				3.50	F10 240 001*	F10 880 000*
				25.00	F10 896 001*	F10 900 000*
				25.00	F10 916 001*	F10 920 000*
				25.00	F10 936 001*	F10 940 000*
				25.00	F10 956 001*	F10 960 000*
				25.00	F10 976 001*	F10 980 000*
				25.00	F10 996 001*	F11 000 000*
				25.00	F11 016 001*	F11 020 000*

(1) All serials for this series continued from previous series serials with the exception of the Richmond star which reverted to 00 000 001

				25.00	F11 036 001*	F11 040 000*
				25.00	F11 056 001*	F11 060 000*
				25.00	F11 076 001*	F11 080 000*
				25.00	F11 096 001*	F11 100 000*
				25.00	F11 116 001*	F11 120 000*
				25.00	F11 136 001*	F11 140 000*
				25.00	F11 156 001*	F11 160 000*
				25.00	F11 176 001*	F11 180 000*
				25.00	F11 196 001*	F11 200 000*
				25.00	F11 216 001*	F11 220 000*
				25.00	F11 236 001*	F11 240 000*
				25.00	F11 256 001*	F11 260 000*
				25.00	F11 276 001*	F11 280 000*
				25.00	F11 296 001*	F11 300 000*
				25.00	F11 316 001*	F11 320 000*
				25.00	F11 336 001*	F11 340 000*
				25.00	F11 356 001*	F11 360 000*
				25.00	F11 376 001*	F11 380 000*
				25.00	F11 396 001*	F11 400 000*
				25.00	F11 416 001*	F11 420 000*
				25.00	F11 436 001*	F11 440 000*
				25.00	F11 456 001*	F11 460 000*

DISTRICT	TOTAL NOTES PRINTED	BLOCKS	ESTIMATED VALUE VG/F	CU	LOW OFFICIAL SERIAL NUMBER	HIGH OFFICIAL SERIAL NUMBER
				25.00	F11 476 001*	F11 480 000*
				25.00	F11 496 001*	F11 500 000*
				25.00	F11 516 001*	F11 520 000*
				25.00	F11 520 001*	F16 000 000*
7 G CHICAGO	83,200,000	G--G		3.00	G16 640 001G	G99 840 000G
	99,840,000	G--H		3.00	G00 000 001H	G99 840 000H
	67,840,000	G--I		3.00	G00 000 001I	G67 840 000I
	1,560,000	G--*		3.50	G10 240 001*	G12 800 000*
8 H ST. LOUIS	99,840,000	H--C		3.00	H00 000 001C	H99 840 000C
	3,840,000	H--D		3.00	H00 000 001D	H03 840 000D
	1,664,000	H--*		3.50	H02 560 001*	H03 200 000*
				25.00	H03 216 001*	H03 220 000*
				25.00	H03 236 001*	H03 240 000*
				25.00	H03 256 001*	H03 260 000*
				25.00	H03 276 001*	H03 280 000*
				25.00	H03 296 001*	H03 300 000*
				25.00	H03 316 001*	H03 320 000*
				25.00	H03 336 001*	H03 340 000*
				25.00	H03 356 001*	H03 360 000*
				25.00	H03 376 001*	H03 380 000*
				25.00	H03 396 001*	H03 400 000*
				25.00	H03 416 001*	H03 420 000*
				25.00	H03 436 001*	H03 440 000*
				25.00	H03 456 001*	H03 460 000*
				25.00	H03 476 001*	H03 480 000*
				25.00	H03 496 001*	H03 500 000*
				25.00	H03 516 001*	H03 520 000*
				25.00	H03 536 001*	H03 540 000*
				25.00	H03 556 001*	H03 560 000*
				25.00	H03 576 001*	H03 580 000*
				25.00	H03 596 001*	H03 600 000*
				25.00	H03 616 001*	H03 620 000*
				25.00	H03 636 001*	H03 640 000*
				25.00	H03 656 001*	H03 660 000*
				25.00	H03 676 001*	H03 680 000*
				25.00	H03 696 001*	H03 700 000*
				25.00	H03 716 001*	H03 720 000*
				25.00	H03 736 001*	H03 740 000*
				25.00	H03 756 001*	H03 760 000*
				25.00	H03 776 001*	H03 780 000*
				25.00	H03 796 001*	H03 800 000*
				25.00	H03 816 001*	H03 820 000*
				25.00	H03 836 001*	H03 840 000*
				25.00	H03 852 001*	H03 860 000*
				25.00	H03 872 001*	H03 880 000*
				25.00	H03 892 001*	H03 900 000*
				25.00	H03 912 001*	H03 920 000*
				25.00	H03 932 001*	H03 940 000*
				25.00	H03 952 001*	H03 960 000*
				25.00	H03 972 001*	H03 980 000*
				25.00	H03 992 001*	H04 000 000*
				25.00	H04 012 001*	H04 020 000*
				25.00	H04 032 001*	H04 040 000*
				25.00	H04 052 001*	H04 060 000*
				25.00	H04 072 001*	H04 080 000*
				25.00	H04 092 001*	H04 100 000*
				25.00	H04 112 001*	H04 120 000*
				25.00	H04 132 001*	H04 140 000*
				25.00	H04 152 001*	H04 160 000*
				25.00	H04 172 001*	H04 180 000*
				25.00	H04 192 001*	H04 200 000*
				25.00	H04 212 001*	H04 220 000*
				25.00	H04 232 001*	H04 240 000*
				25.00	H04 252 001*	H04 260 000*
				25.00	H04 272 001*	H04 280 000*
				25.00	H04 292 001*	H04 300 000*
				25.00	H04 312 001*	H04 320 000*
				25.00	H04 332 001*	H04 340 000*
				25.00	H04 352 001*	H04 360 000*
				25.00	H04 372 001*	H04 380 000*

DISTRICT	TOTAL NOTES PRINTED	BLOCKS	ESTIMATED VALUE VG/F	CU	LOW OFFICIAL SERIAL NUMBER	HIGH OFFICIAL SERIAL NUMBER
				25.00	H04 392 001*	H04 400 000*
				25.00	H04 412 001*	H04 420 000*
				25.00	H04 432 001*	H04 440 000*
				25.00	H04 452 001*	H04 460 000*
				25.00	H04 472 001*	H04 480 000*
				25.00	H04 488 001*	H04 500 000*
				25.00	H04 508 001*	H04 520 000*
				25.00	H04 528 001*	H04 540 000*
				25.00	H04 548 001*	H04 560 000*
				25.00	H04 568 001*	H04 580 000*
				25.00	H04 588 001*	H04 600 000*
				25.00	H04 608 001*	H04 620 000*
				25.00	H04 628 001*	H04 640 000*
				25.00	H04 648 001*	H04 660 000*
				25.00	H04 668 001*	H04 680 000*
				25.00	H04 688 001*	H04 700 000*
				25.00	H04 708 001*	H04 720 000*
				25.00	H04 728 001*	H04 740 000*
				25.00	H04 748 001*	H04 760 000*
				25.00	H04 768 001*	H04 780 000*
				25.00	H04 788 001*	H04 800 000*
				25.00	H04 808 001*	H04 820 000*
				25.00	H04 828 001*	H04 840 000*
				25.00	H04 848 001*	H04 860 000*
				25.00	H04 868 001*	H04 880 000*
				25.00	H04 888 001*	H04 900 000*
				25.00	H04 908 001*	H04 920 000*
				25.00	H04 928 001*	H04 940 000*
				25.00	H04 948 001*	H04 960 000*
				25.00	H04 968 001*	H04 980 000*
				25.00	H04 988 001*	H05 000 000*
				25.00	H05 008 001*	H05 020 000*
				25.00	H05 028 001*	H05 040 000*
				25.00	H05 048 001*	H05 060 000*
				25.00	H05 068 001*	H05 080 000*
				25.00	H05 088 001*	H05 100 000*
				25.00	H05 108 001*	H05 120 000*
				25.00	H05 132 001*	H05 140 000*
				25.00	H05 152 001*	H05 160 000*
				25.00	H05 172 001*	H05 180 000*
				25.00	H05 192 001*	H05 200 000*
				25.00	H05 212 001*	H05 220 000*
				25.00	H05 232 001*	H05 240 000*
				25.00	H05 252 001*	H05 260 000*
				25.00	H05 272 001*	H05 280 000*
				25.00	H05 292 001*	H05 300 000*
				25.00	H05 312 001*	H05 320 000*
				25.00	H05 332 001*	H05 340 000*
				25.00	H05 352 001*	H05 360 000*
				25.00	H05 372 001*	H05 380 000*
				25.00	H05 392 001*	H05 400 000*
				25.00	H05 412 001*	H05 420 000*
				25.00	H05 432 001*	H05 440 000*
				25.00	H05 452 001*	H05 460 000*
				25.00	H05 472 001*	H05 480 000*
				25.00	H05 492 001*	H05 500 000*
				25.00	H05 512 001*	H05 520 000*
				25.00	H05 532 001*	H05 540 000*
				25.00	H05 552 001*	H05 560 000*
				25.00	H05 572 001*	H05 580 000*
				25.00	H05 592 001*	H05 600 000*
				25.00	H05 612 001*	H05 620 000*
				25.00	H05 632 001*	H05 640 000*
				25.00	H05 652 001*	H05 660 000*
				25.00	H05 672 001*	H05 680 000*
				25.00	H05 692 001*	H05 700 000*
				25.00	H05 712 001*	H05 720 000*
				25.00	H05 732 001*	H05 740 000*
				25.00	H05 752 001*	H05 760 000*
9	I MINNEAPOLIS	38,400,000	I--B	3.00	I15 360 001B	I53 760 000B

	DISTRICT	TOTAL NOTES PRINTED	BLOCKS	ESTIMATED VALUE VG/F	CU	LOW OFFICIAL SERIAL NUMBER	HIGH OFFICIAL SERIAL NUMBER
9	I MINNEAPOLIS	1 024 000	I--*		3.50	I02 560 001*	I03 200 000*
					25.00	I03 208 001*	I03 220 000*
					25.00	I03 228 001*	I03 240 000*
					25.00	I03 248 001*	I03 260 000*
					25.00	I03 268 001*	I03 280 000*
					25.00	I03 288 001*	I03 300 000*
					25.00	I03 308 001*	I03 320 000*
					25.00	I03 328 001*	I03 340 000*
					25.00	I03 348 001*	I03 360 000*
					25.00	I03 368 001*	I03 380 000*
					25.00	I03 388 001*	I03 400 000*
					25.00	I03 408 001*	I03 420 000*
					25.00	I03 428 001*	I03 440 000*
					25.00	I03 448 001*	I03 460 000*
					25.00	I03 468 001*	I03 480 000*
					25.00	I03 488 001*	I03 500 000*
					25.00	I03 508 001*	I03 520 000*
					25.00	I03 528 001*	I03 540 000*
					25.00	I03 548 001*	I03 560 000*
					25.00	I03 568 001*	I03 580 000*
					25.00	I03 588 001*	I03 600 000*
					25.00	I03 608 001*	I03 620 000*
					25.00	I03 628 001*	I03 640 000*
					25.00	I03 648 001*	I03 660 000*
					25.00	I03 668 001*	I03 680 000*
					25.00	I03 688 001*	I03 700 000*
					25.00	I03 708 001*	I03 720 000*
					25.00	I03 728 001*	I03 740 000*
					25.00	I03 748 001*	I03 760 000*
					25.00	I03 768 001*	I03 780 000*
					25.00	I03 788 001*	I03 800 000*
					25.00	I03 808 001*	I03 820 000*
					25.00	I03 828 001*	I03 840 000*
10	J KANSAS CITY	76,160,000	J--C		3.00	J23 680 001C	J99 840 000C
		99,840,000	J--D		3.00	J00 000 001D	J99 840 000D
		90,880,000	J--E		3.00	J00 000 001E	J90 880 000E
		4,864,000	J--*		3.50	J05 120 001*	J05 760 000*
					25.00	J05 776 001*	J05 780 000*
					25.00	J05 796 001*	J05 800 000*
					25.00	J05 816 001*	J05 820 000*
					25.00	J05 836 001*	J05 840 000*
					25.00	J05 856 001*	J05 860 000*
					25.00	J05 876 001*	J05 880 000*
					25.00	J05 896 001*	J05 900 000*
					25.00	J05 916 001*	J05 920 000*
					25.00	J05 936 001*	J05 940 000*
					25.00	J05 956 001*	J05 960 000*
					25.00	J05 976 001*	J05 980 000*
					25.00	J05 996 001*	J06 000 000*
					25.00	J06 016 001*	J06 020 000*
					25.00	J06 036 001*	J06 040 000*
					25.00	J06 056 001*	J06 060 000*
					25.00	J06 076 001*	J06 080 000*
					25.00	J06 096 001*	J06 100 000*
					25.00	J06 116 001*	J06 120 000*
					25.00	J06 136 001*	J06 140 000*
					25.00	J06 156 001*	J06 160 000*
					25.00	J06 176 001*	J06 180 000*
					25.00	J06 196 001*	J06 200 000*
					25.00	J06 216 001*	J06 220 000*
					25.00	J06 236 001*	J06 240 000*
					25.00	J06 256 001*	J06 260 000*
					25.00	J06 276 001*	J06 280 000*
					25.00	J06 296 001*	J06 300 000*
					25.00	J06 316 001*	J06 320 000*
					25.00	J06 336 001*	J06 340 000*
					25.00	J06 356 001*	J06 360 000*
					25.00	J06 376 001*	J06 380 000*
					25.00	J06 396 001*	J06 400 000*
					25.00	J06 416 001*	J06 420 000*

DISTRICT	TOTAL NOTES PRINTED	BLOCKS	ESTIMATED VALUE VG/F	CU	LOW OFFICIAL SERIAL NUMBER	HIGH OFFICIAL SERIAL NUMBER
				25.00	J06 436 001*	J06 440 000*
				25.00	J06 456 001*	J06 460 000*
				25.00	J06 476 001*	J06 480 000*
				25.00	J06 496 001*	J06 500 000*
				25.00	J06 516 001*	J06 520 000*
				25.00	J06 536 001*	J06 540 000*
				25.00	J06 556 001*	J06 560 000*
				25.00	J06 576 001*	J06 580 000*
				25.00	J06 596 001*	J06 600 000*
				25.00	J06 616 001*	J06 620 000*
				25.00	J06 636 001*	J06 640 000*
				25.00	J06 656 001*	J06 660 000*
				25.00	J06 676 001*	J06 680 000*
				25.00	J06 696 001*	J06 700 000*
				25.00	J06 716 001*	J06 720 000*
				25.00	J06 736 001*	J06 740 000*
				25.00	J06 756 001*	J06 760 000*
				25.00	J06 776 001*	J06 780 000*
				25.00	J06 796 001*	J06 800 000*
				25.00	J06 816 001*	J06 820 000*
				25.00	J06 836 001*	J06 840 000*
				25.00	J06 856 001*	J06 860 000*
				25.00	J06 876 001*	J06 880 000*
				25.00	J06 896 001*	J06 900 000*
				25.00	J06 916 001*	J06 920 000*
				25.00	J06 936 001*	J06 940 000*
				25.00	J06 956 001*	J06 960 000*
				25.00	J06 976 001*	J06 980 000*
				25.00	J06 996 001*	J07 000 000*
				25.00	J07 016 001*	J07 020 000*
				25.00	J07 036 001*	J07 040 000*
				3.50	J07 040 001*	J08 320 000*
				25.00	J08 336 001*	J08 340 000*
				25.00	J08 356 001*	J08 360 000*
				25.00	J08 376 001*	J08 380 000*
				25.00	J08 396 001*	J08 400 000*
				25.00	J08 416 001*	J08 420 000*
				25.00	J08 436 001*	J08 440 000*
				25.00	J08 456 001*	J08 460 000*
				25.00	J08 476 001*	J08 480 000*
				25.00	J08 496 001*	J08 500 000*
				25.00	J08 516 001*	J08 520 000*
				25.00	J08 536 001*	J08 540 000*
				25.00	J08 556 001*	J08 560 000*
				25.00	J08 576 001*	J08 580 000*
				25.00	J08 596 001*	J08 600 000*
				25.00	J08 616 001*	J08 620 000*
				25.00	J08 636 001*	J08 640 000*
				25.00	J08 656 001*	J08 660 000*
				25.00	J08 676 001*	J08 680 000*
				25.00	J08 696 001*	J08 700 000*
				25.00	J08 716 001*	J08 720 000*
				25.00	J08 736 001*	J08 740 000*
				25.00	J08 756 001*	J08 760 000*
				25.00	J08 776 001*	J08 780 000*
				25.00	J08 796 001*	J08 800 000*
				25.00	J08 816 001*	J08 820 000*
				25.00	J08 836 001*	J08 840 000*
				25.00	J08 856 001*	J08 860 000*
				25.00	J08 876 001*	J08 880 000*
				25.00	J08 896 001*	J08 900 000*
				25.00	J08 916 001*	J08 920 000*
				25.00	J08 936 001*	J08 940 000*
				25.00	J08 956 001*	J08 960 000*
				25.00	J08 972 001*	J08 980 000*
				25.00	J08 992 001*	J09 000 000*
				25.00	J09 012 001*	J09 020 000*
				25.00	J09 032 001*	J09 040 000*
				25.00	J09 052 001*	J09 060 000*
				25.00	J09 072 001*	J09 080 000*

DISTRICT	TOTAL NOTES PRINTED	BLOCKS	ESTIMATED VALUE VG/F	CU	LOW OFFICIAL SERIAL NUMBER	HIGH OFFICIAL SERIAL NUMBER
				25.00	J09 092 001*	J09 100 000*
				25.00	J09 112 001*	J09 120 000*
				25.00	J09 132 001*	J09 140 000*
				25.00	J09 152 001*	J09 160 000*
				25.00	J09 172 001*	J09 180 000*
				25.00	J09 192 001*	J09 200 000*
				25.00	J09 212 001*	J09 220 000*
				25.00	J09 232 001*	J09 240 000*
				25.00	J09 252 001*	J09 260 000*
				25.00	J09 272 001*	J09 280 000*
				25.00	J09 292 001*	J09 300 000*
				25.00	J09 312 001*	J09 320 000*
				25.00	J09 332 001*	J09 340 000*
				25.00	J09 352 001*	J09 360 000*
				25.00	J09 372 001*	J09 380 000*
				25.00	J09 392 001*	J09 400 000*
				25.00	J09 412 001*	J09 420 000*
				25.00	J09 432 001*	J09 440 000*
				25.00	J09 452 001*	J09 460 000*
				25.00	J09 472 001*	J09 480 000*
				25.00	J09 492 001*	J09 500 000*
				25.00	J09 512 001*	J09 520 000*
				25.00	J09 532 001*	J09 540 000*
				25.00	J09 552 001*	J09 560 000*
				25.00	J09 572 001*	J09 580 000*
				25.00	J09 592 001*	J09 600 000*
				3.50	J09 600 001*	J10 880 000*
				25.00	J10 892 001*	J10 900 000*
				25.00	J10 912 001*	J10 920 000*
				25.00	J10 932 001*	J10 940 000*
				25.00	J10 952 001*	J10 960 000*
				25.00	J10 972 001*	J10 980 000*
				25.00	J10 992 001*	J11 000 000*
				25.00	J11 012 001*	J11 020 000*
				25.00	J11 032 001*	J11 040 000*
				25.00	J11 052 001*	J11 060 000*
				25.00	J11 072 001*	J11 080 000*
				25.00	J11 092 001*	J11 100 000*
				25.00	J11 112 001*	J11 120 000*
				25.00	J11 132 001*	J11 140 000*
				25.00	J11 152 001*	J11 160 000*
				25.00	J11 172 001*	J11 180 000*
				25.00	J11 192 001*	J11 200 000*
				25.00	J11 212 001*	J11 220 000*
				25.00	J11 232 001*	J11 240 000*
				25.00	J11 252 001*	J11 260 000*
				25.00	J11 272 001*	J11 280 000*
				25.00	J11 292 001*	J11 300 000*
				25.00	J11 312 001*	J11 320 000*
				25.00	J11 332 001*	J11 340 000*
				25.00	J11 352 001*	J11 360 000*
				25.00	J11 372 001*	J11 380 000*
				25.00	J11 392 001*	J11 400 000*
				25.00	J11 412 001*	J11 420 000*
				25.00	J11 432 001*	J11 440 000*
				25.00	J11 452 001*	J11 460 000*
				25.00	J11 472 001*	J11 480 000*
				25.00	J11 492 001*	J11 500 000*
				25.00	J11 512 001*	J11 520 000*
				25.00	J11 536 001*	J11 540 000*
				25.00	J11 556 001*	J11 560 000*
				25.00	J11 576 001*	J11 580 000*
				25.00	J11 596 001*	J11 600 000*
				25.00	J11 616 001*	J11 620 000*
				25.00	J11 636 001*	J11 640 000*
				25.00	J11 656 001*	J11 660 000*
				25.00	J11 676 001*	J11 680 000*
				25.00	J11 696 001*	J11 700 000*
				25.00	J11 716 001*	J11 720 000*
				25.00	J11 736 001*	J11 740 000*

DISTRICT	TOTAL NOTES PRINTED	BLOCKS	ESTIMATED VALUE VG/F	CU	LOW OFFICIAL SERIAL NUMBER	HIGH OFFICIAL SERIAL NUMBER
				25.00	J11 756 001*	J11 760 000*
				25.00	J11 776 001*	J11 780 000*
				25.00	J11 796 001*	J11 800 000*
				25.00	J11 816 001*	J11 820 000*
				25.00	J11 836 001*	J11 840 000*
				25.00	J11 856 001*	J11 860 000*
				25.00	J11 876 001*	J11 880 000*
				25.00	J11 896 001*	J11 900 000*
				25.00	J11 916 001*	J11 920 000*
				25.00	J11 936 001*	J11 940 000*
				25.00	J11 956 001*	J11 960 000*
				25.00	J11 976 001*	J11 980 000*
				25.00	J11 996 001*	J12 000 000*
				25.00	J12 016 001*	J12 020 000*
				25.00	J12 036 001*	J12 040 000*
				25.00	J12 056 001*	J12 060 000*
				25.00	J12 076 001*	J12 080 000*
				25.00	J12 096 001*	J12 100 000*
				25.00	J12 116 001*	J12 120 000*
				25.00	J12 136 001*	J12 140 000*
				25.00	J12 156 001*	J12 160 000*
				3.50	J12 160 001*	J12 800 000*
11 K DALLAS	10,240,000	K--C		3.00	K89 600 001C	K99 840 000C
	99,840,000	K--D		3.00	K00 000 001D	K99 840 000D
	99,840,000	K--E		3.00	K00 000 001E	K99 840 000E
	99,840,000	K--F		3.00	K00 000 001F	K99 840 000F
	3,840,000	K--G		3.00	K00 000 001G	K03 840 000G
	5,504,000	K--*		3.50	K06 400 001*	K07 040 000*
				25.00	K07 056 001*	K07 060 000*
				25.00	K07 076 001*	K07 080 000*
				25.00	K07 096 001*	K07 100 000*
				25.00	K07 116 001*	K07 120 000*
				25.00	K07 136 001*	K07 140 000*
				25.00	K07 156 001*	K07 160 000*
				25.00	K07 176 001*	K07 180 000*
				25.00	K07 196 001*	K07 200 000*
				25.00	K07 216 001*	K07 220 000*
				25.00	K07 236 001*	K07 240 000*
				25.00	K07 256 001*	K07 260 000*
				25.00	K07 276 001*	K07 280 000*
				25.00	K07 296 001*	K07 300 000*
				25.00	K07 316 001*	K07 320 000*
				25.00	K07 336 001*	K07 340 000*
				25.00	K07 356 001*	K07 360 000*
				25.00	K07 376 001*	K07 380 000*
				25.00	K07 396 001*	K07 400 000*
				25.00	K07 416 001*	K07 420 000*
				25.00	K07 436 001*	K07 440 000*
				25.00	K07 456 001*	K07 460 000*
				25.00	K07 476 001*	K07 480 000*
				25.00	K07 496 001*	K07 500 000*
				25.00	K07 516 001*	K07 520 000*
				25.00	K07 536 001*	K07 540 000*
				25.00	K07 556 001*	K07 560 000*
				25.00	K07 576 001*	K07 580 000*
				25.00	K07 596 001*	K07 600 000*
				25.00	K07 616 001*	K07 620 000*
				25.00	K07 636 001*	K07 640 000*
				25.00	K07 656 001*	K07 660 000*
				25.00	K07 676 001*	K07 680 000*
				25.00	K07 692 001*	K07 700 000*
				25.00	K07 712 001*	K07 720 000*
				25.00	K07 732 001*	K07 740 000*
				25.00	K07 752 001*	K07 760 000*
				25.00	K07 772 001*	K07 780 000*
				25.00	K07 792 001*	K07 800 000*
				25.00	K07 812 001*	K07 820 000*
				25.00	K07 832 001*	K07 840 000*
				25.00	K07 852 001*	K07 860 000*
				25.00	K07 872 001*	K07 880 000*

DISTRICT	TOTAL NOTES PRINTED	BLOCKS	ESTIMATED VALUE VG/F CU	LOW OFFICIAL SERIAL NUMBER	HIGH OFFICIAL SERIAL NUMBER
			25.00	K07 892 001*	K07 900 000*
			25.00	K07 912 001*	K07 920 000*
			25.00	K07 932 001*	K07 940 000*
			25.00	K07 952 001*	K07 960 000*
			25.00	K07 972 001*	K07 980 000*
			25.00	K07 992 001*	K08 000 000*
			25.00	K08 012 001*	K08 020 000*
			25.00	K08 032 001*	K08 040 000*
			25.00	K08 052 001*	K08 060 000*
			25.00	K08 072 001*	K08 080 000*
			25.00	K08 092 001*	K08 100 000*
			25.00	K08 112 001*	K08 120 000*
			25.00	K08 132 001*	K08 140 000*
			25.00	K08 152 001*	K08 160 000*
			25.00	K08 172 001*	K08 180 000*
			25.00	K08 192 001*	K08 200 000*
			25.00	K08 212 001*	K08 220 000*
			25.00	K08 232 001*	K08 240 000*
			25.00	K08 252 001*	K08 260 000*
			25.00	K08 272 001*	K08 280 000*
			25.00	K08 292 001*	K08 300 000*
			25.00	K08 312 001*	K08 320 000*
			3.50	K08 320 001*	K12 800 000*
12 L SAN FRANCISCO	82,560,000	L--F	3.00	L17 280 001F	L99 840 000F
	99,840,000	L--G	3.00	L00 000 001G	L99 840 000G
	99,840,000	L--H	3.00	L00 000 001H	L99 840 000H
	99,840,000	L--I	3.00	L00 000 001I	L99 840 000I
	51,200,000	L--J	3.00	L00 000 001J	L51 200 000J
	5,888,000	L--*	3.50	L08 960 001*	L14 080 000*
			25.00	L14 096 001*	L14 100 000*
			25.00	L14 116 001*	L14 120 000*
			25.00	L12 136 001*	L14 140 000*
			25.00	L14 156 001*	L14 160 000*
			25.00	L14 176 001*	L14 180 000*
			25.00	L14 196 001*	L14 200 000*
			25.00	L14 216 001*	L14 220 000*
			25.00	L14 236 001*	L14 240 000*
			25.00	L14 256 001*	L14 260 000*
			25.00	L14 276 001*	L14 280 000*
			25.00	L14 296 001*	L14 300 000*
			25.00	L14 316 001*	L14 320 000*
			25.00	L14 336 001*	L14 340 000*
			25.00	L14 356 001*	L14 360 000*
			25.00	L14 376 001*	L14 380 000*
			25.00	L14 396 001*	L14 400 000*
			25.00	L14 416 001*	L14 420 000*
			25.00	L14 436 001*	L14 440 000*
			25.00	L14 456 001*	L14 460 000*
			25.00	L14 476 001*	L14 480 000*
			25.00	L14 496 001*	L14 500 000*
			25.00	L14 516 001*	L14 520 000*
			25.00	L14 536 001*	L14 540 000*
			25.00	L14 556 001*	L14 560 000*
			25.00	L14 576 001*	L14 580 000*
			25.00	L14 596 001*	L14 600 000*
			25.00	L14 616 001*	L14 620 000*
			25.00	L14 636 001*	L14 640 000*
			25.00	L14 656 001*	L14 660 000*
			25.00	L14 676 001*	L14 680 000*
			25.00	L14 696 001*	L14 700 000*
			25.00	L14 716 001*	L14 720 000*
			3.50	L14 720 001*	L15 360 000*

The production unit was changed from 20,000 sheets to 40,000 sheets for:

BANK	STARTING WITH SERIAL	BANK	STARTING WITH SERIAL
Boston	A06 400 001D	Chicago	G42 240 001H
New York	B53 760 001J	St. Louis	H84 480 001C
Philadelphia	C29 440 001D	Minneapolis	I37 120 001B
Cleveland	D94 720 001C	Kansas City	J75 520 001D
Richmond	E06 400 001G	Dallas	K42 240 001E
Atlanta	F42 240 001H	San Francisco	L43 520 001H

CAT. NO. IF81
$1.00 FEDERAL RESERVE NOTE (GREEN SEAL) 32 Subject
SERIES 1981

SIGNATURES: Angela M. Buchanan, Treasurer of the United States.
Donald T. Regan, Secretary of the Treasury.

PLATE SERIALS: Both face and back check numbers begin at 1. (See footnote)

SERIAL NUMBERS: All districts begin at 00 000 001.

	DISTRICT	TOTAL NOTES PRINTED	BLOCKS	ESTIMATED VALUE VG/F	CU	LOW OFFICIAL SERIAL NUMBER	HIGH OFFICIAL SERIAL NUMBER
1	A BOSTON		A--A		1.50	A00 000 001A	A28 160 000A
			A--*		2.50	A00 000 001*	A00 640 000*
2	B NEW YORK		B--A		1.50	B00 000 001A	B92 160 000A
			B--*		2.50	B00 000 001*	B01 920 000*
3	C PHILADELPHIA		C--A		1.50	C00 000 001A	C15 360 000A
			C--*		2.50	C00 000 001*	C00 640 000*
					10.00	C00 652 001*	C00 660 000*
					10.00	C00 672 001*	C00 680 000*
					10.00	C00 692 001*	C00 700 000*
					10.00	C00 712 001*	C00 720 000*
					10.00	C00 732 001*	C00 740 000*
					10.00	C00 752 001*	C00 760 000*
					10.00	C00 772 001*	C00 780 000*
					10.00	C00 792 001*	C00 800 000*
					10.00	C00 812 001*	C00 820 000*
					10.00	C00 832 001*	C00 840 000*
					10.00	C00 852 001*	C00 860 000*
					10.00	C00 872 001*	C00 880 000*
					10.00	C00 892 001*	C00 900 000*
					10.00	C00 912 001*	C00 920 000*
					10.00	C00 932 001*	C00 940 000*
					10.00	C00 952 001*	C00 960 000*
					10.00	C00 972 001*	C00 980 000*
					10.00	C00 992 001*	C01 000 000*
					10.00	C01 012 001*	C01 020 000*
					10.00	C01 032 001*	C01 040 000*
					10.00	C01 052 001*	C01 060 000*
					10.00	C01 072 001*	C01 080 000*
					10.00	C01 092 001*	C01 100 000*
					10.00	C01 112 001*	C01 120 000*
					10.00	C01 132 001*	C01 140 000*
					10.00	C01 152 001*	C01 160 000*
					10.00	C01 172 001*	C01 180 000*
					10.00	C01 192 001*	C01 200 000*
					10.00	C01 212 001*	C01 220 000*
					10.00	C01 232 001*	C01 240 000*
					10.00	C01 252 001*	C01 260 000*
					10.00	C01 272 001*	C01 280 000*
4	D CLEVELAND		D--A		1.50	D00 000 001A	D10 240 000A
5	E RICHMOND		E--A		1.50	E00 000 001A	E32 000 000A
			E--*		2.50	E00 000 001*	E00 640 000*
6	F ATLANTA		F--A		1.50	F00 000 001A	F69 120 000A
			F--*		2.50	F00 000 001*	F00 640 000*
7	G CHICAGO		G--A		1.50	G00 000 001A	G52 480 000A
			G--*		2.50	G00 000 001*	G01 280 000*
8	H ST. LOUIS		H--A		1.50	H00 000 001A	H21 760 000A
			H--*		10.00	H00 008 001*	H00 020 000*
					10.00	H00 028 001*	H00 040 000*
					10.00	H00 048 001*	H00 060 000*
					10.00	H00 068 001*	H00 080 000*
					10.00	H00 088 001*	H00 100 000*
					10.00	H00 108 001*	H00 120 000*
					10.00	H00 128 001*	H00 140 000*
					10.00	H00 148 001*	H00 160 000*
					10.00	H00 168 001*	H00 180 000*
					10.00	H00 188 001*	H00 200 000*
					10.00	H00 208 001*	H00 220 000*

DISTRICT	TOTAL NOTES PRINTED	BLOCKS	ESTIMATED VALUE VG/F CU	LOW OFFICIAL SERIAL NUMBER	HIGH OFFICIAL SERIAL NUMBER
			10.00	H00 228 001*	H00 240 000*
			10.00	H00 248 001*	H00 260 000*
			10.00	H00 268 001*	H00 280 000*
			10.00	H00 288 001*	H00 300 000*
			10.00	H00 308 001*	H00 320 000*
			10.00	H00 328 001*	H00 340 000*
			10.00	H00 348 001*	H00 360 000*
			10.00	H00 368 001*	H00 380 000*
			10.00	H00 388 001*	H00 400 000*
			10.00	H00 408 001*	H00 420 000*
			10.00	H00 428 001*	H00 440 000*
			10.00	H00 448 001*	H00 460 000*
			10.00	H00 468 001*	H00 480 000*
			10.00	H00 488 001*	H00 500 000*
			10.00	H00 508 001*	H00 520 000*
			10.00	H00 528 001*	H00 540 000*
			10.00	H00 548 001*	H00 560 000*
			10.00	H00 568 001*	H00 580 000*
			10.00	H00 588 001*	H00 600 000*
			10.00	H00 608 001*	H00 620 000*
			10.00	H00 628 001*	H00 640 000*
9 I MINNEAPOLIS		I--A	1.50	I00 000 001A	I16 640 000A
		I--*	10.00	I00 012 001*	I00 020 000*
			10.00	I00 032 001*	I00 040 000*
			10.00	I00 052 001*	I00 060 000*
			10.00	I00 072 001*	I00 080 000*
			10.00	I00 092 001*	I00 100 000*
			10.00	I00 112 001*	I00 120 000*
			10.00	I00 132 001*	I00 140 000*
			10.00	I00 152 001*	I00 160 000*
			10.00	I00 172 001*	I00 180 000*
			10.00	I00 192 001*	I00 200 000*
			10.00	I00 212 001*	I00 220 000*
			10.00	I00 232 001*	I00 240 000*
			10.00	I00 252 001*	I00 260 000*
			10.00	I00 272 001*	I00 280 000*
			10.00	I00 292 001*	I00 300 000*
			10.00	I00 312 001*	I00 320 000*
			10.00	I00 332 001*	I00 340 000*
			10.00	I00 352 001*	I00 360 000*
			10.00	I00 372 001*	I00 380 000*
			10.00	I00 392 001*	I00 400 000*
			10.00	I00 412 001*	I00 420 000*
			10.00	I00 432 001*	I00 440 000*
			10.00	I00 452 001*	I00 460 000*
			10.00	I00 472 001*	I00 480 000*
			10.00	I00 492 001*	I00 500 000*
			10.00	I00 512 001*	I00 520 000*
			10.00	I00 532 001*	I00 540 000*
			10.00	I00 552 001*	I00 560 000*
			10.00	I00 572 001*	I00 580 000*
			10.00	I00 592 001*	I00 600 000*
			10.00	I00 612 001*	I00 620 000*
			10.00	I00 632 001*	I00 640 000*
10 J KANSAS CITY		J--A	1.50	J00 000 001A	J32 000 000A
		J--*	2.50	J00 000 001*	J00 640 000*
11 K DALLAS		K--A	1.50	K00 000 001A	K17 920 000A
12 L SAN FRANCISCO		L--A	1.50	L00 000 001A	L51 200 000A
		L--*	2.50	L00 000 001*	L00 640 000*

Total Blocks: Twenty two.

(1) Printings through November, 1981.

Footnote: Back check number reverted to #1 (highest back check of the Series 1977A was #2185. Reversion to #1 was caused by a change in the engraving. A new test whereby the engraving is not as deeply cut as in previous series is theoretically hoped to save ink. Collectors are exhorted to look for MULES in the 1981 $1.00 notes, such mules would have back check numbers probably in the 1900 to 2185 range. A report of any such finds would be appreciated.

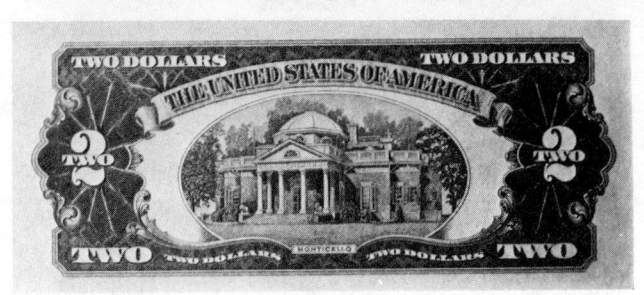

CAT. NO. IIL28B
$2.00 UNITED STATES NOTE — LEGAL TENDER (RED SEAL) (12 Subject)
SERIES 1928B

SERIAL NUMBERS:
   (Low Observed) A88 538 455A B09 004 381A (High Observed)
   Star Notes:
   (Low Observed) *00 943 989A *01 053 286A (High Observed)
PLATE SERIALS: Face check #1 through #6 not used. Face check number range #7 through #42.
SIGNATURES: Walter O. Woods, Treasurer of the United States
   Ogden L. Mills, Secretary of the Treasury.
TOTAL QUANTITY PRINTED: 9,001,632 notes.

ESTIMATED VALUES:

	VG/F	CU
A--A	$150.00	$400.00
B--A	125.00	350.00
*--A	350.00	700.00

TOTAL BLOCKS KNOWN: Three.

CAT. NO. IIL28
$2.00 UNITED STATES NOTE — LEGAL TENDER (RED SEAL) (12 Subject)
SERIES 1928

SERIAL NUMBERS:
   (Low Official) A00 000 001A A55 944 639A (High Observed)
   Star Notes:
   (Low Official) *00 000 001A *00 666 015A (Low Observed)
   *00 675 099A (High Observed)
PLATE SERIALS: Face check #1 was not used. Face check number ranges #2 throuth #103.
   Back check numbers are "micro" type and begin at #1.
SIGNATURES: H.T. Tate, Treasurer of the United States
   Andrew W. Mellon, Secretary of the Treasury
TOTAL QUANTITY PRINTED: 55,889,424 notes
DESIGN: Face design for series 1928 through 1928G has red Treasury seal to left of portrait of Jefferson with large TWO at right. Back shows Monticello. Face and back check numbers doubled in size for series 1928D and later.

ESTIMATED VALUES:

	VG/F	CU
A--A	$17.50	$40.00
*--A	60.00	150.00

TOTAL BLOCKS KNOWN: Two.

CAT. NO. IIL28C
$2.00 UNITED STATES NOTE — LEGAL TENDER (RED SEAL) (12 Subject)
SERIES 1928C

SERIAL NUMBERS:
   (Low Official) B09 008 001A C05 594 680A (High Observed)
   Star Notes:
   (Low Observed) *01 082 940A *01 990 816A (High Observed)
PLATE SERIALS: Face check number range #1 through #181, excluding #56 through #75 which were not used.
   Back check numbers end at #228 (high of the "micro" type).
SIGNATURES: W.A. Julian, Treasurer of the United States
   Henry Morgenthau, Jr., Secretary of the Treasury
TOTAL QUANTITY PRINTED: 86,584,008 notes

ESTIMATED VALUES:

	VG/F	CU
B--A	$8.50	$50.00
C--A	15.00	75.00
*--A	100.00	250.00

TOTAL BLOCKS KNOWN: Three

CAT. NO. IIL28A
$2.00 UNITED STATES NOTE — LEGAL TENDER (RED SEAL) (12 Subject)
SERIES 1928A

SERIAL NUMBERS:
   (Low Observed) A51 112 758A B08 878 777A (High Observed)
   Star Notes:
   (Low Observed) *00 834 244A *01 055 379A (High Observed)
PLATE SERIALS: Face check #1 (master), #2 and #3 were not used. Face check number range #4 through #93.
SIGNATURES: Walter O. Woods, Treasurer of the United States
   Andrew W. Mellon, Secretary of the Treasury
TOTAL QUANTITY PRINTED: 46,859,136 notes.

ESTIMATED VALUES:

	VG/F	CU
A--A	$35.00	100.00
B--A	150.00	350.00

TOTAL BLOCKS KNOWN: Three

CAT. NO. IIL28C
$2.00 UNITED STATES NOTE — LEGAL TENDER (RED SEAL) (12 Subject)
SERIES 1928C MULE

These are Series 1928C notes with the larger back check numbers (#289 or higher), and are actually Series 1928C faces on Series 1928D backs.
SERIAL NUMBERS:
   (Low Observed) B98 598 185A C01 255 480A (High Observed)

ESTIMATED VALUES:

	VG/F
B--A	$500.00
C--A	350.00

TOTAL BLOCKS KNOWN: Two.

101

CAT. NO. IIL28D
$2.00 UNITED STATES NOTE — LEGAL TENDER (RED SEAL) (12 Subject)
SERIES 1928D

SERIAL NUMBERS:
   (Low Official) B83 988 001A D35 443 700A (High Observed)
   (Low Observed) B98 122 371A
   Star Notes:
   (Low Observed) *02 240 015A *03 214 772A (High Observed)
PLATE SERIALS: Face check number range is #182 through #401.
   Back check numbers begin at #289.
SIGNATURES: W.A. Julian, Treasurer of the United States
   Henry Morgenthau, Jr., Secretary of the Treasury
TOTAL QUANTITY PRINTED: 146,381,364 notes.

ESTIMATED VALUES:

	VG/F	CU
B--A	$250.00	
C--A and D--A	7.50	25.00
*--A	25.00	50.00

TOTAL BLOCKS KNOWN: Four

CAT. NO. IIL28D
$2.00 UNITED STATES NOTE — LEGAL TENDER (RED SEAL) (12 Subject)
SERIES 1928D MULE

These are Series 1928D notes with the micro back check numbers (#288 or lower), and are actually Series 1928D faces on Series 1928C backs.
SERIAL NUMBERS:
   (Low Observed) B88 695 447A C55 064 693A (High Observed)
Star Notes:
   (Low Observed) *01 911 287A *02 379 560A (High Observed)

ESTIMATED VALUES:

	VG/F	CU
B--A	$10.00	25.00
C--A	10.00	25.00
D--A		unknown
*--A	25.00	45.00

TOTAL BLOCKS KNOWN: Three

CAT. NO. IIL28E
$2.00 UNITED STATES NOTE — LEGAL TENDER (RED SEAL) (12 Subject)
SERIES 1928E

SERIAL NUMBERS:
   (Low Official) D29 712 001A D39 591 186A (High Observed)
   Star Notes:
   (Low Observed) *03 224 484A (High Observed)
PLATE SERIALS: Face check number range #403 through #414.
SIGNATURES: W.A. Julian, Treasurer of the United States
   Fred M. Vinson, Secretary of the Treasury
TOTAL QUANTITY PRINTED: 5,261,016 notes.

ESTIMATED VALUES:

	VG/F	CU
D--A	$15.00	$50.00
*--A	200.00	1000.00

TOTAL BLOCKS KNOWN: Two

CAT. NO. IIL28F
$2.00 UNITED STATES NOTE — LEGAL TENDER (RED SEAL) (12 Subject)
SERIES 1928F

SERIAL NUMBERS:
   (Low Official) D36 192 001A D81 308 493A (High Observed)
   Star Notes:
   (Low Observed) *03 245 546A *03 642 562A (High Observed)
PLATE SERIALS: Face check number range #440 through #462.
SIGNATURES: W.A. Julian, Treasurer of the United States
   John W. Snyder, Secretary of the Treasury
TOTAL QUANTITY PRINTED: 43,349,292 notes.

ESTIMATED VALUES:

	VG/F	CU
D--A	$8.00	$17.50
*--A	20.00	35.00

TOTAL BLOCKS KNOWN: Two

CAT. NO. IIL28G
$2.00 UNITED STATES NOTE — LEGAL TENDER (RED SEAL) (12 Subject)
SERIES 1928G

SERIAL NUMBERS:
   (Official Range) D78 552 001A through E30 760 000A
   Star Notes:
   (Low Observed) *02 754 165A *04 152 000A (High Official)
PLATE SERIALS: Face check number range #483 through #516. Back check numbers end at #390 (high of 12 subject sheets)
SIGNATURES: Georgia Neese Clark, Treasurer of the United States
   John W. Snyder, Secretary of the Treasury
TOTAL QUANTITY PRINTED: 5,007,912 notes

ESTIMATED VALUES:

	VG/F	CU
D--A and E--A	$5.00	$12.50
*--A	10.00	25.00

TOTAL BLOCKS KNOWN: Three

CAT. NO. IlL53
$2.00 UNITED STATES NOTE — LEGAL TENDER (RED SEAL) (18 Subject)
SERIES 1953

SERIAL NUMBERS:
   (Official Range) A00 000 001A through A45 360 000A
   Star Notes:
   (Low Official) *00 000 001A *02 155 445A (high Observed)
PLATE SERIALS: Face check numbers begin at #1. (#8 was not used).
   Back check numbers begin at #391 (Low of 18 subject sheets).
SIGNATURES: Ivy Baker Priest, Treasurer of the United States
   George M. Humphrey, Secretary of the Treasury
DESIGN: Face design for series 1953 through 1963A has large numeral 2 in grey to left of portrait of Jefferson with smaller red Treasury seal to right printed over TWO. The word "of" is left out of series date which is placed at lower right. "Washington, D.C." is moved up under serial number upper right. Back design remains Monticello. "IN GOD WE TRUST" added for series 1963 and 1963A. $2.00 United States Note was discontinued with series 1963A.

ESTIMATED VALUES: CU
                          A--A $8.50
                          *--A   12.50

TOTAL BLOCKS KNOWN: Two

CAT. NO. IlL53A
$2.00 UNITED STATES NOTE — LEGAL TENDER (RED SEAL) (18 Subject)
SERIES 1953A

SERIAL NUMBERS:
   (Official Range) A45 360 001A through A63 360 000A
   Star Notes:
   (Low Observed) *02 161 547A through *02 859 415A (high observed)
SIGNATURES: Ivy Baker Priest, Treasurer of the United States
   Robert B. Anderson, Secretary of the Treasury

ESTIMATED VALUES: CU
                          A--A $8.00
                          *--A   10.00

TOTAL BLOCKS KNOWN: Two

CAT. NO. IlL53B
$2.00 UNITED STATES NOTE — LEGAL TENDER (RED SEAL) (18 Subject)
SERIES 1953B

SERIAL NUMBERS:
   (Official Range) A63 360 001A through A74 160 000A
   Star Notes:
   (Low Observed) *02 883 215A *03 591 612A (high observed)
SIGNATURES: Elizabeth Rudel Smith, Treasurer of the United States
   C. Douglas Dillon, Secretary of the Treasury

ESTIMATED VALUES: CU
                          A--A $7.00
                          *--A   10.00

TOTAL BLOCKS KNOWN: Two

CAT. NO. IlL53C
$2.00 UNITED STATES NOTE — LEGAL TENDER (RED SEAL) (18 Subject)
SERIES 1953C

SERIAL NUMBERS:
   (Official Range) A74 160 001A through A79 920 000A
   Star Notes:
   (Low Observed) *03 601 348A *03 955 427A (High Observed)
SIGNATURES: Kathryn O'Hay Granahan, Treasurer of the United States
   C. Douglas Dillon, Secretary of the Treasury
PLATE SERIALS: Back check numbers used on 18 subject sheets end at #412.
   Face check numbers used on 18 subject sheets end at #16.

ESTIMATED VALUES: CU
                          A--A $7.00
                          *--A   10.00

TOTAL BLOCKS KNOWN: Two

CAT. NO. IlL63
$2.00 UNITED STATES NOTE — LEGAL TENDER (RED SEAL) (32 Subject)
SERIES 1963

SERIAL NUMBERS:
   (Official Range) A00 000 001A through A15 360 000A
   Star Notes:
   (Official Range) *00 000 001A through *00 640 000A
PLATE SERIALS: Both face and back check numbers on 32 subject sheets begin at #1.
SIGNATURES: Kathryn O'Hay Granahan, Treasurer of the United States
   C. Douglas Dillon, Secretary of the Treasury

ESTIMATED VALUES: CU
                          A--A $7.50
                          *--A   10.00

TOTAL BLOCKS KNOWN: Two

CAT. NO. IIL63A
$2.00 UNITED STATES NOTE — LEGAL TENDER (RED SEAL) (32 Subject)
SERIES 1963A

SERIAL NUMBERS:
 (Official Range) A15 360 001A through A18 560 000A
 Star Notes:
 (Official Range) *00 640 001A through *01 280 000A
PLATE SERIALS: Both face and back check numbers end at #3.
SIGNATURES: Kathryn O'Hay Granahan, Treasurer of the United States
 Henry H. Fowler, Secretary of the Treasury

ESTIMATED VALUES:

	CU
A--A	$7.50
*--A	10.00

TOTAL BLOCKS KNOWN: Two
NOTE: The printing of the $2.00 United States Note terminated with Series 1963A.

$2.00 FEDERAL RESERVE NOTE Series 1976

FACE Portrait: Thomas Jefferson, third President of the United States and author of the Declaration of Independence, was born at Shadwell in Albemarle County, Virginia in 1743. His father, Peter Jefferson was a planter and surveyor of Welsh descent and was a member of the House of Burgesses. His mother was Jane Randolph. Thomas was the third child and eldest son of ten children. At 17 he entered William and Mary College and in 1767 was admitted to the bar. In 1769 he was a delegate to the House of Burgesses and there his first important effort was in support of a motion for the easier emancipation of slaves. Jefferson was a member of the Second Continental Congress which met in Philadelphia in 1775 and took his seat a few days after the Battle of Bunker Hill. He was re-elected to the Third Congress in 1776 and on June 7, 1776, Richard Henry Lee moved that Independence be declared. Jefferson was chairman of a committe of five to prepare the draft declaration. Other committee members were Benjamin Franklin, John Adams, Roger Sherman, and Robert H. Livingston. Jefferson succeeded Patrick Henry as governor of Virginia (1779-1781) and was elected President in 1801.

Artist: Gilbert Stuart. (For biography see $1.00 note.)

Engraver: Charles Kennedy Burt, born in Edinburg, Scotland on November 8, 1823, the son of Charles and Jessee Kennedy Burt. He was a natural artist, starting at the age of 12 attending night classes in drawing while attending his ordinary schooling. When about 17 his class was required to draw Eddystone Light from a verbal description. Burt won the prize and his drawing hung on the walls of Edinburg High School for many years. He studied engraving with W. Holmes, Lizars, a widely known and able engraver of Edinburg. In 1842 he came to New York City and was employed by A.L. Dick, Rawdon, Wright, Hatch and Edson, and the American Banknote Co. for 16 years. He was chief engraver for the U.S. Treasury Department for 20 years. He engraved postage stamps for Italy, Russia, Brazil, Chile, Canada and other foreign countries. Besides engraving 19 plates of the Presidents of the United States, he executed portraits of many of the royalty and other notable persons. He married Margaret Sargeant, daughter of Thomas Sargeant of Parsipanny at Rockaway, N.J. on June 3, 1844. They had one son and seven daughters. He died in Brooklyn, N.Y. on March 25, 1892.

The engraving of Jefferson was completed in June 1867 and first used on the $2.00 Treasury Note Series 1869.

BACK PICTURE: Signing of the Declaration of Independence.
ARTIST: Col. John Trumbull, born at Lebanon, Conn. on 6 June 1756, the son of Rev. Jonathan Trumbull. He graduated from Harvard University in 1773 and later joined the First Connecticut Regiment as adjutant. Gen. George Washington was attracted by the accuracy of Trumbull's drawing of the works around Boston and made Trumbull his aide-de-camp. He advanced rapidly to Colonel, but due to a grievance, retired 22 Feb. 1777. He became a pupil of Benjamin West in London. He was imprisoned for 18 months in retaliation for the execution of Major Andre. On his return from England, he executed many historical paintings, the most famous being the Signing of the Declaration of Independence. His paintings of Washington, done in 1792 was presented to Yale. The Trumbull Gallery at Yale contains 57 paintings and was presented in consideration of a $1,000.00 annuity to be paid during his life. The profits for their exhibition after his death were to be applied to the education of needy students. He died in New York City, 10 Nov. 1843.

Engraver: Charles Schlecht. Engraved in January 1875. In order to maximize security features for present size notes, the vignette was cropped. The present engraving was modified by Edward Archer. Schlecht's engraving was done from the Athenaeum painting now in the Boston Athenaeum Society Museum.

Portrayed in the original are; at far left, George Wythe, Va.; William Whipple, N.H.; Josiah Bartlett, N.H.; Thomas Lynch, Jr., S.C.; Benjamin Harrison, Va.; Standing in back, William Paca, Md.; Samuel Chase, Md.; Richard Stockton, N.J.; Lewis Morris, N.Y.; William Floyd, N.Y.; Arthur Middleton, S.C.; Stephen Hopkins, R.I.; William Ellery, R.I.; George Clymer, Pa.; Seated in first row, Richard Henry Lee, Va.; Samuel Adams, Mass.; George Clinton, N.Y.; Thomas Heyward, Jr., S.C.; Charles Carroll, Md.; Robert Morris, Pa.; Thomas Willing, Pa.; Benjamin Rush, Pa.;

Elbridge Gerry, Mass.; Robert Treat Paine, Mass.; William Hooper, N.C.; George Walton, Ga.; James Wilson, Pa.; Abraham Clark, N.J.; Francis Hopkinson, N.J.

At desk, John Adams, Mass.; Roger Sherman, Conn.; Robert Livingston, N.Y.; Thomas Jefferson, Va.; Benjamin Franklin, Pa.; Charles Thompson, Pa.; John Hancock, Mass.; Seated and standing beyond desk, Thomas Nelson, Jr., Va.; Francis Lewis, N.Y.; John Witherspoon, N.J.; Samuel Huntington, Conn.; William Williams, Conn.; Oliver Woolcott, Conn.; George Read, Del.; John Dickinson, Pa.; Edward Rutledge, S.C.; Thomas McKean, Del.; and Philip Livingston, N.Y.

Those who appear in the original painting but who will not grace the back of the new deuce are George Wythe, Va.; William Whipple, N.H.; Josiah Bartlett, N.H.; and Thomas Lynch, Jr., S.C.; all left off of the left side facing the vignette. Those left off to the right of the vignette are Thomas McKean, Del.; and Philip Livingston, N.Y.

CAT. NO. IIF76
$2.00 FEDERAL RESERVE BANK NOTE (GREEN SEAL) 32 Subject
SERIES 1976

SIGNATURES: Francine I. Neff, Treasurer of the United States
  William E. Simon, Secretary of the Treasury
PLATE SERIALS: Face check numbers 1 through 80, 93 and 94.
  Back check numbers 1 through 78, 87 and 100.

	DISTRICT	TOTAL NOTES PRINTED	BLOCKS	ESTIMATED VALUE VG/F	CU	OFFICIAL LOW SERIAL NUMBER	OFFICIAL HIGH SERIAL NUMBER	
1	A BOSTON		A--A		2.50	A00 000 001A	A10 240 000A	cv
			A--A		2.50	A10 240 001A	A29 440 000A	cp
			A--A		3.50	A00 000 001*	A01 280 000*	cv
2	B NEW YORK		B--A		2.50	B00 000 001A	B08 960 000A	cv
			B--A		2.50	B08 960 001A	B29 440 000A	cp
			B--A		2.50	B29 440 001A	B38 400 000A	cv
			B--A		2.50	B38 400 001A	B67 200 000A	cp
			B--*		3.50	B00 000 001*	B02 560 000*	cv
3	C PHILADELPHIA		C--A		2.50	C00 000 001A	C12 800 000A	cv
			C--A		2.50	C12 800 001A	C33 280 000A	cp
			C--*		3.50	C00 000 001*	C01 280 000*	cv
4	D CLEVELAND		D--A		2.50	D00 000 001A	D08 960 000A	cv
			D--A		2.50	D08 960 001A	D31 360 000A	cp
			D--*		3.50	D00 000 001*	D01 280 000*	cv
5	E RICHMOND		E--A		2.50	E00 000 001A	E56 960 000A	cp
			E--*		3.50	E00 000 001*	E00 640 000*	cv
6	F ATLANTA		F--A		2.50	F00 000 001A	F24 320 000A	cp
			F--A		5.00	F24 320 001A	F26 880 000A	cv
			F--A		2.50	F26 880 001A	F60 800 000A	cp
			F--*		3.50	F00 000 001*	F01 280 000*	cv
7	G CHICAGO		G--A		2.50	G00 000 001A	G37 120 000A	cp
			G--A		2.50	G37 120 001A	G46 720 000A	cv
			G--A		2.50	G46 720 001A	G75 520 000A	cp
			G--*		3.50	G00 000 001*	G01 280 000*	cv
8	H ST. LOUIS		H--A		3.50	H00 000 001A	H04 480 000A	cv
			H--A		2.50	H04 480 001A	H39 040 000A	cp
			H--*		3.50	H00 000 001*	H01 280 000*	cv
9	I MINNEAPOLIS		I--A		2.50	I00 000 001A	I10 880 000A	cv
			I--A		2.50	I10 880 001A	I14 080 000A	cp
			I--*		3.50	I00 000 001*	I00 640 000*	cv
10	J KANSAS CITY		J--A		2.50	J00 000 001A	J07 040 000A	cv
			J--A		2.50	J07 040 001A	J24 960 000A	cp
			J--*		3.50	J00 000 001*	J00 640 000*	cv
11	K DALLAS		K--A		2.50	K00 000 001A	K09 600 000A	cv
			K--A		2.50	K09 600 001A	K41 600 000A	cp
			K--*		3.50	K00 000 001*	K01 280 000*	cv
12	L SAN FRANCISCO		L--A		2.50	L00 000 001A	L82 560 000A	cp
			L--*		3.50	L00 000 001*	L01 920 000*	cv

**TREASURY DEPARTMENT
BUREAU OF ENGRAVING AND PRINTING.**

Washington, D.C.
March 14, 1933.

FOR IMMEDIATE RELEASE

The Bureau of Engraving and printing issued the following statement today:

Late in the day of March 9, 1933, the day that marked the enactment of legislation to provide relief in the banking emergency that had developed, the Bureau of Engraving and Printing was directed to proceed with the physical production of new Federal Reserve Bank notes. These new bank notes were authorized to meet the need for currency resulting from the panic withdrawals from our banks. They are like our National bank notes in appearance, and they are secured by government bonds or by the obligations of member banks in turn secured by good assets.

The first shipment of the new notes, completed twenty-four hours after the order was received, was delivered in New York at the Federal Reserve Bank on the morning of March 11, 1933. The quick action on the part of the Bureau of Engraving and Printing is getting into production was made possible through the fact that much of the preliminary work was being accomplished at the same time that plans were being considered and the Bill being drafted.

There was not sufficient time to engrave new dies and make new plates for the printing of the Federal Reserve bank notes. The standard National bank currency, on which the Bureau of Engraving and Printing was already in production, was therefore pressed into service. First it was necessary to procure facsimile signatures of two officials of each of the twelve Federal Reserve Banks. These were taken from certificates in the files of the Department. Production of special logotype plates, bearing the signature of bank officials, was undertaken at the plant of the American Type Founders Company at Jersey City.

It was necessary to add employees to the staff of the Bureau of Engraving and Printing. On March 13, 1933, 475 persons were recruited in the service. Men who wives were not employed, women whose husbands were not employed, and veterans were given preference in the large number of former employees who applied for positions.

The initial order for Federal Reserve Bank notes amounts to 15,524,000 sheets, or 186,288,000 notes, with an approximate face value of $2,000,000,000.

The production at the Bureau of Engraving and Printing will reach its peak within the next week, if demands require it. At peak production over six million notes will leave the bureau every twenty-four hours. These notes will be shipped to the various Federal Reserve banks throughout the country.

The production program required by the Emergency Bank Act is unprecedented. To meet this program many quick changes had to be made in the methods of handling the currency as it passed from one operation to another. Vaults had to be expanded. The entire staff of the Bureau undertook the task in splendid spirit. Several of the important operations are continuing throughout twenty-four hours of the day.

**CAT. NO. VN29
$5.00 FEDERAL RESERVE BANK NOTE (BROWN SEAL) (12 Subject)
SERIES 1929**

SPECIAL NUMBERS: Figures shown below are the official high numbers. All districts started both regular and star notes with serial 00 000 001. Bureau of Engraving and Printing information is incomplete on star serial numbers, as are reports of High Observed Serial Numbers.

PLATE SERIALS: Face check numbers within the range, #1 through #910.

SIGNATURES: E.E. Jones, Register of the Treasury.
W.O. Woods, Treasurer of the United States.
Also the Federal Reserve Bank Cashier or Controller or the Deputy or Assistant Deputy Governor, with the Governor.

TOTAL BLOCKS KNOWN: Twenty-two. Collectors are kindly requested to supply information on star serial numbers.

	DISTRICT	TOTAL NOTES PRINTED	BLOCKS	ESTIMATED VALUE VG/F	CU	LOW OBSERVED SERIAL NUMBER	HIGH OFFICIAL SERIAL NUMBER HIGH * OBSERVED
1	A BOSTON		A--A	22.50	50.00	A00 000 024A	A03 180 000A
		36,000	A--*	35.00	105.00		
2	B NEW YORK		B--A	22.50	47.50	B00 000 003A	B02 100 000A
		24,000	B--*	35.00	100.00		
3	C PHILADELPHIA		C--A	22.50	50.00	C00 000 070A	C03 096 000A
		36,000	C--*	35.00	105.00	C00 014 413*	C00 022 349*
4	D CLEVELAND		D--A	22.50	47.50	D00 000 040A	D04 236 000A
		60,000	D--*	35.00	100.00	D00 025 600*	D00 035 402*
6	F ATLANTA		F--A	27.50	100.00	F00 000 020A	F01 884 000A
		24,000	F--*	37.50	115.00	F00 002 604*	F00 071 992
7	G CHICAGO		G--A	20.00	45.00	G01 783 316A	G05 988 000A
		84,000	G--*	32.50	100.00	G00 030 317*	G00 030 317*
8	H ST. LOUIS		H--A	100.00	350.00		H00 276 000A
		24,000	H--*	50.00	150.00		
9	I MINNEAPOLIS		I--A	32.50	100.00	I00 000 020A	I00 684 000A
		24,000	I--*	45.00	135.00		
10	J KANSAS CITY		J--A	25.00	65.00	J00 000 008A	J02 460 000A
		48,000	J--*	37.50	110.00		J00 031 617*
11	K DALLAS		K--A	30.00	65.00	K00 790 286A	K00 996 000A
		24,000	K--*	42.50	125.00		
12	L SAN FRANCISCO		L--A	500.00	1500.		L00 360 000A
		24,000	L--*	1375.	5000.		

CAT. NO. VS34
$5.00 SILVER CERTIFICATE (BLUE SEAL) (12 Subject)
SERIES 1934

SERIAL NUMBERS:
  (Low Official) A00 000 001A E51 445 583A (High Observed)
Star Notes:
  (Low Official) *00 000 001A *03 954 635A (High Observed)
PLATE SERIALS: Face check number range #1-#561. Back check numbers below #938 (micro size)

SIGNATURES: W.A. Julian, Treasurer of the United States
  Henry Morgenthau, Jr., Secretary of the Treasury

DESIGN: Face design for series 1934 through 1934D has large blue 5 to left of portrait of Lincoln with blue Treasury seal at right. Back design shows Lincoln Memorial, Washington, D.C. Face and back check numbers doubled in size for series 1934A and later.

TOTAL QUANTITY PRINTED: 393,088,368 notes

ESTIMATED VALUES:

	VG/F	CU
A--A through D--A	$12.00	$20.00
E--A	35.00	75.00
*--A	25.00	50.00

TOTAL BLOCKS KNOWN: Six

CAT. NO. VS34
$5.00 SILVER CERTIFICATE (BLUE SEAL) (12 Subject)
SERIES 1934 MULE

These are Series 1934 notes with the larger back check numbers (#939 or higher), and are actually Series 1934 faces on Series 1934A backs.

SERIAL NUMBERS:
  (Low Observed) E06 094 905A E53 049 647A (High Observed)

ESTIMATED VALUES:

	VG/F	CU
E--A	$500.00	$1200.00

TOTAL BLOCKS KNOWN: One.

Lincoln Photo by Mathew Brady Feb. 9, 1864. Original glass plate negative presented to Library of Congress in 1953 by Louis Rabinowitz.

CAT. NO. VS34A
$5.00 SILVER CERTIFICATE (BLUE SEAL) (12 Subject)
SERIES 1934A

SERIAL NUMBERS:
  (Low Observed) E28 924 120A L26 399 695A (High Observed)
Star Notes:
  (Low Observed) *04 837 313A *11 656 719A (High Observed)

PLATE SERIALS: Face check number range #562-#1765. Back check numbers begin at #939.

SIGNATURES: W.A. Julian, Treasurer of the United States
Henry Morgenthau, Jr., Secretary of the Treasury
TOTAL QUANTITY PRINTED: 656,265,948 notes

ESTIMATED VALUES:	VG/F	CU
E--A through K--A	$10.00	$15.00
L--A	25.00	50.00
*--A	15.00	35.00

TOTAL BLOCKS KNOWN: Nine

CAT. NO. VS34A
$5.00 SILVER CERTIFICATE (BLUE SEAL) (12 Subject)
SERIES 1934A MULE

These are Series 1934A notes with micro back check numbers, and are actually Series 1934A faces on Series 1934 backs.

SERIAL NUMBERS:
(Low Observed) D56 173 786A   L17 092 520A (High Observed)
Star Notes:
(Low Observed) *03 594 833A   *06 414 028A (High Observed)
PLATE SERIALS: Back check numbers 938 or less (micro size).

ESTIMATED VALUES:	VG/F	CU
D--A through G--A	$12.50	$25.00
H--A	20.00	35.00
I--A and J--A	Presently unknown	
K--A and L	100.00	200.00
*--A	50.00	125.00

TOTAL BLOCKS KNOWN: Eight.

CAT. NO VS34A
$5.00 SILVER CERTIFICATE (BLUE SEAL)(Subject)
SERIES 1934A TRIAL NOTE

SERIAL NUMBERS:
(Low Observed) K21 768 367 A through K 52 282 527 A (High Observed)
PLATE SERIAL: Face check number 307.
TOTAL QUANTITY PRINTED: 569,244. (Includes 1934A North Africa below.)
ESTIMATED VALUE: K--A Rare
TOTAL BLOCKS KNOWN: One.

CAT. NO. VS34A
$5.00 SILVER CERTIFICATE (YELLOW SEAL) (12 Subject)
NORTH AFRICA
SERIES 1934A

SERIAL NUMBERS:
(Official Ranges) K34 138 001A through K34 508 000A
K36 420 001A through K36 740 000A
K37 464 001A through K37 784 000A
K40 068 001A through K42 068 000A
K43 152 001A through K44 852 000A
K53 984 001A through K65 984 000A
Star Notes:
(Low Observed) *10 549 061A *11 015 131A (High Observed)

PLATE SERIALS: Back check numbers begin at 939.

ESTIMATED VALUES:	BLOCKS	VG/F	CU
	K--A	17.50	100.00
	*--A	35.00	150.00

TOTAL BLOCKS KNOWN: Two.

CAT. NO. VS34A
$5.00 SILVER CERTIFICATE (YELLOW SEAL) (12 Subject)
SERIES 1934A NORTH AFRICA TRIAL NOTE

SERIAL NUMBERS:
(Low Observed) K54 472 223 A   K62 801 265 A (High Observed)
Star Notes:
(Low Observed) *10 991 486 A   *11 010 487 A (High Observed)
PLATE SERIAL: Face check number 307.

ESTIMATED VALUE:	VG/F	CU
K--A	50.00	150.00
*--A	50.00	200.00

TOTAL BLOCKS KNOWN: Two.

CAT. NO VS34B
$5.00 SILVER CERTIFICATE (BLUE SEAL) (12 Subject)
SERIES 1934B

SERIAL NUMBERS:
(Low Official) K90 375 110A   M33 301 809A (High Observed)
Star Notes:
(Low Observed) *11 412 724A   *12 397 170A (High Observed)
PLATE SERIALS: Face check number range #1769-#1826. Back check #939 and higher.
SIGNATURES: W.A. Julian, Treasurer of the United States   Fred M. Vinson, Secretary of the Treasury
TOTAL QUANTITY PRINTED: 59,128, 500 notes

ESTIMATED VALUES:	VG/F	CU
K--A	$25.00	$50.00
L--A	12.00	35.00
M--A	150.00	300.00
*--A	35.00	100.00

TOTAL BLOCKS KNOWN: Four

Cat. No. VS34B
$5.00 SILVER CERTIFICATE (BLUE SEAL) (12 Subject)
SERIES 1934B MULE

These are Series 1934B notes with micro back check numbers, and are actually Series 1934B faces on Series 1934 backs.
SERIAL NUMBERS:
(Low Observed) K11 692 973A   L84 008 002A (High Observed)
Star Notes:
(Low Observed) *11 665 559A   *11 731 841A (High Observed)
PLATE SERIALS: Back check numbers used #629 and #637 (micro size)

ESTIMATED VALUES:	VG/F	CU
K--A	$250.00	$500.00
L--A	200.00	400.00
*--A	Rare	

TOTAL BLOCKS KNOWN: Three.

CAT. NO. VS34C
$5.00 SILVER CERTIFICATE (BLUE SEAL) (12 Subject)
SERIES 1934C

SERIAL NUMBERS:
(Low Observed) L49 546 170A   Q65 450 107A (High Observed)
Star Notes:
(Low Observed) *12 004 318A   *17 687 718A (High Observed)
PLATE SERIALS: Face check number range #1875-#2031. Back check number 939 and higher.
SIGNATURES: W.A. Julian, Treasurer of the United States
            John W. Snyder, Secretary of the Treasury
TOTAL QUANTITY PRINTED: 403,328, 964 notes

ESTIMATED VALUES:	VG/F	CU
L--A through Q--A	$10.00	$20.00
*--A	17.50	30.00

TOTAL BLOCKS: Six

CAT. NO. VS34C
$5.00 SILVER CERTIFICATE (BLUE SEAL) (12 Subject)
SERIES 1934C MULE

These are Series 1934C notes with micro back check numbers, and are actually Series 1934C faces on Series 1934 Backs.
SERIAL NUMBERS:
(Low Observed) L51 435 522A   P72 850 478A (High Observed)
Star Notes:
(Low Observed) *13 803 080A   *15 047 154A (High Observed)
PLATE SERIALS: Back check numbers used #629 and #637 (micro size).

ESTIMATED VALUES:	VG/F	CU
L--A Through P--A	$35.00	$75.00
*--A	250.00	500.00

TOTAL BLOCKS KNOWN: Five.

CAT. NO VS34D
$5.00 SILVER CERTIFICATE (BLUE SEAL) (12 Subject)
SERIES 1934D

SERIAL NUMBERS:
(Official) Q23 136 001A through V14 796 000A (all varieties)
LOW OBSERVED: *16 884 788A   *23 088 000A HIGH OFFICIAL

SIGNATURES: Georgia Nesse Clark, Treasurer of the United States
            John W. Snyder, Secretary of the Treasury
TOTAL QUANTITY PRINTED: 486,146, 148 (all varieties)

WIDE 1
PLATE SERIALS: Back check number 2007 or lower.
(Low Observed:) Q45 838 633A   V13 492 055A (High Observed)
*16 884 788A   *22 854 814A

ESTIMATED VALUES:	VG/F	CU
Q--A through V--A	$10.00	$15.00
*--A	15.00	25.00

TOTAL BLOCKS KNOWN: Seven

NARROW
Plate Serials: Back check number 2008 through 2066.
LOW OBSERVED: T43 892 772A   HIGH OBSERVED: V13 942 627A
*21 432 006A   *22 469 986A

ESTIMATED VALUES:	VG/F	CU
T--A Through V--A	$15.00	$30.00
	30.00	60.00

TOTAL BLOCKS KNOWN: Four

WIDE II
PLATE SERIALS: Back check number 2067 through 2096.
(Low Observed:) U43 735 577A   V12 325 327A (High Observed)
*22 073 854A   *23 034 317A

ESTIMATED VALUES:	VG/F	CU
U--A and V--A	$25.00	$50.00
*--A	100.00	250.00

TOTAL BLOCKS KNOWN: Three

CAT. NO VS53
$5.00 SILVER CERTIFICATE (BLUE SEAL) (18 Subject)
SERIES 1953

SERIAL NUMBERS:
  (Official Range) A00 000 001A through D39 600 000A
  Star Notes:
  (Low Official) *00 000 001A *15 109 685A (High Observed)
PLATE SERIALS: Face check numbers begin at #1. Back check numbers begin at #2097 (low of 18 subject sheets).
SIGNATURES: Ivy Baker Priest, Treasurer of the United States
  George M. Humphrey, Secretary of the Treasury
DESIGN: Face design series 1953 through 1953B has smaller 5 to left of portrait of Lincoln and smaller blue Treasury seal at right. Back design similar to 1934.
  No $5.00 silver certificates have motto.

ESTIMATED VALUES:		CU
A--A through D--A		$15.00
*--A		25.00

TOTAL BLOCKS KNOWN: Five

CAT. NO. VS53A
$5.00 SILVER CERTIFICATE (BLUE SEAL) (18 Subject)
SERIES 1953A

SERIAL NUMBERS:
  (Official Range) D39 600 001A through F72 000 000A
  Star Notes:
  (Low Observed) *15 162 950A *29 363 003A (High Observed)
SIGNATURES: Ivy Baker Priest, Treasurer of the United States
  Robert B. Anderson, Secretary of the Treasury

ESTIMATED VALUES:		CU
D--A through F--A		$12.00
*--A		15.00

TOTAL BLOCKS KNOWN: Four

CAT. NO. VS53B
$5.00 SILVER CERTIFICATE (BLUE SEAL) (18 Subject)
SERIES 1953B

SERIAL NUMBERS:
  (Official Range) F72 000 001A through G45 000 000A
  Star Notes:
  (Official Range) *28 080 001A through *31 320 000A (High Official)
  (Low Observed) *28 371 579A *28 419 074A (High Observed)
SIGNATURES: Elizabeth Rudel Smith, Treasurer of the United States
  C. Douglas Dillon, Secretary of the Treasury.

ESTIMATED VALUES:	VG/F	CU
F--A		$12.00
*--A	$200.00	350.00

TOTAL BLOCKS KNOWN: Two
Notes in G--A block not released.

CAT. NO. VS53C
$5.00 SILVER CERTIFICATE (BLUE SEAL) (18 Subject)
SERIES 1953C

SERIAL NUMBERS:
  (Official Range) G45 000 001A through H35 640 000A
  Star Notes:
  (Low Observed) *31 320 001A *35 640 000A (High Observed)
PLATE SERIALS: Face check numbers of 18 subject sheets end at #97. Back check numbers on 18 subject sheets end at #2587.
SIGNATURES: Kathryn O'Hay Granahan, Treasurer of the United States
  C. Douglas Dillon, Secretary of the Treasury
NOTE: This series was printed but not released.

CAT. NO. VL28
$5.00 UNITED STATES NOTE - LEGAL Tender (RED SEAL) (12 Subject)
SERIES 1928

SERIAL NUMBERS:
  (Low Official) A00 000 001A D14 577 286A (High Observed)
  Star Notes:
  (Low Official) *00 000 001A *03 104 548A (High Observed)
PLATE SERIALS: Face check range is #5 through #408; face check #1 through #4 were not used. Back check numbers are micro type and begin at #1.
SIGNATURES: Walter O. Woods, Treasurer of the United States
  Andrew W. Mellon, Secretary of the Treasury
TOTAL QUANTITY PRINTED: 267, 209, 616 notes
DESIGN: Face design for series 1928 through 1928F has large red Treasury seal to left of portrait of Lincoln, large FIVE at right. Back design shows Lincoln Memorial, Washington, D.C. Face and back check numbers doubled in size for series 1928C and later.

ESTIMATED VALUES:	VG/F	CU
A--A through C--A	$17.50	$35.00
D--A	25.00	50.00
*--A	100.00	250.00

TOTAL BLOCKS KNOWN: Five

CAT. NO. VL28A
$5.00 UNITED STATES NOTE LEGAL TENDER (RED SEAL) (12 Subject)
SERIES 1928A

SERIAL NUMBERS:
  (Low Observed) C44 916 612A D14 724 105A (High Observed)
  Star Notes:
  (Low Observed) *03 069 369A *03 330 983A (High Observed)
PLATE SERIALS: Face check range is #3 through #122, #174 and #175. (Face check #1, #2, and #123 through #173 were not used).
SIGNATURES: Walter O. Woods, Treasurer of the United States
  Ogden L. Mills, Secretary of the Treasury
TOTAL QUANTITY PRINTED: 58, 194, 600 notes.

ESTIMATED VALUES:	VG/F	CU
C--A and D--A	$25.00	$75.00
*--A	150.00	350.00

TOTAL BLOCKS KNOWN: Three

CAT. NO. VL28B
$5.00 UNITED STATES NOTE -- LEGAL TENDER (RED SEAL) (12 Subject)
SERIES 1928B

SERIAL NUMBERS:
  (Low Official) D15 228 001A E68 016 167A (High Observed)

Star Notes:
 (Low Observed) *02 409 465A *05 014 213A (High Observed)
PLATE SERIALS: Face check range #1 through #287. Back check numbers end at #938 (High of the micro type).
SIGNATURES: W.A. Julian, Treasurer of the United States
 Henry Morgenthau, Jr., Secretary of the Treasury
TOTAL QUANTITY PRINTED: 147, 827, 340 notes.

ESTIMATED VALUES:

	VG/F	CU
D--A and E--A	$12.50	$30.00
*--A	35.00	125.00

TOTAL BLOCKS KNOWN: Three

CAT. NO. VL28B
$5.00 UNITED STATES NOTE--LEGAL TENDER (RED SEAL) (12 Subject)
SERIES 1928B MULE

These are Series 1928B notes with the larger back check numbers (#939 or higher), and are actually Series 1928B faces on Series 1928C backs.
SERIAL NUMBERS:
 (Low Observed) E09 764 160A E77 337 581A (High Observed)
Star Notes:
 (Low Observed) *04 839 268A *A04 890 555A (High Observed)

ESTIMATED VALUES:

	VG/F	CU
E--A	$30.00	$70.00
*--A	150.00	350.00

TOTAL BLOCKS KNOWN: Two.

CAT. NO. VL28C
$5.00 UNITED STATES NOTE — LEGAL TENDER (RED SEAL) (12 Subject)
SERIES 1928C

SERIAL NUMBERS:
 (Low Observed) E50 813 459A through G57 877 893A (High Observed)
Star Notes:
 (Low Observed) *05 232 293A rough *07 074 007 (High Observed)
PLATE SERIALS: Face check range #288 through #522.
 Back check numbers begin at #939
SIGNATURES: W.A. Julian, Treasurer of the United States
 Henry Morgenthau, Jr., Secretary of the Treasury
TOTAL NOTES PRINTED: 214,735,765

ESTIMATED VALUES:

	VG/F	CU
E--A through G--A	$12.50	$25.00
*--A	35.00	75.00

TOTAL BLOCKS KNOWN: Four

CAT. NO. VL28C
$5.00 UNITED STATES NOTE — LEGAL TENDER (RED SEAL) (12 Subject)
SERIES 1928C MULE

These are Series 1928C notes with micro back check numbers, (#938 or lower), and are actually Series 1928C faces on Series 1928B backs.
SERIAL NUMBERS:
 (Low Observed) E44 200 345A G52 180 700A (High Observed)
Star Notes:
 (Low Observed) *04 979 317A *05 479 315A (High Observed)

ESTIMATED VALUES:

	VG/F	CU
E--A	$25.00	$60.00
F--A	50.00	100.00
G--A	200.00	
*--A	75.00	200.00

TOTAL BLOCKS KNOWN: Four

CAT. NO. VL28D
$5.00 UNITED STATES NOTE — LEGAL TENDER (RED SEAL) (12 Subject)
SERIES 1928D

SERIAL NUMBERS:
 (Low Official) G50 628 001A through G66 675 309A (High Observed)
Star Notes:
 (Low Observed) *07 100 070A through *07 159 142A (High Observed)
PLATE SERIALS: Face check range #524 through #550. Back check #939 or higher.
SIGNATURES: W.A. Julian, Treasurer of the United States
 Fred M. Vinson, Secretary of the Treasury
TOTAL NOTES PRINTED: 9,297,120 notes.

ESTIMATED VALUES:

	VG/F	CU
G--A	$35.00	$100.00
*--A	150.00	350.00

TOTAL BLOCKS KNOWN: Two

CAT. NO. VL28D
$5.00 UNITED STATES NOTE — LEGAL TENDER (RED SEAL) (12 Subject)
SERIES 1928D MULE

These are series 1928D notes with micro back check number (#938 or lower), and are actually Series 1928D faces on Series 1928B backs.
SERIAL NUMBERS:
 (Low Observed) G58 008 072A G64 977 445A (High Observed)
PLATE SERIALS: Back check numbers used #629 and #637 (micro size)

ESTIMATED VALUES:

	VG/F
G--A	$500.00

TOTAL BLOCKS KNOWN: One

CAT. NO. VL28E
$5.00 UNITED STATES NOTE — LEGAL TENDER (RED SEAL) (12 Subject)
SERIES 1928E

SERIAL NUMBERS:
 (Low Official) G62 496 001A through H77 577 770A (High Observed)
Star Notes:
 (Low Observed) *07 187 321A through *08 697 470A (High Observed)
PLATE SERIALS: Face check range #566 through #627.
SIGNATURES: W.A. Julian, Treasurer of the United States
 John W. Snyder, Secretary of the Treasury
TOTAL QUANTITY PRINTED: 109,952,760 notes.

ESTIMATED VALUES:

	VG/F	CU
G--A and H--A	$15.00	$27.50
*--A	35.00	65.00

TOTAL BLOCKS KNOWN: Three.

CAT. NO. VL28E
$5.00 UNITED STATES NOTE — LEGAL TENDER (RED SEAL) (12 Subject)
SERIES 1928E MULE

These are Series 1928E Notes with micro back check numbers, and are actually Series 1928E Faces on Series 1928B Backs.
SERIAL NUMBERS:
 (Low Observed) G70 465 356A through H29 177 878A (High Observed)
PLATE SERIALS: Back check numbers used #629 and #637 (micro size).

ESTIMATED VALUES:

	VG/F	CU
G--A and H--A	$100.00	$350.00

TOTAL BLOCKS KNOWN: Two

111

CAT. NO. VL28F
$5.00 UNITED STATES NOTE (RED SEAL) (12 Subject)
SERIES 1928F

SERIAL NUMBERS: (all varieties)
OFFICIAL LOW: H71 592 001A I79 468 000A OFFICIAL HIGH
OBSERVED LOW: *08 456 672A *09 744 000A OFFICIAL HIGH
SIGNATURES: Georgia Neese Clark, Treasurer of the United States
    John W. Snyder, Secretary of the Treasury
TOTAL QUANTITY PRINTED: 104,194,704 (all varieties)
                    WIDE I
PLATE SERIALS: Back check number 2007 or lower.
LOW OBSERVED H72 318 257A I75 262 623A HIGH OBSERVED
(Specimens observed were not recorded, collectors please report.)
LOW OBSERVED *08 551 419A *08 888 366A HIGH OBSERVED

ESTIMATED VALUES:		VG/F	CU
	H--A and I--A	12.50	25.00
	I--A	25.00	60.00

TOTAL BLOCKS KNOWN: Three
                    NARROW
PLATE SERIALS: Back check number 2008 through 2066
LOW OBSERVED: I51 902 306A High observed I74 222 529A
*09 641 024A Collectors please report.

ESTIMATED VALUES:	I--A	35.00	50.00
	*--A	100.00	200.00

TOTAL BLOCKS KNOWN: Two
                    WIDE II
PLATE SERIALS: Back check number 2067 through 2096.
LOW OBSERVED: I70 867 629A High observed I79 394 789A
*09 650 582A Collectors please report.

ESTIMATED VALUES:	I--A	50.00	100.00
	*--A	100.00	200.00

CAT. NO VL53
$5.00 UNITED STATES NOTE — LEGAL TENDER (RED SEAL) (18 Subject)
SERIES 1953

SERIAL NUMBERS:
    (Official Range) A00 000 001 A through B20 880 000A
    Star Notes:
    (Low Official) *00 000 001A *05 717 636A (High Observed)
PLATE SERIALS: Face check numbers begin at #1. Back check numbers
    begin at #2097 (low of 18 subject sheets.)
SIGNATURES: Ivy Baker Priest, Treasurer of the United States
    George M. Humphrey, Secretary of the Treasury
DESIGN: Face design for series 1953 through 1963 has large numeral 5 in
    grey at left of portrait of Lincoln, smaller red Treasury seal over FIVE at
    right. Back design continues Lincoln Memorial. IN GOD WE TRUST
    added for series 1963, $5.00 United States Notes were discontinued
    with series 1963.

ESTIMATED VALUES		VG/F	CU
	A--A	$10.00	$20.00
	B--A	20.00	50.00
	*--A	30.00	75.00

TOTAL BLOCKS KNOWN: Three

CAT. NO. VL53A
$5.00 UNITED STATES NOTE — LEGAL TENDER (RED SEAL) (18 Subject)
SERIES 1953A

SERIAL NUMBERS:
    (Official Range) B20 880 001A through C11 160 000A
    Star Notes:
    (Low Observed) *05 786 055A *11 150 886A (High Observed)
SIGNATURES: Ivy Baker Priest, Treasurer of the United States
    Robert B. Anderson, Secretary of the Treasury

ESTIMATED VALUES:		CU
	B-A and C--A	$15.00
	*--A	25.00

TOTAL BLOCKS KNOWN: Three.

CAT. NO. VL53B
$5.00 UNITED STATES NOTE — LEGAL TENDER (RED SEAL) (18 Subject)
SERIES 1953B

SERIAL NUMBERS:
    (Official Range) C11 160 001A through C55 800 00A
    Star Notes:
    (Low Observed) *11 186 152A *13 297 110A (High Observed)
SIGNATURES: Elizabeth Rudel Smith, Treasurer of the United States
    C. Douglas Dillon, Secretary of the Treasury

ESTIMATED VALUES:		CU
	C--A	$15.00
	*--A	20.00

TOTAL BLOCKS KNOWN: Two.

CAT. NO. VL53C
$5.00 UNITED STATES NOTE — LEGAL TENDER (RED SEAL) (18 Subject)
SERIES 1953C

SERIAL NUMBERS:
    (Official Range) C55 800 001A through C64 440 000A
    Star Notes:
    (Low Observed) *13 333 217A *13 680 000A (High Official)
PLATE SERIALS: Face check numbers on 18 subject sheets end at #44.
    Back check numbers on 18 subject sheets end at #2587.
SIGNATURES: Kathryn O'Hay Granahan, Treasurer of the United States
    C. Douglas Dillon, Secretary of the Treasury

ESTIMATED VALUES:		CU
	C--A	15.00
	*--A	12.00

TOTAL BLOCKS KNOWN: Two.

CAT. NO. VL63
$5.00 UNITED STATES NOTE — LEGAL TENDER (RED SEAL) (32 Subject)
SERIES 1963

SERIAL NUMBERS:
   (Low Official) A00 000 001A though A63 360 000A (High Official)
   Star Notes:
   (Official Range) *00 000 001A through *03 840 000A
PLATE SERIALS: The range of the face check numbers made for 32 subject sheets is # 1 through #10. Back check number range #1 through #9.
SIGNATURES: Kathryn O'Hay Granahan, Treasurer of the United States
   C. Douglas Dillon, Secretary of the Treasury

ESTIMATED VALUES:

		CU
A--A		$10.00
*--A		15.00

TOTAL BLOCKS KNOWN: Two

TREASURY DEPARTMENT
WASHINGTON, D.C.   October 17, 1968
FOR IMMEDIATE RELEASE
TREASURY TO END $5 U.S. NOTE ISSUE:
WILL DISTRIBUTE $100 NOTES INSTEAD

The Treasury Department announced today that it will soon stop issuing $5 United States Notes — the only denomination of such notes now distributed — and begin issuing $100 United States Notes.

The Treasury explained that the change has nothing to do with the amount of currency available to commerce but only with cutting the cost of sorting notes unfit for continued circulation.

The Federal Reserve System, whose currency comprises 99 percent of paper money in circulation, will continue to issue the familiar Federal Reserve Notes in all present denominations. United States Notes make up less than one percent of circulating currency and the change will have no practical effect on money users.

In fiscal year 1967, 340 million unfit $5 notes of both types — United States and Federal Reserve — were retired compared to only 5.5 million in the $100 denomination. With elimination of $5 United States Notes there will be fewer notes to sort by type for retirement and thus a cost saving.

By law, the Treasury must keep $322,539,016 of United States Notes outstanding, but retired notes may be replaced by any denomination. Eventually, $100 will be the only denomination in which both Treasury and the Federal Reserve System issues currency.

Like the current $100 Federal Reserve Note, the new $100 United States Note will bear a portrait of Benjamin Franklin. Differences in the two notes — including designations on the front side and colors in which seals and serial numbers are printed — will make them easily distinguishable.

CAT. NO. VF28
$5.00 FEDERAL RESERVE NOTE (GREEN SEAL) (12 Subject)
SERIES 1928

SERIAL NUMBERS: All districts started both regular and star notes with serial 00 000 001. Bureau of Engraving and Printing information is incomplete on ending serial numbers.
PLATE SERIALS: Both face and back check numbers begin at #1.
SIGNATURES: H.T. Tate, Treasurer of the United States.
   A. W. Mellon, Secretary of the Treasury

ESTIMATED VALUES:

	DISTRICT	TOTAL NOTES PRINTED	BLOCKS	ESTIMATED VALUE VG/F	CU	LOW OBSERVED SERIAL NUMBER	HIGH OBSERVED SERIAL NUMBER
1	A BOSTON	8,025,300	A--A	$14.00	$40.00	A00 000 090A	A07 452 161A
			A--*	25.00	65.00		
2	B NEW YORK	14,701,884	B--A	12.00	35.00	B00 787 007A	B50 764 007A
			B--*	22.50	60.00		
3	C PHILADELPHIA	11,819,712	C--A	12.50	35.00	C09 316 908A	C27 758 611A
			C--*	22.50	60.00		
4	D CLEVELAND	9,049,500	D--A	13.00	37.50	D00 000 385A	D13 179 914A
			D--*	25.00	62.50	D00 088 287*	
5	E RICHMOND	6,027,660	E--A	15.00	42.50	E03 854 699A	E06 022 463A
			E--*	27.50	67.50		E00 085 392*
6	F ATLANTA	10,964,400	F--A	13.50	37.50	F01 886 364A	F10 800 485A
			F--*	25.00	62.50	F00 002 255*	F00 049 866*
7	G CHICAGO	12,326,052	G--A	12.00	35.00	G00 000 112A	G23 387 298A
			G--*	22.50	60.00	G00 201 352*	G00 445 680*

113

	DISTRICT	TOTAL NOTES PRINTED	BLOCKS	ESTIMATED VALUE VG/F	CU	LOW OFFICIAL SERIAL NUMBER	HIGH OFFICIAL SERIAL NUMBER
8	H ST. LOUIS	4,675,200	H--A	15.00	42.50	H00 000 014A	H04 220 853A
			H--*	27.50	67.50	H00 020 486*	H00 113 707
9	I MINNEAPOLIS	4,284,300	I--A	17.50	45.00		
			I--*	30.00	72.50	I02 608 325A	I03 818 066A
10	J KANSAS CITY	4,480,800	J--A	16.50	45.00	J00 477 365A	J05 245 344A
			J--*	30.00	70.00	J00 041 535*	J00 137 993*
11	K DALLAS	8,137,824	K--A	17.50	42.50	K01 708 136A	K05 600 102A
			K--*	30.00	70.00	K00 014 742*	K00 114 746*
12	L SAN FRANCISCO	9,792,000	L--A	14.00	40.00	L08 760 249A	L11 189 914A
			L--*	25.00	62.50		

TOTAL BLOCKS KNOWN: Twenty-four
Collectors are kindly requested to supply any serial numbers which improve on above information.

CAT. NO. VF28A
$5.00 FEDERAL RESERVE NOTE (GREEN SEAL) (12 Subject)
SERIES 1928A

SERIAL NUMBERS: All districts continued sequence from previous series with regular and star notes.
PLATE SERIALS: Face check numbers begin with #1.
SIGNATURES: Walter O. Woods, Treasurer of the United States
    A. W. Mellon, Secretary of the Treasury

	DISTRICT	TOTAL NOTES PRINTED	BLOCKS	ESTIMATED VALUE VG/F	CU	LOW OBSERVED SERIAL NUMBER	HIGH OBSERVED SERIAL NUMBER
1	A BOSTON	9,404,352	A--A	$11.50	$40.00	A07 553 069A	A16 638,789A
			A--*	25.00	67.50	A00 406 454*	
2	B NEW YORK	42,878,196	B--A	10.00	35.00	B10 828 275A	B54 038 970A
			B--*	20.00	57.50	B00 243 238*	
3	C PHILADELPHIA	10,806,012	C--A	11.50	37.50	C06 466 940A	C32 769 554A
			C--*	22.50	62.50	C00 218 478*	C00 350 766*
4	D CLEVELAND	6,822,000	D--A	11.50	37.50	D07 510 464A	D13 179 896A
			D--*	22.50	62.50		
5	E RICHMOND	2,409,900	E--A	14.00	45.00	E05 457 947A	E07 580 362A
			E--*	27.50	72.50	E00 126 303*	
6	F ATLANTA	3,537,600	F--A	12.50	42.50	F08 928 700A	F17 171 469A
			F--A	25.00	42.50		
7	G CHICAGO	37,882,176	G--A	10.00	35.00	G00 687 807A	G49 855 759A
			G--*	20.00	57.50	G00 247 663*	G00 649 815*
8	H ST LOUIS	2,731,824	H--A	12.50	42.50	H05 117 274A	H09 047 974A
			H--*	25.00	70.00		
9	I MINNEAPOLIS	652,800	I--A	16.50	50.00	I04 188 101A	I04 924 161A
			I--*	30.00	80.00		
10	J KANSAS CITY	3,572,400	J--A	14.00	45.00	J04 822 495A	J08 077 220A
			J--*	27.50	72.50		
11	K DALLAS	2,564,400	K--A	15.50	47.50	K05 632 501A	K08 234 307A
			K--*	28.50	75.00	K00 134 737*	
12	L SAN FRANCISCO	6,565,500	L--A	11.50	37.50	L09 694 201A	L14 362 130A
			L--*	23.50	62.50	L00 292 696*	L00 350 766*

TOTAL BLOCKS KNOWN: Twenty-four
Collectors are requested to supply any serial numbers which improve on above information.

CAT. NO VF28B
$5.00 FEDERAL RESERVE NOTE (DARK GREEN SEAL) (12 Subject)
SERIES 1928B

SERIAL NUMBERS: All districts continued sequence from previous series with regular and star notes.
PLATE SERIALS: Face check numbers begin with #1

SIGNATURES: Walter O. Woods, Treasurer of the United States
A. W. Mellon, Secretary of the Treasury

	DISTRICT	TOTAL NOTES PRINTED	BLOCKS	ESTIMATED VALUE VG/F	CU	LOW OBSERVED SERIAL NUMBER	HIGH OBSERVED SERIAL NUMBER
1	A BOSTON	28,430,724	A--A	$11.00	$32.50	A15 921 412A	A29 010 354A
			A--*	21.50	60.00	A00 425 259*	
2	B NEW YORK	51,157,536	B--A	10.00	30.00	B55 838 691A	B69 070 556A
			B--*	20.00	57.50		
3	C PHILADELPHIA	25,698,396	C--A	11.00	32.50	C21 695 184A	C38 171 567A
			C--*	21.50	60.00	C00 401 030*	C00 438 870*
4	D CLEVELAND	24,874,272	D--A	11.00	32.50	D15 828 264A	D30 032 980A
			D--*	21.50	60.00	D00 364 555*	
5	E RICHMOND	15,151,932	E--A	12.50	40.00	E08 343 197A	E13 568 780A
			E--*	25.00	65.00		
6	ATLANTA	13,386,420	F--A	12.00	37.50	F15 387 397A	F23 721 128A
			F--*	25.00	65.00	F00 333 663*	
7	G CHICAGO	17,157,036	G--A	11.00	32.50	G45 649 832A	G48 671 639A
			G--*	21.50	60.00		
8	H ST. LOUIS	20,251,716	H--A	12.00	35.00	H06 221 967A	H25 154 711A
			H--*	22.50	62.50	H00 241 323*	
9	I MINNEAPOLIS	6,954,060	I--A	15.00	45.00	I04 692 029A	I08 295 799A
			I--*	27.50	70.00	I00 101 208*	
10	J KANSAS CITY	10,677,636	J--A	13.50	40.00	J08 602 028A	J09 380 977A
			J--*	25.00	65.00		
11	K DALLAS	4,334,400	K--A	14.50	42.50	K09 827 819A	K12 115 181A
			K--*	27.50	70.00		
12	L SAN FRANCISCO	28,840,080	L--A	11.00	32.50	L17 719 957A	L35 493 749A
			L--*	21.50	60.00		

TOTAL BLOCKS KNOWN: Twenty-four
Collectors are kindly requested to supply any numbers which improve on above information.
(1) Includes both Dark and Light Green Seals.

CAT. NO. VF28B
$5.00 FEDERAL RESERVE NOTE (LIGHT GREEN SEAL) (12 Subject)
SERIES 1928B

SERIAL NUMBERS: All districts continued sequence from previous series.
TOTAL NOTES PRINTED: This information is found on previous page and includes both light and dark seal varieties of Series 1928B.

	DISTRICT	TOTAL NOTES PRINTED	BLOCKS	ESTIMATED VALUE VG/F	CU	LOW OBSERVED SERIAL NUMBER	HIGH OBSERVED SERIAL NUMBER
1	A BOSTON		A--A	$12.00	$37.50		
			A--*	23.50	65.00		
2	B NEW YORK		B--A	11.00	35.00	B62 532 058A	B79 618 320A
			B--*	22.50	62.50		
3	C PHILADELPHIA		C--A	12.00	37.50	C22 263 772A	C39 044 023A
			C--*	23.50	65.00		
4	D CLEVELAND		D--A	12.00	37.50	D21 250 688A	D25 055 270A
			D--*	23.50	65.00	D00 571 523*	
5	E RICHMOND		E--A	13.50	45.00	E38 269 080A	
			E--*	27.50	70.00		
6	F ATLANTA		F--A	13.00	42.50	F14 610 349A	F28 452 147A
			F--*	27.50	70.00		
7	G CHICAGO		G--A	12.00	37.50	G47 473 955A	G48 487 082A
			G--*	23.50	65.00		
8	H ST. LOUIS		H--A	13.00	40.00	H11 280 880A	H27 502 231A
			H--*	25.00	67.50		
9	I MINNEAPOLIS		I--A	16.50	50.00	I07 684 974A	
			I--*	30.00	75.00		
10	J KANSAS CITY		J--A	14.50	45.00	J09 774 705A	
			J--*	27.50	70.00		
11	K DALLAS		K--A	15.50	47.50	K10 827 231A	K11 403 644A
			K--*	30.00	75.00		
12	L SAN FRANCISCO		L--A	12.00	37.50	L18 566 372A	L39 700 819A
			L--*	23.50	65.00		

TOTAL BLOCKS KNOWN: Twenty-four
Collectors are kindly requested to supply any numbers which improve on above information.

CAT. NO. VF28C
$5.00 FEDERAL RESERVE NOTE (GREEN SEAL) (12 Subject)
SERIES 1928C

SERIAL NUMBERS: Districts printed continued sequence from previous series.

PLATE SERIALS: Face check numbers begin with #1.

SIGNATURES: Walter O Woods, Treasurer of the United States
   Ogden L. Mills, Secretary of the Treasury

DISTRICT	TOTAL NOTES PRINTED	BLOCKS	ESTIMATED VALUE VG/F	CU	LOW OBSERVED SERIAL NUMBER	HIGH OBSERVED SERIAL NUMBER
4 D CLEVELAND	3,293,640	D--A	250.00	750.00		
6 F ATLANTA	2,056,200	F--A	250.00	750.00	F23 852 359A	F28 424 033A
12 L SAN FRANCISCO	266,304	L--A	250.00	750.00		

TOTAL BLOCKS KNOWN: Three.

Collectors are kindly requested to supply any numbers which improve on above information.

CAT. NO. VF28D
$5.00 FEDERAL RESERVE NOTE (GREEN SEAL) (12 Subject)
SERIES 1928D

SERIAL NUMBERS: District printed continued sequence from previous series.

PLATE SERIALS: Face check range #1 through #9.

SIGNATURES: Walter O. Woods, Treasurer of the United States
   W.H. Woodin, Secretary of the Treasury

DISTRICT	TOTAL NOTES PRINTED	BLOCKS	ESTIMATED VALUE VG/F	CU	LOW OBSERVED SERIAL NUMBER	HIGH OBSERVED SERIAL NUMBER
6 F ATLANTA	1,281,600	F--A	250.00	1000.	F26 282 729A	F28 617 186A

TOTAL BLOCKS KNOWN: One.

Collectors are kindly requested to supply any numbers which improve on above information.

CAT. NO. VF34
$5.00 FEDERAL RESERVE NOTE (DARK GREEN SEAL) (12 Subject)
SERIES 1934

SERIAL NUMBERS: All districts started both regular and star notes with 00 000 001.

PLATE SERIALS: Back check number 938 and lower.

DISTRICT	TOTAL NOTES PRINTED	BLOCKS	ESTIMATED VALUE VG/F	CU	LOW OBSERVED SERIAL NUMBER	HIGH OBSERVED SERIAL NUMBER
2 B NEW YORK		B--A	35.00	75.00		B15 260 338A

	DISTRICT	TOTAL NOTES PRINTED	BLOCKS	ESTIMATED VALUE VG/F	CU	LOW OFFICIAL SERIAL NUMBER	HIGH OFFICIAL SERIAL NUMBER
3	C PHILADELPHIA		C--A	35.00	75.00	C06 891 512A	C08 029 264A
			C--*	75.00	150.00	C00 095 026*	
4	D CLEVELAND		D--A	35.00	75.00		D02 308 449A
5	E RICHMOND		E--A	35.00	75.00	E00 054 350A	
			E--*	75.00	150.00	E00 640 402*	
6	F ATLANTA		F--A	35.00	75.00	F12 119 799A	
7	G CHICAGO		G--A	35.00	75.00	G00 198 741A	G10 875 488A
8	H ST. LOUIS		H--A	35.00	75.00	H10 671 712A	H46 440 017A
			H--*	100.00	250.00	H00 020 486*	
9	I MINNEAPOLIS		I--A	35.00	75.00	I05 047 277A	I03 900 887A
			I--*	150.00	300.00		I00 083 077*
11	K DALLAS		K--*	100.00	250.00	K00 091 232*	K00 091 576*
12	L SAN FRANCISCO		L--A	35.00	75.00		L10 153 703A
			L--*	100.00	250.00	L00 005 324*	

TOTAL KNOWN BLOCKS: Fifteen.

CAT. NO. VF34
$5.00 FEDERAL RESERVE NOTE (DARK GREEN SEAL)
SERIES 1934 MULE

PLATE SERIALS: Back check number 939 and higher.

	DISTRICT	TOTAL NOTES PRINTED	BLOCKS	ESTIMATED VALUE VG/F	CU	LOW OBSERVED SERIAL NUMBER	HIGH OBSERVED SERIAL NUMBER
1	A BOSTON		A--A	11.50	35.00	A06 190 178A	A37 361 644A
			A--*	22.00	57.50	A00 190 989*	A00 269 453*
2	B NEW YORK		B--A	10.00	32.50	B17 676 495A	
			B--B	10.00	32.50		B72 677 449B
			B--*	20.00	55.00		
3	C PHILADELPHIA		C--A	10.00	32.50	C07 732 843A	C64 460 348A
			C--*	20.00	55.00	C00 086 921*	C00 560 030*
4	D CLEVELAND		D--A	10.00	31.00	D07 651 389A	D57 994 447A
			D--*	20.00	52.50	D00 215 154*	D00 728 450*
5	E RICHMOND		E--A	10.00	31.00	E10 784 859A	E60 059 991A
			E--*	20.00	52.50	E00 139 846*	E00 632 856*
6	F ATLANTA		F--A	10.00	32.50	F16 845 339A	F68 164 863A
			F--*	20.00	55.00	F00 766 237*	F00 766 242*
7	G CHICAGO		G--A	11.00	35.00	G12 120 900A	G58 557 297A
			G--*	21.50	57.50	G00 186 010*	G00 463 570*
8	H ST. LOUIS		H--A	11.00	32.50	H15 045 606A	H50 974 371A
			H--*	21.00	55.00	H00 427 381*	H00 502 768*
9	I MINNEAPOLIS		I--A	12.00	37.50	I06 278 084A	I15 302 244A
			I--*	23.50	62.50		I00 166 514*
10	J KANSAS CITY		J--A	11.50	36.00	J09 085 694A	J31 057 520A
			J--*	22.00	57.50		J00 087 675*
11	K DALLAS		K--A	11.50	36.00	K13 471 807A	K31 181 830A
			K--*	22.00	57.50		K00 348 303*
12	L SAN FRANCISCO		L--A	11.00	35.00	L18 550 641A	L44 890 159A
			L--*	21.50	57.50		

TOTAL KNOWN BLOCKS: Twenty-five.

Collectors are requested to furnish serial numbers and seal color with face and back check numbers which improve on above.

CAT. NO. VF34
$5.00 FEDERAL RESERVE NOTE (LIGHT GREEN SEAL) (12 Subject)
SERIES 1934

PLATE SERIALS: Both face and back check numbers start at #1. Back check #938 and lower.

SIGNATURES: W.A. Julian, Treasurer of the United States
Henry Morgenthau, Jr., Secretary of the Treasury.

	DISTRICT	TOTAL NOTES PRINTED (1)	BLOCKS	ESTIMATED VALUE VG/F	CU	LOW OBSERVED SERIAL NUMBER	HIGH OBSERVED SERIAL NUMBER
1	A BOSTON	30,510,036	A--A	12.50	37.50	A00 918 146A	A17 832 672A
			A--*	22.50	60.00		

	DISTRICT	TOTAL NOTES PRINTED	BLOCKS	ESTIMATED VALUE VG/F	CU	LOW OFFICIAL SERIAL NUMBER	HIGH OFFICIAL SERIAL NUMBER
2	B NEW YORK	47,888,760	B--A	11.00	35.00	B00 000 003A	B14 151 880A
			B--*	21.00	57.50	B00 007 363*	B00 077 576*
3	C PHILADELPHIA	47,327,760	C--A	11.50	35.00	C00 840 196A	C06 756 383A
			C--*	21.00	57.50		C00 043 755*
4	D CLEVELAND	62,273,508	D--A	11.00	33.50	D00 127 499A	D05 130 507A
			D--*	20.00	55.00		
5	E RICHMOND	62,128,452	E--A	11.00	33.50	E02 655 374A	E32 041 748A
			E--*	20.00	55.00	E00 678 292*	
6	F ATLANTA	50,548,608	F--A	11.50	35.00	F03 641 100A	F11 628 314A
			F--*	22.00	57.50	F00 012 697*	F00 766 237*
7	G CHICAGO	31,299,156	G--A	12.00	37.50	G00 020 996A	G10 875 488A
			G--*	22.50	60.00	G00 052 784*	G00 080 750*
8	H ST. LOUIS	48,737,280	H--A	12.50	35.00	H00 440 118A	H09 852 912A
			H--*	22.00	57.50	H00 036 197*	H00 049 487*
9	I MINNEAPOLIS	16,795,392	I--A	15.00	40.00	I00 511 332A	I05 047 277A
			I--*	25.00	65.00	I00 028 690*	I00 083 077*
10	J KANSAS CITY	31,854,432	J--A	13.50	38.50	J00 004 451A	J02 508 558A
			J--*	22.50	60.00		
11	K DALLAS	33,332,208	K--A	13.50	38.50	K00 016 483A	K10 901 395A
			K--*	22.50	60.00		
12	L SAN FRANCISCO	39,324,168	L--A	12.50	37.50	L02 718 182A	L10 400 155A
			L--*	22.50	60.00		

TOTAL KNOWN BLOCKS: Twenty-four

(1) Includes both regular and Mule, Light and Dark seals.

CAT. NO. VF34
$5.00 FEDERAL RESERVE NOTE (LIGHT GREEN SEAL) (12 Subject)
SERIES 1934 MULE

PLATE SERIALS: Back check number 939 and higher.

	DISTRICT	TOTAL NOTES PRINTED	BLOCKS	ESTIMATED VALUE VG/F	CU	LOW OBSERVED SERIAL NUMBER	HIGH OBSERVED SERIAL NUMBER
1	A BOSTON		A--A	25.00	50.00	A13 746 429A	A26 538 310A
2	B NEW YORK		B--A	25.00	50.00		B96 398 526A
3	C PHILADELPHIA		C--A	25.00	50.00	C15 699 990A	C61 918 552A
			C--*	50.00	100.00		C00 219 533*
4	D CLEVELAND		D--A	25.00	50.00	D08 303 983A	D56 873 483A
			D--*	50.00	100.00		D00 351 479*
5	E RICHMOND		E--A	25.00	50.00	E04 399 085A	E61 854 948A
6	F ATLANTA		F--A	25.00	50.00		F54 343 906A
			F--*	50.00	100.00		F00 680 462*
7	G CHICAGO		G--A	25.00	50.00		G47 207 440A
			G--*	50.00	100.00	G00 338 762*	G00 384 961*
8	H ST. LOUIS		H--A	25.00	50.00	H09 814 964A	H38 763 058A
9	I MINNEAPOLIS		I--*	50.00	100.00	I00 091 074*	I08 509 344A
10	J KANSAS CITY		J--A	25.00	50.00	J05 942 922A	J28 188 962A
11	K DALLAS		K--A	25.00	50.00	K04 606 264A	K26 583 039A
12	L SAN FRANCISCO		L--A	25.00	50.00	L18 658 668A	L28 934 630A

TOTAL KNOWN BLOCKS: Sixteen

Collectors are requested to furnish serial numbers and seal color with face and back check numbers which improve on above.

CAT. NO. VF34
$5.00 FEDERAL RESERVE NOTE (BROWN SEAL) (12 Subject) HAWAII
SERIES 1934

SERIAL NUMBERS:
   (Official Ranges) L12 396 001A through L14 996 000A
   L19 776 001A through L20 176 000A

L46 404 001A through L47 804 000A
L54 072 001A through L56 088 000A
L66 132 001A through L69 132 000A
Star Notes:
(Low Observed) L00 129 920*   L00 187 194* (High Observed)

PLATE SERIALS: Back check numbers 938 or lower.
SIGNATURES: Same as Series 1934

ESTIMATED VALUES:

BLOCKS	VG/F	CU
L--A	50.00	250.00
L--*	150.00	500.00

TOTAL BLOCKS KNOWN: Two.

CAT. NO. VF34
$5.00 FEDERAL RESERVE NOTE (BROWN SEAL) (12 Subject)
HAWAII
SERIES 1934 MULE

SERIAL NUMBERS: Same as Series 1934 Hawaii above.
  Star Notes:
   (Low Observed) L00 130 818*   L00 190 469* (High Observed)
PLATE SERIALS: Back check numbers 939 or higher.

ESTIMATED VALUES:

BLOCKS	VG/F	CU
L--A	35.00	200.00
L--*	100.00	200.00

TOTAL BLOCKS KNOWN: Two.

CAT. NO. VF34A
$5.00 FEDERAL RESERVE NOTE (GREEN SEAL) (12 Subject)
SERIES 1934A

SERIAL NUMBERS: All districts continued sequence from previous series.
PLATE SERIALS: Back check numbers begin at 939.
SIGNATURES: W.A. Julian, Treasurer of the United States
   Henry Morgenthau, Jr., Secretary of the Treasury

DISTRICT	TOTAL NOTES PRINTED	BLOCKS	VG/F	CU	LOW OBSERVED SERIAL NUMBER	HIGH OBSERVED SERIAL NUMBER
1 A BOSTON	23,231,568	A--A	11.50	33.50	A21 342 253A	A51 153 931A
		A--*	22.00	55.00	A00 391 563*	A00 597 573*
2 B NEW YORK	143,199,336	B--A	10.50	30.00	B34 173 012A	
		B--B	10.00	27.50		B89 463 392B
		B--*	20.00	50.00	B00 493 247*	B02 092 138*

	DISTRICT	TOTAL NOTES PRINTED	BLOCKS	ESTIMATED VALUE VG/F	CU	LOW OFFICIAL SERIAL NUMBER	HIGH OFFICIAL SERIAL NUMBER
3	C PHILADELPHIA	30,691,632	C--A	11.00	32.00	C27 010 066A	C73 940 411A
			C--*	22.50	55.00	C00 554 825*	C00 925 000*
4	D CLEVELAND	1,610,676	D--A	17.50	40.00	D59 305 799A	D62 128 723A
			D--*	27.50	60.00		
5	E RICHMOND	6,555,168	E--A	15.00	37.50	E46 685 672A	E66 003 920A
			E--*	25.00	57.50	E00 782 182*	
6	F ATLANTA	22,811,916	F--A	11.50	33.50	F17 523 826A	F32 737 123A
			F--*	22.00	55.00	F00 299 341*	
7	G CHICAGO	88,376,376	G--A	10.50	30.00	G22 168 431A	
			G--B	11.50	31.50		G16 084 199B
			G--*	20.00	50.00	G00 382 596*	G01 449 391*
8	H ST. LOUIS	7,843,452	H--A	15.00	37.50	H40 698 437A	H51 718 000A
			H--*	25.00	57.50		
12	L SAN FRANCISCO	72,118,452	L--A	10.50	30.00	L24 794 934A	
			L--B	12.00	32.00		L00 793 914B
			L--*	20.00	50.00	L00 813 730*	L01 219 181*

TOTAL KNOWN BLOCKS: Twenty-one
FOOTNOTE: No regular or star notes were printed for Minneapolis, Kansas City of Dallas.

CAT. NO. VF34A
$5.00 FEDERAL RESERVE NOTE (12 Subject)
SERIES 1934A MULE

PLATE SERIALS: Back check #938 or lower.

	DISTRICT	TOTAL NOTES PRINTED	BLOCKS	ESTIMATED VALUE VG/F	CU	LOW OBSERVED SERIAL NUMBER	HIGH OBSERVED SERIAL NUMBER
2	B NEW YORK		B--A	25.00	50.00	B00 374 463A	
5	E RICHMOND		E--A	25.00	50.00	E00 065 144A	
7	G CHICAGO		G--A	25.00	50.00	G00 280 504A	G80 536 253A
8	H ST. LOUIS		H--A	25.00	50.00	H00 066 126A	H39 621 679A

Collectors are kindly requested to furnish serial number, face and back check numbers of specimens of above.

CAT. NO. VF34A
$5.00 FEDERAL RESERVE NOTE (BROWN SEAL) (12 Subject)
SERIES 1934A HAWAII

SERIAL NUMBERS: Same as Series 1934 Hawaii.
STAR NOTES: (Low Obversed) L00 894 083*
PLATE SERIALS: Back check numbers 939 or higher.
SIGNATURES: Same as Series 1934A

ESTIMATED VALUES:

BLOCKS	VG/F	CU
L--A	17.50	200.00
L--*	50.00	100.00

TOTAL BLOCKS KNOWN: Two.

CAT. NO. VF34B
$5.00 FEDERAL RESERVE NOTE (GREEN SEAL) (12 Subject)
SERIES 1934B

SERIAL NUMBERS: All districts continued sequence from previous series.
PLATE SERIALS: Back check number 939 and higher.
SIGNATURES: W.A. Julian, Treasurer of the United States
  Fred M. Vinson, Secretary of the Treasury

	DISTRICT	TOTAL NOTES PRINTED	BLOCKS	ESTIMATED VALUE VG/F	CU	LOW OBSERVED SERIAL NUMBER	HIGH OBSERVED SERIAL NUMBER
1	A BOSTON	3,457,800	A--A	14.00	40.00	A51 927 351A	A56 200 677A
			A--*	23.50	60.00		
2	B NEW YORK	14,099,580	B--B	11.00	35.00	B76 440 781B	B95 741 965B
			B--*	20.00	50.00	B02 263 343*	
3	C PHILADELPHIA	8,306,820	C--A	12.50	38.50	C72 036 121A	C80 574 996A
			C--*	22.50	55.00	C01 014 938*	C01 026 003*
4	D CLEVELAND	11,348,184	D--A	11.50	35.00	D57 994 351A	D69 721 975A
			D--*	20.00	50.00	D00 756 699*	D00 890 775*
5	E RICHMOND	5,902,848	E--A	13.50	35.00	E67 499 771A	E72 106 406A
			E--*	22.50	60.00		
6	F ATLANTA	4,314,048	F--A	14.00	40.00	F69 413 365A	F72 120 482A
			F--*	23.50	60.00		
7	G CHICAGO	9,070,932	G--B	12.50	38.50	G13 186 858B	G25 042 572B
			G--*	22.50	55.00		
8	H ST. LOUIS	4,307,712	H--A	14.00	42.50	H53 492 931A	H71 547 955A
			H--*	23.50	65.00	H00 682 009*	H00 753 479*
9	I MINNEAPOLIS	2,482,500	I--A	15.00	45.00	I16 618 321A	I17 833 985A
			I--*	25.00	70.00	I00 232 537*	
10	J KANSAS CITY	73,800	J--A	17.50	50.00		
			J--*	30.00	80.00		
12	L SAN FRANCISCO	9,910,296	L--A	13.00	40.00	L95 336 592A	
			L--B	13.50	42.50		L03 750 526B
			L--*	22.50	55.00		

TOTAL KNOWN BLOCKS: Twenty-Three
FOOTNOTE: No regular or star notes were printed for Dallas.

CAT. NO. VF34B
$5.00 FEDERAL RESERVE NOTE (GREEN SEAL) (12 Subject)
SERIES 1934B MULE (Back Check #938 and lower)

These are actually Series 1934B faces on Series 1934 backs.
SERIAL NUMBERS: All districts continued sequence from previous series.

	DISTRICT	TOTAL NOTES PRINTED	BLOCKS	ESTIMATED VALUE VG/F	CU	LOW OFFICIAL SERIAL NUMBER	HIGH OFFICIAL SERIAL NUMBER
2	B NEW YORK		B--A	25.00	100.00	B58 021 649A	
			B--B	25.00	100.00	B80 851 374B	B94 911 759B
7	G CHICAGO		G--A	25.00	100.00	G21 370 363B	
8	H ST. LOUIS		H--A	35.00	100.00	H54 567 383A	
9	I MINNEAPOLIS		I--A	25.00	100.00	I18 105 713A	
12	L SAN FRANCISCO		L--B	25.00	100.00	L01 597 562B	L02 967 122B
			L--*	50.00	150.00	L01 359 866*	L01 359 867*

TOTAL KNOWN BLOCKS: Five.
Collectors are kindly requested to supply any numbers which improve on above information.

CAT. NO. VF34C
$5.00 FEDERAL RESERVE NOTE (GREEN SEAL) (12 Subject)
SERIES 1934C

SERIAL NUMBERS: All districts continued sequence from previous series.
PLATE SERIALS: Back check number 939 and higher.
SIGNATURES: W.A. Julian, Treasurer of the United States
John W. Snyder, Secretary of the Treasury

	DISTRICT	TOTAL NOTES PRINTED	BLOCKS	ESTIMATED VALUE VG/F	CU	LOW OFFICIAL SERIAL NUMBER	HIGH OFFICIAL SERIAL NUMBER
1	A BOSTON	14,463,600	A--A	11.00	25.00	A54 946 387A	A69 278 685A
			A--*	19.00	40.00	A00 904 062*	
2	B NEW YORK	74,383,248	B--B	14.00	27.50	B98 488 573B	
			B--C	10.00	20.00		B61 890 091C
			B--*	17.50	35.00	B02 795 441*	B03 287 613*
3	C PHILADELPHIA	22,879,212	C--A	11.00	25.00	C82 464 358A	
			C--B	14.00	27.50		C05 721 259B
			C--*	18.50	37.50	C01 083 169*	C01 168 967*
4	D CLEVELAND	19,898,256	D--A	11.00	25.00	D69 301 787A	D88 716 575A
			D--*	19.00	37.50	D00 933 393*	D01 060 906*
5	E RICHMOND	23,800,524	E--A	10.50	25.00	E59 821 773A	E93 983 925A
			E--*	18.50	37.50	E00 988 099*	E01 176 380*

	DISTRICT	TOTAL NOTES PRINTED	BLOCKS	ESTIMATED VALUE VG/F	CU	LOW OFFICIAL SERIAL NUMBER	HIGH OFFICIAL SERIAL NUMBER
6	F ATLANTA	23,572,968	F--A	10.50	25.00	F74 457 032A	F95 223 927A
			F--*	18.50	37.50		
7	G CHICAGO	60,598,812	G--B	10.00	22.50	G24 947 581B	G80 425 385B
			G--*	17.50	35.00	G01 709 522*	G02 475 178*
8	H ST. LOUIS	20,393,340	H--A	11.00	25.00	H63 860 635A	
			H--B	17.50	35.00		H07 551 780B
			H--*	19.00	37.50	H00 784 303*	H01 556 190*
9	I MINNEAPOLIS	5,089,200	I--A	15.00	30.00	I18 659 627A	I22 393 332A
			I--*	22.50	45.00		
10	J KANSAS CITY	8,313,504	J--A	12.50	27.50	J31 066 285A	J37 473 472A
			J--*	20.00	42.50	J00 453 442*	
11	K DALLAS	5,107,800	K--A	15.00	30.00	K31 819 270A	K37 276 203A
			K--*	22.50	45.00		
12	L SAN FRANCISCO	9,451,944	L--B	12.50	27.50	L05 994 335B	L11 932 820B
			L--*	20.00	42.50	L01 431 170*	

TOTAL KNOWN BLOCKS: Twenty-seven

CAT. NO. VF34C
$5.00 FEDERAL RESERVE NOTE (GREEN SEAL) (12 Subject)
SERIES 1934C MULE
These are actually Series 1934C faces on Series 1934 backs. (Back check #938 and lower)

	DISTRICT	TOTAL NOTES PRINTED	BLOCKS	ESTIMATED VALUE VG/F	CU	LOW OFFICIAL SERIAL NUMBER	HIGH OFFICIAL SERIAL NUMBER
1	A BOSTON		A--A	25.00	100.00	A54 870 831A	
2	B NEW YORK		B--C	25.00	100.00	B22 594 851C	B45 409 229C
7	G CHICAGO		G--B	25.00	100.00	G31 475 153B	G64 633 087B
8	H ST. LOUIS		H--A	25.00	100.00	H70 831 511A	
9	I MINNEAPOLIS		I--A	25.00	100.00	I20 058 699A	
10	J KANSAS CITY		J--A	25.00	100.00	J31 266 251A	
12	L SAN FRANCISCO		L--A	25.00	100.00	L07 782 787A	

TOTAL KNOWN BLOCKS: Seven

CAT. NO. VF34D
$5.00 FEDERAL RESERVE NOTE (GREEN SEAL) (12 Subject)
SERIES 1934D

SERIAL NUMBERS: All districts continued sequence from previous series.
SIGNATURES: Georgia Neese Clark, Treasurer of the United States
John W. Snyder, Secretary of the Treasury

	DISTRICT	TOTAL NOTES PRINTED	BLOCKS	ESTIMATED VALUE VG/F	CU	LOW OFFICIAL SERIAL NUMBER	HIGH OFFICIAL SERIAL NUMBER
1	A BOSTON	12,660,552	A--A	11.00	25.00	A68 486 900A	A80 384 786A
			A--*	18.00	37.50	A00 937 183*	A01 052 000*
2	B NEW YORK	50,976,576	B--C	10.00	22.50	B57 783 928C	
			B--D	11.00	24.00		B12 352 539D
			B--*	17.50	35.00	B03 455 394*	B03 888 000*
3	C PHILADELPHIA	12,106,740	C--B	11.00	25.00	C02 491 319B	C14 340 094B
			C--*	18.00	37.50		C01 500 000*
4	D CLEVELAND	8,969,052	D--A	12.00	26.50	D65 673 725A	D97 848 456A
			D--B	16.50	30.00		
			D--*	19.00	40.00	D01 209 511*	D01 284 000*
5	E RICHMOND	13,333,032	E--A	11.00	25.00	E94 054 703A	
			E--B	14.00	30.00		E06 944 636B
			E--*	18.00	37.50		E01 428 000*
6	F ATLANTA	9,599,352	F--A	12.00	25.00	F99 169 995A	
			F--B	14.00	30.00		F03 093 944B
			F--*	19.00	38.50		F01 380 000*
7	G CHICAGO	36,601,680	G--B	11.50	23.50	G80 874 865B	
			G--C	11.50	23.50		G16 249 094C
			G--*	17.50	35.00	G02 622 609*	G02 916 000*
8	H ST. LOUIS	8,093,412	H--A	12.00	26.50	H76 423 572A	H77 332 249A
			H--B	15.00	30.00		H18 892 698B
			H--*	19.00	40.00	H01 033 988*	H01 176 000*
9	I MINNEAPOLIS	3,594,900	I--A	15.00	30.00	I23 569 492A	I24 510 891A
			I--*	22.50	42.50		I00 372 000*

	DISTRICT	TOTAL NOTES PRINTED	BLOCKS	ESTIMATED VALUE VG/F	CU	LOW OFFICIAL SERIAL NUMBER	HIGH OFFICIAL SERIAL NUMBER
10	J KANSAS CITY	6,538,740	J--A	12.50	26.50	J38 882 384A	J44 891 392A
			J--*	20.00	40.00		J00 568 000*
11	K DALLAS	4,139,016	K--A	14.00	30.00	K33 950 138A	K40 091 582A
			K--*	22.50	42.50	K00 493 278*	K00 496 000*
12	L SAN FRANCISCO	11,704,200	L--B	11.50	25.00	L19 874 479B	L21 664 370B
			L--*	18.50	37.50		L01 644 000*

TOTAL BLOCKS KNOWN: Thirty.
Collectors are kindly requested to furnish serial numbers, which improve on above information.

CAT. NO. VF50
$5.00 FEDERAL RESERVE NOTE GREEN SEAL (12 Subject)
SERIES 1950 WIDE

SERIAL NUMBERS: All districts started both regular and star notes with serial 00 000 001.
PLATE SERIALS: Face check numbers begin at #1.
  Back check numbers 2007 or lower.
SIGNATURES: Georgia Neese Clark, Treasurer of the United States
  John W. Snyder, Secretary of the Treasury

	DISTRICT	TOTAL NOTES PRINTED	BLOCKS	ESTIMATED VAL VG/F	CU	LOW OBSERVED SERIAL NUMBER	HIGH OBSERVED SERIAL NUMBER	HIGH OFFICIAL SERIAL NUMBER
1	A BOSTON	30,672,000	A--A	10.00	17.50	A09 160 952A	A25 219 300A	A30 672 000A
		408,000	A--*	15.00	27.50			A00 408 000*
2	B NEW YORK	106,768,000	B--A	10.00	13.50	B00 000 018A		
			B--B	12.00	15.00		B05 116 461B	B06 768 000B
		1,464,000	B--*	14.00	22.50	B00 866 227*	B00 870 461*	B01 464 000*
3	C PHILADELPHIA	44,784,000	C--A	10.00	15.00	C04 809 907A	C37 184 087A	C44 784 000A
		600,000	C--*	15.00	25.00	C00 237 838*		C00 600 000*
4	D CLEVELAND	54,000,000	D--A	10.00	15.00	D00 000 005A	D51 068 728A	D54 000 000A
		744,000	D--*	15.00	25.00	D00 459 954*		D00 744 000*
5	E RICHMOND	47,088,000	E--A	10.00	15.00	E00 270 809A	E45 051 958A	E47 088 000A
		684,000	E--*	15.00	25.00	E00 455 400*		E00 684 000*
6	F ATLANTA	52,416,000	F--A	10.00	15.00	F36 132 013A	F50 166 008A	F52 416 000A
		696,000	F--*	15.00	25.00	F00 060 918*		F00 696 000*
7	G CHICAGO	85,104,000	G--A	10.00	13.50	G00 000 500A	G47 126 653A	G85 104 000A
		1,176,000	G--*	14.00	22.50	G00 613 437*		G01 176 000*
8	H ST. LOUIS	36,864,000	H--A	10.00	17.50	H15 222 221A	H35 554 543A	H36 864 000A
		552,000	H--*	15.00	27.50	H00 308 218*		H00 552 000*
9	I MINNEAPOLIS	11,796,000	I--A	12.00	20.00	I00 000 007A	I08 622 432A	I11 796 000A
		144,000	I--*	16.00	30.00	I00 085 003*	I00 117 658*	I00 144 000*
10	J KANSAS CITY	25,428,000	J--A	11.00	17.50	J07 011 107A	J15 713 542A	J25 428 000A
		360,000	J--*	15.00	27.50	J00 011 106*	J00 184 924*	J00 360 000*
11	K DALLAS	22,848,000	K--A	11.00	17.50	K03 116 659A	K07 347 528A	K22 848 000A
		372,000	K--*	15.00	27.50			K00 372 000*
12	L SAN FRANCISCO	55,008,000	L--A	10.00	15.00	L04 051 327A	L34 698 253A	L55 008 000A
		744,000	L--*	15.00	25.00	L00 640 807*		L00 744 000*

TOTAL BLOCKS KNOWN: Twenty-five
FOOTNOTE: Total notes printed and official high serial numbers are for all varieties of this series.
Collectors are kindly requested to furnish serial numbers, face and back check numbers of this variety so that total blocks can be determined.
TREASURY DEPARTMENT, Information Service, IMMEDIATE RELEASE, Thursday, November 9, 1950, S-2503
  The Treasury Department announced today that the first delivery of Federal Reserve notes designated Series of 1950 had been made by the Bureau of Engraving and Printing to the Federal Reserve System. The new series of notes have the signature of the Secretary of the Treasury and the Treasurer of the United States, the series designation, and the identification of the issuing Federal Reserve Bank overprinted in the same manner as the serial numbers and the seal, instead of engraved as heretofore.
  The serial numbers of the notes are slightly reduced from their former size, and are now identical in style with the serial numbers which appear on one dollar silver certificates. The identification of the issuing bank and the Treasury Seal have also been reduced in size.

CAT. NO. VF50
$5.00 FEDERAL RESERVE NOTE (GREEN SEAL) (12 Subject)
SERIES 1950 NARROW

PLATE SERIALS: Back check number range #2008-2066.

	DISTRICT	TOTAL NOTES PRINTED	BLOCKS	ESTIMATED VALUE VG/F	CU	LOW OBSERVED SERIAL NUMBER	HIGH OBSERVED SERIAL NUMBER
1	A BOSTON		A--A	12.50	20.00	A17 738 425A	A29 017 643A
2	B NEW YORK		B--A	12.50	16.00	B68 131 945A	
			B--B	12.50	16.00		B04 242 281B
			B--*	15.00	25.00	B00 824 357*	B01 375 357*

	DISTRICT	TOTAL NOTES PRINTED	BLOCKS	ESTIMATED VALUE VG/F	CU	LOW OFFICIAL SERIAL NUMBER	HIGH OFFICIAL SERIAL NUMBER
3	C PHILADELPHIA		C--A	12.50	17.50	C25 191 174A	C36 710 356A
			C--*	17.50	28.50		C00 429 930*
4	D CLEVELAND		D--A	12.50	17.50	D44 770 860A	D53 997 798A
			D--*	17.50	27.50		D00 717 430*
5	E RICHMOND		E--A	12.50	17.50	E27 648 294A	E46 969 425A
6	F ATLANTA		F--A	12.50	16.00	F36 965 675A	F36 965 676A
7	G CHICAGO		G--A	12.50	17.50	G52 807 564A	G70 350 154A
			G--*	12.50	17.50	G00 964 200*	
8	H ST. LOUIS		H--A	12.50	17.50	H21 533 064A	H36 639 659A
9	I MINNEAPOLIS		I--A	12.50	16.00	I06 328 008A	I09 857 745A
10	J KANSAS CITY		J--A	14.50	22.50	J16 949 700A	J24 466 242A
11	K DALLAS		K--A	12.50	17.50	K19 352 409A	K20 794 697A
12	L SAN FRANCISCO		L--A	13.50	20.00	L38 391 131A	L52 328 092A
			L--*	12.50	17.50	L00 667 972*	

TOTAL BLOCKS KNOWN: Sixteen.
Collectors are kindly requested to furnish serial number, face and back check numbers of this variety so that total blocks can be determined.

CAT. NO VF50
$5.00 FEDERAL RESERVE NOTE (GREEN SEAL) (12 Subject)
SERIES 1950 WIDE II

PLATE SERIALS: Face check numbers end at #144. Back check number range #2067-#2096. Both are highest of 12 subject sheets.

	DISTRICT	TOTAL NOTES PRINTED	BLOCKS	ESTIMATED VALUE VG/F	CU	LOW OBSERVED SERIAL NUMBER	HIGH OBSERVED SERIAL NUMBER
1	A BOSTON		A--A	14.00	20.00	A25 219 890A	A25 366 951A
2	B NEW YORK		B--A	17.50	25.00	B72 080 268A	
			B--B	16.00	23.50		B03 858 598A
4	D CLEVELAND		D--A	14.00	20.00	D39 858 436A	D50 973 519A
5	E RICHMOND		E--A	14.00	20.00	E38 046 676A	
7	G CHICAGO		G--A	13.00	18.50	G57 723 984A	G81 917 195A
8	H ST. LOUIS		H--A	14.00	20.00	H25 443 568A	H36 596 446A
10	J KANSAS CITY		J--A	15.00	22.50	J15 960 799A	J21 041 939A
11	K DALLAS		K--A	15.00	22.50		K20 575 016A
12	L SAN FRANCISCO		L--A	13.00	18.50	L52 328 096A	L52 328 098A

TOTAL BLOCKS KNOWN: Ten.
Collectors are kindly requested to furnish serial number, face and back check numbers of this variety so that total blocks can be determined.

CAT. NO. VF50A
$5.00 FEDERAL RESERVE NOTE (GREEN SEAL) (18 Subject)
SERIES 1950A

SERIAL NUMBERS: All districts continued sequence from previous series.
PLATE SERIALS: Face check numbers begin at #145. Back check numbers begin at #2097. Both lowest of 18 subject sheets.
SIGNATURES: Ivy Baker Priest, Treasurer of the United States
George M. Humphrey, Secretary of the Treasury

ESTIMATED VALUES

	DISTRICT	TOTAL NOTES PRINTED	BLOCKS	ESTIMATED VALUE VG/F	CU	LOW OFF.SERIAL	HIGH OFF.SERIAL
1	A BOSTON	53,568,000	A--A		$13.50	A30 672 001A	A84 240 000A
		2,808,000	A--*		21.50	A00 432 001*	A03 240 000*
2	B NEW YORK	186,472,000	B--B		13.50	B06 768 001B	
			B--C		13.50		B93 240 000C
		9,216,000	B--*		20.00	B01 584 001*	B10 800 000*
3	C PHILADELPHIA	69,616,000	C--A		13.50	C44 784 001A	
			C--B		14.50		C14 400 00B
		4,320,000	C--*		21.50	C00 720 001*	C05 040 000*
4	D CLEVELAND	45,360,000	D--A		13.50	D54 000 001A	D99 360 000A
		2,376,000	D--*		21.50	D00 864 001*	D03 240 000*
5	E RICHMOND	76,672,000	E--A		13.50	E47 088 001A	
			E--B		14.00		E23 760 000B
		5,400,000	E--*		20.00	E00 720 001*	E06 120 000*

	DISTRICT	TOTAL NOTES PRINTED	BLOCKS	ESTIMATED VALUE VG/F	CU	LOW OFFICIAL SERIAL NUMBER	HIGH OFFICIAL SERIAL NUMBER
6	F ATLANTA	86,464,000	F--A		13.50	F52 416 001A	
			F--B		13.50		F38 880 000B
		5,040,000	F--*		20.00	F00 720 001*	F05 760 000*
7	G CHICAGO	129,296,000	G--A		14.50	G85 104 001A	
			G--B		13.00		
			G--C		14.50		G14 400 000C
		6,264,000	G--*		20.00	G01 296 001*	G07 560 000*
8	H ST. LOUIS	54,936,000	H--A		14.00	H36 864 001A	H91 800 000A
		3,384,000	H--*		22.00	H00 576 001	H03 960 000*
9	I MINNEAPOLIS	11,232,000	I--A		15.00	I11 808 001A	I23 040 000A
		864,000	I--*		25.00	I00 144 001*	I01 008 000*
10	J KANSAS CITY	29,952,000	J--A		14.00	J25 488 001A	J55 440 000A
		1,088,000	J--*		22.50	J00 432 001*	J02 520 000*
11	K DALLAS	24,984,000	K--A		14.00	K22 896 001A	K47 880 000A
		1,368,000	K--*		22.50	K00 432 001*	K00 804 723*
12	L SAN FRANCISCO	90,712,000	L--A		13.50	L55 008 001A	
			L--B		13.50		L45 720 000B
			L--*		21.00	L00 864 001*	L07 200 000*

TOTAL BLOCKS KNOWN: Thirty-one.

CAT. NO. VF50B
$5.00 FEDERAL RESERVE NOTE (GREEN SEAL) (18 Subject)
SERIES 1950B

SERIAL NUMBERS: All districts continued sequence from previous series.
SIGNATURES: Ivy Baker Priest, Treasurer of the United States
   Robert B. Anderson, Secretary of the Treasury

ESTIMATED VALUES:

	DISTRICT	TOTAL NOTES PRINTED	BLOCKS	ESTIMATED VALUE VG/F	CU	LOW OFF.SERIAL	HIGH OFF. SERIAL
1	A BOSTON	30,880,000	A--A		$12.50	A84 240 001A	
			A--B		12.50		A15 120 000B
		2,520,000	A--*		18.50	A 03 240 001*	A05 760 000*
2	B NEW YORK	85,960,000	B--C		13.50	B93 240 001C	
			B--D		12.50		B79 200 000D
		4,680,000	B--*		16.50	B10 800 001*	B15 480 000*
3	C PHILADELPHIA	43,560,000	C--B		12.50	C14 400 001B	C57 960 000B
		2,880,000	C--*		17.50	C05 040 001*	C07 920 000*
4	D CLEVELAND	38,800,000	D--A		20.00	D99 360 001A	
			D--B		12.50		D38, 160 000B
		2,880,000	D--*		17.50	D03 240 001*	D06 120 000*
5	E RICHMOND	52,920,000	E--B		12.50	E23 760 001B	E76 680 000B
		2,080,000	E--*		17.50	E06 120 001*	E09 000 000*
6	F ATLANTA	80,560,000	F--B		12.50	F38 880 001B	
			F--C		14.00		F19 440 000C
		3,960,000	F--*		17.50	F05 760 001*	F09 720 000*
7	G CHICAGO	104,320,000	G--C		12.50	G14 400 001C	
			G--D		12.50		G18 720 000D
		6,120,000	G--*		16.50	G07 560 001*	G13 680 000*
8	H ST. LOUIS	25,840,000	H--A		14.00	H91 800 001A	
			H--B		13.00		H17 640 000B
		1,440,000	H--*		18.50	H03 960 001*	H05 400 000*
9	I MINNEAPOLIS	20,880,000	I--A		14.00	I23 040 001A	I43 920 000A
		792,000	I--*		19.00	I01 008 001*	I01 800 000*
10	J KANSAS CITY	32,400,000	J--A		13.00	J55 440 001A	J87 840 000A
		2,520,000	J--*		18.00	J02 520 001*	J05 040 000*
11	K DALLAS	52,120,000	K--A		12.50	K47 880 001A	K99 999 999A
		3,240,000	K--*		17.50	K01 800 001*	K05 040 000*
12	L SAN FRANCISCO	56,080,000	L--B		12.50	L45 720 001B	
			L--C		20.00		L01 800 000C
		3,600,000	L--*		17.50	L07 200 001*	L10 800 000*

TOTAL BLOCKS KNOWN: Thirty-one.

CAT. NO. VF50C
$5.00 FEDERAL RESERVE NOE (GREEN SEAL) (18 Subject)
SERIES 1950C

SERIAL NUMBERS: All districts continued sequence from previous series.
SIGNATURES: Elizabeth Rudel Smith, Treasurer of the United States
   C. Douglas Dillon, Secretary of the Treasury

ESTIMATED VALUES:

	DISTRICT	TOTAL NOTES PRINTED	BLOCKS	ESTIMATED VALUE VG/F	CU	LOW OFF. SERIAL	HIGH OFF. SERIAL
1	A BOSTON	20,880,000	A--B		$12.00	A15 120 001B	A36 000 000B
		720,000	A--*		17.00	A05 760 001*	A06 480 000*
2	B NEW YORK	47,440,000	B--D		11.50	B79 200 001D	
			B--E		11.50		B26 640 000E
		2,880,000	B--*		16.00	B15 480 001*	B18 360 000*
3	C PHILADELPHIA	29,520,000	C--B		11.50	C57 960 001B	C87 480 000B
		1,800,000	C--*		16.50	C07 920 0001*	C09 720 000*
4	D CLEVELAND	33,840,000	D--B		11.50	D38 160 001B	D72 000 000B
		1,800,000	D--*		16.50	D06 120 001*	D07 920 000*
5	E RICHMOND	33,480,000	E--B		11.50	E76 680 001B	
			E--C		12.50		E10 080 000C
		2,160,000	E--*		16.50	E09 000 001*	E11 160 000*
6	F ATLANTA	54,360,000	F--C		11.50	F19 440 001C	F76 500 000C
		3,240,000	F--*		16.50	F09 720 001*	F12 960 000*
7	G CHICAGO	56,880,000	G--D		11.50	G18 720 001D	G75 600 000D
		3,240,000	G--*		16.50	G13 680 001*	G16 920 000*
8	H ST. LOUIS	22,680,000	H--B		12.00	H17 640 001B	H40 320 000B
		720,000	H--*		17.50	H05 400 001*	H06 120 000*
9	I MINNEAPOLIS	12,960,000	I--A		13.00	I43 920 001A	I56 880 000A
		720,000	I--*		18.50	I01 800 001*	I02 520 000*
10	J KANSAS CITY	24,760,000	J--A		12.50	J87 840 001A	
			J--B		12.50		J12 600 000B
		1,800,000	J--*		17.50	J05 040 001*	J06 840 000*
11	K DALLAS	3,960,000	K--B		15.00	K00 000 001B	K03 960 000B
		360,000	K--*		20.00	K05 040 001*	K05 400 000*
12	L SAN FRANCISCO	25,920,000	L--C		12.50	K01 800 001C	L27 720 000C
		1,440,000	L--*		17.50	L10 800 001*	L12 240 000*

TOTAL BLOCKS KNOWN: Twenty seven.

CAT. NO. VF50D
$5.00 FEDERAL RESERVE NOTE (GREEN SEAL) (18 Subject)
SERIES 1950D

SERIAL NUMBERS: All districts sequence from previous series.
SIGNATURES: Kathryn O'Hay Granahan, Treasurer of the United States
   C. Douglas Dillon, Secretary of the Treasury

	DISTRICT	TOTAL NOTES PRINTED	BLOCKS	ESTIMATED VALUE VG/F	CU	LOW OFFICIAL SERIAL NUMBER	HIGH OFFICIAL SERIAL NUMBER
1	A BOSTON	25,200,000	A--B		11.00	A36 000 001B	A61 200 000B
		1,800,000	A--*		15.00	A06 480 001*	A07 560 000*
2	B NEW YORK	102,160,000	B--E		11.00	B26 640 001E	
			B--F		11.50		B28 800 000F
		5,040,000	B--*		14.00	B18 360 001*	B23 400 000*
3	C PHILADELPHIA	21,520,000	C--B		11.50	C87 480 001B	
			C--C		12.00		C09 000 000C
		1,080,000	C--*		15.00	C09 720 001*	C10 800 000*
4	D CLEVELAND	23,400,000	D--B		11.00	D72 000 001B	D95 400 000B
		1,080,000	D--*		15.00	D07 920 001*	D09 000 000*
5	E RICHMOND	42,490,000	E--C		11.00	E10 080 001C	E52 560 000C
		1,800,000	E--*		15.00	E11 160 001*	E12 960 000*
6	F ATLANTA	35,200,000	F--C		11.50	F73 800 001C	
			F--D		12.00		F09 000 000D
		1,800,000	F--*		15.00	F12 960 001*	F14 760 000*
7	G CHICAGO	67,240,000	G--D		11.50	G75 600 001D	
			G--E		11.00		G42 840 000E
		3,600,000	G--*		14.00	G16 920 001*	G20 520 000*

	DISTRICT	TOTAL NOTES PRINTED	BLOCKS	ESTIMATED VALUE VG/F	CU	LOW OFFICIAL SERIAL NUMBER	HIGH OFFICIAL SERIAL NUMBER
8	H ST. LOUIS	20,160,000	H--B		11.00	H40 320 001B	H60 480 000B
		720,000	H--*		15.00	H06 120 001*	H20 520 000*
9	I MINNEAPOLIS	7,920,000	I--A		12.00	I56 880 001A	I64 800 000A
		360,000	I--*		17.50	I02 520 001*	I02 880 000*
10	J KANSAS CITY	11,160,000	J--B		12.00	J12 600 001B	J23 760 000B
		720,000	J--*		16.50	J06 840 001*	J07 560 000*
11	K DALLAS	7,200,000	K--B		12.00	K03 960 001B	K11 160 000B
		360,000	K--*		17.50	K05 400 001*	K05 760 000*
12	L SAN FRANCISCO	53,280,000	L--C		11.00	L27 720 001C	L81 000 000C
		3,600,000	L--*		15.00	L12 240 001*	L15 840 000*

TOTAL BLOCKS KNOWN: Twenty-eight.

CAT. NO. VF50E
$5.00 FEDERAL RESERVE NOTE (GREEN SEAL) (18 Subject)
SERIES 1950E

SERIAL NUMBERS: District printed continued sequence from previous series.
PLATE SERIALS: Face check numbers on 18 subject sheets end at #436.
  Back check numbers of 18 subject sheets end at #2587.
SIGNATURES: Kathryn O'Hay Granahan, Treasurer of the United States.
  Henry H. Fowler, Secretary of the Treasury.

	DISTRICT	TOTAL NOTES PRINTED	BLOCKS	ESTIMATED VALUE VG/F	CU	LOW OFFICIAL SERIAL NUMBER	HIGH OFFICIAL SERIAL NUMBER
2	B NEW YORK	82,000,000	B--F		12.50	B28 800 001F	
			B--G		14.00		B10 800 000G
		6,678,000	B--*		15.00	B23 400 001*	B30 078 000*
7	G CHICAGO	14,760,000	G--E		15.00	G42 840 001E	G57 600 000E
		1,080,000	G--*		17.50	G20 520 001*	G21 600 000*
12	L SAN FRANCISCO	24,400,000	L--C		13.50	L81 000 001C	
			L--D		14.50		L05 400 000D
		1,800,000	L--*		16.50	L15 840 001*	L17 640 000*

TOTAL BLOCKS KNOWN: Eight.

CAT. NO. VF63
$5.00 FEDERAL RESERVE NOTE (GREEN SEAL) (32 Subject)
SERIES 1963

SERIAL NUMBERS: All districts started both regular and star notes with serial 00 000 001.
PLATE SERIALS: Both face and back check numbers begin at #1 with 32 subject sheets.
  Motto IN GOD WE TRUST added to back.
SIGNATURES: Kathryn O'Hay Granahan, Treasurer of the United States
  C. Douglas Dillin, Secretary of the Treasury

	DISTRICT	TOTAL NOTES PRINTED	BLOCKS	ESTIMATED VALUE VG/F	CU	LOW OFFICIAL SERIAL NUMBER	HIGH OFFICIAL SERIAL NUMBER
1	A BOSTON	4,480,000	A--A		14.00		A04 480 000A
		64,000,000	A--*		17.50		A00 640 000*
2	B NEW YORK	12,160,000	B--A		12.50		B12 160 000A
		1,280,000	B--*		16.00		B01 280 000*
3	C PHILADELPHIA	8,320,000	C--A		13.50		C08 320 000A
		1,920,000	C--*		17.00		C01 920 000*
4	D CLEVELAND	10,240,000	D--A		13.00		D10 240 000A
		1,920,000	D--*		16.50		D01 920 000*
6	F ATLANTA	17,920,000	F--A		12.00		F17 920 000A
		2,560,000	F--*		16.00		F02 560 000*
7	G CHICAGO	22,400,000	G--A		12.00		G22 400 000A
		3,200,000	G--*		16.00		G03 200 000*
8	H ST. LOUIS	14,080,000	H--A		12.00		H14 080 000A
		1,920,000	H--*		16.00		H01 920 000*
10	J KANSAS CITY	1,920,000	J--A		15.00		J01 920 000A
		640,000	J--*		19.00		J00 640 000*
11	K DALLAS	5,760,000	K--A		14.00		K05 760 000A
		1,920,000	K--*		17.50		K01 920 000*
12	L SAN FRANCISCO	18,560,000	L--A		12.00		L18 560 000A
		1,920,000	L--*		16.00		L01 920 000*

TOTAL BLOCKS KNOWN: Twenty.
No Richmond or Minneapolis regular or star printed for this series.

CAT. NO. VF63A
$5.00 FEDERAL RESERVE NOTE (GREEN SEAL) (32 Subject)
SERIES 1963A

SERIAL NUMBERS: All districts continued sequence from previous series.
SIGNATURES: Kathryn O'Hay Granahan, Treasuere of the United States
  Henry F. Fowler, Secretary of the Treasury

	DISTRICT	TOTAL NOTES PRINTED	BLOCKS	ESTIMATED VALUE VG/F	CU	LOW OFFICIAL SERIAL NUMBER	HIGH OFFICIAL SERIAL NUMBER
1	A BOSTON	77,440,000	A--A		8.50	A04 480 001A	A81 920 000A
		5,760,000	A--*		10.00	A00 640 001*	A06 400 000*
2	B NEW YORK	98,080,000	G--A		8.50	B12 160 001A	
			B--B		8.50		B10 240 000B
		7,680,000	B--*		10.00	B01 280 001*	B08 320 000*
						B08 480 001*	B08 960 000*
3	C PHILADELPHIA	106,400,000	C--A		8.50	C08 320 001A	
			C--B		8.50		C14 720 000B
		10,240,000	C--*		10.00	C01 920 001*	C10 240 000*
						C10 400 001*	C12 160 000*
4	D CLEVELAND	83,840,000	D--A		8.50	D10 240 001A	D84 080 000A
		7,040,000	D--*		10.00	D01 920 001*	D08 960 000*
5	E RICHMOND	118,560,000	E--A		8.50	$00 000 001A	
			E--B		8.50		E18 560 000B
		10,880,000	E--*		10.00	E00 000 001*	E10 880 000*
6	F ATLANTA	117,920,000	F--A		8.50	F17 920 001A	
			F--B		8.50		F35 840 000B
		9,600,000	F--*		10.00	F02 560 001*	F12 160 000*
7	G CHICAGO	213,440,000	G--A		8.50	G22 400 001A	
			G--B		8.50		
			C--C		8.50		G35 840 000C
		16,640,000	G--*		10.00	G03 200 001*	G19 840 000*
8	H ST. LOUIS	56,960,000	H--A		8.50	H14 080 001A	H71 040 000A
		5,120,000	H--*		10.00	H01 920 001*	H07 040 000*
9	I MINNEAPOLIS	32,640,000	I--A		8.50	I00 000 001A	I32 640 000A
		3,200,000	I--*		10.00	I00 000 001*	I03 200 000*
10	J KANSAS CITY	55,040,000	J--A		8.50	J01 920 001A	J56 960 000A
		5,760,000	J--*		10.00	J00 640 001*	J06 400 000*
12	K DALLAS	64,000,000	K--A		8.50	K05 760 001A	K69 760 000A
		3,840,000	K--*		10.00	K01 920 001*	K05 760 000*
12	L SAN FRANCISCO	128900000	L--A		8.50	L18 560 001A	
			L--B		8.50		L47 360 000B
		12,153,000	L--*		10.00	L01 920 001*	L14 073 000*

TOTAL BLOCKS KNOWN: Thirty-one

CAT. NO. VF69
$5.00 FEDERAL RESERVE NOTE (GREEN SEAL) (32 Subject)
SERIES 1969

SERIAL NUMBERS: All districts started both regular and star note with serial 00 000 001.
PLATE SERIALS: Face check numbers begin at #1.
SIGNATURES: Dorothy Andrews Elston, Treasurer of the United States
  David M. Kennedy, Secretary of the Treasury
ESTIMATED VALUES: All regular notes $8.00 each CU, all star notes $10.00 CU

	DISTRICT	TOTAL NOTES PRINTED	BLOCKS	ESTIMATED VALUE VG/F	CU	LOW OFFICIAL SERIAL NUMBER	HIGH OFFICIAL SERIAL NUMBER
1	A BOSTON	51,200,000	A--A				A51 200 000A
		1,920,000	A--*				A01 920 000*
2	B NEW YORK	198,560,000	B--A				
			B--B				B98 560 000B
		8,960,000	B--*			B00 000 01*	B05 760 000*
			B--*			B05 920 001*	B08 960 000*
3	C PHILADELPHIA	69,120,000	C--A				C69 120 000A
		2,560,000	C--*				C02 560 000*
4	D CLEVELAND	56,320,000	D--A				D56 320 000A
		2,560,000	D--*				D02 560 000*

	DISTRICT	TOTAL NOTES PRINTED	BLOCKS	ESTIMATED VALUE VG/F	CU	LOW OFFICIAL SERIAL NUMBER	HIGH OFFICIAL SERIAL NUMBER
5	E RICHMOND	84,480,000	E--A				E84 480 000A
		3,200,000	E--*				E03 200 000*
6	F ATLANTA	84,480,000	F--A				F84 480 000A
		3,840,000	F--*				F03 840 000*
7	G CHICAGO	125,600,000	G--A				
			G--B				G25 600 000B
		5,120,000	G--*				G05 120 000*
8	H ST. LOUIS	27,520,000	H--A				H27 520 000A
		1,280,000	H--*				H01 280 000*
9	I MINNEAPOLIS	16,640,000	I--A				I16 640 000
		640,000	I--*				I00 640 000*
10	J KANSAS CITY	48,640,000	J--A				J48 640 000A
		3,192,000	J--*				J03 192 000*
11	K DALLAS	39,680,000	K--A				K39 680 000A
		1,920,000	K--*				K01 920 000*
12	L SAN FRANCISCO	103840000	L--A				
			L--B				L03 840 000B
		4,480,000	L--*			L00 000 01*	L03 840 000*
			L--*			L04 000 001*	L04 480 000*

TOTAL KNOWN BLOCKS: Twenty-eight.

CAT. NO. VF69A
$5.00 FEDERAL RESERVE NOTE (GREEN SEAL) (32 Subject)
SERIES 1969A

SIGNATURES: Dorothy Andrews Kabis, Treasurer of the United States
John B. Connaly, Secretary of the Treasury
ESTIMATED VALUES: All regular notes $8.00 each CU, stars $10.00 each CU

	DISTRICT	TOTAL NOTES PRINTED	BLOCKS	ESTIMATED VALUE VG/F	CU	LOW OFFICIAL SERIAL NUMBER	HIGH OFFICIAL SERIAL NUMBER
1	A BOSTON	23,040,000	A--A			A51 200 001A	A74 240 000A
		1,280,000	A--*			A01 920 001*	A03 200 000*
2	B NEW YORK	72,240,000	B--B			B98 560 001B	
			B--C				B60 800 000C
		1,760,000	B--*			B09 120 001*	B10 880 000*
3	C PHILADELPHIA	41,160 000	C--A			C60 120 001A	
			C--B				C01 280 000B
		1,920,000	C--*			C02 560 001*	C03 840 000*
						C04 000 001*	C04 480 000*
4	D CLEVELAND	21,120,000	D--A			D56 320 001A	D77 440 000A
		640,000	D--*			D02 560 001*	D03 200 000*
5	E RICHMOND	37,920,000	E--A			E84 480 001A	
			E--B				E22 400 000B
		1,120,000	E--*			E03 360 001*	E04 480 000*
6	F ATLANTA	25, 120,000	F--A			F84 480 001A	
			F--B				F09 600 000B
		480,000	F--*			F04 000 001A	F04 480 000*
7	G CHICAGO	60,800,000	G--B			G25 600 001B	G86 400 000B
		1,920,000	G--*			G05 120 001*	G07 040 000*
8	H ST. LOUIS	15,360,000	H--A			H27 520 001A	H42 880 000A
		640,000	H--*			H01 280 001*	H01 920 000*
9	I MINNEAPOLIS	8,960,000	I--A			I16 640 001A	I25 600 000A
		640,000	I--*			I00 640 001*	I01 280 000*
10	J KANSAS CITY	17,920,000	J--A			J48 640 001A	J66 560 000A
		640,000	J--*			J03 200 001*	J03 840 000*
11	K DALLAS	21,120,000	K--A			K39 680 001A	K60 800 000A
		640,000	K--*			K01 920 001*	K02 560 000*
12	L SAN FRANCISCO	44,800,000	L--B			L03 840 001B	L48 640 000B
		1,920,000	L--*			L04 480 001*	L06 400 000*

TOTAL BLOCKS: Twenty-eight.

CAT. NO. VF69B
$5.00 FEDERAL RESERVE NOTE (GREEN SEAL) (32 Subject)
SERIES 1969B

SIGNATURES: Romana Acosta Banuelos, Treasurer of the United States
John B. Connally, Secretary of the Treasury
ESTIMATED VALUES: All regular notes $8.00 each CU, stars $10.00 each CU

	DISTRICT	TOTAL NOTES PRINTED	BLOCKS	ESTIMATED VALUE VG/F	CU	LOW OFFICIAL SERIAL NUMBER	HIGH OFFICIAL SERIAL NUMBER
1	A BOSTON	5,760,000	A--A			A74 240 001A	A80 000 000A
						no stars printed	
2	B NEW YORK	34,560,000	B--C			B60 800 001C	B95 360 000C
		634,000	B--*			B10 880 001*	B11 514 000*
3	C PHILDELPHIA	5,120,000	C--B			C01 280 001B	C06 400 000B
						no starsprinted	
4	D CLEVELAND	12,160,000	D--A			D77 440 001A	D89 600 000A
						no stars printed	
5	E RICHMOND	15,360,000	E--B			E22 400 001B	E37 760 000B
		640,000	E--*			E04 480 001*	E05 120 000*
6	F ATLANTA	18,560,000	F--B			F09 600 001B	F28 160 000B
		640,000	F--*			F04 480 001*	F05 120 000*
7	G CHICAGO		G--B			G86 400 001B	
		27,040,000	G--C				G13 440 000C
		480,000	G--*			G07 200 001*	G07 680 000*
8	H ST. LOUIS	5,120,000	H--A			H42 880 001A	H48 000 000A
						no stars printed	
9	I MINNEAPOLIS	8,320,000	I--A			I25 600 001A	I33 920 000A
						no stars printed	
10	J KANSAS CITY	8,320,000	J--A			J66 560 001A	J74 880 000A
		640,000	J--*			J03 840 001*	J04 480 000*
11	K DALLAS	12,160,000	K--A			K60 800 001A	K72 960 000A
						no stars printed	
12	L SAN FRANCISCO	23,160,000	L--B			L48 640 001B	L72 320 000B
		640,000	L--*			L06 400 001*	L07 040 000*

TOTAL BLOCKS: Nineteen

CAT. NO. VF69C
$5.00 FEDERAL RESERVE NOTE (GREEN SEAL) (32 Subject)
SERIES 1969C

SIGNATURES: Romano Acosta Banuelos, Treasurer of the United States
George P. Shultz, Secretary of the Treasury
ESTIMATED VALUES: All regular notes $8.00, stars $10.00 CU

	DISTRICT	TOTAL NOTES PRINTED	BLOCKS	ESTIMATED VALUE VG/F	CU	LOW OFFICIAL SERIAL NUMBER	HIGH OFFICIAL SERIAL NUMBER
1	A BOSTON	50,720,000	A--A			A80 000 001A	
			A--B				A30 720 000B
		1,920,000	A--*			A03 200 001*	A05 120 000*
2	B NEW YORK	120,000,000	B--C			B95 360 001C	
			B--D				
			B--E				B15 360 000E
		2,400,000	B--*			B11 680 001*	B14 080 000*
3	C PHILADELPHIA	53,760,000	C--B			C06 400 001B	C60 160 000B
		1,280,000	C--*			C04 480 001*	C05 760 000*
4	D CLEVELAND	43,680,000	D--A			D89 600 001A	
			D--B				D33 280 000B
		1,120,000	D--*			D03 360 001*	D03 840 000*
5	E RICHMOND	73,760,000	E--B			E37 760 001B	
			E--C				E11 530 000C
		640,000	E--*			E05 120 001*	E05 760 000*
6	F ATLANTA	81,440,000	F--B			F28 160 001B	
			F--C				F09 600 000C
		3,200,000	F--*			F05 120 001*	F08 320 000*
7	G CHICAGO	54,400,000	G--C			G13 440 001C	G67 840 000C
			G--*			none printed	
8	H ST. LOUIS	37,760,000	H--A			H48 000 001A	H86 400 000A
		1,920,000	H--*			H01 920 001*	H03 200 000*
9	I MINNEAPOLIS	11,520,000	I--A			I33 920 001A	I45 440 000A
			I--*			none printed	

	DISTRICT	TOTAL NOTES PRINTED	BLOCKS	ESTIMATED VALUE VG/F	CU	LOW OFFICIAL SERIAL NUMBER	HIGH OFFICIAL SERIAL NUMBER
10	J KANSAS CITY	41,120,000	J--A			J74 880 001A	
			J--B				J16 000 000B
		1,920,000	J--*			J04 480 001*	J06 400 000*
11	K DALLAS	41,120,000	D--A			K72 960 001A	
			K--B				K14 080 000B
		1,920,000	K--*			K02 560 001*	K04 480 000*
12	L SAN FRANCISCO	80,800,000	L--B			L72 320 001B	
			L--C				L57 120 000C
		3,680,000	L--C			L07 200 001*	L10 240 000*

TOTAL BLOCKS: Thirty-one.

CAT. NO. VF74
$5.00 FEDERAL RESERVE NOTE (GREEN SEAL) 32 Subject
SERIES 1974

SIGNATURES: Francine I. Neff, Treasurer of the United States.
 William E. Simon, Secretary of the Treasury.

SERIAL NUMBERS: All districts continue from previous series.

PLATE SERIALS: Face and back check continue from previous series.

	DISTRICT	TOTAL NOTES PRINTED	BLOCKS	ESTIMATED VALUE VG/F	CU	LOW OFFICIAL SERIAL NUMBER	HIGH OFFICIAL SERIAL NUMBER	
1	A BOSTON		A--B		8.00	A30 720 001B	A55 680 000B	cv
					8.00	A55 680 001B	A88 960 000B	cp
			A--*		10.00	A05 120 001*	A06 400 000*	cv
					25.00	A06 416 001*	A06 420 000*	cv
					25.00	A06 436 001*	A06 440 000*	cv
					25.00	A06 456 001*	A06 460 000*	cv
					25.00	A06 476 001*	A06 480 000*	cv
					25.00	A06 496 001*	A06 500 000*	cv
					25.00	A06 516 001*	A06 520 000*	cv
					25.00	A06 536 001*	A06 540 000*	cv
					25.00	A06 556 001*	A06 560 000*	cv
					25.00	A06 576 001*	A06 580 000*	cv
					25.00	A06 596 001*	A06 600 000*	cv
					25.00	A06 616 001*	A06 620 000*	cv
					25.00	A06 636 001*	A06 640 000*	cv
					25.00	A06 656 001*	A06 660 000*	cv
					25.00	A06 676 001*	A06 680 000*	cv
					25.00	A06 696 001*	A06 700 000*	cv
					25.00	A06 716 001*	A06 720 000*	cv
					25.00	A06 736 001*	A06 740 000*	cv
					25.00	A06 756 001*	A06 760 000*	cv
					25.00	A06 776 001*	A06 780 000*	cv
					25.00	A06 796 001*	A06 800 000*	cv
					25.00	A06 816 001*	A06 820 000*	cv
					25.00	A06 836 001*	A06 840 000*	cv
					25.00	A06 856 001*	A06 860 000*	cv
					25.00	A06 876 001*	A06 880 000*	cv
					25.00	A06 896 001*	A06 900 000*	cv
					25.00	A06 916 001*	A06 920 000*	cv
					25.00	A06 936 001*	A06 940 000*	cv
					25.00	A06 956 001*	A06 960 000*	cv
					25.00	A06 976 001*	A06 980 000*	cv
					25.00	A06 996 001*	A07 000 000*	cv
					25.00	A07 016 001*	A07 020 000*	cv
					25.00	A07 036 001*	A07 040 000*	cv
2	B NEW YORK		B--E		8.00	B15 360 001E	B99 999 999E	cv
					12.50	B00 000 001F	B01 920 000F	cv
					8.00	B01 920 001F	B68 480 000F	cp
			B--*		10.00	B14 080 001*	B16 640 000*	cv
					25.00	B16 652 001*	B16 660 000*	cv
					25.00	B16 672 001*	B16 680 000*	cv

DISTRICT	TOTAL NOTES PRINTED	BLOCKS	ESTIMATED VALUE VG/F	VALUE CU	LOW OFFICIAL SERIAL NUMBER	HIGH OFFICIAL SERIAL NUMBER	
				25.00	B16 692 001*	B16 700 000*	cv
				25.00	B16 712 001*	B16 720 000*	cv
				25.00	B16 732 001*	B16 740 000*	cv
				25.00	B16 752 001*	B16 760 000*	cv
				25.00	B16 772 001*	B16 780 000*	cv
				25.00	B16 792 001*	B16 800 000*	cv
				25.00	B16 812 001*	B16 820 000*	cv
				25.00	B16 832 001*	B16 840 000*	cv
				25.00	B16 852 001*	B16 860 000*	cv
				25.00	B16 872 001*	B16 880 000*	cv
				25.00	B16 892 001*	B16 900 000*	cv
				25.00	B16 912 001*	B16 920 000*	cv
				25.00	B16 932 001*	B16 940 000*	cv
				25.00	B16 952 001*	B16 960 000*	cv
				25.00	B16 972 001*	B16 980 000*	cv
				25.00	B16 992 001*	B17 000 000*	cv
				25.00	B17 012 001*	B17 020 000*	cv
				25.00	B17 032 001*	B17 040 000*	cv
				25.00	B17 052 001*	B17 060 000*	cv
				25.00	B17 072 001*	B17 080 000*	cv
				25.00	B17 092 001*	B17 100 000*	cv
				25.00	B17 112 001*	B17 120 000*	cv
				25.00	B17 132 001*	B17 140 000*	cv
				25.00	B17 152 001*	B17 160 000*	cv
				25.00	B17 172 001*	B17 180 000*	cv
				25.00	B17 192 001*	B17 200 000*	cv
				25.00	B17 212 001*	B17 220 000*	cv
				25.00	B17 232 001*	B17 240 000*	cv
				25.00	B17 252 001*	B17 260 000*	cv
				25.00	B17 272 001*	B17 280 000*	cv
3	C PHILADELPHIA	C--B		8.00	C60 160 001B	C99 999 999B	cv
		C--C		8.00	C00 000 001C	C10 880 000C	cv
				12.50	C10 880 001C	C14 080 000C	cp
		C--*		10.00	C05 760 001*	C08 320 000*	cv
4	D CLEVELAND	D--B		8.00	D33 280 001B	D71 680 000B	cv
				8.00	D71 680 001B	D99 840 000B	cp
		D--C		8.00	D00 000 001C	D11 520 000C	cp
		D--*			none printed for this series.		
5	E RICHMOND	E--C		8.00	E11 520 001C	E84 480 000C	cv
				8.00	E84 480 001C	E99 840 000C	cp
				25.00	E99 840 001C	E99 999 999C	cv
		E--D		8.00	E00 000 001D	E46 720 000D	cp
		E--*		10.00	E05 760 001*	E07 680 000*	cv
6	F ATLANTA	F--C		8.00	F09 600 001C	F73 600 000C	cv
				8.00	F73 600 001C	F99 840 000C	cp
				25.00	F99 840 001C	F99 999 999C	cv
		F--D		8.00	F00 000 001D	F37 120 000D	cp
		F--*		10.00	F08 320 001*	F11 520 000*	cv
7	G CHICAGO	G--C		8.00	G67 840 001C	G86 400 000C	cv
				8.00	G86 400 001C	G92 160 000C	cp
				10.00	G92 160 001C	G96 000 000C	cv
				10.00	G96 000 001C	G99 840 000C	cp
				25.00	G99 840 001C	G99 999 999C	cv
		G--D		8.00	G00 000 001D	G63 360 000D	cp
		G--*		10.00	G07 680 001*	G08 960 000*	cv
				25.00	G08 972 001*	G08 980 000*	cv
				25.00	G08 992 001*	G09 000 000*	cv
				25.00	G09 012 001*	G09 020 000*	cv
				25.00	G09 032 001*	G09 040 000*	cv
				25.00	G09 052 001*	G09 060 000*	cv
				25.00	G09 072 001*	G09 080 000*	cv
				25.00	G09 092 001*	G09 100 000*	cv
				25.00	G09 112 001*	G09 120 000*	cv
				25.00	G09 132 001*	G09 140 000*	cv
				25.00	G09 152 001*	G09 160 000*	cv
				25.00	G09 172 001*	G09 180 000*	cv
				25.00	G09 192 001*	G09 200 000*	cv
				25.00	G09 212 001*	G09 220 000*	cv
				25.00	G09 232 001*	G09 240 000*	cv

DISTRICT	TOTAL NOTES PRINTED	BLOCKS	ESTIMATED VALUE VG/F	CU	LOW OFFICIAL SERIAL NUMBER	HIGH OFFICIAL SERIAL NUMBER	
				25.00	G09 252 001*	G09 260 000*	CV
				25.00	G09 272 001*	G09 280 000*	CV
				25.00	G09 292 001*	G09 300 000*	CV
				25.00	G09 312 001*	G09 320 000*	CV
				25.00	G09 332 001*	G09 340 000*	CV
				25.00	G09 352 001*	G09 360 000*	CV
				25.00	G09 372 001*	G09 380 000*	CV
				25.00	G09 392 001*	G09 400 000*	CV
				25.00	G09 412 001*	G09 420 000*	CV
				25.00	G09 432 001*	G09 440 000*	CV
				25.00	G09 452 001*	G09 460 000*	CV
				25.00	G09 472 001*	G09 480 000*	CV
				25.00	G09 492 001*	G09 500 000*	CV
				25.00	G09 512 001*	G09 520 000*	CV
				25.00	G09 532 001*	G09 540 000*	CV
				25.00	G09 552 001*	G09 560 000*	CV
				25.00	G09 572 001*	G09 580 000*	CV
				25.00	G09 592 001*	G09 600 000*	CV
				25.00	G09 612 001*	G09 620 000*	CV
				25.00	G09 632 001*	G09 640 000*	CV
				25.00	G09 652 001*	G09 660 000*	CV
				25.00	G09 672 001*	G09 680 000*	CV
				25.00	G09 692 001*	G09 700 000*	CV
				25.00	G09 712 001*	G09 720 000*	CV
				25.00	G09 732 001*	G09 740 000*	CV
				25.00	G09 752 001*	G09 760 000*	CV
				25.00	G09 772 001*	G09 780 000*	CV
				25.00	G09 792 001*	G09 800 000*	CV
				25.00	G09 812 001*	G09 820 000*	CV
				25.00	G09 832 001*	G09 840 000*	CV
				25.00	G09 852 001*	G09 860 000*	CV
				25.00	G09 872 001*	G09 880 000*	CV
				25.00	G09 892 001*	G09 900 000*	CV
				25.00	G09 912 001*	G09 920 000*	CV
				25.00	G09 932 001*	G09 940 000*	CV
				25.00	G09 952 001*	G09 960 000*	CV
				25.00	G09 972 001*	G09 980 000*	CV
				25.00	G09 992 001*	G10 000 000*	CV
				25.00	G10 012 001*	G10 020 000*	CV
				25.00	G10 032 001*	G10 040 000*	CV
				25.00	G10 052 001*	G10 060 000*	CV
				25.00	G10 072 001*	G10 080 000*	CV
				25.00	G10 092 001*	G10 100 000*	CV
				25.00	G10 112 001*	G10 120 000*	CV
				25.00	G10 132 001*	G10 140 000*	CV
				25.00	G10 152 001*	G10 160 000*	CV
				25.00	G10 172 001*	G10 180 000*	CV
				25.00	G10 192 001*	G10 200 000*	CV
				25.00	G10 212 001*	G10 220 000*	CV
				25.00	G10 232 001*	G10 240 000*	CV
				25.00	G10 256 001*	G10 260 000*	CV
				25.00	G10 276 001*	G10 280 000*	CV
				25.00	G10 296 001*	G10 300 000*	CV
				25.00	G10 316 001*	G10 320 000*	CV
				25.00	G10 336 001*	G10 340 000*	CV
				25.00	G10 356 001*	G10 360 000*	CV
				25.00	G10 376 001*	G10 380 000*	CV
				25.00	G10 396 001*	G10 400 000*	CV
				25.00	G10 416 001*	G10 420 000*	CV
				25.00	G10 436 001*	G10 440 000*	CV
				25.00	G10 456 001*	G10 460 000*	CV
				25.00	G10 476 001*	G10 480 000*	CV
				25.00	G10 496 001*	G10 500 000*	CV
				25.00	G10 516 001*	G10 520 000*	CV
				25.00	G10 536 001*	G10 540 000*	CV
				25.00	G10 556 001*	G10 560 000*	CV
				25.00	G10 576 001*	G10 580 000*	CV
				25.00	G10 596 001*	G10 600 000*	CV
				25.00	G10 616 001*	G10 620 000*	CV

DISTRICT	TOTAL NOTES PRINTED	BLOCKS	ESTIMATED VALUE VG/F	CU	LOW OFFICIAL SERIAL NUMBER	HIGH OFFICIAL SERIAL NUMBER	
				25.00	G10 636 001*	G10 640 000*	cv
				25.00	G10 656 001*	G10 660 000*	cv
				25.00	G10 676 001*	G10 680 000*	cv
				25.00	G10 696 001*	G10 700 000*	cv
				25.00	G10 716 001*	G10 720 000*	cv
				25.00	G10 736 001*	G10 740 000*	cv
				25.00	G10 756 001*	G10 760 000*	cv
				25.00	G10 776 001*	G10 780 000*	cv
				25.00	G10 796 001*	G10 800 000*	cv
				25.00	G10 816 001*	G10 820 000*	cv
				25.00	G10 836 001*	G10 840 000*	cv
				25.00	G10 856 001*	G10 860 000*	cv
				25.00	G10 876 001*	G10 880 000*	cv
8	H ST. LOUIS	H--A		8.00	H86 400 001A	H99 999 999A	cv
		H--B		8.00	H00 000 001B	H14 720 000B	cv
				8.00	H14 720 001B	H51 200 000B	cp
		H--*		10.00	H04 480 001*	H05 120 000*	cv
9	I MINNEAPOLIS	I--A		8.00	I45 440 001A	H66 560 000A	cv
				8.00	I66 560 001A	H87 040 000A	cp
		I--*		10.00	I01 280 001*	I03 840 000*	cv
10	J KANSAS CITY	J--B		8.00	J16 000 001B	J33 920 000B	cv
				8.00	J33 920 001B	J58 240 000B	cp
		J--*		10.00	J06 400 001*	J08 320 000*	cv
				25.00	J08 336 001*	J08 340 000*	cv
				25.00	J08 356 001*	J08 360 000*	cv
				25.00	J08 376 001*	J08 380 000*	cv
				25.00	J08 396 001*	J08 400 000*	cv
				25.00	J08 416 001*	J08 420 000*	cv
				25.00	J08 436 001*	J08 440 000*	cv
				25.00	J08 456 001*	J08 460 000*	cv
				25.00	J08 476 001*	J08 480 000*	cv
				25.00	J08 496 001*	J08 500 000*	cv
				25.00	J08 516 001*	J08 520 000*	cv
				25.00	J08 536 001*	J08 540 000*	cv
				25.00	J08 556 001*	J08 560 000*	cv
				25.00	J08 576 001*	J08 580 000*	cv
				25.00	J08 596 001*	J08 600 000*	cv
				25.00	J08 616 001*	J08 620 000*	cv
				25.00	J08 636 001*	J08 640 000*	cv
				25.00	J08 656 001*	J08 660 000*	cv
				25.00	J08 676 001*	J08 680 000*	cv
				25.00	J08 696 001*	J08 700 000*	cv
				25.00	J08 716 001*	J08 720 000*	cv
				25.00	J08 736 001*	J08 740 000*	cv
				25.00	J09 756 001*	J08 760 000*	cv
				25.00	J08 776 001*	J08 780 000*	cv
				25.00	J08 796 001*	J08 800 000*	cv
				25.00	J08 816 001*	J08 820 000*	cv
				25.00	J08 836 001*	J08 840 000*	cv
				25.00	J08 856 001*	J08 860 000*	cv
				25.00	J08 876 001*	J08 880 000*	cv
				25.00	J08 896 001*	J08 900 000*	cv
				25.00	J08 916 001*	J08 920 000*	cv
				25.00	J08 936 001*	J08 940 000*	cv
				25.00	J08 956 001*	J08 960 000*	cv
				25.00	J08 976 001*	J08 980 000*	cv
				25.00	J08 996 001*	J09 000 000*	cv
				25.00	J09 016 001*	J09 020 000*	cv
				25.00	J09 036 001*	J09 040 000*	cv
				25.00	J09 056 001*	J09 060 000*	cv
				25.00	J09 076 001*	J09 080 000*	cv
				25.00	J09 096 001*	J09 100 000*	cv
				25.00	J09 116 001*	J09 120 000*	cv
				25.00	J09 136 001*	J09 140 000*	cv
				25.00	J09 156 001*	J09 160 000*	cv
				25.00	J09 176 001*	J09 180 000*	cv
				25.00	J09 196 001*	J09 200 000*	cv
				25.00	J09 216 001*	J09 220 000*	cv
				25.00	J09 236 001*	J09 240 000*	cv

DISTRICT	TOTAL NOTES PRINTED	BLOCKS	ESTIMATED VALUE VG/F	VALUE CU	LOW OFFICIAL SERIAL NUMBER	HIGH OFFICIAL SERIAL NUMBER	
				25.00	J09 256 001*	J09 260 000*	cv
				25.00	J09 276 001*	J09 280 000*	cv
				25.00	J09 296 001*	J09 300 000*	cv
				25.00	J09 316 001*	J09 320 000*	cv
				25.00	J09 336 001*	J09 340 000*	cv
				25.00	J09 356 001*	J09 360 000*	cv
				25.00	J09 376 001*	J09 380 000*	cv
				25.00	J09 396 001*	J09 400 000*	cv
				25.00	J09 416 001*	J09 420 000*	cv
				25.00	J09 436 001*	J09 440 000*	cv
				25.00	J09 456 001*	J09 460 000*	cv
				25.00	J09 476 001*	J09 480 000*	cv
				25.00	J09 496 001*	J09 500 000*	cv
				25.00	J09 516 001*	J09 520 000*	cv
				25.00	J09 536 001*	J09 540 000*	cv
				25.00	J09 556 001*	J09 560 000*	cv
				25.00	J09 576 001*	J09 580 000*	cv
				25.00	J09 596 001*	J09 600 000*	cv
11 K DALLAS		K--B		8.00	K14 080 001B	K26 240 000B	cv
				8.00	K26 240 001B	K71 680 000B	cp
		K--*		10.00	K04 480 001*	K05 760 000*	cv
		K--*		25.00	K05 776 001*	K05 780 000*	cv
				25.00	K05 796 001*	K05 800 000*	cv
				25.00	K05 816 001*	K05 820 000*	cv
				25.00	K05 836 001*	K05 840 000*	cv
				25.00	K05 856 001*	K05 860 000*	cv
				25.00	K05 876 001*	K05 880 000*	cv
				25.00	K05 896 001*	K05 900 000*	cv
				25.00	K05 916 001*	K05 920 000*	cv
				25.00	K05 936 001*	K05 940 000*	cv
				25.00	K05 956 001*	K05 960 000*	cv
				25.00	K05 976 001*	K05 980 000*	cv
				25.00	K05 996 001*	K06 000 000*	cv
				25.00	K06 016 001*	K06 020 000*	cv
				25.00	K06 036 001*	K06 040 000*	cv
				25.00	K06 056 001*	K06 060 000*	cv
				25.00	K06 076 001*	K06 080 000*	cv
				25.00	K06 096 001*	K06 100 000*	cv
				25.00	K06 116 001*	K06 120 000*	cv
				25.00	K06 136 001*	K06 140 000*	cv
				25.00	K06 156 001*	K06 160 000*	cv
				25.00	K06 176 001*	K06 180 000*	cv
				25.00	K06 196 001*	K06 200 000*	cv
				25.00	K06 216 001*	K06 220 000*	cv
				25.00	K06 236 001*	K06 240 000*	cv
				25.00	K06 256 001*	K06 260 000*	cv
				25.00	K06 276 001*	K06 280 000*	cv
				25.00	K06 296 001*	K06 300 000*	cv
				25.00	K06 316 001*	K06 320 000*	cv
				25.00	K06 336 001*	K06 340 000*	cv
				25.00	K06 356 001*	K06 360 000*	cv
				25.00	K06 376 001*	K06 380 000*	cv
				25.00	K06 396 001*	K06 400 000*	cv
				25.00	L15 724 001*	L15 740 000*	cv
				25.00	L15 744 001*	L15 760 000*	cv
				25.00	L15 764 001*	L15 780 000*	cv
				25.00	L15 784 001*	L15 800 *000	cv
				25.00	L15 804 001*	L15 820 000*	cv
				25.00	L15 824 001*	L15 840 000*	cv
				25.00	L15 844 001*	L15 860 000*	cv
				25.00	L15 864 001*	L15 880 000*	cv
				25.00	L15 884 001*	L15 900 000*	cv
				25.00	L15 904 001*	L15 920 000*	cp
				25.00	L15 924 001*	L15 940 000*	cv
				25.00	L15 944 001*	L15 960 000*	cv
				25.00	L15 964 001*	L15 980 000*	cv
				25.00	L15 984 001*	L16 000 000*	cv
				25.00	L16 016 001*	L16 020 000*	cv
				25.00	L16 036 001*	L16 040 000*	cv

DISTRICT	TOTAL NOTES PRINTED	BLOCKS	ESTIMATED VALUE VG/F	CU	LOW OFFICIAL SERIAL NUMBER	HIGH OFFICIAL SERIAL NUMBER	
				25.00	L16 056 001*	L16 060 000*	cv
				25.00	L16 076 001*	L16 080 000*	cv
				25.00	L16 096 001*	L16 100 000*	cv
				25.00	L16 116 001*	L16 120 000*	cv
				25.00	L16 136 001*	L16 140 000*	cv
				25.00	L16 156 001*	L16 160 000*	cv
				25.00	L16 176 001*	L16 180 000*	cv
				25.00	L16 196 001*	L16 200 000*	cv
				25.00	L16 216 001*	L16 220 000*	cv
				25.00	L16 236 001*	L16 240 000*	cv
				25.00	L16 256 001*	L16 260 000*	cv
				25.00	L16 276 001*	l16 280 000*	cv
				25.00	L16 296 001*	L16 300 000*	cv
				25.00	L16 316 001*	L16 320 000*	cv
				25.00	L16 336 001*	L16 340 000*	cv
				25.00	L16 356 001*	L16 360 000*	cv
				25.00	L16 376 001*	L16 380 000*	cv
				25.00	L16 396 001*	L16 400 000*	cv
				25.00	L16 416 001*	L16 420 000*	cv
				25.00	L16 436 001*	L16 440 000*	cv
				25.00	L16 456 001*	L16 460 000*	cv
				25.00	L16 476 001*	L16 480 000*	cv
				25.00	L16 496 001*	L16 500 000*	cv
				25.00	L16 516 001*	L16 520 000*	cv
				25.00	L16 536 001*	L16 540 000*	cv
				25.00	L16 556 001*	L16 560 000*	cv
				25.00	L16 576 001*	L16 580 000*	cv
				25.00	L16 596 001*	L16 600 000*	cv
				25.00	L16 616 001*	L16 620 000*	cv
				25.00	L15 636 001*	L16 640 000*	cv
12 L SAN FRANCISCO		L--C		8.00	L53 120 001C	L97 920 000C	cv
				25.00	L97 920 001C	L99 840 000C	cp
				25.00	L99 840 001C	L99 999 999C	cv
		L--D		8.00	L00 000 001D	L92 800 000D	cp
		L--*		10.00	L10 240 001*	L14 720 000*	cv
				25.00	L14 736 001*	L14 740 000*	cv
				25.00	L14 756 001*	L14 760 000*	cv
				25.00	L14 776 001*	L14 780 000*	cv
				25.00	L14 796 001*	L14 800 000*	cv
				25.00	L14 816 001*	L14 820 000*	cv
				25.00	L14 836 001*	L14 840 000*	cv
				25.00	L14 856 001*	L14 860 000*	cv
				25.00	L14 876 001*	L14 880 000*	cv
				25.00	L14 896 001*	L14 900 000*	cv
				25.00	L14 916 001*	L14 920 000*	cv
				25.00	L14 936 001*	L14 940 000*	cv
				25.00	L14 956 001*	L14 960 000*	cv
				25.00	L14 976 001*	L14 980 000*	cv
				25.00	L14 996 001*	L15 000 000*	cv
				25.00	L15 016 001*	L15 020 000*	cv
				25.00	L15 036 001*	L15 040 000*	cv
				25.00	L15 056 001*	L15 060 000*	cv
				25.00	L15 076 001*	L15 080 000*	cv
				25.00	L15 096 001*	L15 100 000*	cv
				25.00	L15 116 001*	L15 120 000*	cv
				25.00	L15 136 001*	L15 140 000*	cv
				25.00	L15 156 001*	L15 160 000*	cv
				25.00	L15 176 001*	L15 180 000*	cv
				25.00	L15 196 001*	L15 200 000*	cv
				25.00	L15 216 001*	L15 220 000*	cv
				25.00	L15 236 001*	L15 240 000*	cv
				25.00	L15 256 001*	L15 260 000*	cv
				25.00	L15 276 001*	L15 280 000*	cv
				25.00	L15 296 001*	L15 300 000*	cv
				25.00	L15 316 001*	L15 320 000*	cv
				25.00	L15 336 001*	L15 340 000*	cv
				25.00	L15 356 001*	L15 360 000*	cv
				25.00	L15 364 001*	L15 380 000*	cv
				25.00	L15 384 001*	L15 400 000*	cv

DISTRICT	TOTAL NOTES PRINTED	BLOCKS	ESTIMATED VALUE VG/F	CU	LOW OFFICIAL SERIAL NUMBER	HIGH OFFICIAL SERIAL NUMBER	
				25.00	L15 404 001*	L15 420 000*	cv
				25.00	L15 424 001*	L15 440 000*	cv
				25.00	L15 444 001*	L15 460 000*	cv
				25.00	L15 464 001*	L15 480 000*	cv
				25.00	L15 484 001*	L15 500 000*	cv
				25.00	L15 504 001*	L15 520 000*	cv
				25.00	L15 524 001*	L15 540 000*	cv
				25.00	L15 544 001*	L15 560 000*	cv
				25.00	L15 564 001*	L15 580 000*	cv
				25.00	L15 584 001*	L15 600 000*	cv
				25.00	L15 604 001*	L15 620 000*	cv
				25.00	L15 624 001*	L15 640 000*	cv
				25.00	L15 644 001*	L15 660 000*	cv
				25.00	L15 664 001*	L15 680 000*	cv
				25.00	L15 684 001*	L15 700 000*	cv
				25.00	L15 704 001*	L15 720 000*	cv

CAT. NO. VF77
$5.00 FEDERAL RESERVE NOTE (GREEN SEAL) 32 Subject
SERIES 1977

SIGNATURES: Azie Taylor Morton, Treasurer of the United States.
W. Michael Blumenthal, Secretary of the Treasury.

SERIAL NUMBERS: All districts, regular and stars revert to 00 000 001.

PLATE SERIALS: Face and back check numbers continue from previous series.

DISTRICT	TOTAL NOTES PRINTED	BLOCKS	ESTIMATED VALUE VG/F	CU	LOW OFFICIAL SERIAL NUMBER	HIGH OFFICIAL SERIAL NUMBER	
1 A BOSTON		A--A		7.50	A00 000 001A	A60 800 000A	cp
		A--*		25.00	A00 016 001*	A00 020 000*	cv
				25.00	A00 036 001*	A00 040 000*	cv
				25.00	A00 056 001*	A00 060 000*	cv
				25.00	A00 076 001*	A00 080 000*	cv
				25.00	A00 096 001*	A00 100 000*	cv
				25.00	A00 116 001*	A00 120 000*	cv
				25.00	A00 136 001*	A00 140 000*	cv
				25.00	A00 156 001*	A00 160 000*	cv
				25.00	A00 176 001*	A00 180 000*	cv
				25.00	A00 196 001*	A00 200 000*	cv
				25.00	A00 216 001*	A00 220 000*	cv
				25.00	A00 236 001*	A00 240 000*	cv
				25.00	A00 256 001*	A00 260 000*	cv
				25.00	A00 276 001*	A00 280 000*	cv
				25.00	A00 296 001*	A00 300 000*	cv
				25.00	A00 316 001*	A00 320 000*	cv
				25.00	A00 336 001*	A00 340 000*	cv
				25.00	A00 356 001*	A00 360 000*	cv
				25.00	A00 376 001*	A00 380 000*	cv
				25.00	A00 396 001*	A00 400 000*	cv
				25.00	A00 416 001*	A00 420 000*	cv
				25.00	A00 436 001*	A00 440 000*	cv
				25.00	A00 456 001*	A00 460 000*	cv
				25.00	A00 476 001*	A00 480 000*	cv
				25.00	A00 496 001*	A00 500 000*	cv
				25.00	A00 516 001*	A00 520 000*	cv
				25.00	A00 536 001*	A00 540 000*	cv
				25.00	A00 556 001*	A00 560 000*	cv
				25.00	A00 576 001*	A00 580 000*	cv
				25.00	A00 596 001*	A00 600 000*	cv
				25.00	A00 616 001*	A00 620 000*	cv
				25.00	A00 636 001*	A00 640 000*	cv
				25.00	A00 656 001*	A00 660 000*	cv
				25.00	A00 676 001*	A00 680 000*	cv
				25.00	A00 696 001*	A00 700 000*	cv
				25.00	A00 716 001*	A00 720 000*	cv
				25.00	A00 736 001*	A00 740 000*	cv
				25.00	A00 756 001*	A00 760 000*	cv
				25.00	A00 776 001*	A00 780 000*	cv

DISTRICT	TOTAL NOTES PRINTED	BLOCKS	ESTIMATED VALUE VG/F	CU	LOW OFFICIAL SERIAL NUMBER	HIGH OFFICIAL SERIAL NUMBER	
				25.00	A00 796 001*	A00 800 000*	cv
				25.00	A00 816 001*	A00 820 000*	cv
				25.00	A00 836 001*	A00 840 000*	cv
				25.00	A00 856 001*	A00 860 000*	cv
				25.00	A00 876 001*	A00 880 000*	cv
				25.00	A00 896 001*	A00 900 000*	cv
				25.00	A00 916 001*	A00 920 000*	cv
				25.00	A00 936 001*	A00 940 000*	cv
				25.00	A00 956 001*	A00 960 000*	cv
				25.00	A00 976 001*	A00 980 000*	cv
				25.00	A00 996 001*	A01 000 000*	cv
				25.00	A01 016 001*	A01 020 000*	cv
				25.00	A01 036 001*	A01 040 000*	cv
				25.00	A01 056 001*	A01 060 000*	cv
				25.00	A01 076 001*	A01 080 000*	cv
				25.00	A01 096 001*	A01 100 000*	cv
				25.00	A01 116 001*	A01 120 000*	cv
				25.00	A01 136 001*	A01 140 000*	cv
				25.00	A01 156 001*	A01 160 000*	cv
				25.00	A01 176 001*	A01 180 000*	cv
				25.00	A01 196 001*	A01 200 000*	cv
				25.00	A01 216 001*	A01 220 000*	cv
				25.00	A01 236 001*	A01 240 000*	cv
				25.00	A01 256 001*	A01 260 000*	cv
				25.00	A01 276 001*	A01 280 000*	cv
				25.00	A01 296 001*	A01 300 000*	cv
				25.00	A01 316 001*	A01 320 000*	cv
				25.00	A01 336 001*	A01 340 000*	cv
				25.00	A01 356 001*	A01 360 000*	cv
				25.00	A01 376 001*	A01 380 000*	cv
				25.00	A01 396 001*	A01 400 000*	cv
				25.00	A01 416 001*	A01 420 000*	cv
				25.00	A01 436 001*	A01 440 000*	cv
				25.00	A01 456 001*	A01 460 000*	cv
				25.00	A01 476 001*	A01 480 000*	cv
				25.00	A01 496 001*	A01 500 000*	cv
				25.00	A01 516 001*	A01 520 000*	cv
				25.00	A01 536 001*	A01 540 000*	cv
				25.00	A01 556 001*	A01 560 000*	cv
				25.00	A01 576 001*	A01 580 000*	cv
				25.00	A01 596 001*	A01 600 000*	cv
				25.00	A01 616 001*	A-1 620 000*	cv
				25.00	A01 636 001*	A01 640 000*	cv
				25.00	A01 656 001*	A01 660 000*	cv
				25.00	A01 676 001*	A01 680 000*	cv
				25.00	A01 696 001*	A01 700 000*	cv
				25.00	A01 716 001*	A01 720 000*	cv
				25.00	A01 736 001*	A01 740 000*	cv
				25.00	A01 756 001*	A01 760 000*	cv
				25.00	A01 776 001*	A01 780 000*	cv
				25.00	A01 796 001*	A01 800 000*	cv
				25.00	A01 816 001*	A01 820 000*	cv
				25.00	A01 836 001*	A01 840 000*	cv
				25.00	A01 856 001*	A01 860 000*	cv
				25.00	A01 876 001*	A01 880 000*	cv
				25.00	A01 896 001*	A01 900 000*	cv
				25.00	A01 916 000*	A01 920 000*	cv
				10.00	A01 920 001*	A03 200 000*	cv
2	B NEW YORK	B--A		7.50	B00 000 001A	B99 840 000A	cp
		B--B		7.50	B00 000 001B	B83 200 000B	cp
		B--*		25.00	B00 016 001*	B00 020 000*	cv
				25.00	B00 036 001*	B00 040 000*	cv
				25.00	B00 056 001*	B00 060 000*	cv
				25.00	B00 076 001*	B00 080 000*	cv
				25.00	B00 096 001*	B00 100 000*	cv
				25.00	B00 116 001*	B00 120 000*	cv
				25.00	B00 136 001*	B00 140 000*	cv
				25.00	B00 156 001*	B00 160 000*	cv
				25.00	B00 176 001*	B00 180 000*	cv

VALUE CU	LOW OFFICIAL SERIAL NUMBER	HIGH OFFICIAL SERIAL NUMBER		VALUE CU	LOW OFFICIAL SERIAL NUMBER	HIGH OFFICIAL SERIAL NUMBER	
25.00	B00 196 001*	B00 200 000*	cv	25.00	B01 596 001*	B01 600 000*	cv
25.00	B00 216 001*	B00 220 000*	cv	25.00	B01 616 001*	B01 620 000*	cv
25.00	B00 236 001*	B00 240 000*	cv	25.00	B01 636 001*	B01 640 000*	cv
25.00	B00 256 001*	B00 260 000*	cv	25.00	B01 656 001*	B01 660 000*	cv
25.00	B00 276 001*	B00 280 000*	cv	25.00	B01 676 001*	B01 680 000*	cv
25.00	B00 296 001*	B00 300 000*	cv	25.00	B01 696 001*	B01 700 000*	cv
25.00	B00 316 001*	B00 320 000*	cv	25.00	B01 716 001*	B01 720 000*	cv
25.00	B00 336 001*	B00 340 000*	cv	25.00	B01 736 001*	B01 740 000*	cv
25.00	B00 356 001*	B00 360 000*	cv	25.00	B01 756 001*	B01 760 000*	cv
25.00	B00 376 001*	B00 380 000*	cv	25.00	B01 776 001*	B01 780 000*	cv
25.00	B00 396 001*	B00 400 000*	cv	25.00	B01 796 001*	B01 800 000*	cv
25.00	B00 416 001*	B00 420 000*	cv	25.00	B01 816 001*	B01 820 000*	cv
25.00	B00 436 001*	B00 440 000*	cv	25.00	B01 836 001*	B01 840 000*	cv
25.00	B00 456 001*	B00 460 000*	cv	25.00	B01 856 001*	B01 860 000*	cv
25.00	B00 476 001*	B00 480 000*	cv	25.00	B01 876 001*	B01 880 000*	cv
25.00	B00 496 001*	B00 500 000*	cv	25.00	B01 896 001*	B01 900 000*	cv
25.00	B00 516 001*	B00 520 000*	cv	25.00	B01 916 001*	B01 920 000*	cv
25.00	B00 536 001*	B00 540 000*	cv	25.00	B01 936 001*	B01 940 000*	cv
25.00	B00 556 001*	B00 560 000*	cv	25.00	B01 956 001*	B01 960 000*	cv
25.00	B00 576 001*	B00 580 000*	cv	25.00	B01 976 001*	B01 980 000*	cv
25.00	B00 596 001*	B00 600 000*	cv	25.00	B01 996 001*	B02 000 000*	cv
25.00	B00 616 001*	B00 620 000*	cv	25.00	B02 016 001*	B02 020 000*	cv
25.00	B00 636 001*	B00 640 000*	cv	25.00	B02 036 001*	B02 040 000*	cv
25.00	B00 648 001*	B00 660 000*	cv	25.00	B02 056 001*	B02 060 000*	cv
25.00	B00 668 001*	B00 680 000*	cv	25.00	B02 076 001*	B02 080 000*	cv
25.00	B00 688 001*	B00 700 000*	cv	25.00	B02 096 001*	B02 100 000*	cv
25.00	B00 708 001*	B00 720 000*	cv	25.00	B02 116 001*	B02 120 000*	cv
25.00	B00 728 001*	B00 740 000*	cv	25.00	B02 136 001*	B02 140 000*	cv
25.00	B00 748 001*	B00 760 000*	cv	25.00	B02 156 001*	B02 160 000*	cv
25.00	B00 768 001*	B00 780 000*	cv	25.00	B02 176 001*	B02 180 000*	cv
25.00	B00 788 001*	B00 800 000*	cv	25.00	B02 196 001*	B02 200 000*	cv
25.00	B00 808 001*	B00 820 000*	cv	25.00	B02 216 001*	B02 220 000*	cv
25.00	B00 828 001*	B00 840 000*	cv	25.00	B02 236 001*	B02 240 000*	cv
25.00	B00 848 001*	B00 860 000*	cv	25.00	B02 256 001*	B02 260 000*	cv
25.00	B00 868 001*	B00 880 000*	cv	25.00	B02 276 001*	B02 280 000*	cv
25.00	B00 888 001*	B00 900 000*	cv	25.00	B02 296 001*	B02 300 000*	cv
25.00	B00 908 001*	B00 920 000*	cv	25.00	B02 316 001*	B02 320 000*	cv
25.00	B00 928 001*	B00 940 000*	cv	25.00	B02 336 001*	B02 340 000*	cv
25.00	B00 948 001*	B00 960 000*	cv	25.00	B02 356 001*	B02 360 000*	cv
25.00	B00 968 001*	B00 980 000*	cv	25.00	B02 376 001*	B02 380 000*	cv
25.00	B00 988 001*	B01 000 000*	cv	25.00	B02 396 001*	B02 400 000*	cv
25.00	B01 008 001*	B01 020 000*	cv	25.00	B02 416 001*	B02 420 000*	cv
25.00	B01 028 001*	B01 040 000*	cv	25.00	B02 436 001*	B02 440 000*	cv
25.00	B01 048 001*	B01 060 000*	cv	25.00	B02 456 001*	B02 460 000*	cv
25.00	B01 068 001*	B01 080 000*	cv	25.00	B02 476 001*	B02 480 000*	cv
25.00	B01 088 001*	B01 100 000*	cv	25.00	B02 496 001*	B02 500 000*	cv
25.00	B01 108 001*	B01 120 000*	cv	25.00	B02 516 001*	B02 520 000*	cv
25.00	B01 128 001*	B01 140 000*	cv	25.00	B02 536 001*	B02 540 000*	cv
25.00	B01 148 001*	B01 160 000*	cv	25.00	B02 556 001*	B02 560 000*	cv
25.00	B01 168 001*	B01 180 000*	cv	10.00	B02 560 001*	B03 200 000*	cp
25.00	B01 188 001*	B01 200 000*	cv	10.00	B03 200 001*	B03 840 000*	cv
25.00	B01 208 001*	B01 220 000*	cv	25.00	B03 848 001*	B03 860 000*	cv
25.00	B01 228 001*	B01 240 000*	cv	25.00	B03 868 001*	B03 880 000*	cv
25.00	B01 248 001*	B01 260 000*	cv	25.00	B03 888 001*	B03 900 000*	cv
25.00	B01 268 001*	B01 280 000*	cv	25.00	B03 908 001*	B03 920 000*	cv
25.00	B01 296 001*	B01 300 000*	cv	25.00	B03 928 001*	B03 940 000*	cv
25.00	B01 316 001*	B01 320 000*	cv	25.00	B03 948 001*	B03 960 000*	cv
25.00	B01 336 001*	B01 340 000*	cv	25.00	B03 968 001*	B03 980 000*	cv
25.00	B01 356 001*	B01 360 000*	cv	25.00	B03 988 001*	B04 000 000*	cv
25.00	B01 376 001*	B01 380 000*	cv	25.00	B04 008 001	B04 020 000*	cv
25.00	B01 396 001*	B01 400 000*	cv	25.00	B04 028 001	B04 040 000*	cv
25.00	B01 416 001*	B01 420 000*	cv	25.00	B04 048 001	B04 060 000*	cv
25.00	B01 436 001*	B01 440 000*	cv	25.00	B04 068 001	B04 080 000*	cv
25.00	B01 456 001*	B01 460 000*	cv	25.00	B04 088 001	B04 100 000*	cv
25.00	B01 476 001*	B01 480 000*	cv	25.00	B04 108 001	B04 120 000*	cv
25.00	B01 496 001*	B01 500 000*	cv	25.00	B04 128 001	B04 140 000*	cv
25.00	B01 516 001*	B01 520 000*	cv	25.00	B04 148 001	B04 160 000*	cv
25.00	B01 536 001*	B01 540 000*	cv	25.00	B04 168 001	B04 180 000*	cv
25.00	B01 556 001*	B01 560 000*	cv	25.00	B04 188 001	B04 200 000*	cv
25.00	B01 576 001*	B01 580 000*	cv	25.00	B04 208 001	B04 220 000*	cv

DISTRICT	TOTAL NOTES PRINTED	BLOCKS	ESTIMATED VALUE VG/F	CU	LOW OFFICIAL SERIAL NUMBER	HIGH OFFICIAL SERIAL NUMBER	
				25.00	B04 228 001*	B04 240 000*	cv
				25.00	B04 248 001*	B04 260 000*	cv
				25.00	B04 268 001*	B04 280 000*	cv
				25.00	B04 288 001*	B04 300 000*	cv
				25.00	B04 308 001*	B04 320 000*	cv
				25.00	B04 328 001*	B04 340 000*	cv
				25.00	B04 348 001*	B04 360 000*	cv
				25.00	B04 368 001*	B04 380 000*	cv
				25.00	B04 388 001*	B04 400 000*	cv
				25.00	B04 408 001*	B04 420 000*	cv
				25.00	B04 428 001*	B04 440 000*	cv
				25.00	B04 448 001*	B04 460 000*	cv
				25.00	B04 468 001*	B04 480 000*	cv
				10.00	B04 480 001*	B05 120 000*	cp
3	C PHILADELPHIA	C--A		7.50	C00 000 001A	C78 280 000A	cp
		C--*		10.00	C00 000 001*	C00 640 000*	cv
		C--*		10.00	C00 640 001*	C01 280 000*	cp
4	D CLEVELAND	D--A		7.50	D00 000 001A	D76 160 000A	cp
		D--*		25.00	D00 016 001*	D00 020 000*	cv
				25.00	D00 036 001*	D00 040 000*	cv
				25.00	D00 056 001*	D00 060 000*	cv
				25.00	D00 076 001*	D00 080 000*	cv
				25.00	D00 096 001*	D00 100 000*	cv
				25.00	D00 116 001*	D00 120 000*	cv
				25.00	D00 136 001*	D00 140 000*	cv
				25.00	D00 156 001*	D00 160 000*	cv
				25.00	D00 176 001*	D00 180 000*	cv
				25.00	D00 196 001*	D00 200 000*	cv
				25.00	D00 216 001*	D00 220 000*	cv
				25.00	D00 236 001*	D00 240 000*	cv
				25.00	D00 256 001*	D00 260 000*	cv
				25.00	D00 276 001*	D00 280 000*	cv
				25.00	D00 296 001*	D00 300 000*	cv
				25.00	D00 316 001*	D00 320 000*	cv
				25.00	D00 336 001*	D00 340 000*	cv
				25.00	D00 356 001*	D00 360 000*	cv
				25.00	D00 376 001*	D00 380 000*	cv
				25.00	D00 396 001*	D00 400 000*	cv
				25.00	D00 416 001*	D00 420 000*	cv
				25.00	D00 436 001*	D00 440 000*	cv
				25.00	D00 456 001*	D00 460 000*	cv
				25.00	D00 476 001*	D00 480 000*	cv
				25.00	D00 496 001*	D00 500 000*	cv
				25.00	D00 516 001*	D00 520 000*	cv
				25.00	D00 536 001*	D00 540 000*	cv
				25.00	D00 556 001*	D00 560 000*	cv
				25.00	D00 576 001*	D00 580 000*	cv
				25.00	D00 596 001*	D00 600 000*	cv
				25.00	D00 616 001*	D00 620 000*	cv
				25.00	D00 636 001*	D00 640 000*	cv
				25.00	D00 652 001*	D00 660 000*	cv
				25.00	D00 672 001*	D00 680 000*	cv
				25.00	D00 692 001*	D00 700 000*	cv
				25.00	D00 712 001*	D00 720 000*	cv
				25.00	D00 732 001*	D00 740 000*	cv
				25.00	D00 752 001*	D00 760 000*	cv
				25.00	D00 772 001*	D00 780 000*	cv
				25.00	D00 792 001*	D00 800 000*	cv
				25.00	D00 812 001*	D00 820 000*	cv
				25.00	D00 832 001*	D00 840 000*	cv
				25.00	D00 852 001*	D00 860 000*	cv
				25.00	D00 872 001*	D00 880 000*	cv
				25.00	D00 892 001*	D00 900 000*	cv
				25.00	D00 912 001*	D00 920 000*	cv
				25.00	D00 932 001*	D00 940 000*	cv
				25.00	D00 952 001*	D00 960 000*	cv
				25.00	D00 972 001*	D00 980 000*	cv
				25.00	D00 992 001*	D01 000 000*	cv
				25.00	D01 012 001*	D01 020 000*	cv
				25.00	D01 032 001*	D01 040 000*	cv

DISTRICT	TOTAL NOTES PRINTED	BLOCKS	ESTIMATED VALUE VG/F	CU	LOW OFFICIAL SERIAL NUMBER	HIGH OFFICIAL SERIAL NUMBER	
				25.00	D01 052 001*	D01 060 000*	cv
				25.00	D01 072 001*	D01 080 000*	cv
				25.00	D01 092 001*	D01 100 000*	cv
				25.00	D01 112 001*	D01 120 000*	cv
				25.00	D01 132 001*	D01 140 000*	cv
				25.00	D01 152 001*	D01 160 000*	cv
				25.00	D01 172 001*	D01 180 000*	cv
				25.00	D01 192 001*	D01 200 000*	cv
				25.00	D01 212 001*	D01 220 000*	cv
				25.00	D01 232 001*	D01 240 000*	cv
				25.00	D01 252 001*	D01 260 000*	cv
				25.00	D01 272 001*	D01 280 000*	cv
				25.00	D01 292 001*	D01 300 000*	cp
				25.00	D01 312 001*	D01 320 000*	cp
				25.00	D01 332 001*	D01 340 000*	cp
				25.00	D01 352 001*	D01 360 000*	cp
				25.00	D01 372 001*	D01 380 000*	cp
				25.00	D01 392 001*	D01 400 000*	cp
				25.00	D01 412 001*	D01 420 000*	cp
				25.00	D01 432 001*	D01 440 000*	cp
				25.00	D01 452 001*	D01 460 000*	cp
				25.00	D01 472 001*	D01 480 000*	cp
				25.00	D01 492 001*	D01 500 000*	cp
				25.00	D01 512 001*	D01 520 000*	cp
				25.00	D01 532 001*	D01 540 000*	cp
				25.00	D01 552 001*	D01 560 000*	cp
				25.00	D01 572 001*	D01 580 000*	cp
				25.00	D01 592 001*	D01 600 000*	cp
				25.00	D01 612 001*	D01 620 000*	cp
				25.00	D01 632 001*	D01 640 000*	cp
				25.00	D01 652 001*	D01 660 000*	cp
				25.00	D01 672 001*	D01 680 000*	cp
				25.00	D01 692 001*	D01 700 000*	cp
				25.00	D01 712 001*	D01 720 000*	cp
				25.00	D01 732 001*	D01 740 000*	cp
				25.00	D01 752 001*	D01 760 000*	cp
				25.00	D01 772 001*	D01 780 000*	cp
				25.00	D01 792 001*	D01 800 000*	cp
				25.00	D01 812 001*	D01 820 000*	cp
				25.00	D01 832 001*	D01 840 000*	cp
				25.00	D01 852 001*	D01 860 000*	cp
				25.00	D01 872 001*	D01 880 000*	cp
				25.00	D01 892 001*	D01 900 000*	cp
				25.00	D01 912 001*	D01 920 000*	cp
				25.00	D01 932 001*	D01 940 000*	cp
				25.00	D01 952 001*	D01 960 000*	cp
				25.00	D01 972 001*	D01 980 000*	cp
				25.00	D01 992 001*	D02 000 000*	cp
				25.00	D02 012 001*	D02 020 000*	cp
				25.00	D02 032 001*	D02 040 000*	cp
				25.00	D02 052 001*	D02 060 000*	cp
				25.00	D02 072 001*	D02 080 000*	cp
				25.00	D02 092 001*	D02 100 000*	cp
				25.00	D02 112 001*	D02 120 000*	cp
				25.00	D02 132 001*	D02 140 000*	cp
				25.00	D02 152 001*	D02 160 000*	cp
				25.00	D02 172 001*	D02 180 000*	cp
				25.00	D02 192 001*	D02 200 000*	cp
				25.00	D02 212 001*	D02 220 000*	cp
				25.00	D02 232 001*	D02 240 000*	cp
				25.00	D02 252 001*	D02 260 000*	cp
				25.00	D02 272 001*	D02 280 000*	cp
				25.00	D02 292 001*	D02 300 000*	cp
				25.00	D02 312 001*	D02 320 000*	cp
				25.00	D02 332 001*	D02 340 000*	cp
				25.00	D02 352 001*	D02 360 000*	cp
				25.00	D02 372 001*	D02 380 000*	cp
				25.00	D02 392 001*	D02 400 000*	cp
				25.00	D02 412 001*	D02 420 000*	cp
				25.00	D02 432 001*	D02 440 000*	cp

DISTRICT	TOTAL NOTES PRINTED	BLOCKS	ESTIMATED VALUE VG/F	CU	LOW OFFICIAL SERIAL NUMBER	HIGH OFFICIAL SERIAL NUMBER	
				25.00	D02 452 001*	D02 460 000*	cp
				25.00	D02 472 001*	D02 480 000*	cp
				25.00	D02 492 001*	D02 500 000*	cp
				25.00	D02 512 001*	D02 520 000*	cp
				25.00	D02 532 001*	D02 540 000*	cp
				25.00	D02 552 001*	D02 560 000*	cp
				25.00	D02 572 001*	D02 580 000*	cp
				25.00	D02 592 001*	D02 600 000*	cp
				25.00	D02 612 001*	D02 620 000*	cp
				25.00	D02 632 001*	D02 640 000*	cp
				25.00	D02 652 001*	D02 660 000*	cp
				25.00	D02 672 001*	D02 680 000*	cp
				25.00	D02 692 001*	D02 700 000*	cp
				25.00	D02 712 001*	D02 720 000*	cp
				25.00	D02 732 001*	D02 740 000*	cp
				25.00	D02 752 001*	D02 760 000*	cp
				25.00	D02 772 001*	D02 780 000*	cp
				25.00	D02 792 001*	D02 800 000*	cp
				25.00	D02 812 001*	D02 820 000*	cp
				25.00	D02 832 001*	D02 840 000*	cp
				25.00	D02 852 001*	D02 860 000*	cp
				25.00	D02 872 001*	D02 880 000*	cp
				25.00	D02 892 001*	D02 900 000*	cp
				25.00	D02 912 001*	D02 920 000*	cp
				25.00	D02 932 001*	D02 940 000*	cp
				25.00	D02 952 001*	D02 960 000*	cp
				25.00	D02 972 001*	D02 980 000*	cp
				25.00	D02 992 001*	D03 000 000*	cp
				25.00	D03 012 001*	D03 020 000*	cp
				25.00	D03 032 001*	D03 040 000*	cp
				25.00	D03 052 001*	D03 060 000*	cp
				25.00	D03 072 001*	D03 080 000*	cp
				25.00	D03 092 001*	D03 100 000*	cp
				25.00	D03 112 001*	D03 120 000*	cp
				25.00	D03 132 001*	D03 140 000*	cp
				25.00	D03 152 001*	D03 160 000*	cp
				25.00	D03 172 001*	D03 180 000*	cp
				25.00	D03 192 001*	D03 200 000*	cp
5	E RICHMOND	E--A		7.50	E00 000 001A	E99 840 000A	cp
		E--B		7.50	E00 000 001B	E10 880 000B	cp
		E--*		25.00	E00 016 001*	E00 020 000*	cv
				25.00	E00 036 001*	E00 040 000*	cv
				25.00	E00 056 001*	E00 060 000*	cv
				25.00	E00 076 001*	E00 080 000*	cv
				25.00	E00 096 001*	E00 100 000*	cv
				25.00	E00 116 001*	E00 120 000*	cv
				25.00	E00 136 001*	E00 140 000*	cv
				25.00	E00 156 001*	E00 160 000*	cv
				25.00	E00 176 001*	E00 180 000*	cv
				25.00	E00 196 001*	E00 200 000*	cv
				25.00	E00 216 001*	E00 220 000*	cv
				25.00	E00 236 001*	E00 240 000*	cv
				25.00	E00 256 001*	E00 260 000*	cv
				25.00	E00 276 001*	E00 280 000*	cv
				25.00	E00 296 001*	E00 300 000*	cv
				25.00	E00 316 001*	E00 320 000*	cv
				25.00	E00 336 001*	E00 340 000*	cv
				25.00	E00 356 001*	E00 360 000*	cv
				25.00	E00 376 001*	E00 380 000*	cv
				25.00	E00 396 001*	E00 400 000*	cv
				25.00	E00 416 001*	E00 420 000*	cv
				25.00	E00 436 001*	E00 440 000*	cv
				25.00	E00 456 001*	E00 460 000*	cv
				25.00	E00 476 001*	E00 480 000*	cv
				25.00	E00 496 001*	E00 500 000*	cv
				25.00	E00 516 001*	E00 520 000*	cv
				25.00	E00 536 001*	E00 540 000*	cv
				25.00	E00 556 001*	E00 560 000*	cv
				25.00	E00 576 001*	E00 580 000*	cv
				25.00	E00 596 001*	E00 600 000*	cv

DISTRICT	TOTAL NOTES PRINTED	BLOCKS	ESTIMATED VALUE VG/F	CU	LOW OFFICIAL SERIAL NUMBER	HIGH OFFICIAL SERIAL NUMBER	
				25.00	E00 616 001*	E00 620 000*	cv
				25.00	E00 636 001*	E00 640 000*	cv
				25.00	E00 656 001*	E00 660 000*	cv
				25.00	E00 676 001*	E00 680 000*	cv
				25.00	E00 696 001*	E00 700 000*	cv
				25.00	E00 716 001*	E00 720 000*	cv
				25.00	E00 736 001*	E00 740 000*	cv
				25.00	E00 756 001*	E00 760 000*	cv
				25.00	E00 776 001*	E00 780 000*	cv
				25.00	E00 796 001*	E00 800 000*	cv
				25.00	E00 816 001*	E00 820 000*	cv
				25.00	E00 836 001*	E00 840 000*	cv
				25.00	E00 856 001*	E00 860 000*	cv
				25.00	E00 876 001*	E00 880 000*	cv
				25.00	E00 896 001*	E00 900 000*	cv
				25.00	E00 916 001*	E00 920 000*	cv
				25.00	E00 936 001*	E00 940 000*	cv
				25.00	E00 956 001*	E00 960 000*	cv
				25.00	E00 976 001*	E00 980 000*	cv
				25.00	E00 996 001*	E01 000 000*	cv
				25.00	E01 016 001*	E01 020 000*	cv
				25.00	E01 036 001*	E01 040 000*	cv
				25.00	E01 056 001*	E01 060 000*	cv
				25.00	E01 076 001*	E01 080 000*	cv
				25.00	E01 096 001*	E01 100 000*	cv
				25.00	E01 116 001*	E01 120 000*	cv
				25.00	E01 136 001*	E01 140 000*	cv
				25.00	E01 156 001*	E01 160 000*	cv
				25.00	E01 176 011*	E01 180 000*	cv
				25.00	E01 196 001*	E01 200 000*	cv
				25.00	E01 216 001*	E01 220 000*	cv
				25.00	E01 236 001*	E01 240 000*	cv
				25.00	E01 256 001*	E01 260 000*	cv
				25.00	E01 276 001*	E01 280 000*	cv
				10.00	E01 280 001*	E02 560 000*	cv
				10.00	E02 560 001*	E03 840 000*	cp
6	F ATLANTA		F--A	7.50	F00 000 001A	F99 840 000A	cp
			F--B	7.50	F00 000 001B	F27 520 000B	cp
			F--*	25.00	F00 012 001*	F00 020 000*	cv
				25.00	F00 032 001*	F00 040 000*	cv
				25.00	F00 052 001*	F00 060 000*	cv
				25.00	F00 072 001*	F00 080 000*	cv
				25.00	F00 092 001*	F00 100 000*	cv
				25.00	F00 112 001*	F00 120 000*	cv
				25.00	F00 132 001*	F00 140 000*	cv
				25.00	F00 152 001*	F00 160 000*	cv
				25.00	F00 172 001*	F00 180 000*	cv
				25.00	F00 192 001*	F00 200 000*	cv
				25.00	F00 212 001*	F00 220 000*	cv
				25.00	F00 232 001*	F00 240 000*	cv
				25.00	F00 252 001*	F00 260 000*	cv
				25.00	F00 272 001*	F00 280 000*	cv
				25.00	F00 292 001*	F00 300 000*	cv
				25.00	F00 312 001*	F00 320 000*	cv
				25.00	F00 332 001*	F00 340 000*	cv
				25.00	F00 352 001*	F00 360 000*	cv
				25.00	F00 372 001*	F00 380 000*	cv
				25.00	F00 392 001*	F00 400 000*	cv
				25.00	F00 412 001*	F00 420 000*	cv
				25.00	F00 432 001*	F00 440 000*	cv
				25.00	F00 452 001*	F00 460 000*	cv
				25.00	F00 472 001*	F00 480 000*	cv
				25.00	F00 492 001*	F00 500 000*	cv
				25.00	F00 512 001*	F00 520 000*	cv
				25.00	F00 532 001*	F00 540 000*	cv
				25.00	F00 552 001*	F00 560 000*	cv
				25.00	F00 572 001*	F00 580 000*	cv
				25.00	F00 592 001*	F00 600 000*	cv
				25.00	F00 612 001*	F00 620 000*	cv
				25.00	F00 632 001*	F00 640 000*	cv

DISTRICT	TOTAL NOTES PRINTED	BLOCKS	ESTIMATED VALUE VG/F	CU	LOW OFFICIAL SERIAL NUMBER	HIGH OFFICIAL SERIAL NUMBER	
				25.00	F00 648 001*	F00 660 000*	cv
				25.00	F00 668 001*	F00 680 000*	cv
				25.00	F00 688 001*	F00 700 000*	cv
				25.00	F00 708 001*	F00 720 000*	cv
				25.00	F00 728 001*	F00 740 000*	cv
				25.00	F00 748 001*	F00 760 000*	cv
				25.00	F00 768 001*	F00 780 000*	cv
				25.00	F00 788 001*	F00 800 000*	cv
				25.00	F00 808 001*	F00 820 000*	cv
				25.00	F00 828 001*	F00 840 000*	cv
				25.00	F00 848 001*	F00 860 000*	cv
				25.00	F00 868 001*	F00 880 000*	cv
				25.00	F00 888 001*	F00 900 000*	cv
				25.00	F00 908 001*	F00 920 000*	cv
				25.00	F00 928 001*	F00 940 000*	cv
				25.00	F00 948 001*	F00 960 000*	cv
				25.00	F00 968 001*	F00 980 000*	cv
				25.00	F00 988 001*	F01 000 000*	cv
				25.00	F01 008 001*	F01 020 000*	cv
				25.00	F01 028 001*	F01 040 000*	cv
				25.00	F01 048 001*	F01 060 000*	cv
				25.00	F01 068 001*	F01 080 000*	cv
				25.00	F01 088 001*	F01 100 000*	cv
				25.00	F01 108 001*	F01 120 000*	cv
				25.00	F01 128 001*	F01 140 000*	cv
				25.00	F01 148 001*	F01 160 000*	cv
				25.00	F01 168 001*	F01 180 000*	cv
				25.00	F01 188 001*	F01 200 000*	cv
				25.00	F01 208 001*	F01 220 000*	cv
				25.00	F01 228 001*	F01 240 000*	cv
				25.00	F01 248 001*	F01 260 000*	cv
				25.00	F01 268 001*	F01 280 000*	cv
				10.00	F01 280 001*	F02 560 000*	cv
7	G CHICAGO	G--A		7.50	G00 000 001A	G99 840 000A	cp
		G--B		7.50	G00 000 001B	G77 440 000B	cp
		G--*		25.00	G00 016 001*	G00 020 000*	cv
				25.00	G00 036 001*	G00 040 000*	cv
				25.00	G00 056 001*	G00 060 000*	cv
				25.00	G00 076 001*	G00 080 000*	cv
				25.00	G00 096 001*	G00 100 000*	cv
				25.00	G00 116 001*	G00 120 000*	cv
				25.00	G00 136 001*	G00 140 000*	cv
				25.00	G00 156 001*	G00 160 000*	cv
				25.00	G00 176 001*	G00 180 000*	cv
				25.00	G00 196 001*	G00 200 000*	cv
				25.00	G00 216 001*	G00 220 000*	cv
				25.00	G00 236 001*	G00 240 000*	cv
				25.00	G00 256 001*	G00 260 000*	cv
				25.00	G00 276 001*	G00 280 000*	cv
				25.00	G00 296 001*	G00 300 000*	cv
				25.00	G00 316 001*	G00 320 000*	cv
				25.00	G00 336 001*	G00 340 000*	cv
				25.00	G00 356 001*	G00 360 000*	cv
				25.00	G00 376 001*	G00 380 000*	cv
				25.00	G00 396 001*	G00 400 000*	cv
				25.00	G00 416 001*	G00 420 000*	cv
				25.00	G00 436 001*	G00 440 000*	cv
				25.00	G00 456 001*	G00 460 000*	cv
				25.00	G00 476 001*	G00 480 000*	cv
				25.00	G00 496 001*	G00 500 000*	cv
				25.00	G00 516 001*	G00 520 000*	cv
				25.00	G00 536 001*	G00 540 000*	cv
				25.00	G00 556 001*	G00 560 000*	cv
				25.00	G00 576 001*	G00 580 000*	cv
				25.00	G00 596 001*	G00 600 000*	cv
				25.00	G00 616 001*	G00 620 000*	cv
				25.00	G00 636 001*	G00 640 000*	cv
				25.00	G00 652 001*	G00 660 000*	cv
				25.00	G00 672 001*	G00 680 000*	cv
				25.00	G00 692 001*	G00 700 000*	cv

DISTRICT	TOTAL NOTES PRINTED	BLOCKS	ESTIMATED VALUE VG/F	CU	LOW OFFICIAL SERIAL NUMBER	HIGH OFFICIAL SERIAL NUMBER	
				25.00	G00 712 001*	G00 720 000*	cv
				25.00	G00 732 001*	G00 740 000*	cv
				25.00	G00 752 001*	G00 760 000*	cv
				25.00	G00 772 001*	G00 780 000*	cv
				25.00	G00 792 001*	G00 800 000*	cv
				25.00	G00 812 001*	G00 820 000*	cv
				25.00	G00 832 001*	G00 840 000*	cv
				25.00	G00 852 001*	G00 860 000*	cv
				25.00	G00 872 001*	G00 880 000*	cv
				25.00	G00 892 001*	G00 900 000*	cv
				25.00	G00 912 001*	G00 920 000*	cv
				25.00	G00 932 001*	G00 940 000*	cv
				25.00	G00 952 001*	G00 960 000*	cv
				25.00	G00 972 001*	G00 980 000*	cv
				25.00	G00 992 001*	G01 000 000*	cv
				25.00	G01 012 001*	G01 020 000*	cv
				25.00	G01 032 001*	G01 040 000*	cv
				25.00	G01 052 001*	G01 060 000*	cv
				25.00	G01 072 001*	G01 080 000*	cv
				25.00	G01 092 001*	G01 100 000*	cv
				25.00	G01 112 001*	G01 120 000*	cv
				25.00	G01 132 001*	G01 140 000*	cv
				25.00	G01 152 001*	G01 160 000*	cv
				25.00	G01 172 001*	G01 180 000*	cv
				25.00	G01 192 001*	G01 200 000*	cv
				25.00	G01 212 001*	G01 220 000*	cv
				25.00	G01 232 001*	G01 240 000*	cv
				25.00	G01 252 001*	G01 260 000*	cv
				25.00	G01 272 001*	G01 280 000*	cv
				10.00	G01 280 001*	G02 560 000*	cv
				10.00	G02 560 001*	G03 840 000*	cp
8	H ST. LOUIS		H--A	7.50	H00 000 001A	H46 080 000A	cp
			H--*	25.00	H00 016 001*	H00 020 000*	cp
				25.00	H00 036 001*	H00 040 000*	cp
				25.00	H00 056 001*	H00 060 000*	cp
				25.00	H00 076 001*	H00 080 000*	cp
				25.00	H00 096 001*	H00 100 000*	cp
				25.00	H00 116 001*	H00 120 000*	cp
				25.00	H00 136 001*	H00 140 000*	cp
				25.00	H00 156 001*	H00 160 000*	cp
				25.00	H00 176 001*	H00 180 000*	cp
				25.00	H00 196 001*	H00 200 000*	cp
				25.00	H00 216 001*	H00 220 000*	cp
				25.00	H00 236 001*	H00 240 000*	cp
				25.00	H00 256 001*	H00 260 000*	cp
				25.00	H00 276 001*	H00 280 000*	cp
				25.00	H00 296 001*	H00 300 000*	cp
				25.00	H00 316 001*	H00 320 000*	cp
				25.00	H00 336 001*	H00 340 000*	cp
				25.00	H00 356 001*	H00 360 000*	cp
				25.00	H00 376 001*	H00 380 000*	cp
				25.00	H00 396 001*	H00 400 000*	cp
				25.00	H00 416 001*	H00 420 000*	cp
				25.00	H00 436 001*	H00 440 000*	cp
				25.00	H00 456 001*	H00 460 000*	cp
				25.00	H00 476 001*	H00 480 000*	cp
				25.00	H00 496 001*	H00 500 000*	cp
				25.00	H00 516 001*	H00 520 000*	cp
				25.00	H00 536 001*	H00 540 000*	cp
				25.00	H00 556 001*	H00 560 000*	cp
				25.00	H00 576 001*	H00 580 000*	cp
				25.00	H00 596 001*	H00 600 000*	cp
				25.00	H00 616 001*	H00 620 000*	cp
				25.00	H00 636 001*	H00 640 000*	cp
9	I MINNEAPOLIS		I--A	7.50	I00 000 001A	I21 760 000A	cp
			I--*	no stars printed for this series.			
10	J KANSAS CITY		J--A	7.50	J00 000 001A	J78 080 000A	cp
			J--*	25.00	J00 008 001*	J00 020 000*	cv
				25.00	J00 028 001*	J00 040 000*	cv

DISTRICT	TOTAL NOTES PRINTED	BLOCKS	ESTIMATED VALUE VG/F	CU	LOW OFFICIAL SERIAL NUMBER	HIGH OFFICIAL SERIAL NUMBER	
				25.00	J00 048 001*	J00 060 000*	cv
				25.00	J00 068 001*	J00 080 000*	cv
				25.00	J00 088 001*	J00 100 000*	cv
				25.00	J00 108 001*	J00 120 000*	cv
				25.00	J00 128 001*	J00 140 000*	cv
				25.00	J00 148 001*	J00 160 000*	cv
				25.00	J00 168 001*	J00 180 000*	cv
				25.00	J00 188 001*	J00 200 000*	cv
				25.00	J00 208 001*	J00 220 000*	cv
				25.00	J00 228 001*	J00 240 000*	cv
				25.00	J00 248 001*	J00 260 000*	cv
				25.00	J00 268 001*	J00 280 000*	cv
				25.00	J00 288 001*	J00 300 000*	cv
				25.00	J00 308 001*	J00 320 000*	cv
				25.00	J00 328 001*	J00 340 000*	cv
				25.00	J00 348 001*	J00 360 000*	cv
				25.00	J00 368 001*	J00 380 000*	cv
				25.00	J00 388 001*	J00 400 000*	cv
				25.00	J00 408 001*	J00 420 000*	cv
				25.00	J00 428 001*	J00 440 000*	cv
				25.00	J00 448 001*	J00 460 000*	cv
				25.00	J00 468 001*	J00 480 000*	cv
				25.00	J00 488 001*	J00 500 000*	cv
				25.00	J00 508 001*	J00 520 000*	cv
				25.00	J00 528 001*	J00 540 000*	cv
				25.00	J00 548 001*	J00 560 000*	cv
				25.00	J00 568 001*	J00 580 000*	cv
				25.00	J00 588 001*	J00 600 000*	cv
				25.00	J00 608 001*	J00 620 000*	cv
				25.00	J00 628 001*	J00 640 000*	cv
				25.00	J00 648 001*	J00 660 000*	cv
				25.00	J00 668 001*	J00 680 000*	cv
				25.00	J00 688 001*	J00 700 000*	cv
				25.00	J00 708 001*	J00 720 000*	cv
				25.00	J00 728 001*	J00 740 000*	cv
				25.00	J00 748 001*	J00 760 000*	cv
				25.00	J00 768 001*	J00 780 000*	cv
				25.00	J00 788 001*	J00 800 000*	cv
				25.00	J00 808 001*	J00 820 000*	cv
				25.00	J00 828 001*	J00 840 000*	cv
				25.00	J00 848 001*	J00 860 000*	cv
				25.00	J00 868 001*	J00 880 000*	cv
				25.00	J00 888 001*	J00 900 000*	cv
				25.00	J00 908 001*	J00 920 000*	cv
				25.00	J00 928 001*	J00 940 000*	cv
				25.00	J00 948 001*	J00 960 000*	cv
				25.00	J00 968 001*	J00 980 000*	cv
				25.00	J00 988 001*	J01 000 000*	cv
				25.00	J01 008 001*	J01 020 000*	cv
				25.00	J01 028 001*	J01 040 000*	cv
				25.00	J01 048 001*	J01 060 000*	cv
				25.00	J01 068 001*	J01 080 000*	cv
				25.00	J01 088 001*	J01 100 000*	cv
				25.00	J01 108 001*	J01 120 000*	cv
				25.00	J01 128 001*	J01 140 000*	cv
				25.00	J01 148 001*	J01 160 000*	cv
				25.00	J01 168 001*	J01 180 000*	cv
				25.00	J01 188 001*	J01 200 000*	cv
				25.00	J01 208 001*	J01 220 000*	cv
				25.00	J01 228 001*	J01 240 000*	cv
				25.00	J01 248 001*	J01 260 000*	cv
				25.00	J01 268 001*	J01 280 000*	cv
				25.00	J01 280 000*	J01 920 000*	cp
11 K DALLAS		K--A	7.50	K00 000 001A	K60 800 000A	cp
		K--*	25.00	K00 016 001*	K00 020 000*	cv
			25.00	K00 036 001*	K00 040 000*	cv
			25.00	K00 056 001*	K00 060 000*	cv
			25.00	K00 076 001*	K00 080 000*	cv
			25.00	K00 096 001*	K00 100 000*	cv
			25.00	K00 116 001*	K00 120 000*	cv

146

DISTRICT	TOTAL NOTES PRINTED	BLOCKS	ESTIMATED VALUE VG/F	CU	LOW OFFICIAL SERIAL NUMBER	HIGH OFFICIAL SERIAL NUMBER	
				25.00	K00 136 001*	K00 140 000*	cv
				25.00	K00 156 001*	K00 160 000*	cv
				25.00	K00 176 001*	K00 180 000*	cv
				25.00	K00 196 001*	K00 200 000*	cv
				25.00	K00 216 001*	K00 220 000*	cv
				25.00	K00 236 001*	K00 240 000*	cv
				25.00	K00 256 001*	K00 260 000*	cv
				25.00	K00 276 001*	K00 280 000*	cv
				25.00	K00 296 001*	K00 300 000*	cv
				25.00	K00 316 001*	K00 320 000*	cv
				25.00	K00 336 001*	K00 340 000*	cv
				25.00	K00 356 001*	K00 360 000*	cv
				25.00	K00 376 001*	K00 380 000*	cv
				25.00	K00 396 001*	K00 400 000*	cv
				25.00	K00 416 001*	K00 420 000*	cv
				25.00	K00 436 001*	K00 440 000*	cv
				25.00	K00 456 001*	K00 460 000*	cv
				25.00	K00 476 001*	K00 480 000*	cv
				25.00	K00 496 001*	K00 500 000*	cv
				25.00	K00 516 001*	K00 520 000*	cv
				25.00	K00 536 001*	K00 540 000*	cv
				25.00	K00 556 001*	K00 560 000*	cv
				25.00	K00 576 001*	K00 580 000*	cv
				25.00	K00 596 001*	K00 600 000*	cv
				25.00	K00 616 001*	K00 620 000*	cv
				25.00	K00 636 001*	K00 640 000*	cv
				25.00	K00 652 001*	K00 660 000*	cv
				25.00	K00 672 001*	K00 680 000*	cv
				25.00	K00 692 001*	K00 700 000*	cv
				25.00	K00 712 001*	K00 720 000*	cv
				25.00	K00 732 001*	K00 740 000*	cv
				25.00	K00 752 001*	K00 760 000*	cv
				25.00	K00 772 001*	K00 780 000*	cv
				25.00	K00 792 001*	K00 800 000*	cv
				25.00	K00 812 001*	K00 820 000*	cv
				25.00	K00 832 001*	K00 840 000*	cv
				25.00	K00 852 001*	K00 860 000*	cv
				25.00	K00 872 001*	K00 880 000*	cv
				25.00	K00 892 001*	K00 900 000*	cv
				25.00	K00 912 001*	K00 920 000*	cv
				25.00	K00 932 001*	K00 940 000*	cv
				25.00	K00 952 001*	K00 960 000*	cv
				25.00	K00 972 001*	K00 980 000*	cv
				25.00	K00 992 001*	K01 000 000*	cv
				25.00	K01 012 001*	K01 020 000*	cv
				25.00	K01 032 001*	K01 040 000*	cv
				25.00	K01 052 001*	K01 060 000*	cv
				25.00	K01 072 001*	K01 080 000*	cv
				25.00	K01 092 001*	K01 100 000*	cv
				25.00	K01 112 001*	K01 120 000*	cv
				25.00	K01 132 001*	K01 140 000*	cv
				25.00	K01 152 001*	K01 160 000*	cv
				25.00	K01 172 001*	K01 180 000*	cv
				25.00	K01 192 001*	K01 200 000*	cv
				25.00	K01 212 001*	K01 220 000*	cv
				25.00	K01 232 001*	K01 240 000*	cv
				25.00	K01 252 001*	K01 260 000*	cv
				25.00	K01 272 001*	K01 280 000*	cv
				10.00	K01 280 001*	K02 560 000*	cp
12 L SAN FRANCISCO		L--A		7.50	L00 000 001A	L99 840 000A	cp
		L--B		7.50	L00 000 001B	L44 800 000B	cp
		L--*		25.00	L00 012 001*	L00 020 000*	cv
				25.00	L00 032 001*	L00 040 000*	cv
				25.00	L00 052 001*	L00 060 000*	cv
				25.00	L00 072 001*	L00 080 000*	cv
				25.00	L00 092 001*	L00 100 000*	cv
				25.00	L00 112 001*	L00 120 000*	cv
				25.00	L00 132 001*	L00 140 000*	cv
				25.00	L00 152 001*	L00 160 000*	cv
				25.00	L00 172 001*	L00 180 000*	cv

VALUE CU	LOW OFFICIAL SERIAL NUMBER	HIGH OFFICIAL SERIAL NUMBER		VALUE CU	LOW OFFICIAL SERIAL NUMBER	HIGH OFFICIAL SERIAL NUMBER	
25.00	L00 192 001*	L00 200 000*	cv	25.00	L01 572 001*	L01 580 000*	cv
25.00	L00 212 001*	L00 220 000*	cv	25.00	L01 592 001*	L01 600 000*	cv
25.00	L00 232 001*	L00 240 000*	cv	25.00	L01 612 001*	L01 620 000*	cv
25.00	L00 252 001*	L00 260 000*	cv	25.00	L01 632 001*	L01 640 000*	cv
25.00	L00 272 001*	L00 280 000*	cv	25.00	L01 652 001*	L01 660 000*	cv
25.00	L00 292 001*	L00 300 000*	cv	25.00	L01 672 001*	L01 680 000*	cv
25.00	L00 312 001*	L00 320 000*	cv	25.00	L01 692 001*	L01 700 000*	cv
25.00	L00 332 001*	L00 340 000*	cv	25.00	L01 712 001*	L01 720 000*	cv
25.00	L00 352 001*	L00 360 000*	cv	25.00	L01 732 001*	L01 740 000*	cv
25.00	L00 372 001*	L00 380 000*	cv	25.00	L01 752 001*	L01 760 000*	cv
25.00	L00 392 001*	L00 400 000*	cv	25.00	L01 772 001*	L01 780 000*	cv
25.00	L00 412 001*	L00 420 000*	cv	25.00	L01 792 001*	L01 800 000*	cv
25.00	L00 432 001*	L00 440 000*	cv	25.00	L01 812 001*	L01 820 000*	cv
25.00	L00 452 001*	L00 460 000*	cv	25.00	L01 832 001*	L01 840 000*	cv
25.00	L00 472 001*	L00 480 000*	cv	25.00	L01 852 001*	L01 860 000*	cv
25.00	L00 492 001*	L00 500 000*	cv	25.00	L01 872 001*	L01 880 000*	cv
25.00	L00 512 001*	L00 520 000*	cv	25.00	L01 892 001*	L01 900 000*	cv
25.00	L00 532 001*	L00 540 000*	cv	25.00	L01 912 001*	L01 920 000*	cv
25.00	L00 552 001*	L00 560 000*	cv	10.00	L01 920 001*	L02 560 000*	cp
25.00	L00 572 001*	L00 580 000*	cv	25.00	L02 576 001*	L02 580 000*	cp
25.00	L00 592 001*	L00 600 000*	cv	25.00	L02 596 001*	L02 600 000*	cp
25.00	L00 612 001*	L00 620 000*	cv	25.00	L02 616 001*	L02 620 000*	cp
25.00	L00 632 001*	L00 640 000*	cv	25.00	L02 636 001*	L02 640 000*	cp
25.00	L00 648 001*	L00 660 000*	cv	25.00	L02 656 001*	L02 660 000*	cp
25.00	L00 668 001*	L00 680 000*	cv	25.00	L02 676 001*	L02 680 000*	cp
25.00	L00 688 001*	L00 700 000*	cv	25.00	L02 696 001*	L02 700 000*	cp
25.00	L00 708 001*	L00 720 000*	cv	25.00	L02 716 001*	L02 720 000*	cp
25.00	L00 728 001*	L00 740 000*	cv	25.00	L02 736 001*	L02 740 000*	cp
25.00	L00 748 001*	L00 760 000*	cv	25.00	L02 756 001*	L02 760 000*	cp
25.00	L00 768 001*	L00 780 000*	cv	25.00	L02 776 001*	L02 780 000*	cp
25.00	L00 788 001*	L00 800 000*	cv	25.00	L02 796 001*	L02 800 000*	cp
25.00	L00 808 001*	L00 820 000*	cv	25.00	L02 816 001*	L02 820 000*	cp
25.00	L00 828 001*	L00 840 000*	cv	25.00	L02 836 001*	L02 840 000*	cp
25.00	L00 848 001*	L00 860 000*	cv	25.00	L02 856 001*	L02 860 000*	cp
25.00	L00 868 001*	L00 880 000*	cv	25.00	L02 876 001*	L02 880 000*	cp
25.00	L00 888 001*	L00 900 000*	cv	25.00	L02 896 001*	L02 900 000*	cp
25.00	L00 908 001*	L00 920 000*	cv	25.00	L02 916 001*	L02 920 000*	cp
25.00	L00 928 001*	L00 940 000*	cv	25.00	L02 936 001*	L02 940 000*	cp
25.00	L00 948 001*	L00 960 000*	cv	25.00	L02 956 001*	L02 960 000*	cp
25.00	L00 968 001*	L00 980 000*	cv	25.00	L02 976 001*	L02 980 000*	cp
25.00	L00 988 001*	L01 000 000*	cv	25.00	L02 996 001*	L03 000 000*	cp
25.00	L01 008 001*	L01 020 000*	cv	25.00	L03 016 001*	L03 020 000*	cp
25.00	L01 028 001*	L01 040 000*	cv	25.00	L03 036 001*	L03 040 000*	cp
25.00	L01 048 001*	L01 060 000*	cv	25.00	L03 056 001*	L03 060 000*	cp
25.00	L01 068 001*	L01 080 000*	cv	25.00	L03 076 001*	L03 080 000*	cp
25.00	L01 088 001*	L01 100 000*	cv	25.00	L03 096 001*	L03 100 000*	cp
25.00	L01 108 001*	L01 120 000*	cv	25.00	L03 116 001*	L03 120 000*	cp
25.00	L01 128 001*	L01 140 000*	cv	25.00	L03 136 001*	L03 140 000*	cp
25.00	L01 148 001*	L01 160 000*	cv	25.00	L03 156 001*	L03 160 000*	cp
25.00	L01 168 001*	L01 180 000*	cv	25.00	L03 176 001*	L03 180 000*	cp
25.00	L01 188 001*	L01 200 000*	cv	25.00	L03 196 001*	L03 200 000*	cp
25.00	L01 208 001*	L01 220 000*	cv	10.00	L03 200 001*	L03 840 000*	cp
25.00	L01 228 001*	L01 240 000*	cv	25.00	L03 856 001*	L03 860 000*	cp
25.00	L01 248 001*	L01 260 000*	cv	25.00	L03 876 001*	L03 880 000*	cp
25.00	L01 268 001*	L01 280 000*	cv	25.00	L03 896 001*	L03 900 000*	cp
25.00	L01 292 001*	L01 300 000*	cv	25.00	L03 916 001*	L03 920 000*	cp
25.00	L01 312 001*	L01 320 000*	cv	25.00	L03 936 001*	L03 940 000*	cp
25.00	L01 332 001*	L01 340 000*	cv	25.00	L03 956 001*	L03 960 000*	cp
25.00	L01 352 001*	L01 360 000*	cv	25.00	L03 976 001*	L03 980 000*	cp
25.00	L01 372 001*	L01 380 000*	cv	25.00	L03 996 001*	L04 000 000*	cp
25.00	L01 392 001*	L01 400 000*	cv	25.00	L04 016 001*	L04 020 000*	cp
25.00	L01 412 001*	L01 420 000*	cv	25.00	L04 036 001*	L04 040 000*	cp
25.00	L01 432 001*	L01 440 000*	cv	25.00	L04 056 001*	L04 060 000*	cp
25.00	L01 452 001*	L01 460 000*	cv	25.00	L04 076 001*	L04 080 000*	cp
25.00	L01 472 001*	L01 480 000*	cv	25.00	L04 096 001*	L04 100 000*	cp
25.00	L01 492 001*	L01 500 000*	cv	25.00	L04 116 001*	L04 120 000*	cp
25.00	L01 512 001*	L01 520 000*	cv	25.00	L04 136 001*	L04 140 000*	cp
25.00	L01 532 001*	L01 540 000*	cv	25.00	L04 156 001*	L04 160 000*	cp
25.00	L01 552 001*	L01 560 000*	cv	25.00	L04 176 001*	L04 180 000*	cp

DISTRICT	TOTAL NOTES PRINTED	BLOCKS	ESTIMATED VALUE VG/F	CU	LOW OFFICIAL SERIAL NUMBER	HIGH OFFICIAL SERIAL NUMBER	
				25.00	L04 196 001*	L04 200 000*	cp
				25.00	L04 216 001*	L04 220 000*	cp
				25.00	L04 236 001*	L04 240 000*	cp
				25.00	L04 256 001*	L04 260 000*	cp
				25.00	L04 276 001*	L04 280 000*	cp
				25.00	L04 296 001*	L04 300 000*	cp
				25.00	L04 316 001*	L04 320 000*	cp
				25.00	L04 336 001*	L04 340 000*	cp
				25.00	L04 356 001*	L04 360 000*	cp
				25.00	L04 376 001*	L04 380 000*	cp
				25.00	L04 396 001*	L04 400 000*	cp
				25.00	L04 416 001*	L04 420 000*	cp
				25.00	L04 436 001*	L04 460 000*	cp
				25.00	L04 456 001*	L04 480 000*	cp

CAT. NO. VF77A
$5.00 FEDERAL RESERVE NOTE (GREEN SEAL) 32 Subject
SERIES 1977A

SIGNATURES: Azie Taylor Morton, Treasurer of the United States.
  G. William Miller, Secretary of the Treasury.
SERIAL NUMBERS: Continue from previous series.
PLATE SERIALS: Continue from previous series.

	DISTRICT	TOTAL NOTES PRINTED	BLOCKS	ESTIMATED VALUE VG/F	CU	LOW OFFICIAL SERIAL NUMBER	HIGH OFFICIAL SERIAL NUMBER
1	A BOSTON		A--A		7.50	A60 800 001A	A99 840 000A
			A--B		7.50	A00 000 001B	A08 960 000B
			A--*		25.00	A03 216 001*	A03 220 000*
					25.00	A03 236 001*	A03 240 000*
					25.00	A03 256 001*	A03 260 000*
					25.00	A03 276 001*	A03 280 000*
					25.00	A03 296 001*	A03 300 000*
					25.00	A03 316 001*	A03 320 000*
					25.00	A03 336 001*	A03 340 000*
					25.00	A03 356 001*	A03 360 000*
					25.00	A03 376 001*	A03 380 000*
					25.00	A03 396 001*	A03 400 000*
					25.00	A03 416 001*	A03 420 000*
					25.00	A03 436 001*	A03 440 000*
					25.00	A03 456 001*	A03460 000*
					25.00	A03 476 001*	A03 480 000*
					25.00	A03 496 001*	A03 500 000*
					25.00	A03 516 001*	A03 520 000*
					25.00	A03 536 001*	A03 540 000*
					25.00	A03 556 001*	A03 560 000*
					25.00	A03 576 001*	A03 580 000*
					25.00	A03 596 001*	A03 600 000*
					25.00	A03 616 001*	A03 620 000*
					25.00	A03 636 001*	A03 640 000*
					25.00	A03 656 001*	A03 660 000*
					25.00	A03 676 001*	A03 680 000*
					25.00	A03 696 001*	A03 700 000*
					25.00	A03 716 001*	A03 720 000*
					25.00	A03 736 001*	A03 740 000*
					25.00	A03 756 001*	A03 760 000*
					25.00	A03 776 001*	A03 780 000*
					25.00	A03 796 001*	A03 800 000*
					25.00	A03 816 001*	A03 820 000*
					25.00	A03 836 001*	A03 840 000*
					25.00	A03 848 001*	A03 860 000*
					25.00	A03 868 001*	A03 880 000*
					25.00	A03 888 001*	A03 900 000*
					25.00	A03 908 001*	A03 920 000*
					25.00	A03 928 001*	A03 940 000*
					25.00	A03 948 001*	A03 960 000*
					25.00	A03 968 001*	A03 980 000*
					25.00	A03 988 001*	A04 000 000*
					25.00	A04 008 001*	A04 020 000*
					25.00	A04 028 001*	A04 040 000*
					25.00	A04 048 001*	A04 060 000*

DISTRICT	TOTAL NOTES PRINTED	BLOCKS	ESTIMATED VALUE VG/F	CU	LOW OFFICIAL SERIAL NUMBER	HIGH OFFICIAL SERIAL NUMBER
				25.00	A04 068 001*	A04 080 000*
				25.00	A04 088 001*	A04 100 000*
				25.00	A04 108 001*	A04 120 000*
				25.00	A04 128 001*	A04 140 000*
				25.00	A04 148 001*	A04 160 000*
				25.00	A04 168 001*	A04 180 000*
				25.00	A04 188 001*	A04 200 000*
				25.00	A04 208 001*	A04 220 000*
				25.00	A04 228 001*	A04 240 000*
				25.00	A04 248 001*	A04 260 000*
				25.00	A04 268 001*	A04 280 000*
				25.00	A04 288 001*	A04 300 000*
				25.00	A04 308 001*	A04 320 000*
				25.00	A04 328 001*	A04 340 000*
				25.00	A04 348 001*	A04 360 000*
				25.00	A04 368 001*	A04 380 000*
				25.00	A04 388 001*	A04 400 000*
				25.00	A04 408 001*	A04 420 000*
				25.00	A04 428 001*	A04 440 000*
				25.00	A04 448 001*	A04 460 000*
				25.00	A04 468 001*	A04 480 000*
2	B NEW YORK	B--B		7.50	B83 200 001B	B99 840 000B
		B--C		7.50	B00 000 001C	B97 280 000C
		B--*		25.00	B05 136 001*	B05 140 000*
				25.00	B05 156 001*	B05 160 000*
				25.00	B05 176 001*	B05 180 000*
				25.00	B05 196 001*	B05 200 000*
				25.00	B05 216 001*	B05 220 000*
				25.00	B05 236 001*	B05 240 000*
				25.00	B05 256 001*	B05 260 000*
				25.00	B05 276 001*	B05 280 000*
				25.00	B05 296 001*	B05 300 000*
				25.00	B05 316 001*	B05 320 000*
				25.00	B05 336 001*	B05 340 000*
				25.00	B05 356 001*	B05 360 000*
				25.00	B05 376 001*	B05 380 000*
				25.00	B05 396 001*	B05 400 000*
				25.00	B05 416 001*	B05 420 000*
				25.00	B05 436 001*	B05 440 000*
				25.00	B05 456 001*	B05 460 000*
				25.00	B05 476 001*	B05 480 000*
				25.00	B05 496 001*	B05 500 000*
				25.00	B05 516 001*	B05 520 000*
				25.00	B05 536 001*	B05 540 000*
				25.00	B05 556 001*	B05 560 000*
				25.00	B05 576 001*	B05 580 000*
				25.00	B05 596 001*	B05 600 000*
				25.00	B05 616 001*	B05 620 000*
				25.00	B05 636 001*	B05 640 000*
				25.00	B05 656 001*	B05 660 000*
				25.00	B05 676 001*	B05 680 000*
				25.00	B05 696 001*	B05 700 000*
				25.00	B05 716 001*	B05 720 000*
				25.00	B05 736 001*	B05 740 000*
				25.00	B05 756 001*	B05 760 000*
				10.00	B05 760 001*	B07 040 000*
				25.00	B07 048 001*	B07 060 000*
				25.00	B07 068 001*	B07 080 000*
				25.00	B07 088 001*	B07 100 000*
				25.00	B07 108 001*	B07 120 000*
				25.00	B07 128 001*	B07 140 000*
				25.00	B07 148 001*	B07 160 000*
				25.00	B07 168 001*	B07 180 000*
				25.00	B07 188 001*	B07 200 000*
				25.00	B07 208 001*	B07 220 000*
				25.00	B07 228 001*	B07 240 000*
				25.00	B07 248 001*	B07 260 000*
				25.00	B07 268 001*	B07 280 000*
				25.00	B07 288 001*	B07 300 000*

DISTRICT	TOTAL NOTES PRINTED	BLOCKS	ESTIMATED VALUE VG/F	CU	LOW OFFICIAL SERIAL NUMBER	HIGH OFFICIAL SERIAL NUMBER
				25.00	B07 308 001*	B07 320 000*
				25.00	B07 328 001*	B07 340 000*
				25.00	B07 348 001*	B07 360 000*
				25.00	B07 368 001*	B07 380 000*
				25.00	B07 388 001*	B07 400 000*
				25.00	B07 408 001*	B07 420 000*
				25.00	B07 428 001*	B07 440 000*
				25.00	B07 448 001*	B07 460 000*
				25.00	B07 468 001*	B07 480 000*
				25.00	B07 488 001*	B07 500 000*
				25.00	B07 508 001*	B07 520 000*
				25.00	B07 528 001*	B07 540 000*
				25.00	B07 548 001*	B07 560 000*
				25.00	B07 568 001*	B07 580 000*
				25.00	B07 588 001*	B07 600 000*
				25.00	B07 608 001*	B07 620 000*
				25.00	B07 628 001*	B07 640 000*
				25.00	B07 648 001*	B07 660 000*
				25.00	B07 668 001*	B07 680 000*
				25.00	B07 684 001*	B07 700 000*
				25.00	B07 704 001*	B07 720 000*
				25.00	B07 724 001*	B07 740 000*
				25.00	B07 744 001*	B07 760 000*
				25.00	B07 764 001*	B07 780 000*
				25.00	B07 784 001*	B07 800 000*
				25.00	B07 804 001*	B07 820 000*
				25.00	B07 824 001*	B07 840 000*
				25.00	B07 844 001*	B07 860 000*
				25.00	B07 864 001*	B07 880 000*
				25.00	B07 884 001*	B07 900 000*
				25.00	B07 904 001*	B07 920 000*
				25.00	B07 924 001*	B07 940 000*
				25.00	B07 944 001*	B07 960 000*
				25.00	B07 964 001*	B07 980 000*
				25.00	B07 984 001*	B08 000 000*
				25.00	B08 004 001*	B08 020 000*
				25.00	B08 024 001*	B08 040 000*
				25.00	B08 044 001*	B08 060 000*
				25.00	B08 064 001*	B08 080 000*
				25.00	B08 084 001*	B08 100 000*
				25.00	B08 104 001*	B08 120 000*
				25.00	B08 124 001*	B08 140 000*
				25.00	B08 144 001*	B08 160 000*
				25.00	B08 164 001*	B08 180 000*
				25.00	B08 184 001*	B08 200 000*
				25.00	B08 204 001*	B08 220 000*
				25.00	B08 224 001*	B08 240 000*
				25.00	B08 244 001*	B08 260 000*
				25.00	B08 264 001*	B08 280 000*
				25.00	B08 284 001*	B08 300 000*
				25.00	B08 304 001*	B08 320 000*
3	C PHILADELPHIA	C--A		7.50	C78 720 000A	C99 840 000A
		C--B		7.50	C00 000 001B	C34 560 000*
		C--*		25.00	C01 292 001*	C01 300 000*
				25.00	C01 312 001*	C01 320 000*
				25.00	C01 332 001*	C01 340 000*
				25.00	C01 352 001*	C01 360 000*
				25.00	C01 372 001*	C01 380 000*
				25.00	C01 392 001*	C01 400 000*
				25.00	C01 412 001*	C01 420 000*
				25.00	C01 432 001*	C01 440 000*
				25.00	C01 452 001*	C01 460 000*
				25.00	C01 472 001*	C01 480 000*
				25.00	C01 492 001*	C01 500 000*
				25.00	C01 512 001*	C01 520 000*
				25.00	C01 532 001*	C01 540 000*
				25.00	C01 552 001*	C01 560 000*
				25.00	C01 572 001*	C01 580 000*
				25.00	C01 592 001*	C01 600 000*
				25.00	C01 612 001*	C01 620 000*

DISTRICT	TOTAL NOTES PRINTED	BLOCKS	ESTIMATED VALUE VG/F	CU	LOW OFFICIAL SERIAL NUMBER	HIGH OFFICIAL SERIAL NUMBER
				25.00	C01 632 001*	C01 640 000*
				25.00	C01 652 001*	C01 660 000*
				25.00	C01 672 001*	C01 680 000*
				25.00	C01 692 001*	C01 700 000*
				25.00	C01 712 001*	C01 720 000*
				25.00	C01 732 001*	C01 740 000*
				25.00	C01 752 001*	C01 760 000*
				25.00	C01 772 001*	C01 780 000*
				25.00	C01 792 001*	C01 800 000*
				25.00	C01 812 001*	C01 820 000*
				25.00	C01 832 001*	C01 840 000*
				25.00	C01 852 001*	C01 860 000*
				25.00	C01 872 001*	C01 880 000*
				25.00	C01 892 001*	C01 900 000*
				25.00	C01 912 001*	C01 920 000*
				25.00	C01 928 001*	C01 940 000*
				25.00	C01 948 001*	C01 960 000*
				25.00	C01 968 001*	C01 980 000*
				25.00	C01 988 001*	C02 000 000*
				25.00	C02 008 001*	C02 020 000*
				25.00	C02 028 001*	C02 040 000*
				25.00	C02 048 001*	C02 060 000*
				25.00	C02 068 001*	C02 080 000*
				25.00	C02 088 001*	C02 100 000*
				25.00	C02 108 001*	C02 120 000*
				25.00	C02 128 001*	C02 140 000*
				25.00	C02 148 001*	C02 160 000*
				25.00	C02 168 001*	C02 180 000*
				25.00	C02 188 001*	C02 200 000*
				25.00	C02 208 001*	C02 220 000*
				25.00	C02 228 001*	C02 240 000*
				25.00	C02 248 001*	C02 260 000*
				25.00	C02 268 001*	C02 280 000*
				25.00	C02 288 001*	C02 300 000*
				25.00	C02 308 001*	C02 320 000*
				25.00	C02 328 001*	C02 340 000*
				25.00	C02 348 001*	C02 360 000*
				25.00	C02 368 001*	C02 380 000*
				25.00	C02 388 001*	C02 400 000*
				25.00	C02 408 001*	C02 420 000*
				25.00	C02 428 001*	C02 440 000*
				25.00	C02 448 001*	C02 460 000*
				25.00	C02 468 001*	C02 480 000*
				25.00	C02 488 001*	C02 500 000*
				25.00	C02 508 001*	C02 520 000*
				25.00	C02 528 001*	C02 540 000*
				25.00	C02 548 001*	C02 560 000*
4	D CLEVELAND	D--A	7.50		D72 096 001A	D99 840 000A
		D--B	7.50		D00 000 001B	D32 000 000B
		D--*		25.00	D03 216 001*	D03 220 000*
				25.00	D03 236 001*	D03 240 000*
				25.00	D03 256 001*	D03 260 000*
				25.00	D03 276 001*	D03 280 000*
				25.00	D03 296 001*	D03 300 000*
				25.00	D03 316 001*	D03 320 000*
				25.00	D03 336 001*	D03 340 000*
				25.00	D03 356 001*	D03 360 000*
				25.00	D03 376 001*	D03 380 000*
				25.00	D03 396 001*	D03 400 000*
				25.00	D03 416 001*	D03 420 000*
				25.00	D03 436 001*	D03 440 000*
				25.00	D03 456 001*	D03 460 000*
				25.00	D03 476 001*	D03 480 000*
				25.00	D03 496 001*	D03 500 000*
				25.00	D03 516 001*	D03 520 000*
				25.00	D03 536 001*	D03 540 000*
				25.00	D03 556 001*	D03 560 000*
				25.00	D03 576 001*	D03 580 000*
				25.00	D03 596 001*	D03 600 000*
				25.00	D03 616 001*	D03 620 000*

VALUE CU	LOW OFFICIAL SERIAL NUMBER	HIGH OFFICIAL SERIAL NUMBER	VALUE CU	LOW OFFICIAL SERIAL NUMBER	HIGH OFFICIAL SERIAL NUMBER
25.00	D03 636 001*	D03 640 000*	25.00	D05 016 001*	D05 020 000*
25.00	D03 656 001*	D03 660 000*	25.00	D05 036 001*	D05 040 000*
25.00	D03 676 001*	D03 680 000*	25.00	D05 056 001*	D05 060 000*
25.00	D03 696 001*	D03 700 000*	25.00	D05 076 001*	D05 080 000*
25.00	D03 716 001*	D03 720 000*	25.00	D05 096 001*	D05 100 000*
25.00	D03 736 001*	D03 740 000*	25.00	D05 116 001*	D05 120 000*
25.00	D03 756 001*	D03 760 000*	25.00	D05 128 001*	D05 140 000*
25.00	D03 776 001*	D03 780 000*	25.00	D05 148 001*	D05 160 000*
25.00	D03 796 001*	D03 800 000*	25.00	D05 168 001*	D05 180 000*
25.00	D03 816 001*	D03 820 000*	25.00	D05 188 001*	D05 200 000*
25.00	D03 836 001*	D03 840 000*	25.00	D05 208 001*	D05 220 000*
25.00	D03 856 001*	D03 860 000*	25.00	D05 228 001*	D05 240 000*
25.00	D03 876 001*	D03 880 000*	25.00	D05 248 001*	D05 260 000*
25.00	D03 896 001*	D03 900 000*	25.00	D05 268 001*	D05 280 000*
25.00	D03 916 001*	D03 920 000*	25.00	D05 288 001*	D05 300 000*
25.00	D03 936 001*	D03 940 000*	25.00	D05 308 001*	D05 320 000*
25.00	D03 956 001*	D03 960 000*	25.00	D05 328 001*	D05 340 000*
25.00	D03 976 001*	D03 980 000*	25.00	D05 348 001*	D05 360 000*
25.00	D03 996 001*	D04 000 000*	25.00	D05 368 001*	D05 380 000*
25.00	D04 016 001*	D04 020 000*	25.00	D05 388 001*	D05 400 000*
25.00	D04 036 001*	D04 040 000*	25.00	D05 408 001*	D05 420 000*
25.00	D04 056 001*	D04 060 000*	25.00	D05 428 001*	D05 440 000*
25.00	D04 076 001*	D04 080 000*	25.00	D05 448 001*	D05 460 000*
25.00	D04 096 001*	D04 100 000*	25.00	D05 468 001*	D05 480 000*
25.00	D04 116 001*	D04 120 000*	25.00	D05 488 001*	D05 500 000*
25.00	D04 136 001*	D04 140 000*	25.00	D05 508 001*	D05 520 000*
25.00	D04 156 001*	D04 160 000*	25.00	D05 528 001*	D05 540 000*
25.00	D04 176 001*	D04 180 000*	25.00	D05 548 001*	D05 560 000*
25.00	D04 196 001*	D04 200 000*	25.00	D05 568 001*	D05 580 000*
25.00	D04 216 001*	D04 220 000*	25.00	D05 588 001*	D05 600 000*
25.00	D04 236 001*	D04 240 000*	25.00	D05 608 001*	D05 620 000*
25.00	D04 256 001*	D04 260 000*	25.00	D05 628 001*	D05 640 000*
25.00	D04 276 001*	D04 280 000*	25.00	D05 648 001*	D05 660 000*
25.00	D04 296 001*	D04 300 000*	25.00	D05 668 001*	D05 680 000*
25.00	D04 316 001*	D04 320 000*	25.00	D05 688 001*	D05 700 000*
25.00	D04 336 001*	D04 340 000*	25.00	D05 708 001*	D05 720 000*
25.00	D04 356 001*	D04 360 000*	25.00	D05 728 001*	D05 740 000*
25.00	D04 376 001*	D04 380 000*	25.00	D05 748 001*	D05 760 000*
25.00	D04 396 001*	D04 400 000*	25.00	D05 764 001*	D05 780 000*
25.00	D04 416 001*	D04 420 000*	25.00	D05 784 001*	D05 800 000*
25.00	D04 436 001*	D04 440 000*	25.00	D05 804 001*	D05 820 000*
25.00	D04 456 001*	D04 460 000*	25.00	D05 824 001*	D05 840 000*
25.00	D04 476 001*	D04 480 000*	25.00	D05 844 001*	D05 860 000*
25.00	D04 496 001*	D04 500 000*	25.00	D05 864 001*	D05 880 000*
25.00	D04 516 001*	D04 520 000*	25.00	D05 884 001*	D05 900 000*
25.00	D04 536 001*	D04 540 000*	25.00	D05 904 001*	D05 920 000*
25.00	D04 556 001*	D04 560 000*	25.00	D05 924 001*	D05 940 000*
25.00	D04 576 001*	D04 580 000*	25.00	D05 944 001*	D05 960 000*
25.00	D04 596 001*	D04 600 000*	25.00	D05 964 001*	D05 980 000*
25.00	D04 616 001*	D04 620 000*	25.00	D05 984 001*	D06 000 000*
25.00	D04 636 001*	D04 640 000*	25.00	D06 004 001*	D06 020 000*
25.00	D04 656 001*	D04 660 000*	25.00	D06 024 001*	D06 040 000*
25.00	D04 676 001*	D04 680 000*	25.00	D06 044 001*	D06 060 000*
25.00	D04 696 001*	D04 700 000*	25.00	D06 064 001*	D06 080 000*
25.00	D04 716 001*	D04 720 000*	25.00	D06 084 001*	D06 100 000*
25.00	D04 736 001*	D04 740 000*	25.00	D06 104 001*	D06 120 000*
25.00	D04 756 001*	D04 760 000*	25.00	D06 124 001*	D06 140 000*
25.00	D04 776 001*	D04 780 000*	25.00	D06 144 001*	D06 160 000*
25.00	D04 796 001*	D04 800 000*	25.00	D06 164 001*	D06 180 000*
25.00	D04 816 001*	D04 820 000*	25.00	D06 184 001*	D06 200 000*
25.00	D04 836 001*	D04 840 000*	25.00	D06 204 001*	D06 220 000*
25.00	D04 856 001*	D04 860 000*	25.00	D06 224 001*	D06 240 000*
25.00	D04 876 001*	D04 880 000*	25.00	D06 244 001*	D06 260 000*
25.00	D04 896 001*	D04 900 000*	25.00	D06 264 001*	D06 280 000*
25.00	D04 916 001*	D04 920 000*	25.00	D06 284 001*	D06 300 000*
25.00	D04 936 001*	D04 940 000*	25.00	D06 304 001*	D06 320 000*
25.00	D04 956 001*	D04 960 000*	25.00	D06 324 001*	D06 340 000*
25.00	D04 976 001*	D04 980 000*	25.00	D06 344 001*	D06 360 000*
25.00	D04 996 001*	D05 000 000*	25.00	D06 364 001*	D06 380 000*

DISTRICT	TOTAL NOTES PRINTED	BLOCKS	ESTIMATED VALUE VG/F CU	LOW OFFICIAL SERIAL NUMBER	HIGH OFFICIAL SERIAL NUMBER
5 E Richmond			25.00	D06 384 001*	D06 400 000*
		E--B	7.50	E10 880 001B	E88 320 000B
		E--*	25.00	E03 856 001*	E03 860 000*
			25.00	E03 876 001*	E03 880 000*
			25.00	E03 896 001*	E03 900 000*
			25.00	E03 916 001*	E03 920 000*
			25.00	E03 936 001*	E03 940 000*
			25.00	E03 956 001*	E03 960 000*
			25.00	E03 976 001*	E03 980 000*
			25.00	E03 996 001*	E04 000 000*
			25.00	E04 016 001*	E04 020 000*
			25.00	E04 036 001*	E04 040 000*
			25.00	E04 056 001*	E04 060 000*
			25.00	E04 076 001*	E04 080 000*
			25.00	E04 096 001*	E04 100 000*
			25.00	E04 116 001*	E04 120 000*
			25.00	E04 136 001*	E04 140 000*
			25.00	E04 156 001*	E04 160 000*
			25.00	E04 176 001*	E04 180 000*
			25.00	E04 196 001*	E04 200 000*
			25.00	E04 216 001*	E04 220 000*
			25.00	E04 236 001*	E04 240 000*
			25.00	E04 256 001*	E04 260 000*
			25.00	E04 276 001*	E04 280 000*
			25.00	E04 296 001*	E04 300 000*
			25.00	E04 316 001*	E04 320 000*
			25.00	E04 336 001*	E04 340 000*
			25.00	E04 356 001*	E04 360 000*
			25.00	E04 376 001*	E04 380 000*
			25.00	E04 396 001*	E04 400 000*
			25.00	E04 416 001*	E04 420 000*
			25.00	E04 436 001*	E04 440 000*
			25.00	E04 456 001*	E04 460 000*
			25.00	E04 476 001*	E04 480 000*
			10.00	E04 480 001*	E05 120 000*
6 F Atlanta		F--B	7.50	F27 520 001B	F99 840 000B
		F--C	7.50	F00 000 001C	F03 840 000C
		F--*	25.00	F02 576 001*	F02 580 000*
			25.00	F02 596 001*	F02 600 000*
			25.00	F02 616 001*	F02 620 000*
			25.00	F02 636 001*	F02 640 000*
			25.00	F02 656 001*	F02 660 000*
			25.00	F02 676 001*	F02 680 000*
			25.00	F02 696 001*	F02 700 000*
			25.00	F02 716 001*	F02 720 000*
			25.00	F02 736 001*	F02 740 000*
			25.00	F02 756 001*	F02 760 000*
			25.00	F02 776 001*	F02 780 000*
			25.00	F02 796 001*	F02 800 000*
			25.00	F02 816 001*	F02 820 000*
			25.00	F02 836 001*	F02 840 000*
			25.00	F02 856 001*	F02 860 000*
			25.00	F02 876 001*	F02 880 000*
			25.00	F02 896 001*	F02 900 000*
			25.00	F02 916 001*	F02 920 000*
			25.00	F02 936 001*	F02 940 000*
			25.00	F02 956 001*	F02 960 000*
			25.00	F02 976 001*	F02 980 000*
			25.00	F02 996 001*	F03 000 000*
			25.00	F03 016 001*	F03 020 000*
			25.00	F03 036 001*	F03 040 000*
			25.00	F03 056 001*	F03 060 000*
			25.00	F03 076 001*	F03 080 000*
			25.00	F03 096 001*	F03 100 000*
			25.00	F03 116 001*	F03 120 000*
			25.00	F03 136 001*	F03 140 000*
			25.00	F03 156 001*	F03 160 000*
			25.00	F03 176 001*	F03 180 000*
			25.00	F03 196 001*	F03 200 000*

DISTRICT	TOTAL NOTES PRINTED	BLOCKS	ESTIMATED VALUE VG/F	CU	LOW OFFICIAL SERIAL NUMBER	HIGH OFFICIAL SERIAL NUMBER
				25.00	F03 216 001*	F03 220 000*
				25.00	F03 236 001*	F03 240 000*
				25.00	F03 256 001*	F03 260 000*
				25.00	F03 276 001*	F03 280 000*
				25.00	F03 296 001*	F03 300 000*
				25.00	F03 316 001*	F03 320 000*
				25.00	F03 336 001*	F03 340 000*
				25.00	F03 356 001*	F03 360 000*
				25.00	F03 376 001*	F03 380 000*
				25.00	F03 396 001*	F03 400 000*
				25.00	F03 416 001*	F03 420 000*
				25.00	F03 436 001*	F03 440 000*
				25.00	F03 456 001*	F03 460 000*
				25.00	F03 476 001*	F03 480 000*
				25.00	F03 496 001*	F03 500 000*
				25.00	F03 516 001*	F03 520 000*
				25.00	F03 536 001*	F03 540 000*
				25.00	F03 556 001*	F03 560 000*
				25.00	F03 576 001*	F03 580 000*
				25.00	F03 596 001*	F03 600 000*
				25.00	F03 616 001*	F03 620 000*
				25.00	F03 636 001*	F03 640 000*
				25.00	F03 656 001*	F03 660 000*
				25.00	F03 676 001*	F03 680 000*
				25.00	F03 696 001*	F03 700 000*
				25.00	F03 716 001*	F03 720 000*
				25.00	F03 736 001*	F03 740 000*
				25.00	F03 756 001*	F03 760 000*
				25.00	F03 776 001*	F03 780 000*
				25.00	F03 796 001*	F03 800 000*
				25.00	F03 816 001*	F03 820 000*
				25.00	F03 836 001*	F03 840 000*
				25.00	F03 852 001*	F03 860 000*
				25.00	F03 872 001*	F03 880 000*
				25.00	F03 892 001*	F03 900 000*
				25.00	F03 912 001*	F03 920 000*
				25.00	F03 932 001*	F03 940 000*
				25.00	F03 952 001*	F03 960 000*
				25.00	F03 972 001*	F03 980 000*
				25.00	F03 992 001*	F04 000 000*
				25.00	F04 012 001*	F04 020 000*
				25.00	F04 032 001*	F04 040 000*
				25.00	F04 052 001*	F04 060 000*
				25.00	F04 072 001*	F04 080 000*
				25.00	F04 092 001*	F04 100 000*
				25.00	F04 112 001*	F04 120 000*
				25.00	F04 132 001*	F04 140 000*
				25.00	F04 152 001*	F04 160 000*
				25.00	F04 172 001*	F04 180 000*
				25.00	F04 192 001*	F04 200 000*
				25.00	F04 212 001*	F04 220 000*
				25.00	F04 232 001*	F04 240 000*
				25.00	F04 252 001*	F04 260 000*
				25.00	F04 272 001*	F04 280 000*
				25.00	F04 292 001*	F04 300 000*
				25.00	F04 312 001*	F04 320 000*
				25.00	F04 332 001*	F04 340 000*
				25.00	F04 352 001*	F04 360 000*
				25.00	F04 372 001*	F04 380 000*
				25.00	F04 392 001*	F04 400 000*
				25.00	F04 412 001*	F04 420 000*
				25.00	F04 432 001*	F04 440 000*
				25.00	F04 452 001*	F04 460 000*
				25.00	F04 472 001*	F04 480 000*
				10.00	F04 480 001*	F05 120 000*
7	G Chicago	G--B		7.50	G77 040 001B	G99 840 000B
		G--C		7.50	G00 000 001C	G58 880 000C
		G--*		25.00	G03 844 001*	G03 860 000*
				25.00	G03 864 001*	G03 880 000*
				25.00	G03 884 001*	G03 900 000*

DISTRICT	TOTAL NOTES PRINTED	BLOCKS	ESTIMATED VALUE VG/F	CU	LOW OFFICIAL SERIAL NUMBER	HIGH OFFICIAL SERIAL NUMBER
				25.00	F03 904 001*	G03 920 000*
				25.00	G03 924 001*	G03 940 000*
				25.00	G03 944 001*	G03 960 000*
				25.00	G03 964 001*	G03 980 000*
				25.00	G03 984 001*	G04 000 000*
				25.00	G04 004 001*	G04 020 000*
				25.00	G04 024 001*	G04 040 000*
				25.00	G04 044 001*	G04 060 000*
				25.00	G04 064 001*	G04 080 000*
				25.00	G04 084 001*	G04 100 000*
				25.00	G04 104 001*	G04 120 000*
				25.00	G04 124 001*	G04 140 000*
				25.00	G04 144 001*	G04 160 000*
				25.00	G04 164 001*	G04 180 000*
				25.00	G04 184 001*	G04 200 000*
				25.00	G04 204 001*	G04 220 000*
				25.00	G04 224 001*	G04 240 000*
				25.00	G04 244 001*	G04 260 000*
				25.00	G04 264 001*	G04 280 000*
				25.00	G04 284 001*	G04 300 000*
				25.00	G04 304 001*	G04 320 000*
				25.00	G04 324 001*	G04 340 000*
				25.00	G04 344 001*	G04 360 000*
				25.00	G04 364 001*	G04 380 000*
				25.00	G04 384 001*	G04 400 000*
				25.00	G04 404 001*	G04 420 000*
				25.00	G04 424 001*	G04 440 000*
				25.00	G04 444 001*	G04 460 000*
				25.00	G04 464 001*	G04 480 000*
				25.00	G04 492 001*	G04 500 000*
				25.00	G04 512 001*	G04 520 000*
				25.00	G04 532 001*	G04 540 000*
				25.00	G04 552 001*	G04 560 000*
				25.00	G04 572 001*	G04 580 000*
				25.00	G04 592 001*	G04 600 000*
				25.00	G04 612 001*	G04 620 000*
				25.00	G04 632 001*	G04 640 000*
				25.00	G04 652 001*	G04 660 000*
				25.00	G04 672 001*	G04 680 000*
				25.00	G04 692 001*	G04 700 000*
				25.00	G04 712 001*	G04 720 000*
				25.00	G04 732 001*	G04 740 000*
				25.00	G04 752 001*	G04 760 000*
				25.00	G04 772 001*	G04 780 000*
				25.00	G04 792 001*	G04 800 000*
				25.00	G04 812 001*	G04 820 000*
				25.00	G04 832 001*	G04 840 000*
				25.00	G04 852 001*	G04 860 000*
				25.00	G04 872 001*	G04 880 000*
				25.00	G04 892 001*	G04 900 000*
				25.00	G04 912 001*	G04 920 000*
				25.00	G04 932 001*	G04 940 000*
				25.00	G04 952 001*	G04 960 000*
				25.00	G04 972 001*	G04 980 000*
				25.00	G04 992 001*	G05 000 000*
				25.00	G05 012 001*	G05 020 000*
				25.00	G05 032 001*	G05 040 000*
				25.00	G05 052 001*	G05 060 000*
				25.00	G05 072 001*	G05 080 000*
				25.00	G05 092 001*	G05 100 000*
				25.00	G05 112 001*	G05 120 000*
				25.00	G05 132 001*	G05 140 000*
				25.00	G05 152 001*	G05 160 000*
				25.00	G05 172 001*	G05 180 000*
				25.00	G05 192 001*	G05 200 000*
				25.00	G05 212 001*	G05 220 000*
				25.00	G05 232 001*	G05 240 000*
				25.00	G05 252 001*	G05 260 000*
				25.00	G05 272 001*	G05 280 000*

DISTRICT	TOTAL NOTES PRINTED	BLOCKS	ESTIMATED VALUE VG/F	VALUE CU	LOW OFFICIAL SERIAL NUMBER	HIGH OFFICIAL SERIAL NUMBER
				25.00	G05 292 001*	G05 300 000*
				25.00	G05 312 001*	G05 320 000*
				25.00	G05 332 001*	G05 340 000*
				25.00	G05 352 001*	G05 360 000*
				25.00	G05 372 001*	G05 380 000*
				25.00	G05 392 001*	G05 400 000*
				25.00	G05 412 001*	G05 420 000*
				25.00	G05 432 001*	G05 440 000*
				25.00	G05 452 001*	G05 460 000*
				25.00	G05 472 001*	G05 480 000*
				25.00	G05 492 001*	G05 500 000*
				25.00	G05 512 001*	G05 520 000*
				25.00	G05 532 001*	G05 540 000*
				25.00	G05 552 001*	G05 560 000*
				25.00	G05 572 001*	G05 580 000*
				25.00	G05 592 001*	G05 600 000*
				25.00	G05 612 001*	G05 620 000*
				25.00	G05 632 001*	G05 640 000*
				25.00	G05 652 001*	G05 660 000*
				25.00	G05 672 001*	G05 680 000*
				25.00	G05 692 001*	G05 700 000*
				25.00	G05 712 001*	G05 720 000*
				25.00	G05 732 001*	G05 740 000*
				25.00	G05 752 001*	G05 760 000*
				25.00	G05 768 001*	G05 780 000*
				25.00	G05 788 001*	G05 800 000*
				25.00	G05 808 001*	G05 820 000*
				25.00	G05 828 001*	G05 840 000*
				25.00	G05 848 001*	G05 860 000*
				25.00	G05 868 001*	G05 880 000*
				25.00	G05 888 001*	G05 900 000*
				25.00	G05 908 001*	G05 920 000*
				25.00	G05 928 001*	G05 940 000*
				25.00	G05 948 001*	G05 960 000*
				25.00	G05 968 001*	G05 980 000*
				25.00	G05 988 001*	G06 000 000*
				25.00	G06 008 001*	G06 020 000*
				25.00	G06 028 001*	G06 040 000*
				25.00	G06 048 001*	G06 060 000*
				25.00	G06 068 001*	G06 080 000*
				25.00	G06 088 001*	G06 100 000*
				25.00	G06 108 001*	G06 120 000*
				25.00	G06 128 001*	G06 140 000*
				25.00	G06 148 001*	G06 160 000*
				25.00	G06 168 001*	G06 180 000*
				25.00	G06 188 001*	G06 200 000*
				25.00	G06 208 001*	G06 220 000*
				25.00	G06 228 001*	G06 240 000*
				25.00	G06 248 001*	G06 260 000*
				25.00	G06 268 001*	G06 280 000*
				25.00	G06 288 001*	G06 300 000*
				25.00	G06 308 001*	G06 320 000*
				25.00	G06 328 001*	G06 340 000*
				25.00	G06 348 001*	G06 360 000*
				25.00	G06 368 001*	G06 380 000*
				25.00	G06 388 001*	G06 400 000*
8 H ST. LOUIS		H--A		7.50	H46 080 001A	H78 080 000A
		H--*		25.00	H00 656 001*	H00 660 000*
				25.00	H00 676 001*	H00 680 000*
				25.00	H00 696 001*	H00 700 000*
				25.00	H00 716 001*	H00 720 000*
				25.00	H00 736 001*	H00 740 000*
				25.00	H00 756 001*	H00 760 000*
				25.00	H00 776 001*	H00 780 000*
				25.00	H00 796 001*	H00 800 000*
				25.00	H00 816 001*	H00 820 000*
				25.00	H00 836 001*	H00 840 000*
				25.00	H00 856 001*	H00 860 000*
				25.00	H00 876 001*	H00 880 000*

DISTRICT	TOTAL NOTES PRINTED	BLOCKS	ESTIMATED VALUE VG/F	CU	LOW OFFICIAL SERIAL NUMBER	HIGH OFFICIAL SERIAL NUMBER
				25.00	H00 896 001*	H00 900 000*
				25.00	H00 916 001*	H00 920 000*
				25.00	H00 936 001*	H00 940 000*
				25.00	H00 956 001*	H00 960 000*
				25.00	H00 976 001*	H00 980 000*
				25.00	H00 996 001*	H01 000 000*
				25.00	H01 016 001*	H01 020 000*
				25.00	H01 036 001*	H01 040 000*
				25.00	H01 056 001*	H01 060 000*
				25.00	H01 076 001*	H01 080 000*
				25.00	H01 096 001*	H01 100 000*
				25.00	H01 116 001*	H01 120 000*
				25.00	H01 136 001*	H01 140 000*
				25.00	H01 156 001*	H01 160 000*
				25.00	H01 176 001*	H01 180 000*
				25.00	H01 196 001*	H01 200 000*
				25.00	H01 216 001*	H01 220 000*
				25.00	H01 236 001*	H01 240 000*
				25.00	H01 256 001*	H01 260 000*
				25.00	H01 276 001*	H01 280 000*
				25.00	H01 292 001*	H01 300 000*
				25.00	H01 312 001*	H01 320 000*
				25.00	H01 332 001*	H03 340 000*
				25.00	H01 352 001*	H01 360 000*
				25.00	H01 372 001*	H01 380 000*
				25.00	H01 392 001*	H01 400 000*
				25.00	H01 412 001*	H01 420 000*
				25.00	H01 432 001*	H01 440 000*
				25.00	H01 452 001*	H01 460 000*
				25.00	H01 472 001*	H01 480 000*
				25.00	H01 492 001*	H01 500 000*
				25.00	H01 512 001*	H01 520 000*
				25.00	H01 532 001*	H01 540 000*
				25.00	H01 552 001*	H01 560 000*
				25.00	H01 572 001*	H01 580 000*
				25.00	H01 592 001*	H01 600 000*
				25.00	H01 612 001*	H01 620 000*
				25.00	H01 632 001*	H01 640 000*
				25.00	H01 652 001*	H01 660 000*
				25.00	H01 672 001*	H01 680 000*
				25.00	H01 692 001*	H01 700 000*
				25.00	H01 712 001*	H01 720 000*
				25.00	H01 732 001*	H01 740 000*
				25.00	H01 752 001*	H01 760 000*
				25.00	H01 772 001*	H01 780 000*
				25.00	H01 792 001*	H01 800 000*
				25.00	H01 812 001*	H01 820 000*
				25.00	H01 832 001*	H01 840 000*
				25.00	H01 852 001*	H01 860 000*
				25.00	H01 872 001*	H01 880 000*
				25.00	H01 892 001*	H01 900 000*
				25.00	H01 912 001*	H01 920 000*
				25.00	H01 932 001*	H01 940 000*
				25.00	H01 952 001*	H01 960 000*
				25.00	H01 972 001*	H01 980 000*
				25.00	H01 992 001*	H02 000 000*
				25.00	H02 012 001*	H02 020 000*
				25.00	H02 032 001*	H02 040 000*
				25.00	H02 052 001*	H02 060 000*
				25.00	H02 072 001*	H02 080 000*
				25.00	H02 092 001*	H02 100 000*
				25.00	H02 112 001*	H02 120 000*
				25.00	H02 132 001*	H02 140 000*
				25.00	H02 152 001*	H02 160 000*
				25.00	H02 172 001*	H02 180 000*
				25.00	H02 192 001*	H02 200 000*
				25.00	H02 212 001*	H02 220 000*
				25.00	H02 232 001*	H02 240 000*
				25.00	H02 252 001*	H02 260 000*
				25.00	H02 272 001*	H02 280 000*

DISTRICT	TOTAL NOTES PRINTED	BLOCKS	ESTIMATED VALUE VG/F	CU	LOW OFFICIAL SERIAL NUMBER	HIGH OFFICIAL SERIAL NUMBER
				25.00	H02 292 001*	H02 300 000*
				25.00	H02 312 001*	H02 320 000*
				25.00	H02 332 001*	H02 340 000*
				25.00	H02 352 001*	H02 360 000*
				25.00	H02 372 001*	H02 380 000*
				25.00	H02 392 001*	H02 400 000*
				25.00	H02 412 001*	H02 420 000*
				25.00	H02 432 001*	H02 440 000*
				25.00	H02 452 001*	H02 460 000*
				25.00	H02 472 001*	H02 480 000*
				25.00	H02 492 001*	H02 500 000*
				25.00	H02 512 001*	H02 520 000*
				25.00	H02 532 001*	H02 540 000*
				25.00	H02 552 001*	H02 560 000*
9	I MINNEAPOLIS	I--A		7.50	I21 760 001A	I32 000 000A
		I--*		25.00	I00 016 001*	I00 020 000*
				25.00	I00 036 001*	I00 040 000*
				25.00	I00 056 001*	I00 060 000*
				25.00	I00 076 001*	I00 080 000*
				25.00	I00 096 001*	I00 100 000*
				25.00	I00 116 001*	I00 120 000*
				25.00	I00 136 001*	I00 140 000*
				25.00	I00 156 001*	I00 160 000*
				25.00	I00 176 001*	I00 180 000*
				25.00	I00 196 001*	I00 200 000*
				25.00	I00 216 001*	I00 220 000*
				25.00	I00 236 001*	I00 240 000*
				25.00	I00 256 001*	I00 260 000*
				25.00	I00 276 001*	I00 280 000*
				25.00	I00 296 001*	I00 300 000*
				25.00	I00 316 001*	I00 320 000*
				25.00	I00 336 001*	I00 340 000*
				25.00	I00 356 001*	I00 360 000*
				25.00	I00 376 001*	I00 380 000*
				25.00	I00 396 001*	I00 400 000*
				25.00	I00 416 001*	I00 420 000*
				25.00	I00 436 001*	I00 440 000*
				25.00	I00 456 001*	I00 460 000*
				25.00	I00 476 001*	I00 480 000*
				25.00	I00 496 001*	I00 500 000*
				25.00	I00 516 001*	I00 520 000*
				25.00	I00 536 001*	I00 540 000*
				25.00	I00 556 001*	I00 560 000*
				25.00	I00 576 001*	I00 580 000*
				25.00	I00 596 001*	I00 600 000*
				25.00	I00 616 001*	I00 620 000*
				25.00	I00 636 001*	I00 640 000*
10	J KANSAS CITY	J--A		7.50	J78 080 001A	J99 840 000A
		J--B		7.50	J00 000 001B	J30 720 000B
		J--*		25.00	J01 928 001*	J01 940 000*
				25.00	J01 948 001*	J01 960 000*
				25.00	J01 968 001*	J01 980 000*
				25.00	J01 988 001*	J02 000 000*
				25.00	J02 008 001*	J02 020 000*
				25.00	J02 028 001*	J02 040 000*
				25.00	J02 048 001*	J02 060 000*
				25.00	J02 068 001*	J02 080 000*
				25.00	J02 088 001*	J02 100 000*
				25.00	J02 108 001*	J02 120 000*
				25.00	J02 128 001*	J02 140 000*
				25.00	J02 148 001*	J02 160 000*
				25.00	J02 168 001*	J02 180 000*
				25.00	J02 188 001*	J02 200 000*
				25.00	J02 208 001*	J02 220 000*
				25.00	J02 228 001*	J02 240 000*
				25.00	J02 248 001*	J02 260 000*
				25.00	J02 268 001*	J02 280 000*
				25.00	J02 288 001*	J02 300 000*
				25.00	J02 308 001*	J02 320 000*
				25.00	J02 328 001*	J02 340 000*

DISTRICT	TOTAL NOTES PRINTED	BLOCKS	ESTIMATED VALUE VG/F	CU	LOW OFFICIAL SERIAL NUMBER	HIGH OFFICIAL SERIAL NUMBER
				25.00	J02 348 001*	J02 360 000*
				25.00	J02 368 001*	J02 380 000*
				25.00	J02 388 001*	J02 400 000*
				25.00	J02 408 001*	J02 420 000*
				25.00	J02 428 001*	J02 440 000*
				25.00	J02 448 001*	J02 460 000*
				25.00	J02 468 001*	J02 480 000*
				25.00	J02 488 001*	J02 500 000*
				25.00	J02 508 001*	J02 520 000*
				25.00	J02 528 001*	J02 540 000*
				25.00	J02 548 001*	J02 560 000*
				10.00	J02 560 001*	J03 200 000*
11 K DALLAS		K--A		7.50	K60 800 001A	K99 840 000A
		K--B		7.50	K00 000 001A	K37 120 000B
		K--*		25.00	K02 576 001*	K02 580 000*
				25.00	K02 596 001*	K02 600 000*
				25.00	K02 616 001*	K02 620 000*
				25.00	K02 636 001*	K02 640 000*
				25.00	K02 656 001*	K02 660 000*
				25.00	K02 676 001*	K02 680 000*
				25.00	K02 696 001*	K02 700 000*
				25.00	k02 716 001*	K02 720 000*
				25.00	K02 736 001*	K02 740 000*
				25.00	K02 756 001*	K02 760 000*
				25.00	K02 776 001*	K02 780 000*
				25.00	K02 796 001*	K02 800 000*
				25.00	K02 816 001*	K02 820 000*
				25.00	K02 836 001*	K02 840 000*
				25.00	K02 856 001*	K02 860 000*
				25.00	K02 876 001*	K02 880 000*
				25.00	K02 896 001*	K02 900 000*
				25.00	K02 916 001*	K02 920 000*
				25.00	K02 936 001*	K02 940 000*
				25.00	K02 956 001*	K02 960 000*
				25.00	K02 976 001*	K02 980 000*
				25.00	K02 996 001*	K03 000 000*
				25.00	K03 016 001*	K03 020 000*
				25.00	K03 036 001*	K03 040 000*
				25.00	K03 056 001*	K03 060 000*
				25.00	K03 076 001*	K03 080 000*
				25.00	K03 096 001*	K03 100 000*
				25.00	K03 116 001*	K03 120 000*
				25.00	K03 136 001*	K03 140 000*
				25.00	K03 156 001*	K03 160 000*
				25.00	K03 176 001*	K03 180 000*
				25.00	K03 196 001*	K03 200 000*
				25.00	K03 212 001*	K03 220 000*
				25.00	K03 232 001*	K03 240 000*
				25.00	K03 252 001*	K03 260 000*
				25.00	K03 272 001*	K03 280 000*
				25.00	K03 292 001*	K03 300 000*
				25.00	K03 312 001*	K03 320 000*
				25.00	K03 332 001*	K03 340 000*
				25.00	K03 352 001*	K03 360 000*
				25.00	K03 372 001*	K03 380 000*
				25.00	K03 392 001*	K03 400 000*
				25.00	K03 412 001*	K03 420 000*
				25.00	K03 432 001*	K03 440 000*
				25.00	K03 452 001*	K03 460 000*
				25.00	K03 472 001*	K03 480 000*
				25.00	K03 492 001*	K03 500 000*
				25.00	K03 512 001*	K03 520 000*
				25.00	K03 532 001*	K03 540 000*
				25.00	K03 552 001*	K03 560 000*
				25.00	K03 572 001*	K03 580 000*
				25.00	K03 592 001*	K03 600 000*
				25.00	K03 612 001*	K03 620 000*
				25.00	K03 632 001*	K03 640 000*
				25.00	K03 652 001*	K03 660 000*
				25.00	K03 672 001*	K03 680 000*

DISTRICT	TOTAL NOTES PRINTED	BLOCKS	ESTIMATED VALUE VG/F	CU	LOW OFFICIAL SERIAL NUMBER	HIGH OFFICIAL SERIAL NUMBER
				25.00	K03 692 001*	K03 700 000*
				25.00	K03 712 001*	K03 720 000*
				25.00	K03 732 001*	K03 740 000*
				25.00	K03 752 001*	K03 760 000*
				25.00	K03 772 001*	K03 780 000*
				25.00	K03 792 001*	K03 800 000*
				25.00	K03 812 001*	K03 820 000*
				25.00	K03 832 001*	K03 840 000*
				25.00	K03 852 001*	K03 860 000*
				25.00	K03 872 001*	K03 880 000*
				25.00	K03 892 001*	K03 900 000*
				25.00	K03 912 001*	K03 920 000*
				25.00	K03 932 001*	K03 940 000*
				25.00	K03 952 001*	K03 960 000*
				25.00	K03 972 001*	K03 980 000*
				25.00	K03 992 001*	K04 000 000*
				25.00	K04 012 001*	K04 020 000*
				25.00	K04 032 001*	K04 040 000*
				25.00	K04 052 001*	K04 060 000*
				25.00	K04 072 001*	K04 080 000*
				25.00	K04 092 001*	K04 100 000*
				25.00	K04 112 001*	K04 120 000*
				25.00	K04 132 001*	K04 140 000*
				25.00	K04 152 001*	K04 160 000*
				25.00	K04 172 001*	K04 180 000*
				25.00	K04 192 001*	K04 200 000*
				25.00	K04 212 001*	K04 220 000*
				25.00	K04 232 001*	K04 240 000*
				25.00	K04 252 001*	K04 260 000*
				25.00	K04 272 001*	K04 280 000*
				25.00	K04 292 001*	K04 300 000*
				25.00	K04 312 001*	K04 320 000*
				25.00	K04 332 001*	K04 340 000*
				25.00	K04 352 001*	K04 360 000*
				25.00	K04 372 001*	K04 380 000*
				25.00	K04 392 001*	K04 400 000*
				25.00	K04 412 001*	K04 420 000*
				25.00	K04 432 001*	K04 440 000*
				25.00	K04 452 001*	K04 460 000*
				25.00	K04 472 001*	K04 480 000*
				25.00	K04 480 001*	K05 760 000*
12 L SAN FRANCISCO		L--B		7.50	L44 800 001B	L99 840 000B
		L--C		7.50	L00 000 001C	L42 240 000C
		L--*		10.00	L04 480 001*	L05 120 000*
		L--*		25.00	L05 132 001*	L05 140 000*
				25.00	L05 152 001*	L05 160 000*
				25.00	L05 172 001*	L05 180 000*
				25.00	L05 192 001*	L05 200 000*
				25.00	L02 212 001*	L05 220 000*
				25.00	L05 232 001*	L05 240 000*
				25.00	L05 252 001*	L05 260 000*
				25.00	L05 272 001*	L05 280 000*
				25.00	L05 292 001*	L05 300 000*
				25.00	L05 312 001*	L05 320 000*
				25.00	L05 332 001*	L05 340 000*
				25.00	L05 352 001*	L05 360 000*
				25.00	L05 372 001*	L05 380 000*
				25.00	L05 392 001*	L05 400 000*
				25.00	L05 412 001*	L05 420 000*
				25.00	L05 432 001*	L05 440 000*
				25.00	L05 452 001*	L05 460 000*
				25.00	L05 472 001*	L05 480 000*
				25.00	L05 492 001*	L05 500 000*
				25.00	L05 512 001*	L05 520 000*
				25.00	L05 532 001*	L05 540 000*
				25.00	L05 552 001*	L05 560 000*
				25.00	L05 572 001*	L05 580 000*
				25.00	L05 592 001*	L05 600 000*
				25.00	L05 612 001*	L05 620 000*
				25.00	L05 632 001*	L05 640 000*

DISTRICT	TOTAL NOTES PRINTED	BLOCKS	ESTIMATED VALUE VG/F	CU	LOW OFFICIAL SERIAL NUMBER	HIGH OFFICIAL SERIAL NUMBER
				25.00	L05 652 001*	L05 660 000*
				25.00	L05 672 001*	L05 680 000*
				25.00	L05 692 001*	L05 700 000*
				25.00	L05 712 001*	L05 720 000*
				25.00	L05 732 001*	L05 740 000*
				25.00	L05 752 001*	L05 760 000*
				25.00	L05 772 001*	L05 780 000*
				25.00	L05 792 001*	L05 800 000*
				25.00	L05 812 001*	L05 820 000*
				25.00	L05 832 001*	L05 840 000*
				25.00	L05 852 001*	L05 860 000*
				25.00	L05 872 001*	L05 880 000*
				25.00	L05 892 001*	L05 900 000*
				25.00	L05 912 001*	L05 920 000*
				25.00	L05 932 001*	L05 940 000*
				25.00	L05 952 001*	L05 960 000*
				25.00	L05 972 001*	L05 980 000*
				25.00	L05 992 001*	L06 000 000*
				25.00	L06 012 001*	L06 020 000*
				25.00	L06 032 001*	L06 040 000*
				25.00	L06 052 001*	L06 060 000*
				25.00	L06 072 001*	L06 080 000*
				25.00	L06 092 001*	L06 100 000*
				25.00	L06 112 001*	L06 120 000*
				25.00	L06 132 001*	L06 140 000*
				25.00	L06 152 001*	L06 160 000*
				25.00	L06 172 001*	L06 180 000*
				25.00	L06 192 001*	L06 200 000*
				25.00	L06 212 001*	L06 220 000*
				25.00	L06 232 001*	L06 240 000*
				25.00	L06 252 001*	L06 260 000*
				25.00	L06 272 001*	L06 280 000*
				25.00	L06 292 001*	L06 300 000*
				25.00	L06 312 001*	L06 320 000*
				25.00	L06 332 001*	L06 340 000*
				25.00	L06 352 001*	L06 360 000*
				25.00	L06 372 001*	L06 380 000*
				25.00	L06 392 001*	L06 400 000*

The production unit was changed from 20,000 sheets to 40,000 sheets for

BANK	STARTING WITH SERIAL	BANK	STARTING WITH SERIAL
Boston	A78 080 001A	Chicago	G10 240 001C
New York	B28 160 001C	St. Louis	H70 400 001A
Philadelphia	C90 880 001A	Minneapolis	I21 760 001A
Cleveland	D02 560 001B	Kansas City	J02 560 001B
Richmond	E40 960 001B	Dallas	K74 720 001A
Atlanta	F62 720 001B	San Francisco	L70 400 001B

CAT. NO. VF81
$5.00 FEDERAL RESERVE NOTE (GREEN SEAL) 32 Subject.
SERIES 1981

SIGNATURES: Angela M. Buchanan, Treasurer of the United States,
  Donald T. Regan, Secretary of the Treasury.
SERIAL NUMBERS: All districts revert to 00 000 001

	DISTRICT	TOTAL NOTES PRINTED	BLOCKS	ESTIMATED VALUE VG/F	CU	LOW OFFICIAL SERIAL NUMBER	HIGH OFFICIAL SERIAL NUMBER
1	A BOSTON		A--A		7.50	A00 000 001A	A08 960 000A
2	B NEW YORK		B--A		7.50	B00 000 001A	B30 720 000A
4	C CLEVELAND		D--A		7.50	D00 000 001A	D16 640 000A
6	F ATLANTA		F--A		7.50	F00 000 001A	F10 240 000A
7	G CHICAGO		G--A		7.50	G00 000 001A	G12 800 000A
10	J Kansas City		J--A		7.50	J00 000 001A	J10 240 000A
11	K Dallas		K--A		7.50	K00 000 001A	K08 960 000A
12	L San Francisco		L--A		7.50	L00 000 001A	L23 040 000A
			L--*		10.00	L00 000 001*	L00 640 000*

Total Blocks: Nine.
(1) Production through November 1981.

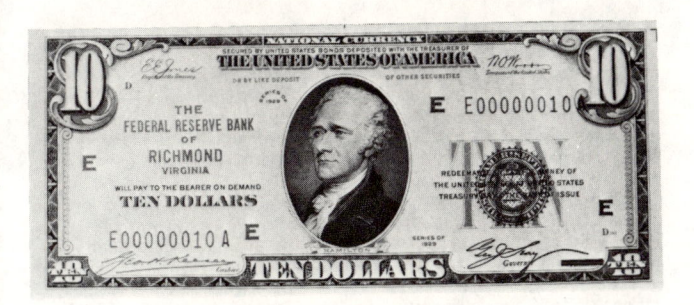

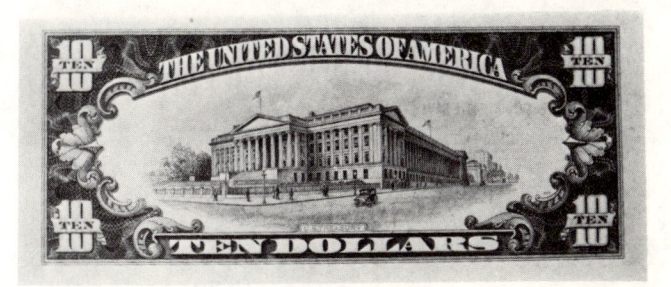

CAT. NO. XN29
$10.00 FEDERAL RESERVE BANK NOTE (BROWN SEAL) (12 Subject)
SERIES 1929

SERIAL NUMBERS: Figures shown below are the official high numbers. All districts started both regular and star notes with serial 00 000 001. Bureau of Engraving and Printing information is incomplete on star serial numbers, as are reports of high observed serial numbers.
PLATE SERIALS: Face check numbers within the range #1 through #290.
SIGNATURES: E.E. Jones, Register of the Treasury.
   W.O. Woods, Treasurer of the United States.
   Also the Federal Reserve Bank Cashier or Controller or the Deputy or Assistant Deputy Governor, with the Governor.

	DISTRICT	TOTAL NOTES PRINTED	BLOCKS	ESTIMATED VALUE VG/F	CU	LOW OBSERVED SERIAL NUMBER	HIGH OBSERVED SERIAL NUMBER
1	A BOSTON	24,000	A--A	25.00	50.00	A00 485 578A	A01 680 000A
			A--*	37.50	95.00		
2	B NEW YORK	76,000	B--A	22.50	45.00	B00 010 111A	B05 556 000A
			B--*	35.00	90.00	B00 006 081*	B00 067 879*
3	C PHILADELPHIA	24,000	C--A	25.00	52.50	C00 213 248A	C01 416 000A
			C--*	37.50	95.00	C00 007 359*	
4	D CLEVELAND	36,000	D--A	25.00	50.00	D01 554 775A	D02 412 000A
			D--*	37.50	90.00	D00 016 222*	D00 023 401*
5	E RICHMOND	24,000	E--A	25.00	55.00	E00 000 021A	E01 356 000A
			E--*	37.50	100.00	E00 015 295*	E00 108 228*
6	F ATLANTA	36,000	F--A	27.50	60.00	F00 080 689A	F01 056 000A
			F--*	40.00	110.00	F00 002 270*	
7	G CHICAGO	12,000	G--A	22.50	45.00	G00 778 488A	G03 156 000A
			G--*	35.00	90.00		
8	H ST. LOUIS	36,000	H--A	25.00	55.00	H00 302 369A	H01 584 000A
			H--*	37.50	100.00	H00 019 593*	H00 024 029*
9	I MINNEAPOLIS	24,000	I--A	30.00	65.00	I00 174 847A	I00 588 000A
			I--*	45.00	125.00		I00 002 601*
10	J KANSAS CITY	36,000	J--A	27.50	57.50	J00 000 010A	J01 284 000A
			J--*	40.00	105.00	J00 022 111*	J00 025 816*
11	K DALLAS	12,000	K--A	32.50	200.00		K00 504 000A
			K--*	47.50	125.00	K00 000 189*	
12	L SAN FRANCISCO	36,000	L--A	27.50	60.00	L00 017 495A	L01 080 000A
			L--*	40.00	110.00	L00 009 913*	L00 013 596*

TOTAL BLOCKS PRINTED: Twenty-four. Collectors are kindly requested to supply information on serial numbers.

CAT. NO. XL28
$10.00 UNITED STATES NOTE (LEGAL TENDER) Red seal
SERIES 1928

SERIAL NUMBERS: No Bureau record of printing.
PLATE SERIALS: Face and back check number 1.
SIGNATURES: Walter O. Woods, Treasurer of the United States.
W.H. Woodin, Secretary of the Treasury.

One specimen of this note has been observed however the owner requests that serial number not be used and that he remain anonymous. we respect his wishes.

CAT. NO. XG28A
$10.00 GOLD CERTIFICATE (GOLD SEAL) 12 Subject
SERIES 1928A

SERIAL NUMBERS: B30 802 001A through B33 346 000A
TOTAL QUANTITY PRINTED: 2,544,000 notes.
SIGNATURES: Walter O. Woods, Treasurer of the United States.
Ogden L. Mills, Secretary of the Treasury.

NOTE: Although BEP records indicate that 2,544,000 notes were DELIVERED, it is believed that all are in storage vaults in basement of Main Treasury Building, Washington, D.C. and that none were released to the public.

TREASURY REMOVES RESTRICTIONS ON UNITED STATES GOLD CERTIFICATES ISSUED BEFORE 1934

On April 24, 1964, the Secretary of the Treasury issued Regulations removing all restrictions on the acquisition or holding of gold certificates which were issued by the United States Government prior to January 30, 1934. The main effect of this action will be to permit collectors to hold this type of currency.

The restrictions which are being eliminated are considered no longer necessary or desirable. Under the laws enacted in 1934, these pre-1934 gold certificates are not redeemable in gold. They will, of course, continue to be exchangeable at face value for other currency of the United States.

The new Regulation authorizing the holding of gold certificates applies only to United States gold certificates isued prior to January 30, 1934. The holding of any other type of gold certificates, including any issued by foreigners against gold held on deposit abroad, continues to be prohibited. Also, the status of the special series gold certificates issued by the U.S. Treasury only to the Federal Reserve system for reserve purposes is not affected.

CAT. NO. XG28
$10.00 GOLD CERTIFICATE (GOLD SEAL) 12 Subject
SERIES 1928

SERIAL NUMBERS:
  (Official Range) A00 000 001A through B30 812 000A
  Star Notes:
  (Low Official) *00 000 001A *01 473 261A (High Observed)
PLATE SERIALS: Face check #1 through #290.
SIGNATURES: Walter O. Woods, Treasurer of the United States.
Andrew W. Mellon, Secretary of the Treasury.

ESTIMATED VALUES:	BLOCKS	VG/F	CU
	A--A	25.00	200.00
	B--A	75.00	350.00
	*--A	100.00	500.00

TOTAL BLOCKS KNOWN: Three.

CAT. NO. XS33
$10.00 SILVER CERTIFICATE (BLUE SEAL) (12 Subject)
SERIES 1933

SERIAL NUMBERS:
  (Official Range) A00 000 001A through A00 216 000A
PLATE SERIALS: Face check #1 only.
SIGNATURES: W.A. Julian, Treasurer of the United States
W.H. Woodin, Secretary of the Treasury
DESIGN: Face design for series 1933 has blue Treasury seal to left of portrait of Hamilton, TEN at right. Back design shows the United States Treasury Building, Washington, D.C.
TOTAL QUANTITY PRINTED: 216,000

ESTIMATED VALUES:		VG/F	CU
	A--A	750.00	5000.00
	*--A	UNKNOWN	

TOTAL BLOCKS KNOWN: One

CAT. NO. XS33A
$10.00 SILVER CERTIFICATE (BLUE SEAL) (12 Subject)
Series 1933A

SERIAL NUMBERS: A00 216 001A through A00 552 000A.
PLATE SERIALS: Face check #1 only.
SIGNATURES: W.A. Julian, Treasurer of the United States
  Henry Morgenthau, Jr. Secretary of the Treasury.
TOTAL QUANTITY PRINTED: 336,000.

ESTIMATED VALUES:
              A--A   UNKNOWN
              A--*   Possibly UNIQUE

In November 1935, 368,000 $10.00 silver certificates were destroyed. Reports indicate that 156,000 Series 1933 and 60,000 Series 1933A were released and that the balance of 60,000 1933 and 308,000 of the 1933A were destroyed, however these reports are believed to be inaccurate since NO 1933A regular notes have ever been reported. It is likely that the destruction included the entire printing of 1933A.

Perhaps the scarcest notes in the small series Silver Certificates are Series of 1933 and 1933A $10.00 notes. Issued in the year 1933, their manufacture was cut short by the Administration's change in the silver policy. These two (1933 and 1933A) are the only certificates mentioning the word "coin" as such. The Series of 1933 were issued just prior to Woodin's retirement (signatures W. A. Julian and W.H. Woodin). This $10.00 differs from all other Silver Certificates, being inscribed "The United States of America — Ten Dollars — payable in silver coin to bearer on demand." No mention is made of the deposit of the silver. Only a few plates were prepared and only face check #1 is known. Later in the year Series 1933A was printed, Morgenthau's name replacing that of Woodin. A single star note is known in Series 1933A, however no regular notes have ever been seen or reported.

CAT. NO. XS34
$10.00 SILVER CERTIFICATE (BLUE SEAL)
SERIES 1934 MULE

These are series 1934 notes with the larger back check numbers (585 or higher), and are actually Series 1934 Face on Series 1934A Back.
SERIAL NUMBERS:
  (Low Observed) A34 998 118A B16 924 554A (High Observed)
  Star Notes:
  (Low Observed) *00 494 654A *01 007 810 (High Observed)

ESTIMATED VALUES:

	VG/F	CU
A--A	$17.50	$35.00
B--A	100.00	200.00
*--A	35.00	75.00

TOTAL BLOCKS KNOWN: Three

CAT. NO. XS34
$10.00 SILVER CERTIFICATE (BLUE SEAL) (12 Subject)
SERIES 1934

SERIAL NUMBERS:
  (Low Official) A00 000 001A A84 946 579A (High Observed)
  Star Notes:
  (Low Official) *00 000 001A *00 939 068A (High Observed)
PLATE SERIALS: Back check numbers #584 (micro size) and lower.
SIGNATURES: W.A. Julian, Treasurer of the United States
  Henry Morgenthau, Jr., Secretary of the Treasury
DESIGN: Face design for series 1934 through 1934D shows large blue 10 to left of portait of Hamilton, blue Treasury seal at right. Back design same as 1933. Face and back check number doubled in size for series 1934A and later.
TOTAL QUANTITY PRINTED: 88,692,864 notes.

ESTIMATED VALUES:

	VG/F	CU
A--A	$17.50	$35.00
*--A	35.00	75.00

TOTAL BLOCKS KNOWN: Two

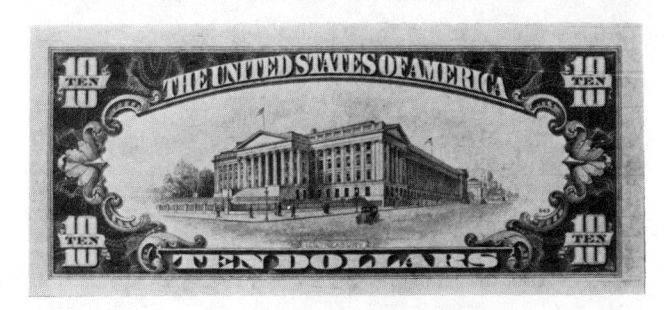

CAT. NO. XS34
$10.00 SILVER CERTIFICATE (YELLOW SEAL) (12 Subject)
NORTH AFRICA
SERIES 1934 MULE (1)

SERIAL NUMBERS:
  (Low Observed) A91 141 810A B07 560 760A (High Observed)
  Star Notes:
  (Low Observed) *01 122 388A
PLATE SERIALS: Back check number 585 or higher.
  Face check number 116, 123, 125, 126, 127.
SIGNATURES: Same as Series 1934.

ESTIMATED VALUES:

Blocks	VG/F	CU
A--A	400.00	2000.00
B--A	400.00	2500.00
*--A	3500.00	

TOTAL BLOCKS KNOWN: Three.
FOOTNOTE: (1) No regular (1934 face on 1934 backs) are known for the 1934 North Africa notes.

CAT. NO. XS34A
$10.00 SILVER CERTIFICATE (BLUE SEAL) (12 Subject)
SERIES 1934A

SERIAL NUMBERS:
  (Low Observed) A 74 862 042 A B 26 053 155 A (High Observed)
  Star Notes
  (Low Observed) *00 951 347 A *01 547 059 A (High Observed)

PLATE SERIALS: Face check number range #129-#210.
  Back check numbers begin at #585.

SIGNATURES: W.A. Julian, Treasurer of the United States
  Henry Morgenthau, Jr., Secretary of the Treasury

TOTAL QUANTITY PRINTED: 42, 346, 428 notes.

ESTIMATED VALUES:

	VG/F	CU
A--A and B--A	$20.00	$45.00
*--A	45.00	90.00

TOTAL BLOCKS KNOWN: Three

CAT. NO. XS34A
$10.00 SILVER CERTIFICATE (BLUE SEAL)
SERIES 1934A MULE

These are Series 1934A notes with the Micro Back Check Numbers, (#584 or lower) and are actually Series 1934A Faces on Series 1934 Backs.

SERIAL NUMBERS:
 (Low Observed) A 74 452 813 A A 90 577 124 A (High Observed)

PLATE SERIALS: Back check numbers used #404, 553, and 578.

ESTIMATED VALUES:

	VG/F	CU
A--A	$50.00	$100.00

TOTAL BLOCKS KNOWN: One

CAT. NO. XS34A
$10.00 SILVER CERTIFICATE (YELLOW SEAL) (12 Subject)
NORTH AFRICA
SERIES 1934A

SERIAL NUMBERS:
 (Official Ranges) A 91 044 001 A through B 00 904 000 A
 B 01 564 001 A through B 13 564 000 A
 Star Notes:
 (Low Observed) * 01 009 385 A through * 01 282 762 A (High Observed)

PLATE SERIALS: Face check #129-209.
 Back check #585 and higher.

SIGNATURES: Sames as Series 1934

ESTIMATED VALUES:

BLOCKS	VG/F	CU
A--A and B--A	17.00	100.00
*--A	30.00	150.00

TOTAL BLOCKS KNOWN: Three.

posed new check number size. They were changed from .02 in. or "micro" to the present day size of .04 in. The check number order was not disturbed, though they were printed during the production run of Series 1934. After these two plates were issued as 1934 A, there was a rush order for $10.00 Silver Certificate faces. These plates were laid aside and more of the 1934 plates were made. This accounts for the staggering of the plate serial (check) numbers.

SERIAL NUMBERS:
 (Low Observed) A 84 958 136 A B 19 469 564 A (High Observed)

STARS (Low Observed) * 00 985 192A *01 485 388 A (High Observed)

PLATE SERIALS: Face check number 86.

TOTAL QUANTITY: 1,203,456 notes (Includes 1934 A Mule and North Africa)

ESTIMATED VALUES:

	VG/F	CU
A--A and B--A	25.00	50.00
*--A	50.00	100.00

TOTAL BLOCKS KNOWN: Three

CAT. NO. XS34A
$10.00 SILVER CERTIFICATE (BLUE SEAL) (12 Subject)
SERIES 1934A MULE TRIAL NOTE

SERIAL NUMBERS:
 (Low Observed) A 84 899 119 A A 90 853 724 A (High Observed)

PLATE SERIALS: Face check number 86. Back check used #404, 553, and 578.

ESTIMATED VALUES:

	VG/F
A--A	100.00

TOTAL BLOCKS KNOWN: One.

CAT. NO. XS34A
$10.00 SILVER CERTIFICATE (BLUE SEAL) (12 Subject)
SERIES 1934A TRIAL NOTE

An important trial group was printed on $10.00 Silver Certificates Series 1934 A, and distinguished by their face check numbers (#86 and #87). These plates, both masters, were made to test the readability of the pro-

CAT. NO. XS34A
$10.00 SILVER CERTIFICATE (BLUE SEAL) 12 Subject
SERIES 1934A TRIAL NOTE

SERIAL NUMBERS:
 (Low Observed) A77 166 224A A90 853 724A (High Observed)
PLATE SERIAL: Face check number 87.
TOTAL QUANTITY PRINTED: 83,100 notes. (Includes 1934A Mule below.)

ESTIMATED VALUE:

	VG/F	CU
A--A	100.00	1000.00

TOTAL BLOCKS KNOWN: One.

CAT. NO. XS34A
$10.00 SILVER CERTIFICATE (BLUE SEAL) 12 Subject
SERIES 1934A MULE TRIAL NOTE

SERIAL NUMBERS:
 (Low Observed) A77 425 715A A78 491 508A (High Observed)
PLATE SERIALS: Face check number 87. Back check # used: 404, 553 and 578.

ESTIMATED VALUE:		VG/F
	A--A	100.00

TOTAL BLOCKS KNOWN: One.

CAT. NO. XS34A
$10.00 SILVER CERTIFICATE (YELLOW SEAL) (12 Subject)
SERIAL 1934A NORTH AFRICA TRIAL NOTE

SERIAL NUMBERS:
 (Low Observed) A 91 816 519 A B 11 643 235 A (High Observed)
STARS (Low Observed) * 01 010 325 A * 01 226 656 A (High Observed)
PLATE SERIAL: Face check number 86.

ESTIMATED VALUES:		VG/F	CU
	A--A and B--A	25.00	50.00
	*--A	50.00	100.00

TOTAL BLOCKS KNOWN: Three.

CAT. NO. XS34B
$10.00 SILVER CERTIFICATE (BLUE SEAL) 12 Subject
SERIES 1934B

SERIAL NUMBERS:
 (Low Official) B15 432 001A B21 521 396A (High Observed)
 Star Notes:
 (Low Observed) *01 333 331A *01 505 683A (High Observed)
PLATE SERIALS: Face check #211 only.
SIGNATURES: W.A. Julian, Treasurer of the United States.
 Fred M. Vinson, Secretary of the Treasury.
TOTAL QUANTITY PRINTED: 337,740 notes.

ESTIMATED VALUES:		VG/F	CU
	B--A	65.00	750.00
	*--A	400.00	1,500.00

TOTAL BLOCKS KNOWN: Two.

CAT. NO. XS34C
$10.00 SILVER CERTIFICATE (BLUE SEAL) 12 Subject
SERIES 1934C

SERIAL NUMBERS:
 (Low Official) B16 848 001A B43 158 586A (High Observed)
 Star Notes:
 (Low Observed) *01 410 277A *01 787 573A (High Observed)
PLATE SERIALS: Face check number range #214-#232.
SIGNATURES: W.A. Julian, Treasurer of the United States.
 John W. Snyder, Secretary of the Treasury.

TOTAL QUANTITY PRINTED: 20,032,632 notes.

ESTIMATED VALUES:		VG/F	CU
	B--A	12.00	25.00
	*--A	15.00	35.00

TOTAL BLOCKS KNOWN: Two.

CAT. NO. XS34D
$10.00 SILVER CERTIFICATE (BLUE SEAL) 12 Subject
SERIES 1934D WIDE

SERIAL NUMBERS:
 (Low Observed) B38 556 671A B50 196 900A (High Official)
 Star Notes:
 (Low Observed) *01 788 051 A *01 980 000A (High Official)
PLATE SERIALS: Face check number range (both groups) #233-#252.
 Back check numbers #1389 or lower.
SIGNATURES: Georgia Neese Clark, Treasurer of the United States.
 John W. Snyder, Secretary of the Treasury.
TOTAL QUANTITY PRINTED: 11,801,112 notes for both varieties.

ESTIMATED VALUES:		VG/F	CU
	B--A	15.00	25.00
	*--A	20.00	40.00

TOTAL BLOCKS KNOWN: Two.

CAT. NO. XS34D
$10.00 SILVER CERTIFICATE (BLUE SEAL) 12 Subject
SERIES 1934D NARROW

SERIAL NUMBERS:
 (Low Observed) B47 556 045A B50 196 900A (High Official)

167

Star Notes:
(Low Observed) *01 932 430A *01 939 976A (High Observed)
PLATE SERIALS: Back check number range #1390-1456 (Highest of 12 subject sheets).

ESTIMATED VALUES:

	VG/F	CU
B--A	100.00	200.00
*--A		rare

TOTAL BLOCKS KNOWN: Two.
(1) Data is for both varieties.
Collectors are requested to report data that would improve on variety serial numbers above.

CAT. NO. XS53
$10.00 SILVER CERTIFICATE (BLUE SEAL) 18 Subject
SERIES 1953

SERIAL NUMBERS:
(Official Range) A00 000 001A through A10 440 000A
Star Notes:
(Low Official) *00 000 001A *00 550 360A (High Observed)
PLATE SERIALS: Face check numbers begin at #1.
Back check numbers begin at #1448 (low of 18 subject sheets).
SIGNATURES: Ivy Baker Priest, Treasurer of the United States.
George M. Humphrey, Secretary of the Treasury.

DESIGN: Face design for series 1953, 1953A, and 1953B has smaller grey 10 to left of portrait of Hamilton, smaller blue Treasury seal at right. Back design unchanged.

ESTIMATED VALUES:

	CU
A--A	35.00
*--A	60.00

TOTAL BLOCKS KNOWN: Two.

CAT. NO. XS53A
$10.00 SILVER CERTIFICATE (BLUE SEAL) 18 Subject
SERIES 1953A

SERIAL NUMBERS:
(Official Range) A10 440 001A through A11 520 000A
Star Notes:
(Low Observed) *00 582 140A *00 720 000A (High Official)
SIGNATURES: Ivy Baker Priest, Treasurer of the United States.
Robert B. Anderson, Secretary of the Treasury.

ESTIMATED VALUES:

	CU
A--A	30.00
*--A	60.00

TOTAL BLOCKS KNOWN: Two.

CAT. NO. XS53B
$10.00 SILVER CERTIFICATE (BLUE SEAL) 18 Subject
SERIES 1953B

SERIAL NUMBERS:
(Official Range) A11 520 000A through A12 240 000A
PLATE SERIALS: Face check numbers on 18 subject sheets end at #5.
Back check numbers on 18 subject sheets end at #1839.
SIGNATURES: Elizabeth Rudel Smith, Treasurer of the United States.
C. Douglas Dillon, Secretary of the Treasury.

ESTIMATED VALUES:

	CU
A--A	50.00

TOTAL BLOCKS KNOWN: One.

CAT. NO. XF28
$10.00 FEDERAL RESERVE NOTE (GREEN SEAL) (12 Subject)
SERIES 1928

SERIAL NUMBERS: All serial numbers both regular and star notes begin with 00 000 001.
PLATE SERIALS: All face and back check numbers begin with 1.
SIGNATURES: H.T. Tate, Treasurer of the United States
A.W. Mellon, Secretary of the Treasury

	DISTRICT	TOTAL NOTES PRINTED	BLOCKS	ESTIMATED VALUE VG/F	CU	LOW OBSERVED SERIAL NUMBER	HIGH OBSERVED SERIAL NUMBER
1	A BOSTON	9,804,552	A--A	$25.00	$50.00	A01 206 873A	A08 690 316A
			A--*	35.00	75.00	A00 066 470*	A00 236 667*

	DISTRICT	TOTAL NOTES PRINTED	BLOCKS	ESTIMATED VALUE VG/F	CU	LOW OFFICIAL SERIAL NUMBER	HIGH OFFICIAL SERIAL NUMBER
2	B NEW YORK	11,295,796	B--A	25.00	50.00	B00 216 177A	B10 035 592A
			B--*	35.00	75.00	B00 012 823*	B00 039 296*
3	C PHILADELPHIA	8,114,412	C--A	25.00	50.00	C04 889 384A	C10 847 487A
			C--*	35.00	75.00		
4	D CLEVELAND	7,570,680	D--A	25.00	50.00	D00 891 166A	D10 155 855A
			D--*	35.00	75.00	D00 158 208*	D00 158 396*
5	E RICHMOND	4,534,800	E--A	27.50	60.00	E01 144 031A	E04 378 311A
			E--*	35.00	75.00		
6	F ATLANTA	6,807,720	F--A	25.00	50.00	F00 303 957A	F08 682 361A
			F--*	35.00	75.00		F00 002 281*
7	G CHICAGO	8,130,000	G--A	25.00	50.00	G02 362 018A	G10 778 287A
			G--*	50.00	75.00	G00 058 367*	G00 304 040*
8	H ST. LOUIS	4,124,100	H--A	27.50	60.00	H00 000 014A	H05 157 636A
			H--*	60.00	90.00	H00 045 491*	H00 146 517*
9	I MINNEAPOLIS	3,874,440	I--A	30.00	65.00	I02 221 078A	I03 679 790A
			I--*	65.00	100.00	I00 044 344*	I00 048 429*
10	J KANSAS CITY	3,620,400	J--A	30.00	65.00	J01 282 021A	J04 655 326A
			J--*	65.00	100.00	J00 004 660*	J00 035 124*
11	K DALLAS	4,855,500	K--A	27.50	60.00	K02 265 722A	K04 557 496A
			K--*	35.00	75.00		
12	L SAN FRANCISCO	7,086,900	L--A	25.00	50.00		L04 918 586A
			L--*	35.00	75.00		

TOTAL BLOCKS: Twenty-four

Collectors are requested to supply any serial numbers that will improve on above information.

CAT. NO. XF28A
$10.00 FEDERAL RESERVE NOTE (GREEN SEAL) (12 Subject)
SERIES 1928A

SERIAL NUMBERS: All districts continued sequence from previous series.
SIGNATURES: Walter O. Woods, Treasurer of the United States
   A.W. Mellon, Secretary of the Treasury

	DISTRICT	TOTAL NOTES PRINTED	BLOCKS	ESTIMATED VALUE VG/F	CU	LOW OBSERVED SERIAL NUMBER	HIGH OBSERVED SERIAL NUMBER
1	A BOSTON	2,893,440	A--A	$17.50	$30.00	A08 555 834A	A11 117 094A
			A--*	25.00	50.00	A00 256 761*	
2	B NEW YORK	18,631,056	B--A	15.00	25.00	B09 601 891A	B27 585 371A
			B--*	20.00	42.50	B00 404 881*	B00 668 377*
3	C PHILADELPHIA	2,710,680	C--A	17.50	30.00	C07 083 912A	C09 798 033A
			C--*	25.00	50.00		
4	D CLEVELAND	5,610,000	D--A	17.50	30.00	D07 270 530A	D15 256 075A
			D--*	22.50	45.00	D00 138 930*	D00 200 157*
5	E RICHMOND	552,300	E--A	27.50	60.00	E05 457 902A	
			E--*	50.00	100.00		
6	F ATLANTA	3,033,480	F--A	17.50	30.00	F05 397 641A	F09 279 060A
			F--*	25.00	50.00	F00 159 856*	
7	G CHICAGO	8,715,000	G--A	17.50	30.00	G08 294 214A	G14 832 230A
			G--*	22.50	45.00	G00 250 073*	
8	H ST. LOUIS	531,600	H--A	27.50	60.00	H03 967 681A	H04 875 354A
			H--*	50.00	100.00	H00 062 759*	H00 108 882*
9	I MINNEAPOLIS	102,600	I--A	75.00	100.00	I03 679 750A	
			I--*	100.00	250.00		
10	J KANSAS CITY	410,400	J--A	27.50	60.00	J04 286 834A	
			J--*	50.00	100.00		
11	K DALLAS	961,800	K--A	22.50	45.00	K04 650 160A	
			K--*	75.00	100.00		
12	L SAN FRANCISCO	2,547,900	L--A	17.50	30.00	L07 670 106A	L09 734 683A
			L--*	25.00	50.00	L00 149 457*	

TOTAL BLOCKS: Twenty-four
Collectors are requested to supply any serial numbers that will improve on above information.

CAT. NO. XF28B
$10.00 FEDERAL RESERVE NOTE (DARK GREEN SEAL) (12 Subject)
SERIES 1928B

SERIAL NUMBERS: All districts continued sequence from previous series.
SIGNATURES: Walter O. Woods, Treasurer of the United States.
  A.W. Mellon, Secretary of the Treasury.

	DISTRICT	TOTAL NOTES PRINTED (1)	BLOCKS	ESTIMATED VALUE VG/F	CU	LOW OBSERVED SERIAL NUMBER	HIGH OBSERVED SERIAL NUMBER
1	A BOSTON	33,218,088	A--A	$17.50	$35.00	A13 166 578A	A35 564 083*
			A--*	30.00	60.00	A00 323 424*	
2	B NEW YORK	44,458,308	B--A	15.00	30.00	B27 480 893A	B69 784 060A
			B--*	25.00	50.00		
3	C PHILADELPHIA	22,689,216	C--A	17.50	35.00	C10 062 953A	C30 514 705A
			C--*	30.00	60.00		
4	D CLEVELAND	17,418,024	D--A	20.00	40.00	D13 089 160A	D24 794 168A
			D--*	35.00	70.00	D00 218 393*	D00 346 433*
5	E RICHMOND	12,714,504	E--A	20.00	40.00	E05 323 470A	E13 569 609A
			E--*	35.00	70.00	E00 124 932*	E00 150 541*
6	F ATLANTA	5,246,700	F--A	22.50	50.00	F09 563 762A	F13 862 358A
			F--*	37.50	80.00		
7	G CHICAGO	38,035,000	G--A	15.00	30.00	G15 708 491A	G53 652 086A
			G--*	25.00	50.00	G00 347 943*	G00 444 009*
8	H ST. LOUIS	10,814,664	H--A	20.00	40.00	H04 350 546A	H11 116 605A
			H--*	35.00	70.00		
9	I MINNEAPOLIS	5,294,460	I--A	22.50	50.00	I03 927 054A	I06 636 587 A
			I--*	37.50	80.00		
10	J KANSAS CITY	7,748,040	J--A	22.50	50.00	J04 478 358A	J08 820 387A
			J--*	37.50	80.00		
11	K DALLAS	3,396,096	K--A	25.00	50.00	K07 487 466A	K08 319 882A
			K--*	40.00	100.00		
12	L SAN FRANCISCO	22,695,300	L--A	17.50	35.00	L09 279 596A	L18 289 932A
			L--*	30.00	60.00		

TOTAL BLOCKS: Twenty-four
Collectors are requested to supply any serial numbers that would improve on above information

(1) Includes both varieties.

CAT. NO. XF28B
$10.00 FEDERAL RESERVE NOTE (LIGHT GREEN SEAL) (12 Subject)
SERIES 1928B

All information same as 1928B dark green seal.

	DISTRICT	TOTAL NOTES PRINTED	BLOCKS	ESTIMATED VALUE VG/F	CU	LOW OFFICIAL SERIAL NUMBER	HIGH OFFICIAL SERIAL NUMBER
1	A BOSTON		A--A	15.00	30.00	A28 888 200A	A42 266 429A
			A--*	27.50	50.00	A00 530 936*	A00 553 066*
2	B NEW YORK		B--A	12.50	25.00	B53 719 374A	B66 656 873A
			B--*	22.50	45.00	B00 738 499*	B00 780 597*
3	C PHILADELPHIA		C--A	15.00	30.00	C22 944 665A	C39 744 939A
			C--*	27.50	50.00		C00 328 478*
4	D CLEVELAND		D--A	17.50	35.00	D15 908 196A	D29 268 477A
			D--*	30.00	60.00	D00 243 657*	D00 353 207*
5	E RICHMOND		E--A	17.50	35.00	E08 979 390A	E16 894 828A
			E--*	30.00	60.00		
6	F ATLANTA		F--A	20.00	35.00	F12 449 218A	F14 176 964A
			F--*	35.00	70.00		
7	G CHICAGO		G--A	12.50	25.00	G31 725 671A	G52 162 793A
			G--*	20.00	35.00	G00 563 830*	G00 605 928*
8	H ST. LOUIS		H--A	17.50	35.00	H09 917 580A	H14 915 400A
			H--*	30.00	60.00	H00 131 528*	H00 161 189*
9	I MINNEAPOLIS		I--A	20.00	35.00	I05 285 001A	I08 017 521A
			I--*	35.00	70.00		I00 085 944*
10	J KANSAS CITY		J--A	20.00	35.00	J08 987 305A	J11 625 049A
			J--*	35.00	70.00		

	DISTRICT	TOTAL NOTES PRINTED	BLOCKS	ESTIMATED VALUE VG/F	CU	LOW OFFICIAL SERIAL NUMBER	HIGH OFFICIAL SERIAL NUMBER
11	K DALLAS		K--A	22.50	45.00		
			K--*	35.00	75.00		
12	L SAN FRANCISCO		L--A	15.00	30.00	L20 679 234A	L23 275 807A
			L--*	25.00	50.00	L00 271 339*	L00 274 127*

TOTAL BLOCKS: Twenty-four

Collectors are requested to supply any serial numbers that improve on above information.

CAT. NO. XF28C
$10.00 FEDERAL RESERVE NOTE (GREEN SEAL) (12 Subject)
SERIES 1928C

SERIAL NUMBERS: Districts printed continued sequence from previous series.

SIGNATURES: Walter O. Woods, Treasurer of the United States
Ogden L. Mills, Secretary of the Treasury

	DISTRICT	TOTAL NOTES PRINTED	BLOCKS	ESTIMATED VALUE VG/F	CU	LOW OFFICIAL SERIAL NUMBER	HIGH OFFICIAL SERIAL NUMBER
1	A BOSTON	NONE					
2	B NEW YORK	2,902,678	B--A	25.00	100.00	B70 031 827A	B73 323 212A
			B--*	35.00	150.00		
3	C PHILADELPHIA	NONE					
4	D CLEVELAND	4,230,428	D--A	20.00	100.00	D29 233 933A	D30 400 271A
			D--*	30.00	150.00		
5	E RICHMOND	304,800	E--A	50.00	100.00		
			E--*	100.00	250.00		
6	F ATLANTA	688,380	F--A	35.00	100.00		
			F--*	75.00	150.00		
7	G CHICAGO	2,423,400	G--A	25.00	100.00	G44 181 072A	G54 852 746A
			G--*	35.00	150.00		
8	H ST. LOUIS	NONE					
9	I MINNEAPOLIS	NONE					
10	J KANSAS CITY	NONE					
11	K DALLAS	NONE					
12	L SAN FRANCISCO	NONE					

TOTAL BLOCKS: Ten

Collectors are requested to supply any serial numbers that improve on above information.

CAT. NO. XF34
$10.00 FEDERAL RESERVE NOTE (DARK GREEN SEAL) (12 Subject)
SERIES 1934

SERIAL NUMBERS: All serial numbers both regular and star notes begin with 00 000 001.

PLATE SERIALS: Face check numbers begin with 1, back check numbers continue from previous series, up to back check number 584.

SIGNATURES: W.A. Julian, Treasurer of the United States
Henry Morgenthau, Jr., Secretary of the Treasury

	DISTRICT	TOTAL NOTES PRINTED (1)	BLOCKS	ESTIMATED VALUE VG/F	CU	LOW OFFICIAL SERIAL NUMBER	HIGH OFFICIAL SERIAL NUMBER
1	A BOSTON	46,276,152	A--A	13.00	27.50	A00 960 273A	A35 378 420A
			A--*	15.00	35.00	A00 404 208*	
2	B NEW YORK	117,298,008	B--A	12.50	25.00	B92 919 607A	
			B--B	12.50	25.00		B04 246 607B
			B--*	13.00	27.50	B00 511 809*	B01 307 634*
3	C PHILADELPHIA	34,770,768	C--A	15.00	30.00	C22 923 114A	C40 023 082A
			C--*	17.50	35.00		C00 226 168*

	DISTRICT	TOTAL NOTES PRINTED	BLOCKS	ESTIMATED VALUE VG/F	CU	LOW OFFICIAL SERIAL NUMBER	HIGH OFFICIAL SERIAL NUMBER
4	D CLEVELAND	28,764,108	D--A	15.00	30.00	D16 492 257A	D25 667 442A
			D--*	17.50	35.00		
5	E RICHMOND	16,437,252	E--A	17.50	32.50	E12 104 720A	E15 181 156A
			E--*	20.00	40.00		
6	F ATLANTA	20,656,872	F--A	15.00	30.00		F28 851 008A
			F--*	17.50	35.00		
7	G CHICAGO	69,962,064	G--A	12.50	25.00	G42 878 550A	G73 692 498A
			G--*	13.00	27.50	G00 379 274*	G00 643 775*
8	H ST. LOUIS	22,593,204	H--A	15.00	30.00	H07 296 150A	H18 263 508A
			H--*	17.50	35.00	H00 005 348*	
9	I MINNEAPOLIS	16,840,980	I--A	17.50	32.50	I00 261 987A	I08 770 469A
			I--*	20.00	40.00	I00 123 464*	
10	J KANSAS CITY	22,627,824	J--A	15.00	30.00	J02 882 622A	J26 262 020A
			J--*	17.50	35.00		J10 891 972*
11	K DALLAS	21,403,488	K--A	15.00	30.00		
			K--*	17.50	35.00		
12	L SAN FRANCISCO	37,402,308	L--A	15.00	30.00	L23 377 981A	L32 120 664A
			L--*	17.50	35.00		

TOTAL BLOCKS: Twenty-five

Collectors are requested to supply serial numbers that improve on above information.

(1) Includes both seal colors and mules.

CAT. NO. XF34
$10.00 FEDERAL RESERVE NOTE MULE (DARK GREEN SEAL) (12 Subject)
SERIES 1934

PLATE SERIALS: Back check number 585 and higher.

	DISTRICT	TOTAL NOTES PRINTED	BLOCKS	ESTIMATED VALUE VG/F	CU	LOW OBSERVED SERIAL NUMBER	HIGH OBSERVED SERIAL NUMBER
1	A BOSTON		A--A				A35 041 268A
			A--A				
2	B NEW YORK		B--A	17.50	35.00	B99 975 344A	
			B--B				
			B--*				
3	C PHILADELPHIA		C--A	17.50	35.00	C26 564 773A	C35 839 892A
			C--B				
4	D CLEVELAND		D--A	17.50	35.00	D47 320 233A	
			D--*				
5	E RICHMOND		E--A				
			E--*				
6	F ATLANTA		F--A	17.50	35.00	F28 849 873A	F89 702 759A
			F--*				
7	G CHICAGO		G--A	15.00	30.00	G54 567 164A	G73 911 416A
			G--*	25.00	50.00	G00 062 146*	G00 778 732*
8	H ST. LOUIS		H--A	17.50	35.00	H18 338 834A	H19 147 939A
			H--*	25.00	50.00		
9	I MINNEAPOLIS		I--A	17.50	35.00	I09 243 549A	I26 815 468A
			I--*				
10	J KANSAS CITY		J--A	17.50	35.00	J20 031 382A	J45 772 513A
			J--*	25.00	50.00	J00 191 894*	J00 623 946*
11	K DALLAS		K--A	17.50	35.00	K10 789 691A	K38 069 498A
			K--*			K00 297 430*	
12	L SAN FRANCISCO		L--A	17.50	35.00	L30 063 979A	L36 866 420A
			L--*				

TOTAL BLOCKS: Twenty-five

Collectors are requested to supply serial numbers that improve on above information.

CAT. NO. XF34
$10.00 FEDERAL RESERVE NOTE (LIGHT GREEN SEAL) (12 Subject)
SERIES 1934

PLATE SERIALS: Face check numbers begin with number 1.
  Back check continues from previous series up to 584.

	DISTRICT	TOTAL NOTES PRINTED	BLOCKS	ESTIMATED VALUE VG/F	CU	LOW OBSERVED SERIAL NUMBER	HIGH OBSERVED SERIAL NUMBER
1	A BOSTON		A--A	11.00	25.00	A00 259 758A	A43 886 186A
			A--*	12.50	30.00	A00 260 362*	A00 260 375*
2	B NEW YORK		B--A	11.00	25.00	B00 000 033A	
			B--B	15.00	30.00		B09 107 657B
			B--*	12.50	25.00	B00 043 761*	
3	C PHILADELPHIA		C--A	12.50	25.00	C00 392 664A	C34 797 147A
			C--*	15.00	30.00	C00 074 117*	C00 360 756*
4	D CLEVELAND		D--A	12.50	25.00	D01 032 237A	D23 339 826A
			D--*	15.00	30.00	D00 007 123*	D00 007 243*
5	E RICHMOND		E--A	12.50	27.50	E01 157 355A	E16 821 578A
			E--*	15.00	30.00		
6	F ATLANTA		F--A	12.50	25.00	F01 217 223A	F10 509 569A
			F--*	15.00	30.00	F00 052 036*	
7	G CHICAGO		G--A	12.50	25.00	G00 045 461A	G62 546 422A
			G--*	15.00	30.00	G00 040 505*	G00 582 079*
8	H ST. LOUIS		H--A	12.50	25.00	H00 565 768A	H19 276 420A
			H--*	15.00	30.00	H00 029 813*	
9	I MINNEAPOLIS		I--A	12.50	25.00	I00 098 036A	I07 499 259A
			I--*	15.00	30.00		
10	J KANSAS CITY		J--A	12.50	25.00	J01 268 426A	J14 134 312A
			J--*	15.00	30.00	J00 178 952*	J00 191 903*
11	K DALLAS		K--A	12.50	25.00	K00 309 695A	K07 952 929A
			K--*	15.00	30.00		
12	L SAN FRANCISCO		L--A	12.50	25.00	L00 242 668A	L30 568 562A
			L--*	15.00	30.00	L00 108 655*	

TOTAL BLOCKS: Twenty-five

Collectors are requested to supply serial numbers that improve on above information.

CAT. NO. XF34
$10.00 FEDERAL RESERVE NOTE MULE (LIGHT GREEN SEAL) (12 Subject)
SERIES 1934

PLATE SERIALS: Back check number 585 and higher.

	DISTRICT	TOTAL NOTES PRINTED	BLOCKS	ESTIMATED VALUE VG/F	CU	LOW OFFICIAL SERIAL NUMBER	HIGH OFFICIAL SERIAL NUMBER
1	A BOSTON		A--A				
			A--*				
2	B NEW YORK		B--A				
			B--B	25.00	60.00	B00 597 809B	
			B--*				
3	C PHILADELPHIA		C--A				C28 085 666A
			C--*				
4	D CLEVELAND		D--A				
			D--*				
5	E RICHMOND		E--A				
			E--*				
6	F ATLANTA		F--A				
			F--*				
7	G CHICAGO		G--A	15.00	50.00	G54 397 265A	G59 259 486A
			G--*	50.00	100.00	G00 812 693*	

	DISTRICT	TOTAL NOTES PRINTED	BLOCKS	ESTIMATED VALUE VG/F	CU	LOW OFFICIAL SERIAL NUMBER	HIGH OFFICIAL SERIAL NUMBER
8	H ST. LOUIS		H--A H--*	15.00	50.00	H19 475 122A	
9	I MINNEAPOLIS		I--A I--*	15.00	50.00	I24 601 254A	
10	J KANSAS CITY		J--A J--*	15.00	50.00	J13 847 733A	J34 988 668A
11	K DALLAS		K--A K--*	15.00	50.00	K24 740 536A	K25 369 666A
12	L SAN FRANCISCO		L--A L--*				L32 120 668A

TOTAL BLOCKS: Twenty-five

Collectors are requested to supply serial numbers that improve on above information.

CAT. NO. XF34A
$10.00 FEDERAL RESERVE NOTE (DARK GREEN SEAL) (12 Subject)
SERIES 1934A

SERIAL NUMBERS: All districts continued sequence from previous series.

PLATE SERIALS: Back check begins at 585

SIGNATURES: W.A. Julian, Treasurer of the United States
Henry Morgenthau, Jr., Secretary of the Treasury.

	DISTRICT	TOTAL NOTES PRINTED (1)	BLOCKS	ESTIMATED VALUE VG/F	CU	LOW OBSERVED SERIAL NUMBER	HIGH OBSERVED SERIAL NUMBER
1	A BOSTON	104,540,088	A--A	11.00	17.50	A53 431 479A	
			A--B	11.00	17.50		A44 222 363B
			A--*	12.50	25.00	A00 898 750*	A01 795 703*
2	B NEW YORK	281,940,996	B--B	11.00	17.50	B21 700 717B	
			B--C	11.00	17.50		
			B--D	11.00	17.50		B90 870 463D
			B--*	12.50	25.00	B02 286 117*	B05 097 302*
3	C PHILADELPHIA	95,338,032	C--A	11.00	17.50	C32 791 370A	
			C--B	11.00	17.50		C27 992 286B
			C--*	12.50	25.00	C00 376 834*	C01 523 585*
4	D CLEVELAND	93,332,004	D--A	11.00	17.50	D38 939 570A	
			D--B	15.00	30.00		D12 473 923B
			D--*	12.50	25.00	D00 717 169*	D01 153 981*
5	E RICHMOND	101,037,912	E--A	11.00	17.50	E17 288 754A	
			E--B	12.50	25.00		E14 497 070B
			E--*	12.50	25.00	E00 369 502*	E01 152 624*
6	F ATLANTA	85,478,160	F--A	11.00	17.50	F18 294 206A	F97 932 586A
			F--B	12.50	25.00		
			F--*	12.50	25.00	F00 428 796*	
7	G CHICAGO	177,285,960	G--A	11.00	17.50	G71 072 584A	
			G--B	11.00	17.50		
			G--C	11.00	17.50		G37 851 417C
			G--*	12.50	25.00	G00 783 328*	G03 144 001*
8	H ST. LOUIS	50,694,312	H--A	11.00	17.50	H23 167 634A	H68 071 995A
			H--*	12.50	25.00	H00 348 164*	H00 857 792*
9	I MINNESPOLIS	16,340,016	I--A	11.00	17.50	I12 334 086A	I27 799 792A
			I--*	12.50	25.00	I00 322 885*	I00 379 905*
10	J KANSAS CITY	31,069,978	J--A	11.00	17.50	J18 160 353A	J52 984 711A
			J--*	12.50	25.00	J00 461 882*	J00 623 948*
11	K DALLAS	28,263,156	K--A	11.00	17.50	K13 954 086A	K44 603 904A
			K--*	12.50	25.00	K00 490 413*	
12	L SAN FRANCISCO	125,537,592	L--A	11.00	17.50	L47 193 506A	
			L--B	11.00	17.50		L44 293 268B
			L--*	12.50	25.00		L01 519 676*

TOTAL BLOCKS: Thirty-four

Collectors are requested to supply serial numbers that improve on above information.

(1) Includes both seal colors and mules.

CAT. NO. XF34A
$10.00 FEDERAL RESERVE NOTE MULE (DARK GREEN SEAL) 12 Subject
SERIES 1934A

PLATE SERIALS: Back check number 584 and lower.

	DISTRICT	TOTAL NOTES PRINTED	BLOCKS	ESTIMATED VALUE VG/F	CU	LOW OFFICIAL SERIAL NUMBER	HIGH OFFICIAL SERIAL NUMBER
1	A BOSTON		A--A			A62 535 662A	
			A--B				
			A--*				
2	B NEW YORK		B--B	15.00	25.00	B14 623 409B	B39 751 390B
			B--C			B01 439 995*	
			B--D				
			B--*	17.50	50.00	B01 376 477*	
3	C PHILADELPHIA		C--A	15.00	25.00	C32 803 388A	C40 083 516A
			C--B				
			C--*				
4	D CLEVELAND		D--A	15.00	25.00	D32 247 202A	D50 366 255A
			D--B				
			D--*				
5	E RICHMOND		E--A	15.00	25.00	E01 910 457A	E22 665 433A
			E--B				
			E--*				
6	F ATLANTA		F--A				
			F--B				
			F--*				
7	G CHICAGO		G--A	15.00	25.00	G61 302 477A	G75 438 444A
			G--B				
			G--C				
			G--*	17.50	50.00	G00 974 185*	G03 003 162*
8	H ST. LOUIS		H--A				
			H--*	17.50	50.00	H00 654 374*	
9	I MINNEAPOLIS		I--A				
			I--*				
10	J KANSAS CITY		J--A				
			J--*				
11	K DALLAS		K--A				
			K--*				
12	L SAN FRANCISCO		L--A				
			L--B				
			L--*				

TOTAL BLOCKS: Thirty-four.
Collectors are requested to provide any serial numbers that improve on above information.

CAT. NO. XF34A
$10.00 FEDERAL RESERVE NOTE (LIGHT GREEN SEAL) 12 Subject
SERIES 1934A

PLATE SERIALS: Back check numbers 585 and higher.

	DISTRICT	TOTAL NOTES PRINTED	BLOCKS	ESTIMATED VALUE VG/F	CU	LOW OFFICIAL SERIAL NUMBER	HIGH OFFICIAL SERIAL NUMBER
1	A BOSTON		A--A	12.00	17.50	A62 787 979A	
			A--B	12.00	17.50		A42 703 626B
			A--*	15.00	30.00	A01 158 180*	A01 245 426*
2	B NEW YORK		B--B	12.00	15.50	B13 772 577B	
			B--C	12.00	17.50		
			B--D	12.00	17.50		B89 961 988D
			B--*	15.00	30.00	B02 517 339*	B05 159 172*
3	C PHILADELPHIA		C--A	12.00	17.50	C32 330 960A	
			C--B	12.00	17.50		C23 02 333B
			C--*	15.00	30.00	C00 664 703*	C01 386 687*
4	D CLEVELAND		D--A	12.00	17.50	D34 296 413A	
			D--B	12.00	17.50		D00 985 494B
			D--*	15.00	17.50	D00 658 044*	D01 200 183*
5	E RICHMOND		E--A	12.00	17.50	E16 914 988A	
			E--B	12.00	17.50		E12 996 893B
			E--*	15.00	30.00	E01 270 366*	E01 304 236*

DISTRICT	TOTAL NOTES PRINTED	BLOCKS	ESTIMATED VALUE VG/F	CU	LOW OFFICIAL SERIAL NUMBER	HIGH OFFICIAL SERIAL NUMBER
6 F ATLANTA		F--A	12.00	17.50	F15 665 042A	F87 670 202A
		F--B	12.50	20.00		
		F--*	15.00	30.00	F00 879 743*	F01 186 759*
7 G CHICAGO		G--A	12.00	17.50	G70 175 527A	
		G--B	12.00	17.50		
		G--C	12.50	20.00		G19 630 194C
		G--*	15.00	30.00	G00 932 628*	G02 997 875*
8 H ST. LOUIS		H--A	12.00	17.50	H24 704 379 A	H64 485 848A
		H--*	15.00	30.00	H00 739 990*	
9 I MINNEAPOLIS		I--A	12.00	17.50	I09 243 570A	I25 768 860A
		I--*	15.00	30.00		
10 J KANSAS CITY		J--A	12.00	17.50	J20 613 278A	J52 095 878A
		J--*	15.00	30.00		
11 K DALLAS		K--A	12.00	17.50	K23 828 062A	K32 330 619A
		K--*	15.00	30.00		
12 L SAN FRANCISCO		L--A	12.00	17.50	L39 870 377A	
		L--B	12.00	17.50		L45 946 108B
		L--*	15.00	30.00		

TOTAL BLOCKS: Thirty-four.
Collectors are requested to supply serial numbers that improve on above information.

CAT. NO. XF34A
$10.00 FEDERAL RESERVE NOTE MULE (LIGHT GREEN SEAL) (12 Subject)
SERIES 1934A

PLATE SERIALS: Back check number 584 and lower.

DISTRICT	TOTAL NOTES PRINTED	BLOCKS	ESTIMATED VALUE VG/F	CU	LOW OBSERVED SERIAL NUMBER	HIGH OBSERVED SERIAL NUMBER
1 A BOSTON		A--A	17.50	17.50	A43 438 366A	
		A--B	17.50	17.50		A45 107 532B
2 B NEW YORK		B--B	17.50	17.50	B07 635 340B	B35 599 754B
3 C PHILADELPHIA		C--A	17.50	17.50	C34 739 596A	C38 622 756A
4 D CLEVELAND		D--A	17.50	17.50	D31 289 689A	D36 045 489A
5 E RICHMOND		E--A	17.50	17.50	E16 728 074A	
7 G CHICAGO		G--A	17.50	17.50	G61 302 477A	G68 136 040A
9 I MINNEAPOLIS		I--A	17.50	17.50	I11 544 301A	I12 530 556A
10 J KANSAS CITY		J--A	17.50	17.50	J04 616 427A	

TOTAL BLOCKS: Nine.
Collectors are requested to supply serials numbers that would improve on above information.

CAT. NO. XF34A
$10.00 FEDERAL RESERVE NOTE (BROWN SEAL) 12 Subject
HAWAII
SERIES 1934A

SERIAL NUMBERS:
(Official Ranges) L65 856 001A through L66 456 000A
L67 476 001A through L69 076 000A
L69 736 001A through L71 336 000A
L77 052 001A through L77 172 000A
L11 160 001B through L12 664 000B
L28 212 001B through L29 712 000B
L43 032 001B through L45 532 000B

L50 292 001B through L51 292 000B
Star Notes:
(Low Observed) L00 905 711* L02 011 363* (High Observed)
SIGNATURES: Same as Series 1934A.

ESTIMATED VALUES: BLOCKS   **VG/F**   **CU**
    L--A and L--B   20.00   200.00
    L--*   50.00   250.00

TOTAL BLOCKS KNOWN: Three.
ILLUSTRATION: See the following page.

CAT. NO. XF34B
$10.00 FEDERAL RESERVE NOTE (GREEN SEAL) (12 Subject)
SERIES 1934B

SERIAL NUMBERS: All districts continued sequence from previous series.
SIGNATURES: W.A. Julian, Treasurer of the United States.
  Fred M. Vinson, Secretary of the Treasury.

	DISTRICT	TOTAL NOTES PRINTED	BLOCKS	VG/F	CU	LOW OBSERVED SERIAL NUMBER	HIGH OBSERVED SERIAL NUMBER
1	A BOSTON	3,999,600	A--B	12.00	20.00	A38 659 831B	A45 794 487B
			A--*	12.50	25.00	A01 820 686*	A01 897 603*
2	B NEW YORK	34,815,948	B--D	12.00	20.00	B75 316 369D	
			B--E	12.00	20.00		B17 311 144E
			B--*	12.50	25.00	B05 092 596*	B05 601 302*
3	C PHILADELPHIA	10,339,020	C--B	12.00	20.00	C22 408 785B	C35 564 386B
			C--*	12.50	25.00	C01 613 493*	C01 660 619*
4	D CLEVELAND	1,394,700	D--B	12.00	20.00	D17 711 381B	D29 697 457B
			D--*	12.50	25.00		
5	E RICHMOND	4,018,272	E--B	12.00	20.00	E11 800 489B	E17 995 646B
			E--*	12.50	25.00		
6	F ATLANTA	6,746,076	F--B	12.00	20.00	F00 347 869B	F08 240 462B
			F--*	12.50	25.00		
7	G CHICAGO	18,130,836	G--C	12.00	20.00	G32 848 555C	G48 703 986C
			G--*	12.50	25.00	G03 032 893*	G03 181 803*
8	H ST. LOUIS	6,849,348	H--A	12.50	25.00	H69 891 088A	H73 815 225A
			H--B	12.00	17.50		
			H--*	12.50	25.00	H00 949 250*	
9	I MINNEAPOLIS	2,254,800	I--A	12.00	20.00	I32 139 319A	I33 647 397A
			I--*	12.50	25.00		
10	J KANSAS CITY	3,835,764	J--A	12.00	20.00	J50 864 742A	J54 163 698A
			J--*	12.50	25.00		
11	K DALLAS	3,085,200	K--A	12.00	20.00	K46 673 651A	K49 034 542A
			K--*	12.50	25.00		
12	L SAN FRANCISCO	9,076,800	L--B	12.00	20.00	L55 870 023B	L63 525 795B
			L--*	12.50	25.00	L02 270 807*	

TOTAL BLOCKS: Twenty-six.
Collectors are requested to supply serial numbers that improve on above information.

CAT. NO. XF34C
$10.00 FEDERAL RESERVE NOTE (GREEN SEAL) (12 Subject)
SERIES 1934C

SERIAL NUMBERS: W.A. Julian, Treasurer of the United States
  John W. Snyder, Secretary of the Treasury

	DISTRICT	TOTAL NOTES PRINTED	BLOCKS	VG/F	CU	LOW OBSERVED SERIAL NUMBER	HIGH OBSERVED SERIAL NUMBER
1	A BOSTON	42,431,404	A--B	12.00	17.50	A46 727 409B	A89 241 775B
			A--*	15.00	25.00	A01 991 691*	A02 188 164*
2	B NEW YORK	115,675,644	B--E	12.00	17.50	B14 341 429E	
			B--F	12.00	17.50		B79 629 354F
			B--*	15.00	25.00	B05 695 448*	B07 813 576*
3	C PHILADELPHIA	46,874,760	C--B	12.00	17.50	C34 226 174B	C81 049 029B
			C--*	15.00	25.00	C01 651 127*	C03 260 509*
4	D CLEVELAND	332,400	D--B	50.00	100.00	D19 581 685B	D58 664 062B
			D--*	75.00	150.00	D00 145 476*	D02 023 589*

177

	DISTRICT	TOTAL NOTES PRINTED	BLOCKS	ESTIMATED VALUE VG/F	CU	LOW OFFICIAL SERIAL NUMBER	HIGH OFFICIAL SERIAL NUMBER
5	E RICHMOND	37,422,600	E--B	12.00	17.50	E18 515 459B	E60 388 949B
			E--*	15.00	25.00	E01 615 677*	E02 123 769*
6	F ATLANTA	44,838,264	F--B	12.00	17.50	F10 012 993B	F51 072 323B
			F--*	15.00	25.00	F01 347 295*	F01 758 281*
7	G CHICAGO	105,875,412	G--C	12.00	17.50	G52 580 795C	
			G--D	12.00	17.50		G52 249 411D
			G--*	15.00	25.00	G03 583 891*	G04 892 293*
8	H ST. LOUIS	36,541,404	H--A	12.00	17.50	H80 584 362A	
			H--B	12.00	17.50		H08 645 013B
			H--*	15.00	25.00	H01 556 190*	H01 213 076*
9	I MINNEAPOLIS	11,944,848	I--A	12.00	17.50	I33 985 183A	I43 165 262A
			I--*	15.00	25.00	I00 526 641*	
10	J KANSAS CITY	20,874,072	J--A	12.00	17.50	J55 102 810A	J76 918 162A
			J--*	15.00	25.00	J00 833 311*	
11	K DALLAS	25,642,620	K--A	12.00	17.50	K50 804 411A	K74 108 012A
			K--*	15.00	25.00		
12	L SAN FRANCISCO	49,164,480	L--B	12.00	17.50	L64 548 208B	
			L--C	12.00	17.50		L07 215 023C
			L--*	15.00	25.00	L02 454 243*	L02 501 521*

TOTAL BLOCKS: Twenty-seven

Collectors are requested to supply serial numbers that improve on above information.

CAT. NO. XF34D
$10.00 FEDERAL RESERVE NOTE (GREEN SEAL) (12 Subject)
SERIES 1934D

SERIAL NUMBERS: All districts continued sequence from previous series.

SIGNATURES: Georgia Neese Clark, Treasurer of the United States
John W. Snyder, Secretary of the Treasury

	DISTRICT	TOTAL NOTES PRINTED	BLOCKS	ESTIMATED VALUE VG/F	CU	LOW OBSERVED SERIAL NUMBER	HIGH OBSERVED SERIAL NUMBER
1	A BOSTON	19,917,900	A--B	12.00	17.50	A89 660 775B	
			A--C	12.00	17.50		A08 687 876C
			A--*	15.00	25.00	A02 798 792*	A02 938 568*
2	B NEW YORK	64,067,904	B--F	12.00	17.50	B24 706 302F	F82 977 478F
			B--G	12.00	17.50		
			B--*	15.00	25.00	B07 813 576*	B08 337 511*
3	C PHILADELPHIA	18,432,000	C--B	12.00	17.50	C75 769 379B	C94 609 249B
			C--C	12.00	17.50		
			C--*	15.00	25.00	C02 425 717*	C02 571 795*
4	D CLEVELAND	20,291,316	D--B	12.00	17.50	D63 592 856B	D76 933 904B
			D--*	15.00	25.00	D02 388 225*	
5	E RICHMOND	18,090,312	E--B	12.00	17.50	E53 277 056B	E68 657 787B
			E--*	15.00	25.00		
6	F ATLANTA	17,064,816	F--B	12.00	17.50	F50 388 847B	F65 958 230B
			F--*	15.00	25.00	F02 236 801*	
7	G CHICAGO	55,943,844	G--D	12.00	17.50	G47 665 115D	
			G--E	12.00	17.50		G01 426 854E
			G--*	15.00	25.00	G05 182 143*	G05 665 693*
8	H ST. LOUIS	15,828,048	H--B	12.00	17.50	H09 348 201B	H21 503 566B
			H--*	15.00	25.00	H01 665 324*	H01 767 546*
9	I MINNEAPOLIS	5,237,220	I--A	12.00	17.50	I44 420 066A	I45 484 854A
			I--*	15.00	25.00		I00 662 768*
10	J KANSAS CITY		J--A	12.00	17.50	J75 180 729A	J79 692 641A
			J--*	15.00	25.00	J01 166 212*	
11	K DALLAS	7,178,196	K--A	12.00	17.50	K73 073 191A	K80 705 334A
			K--*	15.00	25.00		
12	L SAN FRANCISCO	23,956,584	L--C	12.00	17.50	L07 328 128C	L27 559 874C
			L--*	15.00	25.00		

TOTAL BLOCKS: Twenty eight

Collectors are requested to supply serial numbers that improve on above information.

CAT. NO. XF50
$10.00 FEDERAL RESERVE NOTE WIDE (GREEN SEAL) (12 Subject)
SERIES 1950

SERIAL NUMBERS: All districts both regular and star notes begin with 00 000 001 A.

PLATE SERIALS: Back check 1389 and lower.

SIGNATURES: Georgia Neese Clark, Treasurer of the United States.
John W. Snyder, Secretary of the Treasury

	DISTRICT	TOTAL NOTES PRINTED (1)	BLOCKS	ESTIMATED VALUE VG/F	CU	LOW OBSERVED SERIAL NUMBER	HIGH OBSERVED SERIAL NUMBER
1	A BOSTON	70,992,000	A--A	12.00	20.00	A23 473 485A	A70 992 000A
		1,008,000	A--*	12.50	25.00		A01 008 000*
2	B NEW YORK	218,576,000	B--A	12.00	20.00	B00 000 047A	
			B--B	12.00	20.00		
			B--C	12.50	22.50		B18 576 000C
		2,568,000	B--*	12.50	25.00		B03 168 000*
3	C PHILADELPHIA	76,320,000	C--A	12.00	20.00	C00 124 072A	C76 320 000A
		1,008,000	C--*	12.50	25.00		C01 008 000*
4	D CLEVELAND	76,032,000	D--A	12.00	20.00	D34 996 169	D76 032 000A
		1,008,000	D--*	12.50	25.00		D01 008 000*
5	E RICHMOND	61,776,000	E--A	12.00	20.00	E07 264 756A	E41 875 166A
		876,000	E--*	12.50	25.00		E00 876 000*
6	F ATLANTA	63,792,000	F--A	12.00	20.00	F06 102 749A	F63 792 000A
		864,000	F--*	12.50	25.00		F00 864 000*
7	G CHICAGO	161,056,000	G--A	12.00	20.00	G07 525 540A	G50 894 721A
			G--B	12.00	20.00		G61 056 000B
		2,088,000	G--*	12.50	25.00		G02 088 000*
8	H ST. LOUIS	47,808,000	H--A	12.00	20.00	H12 528 106A	H47 808 000A
		648,000	H--*	12.50	25.00		H00 648 000*
9	I MINNEAPOLIS	18,864,000	I--A	12.00	20.00	I01 730 118A	A18 864 000A
		252,000	I--*	12.50	25.00		I00 252 000*
10	J KANSAS CITY	36,332,000	J--A	12.00	20.00	J03 222 124A	J36 332 000A
		456,000	J--*	12.50	25.00		J00 456 000*
11	K DALLAS	33,264,000	K--A	12.00	20.00	K18 202 368A	K33 264 000A
		480,000	K--*	12.50	25.00		K00 480 000*
12	L SAN FRANCISCO	76,896,000	L--A	12.00	20.00	L24 558 682A	L76 896 000A
		1,152,000	L--*	12.50	25.00	L00 877 828*	L01 152 000*

TOTAL BLOCKS: Twenty-seven

(1) Includes varieties

CAT. NO. XF50
$10.00 FEDERAL RESERVE NOTE NARROW (GREEN SEAL) (12 Subject)
SERIES 1950

PLATE SERIALS: Back check number 1390-1456 inclusive

	DISTRICT	TOTAL NOTES PRINTED	BLOCKS	ESTIMATED VALUE VG/F	CU	LOW OBSERVED SERIAL NUMBER	HIGH OBSERVED SERIAL NUMBER
1	A BOSTON		A--A	12.00	20.00	A52 672 720A	A61 479 676A
2	B NEW YORK		B--B	12.00	20.00	B41 715 573B	
			B--C	12.50	22.50		B15 969 729C
3	C PHILADELPHIA		C--A	12.00	20.00	C45 571 678A	C74 610 569A
			C--*	12.50	25.00	C00 612 404*	
4	D CLEVELAND		D--A	12.00	20.00	D59 066 861A	D48 081 316A
5	E RICHMOND		E--A	12.00	20.00	E43 772 722A	E53 905 442A
			E--*	12.50	25.00	E00 765 688*	
6	F ATLANTA		F--A	12.00	20.00	F46 651 804A	
7	G CHICAGO		G--B	12.00	20.00	G19 614 029B	G44 702 685B
8	H ST. LOUIS		H--A	12.00	20.00	H27 407 447A	H44 216 385A
			H--*	12.50	25.00		H00 443 068*
9	I MINNEAPOLIS		I--A	12.00	20.00	I16 828 975A	
10	J KANSAS CITY		J--A	12.00	20.00	J20 978 619A	J29 574 837A
11	K DALLAS		K--A	12.00	20.00	K18 202 369A	K31 415 982A
			K--*	12.50	25.00		
12	L SAN FRANCISCO		L--A	12.00	20.00	L54 597 305A	L65 805 960A

TOTAL BLOCKS KNOWN: Seventeen.

Collectors are requested to supply serial numbers that improve on above information.

CAT. NO. XF50A
$10.00 FEDERAL RESERVE NOTE (GREEN SEAL) (18 Subject)
SERIES 1950A

SIGNATURES: Ivy Baker Priest. Treasurer of the United States
George M. Humphrey, Secretary of the Treasury

	DISTRICT	TOTAL NOTES PRINTED	BLOCKS	ESTIMATED VALUE VG/F	CU	LOW OFFICIAL SERIAL NUMBER	HIGH OFFICIAL SERIAL NUMBER
1	A BOSTON	104,248,000	A--A	12.00	20.00	A70 992 001A	
			A--B	12.00	20.00		A75 240 000B
		5,112,000	A--*	12.50	25.00	A01 008 001*	A06 120 000*
2	B NEW YORK	356,664,000	B--C	12.00	20.00	B18 576 001C	
			B--D	12.00	20.00		
			B--E	12.00	20.00		
			B--F	12.00	20.00		B75 240 000F
		16,992,000	B--*	12.50	25.00	B03 168 001*	B20 160 000*
3	C PHILADELPHIA	71,920,000	C--A	12.00	20.00	C76 320 001A	
			C--B	12.00	20.00		C48 240 000B
		3,672,000	C--*	12.50	25.00	C01 008 001*	C04 680 000*

	DISTRICT	TOTAL NOTES PRINTED	BLOCKS	ESTIMATED VALUE VG/F	CU	LOW OFFICIAL SERIAL NUMBER	HIGH OFFICIAL SERIAL NUMBER
4	D CLEVELAND	75,088,000	D--A	12.00	20.00	D76 032 001A	
			D--B	12.00	20.00		D51 120 000B
		3,672,000	D--*	12.50	25.00	D01 008 001*	D04 680 000*
5	E RICHMOND	82,144,000	E--A	12.00	20.00	E61 776 001A	
			E--B	12.00	20.00		E43 920 000B
		4,392,000	E--*	12.50	25.00	E01 008 001*	E05 400 000*
6	F ATLANTA	73,288,000	F--A	12.00	20.00	F63 792 001A	
			F--B	12.00	20.00		F37 080 000B
		3,816,000	F--*	12.50	25.00	F00 864 001*	F04 680 000*
7	G CHICAGO	235,064,000	G--B	12.00	20.00	G61 056 001B	
			G--C	12.00	20.00		
			G--D	12.00	20.00		G96 120 000D
		11,160,000	G--*	12.50	25.00	G02 160 001*	G13 320 000*
8	H ST. LOUIS	46,512,000	H--A	12.00	20.00	H47 808 001A	H94 320 000A
		2,880,000	H--*	12.50	25.00	H00 720 001*	H03 600 000*
9	I MINNEAPOLIS	8,136,000	I--A	12.00	20.00	I18 864 001A	I27 000 000A
		432,000	I--*	15.00	35.00	I00 288 001*	I00 720 000*
10	J KANSAS CITY	25,488,000	J--A	12.00	20.00	J36 432 001A	J61 920 000A
		2,304,000	J--*	12.50	25.00	J00 576 001*	J02 880 000*
11	K DALLAS	21,816,000	K--A	12.00	20.00	K33 264 001A	K55 080 000A
		1,584,000	K--*	12.50	25.00	K00 576 001*	K02 160 000*
12	L SAN FRANCISCO	101,584,000	L--A	12.00	20.00	L76 896 001A	
			L--B	12.00	20.00		L78 480 000B
		6,408,000	L--*	12.50	25.00	L01 152 001*	L07 560 000*

TOTAL BLOCKS: Thirty five

CAT. NO. XF50B
$10.00 FEDERAL RESERVE NOTE (GREEN SEAL) (18 Subject)
SERIES 1950B

SIGNATURES: Ivy Baker Priest, Treasurer of the United States
 Robert B. Anderson, Secretary of the Treasury

	DISTRICT	TOTAL NOTES PRINTED	BLOCKS	ESTIMATED VALUE VG/F	CU	LOW OFFICIAL SERIAL NUMBER	HIGH OFFICIAL SERIAL NUMBER
1	A BOSTON	49,240,000	A--B		17.50	A75 240 001B	
			A--C		17.50		A24 480 000C
		2,880,000	A--*		22.50	A06 120 001*	A09 000 000*
2	B NEW YORK	170,840,000	B--F		17.50	B75 240 001F	
			B--G		17.50		
			B--H		17.50		B46 080 000H
		8,280,000	B--*		22.50	B20 160 001*	B28 440 000*
3	C PHILADELPHIA	66,880,000	C--B		17.50	C48 240 001B	
			C--C		17.50		C15 120 000C
		3,240,000	C--*		22.50	C04 680 001*	C07 920 000*
4	D CLEVELAND	55,360,000	D--B		17.50	D51 120 001B	
			D--C		17.50		D06 480 000C
		2,880,000	D--*		22.50	D04 680 001*	D07 560 000*
5	E RICHMOND	51,120,000	E--B		17.50	E43 920 001B	E95 040 000B
		2,880,000	E--*		22.50	E05 400 001*	E08 280 000*
6	F ATLANTA	66,520,000	F--B		17.50	F37 080 001B	
			F--C		20.00		F03 600 000C
		2,880,000	F--*		22.50	F04 680 001*	F07 560 000*
7	G CHICAGO	165,080,000	G--D		18.50	G96 120 001D	
			G--E		17.50		
			G--F		17.50		G61 200 000F
		6,480,000	G--*		22.50	G13 680 001*	G20 160 000*
8	H ST. LOUIS	33,040,000	H--A		17.50	H94 320 001A	
			H--B		17.50		H27 360 000B
		1,800,000	H--*		22.50	H03 600 001*	H05 400 000*
9	I MINNEAPOLIS	13,320,000	I--A		17.50	I27 000 001A	I40 320 000A
		720,000	I--*		22.50	I00 720 001*	I01 440 000*
10	J KANSAS CITY	33,480,000	J--A		17.50	J61 920 001A	J95 400 000A
		2,520,000	J--*		22.50	J02 880 001*	J05 400 000*

DISTRICT	TOTAL NOTES PRINTED	BLOCKS	ESTIMATED VALUE VG/F	CU	LOW OFFICIAL SERIAL NUMBER	HIGH OFFICIAL SERIAL NUMBER
11 K DALLAS	26,280,000	K--A		17.50	K55 080 001A	K81 360 000A
	1,440,000	K--*		22.50	K02 160 001*	K03 600 000*
12 L SAN FRANCISCO	55,000,000	L--B		17.50	L78 480 001B	
		L--C		17.50		L33 480 000C
	2,880,000	L--*		22.50	L07 560 001*	L10 440 000*

TOTAL BLOCKS: Thirty four

CAT. NO. XF50C
$10.00 FEDERAL RESERVE NOTE (GREEN SEAL) (18 Subject)
SERIES 1950C

SIGNATURES: Elizabeth Rudel Smith, Treasurer of the United States
C. Douglas Dillon, Secretary of the Treasury

DISTRICT	TOTAL NOTES PRINTED	BLOCKS	ESTIMATED VALUE VG/F	CU	LOW OFFICIAL SERIAL NUMBER	HIGH OFFICIAL SERIAL NUMBER
1 A BOSTON	51,120,000	A--C		15.00	A24 480 001C	A75 600 000C
	2,160,000	A--*		20.00	A09 000 001*	A11 160 000*
2 B NEW YORK	126,520,000	B--H		15.00	B46 080 001H	
		B--I		15.00		B66 600 000I
	6,840,000	B--*		20.00	B28 440 001*	B35 280 000*
3 C PHILADELPHIA	25,200,000	C--C		15.00	C15 120 001C	C40 320 000C
	720,000	C--*		20.00	C07 920 001*	C08 640 000*
4 D CLEVELAND	33,120,000	D--C		15.00	D06 480 001C	D39 600 000C
	1,800,000	D--*		20.00	D07 560 001*	D09 360 000*
5 E RICHMOND	45,640,000	E--B		15.00	E95 040 001B	
		E--C		15.00		E40 680 000C
	1,800,000	E--*		20.00	E08 280 001*	E10 080 000*
6 F ATLANTA	38,880,000	F--C		15.00	F03 600 001C	F42 480 000C
	1,800,000	F--*		20.00	F07 560 001*	F09 360 000*
7 G CHICAGO	69,400,000	G--F		15.00	G61 200 001F	
		G--G		15.00		G30 600 000G
	3,600,000	G--*		20.00	G20 160 001*	G23 760 000*
8 H ST. LOUIS	23,040,000	H--B		15.00	H27 360 001B	H50 400 000B
	1,080,000	H--*		20.00	H05 400 001*	H06 480 000*
9 I MINNEAPOLIS	9,000,000	I--A		15.00	I40 320 001A	I49 320 000A
	720,000	I--*		20.00	I01 440 001*	I02 160 000*
10 J KANSAS CITY	23,320,000	J--A		17.00	J95 400 001A	
		J--B		15.00		J18 720 000B
	800,000	J--*		20.00	J05 680 001*	J06 480 000*
11 K DALLAS	17,640,000	K--A		15.00	K81 360 001A	K99 000 000A
	720,000	K--*		20.00	K03 600 001*	K04 320 000*
12 L SAN FRANCISCO	35,640,000	L--C		15.00	L33 480 001C	L69 120 000C
	1,800,000	L--*		20.00	L10 440 001*	L12 240 000*

TOTAL BLOCKS: Twenty eight.

CAT. NO. XF50D
$10.00 FEDERAL RESERVE NOTE (GREEN SEAL) (18 Subject)
SERIES 1950D

SIGNATURES: Kathryn O'Hay Granahan, Treasurer of the United States
C. Douglas Dillon, Secretary of the Treasury

DISTRICT	TOTAL NOTES PRINTED	BLOCKS	ESTIMATED VALUE VG/F	CU	LOW OFFICIAL SERIAL NUMBER	HIGH OFFICIAL SERIAL NUMBER
1 A BOSTON	38,800,000	A--C		15.00	A75 600 001C	
		A--D		15.00		A14 400 000D
	1,800,000	A--*		20.00	A11 160 001*	A12 960 000*
2 B NEW YORK	150,320,000	B--I		15.00	B66 600 001I	
		B--J		15.00		
		B--K		15.00		B16 920 000K
	6,840,000	B--*		20.00	B35 280 001*	B42 120 000*
3 C PHILADELPHIA	19,080,000	C--C		15.00	C40 320 001C	C59 400 000C
	1,080,000	C--*		20.00	C08 640 001*	C09 720 000*
4 D CLEVELAND	24,120,000	D--C		15.00	D39 600 001C	D63 720 000C
	360,000	D--*		25.00	D09 360 001*	D10 800 000*

	DISTRICT	TOTAL NOTES PRINTED	BLOCKS	ESTIMATED VALUE VG/F	CU	LOW OFFICIAL SERIAL NUMBER	HIGH OFFICIAL SERIAL NUMBER
5	E RICHMOND	33,840,000	E--C		15.00	E40 680 001C	E74 520 000C
		720,000	E--*		20.00	E10 080 001*	E10 800 000*
6	F ATLANTA	36,000,000	F--C		15.00	F42 480 001C	F78 480 000C
		1,440,000	F--*		20.00	F09 360 001*	F10 800 000*
7	G CHICAGO	115,480,000	G--G		15.00	G30 600 001G	
			G--H		15.00		G46 080 000H
		5,040,000	G--*		20.00	G23 760 001*	G28 800 000*
8	H ST. LOUIS	10,440,000	H--B		15.00	H50 400 001B	H60 840 000B
		720,000	H--*		20.00	H06 480 001*	H07 200 000*
9	I MINNEAPOLIS				NONE	None printed	
10	J KANSAS CITY	15,480,000	J--B		15.00	J18 720 001B	J34 200 000B
		1,080,000	J--*		20.00	J06 480 001*	J07 560 000*
11	K DALLAS	18,280,000	K--A		20.00	K99 000 001A	
			K--B		15.00		K17 280 000B
		800,000	K--*		20.00	K04 600 001*	K05 400 000*
12	L SAN FRANCSICO	62,560,000	L--C		15.00	L69 120 001C	
			L--D		15.00		L31 680 000D
		3,600,000	L--*		20.00	L12 240 001*	L15 840 000*

TOTAL BLOCKS: Twenty eight

CAT. NO. XF50E
$10.00 FEDERAL RESERVE NOTE (GREEN SEAL) (18 Subject)
SERIES 1950E

SIGNATURES: Kathryn O'Hay Granahan, Treasurer of the United States
Henry H. Fowler, Secretary of the Treasury

	DISTRICT	TOTAL NOTES PRINTED	BLOCKS	ESTIMATED VALUE VG/F	CU	LOW OFFICIAL SERIAL NUMBER	HIGH OFFICIAL SERIAL NUMBER
2	B NEW YORK	12,600,000	B--K		17.50	B16 920 001K	B54 700 000K
		2,621,000	B--*		25.00	B42 120 001*	B44 741 600*
7	G CHICAGO	65,080,000	G--H		17.50	G46 080 001H	
			G--I		17.50		G11 160 000I
		4,320,000	G--*		25.00	G28 800 001*	G33 120 000*
12	L SAN FRANCISCO	17,280,000	L--D		17.50	L31 680 001D	L48 960 000D
		720,000	L--*		35.00	L15 840 001*	L16 560 000*

TOTAL BLOCKS: Seven

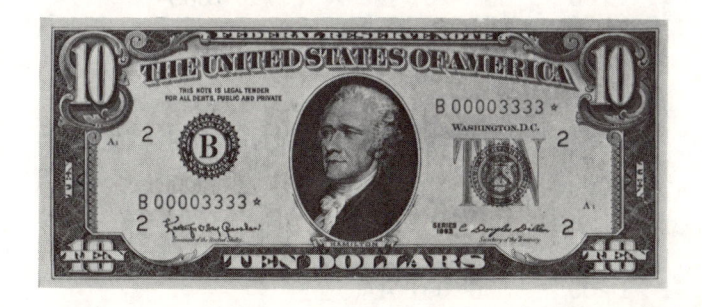

CAT. NO. XF63
$10.00 FEDERAL RESERVE NOTE (GREEN SEAL) (32 Subject)
SERIES 1963

SERIAL NUMBERS: All serial numbers both regular and star notes begin with 00 000 001.

PLATE SERIALS: Face and back check begin with 1. Motto IN GOD WE TRUST added to back.

SIGNATURES: Kathryn O'Hay Granahan, Treasurer of the United States
C. Douglas Dillon, Secretary of the Treasury

	DISTRICT	TOTAL NOTES PRINTED	BLOCKS	ESTIMATED VALUE VG/F	CU	LOW OFFICIAL SERIAL NUMBER	HIGH OFFICIAL SERIAL NUMBER
1	A BOSTON	5,760,000	A--A		15.00		A05 760 000A
			A--*		17.50		A00 640 000*

	DISTRICT	TOTAL NOTES PRINTED	BLOCKS	ESTIMATED VALUE VG/F	CU	LOW OFFICIAL SERIAL NUMBER	HIGH OFFICIAL SERIAL NUMBER
2	B NEW YORK	24,960,000	B--A		15.00		B24 960 000A
			B--*		17.50		B01 920 000*
3	C PHILADELPHIA	6,400,000	C--A		15.00		C06 400 000A
			C--*		17.50		C01 280 000*
4	D CLEVELAND	7,040,000	D--A		15.00		D07 040 000A
			D--*		17.50		D00 640 000*
5	E RICHMOND	4,480,000	E--A		16.00		E04 480 000A
			E--*		17.50		E00 640 000*
6	F ATLANTA	10,880,000	F--A		15.00		F10 880 000A
			F--*		17.50		F01 280 000*
7	G CHICAGO	35,200,000	G--A		15.00		G35 200 000A
			G--*		17.50		G02 560 000*
8	H ST. LOUIS	13,440,000	H--A		15.00		H13 440 000A
			H--*		17.50		H01 280 000*
9	I MINNEAPOLIS	NONE	NONE		NONE		
10	J KANSAS CITY	3,840,000	J--A		17.00		J03 840 000A
			J--*		18.50		J00 640 000*
11	K DALLAS	5,120,000	K--A		15.00		K05 120 000A
			K--*		17.50		K00 640 000*
12	L SAN FRANCISCO	14,080,000	L--A		15.00		L14 080 000A
			L--*		17.50		L01 280 000*

TOTAL BLOCKS: Twenty two

CAT. NO. XF63A
$10.00 FEDERAL RESERVE NOTE (GREEN SEAL) (12 Subject)
SERIES 1963A

SIGNATURES: Kathryn O'Hay Granahan, Treasurer of the United States
Henry H. Fowler, Secretary of the Treasury

	DISTRICT	TOTAL NOTES PRINTED	BLOCKS	ESTIMATED VALUE VG/F	CU	LOW OFFICIAL SERIAL NUMBER	HIGH OFFICIAL SERIAL NUMBER
1	A BOSTON	131,360,000	A--A		14.00	A05 760 001A	
			A--B		14.00		A37 120 000B
		6,400,000	A--*		15.00	A00 640 001*	A07 040 000*
2	B NEW YORK	199,360,000	B--A		14.00	B24 960 001A	
			B--B		14.00		
			B--C		14.00		B24 320 000C
		9,600,000	B--*		15.00	B01 920 001*	B11 520 000*
3	C PHILADELPHIA	100,000,000	C--A		14.00	C06 400 001A	
			C--B		14.00		C06 400 000B
		4,480,000	C--*		15.00	C01 280 001*	C05 760 000*
4	D CLEVELAND	72,960,000	D--A		14.00	D07 040 001A	D80 000 000A
		3,840,000	D--*		15.00	D00 640 001*	D04 480 000*
5	E RICHMOND	114,720,000	E--A		14.00	E04 480 001A	
			E--B		14.00		E19 200 000B
		5,120,000	E--*		15.00	E00 640 001*	E05 760 000*
6	F ATLANTA	80,000,000	F--A		14.00	F10 880 001A	F90 880 000A
		3,840,000	F--*		15.00	F01 280 001*	F05 120 000*
7	G CHICAGO	195,520,000	G--A		14.00	G35 200 001A	
			G--B		14.00		
			G--C		14.00		G30 720 000C
		9,600,000	G--*		15.00	G02 560 001*	G12 160 000*
8	H ST. LOUIS	43,520,000	H--A		14.00	H13 440 001A	H56 960 000A
		1,920,000	H--*		15.00	H01 280 001*	H03 200 000*
9	I MINNEAPOLIS	16,640,000	I--A		14.00	I00 000 001A	I16 640 000A
		640,000	I--*		15.00	I00 000 001*	I00 640 000*
10	J KANSAS CITY	31,360,000	J--A		14.00	J03 840 001A	J35 200 000A
		1,920,000	J--*		15.00	J00 640 001*	J02 560 000*
11	K DALLAS	51,200,000	K--A		14.00	K05 120 001A	K56 320 000A
		1,920,000	K--*		15.00	K00 640 001*	K02 560 000*
12	L SAN FRANCISCO	87,200,000	L--A		14.00	L14 080 001A	
			L--B		17.50		L01 280 000B
		5,120,000	L--*		15.00	L01 280 001*	L06 400 000*

TOTAL BLOCKS: Thirty two

CAT. NO. XF69
$10.00 FEDERAL RESERVE NOTE (GREEN SEAL) (32 Subject)
SERIES 1969

SERIAL NUMBERS: All serial numbers both regular and star notes begin with 00 000 001.
SIGNATURES: Dorothy Andrews Elston, Treasurer of the United States
David M. Kennedy, Secretary of the Treasury

	DISTRICT	TOTAL NOTES PRINTED	BLOCKS	ESTIMATED VALUE VG/F	CU	LOW OFFICIAL SERIAL NUMBER	HIGH OFFICIAL SERIAL NUMBER
1	A BOSTON	74,880,000	A--A		14.00		A74 880 000A
		2,560,000	A--*		15.00		A02 560 000*
2	B NEW YORK	247,360,000	B--A		14.00		
			B--B		14.00		
			B--C		14.00		B47 360 000C
		10,240,000	B--*		15.00		B10 240 000*
3	C PHILADELPHIA	56,960,000	C--A		14.00		C56 960 000A
		2,560,000	C--*		15.00		C01 920 000*
4	D CLEVELAND	57,600,000	D--A		14.00		D57 600 000A
		2,560,000	D--*		15.00		D02 560 000*
5	E RICHMOND	56,960,000	E--A		14.00		E56 960 000A
		2,560,000	E--*		15.00		E02 560 000*
6	F ATLANTA	53,760,000	F--A		14.00		F53 760 000A
		2,560,000	F--*		15.00		F02 560 000*
7	G CHICAGO	142,240,000	G--A		14.00		
			G--B		14.00		G42 240 000B
		6,400,000	G--*		15.00		G06 400 000*
8	H ST. LOUIS	22,400,000	H--A		14.00		H22 400 000A
		640,000	H--*		17.50		H00 640 000*
9	I MINNEAPOLIS	12,800,000	I--A		14.00		I12 800 000A
		1,280,000	I--*		20.00		I01 280 000*
10	J KANSAS CITY	31,360,000	J--A		14.00		J31 360 000A
		1,280,000	J--*		15.00		J01 280 000*
11	K DALLAS	30,080,000	K--A		14.00		K30 080 000A
		1,280,000	K--*		15.00		K01 280 000*
12	SAN FRANCISCO	56,320,000	L--A		14.00		L56 320 000A
		3,185,000	L--*		15.00		L03 185 000*

TOTAL BLOCKS: Twenty seven.

CAT. NO. XF69A
$10.00 FEDERAL RESERVE NOTE (GREEN SEAL) (32 Subject)
SERIES 1969A

SIGNATURES: Dorothy Andrews Kabis, Treasurer of the United States
John B. Connally, Secretary of the Treasury

	DISTRICT	TOTAL NOTES PRINTED	BLOCKS	ESTIMATED VALUE VG/F	CU	LOW OFFICIAL SERIAL NUMBER	HIGH OFFICIAL SERIAL NUMBER
1	A BOSTON	41,120,000	A--A		15.00	A74 880 001A	
			A--B		15.00		A16 000 000B
		1,920,000	A--*		17.50	A02 560 001*	A04 480 000*
2	B NEW YORK	111,840,000	B--C		15.00	B47 360 001C	
			B--D		15.00		B59 520 000D
		3,840,000	B--*		17.50	B10 240 001*	B14 080 000*
3	C PHILADELPHIA	24,320,000	C--A		15.00	C56 960 001A	C81 280 000A
		1,920,000	C--*		17.50	C01 920 001*	C03 840 000*
4	D CLEVELAND	23,680,000	D--A		15.00	D57 600 001A	D81 280 000A
		1,276,000	D--*		17.50	D02 560 001*	D03 836 000*
5	E RICHMOND	25,600,000	E--A		15.00	E56 960,001A	E82 560 000A
		640,000	E--*		20.00	E02 560 001*	E03 200 000*
6	F ATLANTA	20,480,000	F--A		15.00	F53 760 001A	F74 240 000A
		640,000	F--*		20.00	F02 560 000*	F03 200 000*
7	G CHICAGO	80,160,000	G--B		15.00	G42 240 001B	
			G--C		15.00		G22 400 000C
		3,560,000	G--*		17.50	G06 400 001*	G08 960 000*

	DISTRICT	TOTAL NOTES PRINTED	BLOCKS	ESTIMATED VALUE VG/F	CU	LOW OFFICIAL SERIAL NUMBER	HIGH OFFICIAL SERIAL NUMBER
8	H ST. LOUIS	15,360,000	H--A		15.00	H22 400 001A	H37 760 000A
			H--*		20.00	H00 640 001*	H01 280 000*
9	I MINNEAPOLIS	8,320,000	I--A		15.00	I12 800 001A	I21 120 000A
			I--*			none printed	
10	J KANSAS CITY	10,880,000	J--A		15.00	J31 360 001A	J42 240 000A
			J--*			none printed	
11	K DALLAS	20,480,000	K--A		15.00	K30 080 001A	K50 560 000A
		640,000	K--*		20.00	K01 280 001*	K01 920 000*
12	L SAN FRANCISCO	27,520,000	L--A		15.00	L56 320 001A	L83 840 000A
		1,280,000	L--*		17.50	L03 200 001*	L03 840 000*

TOTAL BLOCKS: Twenty-five.

CAT. NO. XF69B
$10.00 FEDERAL RESERVE NOTE (GREEN SEAL) (32 Subject)
SERIES 1969B

SIGNATURES: Romana Acosta Banuelos, Treasurer of the United States
John B. Connally, Secretary of the Treasury

	DISTRICT	TOTAL NOTES PRINTED	BLOCKS	ESTIMATED VALUE VG/F	CU	LOW OFFICIAL SERIAL NUMBER	HIGH OFFICIAL SERIAL NUMBER
1	A BOSTON	16,640,000	A--B		14.00	A16 000 0001B	A32 640 000B
		none	A--*			none printed	
2	B NEW YORK	60,320,000	B--D		14.00	B59 520 001D	
			B--E		14.00		B19 840 000E
		1,920,000	B--*		15.00	B14 080 001*	B16 000 000*
3	C PHILADELPHIA	16,000,000	C--A		14.00	C81 280 001A	C97 280 000A
		none	C--*			none printed	
4	D CLEVELAND	12,800,000	D--A		14.00	D81 280 001A	D94 080 000A
		none	D--*			none printed	
5	E RICHMOND	12,160,000	E--A		14.00	E82 560 001A	E94 720 000A
		640,000	E--*		20.00	E03 200 001*	E03 840 000*
6	F ATLANTA	13,440,000	F--A		14.00	F74 240 001A	F87 680 000A
		640,000	F--*		20.00	F03 200 001*	F03 840 000*
7	G CHICAGO	32,640,000	G--C		14.00	G22 400 001C	G55 040 000C
		1,268,000	G--*		15.00	G08 960 001*	G10 227 000*
8	H ST. LOUIS	8,960,000	H--A		14.00	H37 760 001A	H46 720 000A
		1,280,000	H--*		15.00	H01 280 001*	H02 560 000*
9	I MINNEAPOLIS	3,200,000	I--A		14.00	I21 120 001A	I24 320 000A
		none	I--*			none printed	
10	J KANSAS CITY	5,120,000	J--A		14.00	J42 240 001A	J47 360 000A
		640,000	J--*		20.00	J01 280 001*	J01 920 000*
11	K DALLAS	5,760,000	K--A		14.00	K50 560 001A	K56 320 000A
		none	K--*			none printed	
12	L SAN FRANCISCO	23,840,000	L--A		14.00	L83 840 001A	
			L--B		14.00		L07 680 000B
		640,000	L--*		20.00	L04 000 001*	L05 120 000*

TOTAL BLOCKS: Twenty-one.

CAT. NO. XF69C
$10.00 FEDERAL RESERVE NOTE (GREEN SEAL) (32 Subject)
SERIES 1969C

SIGNATURES: Romano Acosta Banuelos, Treasurer of the United States
George P. Shultz, Secretary of the Treasury
ESTIMATED VALUES: All regular notes $12.50, stars $15.00 CU.

	DISTRICT	TOTAL NOTES PRINTED	BLOCKS	ESTIMATED VALUE VG/F	CU	LOW OFFICIAL SERIAL NUMBER	HIGH OFFICIAL SERIAL NUMBER
1	A BOSTON	44,800,00	A--B			A32 640 001B	A77 440 000B
		640,000	A--*			A04 480 001*	A05 120 000*
2	B NEW YORK	203,200,000	B--E			B19 840 01E	
			B--F				
			B--G				B23 040 000G
		7,040,000	B--*			B16 000 001*	B23 040 000*

	DISTRICT	TOTAL NOTES PRINTED	BLOCKS	ESTIMATED VALUE VG/F	CU	LOW OFFICIAL SERIAL NUMBER	HIGH OFFICIAL SERIAL NUMBER
3	C PHILADELPHIA	69,920,000	C--A			C97 280 000A	
			C--B				C67 200 000B
		1,280,000	C--*			C03 840 001*	C05 120 000*
4	D CLEVELAND	46,880,000	D--A			D94 080 001A	
			D--B				D40 960 000B
		2,400,000	D--*			D04 000 001*	D06 400 000*
5	E RICHMOND	45,600,000	E--A			E94 720 001A	
			E--B				E40 320 000B
		1,120,000	E--*			E04 000 001*	E05 120 000*
6	F ATLANTA	46,240,000	F--A			F87 680 001A	
			F--B				F33 920 000B
		1,920,000	F--*			F03 840 001*	F05 760 000*
7	G CHICAGO	55,200,000	G--C			G55 040 001C	
			G--D				G10 240 000D
		880,000	G--*			G10 000 001*	G10 880 000*
8	H ST. LOUIS	29,800,000	H--A			H46 720 001A	H76 520 000A
		1,280,000	H--*			H02 560 001*	H03 840 000*
9	I MINNEAPOLIS	11,520,000	I--A			I24 320 001A	I35 840 000A
		640,000	I--*			I01 280 001*	I01 920 000*
10	J KANSAS CITY	23,040,000	J--A			J47 360 001A	J70 400 000A
		640,000	J--*			J01 920 001*	J02 560 000*
11	K DALLAS	24,960,000	K--A			K56 320 001A	K81 280 000A
		640,000	K--*			K01 920 000*	K02 560 000*
12	L SAN FRANCISCO	56,960,000	L--B			L07 680 001B	L64 640 000B
		640,000	L--*			L05 120 001*	L05 760 000*

TOTAL BLOCKS: Thirty-one.

CAT. NO. XF74
$10.00 FEDERAL RESERVE NOTE (GREEN SEAL) 32 Subject.
SERIES 1974

SIGNATURES: Francine I. Neff, Treasurer of the United States.
  William E. Simon, Secretary of the Treasury.
SERIAL NUMBERS: Continued from previous series.
PLATE SERIALS: Continued form previous series.

	DISTRICT	TOTAL NOTES PRINTED	BLOCKS	ESTIMATED VALUE VG/F	CU	LOW OFFICIAL SERIAL NUMBER	HIGH OFFICIAL SERIAL NUMBER	
1	A BOSTON		A--B		12.50	A77 440 001B	A99 999 999B	cv
			A--C		12.50	A00 000 001C	A30 080 000C	cv
					12.50	A30 080 001C	A81 920 000C	cp
			A--*		15.00	A05 120 001*	A07 040 000*	cv
					25.00	A07 056 001*	A07 060 000*	cv
					25.00	A07 076 001*	A07 080 000*	cv
					25.00	A07 096 001*	A07 100 000*	cv
					25.00	A07 116 001*	A07 120 000*	cv
					25.00	A07 136 001*	A07 140 000*	cv
					25.00	A07 156 001*	A07 160 000*	cv
					25.00	A07 176 001*	A07 180 000*	cv
					25.00	A07 196 001*	A07 200 000*	cv
					25.00	A07 216 001*	A07 220 000*	cv
					25.00	A07 236 001*	A07 240 000*	cv
					25.00	A07 256 001*	A07 260 000*	cv
					25.00	A07 276 001*	A07 280 000*	cv
					25.00	A07 296 001*	A07 300 000*	cv
					25.00	A07 316 001*	A07 320 000*	cv
					25.00	A07 336 001*	A07 340 000*	cv
					25.00	A07 356 001*	A07 360 000*	cv
					25.00	A07 376 001*	A07 380 000*	cv
					25.00	A07 396 001*	A07 400 000*	cv
					25.00	A07 416 001*	A07 420 000*	cv
					25.00	A07 436 001*	A07 440 000*	cv
					25.00	A07 456 001*	A07 460 000*	cv
					25.00	A07 476 001*	A07 480 000*	cv
					25.00	A07 496 001*	A07 500 000*	cv
					25.00	A07 516 001*	A07 520 000*	cv
					25.00	A07 536 001*	A07 540 000*	cv

DISTRICT	TOTAL NOTES PRINTED	BLOCKS	ESTIMATED VALUE VG/F CU	LOW OFFICIAL SERIAL NUMBER	HIGH OFFICIAL SERIAL NUMBER	
			25.00	A07 556 001*	A07 560 000*	cv
			25.00	A07 576 001*	A07 580 000*	cv
			25.00	A07 596 001*	A07 600 000*	cv
			25.00	A07 616 001*	A07 620 000*	cv
			25.00	A07 636 001*	A07 640 000*	cv
			25.00	A07 656 001*	A07 660 000*	cv
			25.00	A07 676 001*	A07 680 000*	cv
2	B NEW YORK	B--G	12.50	B23 040 001G	B99 999 999G	cv
		B--H	12.50	B00 000 001H	B99 840 000H	cp
			25.00	B99 840 001H	B99 999 999H	cv
		B--I	12.50	B00 000 001I	B62 080 000I	cp
		B--*	15.00	B23 040 001*	B26 240 000*	cv
			15.00	B26 400 001*	B26 880 000*	cv
			25.00	B26 884 001*	B26 900 000*	cv
			25.00	B26 904 001*	B26 920 000*	cv
			25.00	B26 924 001*	B26 940 000*	cv
			25.00	B26 944 001*	B26 960 000*	cv
			25.00	B26 964 001*	B26 980 000*	cv
			25.00	B26 984 001*	B27 000 000*	cv
			25.00	B27 004 001*	B27 020 000*	cv
			25.00	B27 024 001*	B27 040 000*	cv
			25.00	B27 044 001*	B27 060 000*	cv
			25.00	B27 064 001*	B27 080 000*	cv
			25.00	B27 084 001*	B27 100 000*	cv
			25.00	B27 104 001*	B27 120 000*	cv
			25.00	B27 124 001*	B27 140 000*	cv
			25.00	B27 144 001*	B27 160 000*	cv
			25.00	B27 164 001*	B27 180 000*	cv
			25.00	B27 184 001*	B27 200 000*	cv
			25.00	B27 204 001*	B27 220 000*	cv
			25.00	B27 224 001*	B27 240 000*	cv
			25.00	B27 244 001*	B27 260 000*	cv
			25.00	B27 264 001*	B27 280 000*	cv
			25.00	B27 284 001*	B27 300 000*	cv
			25.00	B27 304 001*	B27 320 000*	cv
			25.00	B27 324 001*	B27 340 000*	cv
			25.00	B27 344 001*	B27 360 000*	cv
			25.00	B27 364 001*	B27 380 000*	cv
			25.00	B27 384 001*	B27 400 000*	cv
			25.00	B27 404 001*	B27 420 000*	cv
			25.00	B27 424 001*	B27 440 000*	cv
			25.00	B27 444 001*	B27 460 000*	cv
			25.00	B27 464 001*	B27 480 000*	cv
			25.00	B27 484 001*	B27 500 000*	cv
			25.00	B27 504 001*	B27 520 000*	cv
3	C PHILADELPHIA	C--B	12.50	C67 200 001B	C99 999 999B	cv
		C--C	12.50	C00 000 001C	C30 720 000C	cv
			12.50	C30 720 001C	C36 480 000C	cp
		C--*	15.00	C05 120 001*	C07 680 000*	cv
4	D CLEVELAND	D--B	12.50	D40 960 001B	D99 999 999B	cv
		D--C	12.50	D00 000 001C	D23 040 000C	cp
		D--*	15.00	D06 400 001*	D07 040 000*	cv
5	E RICHMOND	E--B	12.50	E40 320 001B	E98 560 000B	cv
			25.00	E98 560 001B	E99 840 000B	cp
			25.00	E99 840 001B	E99 999 999B	cv
		E--C	12.50	E00 000 001C	E46 080 000C	cp
		E--*	15.00	E05 120 001*	E07 040 000*	cv
6	F ATLANTA	F--B	12.50	F33 920 001B	F78 080 000B	cv
			15.00	F78 080 001B	F99 840 000B	cp
		F--C	12.50	F00 000 001C	F09 600 000C	cp
		F--*	15.00	F05 760 001*	F08 960 000*	cv
7	G CHICAGO	G--D	12.50	G10 240 001D	G36 480 000D	cv
			12.50	G36 480 001D	G 840 000D	cp
		G--E	12.50	G00 000 001E	G14 720 000E	cp
		G--*	15.00	G10 880 001*	G14 080 000*	cv
			15.00	G14 080 001*	G14 720 000*	cv
			25.00	G14 732 001*	G14 740 000*	cv
			25.00	G14 752 001*	G14 760 000*	cv
			25.00	G14 772 001*	G14 780 000*	cv

DISTRICT	TOTAL NOTES PRINTED	BLOCKS	ESTIMATED VALUE VG/F	VALUE CU	LOW OFFICIAL SERIAL NUMBER	HIGH OFFICIAL SERIAL NUMBER	
				25.00	G14 792 001*	G14 800 000*	cv
				25.00	G14 812 001*	G14 820 000*	cv
				25.00	G14 832 001*	G14 840 000*	cv
				25.00	G14 852 001*	G14 860 000*	cv
				25.00	G14 872 001*	G14 880 000*	cv
				25.00	G14 892 001*	G14 900 000*	cv
				25.00	G14 912 001*	G14 920 000*	cv
				25.00	G14 932 001*	G14 940 000*	cv
				25.00	G14 952 001*	G14 960 000*	cv
				25.00	G14 972 001*	G14 980 000*	cv
				25.00	G14 992 001*	G15 000 000*	cv
				25.00	G15 012 001*	G15 020 000*	cv
				25.00	G15 032 001*	G15 040 000*	cv
				25.00	G15 052 001*	G15 060 000*	cv
				25.00	G15 072 001*	G15 080 000*	cv
				25.00	G15 092 001*	G15 100 000*	cv
				25.00	G15 112 001*	G15 120 000*	cv
				25.00	G15 132 001*	G15 140 000*	cv
				25.00	G15 152 001*	G15 160 000*	cv
				25.00	G15 172 001*	G15 180 000*	cv
				25.00	G15 192 001*	G15 200 000*	cv
				25.00	G15 212 001*	G15 220 000*	cv
				25.00	G15 232 001*	G15 240 000*	cv
				25.00	G15 252 001*	G15 260 000*	cv
				25.00	G15 272 001*	G15 280 000*	cv
				25.00	G15 292 001*	G15 300 000*	cv
				25.00	G15 312 001*	G15 320 000*	cv
				25.00	G15 332 001*	G15 340 000*	cv
				25.00	G15 352 001*	G15 360 000*	cv
8 H ST. LOUIS		H--A		12.50	H76 520 001A	H92 800 000A	cv
				12.50	H92 800 001A	H99 840 000A	cp
				25.00	H99 840 001A	H99 999 999A	cv
		H--B		12.50	H00 000 001B	H21 760 000B	cp
		H--*		15.00	H03 840 001*	H05 120 000*	cv
9 I MINNEAPOLIS		I--A		12.50	I35 840 001A	I46 720 000A	cv
				12.50	I46 720 001A	I61 440 000A	cp
		I--*		15.00	I01 920 001*	I02 560 000*	cv
				25.00	I02 576 001*	I02 580 000*	cv
				25.00	I02 596 001*	I02 600 000*	cv
				25.00	I02 616 001*	I02 620 000*	cv
				25.00	I02 636 001*	I02 640 000*	cv
				25.00	I02 656 001*	I02 660 000*	cv
				25.00	I02 676 001*	I02 680 000*	cv
				25.00	I02 696 001*	I02 700 000*	cv
				25.00	I02 716 001*	I02 720 000*	cv
				25.00	I02 736 001*	I02 740 000*	cv
				25.00	I02 756 001*	I02 760 000*	cv
				25.00	I02 776 001*	I02 780 000*	cv
				25.00	I02 796 001*	I02 800 000*	cv
				25.00	I02 816 001*	I02 820 000*	cv
				25.00	I02 836 001*	I02 840 000*	cv
				25.00	I02 856 001*	I02 860 000*	cv
				25.00	I02 876 001*	I02 880 000*	cv
				25.00	I02 896 001*	I02 900 000*	cv
				25.00	I02 916 001*	I02 920 000*	cv
				25.00	I02 936 001*	I02 940 000*	cv
				25.00	I02 956 001*	I02 960 000*	cv
				25.00	I02 976 001*	I02 980 000*	cv
				25.00	I02 996 001*	I03 000 000*	cv
				25.00	I03 016 001*	I03 020 000*	cv
				25.00	I03 036 001*	I03 040 000*	cv
				25.00	I03 056 001*	I03 060 000*	cv
				25.00	I03 076 001*	I03 080 000*	cv
				25.00	I03 096 001*	I03 100 000*	cv
				25.00	I03 116 001*	I03 120 000*	cv
				25.00	I03 136 001*	I03 140 000*	cv
				25.00	I03 156 001*	I03 160 000*	cv
				25.00	I03 176 001*	I03 180 000*	cv
				25.00	I03 196 001*	I03 200 000*	cv

DISTRICT	TOTAL NOTES PRINTED	BLOCKS	ESTIMATED VALUE VG/F	CU	LOW OFFICIAL SERIAL NUMBER	HIGH OFFICIAL SERIAL NUMBER	
				25.00	I03 216 001*	I03 220 000*	cv
				25.00	I03 236 001*	I03 240 000*	cv
				25.00	I03 256 001*	I03 260 000*	cv
				25.00	I03 276 001*	I03 280 000*	cv
				25.00	I03 296 001*	I03 300 000*	cv
				25.00	I03 316 001*	I03 320 000*	cv
				25.00	I03 336 001*	I03 340 000*	cv
				25.00	I03 356 001*	I03 360 000*	cv
				25.00	I03 376 001*	I03 380 000*	cv
				25.00	I03 396 001*	I03 400 000*	cv
				25.00	I03 416 001*	I03 420 000*	cv
				25.00	I03 436 001*	I03 440 000*	cv
				25.00	I03 456 001*	I03 460 000*	cv
				25.00	I03 476 001*	I03 480 000*	cv
				25.00	I03 496 001*	I03 500 000*	cv
				25.00	I03 516 001*	I03 520 000*	cv
				25.00	I03 536 001*	I03 540 000*	cv
				25.00	I03 556 001*	I03 560 000*	cv
				25.00	I03 576 001*	I03 580 000*	cv
				25.00	I03 596 001*	I03 600 000*	cv
				25.00	I03 616 001*	I03 620 000*	cv
				25.00	I03 636 001*	I03 640 000*	cv
				25.00	I03 656 001*	I03 660 000*	cv
				25.00	I03 676 001*	I03 680 000*	cv
				25.00	I03 696 001*	I03 700 000*	cv
				25.00	I03 716 001*	I03 720 000*	cv
				25.00	I03 736 001*	I03 740 000*	cv
				25.00	I03 756 001*	I03 760 000*	cv
				25.00	I03 776 001*	I03 780 000*	cv
				25.00	I03 796 001*	I03 800 000*	cv
				25.00	I03 816 001*	I03 820 000*	cv
				25.00	I03 836 001*	I03 840 000*	cv
10 J KANSAS CITY		J--A		12.50	J70 400 001A	J77 440 000A	cv
				12.50	J77 440 001A	J94 720 000A	cp
		J--*		15.00	J02 560 000*	J03 200 000*	cv
11 K DALLAS		K--A		12.50	K81 280 001A	K95 360 000A	cv
				12.50	K95 360 001A	K99 840 000A	cp
				25.00	K99 840 001A	K99 999 999A	cv
		K--B		12.50	K00 000 001B	K21 120 000B	cp
		K--*		15.00	K02 560 001*	K04 480 000*	cv
12 L SAN FRANCISCO		L--B		12.50	L64 640 001B	L85 120 000B	cv
				12.50	L85 120 001B	L99 840 000B	cp
				25.00	L99 840 001B	L99 999 999B	cv
		L--C		12.50	L00 000 001C	L35 200 000C	cp
		L--*		15.00	L05 760 001*	L07 680 000*	cv

CAT. NO. XF77
$10.00 FEDERAL RESERVE NOTE (GREEN SEAL) 32 Subject
SERIES 1977

SIGNATURES: Azie Taylor Morton, Treasurer of the United States.
 W. Michael Blumenthal, Secretary of the Treasury.

SERIAL NUMBERS: All districts revert to 00 000 001.

PLATE SERIALS: Continue from previus series.

	DISTRICT	TOTAL NOTES PRINTED	BLOCKS	ESTIMATED VALUE VG/F	CU	LOW OFFICIAL SERIAL NUMBER	HIGH OFFICIAL SERIAL NUMBER	
1	A BOSTON		A--A		12.00	A00 000 001A	A96 640 000A	cp
			A--*		25.00	A00 012 001*	A00 020 000*	cv
					25.00	A00 032 001*	A00 040 000*	cv
					25.00	A00 052 001*	A00 060 000*	cv
					25.00	A00 072 001*	A00 080 000*	cv
					25.00	A00 092 001*	A00 100 000*	cv
					25.00	A00 112 001*	A00 120 000*	cv
					25.00	A00 132 001*	A00 140 000*	cv
					25.00	A00 152 001*	A00 160 000*	cv

DISTRICT	TOTAL NOTES PRINTED	BLOCKS	ESTIMATED VALUE VG/F	VALUE CU	LOW OFFICIAL SERIAL NUMBER	HIGH OFFICIAL SERIAL NUMBER	
				25.00	A00 172 001*	A00 180 000*	CV
				25.00	A00 192 001*	A00 200 000*	CV
				25.00	A00 212 001*	A00 220 000*	CV
				25.00	A00 232 001*	A00 240 000*	CV
				25.00	A00 252 001*	A00 260 000*	CV
				25.00	A00 272 001*	A00 280 000*	CV
				25.00	A00 292 001*	A00 300 000*	CV
				25.00	A00 312 001*	A00 320 000*	CV
				25.00	A00 332 001*	A00 340 000*	CV
				25.00	A00 352 001*	A00 360 000*	CV
				25.00	A00 372 001*	A00 380 000*	CV
				25.00	A00 392 001*	A00 400 000*	CV
				25.00	A00 412 001*	A00 420 000*	CV
				25.00	A00 432 001*	A00 440 000*	CV
				25.00	A00 452 001*	A00 460 000*	CV
				25.00	A00 472 001*	A00 480 000*	CV
				25.00	A00 492 001*	A00 500 000*	CV
				25.00	A00 512 001*	A00 520 000*	CV
				25.00	A00 532 001*	A00 540 000*	CV
				25.00	A00 552 001*	A00 560 000*	CV
				25.00	A00 572 001*	A00 580 000*	CV
				25.00	A00 592 001*	A00 600 000*	CV
				25.00	A00 612 001*	A00 620 000*	CV
				25.00	A00 632 001*	A00 640 000*	CV
				15.00	A00 640 001*	A01 290 000*	CV
				25.00	A01 292 001*	A01 300 000*	CV
				25.00	A01 312 001*	A01 320 000*	CV
				25.00	A01 332 001*	A01 340 000*	CV
				25.00	A01 352 001*	A01 360 000*	CV
				25.00	A01 372 001*	A01 380 000*	CV
				25.00	A01 392 001*	A01 400 000*	CV
				25.00	A01 412 001*	A01 420 000*	CV
				25.00	A01 432 001*	A01 440 000*	CV
				25.00	A01 452 001*	A01 460 000*	CV
				25.00	A01 472 001*	A01 480 000*	CV
				25.00	A01 492 001*	A01 500 000*	CV
				25.00	A01 512 001*	A01 520 000*	CV
				25.00	A01 532 001*	A01 540 000*	CV
				25.00	A01 552 001*	A01 560 000*	CV
				25.00	A01 572 001*	A01 580 000*	CV
				25.00	A01 592 001*	A01 600 000*	CV
				25.00	A01 612 001*	A01 620 000*	CV
				25.00	A01 632 001*	A01 640 000*	CV
				25.00	A01 652 001*	A01 660 000*	CV
				25.00	A01 672 001*	A01 680 000*	CV
				25.00	A01 692 001*	A01 700 000*	CV
				25.00	A01 712 001*	A01 720 000*	CV
				25.00	A01 732 001*	A01 740 000*	CV
				25.00	A01 752 001*	A01 760 000*	CV
				25.00	A01 772 001*	A01 780 000*	CV
				25.00	A01 792 001*	A01 800 000*	CV
				25.00	A01 812 001*	A01 820 000*	CV
				25.00	A01 832 001*	A01 840 000*	CV
				25.00	A01 852 001*	A01 860 000*	CV
				25.00	A01 872 001*	A01 880 000*	CV
				25.00	A01 892 001*	A01 900 000*	CV
				25.00	A01 912 001*	A01 920 000*	CV
				15.00	A01 920 001*	A02 560 000*	CV
				25.00	A02 572 001*	A02 580 000*	CV
				25.00	A02 592 001*	A02 600 000*	CV
				25.00	A02 612 001*	A02 620 000*	CV
				25.00	A02 632 001*	A02 640 000*	CV
				25.00	A02 652 001*	A02 660 000*	CV
				25.00	A02 672 001*	A02 680 000*	CV
				25.00	A02 692 001*	A02 700 000*	CV
				25.00	A02 712 001*	A02 720 000*	CV
				25.00	A02 732 001*	A02 740 000*	CV
				25.00	A02 752 001*	A02 760 000*	CV
				25.00	A02 772 001*	A02 780 000*	CV

DISTRICT	TOTAL NOTES PRINTED	BLOCKS	ESTIMATED VALUE VG/F	CU	LOW OFFICIAL SERIAL NUMBER	HIGH OFFICIAL SERIAL NUMBER	
				25.00	A02 792 001*	A02 800 000*	cv
				25.00	A02 812 001*	A02 820 000*	cv
				25.00	A02 832 001*	A02 840 000*	cv
				25.00	A02 852 001*	A02 860 000*	cv
				25.00	A02 872 001*	A02 880 000*	cv
				25.00	A02 892 001*	A02 900 000*	cv
				25.00	A02 912 001*	A02 920 000*	cv
				25.00	A02 932 001*	A02 940 000*	cv
				25.00	A02 952 001*	A02 960 000*	cv
				25.00	A02 972 001*	A02 980 000*	cv
				25.00	A02 992 001*	A03 000 000*	cv
				25.00	A03 012 001*	A03 020 000*	cv
				25.00	A03 032 001*	A03 040 000*	cv
				25.00	A03 052 001*	A03 060 000*	cv
				25.00	A03 072 001*	A03 080 000*	cv
				25.00	A03 092 001*	A03 100 000*	cv
				25.00	A03 112 001*	A03 120 000*	cv
				25.00	A03 132 001*	A03 140 000*	cv
				25.00	A03 152 001*	A03 160 000*	cv
				25.00	A03 172 001*	A03 180 000*	cv
				25.00	A03 192 001*	A03 200 000*	cv
				15.00	A03 200 001*	A03 840 000*	cv
2	B NEW YORK	B--A		12.00	B00 000 001A	B99 840 000A	cp
		B--B		12.00	B00 000 001B	B99 840 000B	cp
		B--C		12.00	B00 000 001C	B77 440 000C	cp
		B--*		25.00	B00 016 001*	B00 020 000*	cv
				25.00	B00 036 001*	B00 040 000*	cv
				25.00	B00 056 001*	B00 060 000*	cv
				25.00	B00 076 001*	B00 080 000*	cv
				25.00	B00 096 001*	B00 100 000*	cv
				25.00	B00 116 001*	B00 120 000*	cv
				25.00	B00 136 001*	B00 140 000*	cv
				25.00	B00 156 001*	B00 160 000*	cv
				25.00	B00 176 001*	B00 180 000*	cv
				25.00	B00 196 001*	B00 200 000*	cv
				25.00	B00 216 001*	B00 220 000*	cv
				25.00	B00 236 001*	B00 240 000*	cv
				25.00	B00 256 001*	B00 260 000*	cv
				25.00	B00 276 001*	B00 280 000*	cv
				25.00	B00 296 001*	B00 300 000*	cv
				25.00	B00 316 001*	B00 320 000*	cv
				25.00	B00 336 001*	B00 340 000*	cv
				25.00	B00 356 001*	B00 360 000*	cv
				25.00	B00 376 001*	B00 380 000*	cv
				25.00	B00 396 001*	B00 400 000*	cv
				25.00	B00 416 001*	B00 420 000*	cv
				25.00	B00 436 001*	B00 440 000*	cv
				25.00	B00 456 001*	B00 460 000*	cv
				25.00	B00 476 001*	B00 480 000*	cv
				25.00	B00 496 001*	B00 500 000*	cv
				25.00	B00 516 001*	B00 520 000*	cv
				25.00	B00 536 001*	B00 540 000*	cv
				25.00	B00 556 001*	B00 560 000*	cv
				25.00	B00 576 001*	B00 580 000*	cv
				25.00	B00 596 001*	B00 600 000*	cv
				25.00	B00 616 001*	B00 620 000*	cv
				25.00	B00 636 001*	B00 640 000*	cv
				25.00	B00 656 001*	B00 660 000*	cv
				25.00	B00 676 001*	B00 680 000*	cv
				25.00	B00 696 001*	B00 700 000*	cv
				25.00	B00 716 001*	B00 720 000*	cv
				25.00	B00 736 001*	B00 740 000*	cv
				25.00	B00 756 001*	B00 760 000*	cv
				25.00	B00 776 001*	B00 780 000*	cv
				25.00	B00 796 001*	B00 800 000*	cv
				25.00	B00 816 001*	B00 820 000*	cv
				25.00	B00 836 001*	B00 840 000*	cv
				25.00	B00 856 001*	B00 860 000*	cv
				25.00	B00 876 001*	B00 880 000*	cv

DISTRICT	TOTAL NOTES PRINTED	BLOCKS	ESTIMATED VALUE VG/F	CU	LOW OFFICIAL SERIAL NUMBER	HIGH OFFICIAL SERIAL NUMBER	
				25.00	B00 896 001*	B00 900 000*	CV
				25.00	B00 916 001*	B00 920 000*	CV
				25.00	B00 936 001*	B00 940 000*	CV
				25.00	B00 956 001*	B00 960 000*	CV
				25.00	B00 976 001*	B00 980 000*	CV
				25.00	B00 996 001*	B01 000 000*	CV
				25.00	B01 016 001*	B01 020 000*	CV
				25.00	B01 036 001*	B01 040 000*	CV
				25.00	B01 056 001*	B01 060 000*	CV
				25.00	B01 076 001*	B01 080 000*	CV
				25.00	B01 096 001*	B01 100 000*	CV
				25.00	B01 116 001*	B01 120 000*	CV
				25.00	B01 136 001*	B01 140 000*	CV
				25.00	B01 156 001*	B01 160 000*	CV
				25.00	B01 176 001*	B01 180 000*	CV
				25.00	B01 196 001*	B01 200 000*	CV
				25.00	B01 216 001*	B01 220 000*	CV
				25.00	B01 236 001*	B01 240 000*	CV
				25.00	B01 256 001*	B01 260 000*	CV
				25.00	B01 276 001*	B01 280 000*	CV
				25.00	B01 288 001*	B01 300 000*	CV
				25.00	B01 308 001*	B01 320 000*	CV
				25.00	B01 328 001*	B01 340 000*	CV
				25.00	B01 348 001*	B01 360 000*	CV
				25.00	B01 368 001*	B01 380 000*	CV
				25.00	B01 388 001*	B01 400 000*	CV
				25.00	B01 408 001*	B01 420 000*	CV
				25.00	B01 428 001*	B01 440 000*	CV
				25.00	B01 448 001*	B01 460 000*	CV
				25.00	B01 468 001*	B01 480 000*	CV
				25.00	B01 488 001*	B01 500 000*	CV
				25.00	B01 508 001*	B01 520 000*	CV
				25.00	B01 528 001*	B01 540 000*	CV
				25.00	B01 548 001*	B01 560 000*	CV
				25.00	B01 568 001*	B01 580 000*	CV
				25.00	B01 588 001*	B01 600 000*	CV
				25.00	B01 608 001*	B01 620 000*	CV
				25.00	B01 628 001*	B01 640 000*	CV
				25.00	B01 648 001*	B01 660 000*	CV
				25.00	B01 668 001*	B01 680 000*	CV
				25.00	B01 688 001*	B01 700 000*	CV
				25.00	B01 708 001*	B01 720 000*	CV
				25.00	B01 728 001*	B01 740 000*	CV
				25.00	B01 748 001*	B01 760 000*	CV
				25.00	B01 768 001*	B01 780 000*	CV
				25.00	B01 788 001*	B01 800 000*	CV
				25.00	B01 808 001*	B01 820 000*	CV
				25.00	B01 828 001*	B01 840 000*	CV
				25.00	B01 848 001*	B01 860 000*	CV
				25.00	B01 868 001*	B01 880 000*	CV
				25.00	B01 888 001*	B01 900 000*	CV
				25.00	B01 908 001*	B01 920 000*	CV
				15.00	B01 920 001*	B02 560 000*	CV
				25.00	B02 572 001*	B02 580 000*	CV
				25.00	B02 592 001*	B02 600 000*	CV
				25.00	B02 612 001*	B02 620 000*	CV
				25.00	B02 632 001*	B02 640 000*	CV
				25.00	B02 652 001*	B02 660 000*	CV
				25.00	B02 672 001*	B02 680 000*	CV
				25.00	B02 692 001*	B02 700 000*	CV
				25.00	B02 712 001*	B02 720 000*	CV
				25.00	B02 732 001*	B02 740 000*	CV
				25.00	B02 752 001*	B02 760 000*	CV
				25.00	B02 772 001*	B02 780 000*	CV
				25.00	B02 792 001*	B02 800 000*	CV
				25.00	B02 812 001*	B02 820 000*	CV
				25.00	B02 832 001*	B02 840 000*	CV
				25.00	B02 852 001*	B02 860 000*	CV
				25.00	B02 872 001*	B02 880 000*	CV

DISTRICT	TOTAL NOTES PRINTED	BLOCKS	ESTIMATED VALUE VG/F	CU	LOW OFFICIAL SERIAL NUMBER	HIGH OFFICIAL SERIAL NUMBER	
				25.00	B02 892 001*	B02 900 000*	cv
				25.00	B02 912 001*	B02 920 000*	cv
				25.00	B02 932 001*	B02 940 000*	cv
				25.00	B02 952 001*	B02 960 000*	cv
				25.00	B02 972 001*	B02 980 000*	cv
				25.00	B02 992 001*	B03 000 000*	cv
				25.00	B03 012 001*	B03 020 000*	cv
				25.00	B03 032 001*	B03 040 000*	cv
				25.00	B03 052 001*	B03 060 000*	cv
				25.00	B03 072 001*	B03 080 000*	cv
				25.00	B03 092 001*	B03 100 000*	cv
				25.00	B03 112 001*	B03 120 000*	cv
				25.00	B03 132 001*	B03 140 000*	cv
				25.00	B03 152 001*	B03 160 000*	cv
				25.00	B03 172 001*	B03 180 000*	cv
				25.00	B03 192 001*	B03 200 000*	cv
				15.00	B03 200 001*	B05 760 000*	cv
				15.00	B05 760 001*	B08 960 000*	cp
3	C PHILADELPHIA	C--A		12.00	C00 000 001A	C83 200 000A	cp
		C--*		15.00	C00 000 001*	C00 640 000*	cp
				25.00	C00 652 001*	C00 660 000*	cp
				25.00	C00 672 001*	C00 680 000*	cp
				25.00	C00 692 001*	C00 700 000*	cp
				25.00	C00 712 001*	C00 720 000*	cp
				25.00	C00 732 001*	C00 740 000*	cp
				25.00	C00 752 001*	C00 760 000*	cp
				25.00	C00 772 001*	C00 780 000*	cp
				25.00	C00 792 001*	C00 800 000*	cp
				25.00	C00 812 001*	C00 820 000*	cp
				25.00	C00 832 001*	C00 840 000*	cp
				25.00	C00 852 001*	C00 860 000*	cp
				25.00	C00 872 001*	C00 880 000*	cp
				25.00	C00 892 001*	C00 900 000*	cp
				25.00	C00 912 001*	C00 920 000*	cp
				25.00	C00 932 001*	C00 940 000*	cp
				25.00	C00 952 001*	C00 960 000*	cp
				25.00	C00 972 001*	C00 980 000*	cp
				25.00	C00 992 001*	C01 000 000*	cp
				25.00	C01 012 001*	C01 020 000*	cp
				25.00	C01 032 001*	C01 040 000*	cp
				25.00	C01 052 001*	C01 060 000*	cp
				25.00	C01 072 001*	C01 080 000*	cp
				25.00	C01 092 001*	C01 100 000*	cp
				25.00	C01 112 001*	C01 120 000*	cp
				25.00	C01 132 001*	C01 140 000*	cp
				25.00	C01 152 001*	C01 160 000*	cp
				25.00	C01 172 001*	C01 180 000*	cp
				25.00	C01 192 001*	C01 200 000*	cp
				25.00	C01 212 001*	C01 220 000*	cp
				25.00	C01 232 001*	C01 240 000*	cp
				25.00	C01 252 001*	C01 260 000*	cp
				25.00	C01 272 001*	C01 280 000*	cp
4	D CLEVELAND	D--A		12.00	D00 000 001A	D83 200 000A	cp
		D--*		25.00	D00 016 001*	D00 020 000*	cv
				25.00	D00 036 001*	D00 040 000*	cv
				25.00	D00 056 001*	D00 060 000*	cv
				25.00	D00 076 001*	D00 080 000*	cv
				25.00	D00 096 001*	D00 100 000*	cv
				25.00	D00 116 001*	D00 120 000*	cv
				25.00	D00 136 001*	D00 140 000*	cv
				25.00	D00 156 001*	D00 160 000*	cv
				25.00	D00 176 001*	D00 180 000*	cv
				25.00	D00 196 001*	D00 200 000*	cv
				25.00	D00 216 001*	D00 220 000*	cv
				25.00	D00 236 001*	D00 240 0008	cv
				25.00	D00 256 001*	D00 260 000*	cv
				25.00	D00 276 001*	D00 280 000*	cv
				25.00	D00 296 001*	D00 300 000*	cv
				25.00	D00 316 001*	D00 320 000*	cv

DISTRICT	TOTAL NOTES PRINTED	BLOCKS	ESTIMATED VALUE VG/F	CU	LOW OFFICIAL SERIAL NUMBER	HIGH OFFICIAL SERIAL NUMBER	
				25.00	D00 336 001*	D00 340 000*	cv
				25.00	D00 356 001*	D00 360 000*	cv
				25.00	D00 376 001*	D00 380 000*	cv
				25.00	D00 396 001*	D00 400 000*	cv
				25.00	D00 416 001*	D00 420 000*	cv
				25.00	D00 436 001*	D00 440 000*	cv
				25.00	D00 456 001*	D00 460 000*	cv
				25.00	D00 476 001*	D00 480 000*	cv
				25.00	D00 496 001*	D00 500 000*	cv
				25.00	D00 516 001*	D00 520 000*	cv
				25.00	D00 536 001*	D00 540 000*	cv
				25.00	D00 556 001*	D00 560 000*	cv
				25.00	D00 576 001*	D00 580 000*	cv
				25.00	D00 596 001*	D00 600 000*	cv
				25.00	D00 616 001*	D00 620 000*	cv
				25.00	D00 636 001*	D00 640 000*	cv
				15.00	D00 640 001*	D01 280 000*	cp
5	E RICHMOND	E--A		12.00	E00 000 001A	E71 040 000A	cp
		E--*		15.00	E00 000 001*	E01 280 000*	cv
				25.00	E01 292 001*	E01 300 000*	cp
				25.00	E01 312 001*	E01 320 000*	cp
				25.00	E01 332 001*	E01 340 000*	cp
				25.00	E01 352 001*	E01 360 000*	cp
				25.00	E01 372 001*	E01 380 000*	cp
				25.00	E01 392 001*	E01 400 000*	cp
				25.00	E01 412 001*	E01 420 000*	cp
				25.00	E01 432 001*	E01 440 000*	cp
				25.00	E01 452 001*	E01 460 000*	cp
				25.00	E01 472 001*	E01 480 000*	cp
				25.00	E01 492 001*	E01 500 000*	cp
				25.00	E01 512 001*	E01 520 000*	cp
				25.00	E01 532 001*	E01 540 000*	cp
				25.00	E01 552 001*	E01 560 000*	cp
				25.00	E01 572 001*	E01 580 000*	cp
				25.00	E01 592 001*	E01 600 000*	cp
				25.00	E01 612 001*	E01 620 000*	cp
				25.00	E01 632 001*	E01 640 000*	cp
				25.00	E01 652 001*	E01 660 000*	cp
				25.00	E01 672 001*	E01 680 000*	cp
				25.00	E01 692 001*	E01 700 000*	cp
				25.00	E01 712 001*	E01 720 000*	cp
				25.00	E01 732 001*	E01 740 000*	cp
				25.00	E01 752 001*	E01 760 000*	cp
				25.00	E01 772 001*	E01 780 000*	cp
				25.00	E01 792 001*	E01 800 000*	cp
				25.00	E01 812 001*	E01 820 000*	cp
				25.00	E01 832 001*	E01 840 000*	cp
				25.00	E01 852 001*	E01 860 000*	cp
				25.00	E01 872 001*	E01 880 000*	cp
				25.00	E01 892 001*	E01 900 000*	cp
				25.00	E01 912 001*	E01 920 000*	cp
				25.00	E01 928 001*	E01 940 000*	cp
				25.00	E01 948 001*	E01 960 000*	cp
				25.00	E01 968 001*	E01 980 000*	cp
				25.00	E01 988 001*	E02 000 000*	cp
				25.00	E02 008 001*	E02 020 000*	cp
				25.00	E02 028 001*	E02 040 000*	cp
				25.00	E02 048 001*	E02 060 000*	cp
				25.00	E02 068 001*	E02 080 000*	cp
				25.00	E02 088 001*	E02 100 000*	cp
				25.00	E02 108 001*	E02 120 000*	cp
				25.00	E02 128 001*	E02 140 000*	cp
				25.00	E02 148 001*	E02 160 000*	cp
				25.00	E02 168 001*	E02 180 000*	cp
				25.00	E02 188 001*	E02 200 000*	cp
				25.00	E02 208 001*	E02 220 000*	cp
				25.00	E02 228 001*	E02 240 000*	cp
				25.00	E02 248 001*	E02 260 000*	cp
				25.00	E02 268 001*	E02 280 000*	cp

DISTRICT	TOTAL NOTES PRINTED	BLOCKS	ESTIMATED VALUE VG/F	CU	LOW OFFICIAL SERIAL NUMBER	HIGH OFFICIAL SERIAL NUMBER	
				25.00	E02 288 001*	E02 300 000*	cp
				25.00	E02 308 001*	E02 320 000*	cp
				25.00	E02 328 001*	E02 340 000*	cp
				25.00	E02 348 001*	E02 360 000*	cp
				25.00	E02 368 001*	E02 380 000*	cp
				25.00	E02 388 001*	E02 400 000*	cp
				25.00	E02 408 001*	E02 420 000*	cp
				25.00	E02 428 001*	E02 440 000*	cp
				25.00	E02 448 001*	E02 460 000*	cp
				25.00	E02 468 001*	E02 480 000*	cp
				25.00	E02 488 001*	E02 500 000*	cp
				25.00	E02 508 001*	E02 520 000*	cp
				25.00	E02 528 001*	E02 540 000*	cp
				25.00	E02 548 001*	E02 560 000*	cp
6	F ATLANTA	F--A		12.00	F00 000 001A	F88 960 000A	cp
		F--*		15.00	F00 000 001*	F01 280 000*	cv
				25.00	F01 292 001*	F01 300 000*	cp
				25.00	F01 312 001*	F01 320 000*	cp
				25.00	F01 332 001*	F01 340 000*	cp
				25.00	F01 352 001*	F01 360 000*	cp
				25.00	F01 372 001*	F01 380 000*	cp
				25.00	F01 392 001*	F01 400 000*	cp
				25.00	F01 412 001*	F01 420 000*	cp
				25.00	F01 432 001*	F01 440 000*	cp
				25.00	F01 452 001*	F01 460 000*	cp
				25.00	F01 472 001*	F01 480 000*	cp
				25.00	F01 492 001*	F01 500 000*	cp
				25.00	F01 512 001*	F01 520 000*	cp
				25.00	F01 532 001*	F01 540 000*	cp
				25.00	F01 552 001*	F01 560 000*	cp
				25.00	F01 572 001*	F01 580 000*	cp
				25.00	F01 592 001*	F01 600 000*	cp
				25.00	F01 612 001*	F01 620 000*	cp
				25.00	F01 632 001*	F01 640 000*	cp
				25.00	F01 652 001*	F01 660 000*	cp
				25.00	F01 672 001*	F01 680 000*	cp
				25.00	F01 692 001*	F01 700 000*	cp
				25.00	F01 712 001*	F01 720 000*	cp
				25.00	F01 732 001*	F01 740 000*	cp
				25.00	F01 752 001*	F01 760 000*	cp
				25.00	F01 772 001*	F01 780 000*	cp
				25.00	F01 792 001*	F01 800 000*	cp
				25.00	F01 812 001*	F01 820 000*	cp
				25.00	F01 832 001*	F01 840 000*	cp
				25.00	F01 852 001*	F01 860 000*	cp
				25.00	F01 872 001*	F01 880 000*	cp
				25.00	F01 892 001*	F01 900 000*	cp
				25.00	F01 912 001*	F01 920 000*	cp
7	G CHICAGO	G--A		12.00	G00 000 001A	G99 840 000A	cp
		G--B		12.00	G00 000 001B	G74 880 000B	cp
		G--*		25.00	G00 016 001*	G00 020 000*	cv
				25.00	G00 036 001*	G00 040 000*	cv
				25.00	G00 056 001*	G00 060 000*	cv
				25.00	G00 076 001*	G00 080 000*	cv
				25.00	G00 096 001*	G00 100 000*	cv
				25.00	G00 116 001*	G00 120 000*	cv
				25.00	G00 136 001*	G00 140 000*	cv
				25.00	G00 156 001*	G00 160 000*	cv
				25.00	G00 176 001*	G00 180 000*	cv
				25.00	G00 196 001*	G00 200 000*	cv
				25.00	G00 216 001*	G00 220 000*	cv
				25.00	G00 236 001*	G00 240 000*	cv
				25.00	G00 256 001*	G00 260 000*	cv
				25.00	G00 276 001*	G00 280 000*	cv
				25.00	G00 296 001*	G00 300 000*	cv
				25.00	G00 316 001*	G00 320 000*	cv
				25.00	G00 336 001*	G00 340 000*	cv
				25.00	G00 356 001*	G00 360 000*	cv
				25.00	G00 376 001*	G00 380 000*	cv

VALUE CU	LOW OFFICIAL SERIAL NUMBER	HIGH OFFICIAL SERIAL NUMBER		VALUE CU	LOW OFFICIAL SERIAL NUMBER	HIGH OFFICIAL SERIAL NUMBER	
25.00	G00 396 001*	G00 400 000*	cv	25.00	G01 776 001*	G01 780 000*	cv
25.00	G00 416 001*	G00 420 000*	cv	25.00	G01 796 001*	G01 800 000*	cv
25.00	G00 436 001*	G00 440 000*	cv	25.00	G01 816 001*	G01 820 000*	cv
25.00	G00 456 001*	G00 460 000*	cv	25.00	G01 836 001*	G01 840 000*	cv
25.00	G00 476 001*	G00 480 000*	cv	25.00	G01 856 001*	G01 860 000*	cv
25.00	G00 496 001*	G00 500 000*	cv	25.00	G01 876 001*	G01 880 000*	cv
25.00	G00 516 001*	G00 520 000*	cv	25.00	G01 896 001*	G01 900 000*	cv
25.00	G00 536 001*	G00 540 000*	cv	25.00	G01 916 001*	G01 920 000*	cv
25.00	G00 556 001*	G00 560 000*	cv	25.00	G01 936 001*	G01 940 000*	cv
25.00	G00 576 001*	G00 580 000*	cv	25.00	G01 956 001*	G01 960 000*	cv
25.00	G00 596 001*	G00 600 000*	cv	25.00	G01 976 001*	G01 980 000*	cv
25.00	G00 616 001*	G00 620 000*	cv	25.00	G01 996 001*	G02 000 000*	cv
25.00	G00 636 001*	G00 640 000*	cv	25.00	G02 016 001*	G02 020 000*	cv
25.00	G00 656 001*	G00 660 000*	cv	25.00	G02 036 001*	G02 040 000*	cv
25.00	G00 676 001*	G00 680 000*	cv	25.00	G02 056 001*	G02 060 000*	cv
25.00	G00 696 001*	G00 700 000*	cv	25.00	G02 076 001*	G02 080 000*	cv
25.00	G00 716 001*	G00 720 000*	cv	25.00	G02 096 001*	G02 100 000*	cv
25.00	G00 736 001*	G00 740 000*	cv	25.00	G02 116 001*	G02 120 000*	cv
25.00	G00 756 001*	G00 760 000*	cv	25.00	G02 136 001*	G02 140 000*	cv
25.00	G00 776 001*	G00 780 000*	cv	25.00	G02 156 001*	G02 160 000*	cv
25.00	G00 796 001*	G00 800 000*	cv	25.00	G02 176 001*	G02 180 000*	cv
25.00	G00 816 001*	G00 820 000*	cv	25.00	G02 196 001*	G02 200 000*	cv
25.00	G00 836 001*	G00 840 000*	cv	25.00	G02 216 001*	G02 220 000*	cv
25.00	G00 856 001*	G00 860 000*	cv	25.00	G02 236 001*	G02 240 000*	cv
25.00	G00 876 001*	G00 880 000*	cv	25.00	G02 256 001*	G02 260 000*	cv
25.00	G00 896 001*	G00 900 000*	cv	25.00	G02 276 001*	G02 280 000*	cv
25.00	G00 916 001*	G00 920 000*	cv	25.00	G02 296 001*	G02 300 000*	cv
25.00	G00 936 001*	G00 940 000*	cv	25.00	G02 316 001*	G02 320 000*	cv
25.00	G00 956 001*	G00 960 000*	cv	25.00	G02 336 001*	G02 340 000*	cv
25.00	G00 976 001*	G00 980 000*	cv	25.00	G02 356 001*	G02 360 000*	cv
25.00	G00 996 001*	G01 000 000*	cv	25.00	G02 376 001*	G02 380 000*	cv
25.00	G01 016 001*	G01 020 000*	cv	25.00	G02 396 001*	G02 400 000*	cv
25.00	G01 036 001*	G01 040 000*	cv	25.00	G02 416 001*	G02 420 000*	cv
25.00	G01 056 001*	G01 060 000*	cv	25.00	G02 436 001*	G02 440 000*	cv
25.00	G01 076 001*	G01 080 000*	cv	25.00	G02 456 001*	G02 460 000*	cv
25.00	G01 096 001*	G01 100 000*	cv	25.00	G02 476 001*	G02 480 000*	cv
25.00	G01 116 001*	G01 120 000*	cv	25.00	G02 496 001*	G02 500 000*	cv
25.00	G01 136 001*	G01 140 000*	cv	25.00	G02 516 001*	G02 520 000*	cv
25.00	G01 156 001*	G01 160 000*	cv	25.00	G02 536 001*	G02 540 000*	cv
25.00	G01 176 001*	G01 180 000*	cv	25.00	G02 556 001*	G02 560 000*	cv
25.00	G01 196 001*	G01 200 000*	cv	15.00	G02 560 001*	G04 480 000*	cv
25.00	G01 216 001*	G01 220 000*	cv	25.00	G04 492 001*	G04 500 000*	cv
25.00	G01 236 001*	G01 240 000*	cv	25.00	G04 512 001*	G04 520 000*	cv
25.00	G01 256 001*	G01 260 000*	cv	25.00	G04 532 001*	G04 540 000*	cv
25.00	G01 276 001*	G01 280 000*	cv	25.00	G04 552 001*	G04 560 000*	cv
25.00	G01 296 001*	G01 300 000*	cv	25.00	G04 572 001*	G04 580 000*	cv
25.00	G01 316 001*	G01 320 000*	cv	25.00	G04 592 001*	G04 600 000*	cv
25.00	G01 336 001*	G01 340 000*	cv	25.00	G04 612 001*	G04 620 000*	cv
25.00	G01 356 001*	G01 360 000*	cv	25.00	G04 632 001*	G04 640 000*	cv
25.00	G01 376 001*	G01 380 000*	cv	25.00	G04 652 001*	G04 660 000*	cv
25.00	G01 396 001*	G01 400 000*	cv	25.00	G04 672 001*	G04 680 000*	cv
25.00	G01 416 001*	G01 420 000*	cv	25.00	G04 692 001*	G04 700 000*	cv
25.00	G01 436 001*	G01 440 000*	cv	25.00	G04 712 001*	G04 720 000*	cv
25.00	G01 456 001*	G01 460 000*	cv	25.00	G04 732 001*	G04 740 000*	cv
25.00	G01 476 001*	G01 480 000*	cv	25.00	G04 752 001*	G04 760 000*	cv
25.00	G01 496 001*	G01 500 000*	cv	25.00	G04 772 001*	G04 780 000*	cv
25.00	G01 516 001*	G01 520 000*	cv	25.00	G04 792 001*	G04 800 000*	cv
25.00	G01 536 001*	G01 540 000*	cv	25.00	G04 812 001*	G04 820 000*	cv
25.00	G01 556 001*	G01 560 000*	cv	25.00	G04 832 001*	G04 840 000*	cv
25.00	G01 576 001*	G01 580 000*	cv	25.00	G04 852 001*	G04 860 000*	cv
25.00	G01 596 001*	G01 600 000*	cv	25.00	G04 872 001*	G04 880 000*	cv
25.00	G01 616 001*	G01 620 000*	cv	25.00	G04 892 001*	G04 900 000*	cv
25.00	G01 636 001*	G01 640 000*	cv	25.00	G04 912 001*	G04 920 000*	cv
25.00	G01 656 001*	G01 660 000*	cv	25.00	G04 932 001*	G04 940 000*	cv
25.00	G01 676 001*	G01 680 000*	cv	25.00	G04 952 001*	G04 960 000*	cv
25.00	G01 696 001*	G01 700 000*	cv	25.00	G04 972 001*	G04 980 000*	cv
25.00	G01 716 001*	G01 720 000*	cv	25.00	G04 992 001*	G05 000 000*	cv
25.00	G01 736 001*	G01 740 000*	cv	25.00	G05 012 001*	G05 020 000*	cv
25.00	G01 756 001*	G01 760 000*	cv	25.00	G05 032 001*	G05 040 000*	cv

DISTRICT	TOTAL NOTES PRINTED	BLOCKS	ESTIMATED VALUE VG/F	VALUE CU	LOW OFFICIAL SERIAL NUMBER	HIGH OFFICIAL SERIAL NUMBER	
				25.00	G05 052 001*	G05 060 000*	cv
				25.00	G05 072 001*	G05 080 000*	cv
				25.00	G05 092 001*	G05 100 000*	cv
				25.00	G05 112 001*	G05 120 000*	cv
				15.00	G05 120 001*	G06 400 000*	cp
8 H ST. LOUIS		H--A		12.00	H00 000 001A	H46 720 000A	cp
		H--*		25.00	H00 012 001*	H00 020 000*	cp
				25.00	H00 032 001*	H00 040 000*	cp
				25.00	H00 052 001*	H00 060 000*	cp
				25.00	H00 072 001*	H00 080 000*	cp
				25.00	H00 092 001*	H00 100 000*	cp
				25.00	H00 112 001*	H00 120 000*	cp
				25.00	H00 132 001*	H00 140 000*	cp
				25.00	H00 152 001*	H00 160 000*	cp
				25.00	H00 172 001*	H00 180 000*	cp
				25.00	H00 192 001*	H00 200 000*	cp
				25.00	H00 212 001*	H00 220 000*	cp
				25.00	H00 232 001*	H00 240 000*	cp
				25.00	H00 252 001*	H00 260 000*	cp
				25.00	H00 272 001*	H00 280 000*	cp
				25.00	H00 292 001*	H00 300 000*	cp
				25.00	H00 312 001*	H00 320 000*	cp
				25.00	H00 332 001*	H00 340 000*	cp
				25.00	H00 352 001*	H00 360 000*	cp
				25.00	H00 372 001*	H00 380 000*	cp
				25.00	H00 392 001*	H00 400 000*	cp
				25.00	H00 412 001*	H00 420 000*	cp
				25.00	H00 432 001*	H00 440 000*	cp
				25.00	H00 452 001*	H00 460 000*	cp
				25.00	H00 472 001*	H00 480 000*	cp
				25.00	H00 492 001*	H00 500 000*	cp
				25.00	H00 512 001*	H00 520 000*	cp
				25.00	H00 532 001*	H00 540 000*	cp
				25.00	H00 552 001*	H00 560 000*	cp
				25.00	H00 572 001*	H00 580 000*	cp
				25.00	H00 592 001*	H00 600 000*	cp
				25.00	H00 612 001*	H00 620 000*	cp
				25.00	H00 632 001*	H00 640 000*	cp
				15.00	H00 640 001*	H01 280 000*	cp
9 I MINNEAPOLIS		I--A		12.00	I00 000 001A	I10 240 000A	cp
				25.00	I00 012 001*	I00 020 000*	cp
				25.00	I00 032 001*	I00 040 000*	cp
				25.00	I00 052 001*	I00 060 000*	cp
				25.00	I00 072 001*	I00 080 000*	cp
				25.00	I00 092 001*	I00 100 000*	cp
				25.00	I00 112 001*	I00 120 000*	cp
				25.00	I00 132 001*	I00 140 000*	cp
				25.00	I00 152 001*	I00 160 000*	cp
				25.00	I00 172 001*	I00 180 000*	cp
				25.00	I00 192 001*	I00 200 000*	cp
				25.00	I00 212 001*	I00 220 000*	cp
				25.00	I00 232 001*	I00 240 000*	cp
				25.00	I00 252 001*	I00 260 000*	cp
				25.00	I00 272 001*	I00 280 000*	cp
				25.00	I00 292 001*	I00 300 000*	cp
				25.00	I00 312 001*	I00 320 000*	cp
				25.00	I00 332 001*	I00 340 000*	cp
				25.00	I00 352 001*	I00 360 000*	cp
				25.00	I00 372 001*	I00 380 000*	cp
				25.00	I00 392 001*	I00 400 000*	cp
				25.00	I00 412 001*	I00 420 000*	cp
				25.00	I00 432 001*	I00 440 000*	cp
				25.00	I00 452 001*	I00 460 000*	cp
				25.00	I00 472 001*	I00 480 000*	cp
				25.00	I00 492 001*	I00 500 000*	cp
				25.00	I00 512 001*	I00 520 000*	cp
				25.00	I00 532 001*	I00 540 000*	cp
				25.00	I00 552 001*	I00 560 000*	cp
				25.00	I00 572 001*	I00 580 000*	cp

DISTRICT	TOTAL NOTES PRINTED	BLOCKS	ESTIMATED VALUE VG/F	CU	LOW OFFICIAL SERIAL NUMBER	HIGH OFFICIAL SERIAL NUMBER	
				25.00	I00 592 001*	I00 600 000*	cp
				25.00	I00 612 001*	I00 620 000*	cp
				25.00	I00 632 001*	I00 640 000*	cp
10 J KANSAS CITY		J--A		12.00	J00 000 001A	J50 560 000A	cp
		J--*		25.00	J00 012 001*	J00 020 000*	cv
				25.00	J00 032 001*	J00 040 000*	cv
				25.00	J00 052 001*	J00 060 000*	cv
				25.00	J00 072 001*	J00 080 000*	cv
				25.00	J00 092 001*	J00 100 000*	cv
				25.00	J00 112 001*	J00 120 000*	cv
				25.00	J00 132 001*	J00 140 000*	cv
				25.00	J00 152 001*	J00 160 000*	cv
				25.00	J00 172 001*	J00 180 000*	cv
				25.00	J00 192 001*	J00 200 000*	cv
				25.00	J00 212 001*	J00 220 000*	cv
				25.00	J00 232 001*	J00 240 000*	cv
				25.00	J00 252 001*	J00 260 000*	cv
				25.00	J00 272 001*	J00 280 000*	cv
				25.00	J00 292 001*	J00 300 000*	cv
				25.00	J00 312 001*	J00 320 000*	cv
				25.00	J00 332 001*	J00 340 000*	cv
				25.00	J00 352 001*	J00 360 000*	cv
				25.00	J00 372 001*	J00 380 000*	cv
				25.00	J00 392 001*	J00 400 000*	cv
				25.00	J00 412 001*	J00 420 000*	cv
				25.00	J00 432 001*	J00 440 000*	cv
				25.00	J00 452 001*	J00 460 000*	cv
				25.00	J00 472 001*	J00 480 000*	cv
				25.00	J00 492 001*	J00 500 000*	cv
				25.00	J00 512 001*	J00 520 000*	cv
				25.00	J00 532 001*	J00 540 000*	cv
				25.00	J00 552 001*	J00 560 000*	cv
				25.00	J00 572 001*	J00 580 000*	cv
				25.00	J00 592 001*	J00 600 000*	cv
				25.00	J00 612 001*	J00 620 000*	cv
				25.00	J00 632 001*	J00 640 000*	cv
				15.00	J00 640 001*	J01 280 000*	cp
11 K DALLAS		K--A		12.00	K00 000 001A	K53 760 000A	cp
		K--*		15.00	K00 000 001*	K00 640 000*	cp
12 L SAN FRANCISCO		L--A		12.00	L00 000 001A	L73 600 000A	cp
		L--*		25.00	L00 012 001*	L00 020 000*	cv
				25.00	L00 032 001*	L00 040 000*	cv
				25.00	L00 052 001*	L00 060 000*	cv
				25.00	L00 072 001*	L00 080 000*	cv
				25.00	L00 092 001*	L00 100 000*	cv
				25.00	L00 112 001*	L00 120 000*	cv
				25.00	L00 132 001*	L00 140 000*	cv
				25.00	L00 152 001*	L00 160 000*	cv
				25.00	L00 172 001*	L00 180 000*	cv
				25.00	L00 192 001*	L00 200 000*	cv
				25.00	L00 212 001*	L00 220 000*	cv
				25.00	L00 232 001*	L00 240 000*	cv
				25.00	L00 252 001*	L00 260 000*	cv
				25.00	L00 272 001*	L00 280 000*	cv
				25.00	L00 292 001*	L00 300 000*	cv
				25.00	L00 312 001*	L00 320 000*	cv
				25.00	L00 332 001*	L00 340 000*	cv
				25.00	L00 352 001*	L00 360 000*	cv
				25.00	L00 372 001*	L00 380 000*	cv
				25.00	L00 392 001*	L00 400 000*	cv
				25.00	L00 412 001*	L00 420 000*	cv
				25.00	L00 432 001*	L00 440 000*	cv
				25.00	L00 452 001*	L00 460 000*	cv
				25.00	L00 472 001*	L00 480 000*	cv
				25.00	L00 492 001*	L00 500 000*	cv
				25.00	L00 512 001*	L00 520 000*	cv
				25.00	L00 532 001*	L00 540 000*	cv
				25.00	L00 552 001*	L00 560 000*	cv
				25.00	L00 572 001*	L00 580 000*	cv

DISTRICT	TOTAL NOTES PRINTED	BLOCKS	ESTIMATED VALUE VG/F	CU	LOW OFFICIAL SERIAL NUMBER	HIGH OFFICIAL SERIAL NUMBER	
				25.00	L00 592 001*	L00 600 000*	cv
				25.00	L00 612 001*	L00 620 000*	cv
				25.00	L00 632 001*	L00 640 000*	cv
				15.00	L00 640 001*	L01 280 000*	cv
				25.00	L01 292 001*	L01 300 000*	cp
				25.00	L01 312 001*	L01 320 000*	cp
				25.00	L01 332 001*	L01 340 000*	cp
				25.00	L01 352 001*	L01 360 000*	cp
				25.00	L01 372 001*	L01 380 000*	cp
				25.00	L01 392 001*	L01 400 000*	cp
				25.00	L01 412 001*	L01 420 000*	cp
				25.00	L01 432 001*	L01 440 000*	cp
				25.00	L01 452 001*	L01 460 000*	cp
				25.00	L01 472 001*	L01 480 000*	cp
				25.00	L01 492 001*	L01 500 000*	cp
				25.00	L01 512 001*	L01 520 000*	cp
				25.00	L01 532 001*	L01 540 000*	cp
				25.00	L01 552 001*	L01 560 000*	cp
				25.00	L01 572 001*	L01 580 000*	cp
				25.00	L01 592 001*	L01 600 000*	cp
				25.00	L01 612 001*	L01 620 000*	cp
				25.00	L01 632 001*	L01 640 000*	cp
				25.00	L01 652 001*	L01 660 000*	cp
				25.00	L01 672 001*	L01 680 000*	cp
				25.00	L01 692 001*	L01 700 000*	cp
				25.00	L01 712 001*	L01 720 000*	cp
				25.00	L01 732 001*	L01 740 000*	cp
				25.00	L01 752 001*	L01 760 000*	cp
				25.00	L01 772 001*	L01 780 000*	cp
				25.00	L01 792 001*	L01 800 000*	cp
				25.00	L01 812 001*	L01 820 000*	cp
				25.00	L01 832 001*	L01 840 000*	cp
				25.00	L01 852 001*	L01 860 000*	cp
				25.00	L01 872 001*	L01 880 000*	cp
				25.00	L01 892 001*	L01 900 000*	cp
				25.00	L01 912 001*	L01 920 000*	cp
				15.00	L01 920 001*	L02 560 000*	cp

XF77A
$10.00 FEDERAL RESERVE NOTE (GREEN SEAL) 32 Subject
SERIES 1977A

SIGNATURES: Azie Taylor Morton, Treasurer of the United States.
  G. William Miller, Secretary of the Treasury.
SERIAL NUMBERS: Continued from previous series.
PLATE SERIALS: Continued from previous series.

	DISTRICT	TOTAL NOTES PRINTED	BLOCKS	ESTIMATED VALUE VG/F	CU	LOW OFFICIAL SERIAL NUMBER	HIGH OFFICIAL SERIAL NUMBER(1)
1	A BOSTON		A--A		12.00	A96 640 000A	A99 840 000A
			A--B		12.00	A00 000 001B	A71 680 000B
			A--*		25.00	A03 848 001*	A03 860 000*
					25.00	A03 868 001*	A03 880 000*
					25.00	A03 888 001*	A03 900 000*
					25.00	A03 908 001*	A03 920 000*
					25.00	A03 928 001*	A03 940 000*
					25.00	A03 948 001*	A03 960 000*
					25.00	A03 968 001*	A03 980 000*
					25.00	A03 988 001*	A03 000 000*
					25.00	A04 008 001*	A04 020 000*
					25.00	A04 028 001*	A04 040 000*
					25.00	A04 048 001*	A04 060 000*
					25.00	A04 068 001*	A04 080 000*
					25.00	A04 088 001*	A04 100 000*
					25.00	A04 108 001*	A04 120 000*
					25.00	A04 128 001*	A04 140 000*
					25.00	A04 148 001*	A04 160 000*
					25.00	A04 168 001*	A04 180 000*

DISTRICT	TOTAL NOTES PRINTED	BLOCKS	ESTIMATED VALUE VG/F	CU	LOW OFFICIAL SERIAL NUMBER	HIGH OFFICIAL SERIAL NUMBER
				25.00	A04 188 001*	A04 200 000*
				25.00	A04 208 001*	A04 220 000*
				25.00	A04 228 001*	A04 240 000*
				25.00	A04 248 001*	A04 260 000*
				25.00	A04 268 001*	A04 280 000*
				25.00	A04 288 001*	A04 300 000*
				25.00	A04 308 001*	A04 320 000*
				25.00	A04 328 001*	A04 340 000*
				25.00	A04 348 001*	A04 360 000*
				25.00	A04 368 001*	A04 380 000*
				25.00	A04 388 001*	A04 400 000*
				25.00	A04 408 001*	A04 420 000*
				25.00	A04 428 001*	A04 440 000*
				25.00	A04 448 001*	A04 460 000*
				25.00	A04 468 001*	A04 480 000*
				15.00	A04 480 001*	A05 120 000*
				25.00	A05 132 001*	A05 140 000*
				25.00	A05 152 001*	A05 160 000*
				25.00	A05 172 001*	A05 180 000*
				25.00	A05 192 001*	A05 200 000*
				25.00	A05 212 001*	A05 220 000*
				25.00	A05 232 001*	A05 240 000*
				25.00	A05 252 001*	A05 260 000*
				25.00	A05 272 001*	A05 280 000*
				25.00	A05 292 001*	A05 300 000*
				25.00	A05 312 001*	A05 320 000*
				25.00	A05 332 001*	A05 340 000*
				25.00	A05 352 001*	A05 360 000*
				25.00	A05 372 001*	A05 380 000*
				25.00	A05 392 001*	A05 400 000*
				25.00	A05 412 001*	A05 420 000*
				25.00	A05 432 001*	A05 440 000*
				25.00	A05 452 001*	A05 460 000*
				25.00	A05 472 001*	A05 480 000*
				25.00	A05 492 001*	A05 500 000*
				25.00	A05 512 001*	A05 520 000*
				25.00	A05 532 001*	A05 540 000*
				25.00	A05 552 001*	A05 560 000*
				25.00	A05 572 001*	A05 580 000*
				25.00	A05 592 001*	A05 600 000*
				25.00	A05 612 001*	A05 620 000*
				25.00	A05 632 001*	A05 640 000*
				25.00	A05 652 001*	A05 660 000*
				25.00	A05 672 001*	A05 680 000*
				25.00	A05 692 001*	A05 700 000*
				25.00	A05 712 001*	A05 720 000*
				25.00	A05 732 001*	A05 740 000*
				25.00	A05 752 001*	A05 760 000*
				25.00	A05 768 001*	A05 780 000*
				25.00	A05 788 001*	A05 800 000*
				25.00	A05 808 001*	A05 820 000*
				25.00	A05 828 001*	A05 840 000*
				25.00	A05 848 001*	A05 860 000*
				25.00	A05 868 001*	A05 880 000*
				25.00	A05 888 001*	A05 900 000*
				25.00	A05 908 001*	A05 920 000*
				25.00	A05 928 001*	A05 940 000*
				25.00	A05 948 001*	A05 960 000*
				25.00	A05 968 001*	A05 980 000*
				25.00	A05 988 001*	A06 000 000*
				25.00	A06 008 001*	A06 020 000*
				25.00	A06 028 001*	A06 040 000*
				25.00	A06 048 001*	A06 060 000*
				25.00	A06 068 001*	A06 080 000*
				25.00	A06 088 001*	A06 100 000*
				25.00	A06 108 001*	A06 120 000*
				25.00	A06 128 001*	A06 140 000*
				25.00	A06 148 001*	A06 160 000*
				25.00	A06 168 001*	A06 180 000*

DISTRICT	TOTAL NOTES PRINTED	BLOCKS	ESTIMATED VALUE VG/F	CU	LOW OFFICIAL SERIAL NUMBER	HIGH OFFICIAL SERIAL NUMBER
				25.00	A06 188 001*	A06 200 000*
				25.00	A06 208 001*	A06 220 000*
				25.00	A06 228 001*	A06 240 000*
				25.00	A06 248 001*	A06 260 000*
				25.00	A06 268 001*	A06 280 000*
				25.00	A06 288 001*	A06 300 000*
				25.00	A06 308 001*	A06 320 000*
				25.00	A06 328 001*	A06 340 000*
				25.00	A06 348 001*	A06 360 000*
				25.00	A06 368 001*	A06 380 000*
				25.00	A06 388 001*	A06 400 000*
2	B NEW YORK	B--C		12.00	B77 440 001C	B99 840 000C
		B--D		12.00	B00 000 001D	B99 840 000D
		B--E		12.00	B00 000 001E	B92 160 000E
		B--*		15.00	B08 960 001*	B14 080 000*
				25.00	B14 096 001*	B14 100 000*
				25.00	B14 116 001*	B14 120 000*
				25.00	B14 136 001*	B14 140 000*
				25.00	B14 156 001*	B14 160 000*
				25.00	B14 176 001*	B14 180 000*
				25.00	B14 196 001*	B14 200 000*
				25.00	B14 216 001*	B14 220 000*
				25.00	B14 236 001*	B14 240 000*
				25.00	B14 256 001*	B14 260 000*
				25.00	B14 276 001*	B14 280 000*
				25.00	B14 296 001*	B14 300 000*
				25.00	B14 316 001*	B14 320 000*
				25.00	B14 336 001*	B14 340 000*
				25.00	B14 356 001*	B14 360 000*
				25.00	B14 376 001*	B14 380 000*
				25.00	B14 396 001*	B14 400 000*
				25.00	B14 416 001*	B14 420 000*
				25.00	B14 436 001*	B14 440 000*
				25.00	B14 456 001*	B14 460 000*
				25.00	B14 476 001*	B14 480 000*
				25.00	B14 496 001*	B14 500 000*
				25.00	B14 516 001*	B14 520 000*
				25.00	B14 536 001*	B14 540 000*
				25.00	B14 556 001*	B14 560 000*
				25.00	B14 576 001*	B14 580 000*
				25.00	B14 596 001*	B14 600 000*
				25.00	B14 616 001*	B14 620 000*
				25.00	B14 636 001*	B14 640 000*
				25.00	B14 656 001*	B14 660 000*
				25.00	B14 676 001*	B14 680 000*
				25.00	B14 696 001*	B14 700 000*
				25.00	B14 716 001*	B14 720 000*
3	C PHILADELPHIA	C--A		12.00	C83 200 001A	C99 840 000A
		C--B		12.00	C00 000 001B	C64 000 000B
		C--*		25.00	C01 296 001*	C01 300 000*
				25.00	C01 316 001*	C01 320 000*
				25.00	C01 336 001*	C01 340 000*
				25.00	C01 356 001*	C01 360 000*
				25.00	C01 376 001*	C01 380 000*
				25.00	C01 396 001*	C01 400 000*
				25.00	C01 416 001*	C01 420 000*
				25.00	C01 436 001*	C01 440 000*
				25.00	C01 456 001*	C01 460 000*
				25.00	C01 476 001*	C01 480 000*
				25.00	C01 496 001*	C01 500 000*
				25.00	C01 516 001*	C01 520 000*
				25.00	C01 536 001*	C01 540 000*
				25.00	C01 556 001*	C01 560 000*
				25.00	C01 576 001*	C01 580 000*
				25.00	C01 596 001*	C01 600 000*
				25.00	C01 616 001*	C01 620 000*
				25.00	C01 636 001*	C01 640 000*
				25.00	C01 656 001*	C01 660 000*
				25.00	C01 676 001*	C01 680 000*

DISTRICT	TOTAL NOTES PRINTED	BLOCKS	ESTIMATED VALUE VG/F	CU	LOW OFFICIAL SERIAL NUMBER	HIGH OFFICIAL SERIAL NUMBER
				25.00	C01 696 001*	C01 700 000*
				25.00	C01 716 001*	C01 720 000*
				25.00	C01 736 001*	C01 740 000*
				25.00	C01 756 001*	C01 760 000*
				25.00	C01 776 001*	C01 780 000*
				25.00	C01 796 001*	C01 800 000*
				25.00	C01 816 001*	C01 820 000*
				25.00	C01 836 001*	C01 840 000*
				25.00	C01 856 001*	C01 860 000*
				25.00	C01 876 001*	C01 880 000*
				25.00	C01 896 001*	C01 900 000*
				25.00	C01 916 001*	C01 920 000*
				15.00	C01 920 001*	C03 840 000*
4	D CLEVELAND	D--A		12.00	D83 200 001A	D99 840 000A
		D--B		12.00	D00 000 001B	D28 160 000B
		D--*		25.00	D01 288 001*	D01 300 000*
				25.00	D01 308 001*	D01 320 000*
				25.00	D01 328 001*	D01 340 000*
				25.00	D01 348 001*	D01 360 000*
				25.00	D01 368 001*	D01 380 000*
				25.00	D01 388 001*	D01 400 000*
				25.00	D01 408 001*	D01 420 000*
				25.00	D01 428 001*	D01 440 000*
				25.00	D01 448 001*	D01 460 000*
				25.00	D01 468 001*	D01 480 000*
				25.00	D01 488 001*	D01 500 000*
				25.00	D01 508 001*	D01 520 000*
				25.00	D01 528 001*	D01 540 000*
				25.00	D01 548 001*	D01 560 000*
				25.00	D01 568 001*	D01 580 000*
				25.00	D01 588 001*	D01 600 000*
				25.00	D01 608 001*	D01 620 000*
				25.00	D01 628 001*	D01 640 000*
				25.00	D01 648 001*	D01 660 000*
				25.00	D01 668 001*	D01 680 000*
				25.00	D01 688 001*	D01 700 000*
				25.00	D01 708 001*	D01 720 000*
				25.00	D01 728 001*	D01 740 000*
				25.00	D01 748 001*	D01 760 000*
				25.00	D01 768 001*	D01 780 000*
				25.00	D01 788 001*	D01 800 000*
				25.00	D01 808 001*	D01 820 000*
				25.00	D01 828 001*	D01 840 000*
				25.00	D01 848 001*	D01 860 000*
				25.00	D01 868 001*	D01 880 000*
				25.00	D01 888 001*	D01 900 000*
				25.00	D01 908 001*	D01 920 000*
				25.00	D01 932 001*	D01 940 000*
				25.00	D01 952 001*	D01 960 000*
				25.00	D01 972 001*	D01 980 000*
				25.00	D01 992 001*	D02 000 000*
				25.00	D02 012 001*	D02 020 000*
				25.00	D02 032 001*	D02 040 000*
				25.00	D02 052 001*	D02 060 000*
				25.00	D02 072 001*	D02 080 000*
				25.00	D02 092 001*	D02 100 000*
				25.00	D02 112 001*	D02 120 000*
				25.00	D02 132 001*	D02 140 000*
				25.00	D02 152 001*	D02 160 000*
				25.00	D02 172 001*	D02 180 000*
				25.00	D02 192 001*	D02 200 000*
				25.00	D02 212 001*	D02 220 000*
				25.00	D02 232 001*	D02 240 000*
				25.00	D02 252 001*	D02 260 000*
				25.00	D02 272 001*	D02 280 000*
				25.00	D02 292 001*	D02 300 000*
				25.00	D02 312 001*	D02 320 000*
				25.00	D02 332 001*	D02 340 000*
				25.00	D02 352 001*	D02 360 000*

DISTRICT	TOTAL NOTES PRINTED	BLOCKS	ESTIMATED VALUE VG/F	CU	LOW OFFICIAL SERIAL NUMBER	HIGH OFFICIAL SERIAL NUMBER
				25.00	D02 372 001*	D02 380 000*
				25.00	D02 392 001*	D02 400 000*
				25.00	D02 412 001*	D02 420 000*
				25.00	D02 432 001*	D02 440 000*
				25.00	D02 452 001*	D02 460 000*
				25.00	D02 472 001*	D02 480 000*
				25.00	D02 492 001*	D02 500 000*
				25.00	D02 512 001*	D02 520 000*
				25.00	D02 532 001*	D02 540 000*
				25.00	D02 552 001*	D02 560 000*
				15.00	D02 560 001*	D03 840 000*
				25.00	D03 856 001*	D03 860 000*
				25.00	D03 876 001*	D03 880 000*
				25.00	D03 896 001*	D03 900 000*
				25.00	D03 916 001*	D03 920 000*
				25.00	D03 936 001*	D03 940 000*
				25.00	D03 956 001*	D03 960 000*
				25.00	D03 976 001*	D03 980 000*
				25.00	D03 996 001*	D04 000 000*
				25.00	D04 016 001*	D04 020 000*
				25.00	D04 036 001*	D04 040 000*
				25.00	D04 056 001*	D04 060 000*
				25.00	D04 076 001*	D04 080 000*
				25.00	D04 096 001*	D04 100 000*
				25.00	D04 116 001*	D04 120 000*
				25.00	D04 136 001*	D04 140 000*
				25.00	D04 156 001*	D04 160 000*
				25.00	D04 176 001*	D04 180 000*
				25.00	D04 196 001*	D04 200 000*
				25.00	D04 216 001*	D04 220 000*
				25.00	D04 236 001*	D04 240 000*
				25.00	D04 256 001*	D04 260 000*
				25.00	D04 276 001*	D04 280 000*
				25.00	D04 296 001*	D04 300 000*
				25.00	D04 316 001*	D04 320 000*
				25.00	D04 336 001*	D04 340 000*
				25.00	D04 356 001*	D04 360 000*
				25.00	D04 376 001*	D04 380 000*
				25.00	D04 396 001*	D04 400 000*
				25.00	D04 416 001*	D04 420 000*
				25.00	D04 436 001*	D04 440 000*
				25.00	D04 456 001*	D04 460 000*
				25.00	D04 476 001*	D04 480 000*
5 E RICHMOND		E--A		12.00	E71 040 001A	E99 840 000A
		E--B		12.00	E00 000 001B	E75 520 000B
		E--*		25.00	E02 576 001*	E02 580 000*
				25.00	E02 596 001*	E02 600 000*
				25.00	E02 616 001*	E02 620 000*
				25.00	E02 636 001*	E02 640 000*
				25.00	E02 656 001*	E02 660 000*
				25.00	E02 676 001*	E02 680 000*
				25.00	E02 696 001*	E02 700 000*
				25.00	E02 716 001*	E02 720 000*
				25.00	E02 736 001*	E02 740 000*
				25.00	E02 756 001*	E02 760 000*
				25.00	E02 776 001*	E02 780 000*
				25.00	E02 796 001*	E02 800 000*
				25.00	E02 816 001*	E02 820 000*
				25.00	E02 836 001*	E02 840 000*
				25.00	E02 856 001*	E02 860 000*
				25.00	E02 876 001*	E02 880 000*
				25.00	E02 896 001*	E02 900 000*
				25.00	E02 916 001*	E02 920 000*
				25.00	E02 936 001*	E02 940 000*
				25.00	E02 956 001*	E02 960 000*
				25.00	E02 976 001*	E02 980 000*
				25.00	E02 996 001*	E03 000 000*
				25.00	E03 016 001*	E03 020 000*
				25.00	E03 036 001*	E03 040 000*

DISTRICT	TOTAL NOTES PRINTED	BLOCKS	ESTIMATED VALUE VG/F	VALUE CU	LOW OFFICIAL SERIAL NUMBER	HIGH OFFICIAL SERIAL NUMBER
				25.00	E03 056 001*	E03 060 000*
				25.00	E03 076 001*	E03 080 000*
				25.00	E03 096 001*	E03 100 000*
				25.00	E03 116 001*	E03 120 000*
				25.00	E03 136 001*	E03 140 000*
				25.00	E03 156 001*	E03 160 000*
				25.00	E03 176 001*	E03 180 000*
				25.00	E03 196 001*	E03 200 000*
				15.00	E03 200 001*	E05 760 000*
				25.00	E05 772 001*	E05 780 000*
				25.00	E05 792 001*	E05 800 000*
				25.00	E05 812 001*	E05 820 000*
				25.00	E05 832 001*	E05 840 000*
				25.00	E05 852 001*	E05 860 000*
				25.00	E05 872 001*	E05 880 000*
				25.00	E05 892 001*	E05 900 000*
				25.00	E05 912 001*	E05 920 000*
				25.00	E05 932 001*	E05 940 000*
				25.00	E05 952 001*	E05 960 000*
				25.00	E05 972 001*	E05 980 000*
				25.00	E05 992 001*	E06 000 000*
				25.00	E06 012 001*	E06 020 000*
				25.00	E06 032 001*	E06 040 000*
				25.00	E06 052 001*	E06 060 000*
				25.00	E06 072 001*	E06 080 000*
				25.00	E06 092 001*	E06 100 000*
				25.00	E06 112 001*	E06 120 000*
				25.00	E06 132 001*	E06 140 000*
				25.00	E06 152 001*	E06 160 000*
				25.00	E06 172 001*	E06 180 000*
				25.00	E06 192 001*	E06 200 000*
				25.00	E06 212 001*	E06 220 000*
				25.00	E06 232 001*	E06 240 000*
				25.00	E06 252 001*	E06 260 000*
				25.00	E06 272 001*	E06 280 000*
				25.00	E06 292 001*	E06 300 000*
				25.00	E06 312 001*	E06 320 000*
				25.00	E06 332 001*	E06 340 000*
				25.00	E06 352 001*	E06 360 000*
				25.00	E06 372 001*	E06 380 000*
				25.00	E06 392 001*	E06 400 000*
				25.00	E06 416 001*	E06 420 000*
				25.00	E06 436 001*	E06 440 000*
				25.00	E06 456 001*	E06 460 000*
				25.00	E06 476 001*	E06 480 000*
				25.00	E06 496 001*	E06 500 000*
				25.00	E06 516 001*	E06 520 000*
				25.00	E06 536 001*	E06 540 000*
				25.00	E06 556 001*	E06 560 000*
				25.00	E06 576 001*	E06 580 000*
				25.00	E06 596 001*	E06 600 000*
				25.00	E06 616 001*	E06 620 000*
				25.00	E06 636 001*	E06 640 000*
				25.00	E06 656 001*	E06 660 000*
				25.00	E06 676 001*	E06 680 000*
				25.00	E06 696 001*	E06 700 000*
				25.00	E06 716 001*	E06 720 000*
				25.00	E06 736 001*	E06 740 000*
				25.00	E06 756 001*	E06 760 000*
				25.00	E06 776 001*	E06 780 000*
				25.00	E06 796 001*	E06 800 000*
				25.00	E06 816 001*	E06 820 000*
				25.00	E06 836 001*	E06 840 000*
				25.00	E06 856 001*	E06 860 000*
				25.00	E06 876 001*	E06 880 000*
				25.00	E06 896 001*	E06 900 000*
				25.00	E06 916 001*	E06 920 000*
				25.00	E06 936 001*	E06 940 000*
				25.00	E06 956 001*	E06 960 000*

DISTRICT	TOTAL NOTES PRINTED	BLOCKS	ESTIMATED VALUE VG/F CU	LOW OFFICIAL SERIAL NUMBER	HIGH OFFICIAL SERIAL NUMBER
			25.00	E06 976 001*	E06 980 000*
			25.00	E06 996 001*	E07 000 000*
			25.00	E07 016 001*	E07 020 000*
			25.00	E07 036 001*	E07 040 000*
6 F ATLANTA		F--A	12.00	F88 960 001A	F99 840 000A
		F--B	12.00	F00 000 001B	F23 040 000B
		F--*	15.00	F01 920 001*	F02 560 000*
7 G CHICAGO		G--B	12.00	G74 880 001B	G99 840 000B
		G--C	12.00	G00 000 001C	G83 200 000C
		G--*	15.00	G06 400 001	G07 680 000
			25.00	G07 692 001*	G07 700 000*
			25.00	G07 712 001*	G07 720 000*
			25.00	G07 732 001*	G07 740 000*
			25.00	G07 752 001*	G07 760 000*
			25.00	G07 772 001*	G07 780 000*
			25.00	G07 792 001*	G07 800 000*
			25.00	G07 812 001*	G07 820 000*
			25.00	G07 832 001*	G07 840 000*
			25.00	G07 852 001*	G07 860 000*
			25.00	G07 872 001*	G07 880 000*
			25.00	G07 892 001*	G07 900 000*
			25.00	G07 912 001*	G07 920 000*
			25.00	G07 932 001*	G07 940 000*
			25.00	G07 952 001*	G07 960 000*
			25.00	G07 972 001*	G07 980 000*
			25.00	G07 992 001*	G08 000 000*
			25.00	G08 012 001*	G08 020 000*
			25.00	G08 032 001*	G08 040 000*
			25.00	G08 052 001*	G08 060 000*
			25.00	G08 072 001*	G08 080 000*
			25.00	G08 092 001*	G08 100 000*
			25.00	G08 112 001*	G08 120 000*
			25.00	G08 132 001*	G08 140 000*
			25.00	G08 152 001*	G08 160 000*
			25.00	G08 172 001*	G08 180 000*
			25.00	G08 192 001*	G08 200 000*
			25.00	G08 212 001*	G08 220 000*
			25.00	G08 232 001*	G08 240 000*
			25.00	G08 252 001*	G08 260 000*
			25.00	G08 272 001*	G08 280 000*
			25.00	G08 292 001*	G08 300 000*
			25.00	G08 312 001*	G08 320 000*
			15.00	G08 320 001*	G08 960 000*
			25.00	G08 968 001*	G08 980 000*
			25.00	G08 988 001*	G09 000 000*
			25.00	G09 008 001*	G09 020 000*
			25.00	G09 028 001*	G09 040 000*
			25.00	G09 048 001*	G09 060 000*
			25.00	G09 068 001*	G09 080 000*
			25.00	G09 088 001*	G09 100 000*
			25.00	G09 108 001*	G09 120 000*
			25.00	G09 128 001C	G09 140 000C
			25.00	G09 148 001*	G09 160 000*
			25.00	G09 168 001*	G09 180 000*
			25.00	G09 188 001*	G09 200 000*
			25.00	G09 208 001*	G09 220 000*
			25.00	G09 228 001*	G09 240 000*
			25.00	G09 248 001*	G09 260 000*
			25.00	G09 268 001*	G09 280 000*
			25.00	G09 288 001*	G09 300 000*
			25.00	G09 308 001*	G09 320 000*
			25.00	G09 328 001*	G09 340 000*
			25.00	G09 348 001*	G09 360 000*
			25.00	G09 368 001*	G09 380 000*
			25.00	G09 388 001*	G09 400 000*
			25.00	G09 408 001*	G09 420 000*
			25.00	G09 428 001*	G09 440 000*
			25.00	G09 448 001*	G09 460 000*
			25.00	G09 468 001*	G09 480 000*

DISTRICT	TOTAL NOTES PRINTED	BLOCKS	ESTIMATED VALUE VG/F	VALUE CU	LOW OFFICIAL SERIAL NUMBER	HIGH OFFICIAL SERIAL NUMBER
				25.00	G09 488 001*	G09 500 000*
				25.00	G09 508 001*	G09 520 000*
				25.00	G09 528 001*	G09 540 000*
				25.00	G09 548 001*	G09 560 000*
				25.00	G09 568 001*	G09 580 000*
				25.00	G09 588 001*	G09 600 000*
				15.00	G09 600 001*	G10 240 000*
8 H ST. LOUIS		H--A		12.00	H46 720 001A	H74 240 000A
		H--*		25.00	H01 292 001*	H01 300 000*
				25.00	H01 312 001*	H01 320 000*
				25.00	H01 332 001*	H01 340 000*
				25.00	H01 352 001*	H01 360 000*
				25.00	H01 372 001*	H01 380 000*
				25.00	H01 392 001*	H01 400 000*
				25.00	H01 412 001*	H01 420 000*
				25.00	H01 432 001*	H01 440 000*
				25.00	H01 452 001*	H01 460 000*
				25.00	H01 472 001*	H01 480 000*
				25.00	H01 492 001*	H01 500 000*
				25.00	H01 512 001*	H01 520 000*
				25.00	H01 532 001*	H01 540 000*
				25.00	H01 552 001*	H01 560 000*
				25.00	H01 572 001*	H01 580 000*
				25.00	H01 592 001*	H01 600 000*
				25.00	H01 612 001*	H01 620 000*
				25.00	H01 632 001*	H01 640 000*
				25.00	H01 652 001*	H01 660 000*
				25.00	H01 672 001*	H01 680 000*
				25.00	H01 692 001*	H01 700 000*
				25.00	H01 712 001*	H01 720 000*
				25.00	H01 732 001*	H01 740 000*
				25.00	H01 752 001*	H01 760 000*
				25.00	H01 772 001*	H01 780 000*
				25.00	H01 792 001*	H01 800 000*
				25.00	H01 812 001*	H01 820 000*
				25.00	H01 832 001*	H01 840 000*
				25.00	H01 852 001*	H01 860 000*
				25.00	H01 872 001*	H01 880 000*
				25.00	H01 892 001*	H01 900 000*
				25.00	H01 912 001*	H01 920 000*
				25.00	H01 928 001*	H01 940 000*
				25.00	H01 948 001*	H01 960 000*
				25.00	H01 968 001*	H01 980 000*
				25.00	H01 988 001*	H02 000 000*
				25.00	H02 008 001*	H02 020 000*
				25.00	H02 028 001*	H02 040 000*
				25.00	H02 048 001*	H02 060 000*
				25.00	H02 068 001*	H02 080 000*
				25.00	H02 088 001*	H02 100 000*
				25.00	H02 108 001*	H02 120 000*
				25.00	H02 128 001*	H02 140 000*
				25.00	H02 148 001*	H02 160 000*
				25.00	H02 168 001*	H02 180 000*
				25.00	H02 188 001*	H02 200 000*
				25.00	H02 208 001*	H02 220 000*
				25.00	H02 228 001*	H02 240 000*
				25.00	H02 248 001*	H02 260 000*
				25.00	H02 268 001*	H02 280 000*
				25.00	H02 288 001*	H02 300 000*
				25.00	H02 308 001*	H02 320 000*
				25.00	H02 328 001*	H02 340 000*
				25.00	H02 348 001*	H02 360 000*
				25.00	H02 368 001*	H02 380 000*
				25.00	H02 388 001*	H02 400 000*
				25.00	H02 408 001*	H02 420 000*
				25.00	H02 428 001*	H02 440 000*
				25.00	H02 448 001*	H02 460 000*
				25.00	H02 468 001*	H02 480 000*
				25.00	H02 488 001*	H02 500 000*

DISTRICT	TOTAL NOTES PRINTED	BLOCKS	ESTIMATED VALUE VG/F	CU	LOW OFFICIAL SERIAL NUMBER	HIGH OFFICIAL SERIAL NUMBER
				25.00	H02 508 001*	H02 520 000*
				25.00	H02 528 001*	H02 540 000*
				25.00	H02 548 001*	H02 560 000*
9 I MINNEAPOLIS		I--A		12.00	I10 240 001A	I17 920 000A
		I--*		25.00	I00 656 001*	I00 660 000*
				25.00	I00 676 001*	I00 680 000*
				25.00	I00 696 001*	I00 700 000*
				25.00	I00 716 001*	I00 720 000*
				25.00	I00 736 001*	I00 740 000*
				25.00	I00 756 001*	I00 760 000*
				25.00	I00 776 001*	I00 780 000*
				25.00	I00 796 001*	I00 800 000*
				25.00	I00 816 001*	I00 820 000*
				25.00	I00 836 001*	I00 840 000*
				25.00	I00 856 001*	I00 860 000*
				25.00	I00 876 001*	I00 880 000*
				25.00	I00 896 001*	I00 900 000*
				25.00	I00 916 001*	I00 920 000*
				25.00	I00 936 001*	I00 940 000*
				25.00	I00 956 001*	I00 960 000*
				25.00	I00 976 001*	I00 980 000*
				25.00	I00 996 001*	I01 000 000*
				25.00	I01 016 001*	I01 020 000*
				25.00	I01 036 001*	I01 040 000*
				25.00	I01 056 001*	I01 060 000*
				25.00	I01 076 001*	I01 080 000*
				25.00	I01 096 001*	I01 100 000*
				25.00	I01 116 001*	I01 120 000*
				25.00	I01 136 001*	I01 140 000*
				25.00	I01 156 001*	I01 160 000*
				25.00	I01 176 001*	I01 180 000*
				25.00	I01 196 001*	I01 200 000*
				25.00	I01 216 001*	I01 220 000*
				25.00	I01 236 001*	I01 240 000*
				25.00	I01 256 001*	I01 260 000*
				25.00	I01 276 001*	I01 280 000*
10 J KANSAS CITY		J--A		12.00	J50 560 001A	J90 880 000A
		J--*		25.00	J01 296 001*	J01 300 000*
				25.00	J01 316 001*	J01 320 000*
				25.00	J01 336 001*	J01 340 000*
				25.00	J01 356 001*	J01 360 000*
				25.00	J01 376 001*	J01 380 000*
				25.00	J01 396 001*	J01 400 000*
				25.00	J01 416 001*	J01 420 000*
				25.00	J01 436 001*	J01 440 000*
				25.00	J01 456 001*	J01 460 000*
				25.00	J01 476 001*	J01 480 000*
				25.00	J01 496 001*	J01 500 000*
				25.00	J01 516 001*	J01 520 000*
				25.00	J01 536 001*	J01 540 000*
				25.00	J01 556 001*	J01 560 000*
				25.00	J01 576 001*	J01 580 000*
				25.00	J01 596 001*	J01 600 000*
				25.00	J01 616 001*	J01 620 000*
				25.00	J01 636 001*	J01 640 000*
				25.00	J01 656 001*	J01 660 000*
				25.00	J01 676 001*	J01 680 000*
				25.00	J01 696 001*	J01 700 000*
				25.00	J01 716 001*	J01 720 000*
				25.00	J01 736 001*	J01 740 000*
				25.00	J01 756 001*	J01 760 000*
				25.00	J01 776 001*	J01 780 000*
				25.00	J01 796 001*	J01 800 000*
				25.00	J01 816 001*	J01 820 000*
				25.00	J01 836 001*	J01 840 000*
				25.00	J01 856 001*	J01 860 000*
				25.00	J01 876 001*	J01 880 000*
				25.00	J01 896 001*	J01 900 000*
				25.00	J01 916 001*	J01 920 000*
				25.00	J01 932 001*	J01 940 000*

VALUE CU	LOW OFFICIAL SERIAL NUMBER	HIGH OFFICIAL SERIAL NUMBER	VALUE CU	LOW OFFICIAL SERIAL NUMBER	HIGH OFFICIAL SERIAL NUMBER
25.00	J01 952 001*	J01 960 000*	25.00	J03 352 001*	J03 360 000*
25.00	J01 972 001*	J01 980 000*	25.00	J03 372 001*	J03 380 000*
25.00	J01 992 001*	J02 000 000*	25.00	J03 392 001*	J03 400 000*
25.00	J02 012 001*	J02 020 000*	25.00	J03 412 001*	J03 420 000*
25.00	J02 032 001*	J02 040 000*	25.00	J03 432 001*	J03 440 000*
25.00	J02 052 001*	J02 060 000*	25.00	J03 452 001*	J03 460 000*
25.00	J02 072 001*	J02 080 000*	25.00	J03 472 001*	J03 480 000*
25.00	J02 092 001*	J02 100 000*	25.00	J03 492 001*	J03 500 000*
25.00	J02 112 001*	J02 120 000*	25.00	J03 512 001*	J03 520 000*
25.00	J02 132 001*	J02 140 000*	25.00	J03 532 001*	J03 540 000*
25.00	J02 152 001*	J02 160 000*	25.00	J03 552 001*	J03 560 000*
25.00	J02 172 001*	J02 180 000*	25.00	J03 572 001*	J03 580 000*
25.00	J02 192 001*	J02 200 000*	25.00	J03 592 001*	J03 600 000*
25.00	J02 212 001*	J02 220 000*	25.00	J03 612 001*	J03 620 000*
25.00	J02 232 001*	J02 240 000*	25.00	J03 632 001*	J03 640 000*
25.00	J02 252 001*	J02 260 000*	25.00	J03 652 001*	J03 660 000*
25.00	J02 272 001*	J02 280 000*	25.00	J03 672 001*	J03 680 000*
25.00	J02 292 001*	J02 300 000*	25.00	J03 692 001*	J03 700 000*
25.00	J02 312 001*	J02 320 000*	25.00	J03 712 001*	J03 720 000*
25.00	J02 332 001*	J02 340 000*	25.00	J03 732 001*	J03 740 000*
25.00	J02 352 001*	J02 360 000*	25.00	J03 752 001*	J03 760 000*
25.00	J02 372 001*	J02 380 000*	25.00	J03 772 001*	J03 780 000*
25.00	J02 392 001*	J02 400 000*	25.00	J03 792 001*	J03 800 000*
25.00	J02 412 001*	J02 420 000*	25.00	J03 812 001*	J03 820 000*
25.00	J02 432 001*	J02 440 000*	25.00	J03 832 001*	J03 840 000*
25.00	J02 452 001*	J02 460 000*	25.00	J03 852 001*	J03 860 000*
25.00	J02 472 001*	J02 480 000*	25.00	J03 872 001*	J03 880 000*
25.00	J02 492 001*	J02 500 000*	25.00	J03 892 001*	J03 900 000*
25.00	J02 512 001*	J02 520 000*	25.00	J03 912 001*	J03 920 000*
25.00	J02 532 001*	J02 540 000*	25.00	J03 932 001*	J03 940 000*
25.00	J02 552 001*	J02 560 000*	25.00	J03 952 001*	J03 960 000*
25.00	J02 576 001*	J02 580 000*	25.00	J03 972 001*	J03 980 000*
25.00	J02 596 001*	J02 600 000*	25.00	J03 992 001*	J04 000 000*
25.00	J02 616 001*	J02 620 000*	25.00	J04 012 001*	J04 020 000*
25.00	J02 636 001*	J02 640 000*	25.00	J04 032 001*	J04 040 000*
25.00	J02 656 001*	J02 660 000*	25.00	J04 052 001*	J04 060 000*
25.00	J02 676 001*	J02 680 000*	25.00	J04 072 001*	J04 080 000*
25.00	J02 696 001*	J02 700 000*	25.00	J04 092 001*	J04 100 000*
25.00	J02 716 001*	J02 720 000*	25.00	J04 112 001*	J04 120 000*
25.00	J02 736 001*	J02 740 000*	25.00	J04 132 001*	J04 140 000*
25.00	J02 756 001*	J02 760 000*	25.00	J04 152 001*	J04 160 000*
25.00	J02 776 001*	J02 780 000*	25.00	J04 172 001*	J04 180 000*
25.00	J02 796 001*	J02 800 000*	25.00	J04 192 001*	J04 200 000*
25.00	J02 816 001*	J02 820 000*	25.00	J04 212 001*	J04 220 000*
25.00	J02 836 001*	J02 840 000*	25.00	J04 232 001*	J04 240 000*
25.00	J02 856 001*	J02 860 000*	25.00	J04 252 001*	J04 260 000*
25.00	J02 876 001*	J02 880 000*	25.00	J04 272 001*	J04 280 000*
25.00	J02 896 001*	J02 900 000*	25.00	J04 292 001*	J04 300 000*
25.00	J02 916 001*	J02 920 000*	25.00	J04 312 001*	J04 320 000*
25.00	J02 936 001*	J02 940 000*	25.00	J04 332 001*	J04 340 000*
25.00	J02 956 001*	J02 960 000*	25.00	J04 352 001*	J04 360 000*
25.00	J02 976 001*	J02 980 000*	25.00	J04 372 001*	J04 380 000*
25.00	J02 996 001*	J03 000 000*	25.00	J04 392 001*	J04 400 000*
25.00	J03 016 001*	J03 020 000*	25.00	J04 412 001*	J04 420 000*
25.00	J03 036 001*	J03 040 000*	25.00	J04 432 001*	J04 440 000*
25.00	J03 056 001*	J03 060 000*	25.00	J04 452 001*	J04 460 000*
25.00	J03 076 001*	J03 080 000*	25.00	J04 472 001*	J04 480 000*
25.00	J03 096 001*	J03 100 000*	25.00	J04 492 001*	J04 500 000*
25.00	J03 116 001*	J03 120 000*	25.00	J04 512 001*	J04 520 000*
25.00	J03 136 001*	J03 140 000*	25.00	J04 532 001*	J04 540 000*
25.00	J03 156 001*	J03 160 000*	25.00	J04 552 001*	J04 560 000*
25.00	J03 176 001*	J03 180 000*	25.00	J04 572 001*	J04 580 000*
25.00	J03 196 001*	J03 200 000*	25.00	J04 592 001*	J04 600 000*
25.00	J03 212 001*	J03 220 000*	25.00	J04 612 001*	J04 620 000*
25.00	J03 232 001*	J03 240 000*	25.00	J04 632 001*	J04 640 000*
25.00	J03 252 001*	J03 260 000*	25.00	J04 652 001*	J04 660 000*
25.00	J03 272 001*	J03 280 000*	25.00	J04 672 001*	J04 680 000*
25.00	J03 292 001*	J03 300 000*	25.00	J04 692 001*	J04 700 000*
25.00	J03 312 001*	J03 320 000*	25.00	J04 712 001*	J04 720 000*
25.00	J03 332 001*	J03 340 000*	25.00	J04 732 001*	J04 740 000*

DISTRICT	TOTAL NOTES PRINTED	BLOCKS	ESTIMATED VALUE VG/F	CU	LOW OFFICIAL SERIAL NUMBER	HIGH OFFICIAL SERIAL NUMBER
				25.00	J04 752 001*	J04 760 000*
				25.00	J04 772 001*	J04 780 000*
				25.00	J04 792 001*	J04 800 000*
				25.00	J04 812 001*	J04 820 000*
				25.00	J04 832 001*	J04 840 000*
				25.00	J04 852 001*	J04 860 000*
				25.00	J04 872 001*	J04 880 000*
				25.00	J04 892 001*	J04 900 000*
				25.00	J04 912 001*	J04 920 000*
				25.00	J04 932 001*	J04 940 000*
				25.00	J04 952 001*	J04 960 000*
				25.00	J04 972 001*	J04 980 000*
				25.00	J04 992 001*	J05 000 000*
				25.00	J05 012 001*	J05 020 000*
				25.00	J05 032 001*	J05 040 000*
				25.00	J05 052 001*	J05 060 000*
				25.00	J05 072 001*	J05 080 000*
				25.00	J05 092 001*	J05 100 000*
				25.00	J05 112 001*	J05 120 000*
				25.00	J05 132 001*	J05 140 000*
				25.00	J05 152 001*	J05 160 000*
				25.00	J05 172 001*	J05 180 000*
				25.00	J05 192 001*	J05 200 000*
				25.00	J05 212 001*	J05 220 000*
				25.00	J05 232 001*	J05 240 000*
				25.00	J05 252 001*	J05 260 000*
				25.00	J05 272 001*	J05 280 000*
				25.00	J05 292 001*	J05 300 000*
				25.00	J05 312 001*	J05 320 000*
				25.00	J05 332 001*	J05 340 000*
				25.00	J05 352 001*	J05 360 000*
				25.00	J05 372 001*	J05 380 000*
				25.00	J05 392 001*	J05 400 000*
				25.00	J05 412 001*	J05 420 000*
				25.00	J05 432 001*	J05 440 000*
				25.00	J05 452 001*	J05 460 000*
				25.00	J05 472 001*	J05 480 000*
				25.00	J05 492 001*	J05 500 000*
				25.00	J05 512 001*	J05 520 000*
				25.00	J05 532 001*	J05 540 000*
				25.00	J05 552 001*	J05 560 000*
				25.00	J05 572 001*	J05 580 000*
				25.00	J05 592 001*	J05 600 000*
				25.00	J05 612 001*	J05 620 000*
				25.00	J05 632 001*	J05 640 000*
				25.00	J05 652 001*	J05 660 000*
				25.00	J05 672 001*	J05 680 000*
				25.00	J05 692 001*	J05 700 000*
				25.00	J05 712 001*	J05 720 000*
				25.00	J05 732 001*	J05 740 000*
				25.00	J05 752 001*	J05 760 000*
11 K DALLAS		K--A		12.00	K53 760 001A	K99 840 000A
		K--B		12.00	K00 000 001B	K14 080 000B
		K--*		15.00	K00 640 001*	K01 920 000*
				25.00	K01 932 001*	K01 940 000*
				25.00	K01 952 001*	K01 960 000*
				25.00	K01 972 001*	K01 980 000*
				25.00	K01 992 001*	K02 000 000*
				25.00	K02 012 001*	K02 020 000*
				25.00	K02 032 001*	K02 040 000*
				25.00	K02 052 001*	K02 060 000*
				25.00	K02 072 001*	K02 080 000*
				25.00	K02 092 001*	K02 100 000*
				25.00	K02 112 001*	K02 120 000*
				25.00	K02 132 001*	K02 140 000*
				25.00	K02 152 001*	K02 160 000*
				25.00	K02 172 001*	K02 180 000*
				25.00	K02 192 001*	K02 200 000*
				25.00	K02 212 001*	K02 220 000*

DISTRICT	TOTAL NOTES PRINTED	BLOCKS	ESTIMATED VALUE VG/F	VALUE CU	LOW OFFICIAL SERIAL NUMBER	HIGH OFFICIAL SERIAL NUMBER
				25.00	K02 232 001*	K02 240 000*
				25.00	K02 252 001*	K02 260 000*
				25.00	K02 272 001*	K02 280 000*
				25.00	K02 292 001*	K02 300 000*
				25.00	K02 312 001*	K02 320 000*
				25.00	K02 332 001*	K02 340 000*
				25.00	K02 352 001*	K02 360 000*
				25.00	K02 372 001*	K02 380 000*
				25.00	K02 392 001*	K02 400 000*
				25.00	K02 412 001*	K02 420 000*
				25.00	K02 432 001*	K02 440 000*
				25.00	K02 452 001*	K02 460 000*
				25.00	K02 472 001*	K02 480 000*
				25.00	K02 492 001*	K02 500 000*
				25.00	K02 512 001*	K02 520 000*
				25.00	K02 532 001*	K02 540 000*
				25.00	K02 552 001*	K02 560 000*
				25.00	K02 576 001*	K02 580 000*
				25.00	K02 596 001*	K02 600 000*
				25.00	K02 616 001*	K02 620 000*
				25.00	K02 636 001*	K02 640 000*
				25.00	K02 656 001*	K02 660 000*
				25.00	K02 676 001*	K02 680 000*
				25.00	K02 696 001*	K02 700 000*
				25.00	K02 716 001*	K02 720 000*
				25.00	K02 736 001*	K02 740 000*
				25.00	K02 756 001*	K02 760 000*
				25.00	K02 776 001*	K02 780 000*
				25.00	K02 796 001*	K02 800 000*
				25.00	K02 816 001*	K02 820 000*
				25.00	K02 836 001*	K02 840 000*
				25.00	K02 856 001*	K02 860 000*
				25.00	K02 876 001*	K02 880 000*
				25.00	K02 896 001*	K02 900 000*
				25.00	K02 916 001*	K02 920 000*
				25.00	K02 936 001*	K02 940 000*
				25.00	K02 956 001*	K02 960 000*
				25.00	K02 976 001*	K02 980 000*
				25.00	K02 996 001*	K03 000 000*
				25.00	K03 016 001*	K03 020 000*
				25.00	K03 036 001*	K03 040 000*
				25.00	K03 056 001*	K03 060 000*
				25.00	K03 076 001*	K03 080 000*
				25.00	K03 096 001*	K03 100 000*
				25.00	K03 116 001*	K03 120 000*
				25.00	K03 136 001*	K03 140 000*
				25.00	K03 156 001*	K03 160 000*
				25.00	K03 176 001*	K03 180 000*
				25.00	K03 196 001*	K03 200 000*
				15.00	K03 200 001*	K05 760 000*
12 L SAN FRANCISCO		L--A		12.00	L73 600 001A	L99 840 000A
		L--B		12.00	L00 000 001B	L33 280 000B
		L--*		25.00	L02 572 001*	L02 580 000*
				25.00	L02 592 001*	L02 600 000*
				25.00	L02 612 001*	L02 620 000*
				25.00	L02 632 001*	L02 640 000*
				25.00	L02 652 001*	L02 660 000*
				25.00	L02 672 001*	L02 680 000*
				25.00	L02 692 001*	L02 700 000*
				25.00	L02 712 001*	L02 720 000*
				25.00	L02 732 001*	L02 740 000*
				25.00	L02 752 001*	L02 760 000*
				25.00	L02 772 001*	L02 780 000*
				25.00	L02 792 001*	L02 800 000*
				25.00	L02 812 001*	L02 820 000*
				25.00	L02 832 001*	L02 840 000*
				25.00	L02 852 001*	L02 860 000*
				25.00	L02 872 001*	L02 880 000*
				25.00	L02 892 001*	L02 900 000*

211

VALUE CU	LOW OFFICIAL SERIAL NUMBER	HIGH OFFICIAL SERIAL NUMBER	VALUE CU	LOW OFFICIAL SERIAL NUMBER	HIGH OFFICIAL SERIAL NUMBER
25.00	L02 912 001*	L02 920 000*	25.00	L04 652 001*	L04 660 000*
25.00	L02 932 001*	L02 940 000*	25.00	L04 672 001*	L04 680 000*
25.00	L02 952 001*	L02 960 000*	25.00	L04 692 001*	L04 700 000*
25.00	L02 972 001*	L02 980 000*	25.00	L04 712 001*	L04 720 000*
25.00	L02 992 001*	L03 000 000*	25.00	L04 732 001*	L04 740 000*
25.00	L03 012 001*	L03 020 000*	25.00	L04 752 001*	L04 760 000*
25.00	L03 032 001*	L03 040 000*	25.00	L04 772 001*	L04 780 000*
25.00	L03 052 001*	L03 060 000*	25.00	L04 792 001*	L04 800 000*
25.00	L03 072 001*	L03 080 000*	25.00	L04 812 001*	L04 820 000*
25.00	L03 092 001*	L03 100 000*	25.00	L04 832 001*	L04 840 000*
25.00	L03 112 001*	L03 120 000*	25.00	L04 852 001*	L04 860 000*
25.00	L03 132 001*	L03 140 000*	25.00	L04 872 001*	L04 880 000*
25.00	L03 152 001*	L03 160 000*	25.00	L04 892 001*	L04 900 000*
25.00	L03 172 001*	L03 180 000*	25.00	L04 912 001*	L04 920 000*
25.00	L03 192 001*	L03 200 000*	25.00	L04 932 001*	L04 940 000*
25.00	L03 212 001*	L03 220 000*	25.00	L04 952 001*	L04 960 000*
25.00	L03 232 001*	L03 240 000*	25.00	L04 972 001*	L04 980 000*
25.00	L03 252 001*	L03 260 000*	25.00	L04 992 001*	L05 000 000*
25.00	L03 272 001*	L03 280 000*	25.00	L05 012 001*	L05 020 000*
25.00	L03 292 001*	L03 300 000*	25.00	L05 032 001*	L05 040 000*
25.00	L03 312 001*	L03 320 000*	25.00	L05 052 001*	L05 060 000*
25.00	L03 332 001*	L03 340 000*	25.00	L05 072 001*	L05 080 000*
25.00	L03 352 001*	L03 360 000*	25.00	L05 092 001*	L05 100 000*
25.00	L03 372 001*	L03 380 000*	25.00	L05 112 000*	L05 120 000*
25.00	L03 392 001*	L03 400 000*	25.00	L05 128 001*	L05 140 000*
25.00	L03 412 001*	L03 420 000*	25.00	L05 148 001*	L05 160 000*
25.00	L03 432 001*	L03 440 000*	25.00	L05 168 001*	L05 180 000*
25.00	L03 452 001*	L03 460 000*	25.00	L05 188 001*	L05 200 000*
25.00	L03 472 001*	L03 480 000*	25.00	L05 208 001*	L05 220 000*
25.00	L03 492 001*	L03 500 000*	25.00	L05 228 001*	L05 240 000*
25.00	L03 512 001*	L03 520 000*	25.00	L05 248 001*	L05 260 000*
25.00	L03 532 001*	L03 540 000*	25.00	L05 268 001*	L05 280 000*
25.00	L03 552 001*	L03 560 000*	25.00	L05 288 001*	L05 300 000*
25.00	L03 572 001*	L03 580 000*	25.00	L05 308 001*	L05 320 000*
25.00	L03 592 001*	L03 600 000*	25.00	L05 328 001*	L05 340 000*
25.00	L03 612 001*	L03 620 000*	25.00	L05 348 001*	L05 360 000*
25.00	L03 632 001*	L03 640 000*	25.00	L05 368 001*	L05 380 000*
25.00	L03 652 001*	L03 660 000*	25.00	L05 388 001*	L05 400 000*
25.00	L03 672 001*	L03 680 000*	25.00	L05 408 001*	L05 420 000*
25.00	L03 692 001*	L03 700 000*	25.00	L05 428 001*	L05 440 000*
25.00	L03 712 001*	L03 720 000*	25.00	L05 448 001*	L05 460 000*
25.00	L03 732 001*	L03 740 000*	25.00	L05 468 001*	L05 480 000*
25.00	L03 752 001*	L03 760 000*	25.00	L05 488 001*	L05 500 000*
25.00	L03 772 001*	L03 780 000*	25.00	L05 508 001*	L05 520 000*
25.00	L03 792 001*	L03 800 000*	25.00	L05 528 001*	L05 540 000*
25.00	L03 812 001*	L03 820 000*	25.00	L05 548 001*	L05 560 000*
25.00	L03 832 001*	L03 840 000*	25.00	L05 568 001*	L05 580 000*
15.00	L03 840 001*	L04 480 000*	25.00	L05 588 001*	L05 600 000*
25.00	L04 492 001*	L04 500 000*	25.00	L05 608 001*	L05 620 000*
25.00	L04 512 001*	L04 520 000*	25.00	L05 628 001*	L05 640 000*
25.00	L04 532 001*	L04 540 000*	25.00	L05 648 001*	L05 660 000*
25.00	L04 552 001*	L04 560 000*	25.00	L05 668 001*	L05 680 000*
25.00	L04 572 001*	L04 580 000*	25.00	L05 688 001*	L05 700 000*
25.00	L04 592 001*	L04 600 000*	25.00	L05 008 001*	L05 720 000*
25.00	L04 612 001*	L04 620 000*	25.00	L05 028 001*	L05 740 000*
25.00	L04 632 001*	L04 640 000*	25.00	L05 048 001*	L05 760 000*

(1) Printed through November 1981.

The production unit was changed from 20,000 sheets to 40,000 sheets for:

BANK	STARTING WITH SERIAL	BANK	STARTING WITH SERIAL
Boston	A28 160 001B	Chicago	G11 520 001C
New York	B55 040 001D	St. Louis	H60 160 001A
Philadelphia	C00 000 001B	Minneapolis	I10 240 001A
Cleveland	D98 560 001A	Kansas City	J64 000 001A
Richmond	E06 400 001B	Dallas	K78 080 001A
Atlanta	F01 280 001B	San Francisco	L90 880 001A

CAT. NO. XXL28
$20.00 UNITED STATES NOTE, LEGAL TENDER (Red Seal)
SERIES 1928

SERIAL NUMBERS: No Bureau record of printing.
PLATE SERIALS: Face and back check number 1.
SIGNATURES: Walter O. Woods, Treasurer of the United States
   W.H. Woodin, Secretary of the Treasury
One specimen of this note has been observed however, the owner requests that serial number not be used and that he remain anonymous. We respect his wishes.

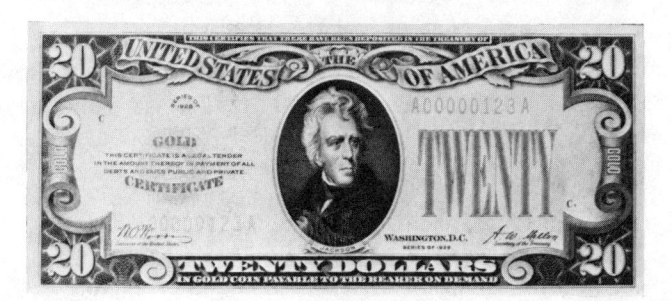

CAT. NO. XXG28
$20.00 GOLD CERTIFICATE (YELLOW SEAL) (12 Subject)
SERIES 1928

SERIAL NUMBERS:
   (Official Range) A00 000 001A through A66 204 000A
      Star Notes:
   (Low Official) *00 000 001A *00 488 307A (High Observed)

PLATE SERIALS: Face check #1 through #174.

SIGNATURES: Walter O. Woods, Treasurer of the United States
   Andrew W. Mellon, Secretary of the Treasury

ESTIMATED VALUES:	BLOCKS	VG/F	CU
	A--A	35.00	250.00

TOTAL BLOCKS KNOWN: Two.

CAT. NO. XXN29
$20.00 FEDERAL RESERVE BANK NOTE (BROWN SEAL)
SERIES 1929

SERIAL NUMBERS: Both regular and star notes start with 00 000 001.
PLATE SERIALS: Face check numbers begin with #1.
SIGNATURES: Same as $5.00 FRBN.

	DISTRICT	TOTAL NOTES PRINTED	BLOCKS	VG/F	CU	LOW OBSERVED SERIAL NUMBER	HIGH OBSERVED SERIAL NUMBER
1	A BOSTON	24,000	A--A	35.00	60.00	A00 120 465A	A00 972 000A
			A--*	47.50	95.00		
2	B NEW YORK	24,000	B--A	30.00	55.00	B00 003 049A	B02 568 000A
			B--*	40.00	92.50	B00 008 474*	B00 018 164*

213

	DISTRICT	TOTAL NOTES PRINTED	BLOCKS	ESTIMATED VALUE VG/F	CU	LOW OFFICIAL SERIAL NUMBER	HIGH OFFICIAL SERIAL NUMBER
3	C PHILADELPHIA	24,000	C--A	32.50	60.00	C00 000 816A	C01 008 000A
			C--*	45.00	95.00	C00 004 432*	C00 006 453*
4	D CLEVELAND	24,000	D--A	32.50	60.00	D00 783 363A	D01 020 000A
			D--*	45.00	95.00	D00 000 899*	D00 005 823*
5	E RICHMOND	24,000	E--A	30.00	57.50	E00 192 997A	E01 632 000A
			E--*	40.00	92.50	E00 003 226*	
6	F ATLANTA	8,000	F--A	35.00	62.50	F00 400 209A	F00 960 000A
			F--*	47.50	100.00	F00 005 880*	
7	G CHICAGO	12,000	G--A	30.00	52.50	G00 118 479A	G02 028 000A
			G--*	40.00	90.00		
8	H ST. LOUIS	24,000	H--A	40.00	80.00	H00 049 375A	H00 444 000A
			H--*	55.00	125.00	H00 001 752*	H00 020 028*
9	I MINNEAPOLIS	12,000	I--A	35.00	62.50	I00 126 110A	I00 864 000A
			I--*	47.50	100.00	I00 000 029*	I00 003 063*
10	J KANSAS CITY	24,000	J--A	37.50	65.00	J00 308 978A	J00 612 000A
			J--*	50.00	105.00	J00 004 527*	J00 005 686*
11	K DALLAS	24,000	K--A	37.50	100.00	K00 098 193A	K00 468 000A
			K--*	50.00	120.00	K00 000 455*	
12	L SAN FRANCISCO	24,000	L--A	35.00	100.00	L00 330 866A	L00 888 000A
			L--*	47.50	150.00	L00 005 691*	

TOTAL BLOCKS PRINTED: Twenty-four. Collectors are kindly requested to supply information on star serial numbers.

CAT. NO. XXF28
$20.00 FEDERAL RESERVE NOTE (GREEN SEAL) (12 Subject)
SERIES 1928

SERIAL NUMBERS: All serial numbers both regular and star notes begin with 00 000 001A.
PLATE SERIALS: Face and back check numbers begin with number 1.
SIGNATURES: H.T. Tate, Treasurer of the United States
　A.W. Mellon, Secretary of the Treasury

	DISTRICT	TOTAL NOTES PRINTED	BLOCKS	ESTIMATED VALUE VG/F	CU	LOW OBSERVED SERIAL NUMBER	HIGH OBSERVED SERIAL NUMBER
1	A BOSTON	3,790,880	A--A	25.00	50.00	A00 167 553A	A00 763 278A
			A--*	35.00	75.00		A00 066 529*
2	B NEW YORK	12,797,200	B--A	25.00	40.00	B08 290 128A	B11 940 078A
			B--*	30.00	70.00	B00 006 020*	
3	C PHILADELPHIA	3,797,200	C--A	25.00	50.00	C00 073 516A	C03 721 622A
			C--*	35.00	75.00		
4	D CLEVELAND	10,626,900	D--A	25.00	40.00	D00 420 010A	D10 862 368A
			D--*	30.00	70.00	D00 058 881*	D00 106 262*
5	E RICHMOND	4,119,600	E--A	25.00	50.00	E00 618 588A	E02 894 722A
			E--*	35.00	75.00		E00 047 239*
6	F ATLANTA	3,842,388	F--A	25.00	50.00	F00 812 377A	F03 833 076A
			F--*	35.00	75.00	F00 009 490*	F00 056 839*
7	G CHICAGO	10,891,740	G--A	25.00	40.00	G03 986 743A	G11 885 003A
			G--*	35.00	75.00	G00 025 459*	G00 155 280*
8	H ST. LOUIS	2,523,300	H--A	25.00	60.00	H00 000 014A	H02 252 609A
			H--*	35.00	75.00		H00 026 811*
9	I MINNEAPOLIS	2,633,100	I--A	25.00	60.00	I00 065 999A	I03 383 699A
			I--*	35.00	75.00	I00 011 654*	I00 030 746*
10	J KANSAS CITY	2,584,500	J--A	25.00	60.00	J00 444 079A	J02 565 449A
			J--*	35.00	75.00		
11	K DALLAS	1,568,500	K--A	25.00	65.00	K00 415 333A	K01 354 612A
			K--*	40.00	100.00		K00 014 063*

	DISTRICT	TOTAL NOTES PRINTED	BLOCKS	ESTIMATED VALUE VG/F	CU	LOW OFFICIAL SERIAL NUMBER	HIGH OFFICIAL SERIAL NUMBER
12	L SAN FRANCISCO	8,404,800	L--A	25.00	50.00	L01 143 913A	L07 376 739A
			L--*	35.00	75.00	L00 060 471*	L00 072 313*

TOTAL BLOCKS: Twenty four
Collectors are requested to supply serial numbers that improve on above information.

CAT. NO. XXF28A
$20.00 FEDERAL RESERVE NOTE (GREEN SEAL) (12 Subject)
SERIES 1928A

SERIAL NUMBERS: All districts continued sequence from previous series.
SIGNATURES: Walter O. Woods, Treasurer of the United States
  A. W. Mellon, Secretary of the Treasury

	DISTRICT	TOTAL NOTES PRINTED	BLOCKS	ESTIMATED VALUE VG/F	CU	LOW OBSERVED SERIAL NUMBER	HIGH OBSERVED SERIAL NUMBER
1	A BOSTON	1,293,900	A--A	30.00	60.00	A04 429 839A	A05 222 537A
			A--*	37.50	85.00		
2	B NEW YORK	1,055,800	B--A	30.00	60.00	B09 712 435A	B12 004 673A
			B--*	37.50	85.00		
3	C PHILADELPHIA	1,717,200	C--A	30.00	60.00	C03 929 993A	C05 197 920A
			C--*	37.50	85.00		
4	D CLEVELAND	625,200	D--A	37.50	75.00	D10 677 322A	D10 718 105A
			D--*	50.00	125.00		
5	E RICHMOND	1,534,500	E--A	30.00	60.00	E03 274 876A	E04 841 357A
			E--*	37.50	85.00		
6	F ATLANTA	1,442,400	F--A	30.00	60.00	F03 825 719A	F04 892 700A
			F--*	37.50	85.00		
7	G CHICAGO	822,000	G--A	37.50	75.00	G10 141 524A	G13 654 684A
			G--*	50.00	100.00		
8	H ST. LOUIS	573,300	H--A	37.50	75.00	H02 678 264A	H02 678 639A
			H--*	60.00	125.00		
10	J KANSAS CITY	113,900	J--A	75.00	125.00	J02 565 109A	J02 708 315A
			J--*	100.00	150.00		
11	K DALLAS	1,032,000	K--A	30.00	60.00	K01 522 525A	K02 211 622A
			K--*	37.50	85.00		

TOTAL BLOCKS: Twenty
Collectors are requested to supply serial numbers that improve on above information.

CAT. NO. XXF28B
$20.00 FEDERAL RESERVE NOTE (GREEN SEAL) (12 Subject)
SERIES 1928B

SERIAL NUMBERS: All districts continued from previous series.
SIGNATURES: Walter O. Woods, Treasurer of the United States
  A. W. Mellon, Secretary of the Treasury

	DISTRICT	TOTAL NOTES PRINTED (1)	BLOCKS	ESTIMATED VALUE VG/F	CU	LOW OBSERVED SERIAL NUMBER	HIGH OBSERVED SERIAL NUMBER
1	A BOSTON	7,749,636	A--A	25.00	50.00	A05 366 760A	A08 272 736A
			A--*	35.00	75.00		
2	B NEW YORK	19,448,436	B--A	25.00	50.00	B28 267 173A	B30 238 010A
			B--*	35.00	75.00	B00 196 360*	

215

	DISTRICT	TOTAL NOTES PRINTED	BLOCKS	ESTIMATED VALUE VG/F	CU	LOW OFFICIAL SERIAL NUMBER	HIGH OFFICIAL SERIAL NUMBER
3	C PHILADELPHIA	8,095,548	C--A	25.00	50.00	C05 732 443A	C10 620 164A
			C--*	35.00	75.00		
4	D CLEVELAND	11,684,196	D--A	25.00	50.00	D11 857 190A	D16 341 689A
			D--*	35.00	75.00		
5	E RICHMOND	4,413,900	E--A	25.00	50.00	E05 410 008A	E09 501 081A
			E--*	35.00	75.00		
6	F ATLANTA	2,390,240	F--A	27.50	60.00	F05 497 242A	
			F--*	37.50	85.00		
7	G CHICAGO	17,220,276	G--A	25.00	50.00	G10 938 122A	G22 234 808A
			G--*	35.00	75.00	G00 400 902*	
8	H ST. LOUIS	3,834,600	H--A	27.50	55.00	H03 003 293A	H03 578 337A
			H--*	35.00	75.00		
9	I MINNEAPOLIS	3,298,920	I--A	27.50	55.00	I02 774 443A	I03 695 973A
			I--*	35.00	75.00		
10	J KANSAS CITY	4,941,252	J--A	25.00	50.00	J02 758 206A	J09 964 305A
			J--*	35.00	75.00		
11	K DALLAS	2,406,060	K--A	27.50	60.00	K02 643 964A	
			K--*	37.50	85.00		
12	L SAN FRANCISCO	9,689,124	L--A	25.00	50.00	L09 106 860A	L11 934 354A
			L--*	35.00	75.00		

TOTAL BLOCKS: Twenty four
Collectors are requested to supply serial numbers that improve on above information.
(1) Includes both varieties.

CAT. NO. XXF28B
$20.00 FEDERAL RESERVE NOTE (LIGHT GREEN SEAL) (12 Subject)
SERIES 1928B

	DISTRICT	TOTAL NOTES PRINTED	BLOCKS	ESTIMATED VALUE VG/F	CU	LOW OBSERVED SERIAL NUMBER	HIGH OBSERVED SERIAL NUMBER
1	A BOSTON		A--A	30.00	65.00	A07 231 931A	A09 183 361A
			A--*	42.50	100.00	A00 086 912*	
2	B NEW YORK		B--A	30.00	65.00	B24 212 797A	B29 236 741A
			B--*				
3	C PHILADELPHIA		C--A	30.00	65.00	C08 000 640A	C10 740 129A
			C--*				
4	D CLEVELAND		D--A	30.00	65.00	D12 375 176A	D17 005 964A
			D--*				
7	G CHICAGO		G--A	30.00	65.00	G13 045 239A	G25 194 159A
			G--*	42.50	100.00	G00 170 621*	
8	H ST. LOUIS		H--A	32.50	70.00	H04 167 416A	H06 348 822A
			H--*				
9	I MINNEAPOLIS		I--A			I03 125 342A	I04 073 462A
10	J KANSAS CITY		J--A	30.00	65.00	J03 389 449A	J05 933 447A
			J--*				
12	L SAN FRANCISCO		L--A	30.00	65.00	L14 929 936A	L16 013 701A
			L--*	42.50	100.00	L00 146 938*	

TOTAL BLOCKS KNOWN: Ten. PROBABLE: Twenty-four
Collectors are requested to supply serial numbers that improve on above information.

CAT. NO. XXF28C
$20.00 FEDERAL RESERVE NOTE (DARK GREEN SEAL) (12 Subject)
SERIES 1928C

SERIAL NUMBERS: All districts continued sequence from previous series.
SIGNATURES: Walter O. Woods, Treasurer of the United States.
  Ogden L. Mills, Secretary of the Treasury.

	DISTRICT	TOTAL NOTES PRINTED	BLOCKS	VG/F	CU	LOW OBSERVED SERIAL NUMBER	HIGH OBSERVED SERIAL NUMBER
7	G CHICAGO	3,363,300	G--A	60.00	125.00	G24 123 209A	G25 181 247A
12	L SAN FRANCISCO	1,420,200	L--A	65.00	150.00	L15 631 459A	L16 434 325A

TOTAL BLOCKS KNOWN: Two.   Probable: Four.
Collectors are requested to supply serial numbers that improve on above information.
Especially wanted is ANY serial number for STAR notes as none are known in this series.

CAT. NO. XXF28C
$20.00 FEDERAL RESERVE NOTE (LIGHT GREEN SEAL) (12 Subject)
SERIES 1928C

	DISTRICT	TOTAL NOTES PRINTED	BLOCKS	VG/F	CU	LOW OBSERVED SERIAL NUMBER	HIGH OBSERVED SERIAL NUMBER
12	L SAN FRANCISCO		L--A	75.00		L15 777 609A	L16 434 325A

TOTAL BLOCKS KNOWN: One.

CAT. NO. XXF34
$20.00 FEDERAL RESERVE NOTE (DARK GREEN SEAL) (12 Subject)
SERIES 1934

SERIAL NUMBERS: All serial numbers both regular and star notes begin with 00 000 001A.
PLATE SERIALS: Face check numbers begin with 1. Back check numbers continue from previous series, up to 317.
SIGNATURES: W.A. Julian, Treasurer of the United States.
  Henry Morgenthau, Jr., Secretary of the Treasury.

	DISTRICT	TOTAL NOTES PRINTED(1)	BLOCKS	VG/F	CU	LOW OBSERVED SERIAL NUMBER	HIGH OBSERVED SERIAL NUMBER
1	A BOSTON	37,673,068	A--A	25.00	40.00	A09 464 557A	A13 582 164A
			A--*	30.00	60.00		
2	B NEW YORK	27,573,264	B--A	25.00	40.00	B16 712 592A	B23 945 422A
			B--*	30.00	60.00		B00 162 424*
3	C PHILADELPHIA	53,209,968	C--A	25.00	37.50	C08 515 738A	C70 548 540A
			C--*	27.50	55.00	C00 039 610*	
4	D CLEVELAND	48,301,416	D--A	25.00	37.50	D21 367 432A	D36 658 559A
			D--*	27.50	55.00		
5	E RICHMOND	36,259,224	E--A	25.00	40.00		E18 390 497A
			E--*	30.00	60.00		
6	F ATLANTA	41,547,660	F--A	25.00	40.00	F06 169 531A	F40 500 918A
			F--*	30.00	60.00		
7	G CHICAGO	20,777,832	G--A	25.00	40.00	G18 182 418A	G23 964 876A
			G--*	30.00	60.00	G00 169 123*	
8	H ST. LOUIS	27,174,552	H--A	25.00	40.00	H06 576 919A	H07 694 939A
			H--*	30.00	60.00	H00 189 324*	
9	I MINNEAPOLIS	16,795,116	I--A	25.00	50.00	I06 000 465A	I07 101 896A
			I--*	30.00	60.00	I00 046 713*	
10	J KANSAS CITY	28,865,304	J--A	25.00	50.00	J08 454 037A	J20 698 888A
			J--*	30.00	60.00		J00 113 509*
11	K DALLAS	20,852,160	K--A	25.00	50.00	K04 170 661A	K16 599 659A
			K--*	30.00	60.00	K00 000 001*	
12	L SAN FRANCISCO	32,203,956	L--A	25.00	40.00	L12 816 206A	L57 438 102A
			L--*	30.00	60.00		

(1) All Varieties.
TOTAL BLOCKS: Twenty-four.
Collectors are requested to supply serial numbers that improve on above information.

CAT. NO. XXF34
$20.00 FEDERAL RESERVE NOTE MULE (DARK GREEN SEAL) (12 Subject)
SERIES 1934

PLATE SERIALS: Back check #318 or higher.

	DISTRICT	TOTAL NOTES PRINTED	BLOCKS	VG/F	CU	LOW OBSERVED SERIAL NUMBER	HIGH OBSERVED SERIAL NUMBER
1	A BOSTON		A--A	25.00	40.00	A14 861 928A	A39 229 242A
			A--*			A00 360 734*	A00 364 157*
3	C PHILADELPHIA		C--A	25.00	37.50	C17 025 718A	C46 581 327A
			C--*	27.50	55.00	C00 039 610*	C00 464 657*
4	D CLEVELAND		D--A	25.00	37.50	D31 686 002A	D65 310 934A
5	E RICHMOND		E--A	25.00	37.50	E40 639 850A	E48 966 903A
6	F ATLANTA		F--A	25.00	37.50	F13 985 788A	F41 813 110A
			F--*			F00 467 620*	
8	H ST. LOUIS		H--A	25.00	37.50	H15 690 426A	H27 087 449A
			H--*	27.50	55.00		H00 216 162*
9	I MINNEAPOLIS		I--A	25.00	40.00	I07 925 554A	I15 121 383A
			I--*	30.00	60.00		I00 193 808*
10	J KANSAS CITY		J--A	25.00	45.00	J08 858 537A	J29 785 870A
			J--*	30.00	57.50		J00 251 124*
11	K DALLAS		K--A	25.00	45.00	K02 533 586A	K18 398 887A
			K--*	30.00	57.50		K00 040 468*
12	L SAN FRANCISCO		L--A	25.00	37.50	L36 957 275A	L98 839 050A
			L--B	25.00	37.50		L00 856 878B
			L--*	30.00	57.50		L01 057 275*

TOTAL BLOCKS KNOWN: Sixteen. PROBABLE: Twenty four.
Collectors are requested to supply serial numbers that improve on above information.

CAT. NO. XXF34
$20.00 FEDERAL RESERVE NOTE (LIGHT GREEN SEAL) (12 Subject)
SERIES 1934

PLATE SERIALS: Back check number up to #317.

	DISTRICT	TOTAL NOTES PRINTED	BLOCKS	VG/F	CU	LOW OBSERVED SERIAL NUMBER	HIGH OBSERVED SERIAL NUMBER
1	A BOSTON		A--A	25.00	40.00	A01 957 256A	A38 260 542A
			A--*	30.00	60.00		
2	B NEW YORK		B--A	25.00	40.00	B01 614 934A	B22 729 948A
			B--*	30.00	60.00		B00 123 819*
3	C PHILADELPHIA		C--A	25.00	37.50	C00 050 443A	C44 923 210A
			C--*	27.50	55.00	C00 022 502*	C00 132 242*
4	D CLEVELAND		D--A	25.00	37.50	D00 320 919A	D32 383 464A
			D--*	27.50	55.00		D00 248 698*
5	E RICHMOND		E--A	25.00	40.00	E02 723 146A	E10 801 410A
			E--*	30.00	60.00		E00 037 768*
6	F ATLANTA		F--A	25.00	40.00	F01 340 538A	F38 061 182A
			F--*	30.00	60.00		
7	G CHICAGO		G--A	25.00	40.00	G01 012 343A	G19 194 157A
			G--*	30.00	60.00	G00 178 557*	
8	H ST. LOUIS		H--A	25.00	40.00	H02 958 539A	H26 117 430A
			H--*	30.00	60.00		H00 061 763*
9	I MINNEAPOLIS		I--A	25.00	50.00	I00 076 074A	I05 432 083A
			I--*	30.00	60.00	I00 006 424*	I00 007 756*
10	J KANSAS CITY		J--A	25.00	50.00	J06 103 743A	J20 429 324A
			J--*	30.00	60.00	J00 010 849*	J00 041 882*

DISTRICT	TOTAL NOTES PRINTED	BLOCKS	ESTIMATED VALUE VG/F	CU	LOW OFFICIAL SERIAL NUMBER	HIGH OFFICIAL SERIAL NUMBER
11 K DALLAS		K--A	25.00	50.00	K08 741 389A	K29 683 233A
		K--*	30.00	60.00		K00 011 988*
12 L SAN FRANCISCO		L--A	25.00	40.00	L03 054 730A	L11 215 181A
		L--*	30.00	60.00	L00 065 413*	

TOTAL BLOCKS KNOWN: Eighteen. PROBABLE: Twenty four.
Collectors are requested to supply serial numbers that improve on above information.

CAT. NO. XXF34
$20.00 FEDERAL RESERVE NOTE MULE (LIGHT GREEN SEAL) (12 Subject)
SERIES 1934

PLATE SERIALS: Back check number 318 or higher.

	DISTRICT	TOTAL NOTES PRINTED	BLOCKS	ESTIMATED VALUE VG/F	CU	LOW OBSERVED SERIAL NUMBER	HIGH OBSERVED SERIAL NUMBER
1	A BOSTON		A--A	25.00	50.00	A30 069 536A	A38 185 336A
3	C PHILADELPHIA		C--A	25.00	50.00		C43 970 479A
4	D CLEVELAND		D--A	25.00	50.00	D32 933 942A	D66 926 117A
6	F ATLANTA		F--A	25.00	50.00	F23 972 567A	F40 855 958A
8	H ST. LOUIS		H--*	60.00	125.00	H00 115 790*	
9	I MINNEAPOLIS		I--A	25.00	50.00	I02 112 538A	I13 872 962A
11	K DALLAS		K--A	25.00	50.00	K18 452 832A	

TOTAL BLOCKS KNOWN: Four. PROBABLE: Twenty four.
Collectors are requested to supply serial numbers that improve on above information.

CAT. NO. XXF34
$20.00 FEDERAL RESERVE NOTE HAWAII (BROWN SEAL) (12 Subject)
SERIES 1934

SERIAL NUMBERS: (1) Low Observed High Observed.
   (Official Ranges) L30 540 001A through L31 090 000A
   L31 632 001A through L32 032 000A
   L33 420 001A through L34 220 000A
   L56 412 001A through L56 912 000A
   L60 588 001A through L61 592 000A
   L67 984 001A through L69 976 000A
   L76 980 001A through L78 480 000A
   L85 536 001A through L90 036 000A
PLATE SERIALS: Back check numbers 317 or lower.
SIGNATURES: W.A. Julian, Treasurer of the United States.
   Henry Morgenthau, Jr., Secretary of the Treasury.

ESTIMATED VALUES:	BLOCKS	VG/F	CU
	L--A	150.00	800.00
	L--*	300.00	1250.00

TOTAL KNOWN BLOCKS: Two. This note is much rarer than Mule.

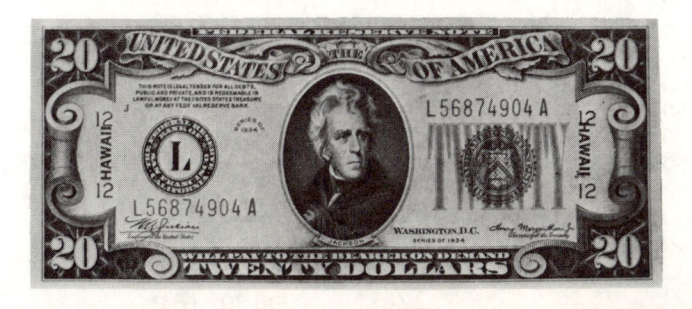

CAT. NO. XXF34
$20.00 FEDERAL RESERVE NOTE
SERIES 1934 MULE--HAWAII

SERIAL NUMBERS: Same as Series 1934 Hawaii above.

Star Notes: (Low Observed) L56 753 946A (High Observed)
   (Low Observed) L00 361 734* L00 866 396* (High Observed)

219

PLATE SERIALS: Back check numbers 318 or higher.

ESTIMATED VALUES:

BLOCKS	VG/F	CU
L--A	100.00	700.00
L--*	250.00	1000.00

TOTAL BLOCKS KNOWN: Two.
Footnote:
(1) Serial numbers include bothe Series 1934 and 1934A.

CAT. NO. XXF34
$20.00 FEDERAL RESERVE NOTE MULE (12 Subject)
SERIES 1934 TRIAL NOTE

PLATE SERIAL: Back check 204.
TOTAL QUANTITY PRINTED: 3,328,728 (Includes 1934 and 1934A both green seal and Hawaii brown seal.)

	DISTRICT	TOTAL NOTES PRINTED	BLOCKS	ESTIMATED VALUE VG/F	CU	LOW OBSERVED SERIAL NUMBER	HIGH OBSERVED SERIAL NUMBER
4	D CLEVELAND		D--A	50.00	100.00	D66 550 471A	D67 074 936A
5	E RICHMOND		E--A	50.00	100.00	E48 287 195A	
6	F ATLANTA		F--A	50.00	100.00	F34 119 489A	
8	H ST. LOUIS		H--A	60.00	125.00	H20 309 291A	
10	J KANSAS CITY		J--A	60.00	125.00	J19 436 527A	
12	L SAN FRANCISCO		L--A	60.00	125.00	L88 493 577A	

Probably exists for all districts. Collectors are requested to supply serial numbers for census of this note.

CAT. NO. XXF34A
$20.00 FEDERAL RESERVE NOTE (DARK GREEN SEAL) (12 Subject)
SERIES 1934A

SERIAL NUMBERS: All districts continued sequence from previous series.
PLATE SERIALS: Back check numbers begin at 318.
SIGNATURES: W.A. Julian, Treasurer of the United States
  Henry Morgenthau, Jr., Secretary of the Treasury

	DISTRICT	TOTAL NOTES PRINTED	BLOCKS	ESTIMATED VALUE VG/F	CU	LOW OBSERVED SERIAL NUMBER	HIGH OBSERVED SERIAL NUMBER
1	A BOSTON	3,202,416	A--A	30.00	50.00	A23 329 725A	
			A--*	35.00	75.00		
2	B NEW YORK	102,555,538	B--A	25.00	40.00	B41 420 317A	
			B--B	25.00	40.00		B31 418 413B
			B--*	30.00	50.00	B00 468 332*	B01 362 303*
3	C PHILADELPHIA	3,371,316	C--A	30.00	50.00	C21 827 204A	C50 540 853A
			C--*	35.00	75.00	C00 404 209*	
4	D CLEVELAND	23,475,108	D--A	25.00	40.00	D29 820 586A	D60 532 980A
			D--*	30.00	50.00	D00 484 888*	
5	E RICHMOND	46,816,224	E--A	25.00	40.00	E25 881 754A	E76 376 415A
			E--*	25.00	40.00		
6	F ATLANTA	6,756,816	F--A	27.50	45.00	F27 620 753A	F47 661 653A
			F--*	32.50	60.00	F00 498 074*	
7	G CHICAGO	91,141,452	G--A	25.00	40.00	G01 024 925A	
			G--B	27.50	45.00		G08 550 326B
			G--*	30.00	50.00	G00 383 825*	G01 108 953*
8	H ST. LOUIS	3,701,568	H--A	30.00	50.00	H12 277 508A	H35 769 437A
			H--*	35.00	75.00		
9	I MINNEAPOLIS	1,162,500	I--A	35.00	60.00	I09 487 367A	
			I--*	50.00	85.00		
10	J KANSAS CITY	3,221,184	J--A	30.00	50.00	J12 541 711A	
			J--*	35.00	75.00	J00 292 767*	J00 302 164*
11	K DALLAS	2,531,700	K--A	30.00	50.00	K18 964 817A	K20 963 608A
			K--*	35.00	75.00		
12	L SAN FRANCISCO	94,454,112	L--A	25.00	40.00	L25 612 260A	
			L--B	25.00	40.00		L16 035 873B
			L--*	30.00	50.00	L00 564 087*	L01 215 376*

TOTAL BLOCKS: Twenty seven.
Collectors are requested to supply serial numbers that improve on above information.
(1) Includes both seal colors and mules.

CAT. NO. XXF34A
$20.00 FEDERAL RESERVE NOTE MULE (DARK GREEN SEAL) (12 Subject)
SERIES 1934A

PLATE SERIALS: Back check number 317 and lower.

	DISTRICT	TOTAL NOTES PRINTED	BLOCKS	VG/F	CU	LOW OBSERVED SERIAL NUMBER	HIGH OBSERVED SERIAL NUMBER
2	B NEW YORK		B--A	25.00	50.00	B26 852 795A	B51 129 24 A
			B--*	35.00	75.00	B01 330 215*	
4	D CLEVELAND		D--A	25.00	50.00	D21 682 289A	D29 656 473A
5	E RICHMOND		E--A	25.00	50.00	E20 304 160A	E31 617 341A
7	G CHICAGO		G--A	25.00	50.00	G20 229 129A	G46 448 684A
			G--*	35.00	75.00	G00 383 825*	G00 433 238*
9	I MINNEAPOLIS		I--A	35.00	65.00	I09 689 683A	
12	L SAN FRANCISCO		L--A	25.00	50.00	L18 235 793A	L24 952 726A
			L--*	35.00	75.00	L00 176 920*	

TOTAL BLOCKS KNOWN: Five. PROBABLE: Twenty seven.
Collectors are requested to supply serial numbers that improve on above information.

CAT. NO. XXF34A
$20.00 FEDERAL RESERVE NOTE (LIGHT GREEN SEAL) (12 Subject)
SERIES 1934A

PLATE SERIALS: Back check number 318 and higher.

	DISTRICT	TOTAL NOTES PRINTED	BLOCKS	VG/F	CU	LOW OBSERVED SERIAL NUMBER	HIGH OBSERVED SERIAL NUMBER
1	A BOSTON		A--*	40.00	80.00	A00 245 112*	
2	B NEW YORK		B--A	25.00	50.00	B48 668 917A	
			B--B	25.00	50.00		B23 711 116B
3	C PHILADELPHIA		C--A	25.00	50.00	C34 903 115A	C39 980 888A
4	D CLEVELAND		D--A	25.00	50.00	D38 332 895A	D50 384 657A
5	E RICHMOND		E--A	25.00	50.00	E18 390 488A	E67 356 195A
			E--*	35.00	75.00	E00 448 266*	
6	F ATLANTA		F--A	25.00	50.00	F46 002 245A	F47 436 716A
7	G CHICAGO		G--A	25.00	50.00	G51 833 755A	G86 607 009A
8	H ST. LOUIS		H--A	25.00	50.00	H11 841 224A	
12	L SAN FRANCISCO		L--A	25.00	50.00	L17 570 455A	
			L--B	25.00	50.00	L35 579 756B	
			L--*	40.00	80.00		L00 441 242*

TOTAL BLOCKS KNOWN: Eleven. PROBABLE: Twenty seven.
Collectors are requested to supply serial numbers that improve on above information.

CAT. NO. XXF34A
$20.00 FEDERAL RESERVE NOTE MULE (LIGHT GREEN SEAL) (12 Subject)
SERIES 1934A

PLATE SERIALS: Back check number 317 and lower.

	DISTRICT	TOTAL NOTES PRINTED	BLOCKS	VG/F	CU	LOW OBSERVED SERIAL NUMBER	HIGH OBSERVED SERIAL NUMBER
2	B NEW YORK		B--A	35.00	70.00	B24 979 631A	B41 148 196A
4	D CLEVELAND		D--A	35.00	70.00	D25 567 521A	D29 236 526A
7	G CHICAGO		G--A	35.00	70.00	G20 435 621A	G42 937 767A
12	L SAN FRANCISCO		L--A	35.00	70.00	L22 088 801A	

TOTAL BLOCKS KNOWN: Four: PROBABLE: Twenty seven.
Collectors are requested to supply serial numbers that improve on above information.

CAT. NO. XXF34A
SERIES 1934A — HAWAII (BROWN SEAL) (12 Subject)

SERIAL NUMBERS: Same as Series 1934 Hawaii above.
Star Notes: (Low Observed) L00 437 367* L00 972 402* (High Observed)
PLATE SERIALS: Back check numbers 318 or higher.
SIGNATURES: Same as Series 1934 Hawaii Above.

ESTIMATED VALUES:	BLOCK	VG/F	CU
	L--A	35.00	250.00
	L--*	75.00	350.00

TOTAL BLOCKS KNOWN: Two.

CAT. NO. XXF34A
SERIES 1934A MULE — HAWAII (BROWN SEAL)

SERIAL NUMBERS:
   (Low Observed) L30 567 214A L34 174 516A (High Observed)
   L00 361 329* L00 441 242*
PLATE SERIALS: Back check numbers 317 or lower.
SIGNATURES: Same as Series 1934.

ESTIMATED VALUES:	BLOCK	VG/F	CU
	L--A	50.00	250.00
	L--*	500.00	1500.00

TOTAL BLOCKS KNOWN: Two.
Collectors are kindly requested to supply serial number, face and back check numbers on star notes listed here so that range can be determined.

CAT. NO. XXF34A
$20.00 FEDERAL RESERVE NOTE (GREEN SEAL) (12 Subject)
SERIES 1934A TRIAL NOTE

PLATE SERIAL: Back check #204.

DISTRICT	TOTAL NOTES PRINTED	BLOCKS	VG/F	CU	LOW OBSERVED SERIAL NUMBER	HIGH OBSERVED SERIAL NUMBER
		B--A	50.00	100.00	B98 418 083A	
		B--B	60.00	125.00		B14 661 059B
		C--A	50.00	100.00	C40 351 306A	
		E--A	50.00	100.00	E52 293 180A	E76 690 574A
		E--*		Rare	E00 530 871*	

TOTAL BLOCKS KNOWN: Two. Probably others exist.

CAT. NO. XXF34A
$20.00 FEDERAL RESERVE NOTE HAWAII (BROWN SEAL)
SERIES 1934A TRIAL NOTE

PLATE SERIAL: Back check #204.
SERIAL NUMBERS:
   (LOW OBSERVED) L85 718 843A L89 660 095A (HIGH OBSERVED)

ESTIMATED VALUE		VG/F	CU
	L--A	60.00	500.00

TOTAL BLOCKS KNOWN: One.
Collectors are requested to supply series, serial number, face and back check numbers for all notes with Back check number 204.

CAT. NO. XXF34B
$20.00 FEDERAL RESERVE NOTE (GREEN SEAL) (12 Subject)
SERIES 1934B

SERIAL NUMBERS: All districts continued sequence from previous series.
PLATE SERIALS: Back check 318 and higher.
SIGNATURES: W.A. Julian, Treasurer of the United States.
   Fred M. Vinson, Secretary of the Treasury.

	DISTRICT	TOTAL NOTES PRINTED	BLOCKS	ESTIMATED VALUE VG/F	CU	LOW OBSERVED SERIAL NUMBER	HIGH OBSERVED SERIAL NUMBER
1	A BOSTON	3,904,800	A--A	30.00	50.00	A38 734 966A	A42 242 548A
			A--*	35.00	75.00	A00 398 858*	
2	B NEW YORK	14,876,436	B--B	27.50	40.00	B17 408 148B	B39 373 235B
			B--*	30.00	65.00	B01 318 080*	B01 492 277*
3	C PHILADELPHIA	3,271,452	C--A	30.00	50.00	C46 212 262A	C52 312 048A
			C--*	35.00	75.00	C00 469 975*	C00 521 662*
4	D CLEVELAND	2,814,600	D--A	30.00	50.00	D68 539 173A	D70 976 182A
			D--*	35.00	75.00	D00 695 683*	
5	E RICHMOND	9,451,632	E--A	27.50	40.00	E73 674 466A	E82 979 964A
			E--*	30.00	65.00	E00 758 543*	E00 845 951*
6	F ATLANTA	6,887,640	F--A	30.00	50.00	F46 830 144A	F53 624 199A
			F--*	30.00	65.00	F00 560 062*	F53 624 199A
7	G CHICAGO	9,084,600	G--B	27.50	40.00	G06 189 141B	G16 105 041B
			G--*	30.00	65.00	G01 124 759*	G01 245 500*
8	H ST. LOUIS	5,817,300	H--A	30.00	50.00	H29 885 020A	H34 659 086A
			H--*	30.00	65.00	H00 345 273*	H00 355 784*
9	I MINNEAPOLIS	2,304,800	I--A	30.00	50.00	I17 021 710A	I19 150 206A
			I--*	35.00	75.00		
10	J KANSAS CITY	3,524,244	J--A	30.00	50.00	J30 057 079A	J32 702 051A
			J--*	35.00	75.00	J00 322 642*	J00 387 184*
11	K DALLAS	2,807,388	K--A	30.00	50.00	K22 526 344A	K25 495 160A
			K--*	35.00	75.00	K00 243 500*	
12	L SAN FRANCISCO	5,289,540	L--B	30.00	50.00	L08 554 084B	L22 243 980B
			L--*	30.00	65.00		

TOTAL BLOCKS: Twenty four.
Collectors are requested to supply serial numbers that improve on above information.
Although none are known it is quite possible mules (back check below 317) exist in this series.

CAT. NO. XXF34B
$20.00 FEDERAL RESERVE NOTE (GREEN SEAL) 12 Subject
SERIES 1934B TRIAL NOTE

PLATE SERIAL: Back check #204.
SERIAL NUMBERS:
(Low Observed) B01 496 889*
ESTIMATED VALUE: Rare (possibly unique)
TOTAL BLOCKS KNOWN: One.

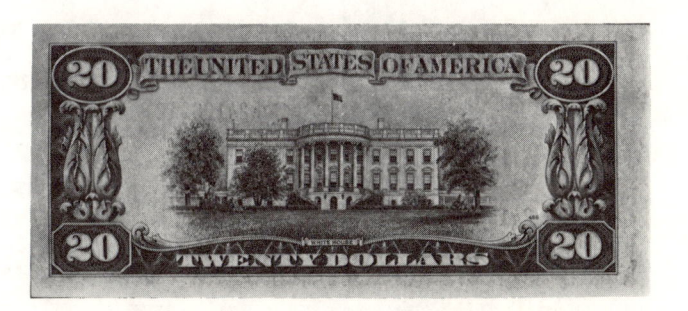

CAT. NO. XXF34F
$20.00 FEDERAL RESERVE NOTE (OLD BACK) (GREEN SEAL) (12 Subject)
SERIES 1934C

SERIAL NUMBERS: All districts continued sequence from previous series.
PLATE SERIALS: Back check numbers up to 587. (See footnote)
SIGNATURES: W.A. Julian, Treasurer of the United States,
  John W. Snyder, Secretary of the Treasury.

	DISTRICT	TOTAL NOTES PRINTED(1)	BLOCKS	ESTIMATED VALUE VG/F	CU	LOW OBSERVED SERIAL NUMBER	HIGH OBSERVED SERIAL NUMBER
1	A BOSTON	7,397,352	A--A	22.50	35.00	A42 295 063A	A46 373 548A
			A--*	25.00	40.00	A00 470 557*	

	DISTRICT	TOTAL NOTES PRINTED	BLOCKS	ESTIMATED VALUE VG/F	CU	LOW OFFICIAL SERIAL NUMBER	HIGH OFFICIAL SERIAL NUMBER
2	B NEW YORK	18,668,148	B--B	22.50	35.00	B38 954 761B	B50 152 113B
			B--*	25.00	40.00		
3	C PHILADELPHIA	11,590,752	C--A	22.50	35.00	C50 572 816A	C55 761 440A
			C--*	25.00	40.00	C00 586 136*	C00 586 380*
4	D CLEVELAND	17,912,424	D--A	22.50	35.00	D71 831 215A	D77 433 529A
			D--*	25.00	40.00	D00 733 432*	
5	E RICHMOND	22,526,568	E--A	22.50	35.00	E82 696 020A	
			E--B	30.00	45.00		E01 832 138B
			E--*	25.00	40.00	E00 784 409*	E00 986 454*
6	F ATLANTA	18,858,876	F--A	22.50	35.00	F55 358 468A	F60 531 129A
			F--*	25.00	40.00	F00 642 722*	F00 662 748*
7	G CHICAGO	26,031,660	G--B	22.50	35.00	G16 185 385B	G25 570 747B
			G--*	25.00	40.00	G01 263 515*	G01 455 294*
8	H ST. LOUIS	13,276,984	H--A	22.50	35.00	H35 698 773A	H39 850 187A
			H--*	25.00	40.00		
9	I MINNEAPOLIS	3,490,200	I--A	30.00	50.00	I19 561 112A	I19 614 220A
			I--*	35.00	75.00		
10	J KANSAS CITY	9,675,468	J--A	22.50	35.00	J34 502 275A	J35 100 540A
			J--*	25.00	40.00		
11	K DALLAS	10,205,364	K--A	22.50	35.00	K25 413 849A	K27 290 340A
			K--*	25.00	40.00	K00 304 910*	
12	L SAN FRANCISCO	20,580,828	L--B	22.50	35.00	L22 220 528B	L29 732 364B
			L--*	25.00	40.00		

TOTAL BLOCKS: Twenty five.
Collectors are requested to supply serial numbers that improve on above information.
(1) Includes both type backs.
Footnote: The early design has small shrubbery, no balcony. The later (new) design has a balcony added to the White House and tall shrubbery.

CAT. NO. VVF34C
$20.00 FEDERAL RESERVE NOTE (NEW BACK) (GREEN SEAL) (12 Subject)
SERIES 1934C

PLATE SERIALS: Back check numbers 588 and higher. (See footnote)

	DISTRICT	TOTAL NOTES PRINTED	BLOCKS	ESTIMATED VALUE VG/F	CU	LOW OBSERVED SERIAL NUMBER	HIGH OBSERVED SERIAL NUMBER
1	A BOSTON		A--A	22.50	35.00	A46 733 962A	A52 528 286A
			A--*	25.00	40.00	A00 515 662*	
2	B NEW YORK		B--B	22.50	35.00	B50 380 463B	B55 063 435B
			B--*	25.00	40.00	B01 740 308*	
3	C PHILADELPHIA		C--A	22.50	35.00	C54 515 243A	C66 038 494A
			C--*	25.00	40.00	C00 629 979*	C00 670 473*
4	D CLEVELAND		D--A	22.50	35.00	D79 037 088A	
			D--B	22.50	35.00		D44 300 344B
			D--*	25.00	40.00		
5	E RICHMOND		E--A	22.50	35.00	E93 104 022A	
			E--B	30.00	45.00		E06 256 305B
			E--*	25.00	40.00	E01 142 664*	
6	F ATLANTA		F--A	22.50	35.00	F61 618 982A	F73 332 888A
			F--*	25.00	40.00		
7	G CHICAGO		G--B	22.50	35.00	G26 178 543B	G40 414 253B
			G--*	25.00	40.00	G01 409 960*	G01 557 975*
8	H ST. LOUIS		H--A	22.50	35.00	H41 535 478A	H48 706 748A
			H--*	25.00	40.00	H00 459 889*	H00 467 580*

	DISTRICT	TOTAL NOTES PRINTED	BLOCKS	ESTIMATED VALUE VG/F	CU	LOW OFFICIAL SERIAL NUMBER	HIGH OFFICIAL SERIAL NUMBER
9	I MINNEAPOLIS		I--A	30.00	50.00	I21 298 486A	I22 286 317A
			I--*	35.00	75.00	I00 232 454*	
10	J KANSAS CITY		J--A	22.50	35.00	J36 547 970A	J41 600 886A
			J--*	25.00	40.00	J00 430 491*	
11	K DALLAS		K--A	22.50	35.00	K31 042 702A	K34 625 505A
			K--*	25.00	40.00	K00 354 202*	K00 367 773*
12	L SAN FRANCISCO		L--B	22.50	35.00	L31 288 124B	L43 266 556B
			L--*	25.00	40.00	L01 503 904*	

TOTAL BLOCKS: Twenty five.
Collectors are requested to supply serial numbers that improve on above information.
Footnote: New design has balcony added to the White House.

CAT. NO. XXF34D
$20.00 FEDERAL RESERVE NOTE (GREEN SEAL) (12 Subject)
SERIES 1934D

SERIAL NUMBERS: All districts continued sequence from previous series.
SIGNATURES: Georgia Neese Clark, Treasurer of the United States.
   John W. Snyder, Secretary of the Treasury.

	DISTRICT	TOTAL NOTES PRINTED	BLOCKS	ESTIMATED VALUE VG/F	CU	LOW OBSERVED SERIAL NUMBER	HIGH OBSERVED SERIAL NUMBER
1	A BOSTON	4,520,000	A--A	22.50	35.00	A41 971 456A	A53 790 164A
			A--*	25.00	40.00		
2	B NEW YORK	27,894,260	B--B	22.50	35.00	B55 961 199B	B69 083 642B
			B--*	25.00	40.00	B01 750 367*	B01 762 702*
3	C PHILADELPHIA	6,022,428	C--A	22.50	35.00	C62 289 525A	C67 670 832A
			C--*	25.00	40.00	C00 667 406*	C00 725 518*
4	D CLEVELAND	8,981,688	D--A	22.50	35.00	D89 321 411A	D96 558 114A
			D--B	35.00	50.00		
			D--*	25.00	40.00	D00 996 177*	
5	E RICHMOND	14,055,984	E--B	22.50	35.00	E04 865 511B	E18 131 889B
			E--*	25.00	40.00	E00 784 409*	
6	F ATLANTA	7,495,440	F--A	22.50	35.00	F72 747 317A	F79 492 323A
			F--*	25.00	40.00	F00 824 781*	
7	G CHICAGO	15,187,596	G--B	22.50	35.00	G41 576 352B	G53 814 518B
			G--*	25.00	40.00	G01 667 671*	
8	H ST. LOUIS	5,923,248	H--A	22.50	35.00	H34 055 557A	H52 933 080A
			H--*	25.00	40.00	H00 622 934*	H00 625 589*
9	I MINNEAPOLIS	2,422,416	I--A	25.00	40.00		I24 318 690A
			I--*	30.00	50.00		
10	J KANSAS CITY	4,211,904	J--A	22.50	35.00	J43 071 668A	J45 481 126A
			J--*	25.00	40.00		
11	K DALLAS	3,707,364	K--A	22.50	35.00	K35 095 524A	K38 559 440A
			K--*	25.00	40.00		
12	L SAN FRANCISCO	12,015,228	L--B	22.50	35.00	L43 679 344B	L53 849 217B
			L--*	25.00	40.00		

TOTAL BLOCKS: Twenty six.
Collectors are requested to supply serial numbers that improve above information.

CAT. NO. XXF50
$20.00 FEDERAL RESERVE NOTE (GREEN SEAL) (12 Subject)
SERIES 1950

SERIAL NUMBERS: All serial numbers both regular and star notes begin with 00 000 001.
SIGNATURES: Georgia Neese Clark, Treasurer of the United States.
   John W. Snyder, Secretary of the Treasury.

	DISTRICT	TOTAL NOTES PRINTED	BLOCKS	ESTIMATED VALUE VG/F	CU	LOW OFFICIAL SERIAL NUMBER	HIGH OFFICIAL SERIAL NUMBER
1	A BOSTON	23,184,000	A--A		30.00		A23 184 000A
			A--*		40.00		
2	B NEW YORK	80,064,000	B--A		30.00		B80 064 000A
			B--*		40.00		B00 927 711*(2)
3	C PHILADELPHIA	29,520,000	C--A		30.00		C29 520 000A
			C--*		40.00		

	DISTRICT	TOTAL NOTES PRINTED	BLOCKS	ESTIMATED VALUE VG/F	CU	LOW OFFICIAL SERIAL NUMBER	HIGH OFFICIAL SERIAL NUMBER
4	D CLEVELAND	51,120,000	D--A		30.00		D51 120 000A
			D--*		40.00		D00 043 082*(2)
5	E RICHMOND	67,536,000	E--A		30.00		E67 536 000A
			E--*		40.00	E00 442 052*	E00 685 052*(2)
6	F ATLANTA	39,312,000	F--A		30.00		F39 312 000A
			F--*		40.00		
7	G CHICAGO	70,464,000	G--A		30.00		G70 464 000A
			G--*		40.00		
8	H ST. LOUIS	27,352,000	H--A		30.00		H27 352 000A
			H--*		40.00		
9	I MINNEAPOLIS	9,216,000	I--A		35.00		I09 216 000A
			I--*		50.00		
10	J KANSAS CITY	22,752,000	J--A		30.00		J22 752 000A
			J--*		40.00		
11	K DALLAS	22,656,000	K--A		30.00		K22 656 000A
			K--*		40.00		
12	L SAN FRANCISCO	70,272,000	L--A		30.00		L70 272 000A
			L--*		40.00	L00 608 911*	

TOTAL BLOCKS: Twenty-four.

(1) Serial nos. G 70 464 001 A thru G 70 560 000 A, H 27 352 001 A thru H 27 360 000 A and K 22 656 001 A thru K 22 752 000 A were assigned for Chicago, St. Louis and Dallas respectively, but were never used.
(2) High Star Observed.

CAT. NO. XXF50A
$20.00 FEDERAL RESERVE NOTE (GREEN SEAL) (18 Subject)
SERIES 1950A

SIGNATURES: Ivy Baker Priest, Treasurer of the United States.
George M. Humphrey, Secretary of the Treasury.

	DISTRICT	TOTAL NOTES PRINTED	BLOCKS	ESTIMATED VALUE VG/F	CU	LOW OFFICIAL SERIAL NUMBER	HIGH OFFICIAL SERIAL NUMBER
1	A BOSTON	19,656,000	A--A		30.00	A23 184 001A	A42 840 000A
			A--*		40.00	A00 488 035*	
2	B NEW YORK	82,568,000(1)	B--A		30.00	B80 064 001A	
			B--B		30.00		B62 640 000B
			B--*		40.00		
3	C PHILADELPHIA	16,560,000	C--A		30.00	C29 520 001A	C46 080 000A
			C--*		40.00	C00 491 484*	
4	D CLEVELAND	50,320,000	D--A		30.00	D51 120 001A	
			D--B		35.00		D01 440 000B
			D--*		40.00		
5	E RICHMOND	69,544,000	E--A		30.00	E67 536 001A	
			E--B		30.00		E37 080 000B
			E--*		40.00	E02 006 676*	E04 717 304*(2)
6	F ATLANTA	27,648,000	F--A		30.00	F39 312 001A	F66 960 000A
			F--*		40.00	F01 017 800*	
7	G CHICAGO	73,720,000	G--A		30.00	G70 560 001A	
			G--B		30.00		G44 280 000B
			G--*		40.00	G02 044 082*	
8	H ST. LOUIS	22,680,000	H--A		30.00	H27 360 001A	H50 040 000A
			H--*		40.00	H00 499 568*	
9	I MINNEAPOLIS	5,544,000	I--A		35.00	I09 216 001A	I14 760 000A
			I--*		50.00		
10	J KANSAS CITY	22,968,000	J--A		30.00	J22 752 001A	J45 720 000A
			J--*		40.00	J01 678 569*	
11	K DALLAS	10,728,000	K--A		32.50	K22 752 001A	K33 480 000A
			K--*		45.00	K00 941 803*	
12	L SAN FRANCISCO	85,528,000	L--A		30.00	L70 272 001A	
			L--B		30.00		L55 800 000B
			L--*		40.00		

TOTAL BLOCKS: Twenty-nine.

(1) B 90 236 001 A to B 90 240 000 A and B 90 252 001 A to B 90 256 000 A were reported missing because of theft. When recovered they were destroyed.
(2) Low 2nd High Star Observed.

CAT. NO. XXF50B
$20.00 FEDERAL RESERVE NOTE (GREEN SEAL) (18 Subject)
SERIES 1950B

SIGNATURES: Ivy Baker Priest, Treasurer of the United States.
Robert B. Anderson, Secretary of the Treasury.

	DISTRICT	TOTAL NOTES PRINTED	BLOCKS	ESTIMATED VALUE VG/F	CU	LOW OFFICIAL SERIAL NUMBER	HIGH OFFICIAL SERIAL NUMBER
1	A BOSTON	5,040,000	A--A		32.50	A42 840 001A	A47 880 000A
			A--*		40.00		
2	B NEW YORK	49,960,000	B--B		30.00	B62 640 001B	
			B--C		30.00		B12 600 000C
			B--*		37.50		B07 537 779*[1]
3	C PHILADELPHIA	7,920,000	C--A		32.50	C46 080 001A	C54 000 000A
			C--*		40.00		
4	D CLEVELAND	38,160,000	D--B		30.00	D01 440 001B	D39 600 000B
			D--*		37.50	D03 818 415*	
5	E RICHMOND	42,120,000	E--B		30.00	E37 080 001B	E79 200 000B
			E--*		37.50		
6	F ATLANTA	40,240,000	F--A		30.00	F66 960 001A	
			F--B		32.50		F07 200 000B
			F--*		37.50		
7	G CHICAGO	80,560,000	G--B		30.00	G44 280 001B	
			G--C		30.00		G24 840 000C
			G--*		37.50		G06 727 379*
8	H ST. LOUIS	19,440,000	H--A		30.00	H50 040 001A	H69 480 000A
			H--*		37.50		
9	I MINNEAPOLIS	12,240,000	I--A		30.00	I14 760 001A	I27 000 000A
			I--*		37.50	I00 749 542*	
10	J KANSAS CITY	28,440,000	J--A		30.00	J45 720 001A	J74 160 000A
			J--*		37.50		
11	K DALLAS	11,880,000	K--A		30.00	K33 840 001A	K45 360 000A
			K--*		40.00	K01 578 478*	
12	L SAN FRANCISCO	51,040,000	L--B		30.00	L55 800 001B	
			L--C		32.50		L06 840 000C
			L--*		40.00	L08 202 036*	L08 946 721*(1)

TOTAL BLOCKS: Twenty-eight.
Footnote: (1) Observed Serial Numbers

E02 006 676*(2)
L08 202 036(1)

CAT. NO. XXF50C
$20.00 FEDERAL RESERVE NOTE (GREEN SEAL) (18 Subject)
SERIES 1950C

SIGNATURES: Elizabeth Rudel Smith, Treasurer of the United States
C. Douglas Dillon, Secretary of the Treasury

	DISTRICT	TOTAL NOTES PRINTED	BLOCKS	ESTIMATED VALUE VG/F	CU	LOW OFFICIAL SERIAL NUMBER	HIGH OFFICIAL SERIAL NUMBER
1	A BOSTON	7,200,000	A--A		32.50	A47 880 001A	A55 080 000A
			A--*		40.00		A02 087 540*
2	B NEW YORK	43,200,000	B--C		30.00	B12 600 001C	B55 800 000C
			B--*		37.50		
3	C PHILADELPHIA	7,560,000	C--A		32.50	C54 000 001A	C61 560 000A
			C--*		40.00		
4	D CLEVELAND	28,440,000	D--B		30.00	D39 600 001B	D68 040 000B
			D--*		37.50		
5	E RICHMOND	37,000,000	E--B		30.00	E79 200 001B	
			E--C		30.00		E16 200 000C
			E--*		37.50		
6	F ATLANTA	19,080,000	F--B		30.00	F07 200 001B	F26 280 000B
			F--*		37.50		
7	G CHICAGO	29,160,000	G--C		30.00	G24 840 001C	G54 000 000C
			G--*		37.50	G09 770 435*	G09 770 455*
8	H ST. LOUIS	12,960,000	H--A		30.00	H69 480 001A	H82 440 000A
			H--*		37.50		

	DISTRICT	TOTAL NOTES PRINTED	BLOCKS	ESTIMATED VALUE VG/F	CU	LOW OFFICIAL SERIAL NUMBER	HIGH OFFICIAL SERIAL NUMBER
9	I MINNEAPOLIS	6,480,000	I--A		35.00	I27 000 001A	I33 480 000A
			I--*		42.50	I01 433 220*	
10	J KANSAS CITY	18,360,000	J--A		30.00	J74 160 001A	J92 520 000A
			J--*		37.50	J04 596 837*	
11	K DALLAS	9,000,000	K--A		32.50	K45 360 001A	K54 360 000A
			K--*		40.00	K02 010 051*	
12	L SAN FRANCISCO	45,360,000	L--C		30.00	L06 840 001C	L52 200 000C
			L--*		37.50		

TOTAL BLOCKS: Twenty-five

CAT. NO. XXF50D
$20.00 FEDERAL RESERVE NOTE (GREEN SEAL) (18 Subject)
SERIES 1950D

SIGNATURES: Kathryn O'Hay Granahan, Treasurer of the United States.
C. Douglas Dillon, Secretary of the Treasury.

	DISTRICT	TOTAL NOTES PRINTED	BLOCKS	ESTIMATED VALUE VG/F	CU	LOW OFFICIAL SERIAL NUMBER	HIGH OFFICIAL SERIAL NUMBER
1	A BOSTON	9,320,000	A--A		27.50	A55 080 001A	A64 440 000A
			A--*		35.00	A02 463 533*	
2	B NEW YORK	64,280,000	B--C		27.50	B55 800 001C	
			B--D		27.50		B10 080 000D
			B--*		35.00		
3	C PHILADELPHIA	5,400,000	C--A		27.50	C61 560 001A	C66 960 000A
			C--*		35.00	C02 572 171*	C02 869 202*
4	D CLEVELAND	23,760,000	D--B		27.50	D68 040 001B	D91 800 000B
			D--*		35.00		D06 050 490*
5	E RICHMOND	30,240,000	E--C		27.50	E16 200 001C	E46 440 000C
			E--*		35.00		
6	F ATLANTA	22,680,000	F--B		27.50	F26 280 001B	F48 960 000B
			F--*		35.00		
7	G CHICAGO	67,960,000	G--C		27.50	G54 000 001C	
			G--D		27.50		G21 960 000D
			G--*		35.00		
8	H ST. LOUIS	6,120,000	H--A		27.50	H82 440 001A	H88 560 000A
			H--*		35.00		
9	I MINNEAPOLIS	3,240,000	I--A		30.00	I33 480 001A	I36 720 000A
			I--*		37.50		
10	J KANSAS CITY	8,200,000	J--A		27.50	J92 520 001A	
			J--B		35.00		J00 720 000B
			J--*		35.00	J05 007 683*	
11	K DALLAS	6,480,000	K--A		27.50	K54 360 001A	K60 840 000A
			K--*		35.00	K02 393 123*	
12	L SAN FRANCISCO	69,400,000	L--C		27.50	L52 200 001C	
			L--D		27.50		L21 600 000D
			L--*		35.00		

TOTAL BLOCKS: Twenty eight.

CAT. NO. XXF50E
$20.00 FEDERAL RESERVE NOTE (GREEN SEAL) (18 Subject)
SERIES 1950E

SIGNATURES: Kathryn O'Hay Granahan, Treasurer of the United States.
Henry H. Fowler, Secretary of the Treasury.

	DISTRICT	TOTAL NOTES PRINTED	BLOCKS	ESTIMATED VALUE VG/F	CU	LOW OFFICIAL SERIAL NUMBER	HIGH OFFICIAL SERIAL NUMBER
2	B NEW YORK	8,640,000	B--D		32.50	B10 080 001D	B18 720 000D
			B--*		45.00	B12 389 340* (1)	B13 025 214* (2)
7	G CHICAGO	9,360,000	G--D		32.50	G21 960 001D	G31 320 000D
			G--*		45.00	G12 764 186*	
12	L SAN FRANCISCO	8,640,000	L--D		32.50	L21 600 001D	L30 240 000D
			L--*		45.00	L14 327 992*	

TOTAL BLOCKS: Six.
(1) Low Observed. (2) High Observed.

CAT. NO. XXF63
$20.00 FEDERAL RESERVE NOTE (GREEN SEAL) (32 Subject)
SERIES 1963

SERIAL NUMBERS: All serial numbers both regular and star notes begin with 00 000 001.
PLATE SERIALS: Face and back check begin with 1. Motto IN GOD WE TRUST added to back.
SIGNATURES: Kathryn O'Hay Granahan, Treasurer of the United States.
  C. Douglas Dillon, Secretary of the Treasury.

	DISTRICT	TOTAL NOTES PRINTED	BLOCKS	ESTIMATED VALUE VG/F	ESTIMATED VALUE CU	LOW OFFICIAL SERIAL NUMBER	HIGH OFFICIAL SERIAL NUMBER
1	A BOSTON	2,560,000	A--A		30.00		A02 560 000A
			A--*		40.00		A00 640 000*
2	B NEW YORK	16,640,000	B--A		25.00		B16 640 000A
			B--*		35.00		B01 920 000*
3	C PHILADELPHIA	none					
4	D CLEVELAND	7,680,000	D--A		25.00		D07 680 000A
			D--*		35.00		
5	E RICHMOND	4,480,000	E--A		25.00		E04 480 000A
			E--*		40.00		E00 000 010* (1)
6	F ATLANTA	10,240,000	F--A		25.00		F10 240 000A
			F--*		35.00		F01 279 114* (1)
7	G CHICAGO	2,560,000	G--A		30.00		G02 560 000A
			G--*		40.00		
8	H ST. LOUIS	3,200,000	H--A		27.50		H03 200 000A
			H--*		40.00		
9	I MINNEAPOLIS	none					
10	J KANSAS CITY	3,840,000	J--A		27.50		J03 840 000A
			J--*		40.00		
11	K DALLAS	2,560,000	K--A		30.00		K02 560 000A
			K--*		40.00		K00 042 427*
12	L SAN FRANCISCO	7,040,000	L--A		25.00		L97 040 000A
			L--*		35.00		L00 632 584*

TOTAL BLOCKS: Twenty.
(1) High Observed

CAT. NO. XXF63A
$20.00 FEDERAL RESERVE NOTE (GREEN SEAL) (32 Subject)
SERIES 1963A

SIGNATURES: Kathryn O'Hay Granahan, Treasurer of the United States.
  Henry H. Fowler, Secretary of the Treasury.

	DISTRICT	TOTAL NOTES PRINTED	BLOCKS	ESTIMATED VALUE VG/F	ESTIMATED VALUE CU	LOW OFFICIAL SERIAL NUMBER	HIGH OFFICIAL SERIAL NUMBER
1	A BOSTON	23,680,000	A--A		25.00	A02 560 001A	A26 240 000A
		1,280,000	A--*		30.00	A00 640 001*	A01 920 000*
2	B NEW YORK	93,600,000	B--A		25.00	B16 640 001A	
			B--B		25.00		B10 240 000B
		3,840,000	B--*		30.00	B01 920 001*	B05 760 000*
3	C PHILADELPHIA	17,920,000	C--A		25.00	C00 000 001A	C17 920 000A
		640,000	C--*		30.00	C00 000 001*	C00 640 000*
4	D CLEVELAND	68,480,000	D--A		25.00	D07 690 001A	D76 160 000A
		2,560,000	D--*		30.00	D01 280 001*	D03 840 000*

	DISTRICT	TOTAL NOTES PRINTED	BLOCKS	ESTIMATED VALUE VG/F	CU	LOW OFFICIAL SERIAL NUMBER	HIGH OFFICIAL SERIAL NUMBER
5	E RICHMOND	128,800,000	E--A		25.00	E04 480 001A	
			E--B		25.00		E33 280 000B
		5,760,000	E--*		30.00	E00 640 001*	E06 400 000*
6	F ATLANTA	42,880,000	F--A		25.00	F10 240 001A	F53 120 000A
		1,920,000	F--*		30.00	F01 280 001*	F03 200 000*
7	G CHICAGO	156,320,000	G--A		25.00	G02 560 001A	
			G--B		25.00		G58 880 000B
		7,040,000	G--*		30.00	G00 640 001*	G07 680 000*
8	H ST. LOUIS	34,560,000	H--A		25.00	H03 200 001A	H37 760 000A
		1,920,000	H--*		30.00	H00 640 001*	H02 560 000*
9	I MINNEAPOLIS	10,240,000	I--A		25.00	I00 000 001A	I10 240 000A
		640,000	I--*		30.00	I00 000 001*	I00 640 000*
10	J KANSAS CITY	37,120,000	J--A		25.00	J03 840 001A	J40 960 000A
		1,920,000	J--*		30.00	J00 640 001*	J02 560 000*
11	K DALLAS	38,400,000	K--A		25.00	K02 560 001A	K40 960 000A
		1,280,000	K--*		30.00	K00 640 001*	K01 920 000*
12	L SAN FRANCISCO	169,120,000	L--A		25.00	L07 040 001A	
			L--B		25.00		L76 160 000B
		8,320,000	L--*		30.00	L01 280 001*	L09 600 000*

TOTAL BLOCKS: Twenty eight.

CAT. NO. XXF69
$20.00 FEDERAL RESERVE NOTE (GREEN SEAL) (32 Subject)
SERIES 1969

SERIAL NUMBERS: All serial numbers both regular and star notes begin with 00 000 001.
SIGNATURES: Dorothy Andrews Elston, Treasurer of the United States.
David M. Kennedy, Secretary of the Treasury.

	DISTRICT	TOTAL NOTES PRINTED	BLOCKS	ESTIMATED VALUE VG/F	CU	LOW OFFICIAL SERIAL NUMBER	HIGH OFFICIAL SERIAL NUMBER
1	A BOSTON	19,200,000	A--A		25.00		A19 200 00A
		1,280,000	A--*		30.00		A01 280 000*
2	B NEW YORK	106,400,000	B--A		25.00		
			B--B		26.00		B06 400 000B
		5,106,000	B--*		30.00		B05 106 000*
3	C PHILADELPHIA	10,880,000	C--A		25.00		C10 880 000A
		1,280,000	C--*		30.00		C01 280 000*
4	D CLEVELAND	60,160,000	D--A		25.00		D60 160 000A
		2,560,000	D--*		30.00		D02 560 000*
5	E RICHMOND	66,560,000	E--A		25.00		E66 560 000A
		2,560,000	E--*		30.00		E02 560 000*
6	F ATLANTA	36,480,000	F--A		25.00		F36 480 000A
		1,280,000	F--*		30.00		F01 280 000*
7	G CHICAGO	107,680,000	G--A		25.00		
			G--B		26.00		G07 680 000B
		3,200,000	G--*		30.00		G03 200 000*
8	H ST. LOUIS	19,200,000	H--A		25.00		H19 200 000A
		640,000	H--*		35.00		H00 640 000*
9	I MINNEAPOLIS	12,160,000	I--A		25.00		I12 160 000A
		640,000	I--*		35.00		I00 640 000*
10	J KANSAS CITY	39,040,000	J--A		25.00		J39 040 000A
		1,280,000	J--*		30.00		J01 280 000*
11	K DALLAS	25,600,000	K--A		25.00		K25 600 000A
		640,000	K--*		35.00		K01 280 000*
12	L SAN FRANCISCO	103,840,000	L--A		25.00		
			L--B		27.50		L03 840 000B
		5,120,000	L--*		30.00		L05 120 000*

TOTAL BLOCKS: Twenty seven.

CAT. NO. XXF69A
$20.00 FEDERAL RESERVE NOTE (GREEN SEAL) (32 Subject)
SERIES 1969A

SIGNATURES: Dorothy Andrews Kabis, Treasurer of the United States.
John B. Connally, Secretary of the Treasury.

	DISTRICT	TOTAL NOTES PRINTED	BLOCKS	ESTIMATED VALUE VG/F	CU	LOW OFFICIAL SERIAL NUMBER	HIGH OFFICIAL SERIAL NUMBER
1	A BOSTON	13,440,000 stars — none	A--A		25.00	A19 200 001A	A32 640 000A
2	B NEW YORK	69,760,000	B--B		25.00	B06 400 001B	B76 160 000B
		2,460,000	B--*		30.00	B05 120 001*	B07 680 000*
3	C PHILADELPHIA	13,440,000 stars — none	C--A		25.00	C10 880 001A	C24 320 000A
4	D CLEVELAND	29,440,000	D--A		25.00	D60 160 001A	D89 600 000A
		640,000	D--*		35.00	D02 560 001*	D03 200 000*
5	E RICHMOND	42,400,000	E--A		25.00	E66 560 001A	
			E--B		25.00		E08 960 000B
		1,920,000	E--*		30.00	E02 560 001*	E04 480 000*
6	F ATLANTA	13,440,000 stars — none	F--A		25.00	F36 480 001A	F49 920 000A
7	G CHICAGO	81,640,000	G--B		25.00	G07 680 001B	G88 320 000B
		1,920,000	G--*		30.00	G03 200 001*	G05 120 000*
8	H ST. LOUIS	14,080,000	H--A		25.00	H19 200 001A	H33 280 000A
		640,000	H--*		35.00	H00 640 001&	H01 280 000*
9	I MINNEAPOLIS	7,040,000 stars — none	I--A		25.00	I12 160 001A	I19 200 000A
10	J KANSAS CITY	16,040,000 stars — none	J--A		25.00	J39 040 001A	J55 680 000A
11	K DALLAS	14,720,000	K--A		25.00	K25 600 001A	K40 320 000A
		640,000	K--*		35.00	K00 640 001*	K01 280 000*
12	L SAN FRANCISCO	50,560,000	L--B		25.00	L03 840 001B	L54 400 000B
		1,280,000	L--*		30.00	L05 120 001*	L06 400 000*

TOTAL BLOCKS: Twenty.

CAT. NO. XXF69B
$20.00 FEDERAL RESERVE NOTE (GREEN SEAL) (32 Subject)
SERIES 1969B

SIGNATURES: Romana A. Banuelos, Treasurer of the United States.
John B. Connally, Secretary of the Treasury.

	DISTRICT	TOTAL NOTES PRINTED	BLOCKS	ESTIMATED VALUE VG/F	CU	LOW OFFICIAL SERIAL NUMBER	HIGH OFFICIAL SERIAL NUMBER
2	B NEW YORK	39,200,000	B--B		25.00	B76 160 001B	
			B--C		25.00		B15 360 000C
			B--*		35.00	B07 200 001*	B07 680 000*
4	D CLEVELAND	6,400,000	D--A		25.00	D89 600 001A	D96 000 000A
5	E RICHMOND	27,520,000	E--B		25.00	E08 960 001B	E36 480 000B
6	F ATLANTA	14,080,000	F--A		25.00	F49 920 001A	F64 000 000A
		640,000	F--*		35.00	F01 280 001*	F01 920 000*
7	G CHICAGO	14,240,000	G--B		25.00	G88 320 001B	
			G--C		27.50		G02 560 000C
8	H ST. LOUIS	1,112,000	G--*		30.00	G05 280 001*	G06 392 999*
		5,120,000	H--A		25.00	H33 280 001A	H38 400 000A
9	I MINNEAPOLIS	2,560,000	I--A		25.00	I19 200 001A	I21 760 000A
10	J KANSAS CITY	3,840,000	J--A		25.00	J55 680 001A	J59 520 000A
		640,000	J--*		35.00	J01 280 001*	J01 920 000*
11	K DALLAS	12,160,000	K--A		25.00	K40 320 001A	K52 480 000A
12	L SAN FRANCISCO	26,000,000	L--B		25.00	L54 400 001B	L80 640 000B
		640,000	L--*		35.00	L06 400 001*	L07 040 000*

TOTAL BLOCKS: Sixteen. Districts and stars not shown above were not printed.

CAT. NO. XXF69C
$20.00 FEDERAL RESERVE NOTE (GREEN SEAL) 32 Subject
SERIES 1969C

SIGNATURES: Romano Acosta Banuelos, Treasurer of the United States.
William E. Simon, Secretary of the Treasury.
PLATE SERIALS: All districts continue from previous series.
SERIAL NUMBERS: All districts continue from previous series.
ESTIMATED VALUES: All regular notes $25.00, all stars $27.50 CU only.

	DISTRICT	TOTAL NOTES PRINTED	BLOCKS	ESTIMATED VALUE VG/F	CU	LOW OFFICIAL SERIAL NUMBER	HIGH OFFICIAL SERIAL NUMBER
1	A BOSTON	17,280,000	A--A			A32 640 001A	A49 920 000A
		640,000	A--*			A01 280 001*	A01 920 000*
2	B NEW YORK	135,200,000	B--C			B15 360 001C	
			B--D				B50 560 000D
		1,640,000	B--*			B07 320 001*	B08 960 000*
3	C PHILADELPHIA	40,960,000	C--A			C24 320 001A	C65 280 000A
		640,000	C--*			C01 280 001*	C01 920 000*
4	D CLEVELAND	57,876,000	D--A			D96 000 001A	
			D--B				D53 760 000B
		480,000	D--*			D03 360 001*	D03 840 000*
5	E RICHMOND	80,160,000	E--B			E36 480 001B	
			E--C				E16 640 000C
		1,920,000	E--*			E04 480 001*	E06 400 000*
6	F ATLANTA	35,840,000	F--A			F64 000 001A	F99 840 000A
		896,000	F--*			F01 024 001*	F01 920 000*
			F--*			F01 920 001*	F02 560 000*
7	G CHICAGO	78,720,000	G--C			G02 560 001C	G81 280 000C
		640,000	G--*			G06 400 001*	G07 040 000*
8	H ST. LOUIS	33,920,000	H--A			H38 400 001A	H72 320 000A
		640,000	H--*			H01 280 001*	H01 920 000*
9	I MINNEAPOLIS	14,080,000	I--A			I21 760 001A	I35 840 000A
		640,000	I--*			I00 640 001*	I01 280 000*
10	J KANSAS CITY	32,000,000	J--A			J59 520 001A	J91 520 000A
		640,000	J--*			J01 920 001*	J02 560 000*
11	K DALLAS	31,360,000	K--A			K52 480 001A	K83 840 000A
		1,920,000	K--*			K01 280 001*	K03 200 000*
12	L SAN FRANCISCO	82,080,000	L--B			L80 640 001B	
			L--C				L62 720 000C
		1,120,000	L--*			L07 200 001*	L08 320 000*

TOTAL BLOCKS: Twenty-eight.

CAT. NO. XXF74
$20.00 FEDERAL RESERVE NOTE (GREEN SEAL) 32 Subject
SERIES 1974

SIGNATURES: Francine I. Neff, Treasurer of the United States.
William E. Simon, Secretary of the Treasury.
SERIAL NUMBERS: Continue from previous series.
PLATE SERIALS: Continue from previous series.

DISTRICT	TOTAL NOTES PRINTED	BLOCKS	ESTIMATED VALUE VG/F	CU	LOW OFFICIAL SERIAL NUMBER	HIGH OFFICIAL SERIAL NUMBER	
1 A BOSTON		A--A		22.50	A49 920 001A	A66 560 000A	cv
		A--A		22.50	A66 560 001A	A99 840 000A	cp
		A--B		22.50	A00 000 001B	A07 040 000B	cp
		A--*		25.00	A01 920 001*	A02 560 000*	cv
				35.00	A02 576 001*	A02 580 000*	cv
				35.00	A02 596 001*	A02 600 000*	cv
				25.00	A02 616 001*	A02 620 000*	cv
				25.00	A02 636 001*	A02 640 000*	cv
				35.00	A02 656 001*	A02 660 000*	cv
				35.00	A02 676 001*	A02 680 000*	cv
				35.00	A02 696 001*	A02 700 000*	cv
				35.00	A02 716 001*	A02 720 000*	cv
				35.00	A02 736 001*	A02 740 000*	cv
				35.00	A02 756 001*	A02 760 000*	cv
				35.00	A02 776 001*	A02 780 000*	cv
				35.00	A02 796 001*	A02 800 000*	cv
				35.00	A02 816 001*	A02 820 000*	cv
				35.00	A02 836 001*	A02 840 000*	cv
				35.00	A02 856 001*	A02 860 000*	cv
				35.00	A02 876 001*	A02 880 000*	cv
				35.00	A02 896 001*	A02 900 000*	cv
				35.00	A02 916 001*	A02 920 000*	cv
				35.00	A02 936 001*	A02 940 000*	cv
				35.00	A02 956 001*	A02 960 000*	cv
				35.00	A02 976 001*	A02 980 000*	cv
				35.00	A02 996 001*	A03 000 000*	cv
				35.00	A03 016 001*	A03 020 000*	cv
				35.00	A03 036 001*	A03 040 000*	cv
				35.00	A03 056 001*	A03 060 000*	cv
				35.00	A03 076 001*	A03 080 000*	cv
				35.00	A03 096 001*	A03 100 000*	cv
				35.00	A03 116 001*	A03 120 000*	cv
				35.00	A03 136 001*	A03 140 000*	cv
				35.00	A03 156 001*	A03 160 000*	cv
				35.00	A03 176 001*	A03 180 000*	cv
				35.00	A03 196 001*	A03 200 000*	cv
2 B NEW YORK		B--D		22.50	B50 560 001D	B99 999 999D	cv
		B--E		22.50	B00 000 001E	B99 999 999D	cv
		B--F		25.00	B00 000 001F	B05 120 000F	cv
				22.50	B05 120 001F	B99 840 000F	cp
		B--G		22.50	B00 000 001G	B47 360 000G	cp
		B--*		25.00	B08 960 001*	B10 240 000*	cv
				25.00	B10 400 001*	B12 160 000*	cv
				25.00	B12 320 001*	B14 720 000*	cv
				50.00	B14 732 001*	B14 740 000*	cv
				50.00	B14 752 001*	B14 760 000*	cv
				50.00	B14 772 001*	B14 780 000*	cv
				50.00	B14 792 001*	B14 800 000*	cv
				50.00	B14 812 001*	B14 820 000*	cv
				50.00	B14 832 001*	B14 840 000*	cv
				50.00	B14 852 001*	B14 860 000*	cv
				50.00	B14 872 001*	B14 880 000*	cv
				50.00	B14 892 001*	B14 900 000*	cv
				50.00	B14 912 001*	B14 920 000*	cv
				50.00	B14 932 001*	B14 940 000*	cv
				50.00	B14 952 001*	B14 960 000*	cv
				50.00	B14 972 001*	B14 980 000*	cv
				50.00	B14 992 001*	B15 000 000*	cv
				50.00	B15 012 001*	B15 020 000*	cv
				50.00	B15 032 001*	B15 040 000*	cv

DISTRICT	TOTAL NOTES PRINTED	BLOCKS	ESTIMATED VALUE VG/F	CU	LOW OFFICIAL SERIAL NUMBER	HIGH OFFICIAL SERIAL NUMBER	
				50.00	B15 052 001*	B15 060 000*	cv
				50.00	B15 072 001*	B15 080 000*	cv
				50.00	B15 092 001*	B15 100 000*	cv
				50.00	B15 112 001*	B15 120 000*	cv
				50.00	B15 132 001*	B15 140 000*	cv
				50.00	B15 152 001*	B15 160 000*	cv
				50.00	B15 172 001*	B15 180 000*	cv
				50.00	B15 192 001*	B15 200 000*	cv
				50.00	B15 212 001*	B15 220 000*	cv
				50.00	B15 232 001*	B15 240 000*	cv
				50.00	B15 252 001*	B15 260 000*	cv
				50.00	B15 272 001*	B15 280 000*	cv
				50.00	B15 292 001*	B15 300 000*	cv
				50.00	B15 312 001*	B15 320 000*	cv
				50.00	B15 332 001*	B15 340 000*	cv
				50.00	B15 352 001*	B15 360 000*	cv
				25.00	B15 360 001*	B17 280 000*	cv
3	C PHILADELPHIA	C--A		22.50	C65 280 001A	C99 200 000A	cv
				25.00	C99 200 001A	C99 840 000A	cp
				25.00	C99 840 001A	C99 999 999A	cv
		C--B		22.50	C00 000 001B	C24 960 000B	cp
		C--*		25.00	C01 920 001*	C03 840 000*	cv
4	D CLEVELAND	D--B		22.50	D53 760 001B	D99 999 999B	cv
		D--C		22.50	D00 000 001C	D27 520 000C	cv
				22.50	D27 520 001C	D99 840 000C	cp
		D--*		25.00	D03 840 001*	D05 120 000*	cv
				25.00	D05 280 001*	D07 040 000*	cv
				50.00	D07 056 001*	D07 060 000*	cv
				50.00	D07 076 001*	D07 080 000*	cv
				50.00	D07 096 001*	D07 100 000*	cv
				50.00	D07 116 001*	D07 120 000*	cv
				50.00	D07 136 001*	D07 140 000*	cv
				50.00	D07 156 001*	D07 160 000*	cv
				50.00	D07 176 001*	D07 180 000*	cv
				50.00	D07 196 001*	D07 200 000*	cv
				50.00	D07 216 001*	D07 220 000*	cv
				50.00	D07 236 001*	D07 240 000*	cv
				50.00	D07 256 001*	D07 260 000*	cv
				50.00	D07 276 001*	D07 280 000*	cv
				50.00	D07 296 001*	D07 300 000*	cv
				50.00	D07 316 001*	D07 320 000*	cv
				50.00	D07 336 001*	D07 340 000*	cv
				50.00	D07 356 001*	D07 360 000*	cv
				50.00	D07 376 001*	D07 380 000*	cv
				50.00	D07 396 001*	D07 400 000*	cv
				50.00	D07 416 001*	D07 420 000*	cv
				50.00	D07 436 001*	D07 440 000*	cv
				50.00	D07 456 001*	D07 460 000*	cv
				50.00	D07 476 001*	D07 480 000*	cv
				50.00	D07 496 001*	D07 500 000*	cv
				50.00	D07 516 001*	D07 520 000*	cv
				50.00	D07 536 001*	D07 540 000*	cv
				50.00	D07 556 001*	D07 560 000*	cv
				50.00	D07 576 001*	D07 580 000*	cv
				50.00	D07 596 001*	D07 600 000*	cv
				50.00	D07 616 001*	D07 620 000*	cv
				50.00	D07 636 001*	D07 640 000*	cv
				50.00	D07 656 001*	D07 660 000*	cv
				50.00	D07 676 001*	D07 680 000*	cv
				50.00	D07 696 001*	D07 700 000*	cp
				50.00	D07 716 001*	D07 720 000*	cp
				50.00	D07 736 001*	D07 740 000*	cp
				50.00	D07 756 001*	D07 760 000*	cp
				50.00	D07 776 001*	D07 780 000*	cp
				50.00	D07 796 001*	D07 800 000*	cp
				50.00	D07 816 001*	D07 820 000*	cp
				50.00	D07 836 001*	D07 840 000*	cp
				50.00	D07 856 001*	D07 860 000*	cp
				50.00	D07 876 001*	D07 880 000*	cp

DISTRICT	TOTAL NOTES PRINTED	BLOCKS	ESTIMATED VALUE VG/F CU	LOW OFFICIAL SERIAL NUMBER	HIGH OFFICIAL SERIAL NUMBER	
			50.00	D07 896 001*	D07 900 000*	cp
			50.00	D07 916 001*	D07 920 000*	cp
			50.00	D07 936 001*	D07 940 000*	cp
			50.00	D07 956 001*	D07 960 000*	cp
			50.00	D07 976 001*	D07 980 000*	cp
			50.00	D07 996 001*	D08 000 000*	cp
			50.00	D08 016 001*	D08 020 000*	cp
			50.00	D08 036 001*	D08 040 000*	cp
			50.00	D08 056 001*	D08 060 000*	cp
			50.00	D08 076 001*	D08 080 000*	cp
			50.00	D08 096 001*	D08 100 000*	cp
			50.00	D08 116 001*	D08 120 000*	cp
			50.00	D08 136 001*	D08 140 000*	cp
			50.00	D08 156 001*	D08 160 000*	cp
			50.00	D08 176 001*	D08 180 000*	cp
			50.00	D08 196 001*	D08 200 000*	cp
			50.00	D08 216 001*	D08 220 000*	cp
			50.00	D08 236 001*	D08 240 000*	cp
			50.00	D08 256 001*	D08 260 000*	cp
			50.00	D08 276 001*	D08 280 000*	cp
			50.00	D08 296 001*	D08 300 000*	cp
			50.00	D08 316 001*	D08 320 000*	cp
5	E RICHMOND	E--C	22.50	E16 640 001C	E96 640 000C	cv
			25.00	E96 640 001C	E99 840 000C	cp
			25.00	E99 840 001C	E99 999 999C	cv
		E--D	22.50	E00 000 001D	E66 560 000D	cp
		E--*	25.00	E06 400 001*	E08 320 000*	cv
			25.00	E08 480 001*	E08 960 000*	cv
			50.00	E08 976 001*	E08 980 000*	cv
			50.00	E08 996 001*	E09 000 000*	cv
			50.00	E09 016 001*	E09 020 000*	cv
			50.00	E09 036 001*	E09 040 000*	cv
			50.00	E09 056 001*	E09 060 000*	cv
			50.00	E09 076 001*	E09 080 000*	cv
			50.00	E09 096 001*	E09 100 000*	cv
			50.00	E09 116 001*	E09 120 000*	cv
			50.00	E09 136 001*	E09 140 000*	cv
			50.00	E09 156 001*	E09 160 000*	cv
			50.00	E09 176 001*	E09 180 000*	cv
			50.00	E09 196 001*	E09 200 000*	cv
			50.00	E09 216 001*	E09 220 000*	cv
			50.00	E09 236 001*	E09 240 000*	cv
			50.00	E09 256 001*	E09 260 000*	cv
			50.00	E09 276 001*	E09 280 000*	cv
			50.00	E09 296 001*	E09 300 000*	cv
			50.00	E09 316 001*	E09 320 000*	cv
			50.00	E09 336 001*	E09 340 000*	cv
			50.00	E09 356 001*	E09 360 000*	cv
			50.00	E09 376 001*	E09 380 000*	cv
			50.00	E09 396 001*	E09 400 000*	cv
			50.00	E09 416 001*	E09 420 000*	cv
			50.00	E09 436 001*	E09 440 000*	cv
			50.00	E09 456 001*	E09 460 000*	cv
			50.00	E09 476 001*	E09 480 000*	cv
			50.00	E09 496 001*	E09 500 000*	cv
			50.00	E09 516 001*	E09 520 000*	cv
			50.00	E09 536 001*	E09 540 000*	cv
			50.00	E09 556 001*	E09 560 000*	cv
			50.00	E09 576 001*	E09 580 000*	cv
			50.00	E09 596 001*	E09 600 000*	cv
			50.00	E09 612 001*	E09 620 000*	cv
			50.00	E09 632 001*	E09 640 000*	cv
			50.00	E09 652 001*	E09 660 000*	cv
			50.00	E09 672 001*	E09 680 000*	cv
			50.00	E09 692 001*	E09 700 000*	cv
			50.00	E09 712 001*	E09 720 000*	cv
			50.00	E09 732 001*	E09 740 000*	cv
			50.00	E09 752 001*	E09 760 000*	cv
			50.00	E09 772 001*	E09 780 000*	cv

DISTRICT	TOTAL NOTES PRINTED	BLOCKS	ESTIMATED VALUE VG/F	CU	LOW OFFICIAL SERIAL NUMBER	HIGH OFFICIAL SERIAL NUMBER	
				50.00	E09 792 001*	E09 800 000*	CV
				50.00	E09 812 001*	E09 820 000*	CV
				50.00	E09 832 001*	E09 840 000*	CV
				50.00	E09 852 001*	E09 860 000*	CV
				50.00	E09 872 001*	E09 880 000*	CV
				50.00	E09 892 001*	E09 900 000*	CV
				50.00	E09 912 001*	E09 920 000*	CV
				50.00	E09 932 001*	E09 940 000*	CV
				50.00	E09 952 001*	E09 960 000*	CV
				50.00	E09 972 001*	E09 980 000*	CV
				50.00	E09 992 001*	E10 000 000*	CV
				50.00	E10 012 001*	E10 020 000*	CV
				50.00	E10 032 001*	E10 040 000*	CV
				50.00	E10 052 001*	E10 060 000*	CV
				50.00	E10 072 001*	E10 080 000*	CV
				50.00	E10 092 001*	E10 100 000*	CV
				50.00	E10 112 001*	E10 120 000*	CV
				50.00	E10 132 001*	E10 140 000*	CV
				50.00	E10 152 001*	E10 160 000*	CV
				50.00	E10 172 001*	E10 180 000*	CV
				50.00	E10 192 001*	E10 200 000*	CV
				50.00	E10 212 001*	E10 220 000*	CV
				50.00	E10 232 001*	E10 240 000*	CV
				50.00	E10 256 001*	E10 260 000*	CV
				50.00	E10 276 001*	E10 280 000*	CV
				50.00	E10 296 001*	E10 300 000*	CV
				50.00	E10 316 001*	E10 320 000*	CV
				50.00	E10 336 001*	E10 340 000*	CV
				50.00	E10 356 001*	E10 360 000*	CV
				50.00	E10 376 001*	E10 380 000*	CV
				50.00	E10 396 001*	E10 400 000*	CV
				50.00	E10 416 001*	E10 420 000*	CV
				50.00	E10 436 001*	E10 440 000*	CV
				50.00	E10 456 001*	E10 460 000*	CV
				50.00	E10 476 001*	E10 480 000*	CV
				50.00	E10 496 001*	E10 500 000*	CV
				50.00	E10 516 001*	E10 520 000*	CV
				50.00	E10 536 001*	E10 540 000*	CV
				50.00	E10 556 001*	E10 560 000*	CV
				50.00	E10 576 001*	E10 580 000*	CV
				50.00	E10 596 001*	E10 600 000*	CV
				50.00	E10 616 001*	E10 620 000*	CV
				50.00	E10 636 001*	E10 640 000*	CV
				50.00	E10 656 001*	E10 660 000*	CV
				50.00	E10 676 001*	E10 680 000*	CV
				50.00	E10 696 001*	E10 700 000*	CV
				50.00	E10 716 001*	E10 720 000*	CV
				50.00	E10 736 001*	E10 740 000*	CV
				50.00	E10 756 001*	E10 760 000*	CV
				50.00	E10 776 001*	E10 780 000*	CV
				50.00	E10 796 001*	E10 800 000*	CV
				50.00	E10 816 001*	E10 820 000*	CV
				50.00	E10 836 001*	E10 840 000*	CV
				50.00	E10 856 001*	E10 860 000*	CV
				50.00	E10 876 001*	E10 880 000*	CV
				50.00	E10 896 001*	E10 900 000*	CV
				50.00	E10 916 001*	E10 920 000*	CV
				50.00	E10 936 001*	E10 940 000*	CV
				50.00	E10 956 001*	E10 960 000*	CV
				50.00	E10 976 001*	E10 980 000*	CV
				50.00	E10 996 001*	E11 000 000*	CV
				50.00	E11 016 001*	E11 020 000*	CV
				50.00	E11 036 001*	E11 040 000*	CV
				50.00	E11 056 001*	E11 060 000*	CV
				50.00	E11 076 001*	E11 080 000*	CV
				50.00	E11 096 001*	E11 100 000*	CV
				50.00	E11 116 001*	E11 120 000*	CV
				50.00	E11 136 001*	E11 140 000*	CV
				50.00	E11 156 001*	E11 160 000*	CV

DISTRICT	TOTAL NOTES PRINTED	BLOCKS	ESTIMATED VALUE VG/F	CU	LOW OFFICIAL SERIAL NUMBER	HIGH OFFICIAL SERIAL NUMBER	
				50.00	E11 176 001*	E11 180 000*	cv
				50.00	E11 196 001*	E11 200 000*	cv
				50.00	E11 216 001*	E11 220 000*	cv
				50.00	E11 236 001*	E11 240 000*	cv
				50.00	E11 256 001*	E11 260 000*	cv
				50.00	E11 276 001*	E11 280 000*	cv
				50.00	E11 296 001*	E11 300 000*	cv
				50.00	E11 316 001*	E11 320 000*	cv
				50.00	E11 336 001*	E11 340 000*	cv
				50.00	E11 356 001*	E11 360 000*	cv
				50.00	E11 376 001*	E11 380 000*	cv
				50.00	E11 396 001*	E11 400 000*	cv
				50.00	E11 416 001*	E11 420 000*	cv
				50.00	E11 436 001*	E11 440 000*	cv
				50.00	E11 456 001*	E11 460 000*	cv
				50.00	E11 476 001*	E11 480 000*	cv
				50.00	E11 496 001*	E11 500 000*	cv
				50.00	E11 516 001*	E11 520 000*	cv
6	F ATLANTA	F--A		25.00	F99 840 001A	F99 999 999A	cv
		F--B		22.50	F00 000 001B	F53 120 000B	cp
		F--*		25.00	F02 560 001*	F03 200 000*	cv
				25.00	F03 360 001*	F03 840 000*	cv
7	G CHICAGO	G--C		22.50	G81 280 001C	G99 999 999C	cv
		G--D		22.50	G00 000 001D	G66 560 000D	cv
				22.50	G66 560 001D	G99 840 000D	cp
				25.00	G99 840 001D	G99 999 999D	cv
		G--E		22.50	G00 000 001E	G99 840 000E	cp
		G--F		22.50	G00 000 001F	G31 360 000F	cp
		G--*		25.00	G07 200 001*	G10 240 000*	cv
				25.00	G10 400 001*	G10 880 000*	cv
				50.00	G10 896 001*	G10 900 000*	cv
				50.00	G10 916 001*	G10 920 000*	cv
				50.00	G10 936 001*	G10 940 000*	cv
				50.00	G10 956 001*	G10 960 000*	cv
				50.00	G10 976 001*	G10 980 000*	cv
				50.00	G10 996 001*	G11 000 000*	cv
				50.00	G11 016 001*	G11 020 000*	cv
				50.00	G11 036 001*	G11 040 000*	cv
				50.00	G11 056 001*	G11 060 000*	cv
				50.00	G11 076 001*	G11 080 000*	cv
				50.00	G11 096 001*	G11 100 000*	cv
				50.00	G11 116 001*	G11 120 000*	cv
				50.00	G11 136 001*	G11 140 000*	cv
				50.00	G11 156 001*	G11 160 000*	cv
				50.00	G11 176 001*	G11 180 000*	cv
				50.00	G11 196 001*	G11 200 000*	cv
				50.00	G11 216 001*	G11 220 000*	cv
				50.00	G11 236 001*	G11 240 000*	cv
				50.00	G11 256 001*	G11 260 000*	cv
				50.00	G11 276 001*	G11 280 000*	cv
				50.00	G11 296 001*	G11 300 000*	cv
				50.00	G11 316 001*	G11 320 000*	cv
				50.00	G11 336 001*	G11 340 000*	cv
				50.00	G11 356 001*	G11 360 000*	cv
				50.00	G11 376 001*	G11 380 000*	cv
				50.00	G11 396 001*	G11 400 000*	cv
				50.00	G11 416 001*	G11 420 000*	cv
				50.00	G11 436 001*	G11 440 000*	cv
				50.00	G11 456 001*	G11 460 000*	cv
				50.00	G11 476 001*	G11 480 000*	cv
				50.00	G11 496 001*	G11 500 000*	cv
				50.00	G11 516 001*	G11 520 000*	cv
				50.00	G11 536 001*	G11 540 000*	cv
				50.00	G11 556 001*	G11 560 000*	cv
				50.00	G11 576 001*	G11 580 000*	cv
				50.00	G11 596 001*	G11 600 000*	cv
				50.00	G11 616 001*	G11 620 000*	cv
				50.00	G11 636 001*	G11 640 000*	cv
				50.00	G11 656 001*	G11 660 000*	cv

DISTRICT	TOTAL NOTES PRINTED	BLOCKS	ESTIMATED VALUE VG/F	CU	LOW OFFICIAL SERIAL NUMBER	HIGH OFFICIAL SERIAL NUMBER	
				50.00	G11 676 001*	G11 680 000*	CV
				50.00	G11 696 001*	G11 700 000*	CV
				50.00	G11 716 001*	G11 720 000*	CV
				50.00	G11 736 001*	G11 740 000*	CV
				50.00	G11 756 001*	G11 760 000*	CV
				50.00	G11 776 001*	G11 780 000*	CV
				50.00	G11 796 001*	G11 800 000*	CV
				50.00	G11 816 001*	G11 820 000*	CV
				50.00	G11 836 001*	G11 840 000*	CV
				50.00	G11 856 001*	G11 860 000*	CV
				50.00	G11 876 001*	G11 880 000*	CV
				50.00	G11 896 001*	G11 900 000*	CV
				50.00	G11 916 001*	G11 920 000*	CV
				50.00	G11 936 001*	G11 940 000*	CV
				50.00	G11 956 001*	G11 960 000*	CV
				50.00	G11 976 001*	G11 980 000*	CV
				50.00	G11 996 001*	G12 000 000*	CV
				50.00	G12 016 001*	G12 020 000*	CV
				50.00	G12 036 001*	G12 040 000*	CV
				50.00	G12 056 001*	G12 060 000*	CV
				50.00	G12 076 001*	G12 080 000*	CV
				50.00	G12 096 001*	G12 100 000*	CV
				50.00	G12 116 001*	G12 120 000*	CV
				50.00	G12 136 001*	G12 140 000*	CV
				50.00	G12 156 001*	G12 160 000*	CV
				50.00	G12 172 001*	G12 180 000*	CV
				50.00	G12 192 001*	G12 200 000*	CV
				50.00	G12 212 001*	G12 220 000*	CV
				50.00	G12 232 001*	G12 240 000*	CV
				50.00	G12 252 001*	G12 260 000*	CV
				50.00	G12 272 001*	G12 280 000*	CV
				50.00	G12 292 001*	G12 300 000*	CV
				50.00	G12 312 001*	G12 320 000*	CV
				50.00	G12 332 001*	G12 340 000*	CV
				50.00	G12 352 001*	G12 360 000*	CV
				50.00	G12 372 001*	G12 380 000*	CV
				50.00	G12 392 001*	G12 400 000*	CV
				50.00	G12 412 001*	G12 420 000*	CV
				50.00	G12 432 001*	G12 440 000*	CV
				50.00	G12 452 001*	G12 460 000*	CV
				50.00	G12 472 001*	G12 480 000*	CV
				50.00	G12 492 001*	G12 500 000*	CV
				50.00	G12 512 001*	G12 520 000*	CV
				50.00	G12 532 001*	G12 540 000*	CV
				50.00	G12 552 001*	G12 560 000*	CV
				50.00	G12 572 001*	G12 580 000*	CV
				50.00	G12 592 001*	G12 600 000*	CV
				50.00	G12 612 001*	G12 620 000*	CV
				50.00	G12 632 001*	G12 640 000*	CV
				50.00	G12 652 001*	G12 660 000*	CV
				50.00	G12 672 001*	G12 680 000*	CV
				50.00	G12 692 001*	G12 700 000*	CV
				50.00	G12 712 001*	G12 720 000*	CV
				50.00	G12 732 001*	G12 740 000*	CV
				50.00	G12 752 001*	G12 760 000*	CV
				50.00	G12 772 001*	G12 780 000*	CV
				50.00	G12 792 001*	G12 800 000*	CV
				50.00	G12 812 001*	G12 820 000*	CV
				50.00	G12 832 001*	G12 840 000*	CV
				50.00	G12 852 001*	G12 860 000*	CV
				50.00	G12 872 001*	G12 880 000*	CV
				50.00	G12 892 001*	G12 900 000*	CV
				50.00	G12 912 001*	G12 920 000*	CV
				50.00	G12 932 001*	G12 940 000*	CV
				50.00	G12 952 001*	G12 960 000*	CV
				50.00	G12 972 001*	G12 980 000*	CV
				50.00	G12 992 001*	G13 000 000*	CV
				50.00	G13 012 001*	G13 020 000*	CV
				50.00	G13 032 001*	G13 040 000*	CV

DISTRICT	TOTAL NOTES PRINTED	BLOCKS	ESTIMATED VALUE VG/F	VALUE CU	LOW OFFICIAL SERIAL NUMBER	HIGH OFFICIAL SERIAL NUMBER	
				50.00	G13 052 001*	G13 060 000*	cv
				50.00	G13 072 001*	G13 080 000*	cv
				50.00	G13 092 001*	G13 100 000*	cv
				50.00	G13 112 001*	G13 120 000*	cv
				50.00	G13 132 001*	G13 140 000*	cv
				50.00	G13 152 001*	G13 160 000*	cv
				50.00	G13 172 001*	G13 180 000*	cv
				50.00	G13 192 001*	G13 200 000*	cv
				50.00	G13 212 001*	G13 220 000*	cv
				50.00	G13 232 001*	G13 240 000*	cv
				50.00	G13 252 001*	G13 260 000*	cv
				50.00	G13 272 001*	G13 280 000*	cv
				50.00	G13 292 001*	G13 300 000*	cv
				50.00	G13 312 001*	G13 320 000*	cv
				50.00	G13 332 001*	G13 340 000*	cv
				50.00	G13 352 001*	G13 360 000*	cv
				50.00	G13 372 001*	G13 380 000*	cv
				50.00	G13 392 001*	G13 400 000*	cv
				50.00	G13 412 001*	G13 420 000*	cv
				50.00	G13 432 001*	G13 440 000*	cv
				25.00	G13 440 001*	G14 080 000*	cv
8	H ST. LOUIS	H--A		22.50	H72 320 001A	H99 999 999A	cv
		H--B		22.50	H00 000 001B	H03 200 000B	cv
				22.50	H03 200 001B	H45 440 000B	cp
		H--*		25.00	H01 920 001*	H02 560 000*	cv
				25.00	H02 720 001*	H03 200 000*	cv
9	I MINNEAPOLIS	I--A		22.50	I35 840 001A	I 000A	cv
				22.50	I 001A	I71 680 000A	cp
				25.00	I01 280 001*	I02 560 000*	cv
10	J KANSAS CITY	J--A		22.50	J91 520 001A	J99 999 999A	cv
		J--B		22.50	J00 000 001B	J17 280 000B	cv
				22.50	J17 280 001B	J65 920 000B	cp
		J--*		25.00	J02 720 001I	J03 200 000*	cv
				50.00	J03 216 001*	J03 220 000*	cv
				50.00	J03 236 001*	J03 240 000*	cv
				50.00	J03 256 001*	J03 260 000*	cv
				50.00	J03 276 001*	J03 280 000*	cv
				50.00	J03 296 001*	J03 300 000*	cv
				50.00	J03 316 001*	J03 320 000*	cv
				50.00	J03 336 001*	J03 340 000*	cv
				50.00	J03 356 001*	J03 360 000*	cv
				50.00	J03 376 001*	J03 380 000*	cv
				50.00	J03 396 001*	J03 400 000*	cv
				50.00	J03 416 001*	J03 420 000*	cv
				50.00	J03 436 001*	J03 440 000*	cv
				50.00	J03 456 001*	J03 460 000*	cv
				50.00	J03 476 001*	J03 480 000*	cv
				50.00	J03 496 001*	J03 500 000*	cv
				50.00	J03 516 001*	J03 520 000*	cv
				50.00	J03 536 001*	J03 540 000*	cv
				50.00	J03 556 001*	J03 560 000*	cv
				50.00	J03 576 001*	J03 580 000*	cv
				50.00	J03 596 001*	J03 600 000*	cv
				50.00	J03 616 001*	J03 620 000*	cv
				50.00	J03 636 001*	J03 640 000*	cv
				50.00	J03 656 001*	J03 660 000*	cv
				50.00	J03 676 001*	J03 680 000*	cv
				50.00	J03 696 001*	J03 700 000*	cv
				50.00	J03 716 001*	J03 720 000*	cv
				50.00	J03 736 001*	J03 740 000*	cv
				50.00	J03 756 001*	J03 760 000*	cv
				50.00	J03 776 001*	J03 780 000*	cv
				50.00	J03 796 001*	J03 800 000*	cv
				50.00	J03 816 001*	J03 820 000*	cv
				50.00	J03 836 001*	J03 840 000*	cv
				50.00	J03 856 001*	J03 860 000*	cv
				50.00	J03 876 001*	J03 880 000*	cv
				50.00	J03 896 001*	J03 900 000*	cv
				50.00	J03 916 001*	J03 920 000*	cv

DISTRICT	TOTAL NOTES PRINTED	BLOCKS	ESTIMATED VALUE VG/F	CU	LOW OFFICIAL SERIAL NUMBER	HIGH OFFICIAL SERIAL NUMBER	
				50.00	J03 936 001*	J03 940 000*	cv
				50.00	J03 956 001*	J03 960 000*	cv
				50.00	J03 976 001*	J03 980 000*	cv
				50.00	J03 996 001*	J04 000 000*	cv
				50.00	J04 016 001*	J04 020 000*	cv
				50.00	J04 036 001*	J04 040 000*	cv
				50.00	J04 056 001*	J04 060 000*	cv
				50.00	J04 076 001*	J04 080 000*	cv
				50.00	J04 096 001*	J04 100 000*	cv
				50.00	J04 116 001*	J04 120 000*	cv
				50.00	J04 136 001*	J04 140 000*	cv
				50.00	J04 156 001*	J04 160 000*	cv
				50.00	J04 176 001*	J04 180 000*	cv
				50.00	J04 196 001*	J04 200 000*	cv
				50.00	J04 216 001*	J04 220 000*	cv
				50.00	J04 236 001*	J04 240 000*	cv
				50.00	J04 256 001*	J04 260 000*	cv
				50.00	J04 276 001*	J04 280 000*	cv
				50.00	J04 296 001*	J04 300 000*	cv
				50.00	J04 316 001*	J04 320 000*	cv
				50.00	J04 336 001*	J04 340 000*	cv
				50.00	J04 356 001*	J04 360 000*	cv
				50.00	J04 376 001*	J04 380 000*	cv
				50.00	J04 396 001*	J04 400 000*	cv
				50.00	J04 416 001*	J04 420 000*	cv
				50.00	J04 436 001*	J04 440 000*	cv
				50.00	J04 456 001*	J04 460 000*	cv
				50.00	J04 476 001*	J04 480 000*	cv
11 K DALLAS		K--A		22.50	K83 840 001A	K96 000 000A	cv
				25.00	K96 000 001A	K99 840 000A	cp
				25.00	K99 840 001A	K99 999 999A	cv
		K--B		22.50	K00 000 001B	K52 480 000B	cp
		K--*		25.00	K03 360 001*	K03 840 000*	cv
				50.00	K03 856 001*	K03 860 000*	cv
				50.00	K03 876 001*	K03 880 000*	cv
				50.00	K03 896 001*	K03 900 000*	cv
				50.00	K03 916 001*	K03 920 000*	cv
				50.00	K03 936 001*	K03 940 000*	cv
				50.00	K03 956 001*	K03 960 000*	cv
				50.00	K03 976 001*	K03 980 000*	cv
				50.00	K03 996 001*	K04 000 000*	cv
				50.00	K04 016 001*	K04 020 000*	cv
				50.00	K04 036 001*	K04 040 000*	cv
				50.00	K04 056 001*	K04 060 000*	cv
				50.00	K04 076 001*	K04 080 000*	cv
				50.00	K04 096 001*	K04 100 000*	cv
				50.00	K04 116 001*	K04 120 000*	cv
				50.00	K04 136 001*	K04 140 000*	cv
				50.00	K04 156 001*	K04 160 000*	cv
				50.00	K04 176 001*	K04 180 000*	cv
				50.00	K04 196 001*	K04 200 000*	cv
				50.00	K04 216 001*	K04 220 000*	cv
				50.00	K04 236 001*	K04 240 000*	cv
				50.00	K04 256 001*	K04 260 000*	cv
				50.00	K04 276 001*	K04 280 000*	cv
				50.00	K04 296 001*	K04 300 000*	cv
				50.00	K04 316 001*	K04 320 000*	cv
				50.00	K04 336 001*	K04 340 000*	cv
				50.00	K04 356 001*	K04 360 000*	cv
				50.00	K04 376 001*	K04 380 000*	cv
				50.00	K04 396 001*	K04 400 000*	cv
				50.00	K04 416 001*	K04 420 000*	cv
				50.00	K04 436 001*	K04 440 000*	cv
				50.00	K04 456 001*	K04 460 000*	cv
				50.00	K04 476 001*	K04 480 000*	cv
12 L SAN FRANCISCO		L--C		22.50	L62 720 001C	L99 999 999C	cv
		L--D		22.50	L00 000 001D	L06 400 000D	cv
				22.50	L06 400 001D	L90 880 000D	cp
		L--*		25.00	L08 320 001*	L10 880 000*	cv

DISTRICT	TOTAL NOTES PRINTED	BLOCKS	ESTIMATED VALUE VG/F	VALUE CU	LOW OFFICIAL SERIAL NUMBER	HIGH OFFICIAL SERIAL NUMBER	
				25.00	L11 040 001*	L12 160 000*	CV
				50.00	L12 172 001*	L12 180 000*	CV
				50.00	L12 192 001*	L12 200 000*	CV
				50.00	L12 212 001*	L12 220 000*	CV
				50.00	L12 232 001*	L12 240 000*	CV
				50.00	L12 252 001*	L12 260 000*	CV
				50.00	L12 272 001*	L12 280 000*	CV
				50.00	L12 292 001*	L12 300 000*	CV
				50.00	L12 312 000*	L12 320 000*	CV
				50.00	L12 332 001*	L12 340 000*	CV
				50.00	L12 353 001*	L12 360 000*	CV
				50.00	L12 372 001*	L12 380 000*	CV
				50.00	L12 392 001*	L12 400 000*	CV
				50.00	L12 412 001*	L12 420 000*	CV
				50.00	L12 432 001*	L12 440 000*	CV
				50.00	L12 452 001*	L12 460 000*	CV
				50.00	L12 472 001*	L12 480 000*	CV
				50.00	L12 492 001*	L12 500 000*	CV
				50.00	L12 512 001*	L12 520 000*	CV
				50.00	L12 532 001*	L12 540 000*	CV
				50.00	L12 552 001*	L12 560 000*	CV
				50.00	L12 572 001*	L12 580 000*	CV
				50.00	L12 592 001*	L12 600 000*	CV
				50.00	L12 612 001*	L12 620 000*	CV
				50.00	L12 632 001*	L12 640 000*	CV
				50.00	L12 652 001*	L12 660 000*	CV
				50.00	L12 672 001*	L12 680 000*	CV
				50.00	L12 692 001*	L12 700 000*	CV
				50.00	L12 712 001*	L12 720 000*	CV
				50.00	L12 732 001*	L12 740 000*	CV
				50.00	L12 752 001*	L12 760 000*	CV
				50.00	L12 772 001*	L12 780 000*	CV
				50.00	L12 792 001*	L12 800 000*	CV
				50.00	L12 816 001*	L12 820 000*	CV
				50.00	L12 836 001*	L12 840 000*	CV
				50.00	L12 856 001*	L12 860 000*	CV
				50.00	L12 876 001*	L12 880 000*	CV
				50.00	L12 896 001*	L12 900 000*	CV
				50.00	L12 916 001*	L12 920 000*	CV
				50.00	L12 936 001*	L12 940 000*	CV
				50.00	L12 956 001*	L12 960 000*	CV
				50.00	L12 976 001*	L12 980 000*	CV
				50.00	L12 996 001*	L13 000 000*	CV
				50.00	L13 016 001*	L13 020 000*	CV
				50.00	L13 036 001*	L13 040 000*	CV
				50.00	L13 056 001*	L13 060 000*	CV
				50.00	L13 076 001*	L13 080 000*	CV
				50.00	L13 096 001*	L13 100 000*	CV
				50.00	L13 116 001*	L13 120 000*	CV
				50.00	L13 136 001*	L13 140 000*	CV
				50.00	L13 156 001*	L13 160 000*	CV
				50.00	L13 176 001*	L13 180 000*	CV
				50.00	L13 196 001*	L13 200 000*	CV
				50.00	L13 216 001*	L13 220 000*	CV
				50.00	L13 236 001*	L13 240 000*	CV
				50.00	L13 256 001*	L13 260 000*	CV
				50.00	L13 276 001*	L13 280 000*	CV
				50.00	L14 296 001*	L13 300 000*	CV
				50.00	L13 316 001*	L13 320 000*	CV
				50.00	L13 336 001*	L13 340 000*	CV
				50.00	L13 356 001*	L13 360 000*	CV
				50.00	L13 376 001*	L13 380 000*	CV
				50.00	L13 396 001*	L13 400 000*	CV
				50.00	L13 416 001*	L13 420 000*	CV
				50.00	L13 436 001*	L13 440 000*	CV
				50.00	L13 453 001*	L13 460 000*	CV
				50.00	L13 472 001*	L13 480 000*	CV
				50.00	L13 492 001*	L13 500 000*	CV
				50.00	L13 512 001*	L13 520 000*	CV

VALUE CU	LOW OFFICIAL SERIAL NUMBER	HIGH OFFICIAL SERIAL NUMBER		VALUE CU	LOW OFFICIAL SERIAL NUMBER	HIGH OFFICIAL SERIAL NUMBER	
50.00	L13 532 001*	L13 540 000*	cv	50.00	L13 812 001*	L13 820 000*	cv
50.00	L13 552 001*	L13 560 000*	cv	50.00	L13 832 001*	L13 840 000*	cv
50.00	L13 572 001*	L13 580 000*	cv	50.00	L13 852 001*	L13 860 000*	cv
50.00	L13 592 001*	L13 600 000*	cv	50.00	L13 872 001*	L13 880 000*	cv
50.00	L13 612 001*	L13 620 000*	cv	50.00	L13 892 001*	L13 900 000*	cv
50.00	L13 632 001*	L13 640 000*	cv	50.00	L13 912 001*	L13 920 000*	cv
50.00	L13 652 001*	L13 660 000*	cv	50.00	L13 932 001*	L13 940 000*	cv
50.00	L13 672 001*	L13 680 000*	cv	50.00	L13 952 001*	L13 960 000*	cv
50.00	L13 692 001*	L13 700 000*	cv	50.00	L13 972 001*	L13 980 000*	cv
50.00	L13 712 001*	L13 720 000*	cv	50.00	L13 992 001*	L14 000 000*	cv
50.00	L13 732 001*	L13 740 000*	cv	50.00	L14 012 001*	L14 020 000*	cv
50.00	L13 752 001*	L13 760 000*	cv	50.00	L14 032 001*	L14 040 000*	cv
50.00	L13 772 001*	L13 780 000*	cv	50.00	L14 052 001*	L14 060 000*	cv
50.00	L13 792 001*	L13 800 000*	cv	50.00	L14 072 001*	L14 080 000*	cv

CAT. NO. XXF77
$20.00 FEDERAL RESERVE NOTE (GREEN SEAL) 32 Subject
SERIES 1977

SIGNATURES: Azie Taylor Morton, Treasurer of the United States.
W. Michael Blumenthal, Secretary of the Treasury.
SERIAL NUMBERS: All districts revert to 00 000 001
PLATE SERIALS: Both face and back check continue from previous series.

	DISTRICT	TOTAL NOTES PRINTED	BLOCKS	ESTIMATED VALUE VG/F	CU	LOW OFFICIAL SERIAL NUMBER	HIGH OFFICIAL SERIAL NUMBER	
1	A BOSTON		A--A		22.50	A00 000 001A	A94 720 000A	cp
			A--*		35.00	A00 008 001*	A00 020 000*	cv
					35.00	A00 028 001*	A00 040 000*	cv
					35.00	A00 048 001*	A00 060 000*	cv
					35.00	A00 068 001*	A00 080 000*	cv
					35.00	A00 088 001*	A00 100 000*	cv
					35.00	A00 108 001	A00 120 000*	cv
					35.00	A00 128 001*	A00 140 000*	cv
					35.00	A00 148 001*	A00 160 000*	cv
					35.00	A00 168 001*	A00 180 000*	cv
					35.00	A00 188 001*	A00 200 000*	cv
					35.00	A00 208 001*	A00 220 000*	cv
					35.00	A00 228 001*	A00 240 000*	cv
					35.00	A00 248 001*	A00 260 000*	cv
					35.00	A00 268 001*	A00 280 000*	cv
					35.00	A00 288 001*	A00 300 000*	cv
					35.00	A00 308 001*	A00 320 000*	cv
					35.00	A00 328 001*	A00 340 000*	cv
					35.00	A00 348 001*	A00 360 000*	cv
					35.00	A00 368 001*	A00 380 000*	cv
					35.00	A00 388 001*	A00 400 000*	cv
					35.00	A00 408 001*	A00 420 000*	cv
					35.00	A00 428 001*	A00 440 000*	cv
					35.00	A00 448 001*	A00 460 000*	cv
					35.00	A00 468 001*	A00 480 000*	cv
					35.00	A00 488 001*	A00 500 000*	cv
					35.00	A00 508 001*	A00 520 000*	cv
					35.00	A00 528 001*	A00 540 000*	cv
					35.00	A00 548 001*	A00 560 000*	cv
					35.00	A00 568 001*	A00 580 000*	cv
					35.00	A00 588 011*	A00 600 000*	cv
					35.00	A00 608 001*	A00 620 000*	cv
					35.00	A00 628 001*	A00 640 000*	cv
					25.00	A00 640 001*	A01 280 000*	cv
					25.00	A01 280 001*	A01 920 000*	cp
					50.00	A01 932 001*	A01 940 000*	cp
					50.00	A01 952 001*	A01 960 000*	cp
					50.00	A01 972 001*	A01 980 000*	cp
					50.00	A01 992 001*	A02 000 000*	cp
					50.00	A02 012 001*	A02 020 000*	cp
					50.00	A02 032 001*	A02 040 000*	cp
					50.00	A02 052 001*	A02 060 000*	cp

DISTRICT	TOTAL NOTES PRINTED	BLOCKS	ESTIMATED VALUE VG/F	CU	LOW OFFICIAL SERIAL NUMBER	HIGH OFFICIAL SERIAL NUMBER	
				50.00	A02 072 001*	A02 080 000*	cp
				50.00	A02 092 001*	A02 100 000*	cp
				50.00	A02 112 001*	A02 120 000*	cp
				50.00	A02 132 001*	A02 140 000*	cp
				50.00	A02 152 001*	A02 160 000*	cp
				50.00	A02 172 001*	A02 180 000*	cp
				50.00	A02 192 001*	A02 200 000*	cp
				50.00	A02 212 001*	A02 220 000*	cp
				50.00	A02 232 001*	A02 240 000*	cp
				50.00	A02 252 001*	A02 260 000*	cp
				50.00	A02 272 001*	A02 280 000*	cp
				50.00	A02 292 001*	A02 300 000*	cp
				50.00	A02 312 001*	A02 320 000*	cp
				50.00	A02 332 001*	A02 340 000*	cp
				50.00	A02 352 001*	A02 360 000*	cp
				50.00	A02 372 001*	A02 380 000*	cp
				50.00	A02 392 001*	A02 400 000*	cp
				50.00	A02 412 001*	A02 420 000*	cp
				50.00	A02 432 001*	A02 440 000*	cp
				50.00	A02 452 001*	A02 460 000*	cp
				50.00	A02 472 001*	A02 480 000*	cp
				50.00	A02 492 001*	A02 500 000*	cp
				50.00	A02 512 001*	A02 520 000*	cp
				50.00	A02 532 001*	A02 540 000*	cp
				50.00	A02 552 001*	A02 560 000*	cp
				50.00	A02 568 001*	A02 580 000*	cp
				50.00	A02 588 001*	A02 600 000*	cp
				50.00	A02 608 001*	A02 620 000*	cp
				50.00	A02 628 001*	A02 640 000*	cp
				50.00	A02 648 001*	A02 660 000*	cp
				50.00	A02 668 001*	A02 680 000*	cp
				50.00	A02 688 001*	A02 700 000*	cp
				50.00	A02 708 001*	A02 720 000*	cp
				50.00	A02 728 001*	A02 740 000*	cp
				50.00	A02 748 001*	A02 760 000*	cp
				50.00	A02 768 001*	A02 780 000*	cp
				50.00	A02 788 001*	A02 800 000*	cp
				50.00	A02 808 001*	A02 820 000*	cp
				50.00	A02 828 001*	A02 840 000*	cp
				50.00	A02 848 001*	A02 860 000*	cp
				50.00	A02 868 001*	A02 880 000*	cp
				50.00	A02 888 001*	A02 900 000*	cp
				50.00	A02 908 001*	A02 920 000*	cp
				50.00	A02 928 001*	A02 940 000*	cp
				50.00	A02 948 001*	A02 960 000*	cp
				50.00	A02 968 001*	A02 980 000*	cp
				50.00	A02 988 001*	A03 000 000*	cp
				50.00	A03 008 001*	A03 020 000*	cp
				50.00	A03 028 001*	A03 040 000*	cp
				50.00	A03 048 001*	A03 060 000*	cp
				50.00	A03 068 001*	A03 080 000*	cp
				50.00	A03 088 001*	A03 100 000*	cp
				50.00	A03 108 001*	A03 120 000*	cp
				50.00	A03 128 001*	A03 140 000*	cp
				50.00	A03 148 001*	A03 160 000*	cp
				50.00	A03 168 001*	A03 180 000*	cp
				50.00	A03 188 001*	A03 200 000*	cp
				50.00	A03 208 001*	A03 220 000*	cp
				50.00	A03 228 001*	A03 240 000*	cp
				50.00	A03 248 001*	A03 260 000*	cp
				50.00	A03 268 001*	A03 280 000*	cp
				50.00	A03 288 001*	A03 300 000*	cp
				50.00	A03 308 001*	A03 320 000*	cp
				50.00	A03 328 001*	A03 340 000*	cp
				50.00	A03 348 001*	A03 360 000*	cp
				50.00	A03 368 001*	A03 380 000*	cp
				50.00	A03 388 001*	A03 400 000*	cp
				50.00	A03 408 001*	A03 420 000*	cp
				50.00	A03 428 001*	A03 440 000*	cp

DISTRICT	TOTAL NOTES PRINTED	BLOCKS	ESTIMATED VALUE VG/F CU	LOW OFFICIAL SERIAL NUMBER	HIGH OFFICIAL SERIAL NUMBER	
			50.00	A03 448 001*	A03 460 000*	cp
			50.00	A03 468 001*	A03 480 000*	cp
			50.00	A03 488 001*	A03 500 000*	cp
			50.00	A03 508 001*	A03 520 000*	cp
			50.00	A03 528 001*	A03 540 000*	cp
			50.00	A03 548 001*	A03 560 000*	cp
			50.00	A03 568 001*	A03 580 000*	cp
			50.00	A03 588 001*	A03 600 000*	cp
			50.00	A03 608 001*	A03 620 000*	cp
			50.00	A03 628 001*	A03 640 000*	cp
			50.00	A03 648 001*	A03 660 000*	cp
			50.00	A03 668 001*	A03 680 000*	cp
			50.00	A03 688 001*	A03 700 000*	cp
			50.00	A03 708 001*	A03 720 000*	cp
			50.00	A03 728 001*	A03 740 000*	cp
			50.00	A03 748 001*	A03 760 000*	cp
			50.00	A03 768 001*	A03 780 000*	cp
			50.00	A03 788 001*	A03 800 000*	cp
			50.00	A03 808 001*	A03 820 000*	cp
			50.00	A03 828 001*	A03 840 000*	cp
2	B NEW YORK	B--A	22.50	B00 000 001A	B99 840 000A	cp
		B--B	22.50	B00 000 001B	B99 840 000B	cp
		B--C	22.50	B00 000 001C	B99 840 000C	cp
		B--D	22.50	B00 000 001D	B99 840 000D	cp
		B--E	22.50	B00 000 001E	B99 840 000E	cp
		B--F	22.50	B00 000 001F	B70 400 000F	cp
		B--*	25.00	B00 000 001*	B02 560 000*	cv
			25.00	B02 560 001*	B07 040 000*	cp
			50.00	B07 056 001*	B07 060 000*	cp
			50.00	B07 076 001*	B07 080 000*	cp
			50.00	B07 096 001*	B07 100 000*	cp
			50.00	B07 116 001*	B07 120 000*	cp
			50.00	B07 136 001*	B07 140 000*	cp
			50.00	B07 156 001*	B07 160 000*	cp
			50.00	B07 176 001*	B07 180 000*	cp
			50.00	B07 196 001*	B07 200 000*	cp
			50.00	B07 216 001*	B07 220 000*	cp
			50.00	B07 236 001*	B07 240 000*	cp
			50.00	B07 256 001*	B07 260 000*	cp
			50.00	B07 276 001*	B07 280 000*	cp
			50.00	B07 296 001*	B07 300 000*	cp
			50.00	B07 316 001*	B07 320 000*	cp
			50.00	B07 336 001*	B07 340 000*	cp
			50.00	B07 356 001*	B07 360 000*	cp
			50.00	B07 376 001*	B07 380 000*	cp
			50.00	B07 396 001*	B07 400 000*	cp
			50.00	B07 416 001*	B07 420 000*	cp
			50.00	B07 436 001*	B07 440 000*	cp
			50.00	B07 456 001*	B07 460 000*	cp
			50.00	B07 476 001*	B07 480 000*	cp
			50.00	B07 496 001*	B07 500 000*	cp
			50.00	B07 516 001*	B07 520 000*	cp
			50.00	B07 536 001*	B07 540 000*	cp
			50.00	B07 556 001*	B07 560 000*	cp
			50.00	B07 576 001*	B07 580 000*	cp
			50.00	B07 596 001*	B07 600 000*	cp
			50.00	B07 616 001*	B07 620 000*	cp
			50.00	B07 636 001*	B07 640 000*	cp
			50.00	B07 656 001*	B07 660 000*	cp
			50.00	B07 676 001*	B07 680 000*	cp
			25.00	B07 680 001*	B12 160 000*	cp
			50.00	B12 176 001*	B12 180 000*	cp
			50.00	B12 196 001*	B12 200 000*	cp
			50.00	B12 216 001*	B12 220 000*	cp
			50.00	B12 236 001*	B12 240 000*	cp
			50.00	B12 256 001*	B12 260 000*	cp
			50.00	B12 276 001*	B12 280 000*	cp
			50.00	B12 296 001*	B12 300 000*	cp
			50.00	B12 316 001*	B12 320 000*	cp

DISTRICT	TOTAL NOTES PRINTED	BLOCKS	ESTIMATED VALUE VG/F	CU	LOW OFFICIAL SERIAL NUMBER	HIGH OFFICIAL SERIAL NUMBER	
				50.00	B12 336 001*	B12 340 000*	cp
				50.00	B12 356 001*	B12 360 000*	cp
				50.00	B12 376 001*	B12 380 000*	cp
				50.00	B12 396 001*	B12 400 000*	cp
				50.00	B12 416 001*	B12 420 000*	cp
				50.00	B12 436 001*	B12 440 000*	cp
				50.00	B12 456 001*	B12 460 000*	cp
				50.00	B12 476 001*	B12 480 000*	cp
				50.00	B12 496 001*	B12 500 000*	cp
				50.00	B12 516 001*	B12 520 000*	cp
				50.00	B12 536 001*	B12 540 000*	cp
				50.00	B12 556 001*	B12 560 000*	cp
				50.00	B12 576 001*	B12 580 000*	cp
				50.00	B12 596 001*	B12 600 000*	cp
				50.00	B12 616 001*	B12 620 000*	cp
				50.00	B12 636 001*	B12 640 000*	cp
				50.00	B12 656 001*	B12 660 000*	cp
				50.00	B12 676 001*	B12 680 000*	cp
				50.00	B12 696 001*	B12 700 000*	cp
				50.00	B12 716 001*	B12 720 000*	cp
				50.00	B12 736 001*	B12 740 000*	cp
				50.00	B12 756 001*	B12 760 000*	cp
				50.00	B12 776 001*	B12 780 000*	cp
				50.00	B12 796 001*	B12 800 000*	cp
				25.00	B12 800 001*	B13 440 000*	cp
3	C PHILADELPHIA	C--A		22.50	C00 000 001A	C99 840 000A	cp
		C--B		22.50	C00 000 001B	C17 920 000B	cp
		C--*		50.00	C00 012 001*	C00 020 000*	cv
				50.00	C00 032 001*	C00 040 000*	cv
				50.00	C00 052 001*	C00 060 000*	cv
				50.00	C00 072 001*	C00 080 000*	cv
				50.00	C00 092 001*	C00 100 000*	cv
				50.00	C00 112 001*	C00 120 000*	cv
				50.00	C00 132 001*	C00 140 000*	cv
				50.00	C00 152 001*	C00 160 000*	cv
				50.00	C00 172 001*	C00 180 000*	cv
				50.00	C00 192 001*	C00 200 000*	cv
				50.00	C00 212 001*	C00 220 000*	cv
				50.00	C00 232 001*	C00 240 000*	cv
				50.00	C00 252 001*	C00 260 000*	cv
				50.00	C00 272 001*	C00 280 000*	cv
				50.00	C00 292 001*	C00 300 000*	cv
				50.00	C00 312 001*	C00 320 000*	cv
				50.00	C00 332 001*	C00 340 000*	cv
				50.00	C00 352 001*	C00 360 000*	cv
				50.00	C00 372 001*	C00 380 000*	cv
				50.00	C00 392 001*	C00 400 000*	cv
				50.00	C00 412 001*	C00 420 000*	cv
				50.00	C00 432 001*	C00 440 000*	cv
				50.00	C00 452 001*	C00 460 000*	cv
				50.00	C00 472 001*	C00 480 000*	cv
				50.00	C00 492 001*	C00 500 000*	cv
				50.00	C00 512 001*	C00 520 000*	cv
				50.00	C00 532 001*	C00 540 000*	cv
				50.00	C00 552 001*	C00 560 000*	cv
				50.00	C00 572 001*	C00 580 000*	cv
				50.00	C00 592 001*	C00 600 000*	cv
				50.00	C00 612 001*	C00 620 000*	cv
				50.00	C00 632 001*	C00 640 000*	cv
				25.00	C00 640 001*	C01 280 000*	cp
				50.00	C01 288 001*	C01 300 000*	cp
				50.00	C01 308 001*	C01 320 000*	cp
				50.00	C01 328 001*	C01 340 000*	cp
				50.00	C01 348 001*	C01 360 000*	cp
				50.00	C01 368 001*	C01 380 000*	cp
				50.00	C01 388 001*	C01 400 000*	cp
				50.00	C01 408 001*	C01 420 000*	cp
				50.00	C01 428 001*	C01 440 000*	cp
				50.00	C01 448 001*	C01 460 000*	cp

DISTRICT	TOTAL NOTES PRINTED	BLOCKS	ESTIMATED VALUE VG/F	CU	LOW OFFICIAL SERIAL NUMBER	HIGH OFFICIAL SERIAL NUMBER	
				50.00	C01 468 001*	C01 480 000*	cp
				50.00	C01 488 001*	C01 500 000*	cp
				50.00	C01 508 001*	C01 520 000*	cp
				50.00	C01 528 001*	C01 540 000*	cp
				50.00	C01 548 001*	C01 560 000*	cp
				50.00	C01 568 001*	C01 580 000*	cp
				50.00	C01 588 001*	C01 600 000*	cp
				50.00	C01 608 001*	C01 620 000*	cp
				50.00	C01 628 001*	C01 640 000*	cp
				50.00	C01 648 001*	C01 660 000*	cp
				50.00	C01 668 001*	C01 680 000*	cp
				50.00	C01 688 001*	C01 700 000*	cp
				50.00	C01 708 001*	C01 720 000*	cp
				50.00	C01 728 001*	C01 740 000*	cp
				50.00	C01 748 001*	C01 760 000*	cp
				50.00	C01 768 001*	C01 780 000*	cp
				50.00	C01 788 001*	C01 800 000*	cp
				50.00	C01 808 001*	C01 820 000*	cp
				50.00	C01 828 001*	C01 840 000*	cp
				50.00	C01 848 001*	C01 860 000*	cp
				50.00	C01 868 001*	C01 880 000*	cp
				50.00	C01 888 001*	C01 900 000*	cp
				50.00	C01 908 001*	C01 920 000*	cp
				50.00	C01 936 001*	C01 940 000*	cp
				50.00	C01 956 001*	C01 960 000*	cp
				50.00	C01 976 001*	C01 980 000*	cp
				50.00	C01 996 001*	C02 000 000*	cp
				50.00	C02 016 001*	C02 020 000*	cp
				50.00	C02 036 001*	C02 040 000*	cp
				50.00	C02 056 001*	C02 060 000*	cp
				50.00	C02 076 001*	C02 080 000*	cp
				50.00	C02 096 001*	C02 100 000*	cp
				50.00	C02 116 001*	C02 120 000*	cp
				50.00	C02 136 001*	C02 140 000*	cp
				50.00	C02 156 001*	C02 160 000*	cp
				50.00	C02 176 001*	C02 180 000*	cp
				50.00	C02 196 001*	C02 200 000*	cp
				50.00	C02 216 001*	C02 220 000*	cp
				50.00	C02 236 001*	C02 240 000*	cp
				50.00	C02 256 001*	C02 260 000*	cp
				50.00	C02 276 001*	C02 280 000*	cp
				50.00	C02 296 001*	C02 300 000*	cp
				50.00	C02 316 001*	C02 320 000*	cp
				50.00	C02 336 001*	C02 340 000*	cp
				50.00	C02 356 001*	C02 360 000*	cp
				50.00	C02 376 001*	C02 380 000*	cp
				50.00	C02 396 001*	C02 400 000*	cp
				50.00	C02 416 001*	C02 420 000*	cp
				50.00	C02 436 001*	C02 440 000*	cp
				50.00	C02 456 001*	C02 460 000*	cp
				50.00	C02 476 001*	C02 480 000*	cp
				50.00	C02 496 001*	C02 500 000*	cp
				50.00	C02 516 001*	C02 520 000*	cp
				50.00	C02 536 001*	C02 540 000*	cp
				50.00	C02 556 001*	C02 560 000*	cp
				25.00	C02 560 001*	C03 200 000*	cp
				50.00	C03 216 001*	C03 220 000*	cp
				50.00	C03 236 001*	C03 240 000*	cp
				50.00	C03 256 001*	C03 260 000*	cp
				50.00	C03 276 001*	C03 280 000*	cp
				50.00	C03 296 001*	C03 300 000*	cp
				50.00	C03 316 001*	C03 320 000*	cp
				50.00	C03 336 001*	C03 340 000*	cp
				50.00	C03 356 001*	C03 360 000*	cp
				50.00	C03 376 001*	C03 380 000*	cp
				50.00	C03 396 001*	C03 400 000*	cp
				50.00	C03 416 001*	C03 420 000*	cp
				50.00	C03 436 001*	C03 440 000*	cp
				50.00	C03 456 001*	C03 460 000*	cp

DISTRICT	TOTAL NOTES PRINTED	BLOCKS	ESTIMATED VALUE VG/F	CU	LOW OFFICIAL SERIAL NUMBER	HIGH OFFICIAL SERIAL NUMBER	
				50.00	C03 476 001*	C03 480 000*	cp
				50.00	C03 496 001*	C03 500 000*	cp
				50.00	C03 516 001*	C03 520 000*	cp
				50.00	C03 536 001*	C03 540 000*	cp
				50.00	C 03 556 001*	C03 560 000*	cp
				50.00	C03 576 001*	C03 580 000*	cp
				50.00	C03 596 001*	C03 600 000*	cp
				50.00	C03 616 001*	C03 620 000*	cp
				50.00	C03 636 001*	C03 640 000*	cp
				50.00	C03 656 001*	C03 660 000*	cp
				50.00	C03 676 001*	C03 680 000*	cp
				50.00	C03 696 001*	C03 700 000*	cp
				50.00	C03 716 001*	C03 720 000*	cp
				50.00	C03 736 001*	C03 740 000*	cp
				50.00	C03 756 001*	C03 760 000*	cp
				50.00	C03 776 001*	C03 780 000*	cp
				50.00	C03 796 001*	C03 800 000*	cp
				50.00	C03 816 001*	C03 820 000*	cp
				50.00	C03 836 001*	C03 840 000*	cp
				25.00	C03 840 001*	C04 480 000*	cp
4	D CLEVELAND	D--A		22.50	D00 000 001A	D99 840 000A	cp
		D--B		22.50	D00 000 001B	D89 600 000B	cp
		D--*		50.00	D00 016 001*	D00 020 000*	cv
				50.00	D00 036 001*	D00 040 000*	cv
				50.00	D00 056 001*	D00 060 000*	cv
				50.00	D00 076 001*	D00 080 000*	cv
				50.00	D00 096 001*	D00 100 000*	cv
				50.00	D00 116 001*	D00 120 000*	cv
				50.00	D00 136 001*	D00 140 000*	cv
				50.00	D00 156 001*	D00 160 000*	cv
				50.00	D00 176 001*	D00 180 000*	cv
				50.00	D00 196 001*	D00 200 000*	cv
				50.00	D00 216 001*	D00 220 000*	cv
				50.00	D00 236 001*	D00 240 000*	cv
				50.00	D00 256 001*	D00 260 000*	cv
				50.00	D00 276 001*	D00 280 000*	cv
				50.00	D00 296 001*	D00 300 000*	cv
				50.00	D00 316 001*	D00 320 000*	cv
				50.00	D00 336 001*	D00 340 000*	cv
				50.00	D00 356 001*	D00 360 000*	cv
				50.00	D00 376 001*	D00 380 000*	cv
				50.00	D00 396 001*	D00 400 000*	cv
				50.00	D00 416 001*	D00 420 000*	cv
				50.00	D00 436 001*	D00 440 000*	cv
				50.00	D00 456 001*	D00 460 000*	cv
				50.00	D00 476 001*	D00 480 000*	cv
				50.00	D00 496 001*	D00 500 000*	cv
				50.00	D00 516 001*	D00 520 000*	cv
				50.00	D00 536 001*	D00 540 000*	cv
				50.00	D00 556 001*	D00 560 000*	cv
				50.00	D00 576 001*	D00 580 000*	cv
				50.00	D00 596 001*	D00 600 000*	cv
				50.00	D 00 616 001*	D00 620 000*	cv
				50.00	D00 636 001*	D00 640 000*	cv
				25.00	D00 640 001*	D01 280 000*	cv
				50.00	D01 288 001*	D01 300 000*	cv
				50.00	D01 308 000*	D01 320 000*	cv
				50.00	D01 328 001*	D01 340 000*	cv
				50.00	D01 348 001*	D01 360 000*	cv
				50.00	D01 368 001*	D01 380 000*	cv
				50.00	D01 388 001*	D01 400 000*	cv
				50.00	D01 408 001*	D01 420 000*	cv
				50.00	D01 428 001*	D01 440 000*	cv
				50.00	D01 448 001*	D01 460 000*	cv
				50.00	D01 468 001*	D01 480 000*	cv
				50.00	D01 488 001*	D01 500 000*	cv
				50.00	D01 508 001*	D01 520 000*	cv
				50.00	D01 528 001*	D01 540 000*	cv
				50.00	D01 548 001*	D01 560 000*	cv

VALUE CU	LOW OFFICIAL SERIAL NUMBER	HIGH OFFICIAL SERIAL NUMBER		VALUE CU	LOW OFFICIAL SERIAL NUMBER	HIGH OFFICIAL SERIAL NUMBER	
50.00	D01 568 001*	D01 580 000*	cv	50.00	D04 808 001*	D04 820 000*	cp
50.00	D01 588 001*	D01 600 000*	cv	50.00	D04 828 001*	D04 840 000*	cp
50.00	D01 608 001*	D01 620 000*	cv	50.00	D04 848 001*	D04 860 000*	cp
50.00	D01 628 001*	D01 640 000*	cv	50.00	D04 868 001*	D04 880 000*	cp
50.00	D01 648 001*	D01 660 000*	cv	50.00	D04 888 001*	D04 900 000*	cp
50.00	D01 668 001*	D01 680 000*	cv	50.00	D04 908 001*	D04 920 000*	cp
50.00	D01 688 001*	D01 700 000*	cv	50.00	D04 928 001*	D04 940 000*	cp
50.00	D01 708 001*	D01 720 000*	cv	50.00	D04 948 001*	D04 960 000*	cp
50.00	D01 728 001*	D01 740 000*	cv	50.00	D04 968 001*	D04 980 000*	cp
50.00	D01 748 001*	D01 760 000*	cv	50.00	D04 988 001*	D05 000 000*	cp
50.00	D01 768 001*	D01 780 000*	cv	50.00	D05 008 001*	D05 020 000*	cp
50.00	D01 788 001*	D01 800 000*	cv	50.00	D05 028 001*	D05 040 000*	cp
50.00	D01 808 001*	D01 820 000*	cv	50.00	D05 048 001*	D05 060 000*	cp
50.00	D01 828 001*	D01 840 000*	cv	50.00	D05 068 001*	D05 080 000*	cp
50.00	D01 848 001*	D01 860 000*	cv	50.00	D05 088 001*	D05 100 000*	cp
50.00	D01 868 001*	D01 880 000*	cv	50.00	D05 108 001*	D05 120 000*	cp
50.00	D01 888 001*	D01 900 000*	cv	50.00	D05 132 001*	D05 140 000*	cp
50.00	D01 908 001*	D01 920 000*	cv	50.00	D05 152 001*	D05 160 000*	cp
25.00	D01 920 001*	D02 560 000*	cv	50.00	D05 172 001*	D05 180 000*	cp
25.00	D02 560 001*	D03 200 000*	cp	50.00	D05 192 001*	D05 200 000*	cp
50.00	D03 212 001*	D03 220 000*	cp	50.00	D05 212 001*	D05 220 000*	cp
50.00	D03 232 001*	D03 240 000*	cp	50.00	D05 232 001*	D05 240 000*	cp
50.00	D03 252 001*	D03 260 000*	cp	50.00	D05 252 001*	D05 260 000*	cp
50.00	D03 272 001*	D03 280 000*	cp	50.00	D05 272 001*	D05 280 000*	cp
50.00	D03 292 001*	D03 300 000*	cp	50.00	D05 292 001*	D05 300 000*	cp
50.00	D03 212 001*	D03 320 000*	cp	50.00	D05 312 001*	D05 320 000*	cp
50.00	D03 332 001*	D03 340 000*	cp	50.00	D05 332 001*	D05 340 000*	cp
50.00	D03 352 001*	D03 360 000*	cp	50.00	D05 352 001*	D05 360 000*	cp
50.00	D03 372 001*	D03 380 000*	cp	50.00	D05 372 001*	D05 380 000*	cp
50.00	D03 392 001*	D03 400 000*	cp	50.00	D05 392 001*	D05 400 000*	cp
50.00	D03 412 001*	D03 420 000*	cp	50.00	D05 412 001*	D05 420 000*	cp
50.00	D03 432 001*	D03 440 000*	cp	50.00	D05 432 001*	D05 440 000*	cp
50.00	D03 452 001*	D03 460 000*	cp	50.00	D05 452 001*	D05 460 000*	cp
50.00	D03 472 001*	D03 480 000*	cp	50.00	D05 472 001*	D05 480 000*	cp
50.00	D03 492 001*	D03 500 000*	cp	50.00	D05 492 001*	D05 500 000*	cp
50.00	D03 512 001*	D03 520 000*	cp	50.00	D05 512 001*	D05 520 000*	cp
50.00	D03 532 001*	D03 540 000*	cp	50.00	D05 532 001*	D05 540 000*	cp
50.00	D 03 552 001*	D03 560 000*	cp	50.00	D05 552 001*	D05 560 000*	cp
50.00	D03 572 001*	D03 580 000*	cp	50.00	D05 572 001*	D05 580 000*	cp
50.00	D03 592 001*	D03 600 000*	cp	50.00	D05 592 001*	D05 600 000*	cp
50.00	D03 612 001*	D03 620 000*	cp	50.00	D05 612 001*	D05 620 000*	cp
50.00	D03 632 001*	D03 640 000*	cp	50.00	D05 632 001*	D05 640 000*	cp
50.00	D03 652 001*	D03 660 000*	cp	50.00	D05 652 001*	D05 660 000*	cp
50.00	D03 672 001*	D03 680 000*	cp	50.00	D05 672 001*	D05 680 000*	cp
50.00	D03 692 001*	D03 700 000*	cp	50.00	D05 692 001*	D05 700 000*	cp
50.00	D03 712 001*	D03 720 000*	cp	50.00	D05 712 001*	D05 720 000*	cp
50.00	D03 732 001*	D03 740 000*	cp	50.00	D05 732 001*	D05 740 000*	cp
50.00	D03 752 001*	D03 760 000*	cp	50.00	D05 752 001*	D05 760 000*	cp
50.00	D03 772 001*	D03 780 000*	cp	25.00	D05 760 001*	D06 400 000*	cp
50.00	D03 792 001*	D03 800 000*	cp	50.00	D06 408 001*	D06 420 000*	cp
50.00	D03 812 001*	D03 820 000*	cp	50.00	D06 428 001*	D06 440 000*	cp
50.00	D03 832 001*	D03 840 000*	cp	50.00	D06 448 001*	D06 460 000*	cp
25.00	D03 840 001*	D04 480 000*	cp	50.00	D06 468 001*	D06 480 000*	cp
50.00	D04 488 001*	D04 500 000*	cp	50.00	D06 488 001*	D06 500 000*	cp
50.00	D04 508 001*	D04 520 000*	cp	50.00	D06 508 001*	D06 520 000*	cp
50.00	D04 528 001*	D04 540 000*	cp	50.00	D06 528 001*	D06 540 000*	cp
50.00	D04 548 001*	D04 560 000*	cp	50.00	D06 548 001*	D06 560 000*	cp
50.00	D04 568 001*	D04 580 000*	cp	50.00	D06 568 001*	D06 580 000*	cp
50.00	D04 588 001*	D04 600 000*	cp	50.00	D06 588 001*	D06 600 000*	cp
50.00	D04 608 001*	D04 620 000*	cp	50.00	D06 608 001*	D06 620 000*	cp
50.00	D04 628 001*	D04 640 000*	cp	50.00	D06 628 001*	D06 640 000*	cp
50.00	D04 648 001*	D04 660 000*	cp	50.00	D06 648 001*	D06 660 000*	cp
50.00	D04 668 001*	D04 680 000*	cp	50.00	D06 668 001*	D06 680 000*	cp
50.00	D04 688 001*	D04 700 000*	cp	50.00	D06 688 001*	D06 700 000*	cp
50.00	D04 708 001*	D04 720 000*	cp	50.00	D06 708 001*	D06 720 000*	cp
50.00	D04 728 001*	D04 740 000*	cp	50.00	D06 728 001*	D06 740 000*	cp
50.00	D04 748 001*	D04 760 000*	cp	50.00	D06 748 001*	D06 760 000*	cp
50.00	D04 768 001*	D04 780 000*	cp	50.00	D06 768 001*	D06 780 000*	cp
50.00	D04 788 001*	D04 800 000*	cp	50.00	D06 788 001*	D06 800 000*	cp

DISTRICT	TOTAL NOTES PRINTED	BLOCKS	ESTIMATED VALUE VG/F	CU	LOW OFFICIAL SERIAL NUMBER	HIGH OFFICIAL SERIAL NUMBER	
				50.00	D06 808 001*	D06 820 000*	cp
				50.00	D06 828 001*	D06 840 000*	cp
				50.00	D06 848 001*	D06 860 000*	cp
				50.00	D06 868 001*	D06 880 000*	cp
				50.00	D06 888 001*	D06 900 000*	cp
				50.00	D06 908 001*	D06 920 000*	cp
				50.00	D06 928 001*	D06 940 000*	cp
				50.00	D06 948 001*	D06 960 000*	cp
				50.00	D06 968 001*	D06 980 000*	cp
				50.00	D06 988 001*	D07 000 000*	cp
				50.00	D07 008 001*	D07 020 000*	cp
				50.00	D07 028 001*	D07 040 000*	cp
				25.00	D07 040 001*	D07 680 000*	cp
5	E RICHMOND	E--A		22.50	E00 000 001A	E99 840 000A	cp
		E--B		22.50	E00 000 001B	E99 840 000B	cp
		E--C		22.50	E00 000 001C	E58 880 000C	cp
		E--*		25.00	E00 000 001*	E00 640 000*	cv
				50.00	E00 652 001*	E00 660 000*	cv
				50.00	E00 672 001*	E00 680 000*	cv
				50.00	E00 692 001*	E00 700 000*	cv
				50.00	E00 712 001*	E00 720 000*	cv
				50.00	E00 732 001*	E00 740 000*	cv
				50.00	E00 752 001*	E00 760 000*	cv
				50.00	E00 772 001*	E00 780 000*	cv
				50.00	E00 792 001*	E00 800 000*	cv
				50.00	E00 812 001*	E00 820 000*	cv
				50.00	E00 832 001*	E00 840 000*	cv
				50.00	E00 852 001*	E00 860 000*	cv
				50.00	E00 872 001*	E00 880 000*	cv
				50.00	E00 892 001*	E00 900 000*	cv
				50.00	E00 912 001*	E00 920 000*	cv
				50.00	E00 932 001*	E00 940 000*	cv
				50.00	E00 952 001*	E00 960 000*	cv
				50.00	E00 972 001*	E00 980 000*	cv
				50.00	E00 992 001*	E01 000 000*	cv
				50.00	E01 012 001*	E01 020 000*	cv
				50.00	E01 032 001*	E01 040 000*	cv
				50.00	E01 052 001*	E01 060 000*	cv
				50.00	E01 072 001*	E01 080 000*	cv
				50.00	E01 092 001*	E01 100 000*	cv
				50.00	E01 112 001*	E01 120 000*	cv
				50.00	E01 132 001*	E01 140 000*	cv
				50.00	E01 152 001*	E01 160 000*	cv
				50.00	E01 172 001*	E01 180 000*	cv
				50.00	E01 192 001*	E01 200 000*	cv
				50.00	E01 212 001*	E01 220 000*	cv
				50.00	E01 232 001*	E01 240 000*	cv
				50.00	E01 252 001*	E01 260 000*	cv
				50.00	E01 272 001*	E01 280 000*	cv
				25.00	E01 280 001*	E01 920 000*	cp
				50.00	E01 932 001*	E01 940 000*	cp
				50.00	E01 952 001*	E01 960 000*	cp
				50.00	E01 972 001*	E01 980 000*	cp
				50.00	E01 992 001*	E02 000 000*	cp
				50.00	E02 012 001*	E02 020 000*	cp
				50.00	E02 032 001*	E02 040 000*	cp
				50.00	E02 052 001*	E02 060 000*	cp
				50.00	E02 072 001*	E02 080 000*	cp
				50.00	E02 092 001*	E02 100 000*	cp
				50.00	E02 112 001*	E02 120 000*	cp
				50.00	E02 132 001*	E02 140 000*	cp
				50.00	E02 152 001*	E02 160 000*	cp
				50.00	E02 172 001*	E02 180 000*	cp
				50.00	E02 192 001*	E02 200 000*	cp
				50.00	E02 212 001*	E02 220 000*	cp
				50.00	E02 232 001*	E02 240 000*	cp
				50.00	E02 252 001*	E02 260 000*	cp
				50.00	E02 272 001*	E02 280 000*	cp
				50.00	E02 292 001*	E02 300 000*	cp

DISTRICT	TOTAL NOTES PRINTED	BLOCKS	ESTIMATED VALUE VG/F	CU	LOW OFFICIAL SERIAL NUMBER	HIGH OFFICIAL SERIAL NUMBER	
				50.00	E02 312 001*	E02 320 000*	cp
				50.00	E02 332 001*	E02 340 000*	cp
				50.00	E02 352 001*	E02 360 000*	cp
				50.00	E02 372 001*	E02 380 000*	cp
				50.00	E02 392 001*	E02 400 000*	cp
				50.00	E02 412 001*	E02 420 000*	cp
				50.00	E02 432 001*	E02 440 000*	cp
				50.00	E02 452 001*	E02 460 000*	cp
				50.00	E02 472 001*	E02 480 000*	cp
				50.00	E02 492 001*	E02 500 000*	cp
				50.00	E02 512 001*	E02 520 000*	cp
				50.00	E02 532 001*	E02 540 000*	cp
				50.00	E02 552 001*	E02 560 000*	cp
				25.00	E02 560 001*	E07 040 000*	cp
6	F ATLANTA	F--A		22.50	F00 000 001A	F70 400 000A	cp
		F--*		25.00	F00 000 001	F01 280 000*	cv
				50.00	F01 296 001*	F01 300 000*	cv
				50.00	F01 316 001*	F01 320 000*	cv
				50.00	F01 336 001*	F01 340 000*	cv
				50.00	F01 356 001*	F01 360 000*	cv
				50.00	F01 376 001*	F01 380 000*	cv
				50.00	F01 396 001*	F01 400 000*	cv
				50.00	F01 416 001*	F01 420 000*	cv
				50.00	F01 436 001*	F01 440 000*	cv
				50.00	F01 456 001*	F01 460 000*	cv
				50.00	F01 476 001*	F01 480 000*	cv
				50.00	F01 496 001*	F01 500 000*	cv
				50.00	F01 516 001*	F01 520 000*	cv
				50.00	F01 536 001*	F01 540 000*	cv
				50.00	F01 556 001*	F01 560 000*	cv
				50.00	F01 576 001*	F01 580 000*	cv
				50.00	F01 596 001*	F01 600 000*	cv
				50.00	F01 616 001*	F01 620 000*	cv
				50.00	F01 636 001*	F01 640 000*	cv
				50.00	F01 656 001*	F01 660 000*	cv
				50.00	F01 676 001*	F01 680 000*	cv
				50.00	F01 696 001*	F01 700 000*	cv
				50.00	F01 716 001*	F01 720 000*	cv
				50.00	F01 736 001*	F01 740 000*	cv
				50.00	F01 756 001*	F01 760 000*	cv
				50.00	F01 776 001*	F01 780 000*	cv
				50.00	F01 796 001*	F01 800 000*	cv
				50.00	F01 816 001*	F01 820 000*	cv
				50.00	F01 836 001*	F01 840 000*	cv
				50.00	F01 856 001*	F01 860 000*	cv
				50.00	F01 876 001*	F01 880 000*	cv
				50.00	F01 896 001*	F01 900 000*	cv
				50.00	F01 916 001*	F01 920 000*	cv
				50.00	F01 932 001*	F01 940 000*	cp
				50.00	F01 952 001*	F01 960 000*	cp
				50.00	F01 972 001*	F01 980 000*	cp
				50.00	F01 992 001*	F02 000 000*	cp
				50.00	F02 012 001*	F02 020 000*	cp
				50.00	F02 032 001*	F02 040 000*	cp
				50.00	F02 052 001*	F02 060 000*	cp
				50.00	F02 072 001*	F02 080 000*	cp
				50.00	F02 092 001*	F02 100 000*	cp
				50.00	F02 112 001*	F02 120 000*	cp
				50.00	F02 132 001*	F02 140 000*	cp
				50.00	F02 152 001*	F02 160 000*	cp
				50.00	F02 172 001*	F02 180 000*	cp
				50.00	F02 192 001*	F02 200 000*	cp
				50.00	F02 212 001*	F02 220 000*	cp
				50.00	F02 232 001*	F02 240 000*	cp
				50.00	F02 252 001*	F02 260 000*	cp
				50.00	F02 272 001*	F02 280 000*	cp
				50.00	F02 292 001*	F02 300 000*	cp
				50.00	F02 312 001*	F02 320 000*	cp
				50.00	F02 332 001*	F02 340 000*	cp

DISTRICT	TOTAL NOTES PRINTED	BLOCKS	ESTIMATED VALUE VG/F	VALUE CU	LOW OFFICIAL SERIAL NUMBER	HIGH OFFICIAL SERIAL NUMBER	
				50.00	F02 352 001*	F02 360 000*	cp
				50.00	F02 372 001*	F02 380 000*	cp
				50.00	F02 392 001*	F02 400 000*	cp
				50.00	F02 412 001*	F02 420 000*	cp
				50.00	F02 432 001*	F02 440 000*	cp
				50.00	F02 452 001*	F02 460 000*	cp
				50.00	F02 472 001*	F02 480 000*	cp
				50.00	F02 492 001*	F02 500 000*	cp
				50.00	F02 512 001*	F02 520 000*	cp
				50.00	F02 532 001*	F02 540 000*	cp
				50.00	F02 552 001*	F02 560 000*	cp
				50.00	F02 568 001*	F02 580 000*	cp
				50.00	F02 588 001*	F02 600 000*	cp
				50.00	F02 608 001*	F02 620 000*	cp
				50.00	F02 628 001*	F02 640 000*	cp
				50.00	F02 648 001*	F02 660 000*	cp
				50.00	F02 668 001*	F02 680 000*	cp
				50.00	F02 688 001*	F02 700 000*	cp
				50.00	F02 708 001*	F02 720 000*	cp
				50.00	F02 728 001*	F02 740 000*	cp
				50.00	F02 748 001*	F02 760 000*	cp
				50.00	F02 768 001*	F02 780 000*	cp
				50.00	F02 788 001*	F02 800 000*	cp
				50.00	F02 808 001*	F02 820 000*	cp
				50.00	F02 828 001*	F02 840 000*	cp
				50.00	F02 848 001*	F02 860 000*	cp
				50.00	F02 868 001*	F02 880 000*	cp
				50.00	F02 888 001*	F02 900 000*	cp
				50.00	F02 908 001*	F02 920 000*	cp
				50.00	F02 928 001*	F02 940 000*	cp
				50.00	F02 948 001*	F02 960 000*	cp
				50.00	F02 968 001*	F02 980 000*	cp
				50.00	F02 988 001*	F03 000 000*	cp
				50.00	F03 008 001*	F03 020 000*	cp
				50.00	F03 028 001*	F03 040 000*	cp
				50.00	F03 048 001*	F03 060 000*	cp
				50.00	F03 068 001*	F03 080 000*	cp
				50.00	F03 088 001*	F03 100 000*	cp
				50.00	F03 108 001*	F03 120 000*	cp
				50.00	F03 128 001*	F03 140 000*	cp
				50.00	F03 148 001*	F03 160 000*	cp
				50.00	F03 168 001*	F03 180 000*	cp
				50.00	F03 188 001*	F03 200 000*	cp
				25.00	F03 200 001*	F03 840 000*	cp
7	G CHICAGO	G--A		22.50	G00 000 001A	G99 840 000A	cp
		G--B		22.50	G00 000 001B	G99 840 000B	cp
		G--C		22.50	G00 000 001C	G99 840 000C	cp
		G--D		22.50	G00 000 001D	G58 880 000D	cp
		G--*		50.00	G00 012 001*	G00 020 000*	cv
				50.00	G00 032 001*	G00 040 000*	cv
				50.00	G00 052 001*	G00 060 000*	cv
				50.00	G00 072 001*	G00 080 000*	cv
				50.00	G00 092 001*	G00 100 000*	cv
				50.00	G00 112 001*	G00 120 000*	cv
				50.00	G00 132 001*	G00 140 000*	cv
				50.00	G00 152 001*	G00 160 000*	cv
				50.00	G00 172 001*	G00 180 000*	cv
				50.00	G00 192 001*	G00 200 000*	cv
				50.00	G00 212 001*	G00 220 000*	cv
				50.00	G00 232 001*	G00 240 000*	cv
				50.00	G00 252 001*	G00 260 000*	cv
				50.00	G00 272 001*	G00 280 000*	cv
				50.00	G00 292 001*	G00 300 000*	cv
				50.00	G00 312 001*	G00 320 000*	cv
				50.00	G00 332 001*	G00 340 000*	cv
				50.00	G00 352 001*	G00 360 000*	cv
				50.00	G00 372 001*	G00 380 000*	cv
				50.00	G00 392 001*	G00 400 000*	cv
				50.00	G00 412 001*	G00 420 000*	cv

DISTRICT	TOTAL NOTES PRINTED	BLOCKS	ESTIMATED VALUE VG/F	CU	LOW OFFICIAL SERIAL NUMBER	HIGH OFFICIAL SERIAL NUMBER	
				50.00	G00 432 001*	G00 440 000*	cv
				50.00	G00 452 001*	G00 460 000*	cv
				50.00	G00 472 001*	G00 480 000*	cv
				50.00	G00 492 001*	G00 500 000*	cv
				50.00	G00 512 001*	G00 520 000*	cv
				50.00	G00 532 001*	G00 540 000*	cv
				50.00	G00 552 001*	G00 560 000*	cv
				50.00	G00 572 001*	G00 580 000*	cv
				50.00	G00 592 001*	G00 600 000*	cv
				50.00	G00 612 001*	G00 620 000*	cv
				50.00	G00 632 001*	G00 640 000*	cv
				50.00	G00 648 001*	G00 660 000*	cv
				50.00	G00 668 001*	G00 680 000*	cv
				50.00	G00 688 001*	G00 700 000*	cv
				50.00	G00 708 001*	G00 720 000*	cv
				50.00	G00 728 001*	G00 740 000*	cv
				50.00	G00 748 001*	G00 760 000*	cv
				50.00	G00 768 001*	G00 780 000*	cv
				50.00	G00 788 001*	G00 800 000*	cv
				50.00	G00 808 001*	G00 820 000*	cv
				50.00	G00 828 001*	G00 840 000*	cv
				50.00	G00 848 001*	G00 860 000*	cv
				50.00	G00 868 001*	G00 880 000*	cv
				50.00	G00 888 001*	G00 900 000*	cv
				50.00	G00 908 001*	G00 920 000*	cv
				50.00	G00 928 001*	G00 940 000*	cv
				50.00	G00 948 001*	G00 960 000*	cv
				50.00	G00 968 001*	G00 980 000*	cv
				50.00	G00 988 001*	G01 000 000*	cv
				50.00	G01 008 001*	G01 020 000*	cv
				50.00	G01 028 001*	G01 040 000*	cv
				50.00	G01 048 001*	G01 060 000*	cv
				50.00	G01 068 001*	G01 080 000*	cv
				50.00	G01 088 001*	G01 100 000*	cv
				50.00	G01 108 001*	G01 120 000*	cv
				50.00	G01 128 001*	G01 140 000*	cv
				50.00	G01 148 001*	G01 160 000*	cv
				50.00	G01 168 001*	G01 180 000*	cv
				50.00	G01 188 001*	G01 200 000*	cv
				50.00	G01 208 001*	G01 220 000*	cv
				50.00	G01 228 001*	G01 240 000*	cv
				50.00	G01 248 001*	G01 260 000*	cv
				50.00	G01 268 001*	G01 280 000*	cv
				50.00	G01 292 001*	G01 300 000*	cv
				50.00	G01 312 001*	G01 320 000*	cv
				50.00	G01 332 001*	G01 340 000*	cv
				50.00	G01 352 001*	G01 360 000*	cv
				50.00	G01 372 001*	G01 380 000*	cv
				50.00	G01 392 001*	G01 400 000*	cv
				50.00	G01 412 001*	G01 420 000*	cv
				50.00	G01 432 001*	G01 440 000*	cv
				50.00	G01 452 001*	G01 460 000*	cv
				50.00	G01 472 001*	G01 480 000*	cv
				50.00	G01 492 001*	G01 500 000*	cv
				50.00	G01 512 001*	G01 520 000*	cv
				50.00	G01 532 001*	G01 540 000*	cv
				50.00	G01 552 001*	G01 560 000*	cv
				50.00	G01 572 001*	G01 580 000*	cv
				50.00	G01 592 001*	G01 600 000*	cv
				50.00	G01 612 001*	G01 620 000*	cv
				50.00	G01 632 001*	G01 640 000*	cv
				50.00	G01 652 001*	G01 660 000*	cv
				50.00	G01 672 001*	G01 680 000*	cv
				50.00	G01 692 001*	G01 700 000*	cv
				50.00	G01 712 001*	G01 720 000*	cv
				50.00	G01 732 001*	G01 740 000*	cv
				50.00	G01 752 001*	G01 760 000*	cv
				50.00	G01 772 001*	G01 780 000*	cv
				50.00	G01 792 001*	G01 800 000*	cv

VALUE CU	LOW OFFICIAL SERIAL NUMBER	HIGH OFFICIAL SERIAL NUMBER		VALUE CU	LOW OFFICIAL SERIAL NUMBER	HIGH OFFICIAL SERIAL NUMBER	
50.00	G01 812 001*	G01 820 000*	cv	50.00	G03 188 001*	G03 200 000*	cv
50.00	G01 832 001*	G01 840 000*	cv	25.00	G03 200 001*	G05 120 000*	cp
50.00	G01 852 001*	G01 860 000*	cv	50.00	G05 128 001*	G05 140 000*	cp
50.00	G01 872 001*	G01 880 000*	cv	50.00	G05 148 001*	G05 160 000*	cp
50.00	G01 892 001*	G01 900 000*	cv	50.00	G05 168 001*	G05 180 000*	cp
50.00	G01 912 001*	G01 920 000*	cv	50.00	G05 188 001*	G05 200 000*	cp
50.00	G01 932 001*	G01 940 000*	cv	50.00	G05 208 001*	G05 220 000*	cp
50.00	G01 952 001*	G01 960 000*	cv	50.00	G05 228 001*	G05 240 000*	cp
50.00	G01 972 001*	G01 980 000*	cv	50.00	G05 248 001*	G05 260 000*	cp
50.00	G01 992 001*	G02 000 000*	cv	50.00	G05 268 001*	G05 280 000*	cp
50.00	G02 012 001*	G02 020 000*	cv	50.00	G05 288 001*	G05 300 000*	cp
50.00	G02 032 001*	G02 040 000*	cv	50.00	G05 308 001*	G05 320 000*	cp
50.00	G02 052 001*	G02 060 000*	cv	50.00	G05 328 001*	G05 340 000*	cp
50.00	G02 072 001*	G02 080 000*	cv	50.00	G05 348 001*	G05 360 000*	cp
50.00	G02 092 001*	G02 100 000*	cv	50.00	G05 368 001*	G05 380 000*	cp
50.00	G02 112 001*	G02 120 000*	cv	50.00	G05 388 001*	G05 400 000*	cp
50.00	G02 132 001*	G02 140 000*	cv	50.00	G05 408 001*	G05 420 000*	cp
50.00	G02 152 001*	G02 160 000*	cv	50.00	G05 428 001*	G05 440 000*	cp
50.00	G02 172 001*	G02 180 000*	cv	50.00	G05 448 001*	G05 460 000*	cp
50.00	G02 192 001*	G02 200 000*	cv	50.00	G05 468 001*	G05 480 000*	cp
50.00	G02 212 001*	G02 220 000*	cv	50.00	G05 488 001*	G05 500 000*	cp
50.00	G02 232 001*	G02 240 000*	cv	50.00	G05 508 001*	G05 520 000*	cp
50.00	G02 252 001*	G02 260 000*	cv	50.00	G05 528 001*	G05 540 000*	cp
50.00	G02 272 001*	G02 280 000*	cv	50.00	G05 548 001*	G05 560 000*	cp
50.00	G02 292 001*	G02 300 000*	cv	50.00	G05 568 001*	G05 580 000*	cp
50.00	G02 312 001*	G02 320 000*	cv	50.00	G05 588 001*	G05 600 000*	cp
50.00	G02 332 001*	G02 340 000*	cv	50.00	G05 608 001*	G05 620 000*	cp
50.00	G02 352 001*	G02 360 000*	cv	50.00	G05 628 001*	G05 640 000*	cp
50.00	G02 372 001*	G02 380 000*	cv	50.00	G05 648 001*	G05 660 000*	cp
50.00	G02 392 001*	G02 400 000*	cv	50.00	G05 668 001*	G05 680 000*	cp
50.00	G02 412 001*	G02 420 000*	cv	50.00	G05 688 001*	G05 700 000*	cp
50.00	G02 432 001*	G02 440 000*	cv	50.00	G05 708 001*	G05 720 000*	cp
50.00	G02 452 001*	G02 460 000*	cv	50.00	G05 728 001*	G05 740 000*	cp
50.00	G02 472 001*	G02 480 000*	cv	50.00	G05 748 001*	G05 760 000*	cp
50.00	G02 492 001*	G02 500 000*	cv	50.00	G05 776 001*	G05 780 000*	cp
50.00	G02 512 001*	G02 520 000*	cv	50.00	G05 796 001*	G05 800 000*	cp
50.00	G02 532 001*	G02 540 000*	cv	50.00	G05 816 001*	G05 820 000*	cp
50.00	G02 552 001*	G02 560 000*	cv	50.00	G05 836 001*	G05 840 000*	cp
50.00	G02 568 001*	G02 580 000*	cv	50.00	G05 856 001*	G05 860 000*	cp
50.00	G02 588 001*	G02 600 000*	cv	50.00	G05 876 001*	G05 880 000*	cp
50.00	G02 608 001*	G02 620 000*	cv	50.00	G05 896 001*	G05 900 000*	cp
50.00	G02 628 001*	G02 640 000*	cv	50.00	G05 916 001*	G05 920 000*	cp
50.00	G02 648 001*	G02 660 000*	cv	50.00	G05 936 001*	G05 940 000*	cp
50.00	G02 668 001*	G02 680 000*	cv	50.00	G05 956 001*	G05 960 000*	cp
50.00	G02 688 001*	G02 700 000*	cv	50.00	G05 976 001*	G05 980 000*	cp
50.00	G02 708 001*	G02 720 000*	cv	50.00	G05 996 001*	G06 000 000*	cp
50.00	G02 728 001*	G02 740 000*	cv	50.00	G06 016 001*	G06 020 000*	cp
50.00	G02 748 001*	G02 760 000*	cv	50.00	G06 036 001*	G06 040 000*	cp
50.00	G02 768 001*	G02 780 000*	cv	50.00	G06 056 001*	G06 060 000*	cp
50.00	G02 788 001*	G02 800 000*	cv	50.00	G06 076 001*	G06 080 000*	cp
50.00	G02 808 001*	G02 820 000*	cv	50.00	G06 096 001*	G06 100 000*	cp
50.00	G02 828 001*	G02 840 000*	cv	50.00	G06 116 001*	G06 120 000*	cp
50.00	G02 848 001*	G02 860 000*	cv	50.00	G06 136 001*	G06 140 000*	cp
50.00	G02 868 001*	G02 880 000*	cv	50.00	G06 156 001*	G06 160 000*	cp
50.00	G02 888 001*	G02 900 000*	cv	50.00	G06 176 001*	G06 180 000*	cp
50.00	G02 908 001*	G02 920 000*	cv	50.00	G06 196 001*	G06 200 000*	cp
50.00	G02 928 001*	G02 940 000*	cv	50.00	G06 216 001*	G06 220 000*	cp
50.00	G02 948 001*	G02 960 000*	cv	50.00	G06 236 001*	G06 240 000*	cp
50.00	G02 968 001*	G02 980 000*	cv	50.00	G06 256 001*	G06 260 000*	cp
50.00	G02 988 001*	G03 000 000*	cv	50.00	G06 276 001*	G06 280 000*	cp
50.00	G03 008 001*	G03 020 000*	cv	50.00	G06 296 001*	G06 300 000*	cp
50.00	G03 028 001*	G03 040 000*	cv	50.00	G06 316 001*	G06 320 000*	cp
50.00	G03 048 001*	G03 060 000*	cv	50.00	G06 336 001*	G06 340 000*	cp
50.00	G03 068 001*	G03 080 000*	cv	50.00	G06 356 001*	G06 360 000*	cp
50.00	G03 088 001*	G03 100 000*	cv	50.00	G06 376 001*	G06 380 000*	cp
50.00	G03 108 001*	G03 120 000*	cv	50.00	G06 396 001*	G06 400 000*	cp
50.00	G03 128 001*	G03 140 000*	cv	25.00	G06 400 001*	G07 040 000*	cp
50.00	G03 148 001*	G03 160 000*	cv	50.00	G07 048 001*	G07 060 000*	cp
50.00	G03 168 001*	G03 180 000*	cv	50.00	G07 068 001*	G07 080 000*	cp

DISTRICT	TOTAL NOTES PRINTED	BLOCKS	ESTIMATED VALUE VG/F	CU	LOW OFFICIAL SERIAL NUMBER	HIGH OFFICIAL SERIAL NUMBER	
				50.00	G07 088 001*	G07 100 000*	cp
				50.00	G07 108 001*	G07 120 000*	cp
				50.00	G07 128 001*	G07 140 000*	cp
				50.00	G07 148 001*	G07 160 000*	cp
				50.00	G07 168 001*	G07 180 000*	cp
				50.00	G07 188 001*	G07 200 000*	cp
				50.00	G07 208 001*	G07 220 000*	cp
				50.00	G07 228 001*	G07 240 000*	cp
				50.00	G07 248 001*	G07 260 000*	cp
				50.00	G07 268 001*	G07 280 000*	cp
				50.00	G07 288 001*	G07 300 000*	cp
				50.00	G07 308 001*	G07 320 000*	cp
				50.00	G07 328 001*	G07 340 000*	cp
				50.00	G07 348 001*	G07 360 000*	cp
				50.00	G07 368 001*	G07 380 000*	cp
				50.00	G07 388 001*	G07 400 000*	cp
				50.00	G07 408 001*	G07 420 000*	cp
				50.00	G07 428 001*	G07 440 000*	cp
				50.00	G07 448 001*	G07 460 000*	cp
				50.00	G07 468 001*	G07 480 000*	cp
				50.00	G07 488 001*	G07 500 000*	cp
				50.00	G07 508 001*	G07 520 000*	cp
				50.00	G07 528 001*	G07 540 000*	cp
				50.00	G07 548 001*	G07 560 000*	cp
				50.00	G07 568 001*	G07 580 000*	cp
				50.00	G07 588 001*	G07 600 000*	cp
				50.00	G07 608 001*	G07 620 000*	cp
				50.00	G07 628 001*	G07 640 000*	cp
				50.00	G07 648 001*	G07 660 000*	cp
				50.00	G07 668 001*	G07 680 000*	cp
				25.00	G07 680 001*	G10 240 000*	cp
8	H ST. LOUIS	H--A		22.50	H00 000 001A	H98 560 000A	cp
		H--*		50.00	H00 012 001*	H00 020 000*	cv
				50.00	H00 032 001*	H00 040 000*	cv
				50.00	H00 052 001*	H00 060 000*	cv
				50.00	H00 072 001*	H00 080 000*	cv
				50.00	H00 092 001*	H00 100 000*	cv
				50.00	H00 132 001*	H00 120 000*	cv
				50.00	H00 132 001*	H00 140 000*	cv
				50.00	H00 152 001*	H00 160 000*	cv
				50.00	H00 172 001*	H00 180 000*	cv
				50.00	H00 192 001*	H00 200 000*	cv
				50.00	H00 212 001*	H00 220 000*	cv
				50.00	H00 232 001*	H00 240 000*	cv
				50.00	H00 252 001*	H00 260 000*	cv
				50.00	H00 272 001*	H00 280 000*	cv
				50.00	H00 292 001*	H00 300 000*	cv
				50.00	H00 312 001*	H00 320 000*	cv
				50.00	H00 332 001*	H00 340 000*	cv
				50.00	H00 352 001*	H00 360 000*	cv
				50.00	H00 372 001*	H00 380 000*	cv
				50.00	H00 392 001*	H00 400 000*	cv
				50.00	H00 412 001*	H00 420 000*	cv
				50.00	H00 432 001*	H00 440 000*	cv
				50.00	H00 452 001*	H00 460 000*	cv
				50.00	H00 472 001*	H00 480 000*	cv
				50.00	H00 492 001*	H00 500 000*	cv
				50.00	H00 512 001*	H00 520 000*	cv
				50.00	H00 532 001*	H00 540 000*	cv
				50.00	H00 552 001*	H00 560 000*	cv
				50.00	H00 572 001*	H00 580 000*	cv
				50.00	H00 592 001*	H00 600 000*	cv
				50.00	H00 612 001*	H00 620 000*	cv
				50.00	H00 632 001*	H00 640 000*	cv
				25.00	H00 640 001*	H01 280 000*	cv
				25.00	H01 280 001*	H01 920 000*	cp
				50.00	H01 936 001*	H01 940 000*	cp
				50.00	H01 956 001*	H01 960 000*	cp
				50.00	H01 976 001*	H01 980 000*	cp

DISTRICT	TOTAL NOTES PRINTED	BLOCKS	ESTIMATED VALUE VG/F	VALUE CU	LOW OFFICIAL SERIAL NUMBER	HIGH OFFICIAL SERIAL NUMBER	
				50.00	H01 996 001*	H02 000 000*	cp
				50.00	H02 016 001*	H02 020 000*	cp
				50.00	H02 036 001*	H02 040 000*	cp
				50.00	H02 056 001*	H02 060 000*	cp
				50.00	H02 076 001*	H02 080 000*	cp
				50.00	H02 096 001*	H02 100 000*	cp
				50.00	H02 116 001*	H02 120 000*	cp
				50.00	H02 136 001*	H02 140 000*	cp
				50.00	H02 156 001*	H02 160 000*	cp
				50.00	H02 176 001*	H02 180 000*	cp
				50.00	H02 196 001*	H02 200 000*	cp
				50.00	H02 216 001*	H02 220 000*	cp
				50.00	H02 236 001*	H02 240 000*	cp
				50.00	H02 256 001*	H02 260 000*	cp
				50.00	H02 276 001*	H02 280 000*	cp
				50.00	H02 296 001*	H02 300 000*	cp
				50.00	H02 316 001*	H02 320 000*	cp
				50.00	H02 336 001*	H02 340 000*	cp
				50.00	H02 356 001*	H02 360 000*	cp
				50.00	H02 376 001*	H02 380 000*	cp
				50.00	H02 396 001*	H02 400 000*	cp
				50.00	H02 416 001*	H02 420 000*	cp
				50.00	H02 436 001*	H02 440 000*	cp
				50.00	H02 456 001*	H02 460 000*	cp
				50.00	H02 476 001*	H02 480 000*	cp
				50.00	H02 496 001*	H02 500 000*	cp
				50.00	H02 516 001*	H02 520 000*	cp
				50.00	H02 536 001*	H02 540 000*	cp
				50.00	H02 556 001*	H02 560 000*	cp
				50.00	H02 576 001*	H02 580 000*	cp
				50.00	H02 596 001*	H02 600 000*	cp
				50.00	H02 616 001*	H02 620 000*	cp
				50.00	H02 636 001*	H02 640 000*	cp
				50.00	H02 656 001*	H02 660 000*	cp
				50.00	H02 676 001*	H02 680 000*	cp
				50.00	H02 696 001*	H02 700 000*	cp
				50.00	H02 716 001*	H02 720 000*	cp
				50.00	H02 736 001*	H02 740 000*	cp
				50.00	H02 756 001*	H02 760 000*	cp
				50.00	H02 776 001*	H02 780 000*	cp
				50.00	H02 796 001*	H02 800 000*	cp
				50.00	H02 816 001*	H02 820 000*	cp
				50.00	H02 836 001*	H02 840 000*	cp
				50.00	H02 856 001*	H02 860 000*	cp
				50.00	H02 876 001*	H02 880 000*	cp
				50.00	H02 896 001*	H02 900 000*	cp
				50.00	H02 916 001*	H02 920 000*	cp
				50.00	H02 936 001*	H02 940 000*	cp
				50.00	H02 956 001*	H02 960 000*	cp
				50.00	H02 976 001*	H02 980 000*	cp
				50.00	H02 996 001*	H03 000 000*	cp
				50.00	H03 016 001*	H03 020 000*	cp
				50.00	H03 036 001*	H03 040 000*	cp
				50.00	H03 056 001*	H03 060 000*	cp
				50.00	H03 076 001*	H03 080 000*	cp
				50.00	H03 096 001*	H03 100 000*	cp
				50.00	H03 116 001*	H03 120 000*	cp
				50.00	H03 136 001*	H03 140 000*	cp
				50.00	H03 156 001*	H03 160 000*	cp
				50.00	H03 176 001*	H03 180 000*	cp
				50.00	H03 196 001*	H03 200 000*	cp
9	I MINNEAPOLIS	I--A		22.50	I00 000 001A	I15 360 000A	cp
		I--*		50.00	I00 008 001*	I00 020 000*	cv
				50.00	I00 028 001*	I00 040 000*	cv
				50.00	I00 048 001*	I00 060 000*	cv
				50.00	I00 068 001*	I00 080 000*	cv
				50.00	I00 088 001*	I00 100 000*	cv
				50.00	I00 108 001*	I00 120 000*	cv
				50.00	I00 128 001*	I00 140 000*	cv

255

DISTRICT	TOTAL NOTES PRINTED	BLOCKS	ESTIMATED VALUE VG/F	CU	LOW OFFICIAL SERIAL NUMBER	HIGH OFFICIAL SERIAL NUMBER	
				50.00	I00 148 001*	I00 160 000*	cv
				50.00	I00 168 001*	I00 180 000*	cv
				50.00	I00 188 001*	I00 200 000*	cv
				50.00	I00 208 001*	I00 220 000*	cv
				50.00	I00 228 001*	I00 240 000*	cv
				50.00	I00 248 001*	I00 260 000*	cv
				50.00	I00 268 001*	I00 280 000*	cv
				50.00	I00 288 001*	I00 300 000*	cv
				50.00	I00 308 001*	I00 320 000*	cv
				50.00	I00 328 001*	I00 340 000*	cv
				50.00	I00 348 001*	I00 360 000*	cv
				50.00	I00 368 001*	I00 380 000*	cv
				50.00	I00 388 001*	I00 400 000*	cv
				50.00	I00 408 001*	I00 420 000*	cv
				50.00	I00 428 001*	I00 440 000*	cv
				50.00	I00 448 001*	I00 460 000*	cv
				50.00	I00 468 001*	I00 480 000*	cv
				50.00	I00 488 001*	I00 500 000*	cv
				50.00	I00 508 001*	I00 520 000*	cv
				50.00	I00 528 001*	I00 540 000*	cv
				50.00	I00 548 001*	I00 560 000*	cv
				50.00	I00 568 001*	I00 580 000*	cv
				50.00	I00 588 001*	I00 600 000*	cv
				50.00	I00 608 001*	I00 620 000*	cv
				50.00	I00 628 001*	I00 640 000*	cv
				50.00	I00 656 001*	I00 660 000*	cp
				50.00	I00 676 001*	I00 680 000*	cp
				50.00	I00 696 001*	I00 700 000*	cp
				50.00	I00 716 001*	I00 720 000*	cp
				50.00	I00 736 001*	I00 740 000*	cp
				50.00	I00 756 001*	I00 760 000*	cp
				50.00	I00 776 001*	I00 780 000*	cp
				50.00	I00 796 001*	I00 800 000*	cp
				50.00	I00 816 001*	I00 820 000*	cp
				50.00	I00 836 001*	I00 840 000*	cp
				50.00	I00 856 001*	I00 860 000*	cp
				50.00	I00 876 001*	I00 880 000*	cp
				50.00	I00 896 001*	I00 900 000*	cp
				50.00	I00 916 001*	I00 920 000*	cp
				50.00	I00 936 001*	I00 940 000*	cp
				50.00	I00 956 001*	I00 960 000*	cp
				50.00	I00 976 001*	I00 980 000*	cp
				50.00	I00 996 001*	I01 000 000*	cp
				50.00	I01 016 001*	I01 020 000*	cp
				50.00	I01 036 001*	I01 040 000*	cp
				50.00	I01 056 001*	I01 060 000*	cp
				50.00	I01 076 001*	I01 080 000*	cp
				50.00	I01 096 001*	I01 100 000*	cp
				50.00	I01 116 001*	I01 120 000*	cp
				50.00	I01 136 001*	I01 140 000*	cp
				50.00	I01 156 001*	I01 160 000*	cp
				50.00	I01 176 001*	I01 180 000*	cp
				50.00	I01 196 001*	I01 200 000*	cp
				50.00	I01 216 001*	I01 220 000*	cp
				50.00	I01 236 001*	I01 240 000*	cp
				50.00	I01 256 001*	I01 260 000*	cp
				50.00	I01 276 001*	I01 280 000*	cp
10 J KANSAS CITY		J--A		22.50	J00 000 001A	J99 840 000A	cp
		J--B		22.50	J00 000 001B	J48 640 000B	cp
		J--*		50.00	J00 008 001*	J00 020 000*	cv
				50.00	J00 028 001*	J00 040 000*	cv
				50.00	J00 048 001*	J00 060 000*	cv
				50.00	J00 068 001*	J00 080 000*	cv
				50.00	J00 088 001*	J00 100 000*	cv
				50.00	J00 108 001*	J00 120 000*	cv
				50.00	J00 128 001*	J00 140 000*	cv
				50.00	J00 148 001*	J00 160 000*	cv
				50.00	J00 168 001*	J00 180 000*	cv
				50.00	J00 188 001*	J00 200 000*	cv

VALUE CU	LOW OFFICIAL SERIAL NUMBER	HIGH OFFICIAL SERIAL NUMBER		VALUE CU	LOW OFFICIAL SERIAL NUMBER	HIGH OFFICIAL SERIAL NUMBER	
50.00	J00 208 001*	J00 220 000*	cv	50.00	J02 832 001*	J02 840 000*	cp
50.00	J00 228 001*	J00 240 000*	cv	50.00	J02 852 001*	J02 860 000*	cp
50.00	J00 248 001*	J00 260 000*	cv	50.00	J02 872 001*	J02 880 000*	cp
50.00	J00 268 001*	J00 280 000*	cv	50.00	J02 892 001*	J02 900 000*	cp
50.00	J00 288 001*	J00 300 000*	cv	50.00	J02 912 001*	J02 920 000*	cp
50.00	J00 308 001*	J00 320 000*	cv	50.00	J02 932 001*	J02 940 000*	cp
50.00	J00 328 001*	J00 340 000*	cv	50.00	J02 952 001*	J02 960 000*	cp
50.00	J00 348 001*	J00 360 000*	cv	50.00	J02 972 001*	J02 980 000*	cp
50.00	J00 368 001*	J00 380 000*	cv	50.00	J02 992 001*	J03 000 000*	cp
50.00	J00 388 001*	J00 400 000*	cv	50.00	J03 012 001*	J03 020 000*	cp
50.00	J00 408 001*	J00 420 000*	cv	50.00	J03 032 001*	J03 040 000*	cp
50.00	J00 428 001*	J00 440 000*	cv	50.00	J03 052 001*	J03 060 000*	cp
50.00	J00 448 001*	J00 460 000*	cv	50.00	J03 072 001*	J03 080 000*	cp
50.00	J00 468 001*	J00 480 000*	cv	50.00	J03 092 001*	J03 100 000*	cp
50.00	J00 488 001*	J00 500 000*	cv	50.00	J03 112 001*	J03 120 000*	cp
50.00	J00 508 001*	J00 520 000*	cv	50.00	J03 132 001*	J03 140 000*	cp
50.00	J00 528 001*	J00 540 000*	cv	50.00	J03 152 001*	J03 160 000*	cp
50.00	J00 548 001*	J00 560 000*	cv	50.00	J03 172 001*	J03 180 000*	cp
50.00	J00 568 001*	J00 580 000*	cv	50.00	J03 192 001*	J03 200 000*	cp
50.00	J00 588 001*	J00 600 000*	cv	25.00	J03 200 001*	J05 120 000*	cp
50.00	J00 608 001*	J00 620 000*	cv	50.00	J05 128 001*	J05 140 000*	cp
50.00	J00 628 001*	J00 640 000*	cv	50.00	J05 148 001*	J05 160 000*	cp
25.00	J00 640 001*	J01 280 000*	cv	50.00	J05 168 001*	J05 180 000*	cp
50.00	J01 292 001*	J01 300 00*	cv	50.00	J05 188 001*	J05 200 000*	cp
50.00	J01 312 001*	J01 320 000*	cv	50.00	J05 208 001*	J05 220 000*	cp
50.00	J01 332 001*	J01 340 000*	cv	50.00	J05 228 001*	J05 240 000*	cp
50.00	J01 352 001*	J01 360 000*	cv	50.00	J05 248 001*	J05 260 000*	cp
50.00	J01 372 001*	J01 380 000*	cv	50.00	J05 268 001*	J05 280 000*	cp
50.00	J01 392 001*	J01 400 000*	cv	50.00	J05 288 001*	J05 300 000*	cp
50.00	J01 412 001*	J01 420 000*	cv	50.00	J05 308 001*	J05 320 000*	cp
50.00	J01 432 001*	J01 440 000*	cv	50.00	J05 328 001*	J05 340 000*	cp
50.00	J01 452 001*	J01 460 000*	cv	50.00	J05 348 001*	J05 360 000*	cp
50.00	J01 472 001*	J01 480 000*	cv	50.00	J05 368 001*	J05 380 000*	cp
50.00	J01 492 001*	J01 500 000*	cv	50.00	J05 388 001*	J05 400 000*	cp
50.00	J01 512 001*	J01 520 000*	cv	50.00	J05 408 001*	J05 420 000*	cp
50.00	J01 532 001*	J01 540 000*	cv	50.00	J05 428 001*	J05 440 000*	cp
50.00	J01 552 001*	J01 560 000*	cv	50.00	J05 448 001*	J05 460 000*	cp
50.00	J01 572 001*	J01 580 000*	cv	50.00	J05 468 001*	J05 480 000*	cp
50.00	J01 592 001*	J01 600 000*	cv	50.00	J05 488 001*	J05 500 000*	cp
50.00	J01 612 001*	J01 620 000*	cv	50.00	J05 508 001*	J05 520 000*	cp
50.00	J01 632 001*	J01 640 000*	cv	50.00	J05 528 001*	J05 540 000*	cp
50.00	J01 652 001*	J01 660 000*	cv	50.00	J05 548 001*	J05 560 000*	cp
50.00	J01 672 001*	J01 680 000*	cv	50.00	J05 568 001*	J05 580 000*	cp
50.00	J01 692 001*	J01 700 000*	cv	50.00	J05 588 001*	J05 600 000*	cp
50.00	J01 712 001*	J01 720 000*	cv	50.00	J05 608 001*	J05 620 000*	cp
50.00	J01 732 001*	J02 740 000*	cv	50.00	J05 628 001*	J05 640 000*	cp
50.00	J01 752 001*	J01 760 000*	cv	50.00	J05 648 001*	J05 660 000*	cp
50.00	J01 772 001*	J01 780 000*	cv	50.00	J05 668 001*	J05 680 000*	cp
50.00	J01 792 001*	J01 800 000*	cv	50.00	J05 688 001*	J05 700 000*	cp
50.00	J01 812 001*	J01 820 000*	cv	50.00	J05 708 001*	J05 720 000*	cp
50.00	J01 832 001*	J01 840 000*	cv	50.00	J05 728 001*	J05 740 000*	cp
50.00	J01 852 001*	J01 860 000*	cv	50.00	J05 748 001*	J05 760 000*	cp
50.00	J01 872 001*	J01 880 000*	cv	50.00	J05 772 001*	J05 780 000*	cp
50.00	J01 892 001*	J01 900 000*	cv	50.00	J05 792 001*	J05 800 000*	cp
50.00	J01 912 001*	J01 920 000*	cv	50.00	J05 812 001*	J05 820 000*	cp
25.00	J01 920 001*	J02 560 000*	cv	50.00	J05 832 001*	J05 840 000*	cp
50.00	J02 572 001*	J02 580 000*	cp	50.00	J05 852 001*	J05 860 000*	cp
50.00	J02 592 001*	J02 600 000*	cp	50.00	J05 872 001*	J05 880 000*	cp
50.00	J02 612 001*	J02 620 000*	cp	50.00	J05 892 001*	J05 900 000*	cp
50.00	J02 632 001*	J02 640 000*	cp	50.00	J05 912 001*	J05 920 000*	cp
50.00	J02 652 001*	J02 660 000*	cp	50.00	J05 932 001*	J05 940 000*	cp
50.00	J02 672 001*	J02 680 000*	cp	50.00	J05 952 001*	J05 960 000*	cp
50.00	J02 692 001*	J02 700 000*	cp	50.00	J05 972 001*	J05 980 000*	cp
50.00	J02 712 001*	J02 720 000*	cp	50.00	J05 992 001*	J06 000 000*	cp
50.00	J02 732 001*	J02 740 000*	cp	50.00	J06 012 001*	J06 020 000*	cp
50.00	J02 752 001*	J02 760 000*	cp	50.00	J06 032 001*	J06 040 000*	cp
50.00	J02 772 001*	J02 780 000*	cp	50.00	J06 052 001*	J06 060 000*	cp
50.00	J02 792 001*	J02 800 000*	cp	50.00	J06 072 001*	J06 080 000*	cp
50.00	J02 812 001*	J02 820 000*	cp	50.00	J06 092 001*	J06 100 000*	cp

DISTRICT	TOTAL NOTES PRINTED	BLOCKS	ESTIMATED VALUE VG/F	VALUE CU	LOW OFFICIAL SERIAL NUMBER	HIGH OFFICIAL SERIAL NUMBER	
				50.00	J06 112 001*	J06 120 000*	cp
				50.00	J06 132 001*	J06 140 000*	cp
				50.00	J06 152 001*	J06 160 000*	cp
				50.00	J06 172 001*	J06 180 000*	cp
				50.00	J06 192 001*	J06 200 000*	cp
				50.00	J06 212 001*	J06 220 000*	cp
				50.00	J06 232 001*	J06 240 000*	cp
				50.00	J06 252 001*	J06 260 000*	cp
				50.00	J06 272 001*	J06 280 000*	cp
				50.00	J06 292 001*	J06 300 000*	cp
				50.00	J06 312 001*	J06 320 000*	cp
				50.00	J06 332 001*	J06 340 000*	cp
				50.00	J06 352 001*	J06 360 000*	cp
				50.00	J06 372 001*	J06 380 000*	cp
				50.00	J06 392 001*	J06 400 000*	cp
11 K DALLAS		K--A		22.50	K00 000 001A	K99 840 000A	cp
		K--B		22.50	K00 000 001B	K64 000 000B	cp
		K--*		50.00	K00 008 001*	K00 020 000*	cv
				50.00	K00 028 001*	K00 040 000*	cv
				50.00	K00 048 001*	K00 060 000*	cv
				50.00	K00 068 001*	K00 080 000*	cv
				50.00	K00 088 001*	K00 100 000*	cv
				50.00	K00 108 001*	K00 120 000*	cv
				50.00	K00 128 001*	K00 140 000*	cv
				50.00	K00 148 001*	K00 160 000*	cv
				50.00	K00 168 001*	K00 180 000*	cv
				50.00	K00 188 001*	K00 200 000*	cv
				50.00	K00 208 001*	K00 220 000*	cv
				50.00	K00 228 001*	K00 240 000*	cv
				50.00	K00 248 001*	K00 260 000*	cv
				50.00	K00 268 001*	K00 280 000*	cv
				50.00	K00 288 001*	K00 300 000*	cv
				50.00	K00 308 001*	K00 320 000*	cv
				50.00	K00 328 001*	K00 340 000*	cv
				50.00	K00 348 001*	K00 360 000*	cv
				50.00	K00 368 001*	K00 380 000*	cv
				50.00	K00 388 001*	K00 400 000*	cv
				50.00	K00 408 001*	K00 420 000*	cv
				50.00	K00 428 001*	K00 440 000*	cv
				50.00	K00 448 001*	K00 460 000*	cv
				50.00	K00 468 001*	K00 480 000*	cv
				50.00	K00 488 001*	K00 500 000*	cv
				50.00	K00 508 001*	K00 520 000*	cv
				50.00	K00 528 001*	K00 540 000*	cv
				50.00	K00 548 001*	K00 560 000*	cv
				50.00	K00 568 001*	K00 580 000*	cv
				50.00	K00 588 001*	K00 600 000*	cv
				50.00	K00 608 001*	K00 620 000*	cv
				50.00	K00 628 001*	K00 640 000*	cv
				50.00	K00 656 001*	K00 660 000*	cv
				50.00	K00 676 001*	K00 680 000*	cv
				50.00	K00 696 001*	K00 700 000*	cv
				50.00	K00 716 001*	K00 720 000*	cv
				50.00	K00 736 001*	K00 740 000*	cv
				50.00	K00 756 001*	K00 760 000*	cv
				50.00	K00 776 001*	K00 780 000*	cv
				50.00	K00 796 001*	K00 800 000*	cv
				50.00	K00 816 001*	K00 820 000*	cv
				50.00	K00 836 001*	K00 840 000*	cv
				50.00	K00 856 001*	K00 860 000*	cv
				50.00	K00 876 001*	K00 880 000*	cv
				50.00	K00 896 001*	K00 900 000*	cv
				50.00	K00 916 001*	K00 920 000*	cv
				50.00	K00 936 001*	K00 940 000*	cv
				50.00	K00 956 001*	K00 960 000*	cv
				50.00	K00 976 001*	K00 980 000*	cv
				50.00	K00 996 001*	K01 000 000*	cv
				50.00	K01 016 001*	K01 020 000*	cv
				50.00	K01 036 001*	K01 040 000*	cv

DISTRICT	TOTAL NOTES PRINTED	BLOCKS	ESTIMATED VALUE VG/F	CU	LOW OFFICIAL SERIAL NUMBER	HIGH OFFICIAL SERIAL NUMBER	
				50.00	K01 056 001*	K01 060 000*	CV
				50.00	K01 076 001*	K01 080 000*	CV
				50.00	K01 096 001*	K01 100 000*	CV
				50.00	K01 116 001*	K01 120 000*	CV
				50.00	K01 136 001*	K01 140 000*	CV
				50.00	K01 156 001*	K01 160 000*	CV
				50.00	K01 176 001*	K01 180 000*	CV
				50.00	K01 196 001*	K01 200 000*	CV
				50.00	K01 216 001*	K01 220 000*	CV
				50.00	K01 236 001*	K01 240 000*	CV
				50.00	K01 256 001*	K01 260 000*	CV
				50.00	K01 276 001*	K01 280 000*	CV
				50.00	K01 292 000*	K01 300 000*	CV
				50.00	K01 312 001*	K01 320 000*	CV
				50.00	K01 332 001*	K01 340 000*	CV
				50.00	K01 352 001*	K01 360 000*	CV
				50.00	K01 372 001*	K01 380 000*	CV
				50.00	K01 392 001*	K01 400 000*	CV
				50.00	K01 412 001*	K01 420 000*	CV
				50.00	K01 432 001*	K01 440 000*	CV
				50.00	K01 452 001*	K01 460 000*	CV
				50.00	K01 472 001*	K01 480 000*	CV
				50.00	K01 492 001*	K01 500 000*	CV
				50.00	K01 512 001*	K01 520 000*	CV
				50.00	K01 532 001*	K01 540 000*	CV
				50.00	K01 552 001*	K01 560 000*	CV
				50.00	K01 572 001*	K01 580 000*	CV
				50.00	K01 592 001*	K01 600 000*	CV
				50.00	K01 612 001*	K01 620 000*	CV
				50.00	K01 632 001*	K01 640 000*	CV
				50.00	K01 652 001*	K01 660 000*	CV
				50.00	K01 672 001*	K01 680 000*	CV
				50.00	K01 692 001*	K01 700 000*	CV
				50.00	K01 712 001*	K01 720 000*	CV
				50.00	K01 732 001*	K01 740 000*	CV
				50.00	K01 752 001*	K01 760 000*	CV
				50.00	K01 772 001*	K01 780 000*	CV
				50.00	K01 792 001*	K01 800 000*	CV
				50.00	K01 812 001*	K01 820 000*	CV
				50.00	K01 832 001*	K01 840 000*	CV
				50.00	K01 852 001*	K01 860 000*	CV
				50.00	K01 872 001*	K01 880 000*	CV
				50.00	K01 892 001*	K01 900 000*	CV
				50.00	K01 912 001*	K01 920 000*	CV
				25.00	K01 920 001*	K02 560 000*	CV
				50.00	K02 576 001*	K02 580 000*	CV
				50.00	K02 596 001*	K02 600 000*	CV
				50.00	K02 616 001*	K02 620 000*	CV
				50.00	K02 636 001*	K02 640 000*	CV
				50.00	K02 656 001*	K02 660 000*	CV
				50.00	K02 676 001*	K02 680 000*	CV
				50.00	K02 696 001*	K02 700 000*	CV
				50.00	K02 716 001*	K02 720 000*	CV
				50.00	K02 736 001*	K02 740 000*	CV
				50.00	K02 756 001*	K02 760 000*	CV
				50.00	K02 776 001*	K02 780 000*	CV
				50.00	K02 796 001*	K02 800 000*	CV
				50.00	K02 816 001*	K02 820 000*	CV
				50.00	K02 836 001*	K02 840 000*	CV
				50.00	K02 856 001*	K02 860 000*	CV
				50.00	K02 876 001*	K02 880 000*	CV
				50.00	K02 896 001*	K02 900 000*	CV
				50.00	K02 916 001*	K02 920 000*	CV
				50.00	K02 936 001*	K02 940 000*	CV
				50.00	K02 956 001*	K02 960 000*	CV
				50.00	K02 976 001*	K02 980 000*	CV
				50.00	K02 996 001*	K03 000 000*	CV
				50.00	K03 016 001*	K03 020 000*	CV
				50.00	K03 036 001*	K03 040 000*	CV

DISTRICT	TOTAL NOTES PRINTED	BLOCKS	ESTIMATED VALUE VG/F	CU	LOW OFFICIAL SERIAL NUMBER	HIGH OFFICIAL SERIAL NUMBER	
				50.00	K03 056 001*	K03 060 000*	cv
				50.00	K03 076 001*	K03 080 000*	cv
				50.00	K03 096 001*	K03 100 000*	cv
				50.00	K03 116 001*	K03 120 000*	cv
				50.00	K03 136 001*	K03 140 000*	cv
				50.00	K03 156 001*	K03 160 000*	cv
				50.00	K03 176 001*	K03 180 000*	cv
				50.00	K03 196 001*	K03 200 000*	cv
				50.00	K03 208 001*	K03 220 000*	cp
				50.00	K03 228 001*	K03 240 000*	cp
				50.00	K03 248 001*	K03 260 000*	cp
				50.00	K03 268 001*	K03 280 000*	cp
				50.00	K03 288 001*	K03 300 000*	cp
				50.00	K03 308 001*	K03 320 000*	cp
				50.00	K03 328 001*	K03 340 000*	cp
				50.00	K03 348 001*	K03 360 000*	cp
				50.00	K03 368 001*	K03 380 000*	cp
				50.00	K03 388 001*	K03 400 000*	cp
				50.00	K03 408 001*	K03 420 000*	cp
				50.00	K03 428 001*	K03 440 000*	cp
				50.00	K03 448 001*	K03 460 000*	cp
				50.00	K03 468 001*	K03 480 000*	cp
				50.00	K03 488 001*	K03 500 000*	cp
				50.00	K03 508 001*	K03 520 000*	cp
				50.00	K03 528 001*	K03 540 000*	cp
				50.00	K03 548 001*	K03 560 000*	cp
				50.00	K03 568 001*	K03 580 000*	cp
				50.00	K03 588 001*	K03 600 000*	cp
				50.00	K03 608 001*	K03 620 000*	cp
				50.00	K03 628 001*	K03 640 000*	cp
				50.00	K03 648 001*	K03 660 000*	cp
				50.00	K03 668 001*	K03 680 000*	cp
				50.00	K03 688 001*	K03 700 000*	cp
				50.00	K03 708 001*	K03 720 000*	cp
				50.00	K03 728 001*	K03 740 000*	cp
				50.00	K03 748 001*	K03 760 000*	cp
				50.00	K03 768 001*	K03 780 000*	cp
				50.00	K03 788 001*	K03 800 000*	cp
				50.00	K03 808 001*	K03 820 000*	cp
				50.00	K03 828 001*	K03 840 000*	cp
				50.00	K03 852 001*	K03 860 000*	cp
				50.00	K03 872 001*	K03 880 000*	cp
				50.00	K03 892 001*	K03 900 000*	cp
				50.00	K03 912 001*	K03 920 000*	cp
				50.00	K03 932 001*	K03 940 000*	cp
				50.00	K03 952 001*	K03 960 000*	cp
				50.00	K03 972 001*	K03 980 000*	cp
				50.00	K03 992 001*	K04 000 000*	cp
				50.00	K04 012 001*	K04 020 000*	cp
				50.00	K04 032 001*	K04 040 000*	cp
				50.00	K04 052 001*	K04 060 000*	cp
				50.00	K04 072 001*	K04 080 000*	cp
				50.00	K04 092 001*	K04 100 000*	cp
				50.00	K04 112 001*	K04 120 000*	cp
				50.00	K04 132 001*	K04 140 000*	cp
				50.00	K04 152 001*	K04 160 000*	cp
				50.00	K04 172 001*	K04 180 000*	cp
				50.00	K04 192 001*	K04 200 000*	cp
				50.00	K04 212 001*	K04 220 000*	cp
				50.00	K04 232 001*	K04 240 000*	cp
				50.00	K04 252 001*	K04 260 000*	cp
				50.00	K04 272 001*	K04 280 000*	cp
				50.00	K04 292 001*	K04 300 000*	cp
				50.00	K04 312 001*	K04 320 000*	cp
				50.00	K04 332 001*	K04 340 000*	cp
				50.00	K04 352 001*	K04 360 000*	cp
				50.00	K04 372 001*	K04 380 000*	cp
				50.00	K04 392 001*	K04 400 000*	cp
				50.00	K04 412 001*	K04 420 000*	cp

DISTRICT	TOTAL NOTES PRINTED	BLOCKS	ESTIMATED VALUE VG/F	CU	LOW OFFICIAL SERIAL NUMBER	HIGH OFFICIAL SERIAL NUMBER	
				50.00	K04 432 001*	K04 440 000*	cp
				50.00	K04 452 001*	K04 460 000*	cp
				50.00	K04 472 001*	K04 480 000*	cp
				25.00	K04 480 001*	K05 760 000*	cp
12 L SAN FRANCISCO		L--A		22.50	L00 000 001A	L99 840 000A	cp
		L--B		22.50	L00 000 001B	L99 840 000B	cp
		L--C		22.50	L00 000 001C	L64 000 000C	cp
		L--*		50.00	L00 012 001*	L00 020 000*	cv
				50.00	L00 032 001*	L00 040 000*	cv
				50.00	L00 052 001*	L00 060 000*	cv
				50.00	L00 072 001*	L00 080 000*	cv
				50.00	L00 092 001*	L00 100 000*	cv
				50.00	L00 112 001*	L00 120 000*	cv
				50.00	L00 132 001*	L00 140 000*	cv
				50.00	L00 152 001*	L00 160 000*	cv
				50.00	L00 172 001*	L00 180 000*	cv
				50.00	L00 192 001*	L00 200 000*	cv
				50.00	L00 212 001*	L00 220 000*	cv
				50.00	L00 232 001*	L00 240 000*	cv
				50.00	L00 252 001*	L00 260 000*	cv
				50.00	L00 272 001*	L00 280 000*	cv
				50.00	L00 292 001*	L00 300 000*	cv
				50.00	L00 312 001*	L00 320 000*	cv
				50.00	L00 332 001*	L00 340 000*	cv
				50.00	L00 352 001*	L00 360 000*	cv
				50.00	L00 372 001*	L00 380 000*	cv
				50.00	L00 392 001*	L00 400 000*	cv
				50.00	L00 412 001*	L00 420 000*	cv
				50.00	L00 432 001*	L00 440 000*	cv
				50.00	L00 452 001*	L00 460 000*	cv
				50.00	L00 472 001*	L00 480 000*	cv
				50.00	L00 492 001*	L00 500 000*	cv
				50.00	L00 512 001*	L00 520 000*	cv
				50.00	L00 532 001*	L00 540 000*	cv
				50.00	L00 552 001*	L00 560 000*	cv
				50.00	L00 572 001*	L00 580 000*	cv
				50.00	L00 592 001*	L00 600 000*	cv
				50.00	L00 612 001*	L00 620 000*	cv
				50.00	L00 632 001*	L00 640 000*	cv
				50.00	L00 656 001*	L00 660 000*	cv
				50.00	L00 676 001*	L00 680 000*	cv
				50.00	L00 696 001*	L00 700 000*	cv
				50.00	L00 716 001*	L00 720 000*	cv
				50.00	L00 736 001*	L00 740 000*	cv
				50.00	L00 756 001*	L00 760 000*	cv
				50.00	L00 776 001*	L00 780 000*	cv
				50.00	L00 796 001*	L00 800 000*	cv
				50.00	L00 816 001*	L00 820 000*	cv
				50.00	L00 836 001*	L00 840 000*	cv
				50.00	L00 856 001*	L00 860 000*	cv
				50.00	L00 876 001*	L00 880 000*	cv
				50.00	L00 896 001*	L00 900 000*	cv
				50.00	L00 916 001*	L00 920 000*	cv
				50.00	L00 936 001*	L00 940 000*	cv
				50.00	L00 956 001*	L00 960 000*	cv
				50.00	L00 976 001*	L00 980 000*	cv
				50.00	L00 996 001*	L01 000 000*	cv
				50.00	L01 016 001*	L01 020 000*	cv
				50.00	L01 036 001*	L01 040 000*	cv
				50.00	L01 056 001*	L01 060 000*	cv
				50.00	L01 076 001*	L01 080 000*	cv
				50.00	L01 096 001*	L01 100 000*	cv
				50.00	L01 116 001*	L01 120 000*	cv
				50.00	L01 136 001*	L01 140 000*	cv
				50.00	L01 156 001*	L01 160 000*	cv
				50.00	L01 176 001*	L01 180 000*	cv
				50.00	L01 196 001*	L01 200 000*	cv
				50.00	L01 216 001*	L01 220 000*	cv
				50.00	L01 236 001*	L01 240 000*	cv

VALUE CU	LOW OFFICIAL SERIAL NUMBER	HIGH OFFICIAL SERIAL NUMBER		VALUE CU	LOW OFFICIAL SERIAL NUMBER	HIGH OFFICIAL SERIAL NUMBER	
50.00	L01 256 001*	L01 260 000*	cv	50.00	L04 516 001*	L04 520 000*	cp
50.00	L01 276 001*	L01 280 000*	cv	50.00	L04 536 001*	L04 540 000*	cp
50.00	L01 292 001*	L01 300 000*	cv	50.00	L04 556 001*	L04 560 000*	cp
50.00	L01 312 001*	L01 320 000*	cv	50.00	L04 576 001*	L04 580 000*	cp
50.00	L01 332 001*	L01 340 000*	cv	50.00	L04 596 001*	L04 600 000*	cp
50.00	L01 352 001*	L01 360 000*	cv	50.00	L04 616 001*	L04 620 000*	cp
50.00	L01 372 001*	L01 380 000*	cv	50.00	L04 636 001*	L04 640 000*	cp
50.00	L01 392 001*	L01 400 000*	cv	50.00	L04 656 001*	L04 660 000*	cp
50.00	L01 412 001*	L01 420 000*	cv	50.00	L04 676 001*	L04 680 000*	cp
50.00	L01 432 001*	L01 440 000*	cv	50.00	L04 696 001*	L04 700 000*	cp
50.00	L01 452 001*	L01 460 000*	cv	50.00	L04 716 001*	L04 720 000*	cp
50.00	L01 472 001*	L01 480 000*	cv	50.00	L04 736 001*	L04 740 000*	cp
50.00	L01 492 001*	L01 500 000*	cv	50.00	L04 756 001*	L04 760 000*	cp
50.00	L01 512 001*	L01 520 000*	cv	50.00	L04 776 001*	L04 780 000*	cp
50.00	L01 532 001*	L01 540 000*	cv	50.00	L04 796 001*	L04 800 000*	cp
50.00	L01 552 001*	L01 560 000*	cv	50.00	L04 816 001*	L04 820 000*	cp
50.00	L01 572 001*	L01 580 000*	cv	50.00	L04 836 001*	L04 840 000*	cp
50.00	L01 592 001*	L01 600 000*	cv	50.00	L04 856 001*	L04 860 000*	cp
50.00	L01 612 001*	L01 620 000*	cv	50.00	L04 876 001*	L04 880 000*	cp
50.00	L01 632 001*	L01 640 000*	cv	50.00	L04 896 001*	L04 900 000*	cp
50.00	L01 652 001*	L01 660 000*	cv	50.00	L04 916 001*	L04 920 000*	cp
50.00	L01 672 001*	L01 680 000*	cv	50.00	L04 936 001*	L04 940 000*	cp
50.00	L01 692 001*	L01 700 000*	cv	50.00	L04 956 001*	L04 960 000*	cp
50.00	L01 712 001*	L01 720 000*	cv	50.00	L04 976 001*	L04 980 000*	cp
50.00	L01 732 001*	L01 740 000*	cv	50.00	L04 996 001*	L05 000 000*	cp
50.00	L01 752 001*	L01 760 000*	cv	50.00	L05 016 001*	L05 020 000*	cp
50.00	L01 772 001*	L01 780 000*	cv	50.00	L05 036 001*	L05 040 000*	cp
50.00	L01 792 001*	L01 800 000*	cv	50.00	L05 056 001*	L05 060 000*	cp
50.00	L01 812 001*	L01 820 000*	cv	50.00	L05 076 001*	L05 080 000*	cp
50.00	L01 832 001*	L01 840 000*	cv	50.00	L05 096 001*	L05 100 000*	cp
50.00	L01 852 001*	L01 860 000*	cv	50.00	L05 116 001*	L05 120 000*	cp
50.00	L01 872 001*	L01 880 000*	cv	25.00	L05 120 001*	L07 040 000*	cp
50.00	L01 892 001*	L01 900 000*	cv	50.00	L07 056 001*	L07 060 000*	cp
50.00	L01 912 001*	L01 920 000*	cv	50.00	L07 076 001*	L07 080 000*	cp
25.00	L01 920 001*	L03 200 000*		50.00	L07 096 001*	L07 100 000*	cp
25.00	L03 200 001*	L03 840 000*	cp	50.00	L07 116 001*	L07 120 000*	cp
50.00	L03 848 001*	L03 860 000*	cp	50.00	L07 136 001*	L07 140 000*	cp
50.00	L03 868 001*	L03 880 000*	cp	50.00	L07 156 001*	L07 160 000*	cp
50.00	L03 888 001*	L03 900 000*	cp	50.00	L07 176 001*	L07 180 000*	cp
50.00	L03 908 001*	L03 920 000*	cp	50.00	L07 196 001*	L07 200 000*	cp
50.00	L03 928 001*	L03 940 000*	cp	50.00	L07 216 001*	L07 220 000*	cp
50.00	L03 948 001*	L03 960 000*	cp	50.00	L07 236 001*	L07 240 000*	cp
50.00	L03 968 001*	L03 980 000*	cp	50.00	L07 256 001*	L07 260 000*	cp
50.00	L03 988 001*	L04 000 000*	cp	50.00	L07 276 001*	L07 280 000*	cp
50.00	L04 008 001*	L04 020 000*	cp	50.00	L07 296 001*	L07 300 000*	cp
50.00	L04 028 001*	L04 040 000*	cp	50.00	L07 316 001*	L07 320 000*	cp
50.00	L04 048 001*	L04 060 000*	cp	50.00	L07 336 001*	L07 340 000*	cp
50.00	L04 068 001*	L04 080 000*	cp	50.00	L07 356 001*	L07 360 000*	cp
50.00	L04 088 001*	L04 100 000*	cp	50.00	L07 376 001*	L07 380 000*	cp
50.00	L04 108 001*	L04 120 000*	cp	50.00	L07 396 001*	L07 400 000*	cp
50.00	L04 128 001*	L04 140 000*	cp	50.00	L07 416 001*	L07 420 000*	cp
50.00	L04 148 001*	L04 160 000*	cp	50.00	L07 436 001*	L07 440 000*	cp
50.00	L04 168 001*	L04 180 000*	cp	50.00	L07 456 001*	L07 460 000*	cp
50.00	L04 188 001*	L04 200 000*	cp	50.00	L07 476 001*	L07 480 000*	cp
50.00	L04 208 001*	L04 220 000*	cp	50.00	L07 496 001*	L07 500 000*	cp
50.00	L04 228 001*	L04 240 000*	cp	50.00	L07 516 001*	L07 520 000*	cp
50.00	L04 248 001*	L04 260 000*	cp	50.00	L07 536 001*	L07 540 000*	cp
50.00	L04 268 001*	L04 280 000*	cp	50.00	L07 556 001*	L07 560 000*	cp
50.00	L04 288 001*	L04 300 000*	cp	50.00	L07 576 001*	L07 580 000*	cp
50.00	L04 308 001*	L04 320 000*	cp	50.00	L07 596 001*	L07 600 000*	cp
50.00	L04 328 001*	L04 340 000*	cp	50.00	L07 616 001*	L07 620 000*	cp
50.00	L04 348 001*	L04 360 000*	cp	50.00	L07 636 001*	L07 640 000*	cp
50.00	L04 368 001*	L04 380 000*	cp	50.00	L07 656 001*	L07 660 000*	cp
50.00	L04 388 001*	L04 400 000*	cp	50.00	L07 676 001*	L07 680 000*	cp
50.00	L04 408 001*	L04 420 000*		50.00	L07 696 001*	L07 700 000*	cp
50.00	L04 428 001*	L04 440 000*	cp	50.00	L07 716 001*	L07 720 000*	cp
50.00	L04 448 001*	L04 460 000*	cp	50.00	L07 736 001*	L07 740 000*	cp
50.00	L04 468 001*	L04 480 000*	cp	50.00	L07 756 001*	L07 760 000*	cp
50.00	L04 496 001*	L04 500 000*	cp	50.00	L07 776 001*	L07 780 000*	cp

VALUE CU	LOW OFFICIAL SERIAL NUMBER	HIGH OFFICIAL SERIAL NUMBER		VALUE CU	LOW OFFICIAL SERIAL NUMBER	HIGH OFFICIAL SERIAL NUMBER	
50.00	L07 796 001*	L07 800 000*	cp	50.00	L08 076 001*	L08 080 000*	cp
50.00	L07 816 001*	L07 820 000*	cp	50.00	L08 096 001*	L08 100 000*	cp
50.00	L07 836 001*	L07 840 000*	cp	50.00	L08 116 001*	L08 120 000*	cp
50.00	L07 856 001*	L07 860 000*	cp	50.00	L08 136 001*	L08 140 000*	cp
50.00	L07 876 001*	L07 880 000*	cp	50.00	L08 156 001*	L08 160 000*	cp
50.00	L07 896 001*	L07 900 000*	cp	50.00	L08 176 001*	L08 180 000*	cp
50.00	L07 916 001*	L07 920 000*	cp	50.00	L08 196 001*	L08 200 000*	cp
50.00	L07 936 001*	L07 940 000*	cp	50.00	L08 216 001*	L08 220 000*	cp
50.00	L07 956 001*	L07 960 000*	cp	50.00	L08 236 001*	L08 240 000*	cp
50.00	L07 976 001*	L07 980 000*	cp	50.00	L08 256 001*	L08 260 000*	cp
50.00	L07 996 001*	L08 000 000*	cp	50.00	L08 276 001*	L08 280 000*	cp
50.00	L08 016 001*	L08 020 000*	cp	50.00	L08 296 001*	L08 300 000*	cp
50.00	L08 036 001*	L08 040 000*	cp	50.00	L08 316 001*	L08 320 000*	cp
50.00	L08 056 001*	L08 060 000*	cp	25.00	L08 320 001*	L09 600 000*	cp

The production unit was changed from 20,000 sheets to 40,000 sheets for:

BANK	STARTING WITH SERIAL	BANK	STARTING WITH SERIAL
Boston	A66 560 001A	Chicago	G60 160 001C
New York	B62 720 001D	St. Louis	H85 760 001A
Philadelphia	C60 160 001A	Minneapolis	I12 800 001A
Cleveland	D46 080 001B	Kansas City	J07 680 001B
Richmond	E69 120 001B	Dallas	K08 960 001B
Atlanta	F55 040 001A	San Francisco	L67 840 001B

CAT. NO. XXF81
$20.00 FEDERAL RESERVE NOTE (GREEN SEAL) 32 Subject
SERIES 1981

SIGNATURES: Angela M. Buchanan, Treasurer of the United States.
Donald T. Regan, Secretary of the Treasury.
SERIAL NUMERS: All serial numbers revert to 00 000 001A.
PLATE SERIALS: Continue from previous series on both face and back.

DISTRICT	TOTAL NOTES PRINTED	BLOCKS	ESTIMATED VALUE VG/F	CU	LOW OFFICIAL SERIAL NUMBER	HIGH OFFICIAL (1) SERIAL NUMBER
5 E RICHMOND		E--A		22.50	E00 000 001A	E15 360 000A
8 H. ST. LOUIS		H--A		22.50	H00 000 001A	H10 240 000A
		H--*		35.00	H00 012 001*	H00 020 000*
				35.00	H00 032 001*	H00 040 000*
				35.00	H00 052 001*	H00 060 000*
				35.00	H00 072 001*	H00 080 000*
				35.00	H00 092 001*	H00 100 000*
				35.00	H00 112 001*	H00 120 000*
				35.00	H00 132 001*	H00 140 000*
				35.00	H00 152 001*	H00 160 000*
				35.00	H00 172 001*	H00 180 000*
				35.00	H00 192 001*	H00 200 000*
				35.00	H00 212 001*	H00 220 000*
				35.00	H00 232 001*	H00 240 000*
				35.00	H00 252 001*	H00 260 000*
				35.00	H00 272 001*	H00 280 000*
				35.00	H00 292 001*	H00 300 000*
				35.00	H00 312 001*	H00 320 000*
				35.00	H00 332 001*	H00 340 000*
				35.00	H00 352 001*	H00 360 000*
				35.00	H00 372 001*	H00 380 000*
				35.00	H00 392 001*	H00 400 000*
				35.00	H00 412 001*	H00 420 000*
				35.00	H00 432 001*	H00 440 000*
				35.00	H00 452 001*	H00 460 000*
				35.00	H00 472 001*	H00 480 000*
				35.00	H00 492 001*	H00 500 000*
				35.00	H00 512 001*	H00 520 000*
				35.00	H00 532 001*	H00 540 000*
				35.00	H00 552 001*	H00 560 000*
				35.00	H00 572 001*	H00 580 000*
				35.00	H00 592 001*	H00 600 000*
				35.00	H00 612 001*	H00 620 000*
				35.00	H00 632 001*	H00 640 000*
				25.00	H00 640 001*	H01 280 000*

(1) Currently in print.

CAT. NO. LG28
$50.00 GOLD CERTIFICATE (YELLOW SEAL) (12 Subject)
SERIES 1928

SERIAL NUMBERS:
  (Official Range) A 00 000 001A through A 05 520 000A
  Star Notes:
  (Low Official) * 00 000 001 A * 00 028 165 A (High Observed)
PLATE SERIALS: Face check #1 through #41.
SIGNATURES: Walter O. Woods, Treasurer of the United States.
  Andrew W. Mellon, Secretary of the Treasury.

ESTIMATED VALUES:	BLOCKS	VG/F	CU
	A--A	100.00	500.00
	*--A	rare	

TOTAL BLOCKS KNOWN: Two.

CAT. NO. LN29
$50.00 FEDERAL RESERVE BANK NOTE (BROWN SEAL)
SERIES 1929

SERIAL NUMBERS: Both regular and star notes start with 00 000 001.
PLATE SERIALS: Face check numbers begin with #1.
SIGNATURES: Same as $5.00 FRBN.

	DISTRICT	TOTAL NOTES PRINTED	BLOCKS	VG/F	CU	LOW OFFICIAL SERIAL NUMBER	HIGH OFFICIAL SERIAL NUMBER
1	A BOSTON		Unkn				
2	B NEW YORK		B--A	75.00	150.00		B00 636 000A
		24,000	B--*	100.00	250.00		B00 015 571*
3	C PHILADELPHIA		Unkn				
4	D CLEVELAND		D--A	75.00	150.00		D00 684 000A
		12,000	D--*	100.00	250.00		D00 005 823*
5	E RICHMOND		Unkn				
6	F ATLANTA		Unkn				
7	G CHICAGO		G--A	85.00	175.00		G00 300 000A
		4,000	G--*	125.00	300.00		
8	H ST. LOUIS		Unkn				
9	I MINNEAPOLIS		I--A	90.00	200.00		I00 132 000A
		12,000	I--*	150.00	400.00		
10	J KANSAS CITY		J--A	85.00	175.00		J00 276 000A
		12,000	J--*	135.00	350.00		J00 003 614*
11	K DALLAS		K--A	90.00	200.00		K00 168 000A
		12,000	K--*	150.00	375.00		
12	L SAN FRANCISCO		L--A	75.00	150.00		L00 576 000A
		12,000	L--*	100.00	250.00		

TOTAL BLOCKS: Fourteen.
Collectors are requested to supply any information that will improve on above data.

CAT. NO. LF28
$50.00 FEDERAL RESERVE NOTE (GREEN SEAL) (12 Subject)
SERIES 1928

SERIAL NUMBERS: All serial numbers both regular and star notes begin with 00 000 001.
PLATE SERIALS: Both face and back checks start with number 1.
SIGNATURES: Walter O. Woods, Treasurer of the United States.
   A. W. Mellon, Secretary of the Treasury.

	DISTRICT	TOTAL NOTES PRINTED	BLOCKS	VG/F	CU	LOW OBSERVED SERIAL NUMBER	HIGH OBSERVED SERIAL NUMBER
1	A BOSTON	265,200	A--A	75.00	125.00		
			A--*	90.00	175.00	A00 010 509*	
2	B NEW YORK	1,351,800	B--A	60.00	90.00	B00 576 777A	B01 199 158A
			B--*	85.00	125.00		B00 019 980*
3	C PHILADELPHIA	997,056	C--A	60.00	90.00	C00 573 650A	C00 792 468A
			C--*	85.00	125.00		
4	D CLEVELAND	1,161,900	D--A	60.00	90.00	D00 263 927A	D01 095 187A
			D--*	85.00	125.00		
5	E RICHMOND	539,400	E--A	65.00	100.00		E00 167 065A
			E--*	90.00	135.00		
6	F ATLANTA	538,800	F--A	65.00	100.00		F00 282 423A
			F--*	90.00	135.00	F00 006 494*	
7	G CHICAGO	1,348,620	G--A	60.00	90.00	G00 813 731A	G02 662 453A
			G--*	85.00	125.00	G00 015 972*	G00 023 615*
8	H ST. LOUIS	627,300	H--A	65.00	100.00	H00 152 967A	H00 315 651A
			H--*	90.00	135.00	H00 002 366*	
9	I MINNEAPOLIS	106,200	I--A	100.00	200.00		I00 017 769A
			I--*	150.00	300.00		
10	J KANSAS CITY	252,600	J--A	75.00	125.00	J00 070 582A	J00 164 328A
			J--*	90.00	175.00	J00 000 845*	
11	K DALLAS	109,920	K--A	100.00	200.00		K00 081 870A
			K--*	150.00	300.00		
12	L SAN FRANCISCO	447,600	L--A	65.00	100.00	L00 096 039A	L00 366 666A
			L--*	90.00	135.00		

TOTAL BLOCKS: Twenty four.
Collectors are requested to supply any serial numbers that improve on above information.

CAT. NO. LF28A
$50.00 FEDERAL RESERVE NOTE (GREEN SEAL) (12 Subject)
SERIES 1928A

DESIGN CHANGE: District letter in seal replaced by numeral. Face check begins with 1.
SIGNATURES: Walter O. Woods, Treasurer of the United States.
   A.W. Mellon, Secretary of the Treasury.

	DISTRICT	TOTAL NOTES PRINTED	BLOCKS	VG/F	CU	LOW OBSERVED SERIAL NUMBER	HIGH OBSERVED SERIAL NUMBER
1	A BOSTON	1,834,989	A--A	60.00	85.00	A00 379 227A	A00 711 856A
			A--*	65.00	100.00		

	DISTRICT	TOTAL NOTES PRINTED	BLOCKS	ESTIMATED VALUE VG/F	CU	LOW OFFICIAL SERIAL NUMBER	HIGH OFFICIAL SERIAL NUMBER	
2	B NEW YORK	3,392,328	B--A	60.00	85.00	B01 392 109A	B01 758 494A	(1)
			B--*	65.00	100.00			
3	C PHILADELPHIA	3,078,944	C--A	60.00	85.00	C00 875 752A	C01 494 599A	
			C--*	65.00	100.00			
4	D CLEVELAND	2,453,364	D--A	60.00	85.00	D01 207 831A	D01 537 299A	
			D--*	65.00	100.00			
5	E RICHMOND	1,516,500	E--A	60.00	85.00	E00 614 252A		
			E--*	65.00	100.00			
6	F ATLANTA	338,400	F--A	80.00	150.00	F00 455 749A		
7	G CHICAGO	5,263,956	G--A	60.00	85.00	G01 894 713A	G03 750 686A	(2)
			G--*	65.00	100.00			
8	H ST. LOUIS	880,500	H--A	67.50	90.00	H00 280 205A	H00 626 709A	
			H--*	75.00	125.00			
9	I MINNEAPOLIS	780,240	I--A	67.50	90.00			
			I--*	75.00	125.00			
10	J KANSAS CITY	791,604	J--A	67.50	90.00			
			J--*	75.00	125.00			
11	K DALLAS	701,496	K--A	55.00	90.00	K00 133 819A		
			K--*	75.00	125.00			
12	L SAN FRANCISCO	1,522,620	L--A	60.00	85.00	L00 744 400A		
			L--*	65.00	100.00			

TOTAL BLOCKS: Twenty four.
Collectors are requested to supply serial numbers that improve on above information.
Note: Both light and dark third printings have been reported but because of the lack of information this edition does not differentiate except as noted. Owners of listed serials or improvements are kindly requested to report whether seals and serials are light or dark together with face and back check.
(1) Reported dark
(2) Reported light

CAT. NO. LF34
$50.00 FEDERAL RESERVE NOTE (DARK GREEN SEAL) (12 Subject)
SERIES 1934

SERIAL NUMBERS: All serial numbers both regular and star begin with 00 000 001.
PLATE SERIALS: Back check number up to 162.
SIGNATURES: W.A. Julian, Treasurer of the United States.
　Henry Morgenthau, Jr. Secretary of the Treasury.

	DISTRICT	TOTAL NOTES PRINTED (1)	BLOCKS	ESTIMATED VALUE VG/F	CU	LOW OBSERVED SERIAL NUMBER	HIGH OBSERVED SERIAL NUMBER
1	A BOSTON	2,729,400	A--A	55.00	70.00		A00 992 807A
			A--*	60.00	90.00		
2	B NEW YORK	17,894,676	B--A	55.00	70.00	B04 418 714A	B16 128 828A
			B--*	60.00	90.00	B00 033 922*	B00 132 401*
3	C PHILADELPHIA	5,833,200	C--A	55.00	70.00	C01 300 551A	C05 377 316A
			C--*	60.00	90.00		C00 043 527*
4	D CLEVELAND	8,817,720	D--A	55.00	70.00	D02 165 562A	D09 374 113A
			D--*	60.00	90.00	D00 022 997*	D00 041 254*
5	E RICHMOND	4,826,628	E--A	55.00	70.00	E03 318 375A	E05 941 655A
			E--*	60.00	90.00		
6	F ATLANTA	3,069,348	F--A	55.00	70.00	F01 486 452A	F03 528 759A
			F--*	60.00	90.00	F00 005 876*	
7	G CHICAGO	8,675,940	G--A	55.00	70.00	G02 437 826A	G08 288 483A
			G--*	60.00	90.00		G00 046 310*
8	H ST. LOUIS	1,497,144	H--A	57.50	75.00	H00 945 828A	H01 617 967A
			H--*	62.50	100.00		
9	I MINNEAPOLIS	539,700	I--A	65.00	90.00	I00 151 503A	I00 564 731A
			I--*	75.00	125.00		
10	J KANSAS CITY	1,133,520	J--A	57.50	75.00	J00 538 925A	J01 148 956A
			J--*	62.50	100.00		J00 006 055
11	K DALLAS	1,194,876	K--A	57.50	75.00	K00 613 277A	K01 172 484A
			K--*	62.50	100.00		K00 009 695*
12	L SAN FRANCISCO	8,101,200	L--A	55.00	70.00	L02 095 464A	L07 568 656A
			L--*	60.00	90.00		L00 080 817*

TOTAL BLOCKS: Twenty four.
Collectors are requested to supply serial numbers that improve on above information.
(1) Includes both seal colors and mules.

CAT. NO. LF34
$50.00 FEDERAL RESERVE NOTE MULE (DARK GREEN SEAL) (12 Subject)
SERIES 1934

PLATE SERIALS: Back check number begins with 163.

	DISTRICT	TOTAL NOTES PRINTED	BLOCKS	ESTIMATED VALUE VG/F	CU	LOW OBSERVED SERIAL NUMBER	HIGH OBSERVED SERIAL NUMBER
1	A BOSTON		A--A				A00 821 285A
			A--*	60.00	90.00		
2	B NEW YORK		B--A	55.00	70.00		B19 028 213A
			B--*				
3	C PHILADELPHIA		C--A	55.00	70.00		C03 030 503A
			C--*				
4	D CLEVELAND		D--A	55.00	70.00		D03 122 704A
			D--*				
5	E RICHMOND		E--A				
			E--*				
6	F ATLANTA		F--*				
7	G CHICAGO		G--A	55.00	70.00		G06 657 429A
			G--*				
8	H ST. LOUIS		H--A	57.50	75.00		H00 945 828A
			H--*				
9	I MINNEAPOLIS		I--A				
			I--*				
10	J KANSAS CITY		J--A				
			J--*				
11	K DALLAS		K--A	57.50	75.00		K01 003 195A
12	L SAN FRANCISCO		L--A				L14 696 723A
			L--*				

TOTAL BLOCKS: Twenty four.
Collectors are requested to supply serial numbers that improve on above information.

CAT. NO. LF34
$50.00 FEDERAL RESERVE NOTE (LIGHT GREEN SEAL) (12 Subject)
SERIES 1934

PLATE SERIALS: Back check number up to 162.

	DISTRICT	TOTAL NOTES PRINTED	BLOCKS	ESTIMATED VALUE VG/F	CU	LOW OBSERVED SERIAL NUMBER	HIGH OBSERVED SERIAL NUMBER
1	A BOSTON		A--A	55.00	70.00	A00 200 420A	A00 636 068A
			A--*	60.00	90.00		A00 009 960*
2	B NEW YORK		B--A	55.00	70.00	B00 446 569A	B04 683 757A
			B--*	60.00	90.00		B00 001 207*
3	C PHILADELPHIA		C--A	55.00	70.00	C00 189 154A	C01 284 007A
			C--*	60.00	90.00		
4	D CLEVELAND		D--A	55.00	70.00	D00 307 324A	D08 204 544A
			D--*	60.00	90.00		
5	E RICHMOND		E--A	55.00	70.00	E00 373 055A	E06 647 594A
			E--*	60.00	90.00		
6	F ATLANTA		F--A	55.00	70.00		
			F--*	60.00	90.00		

	DISTRICT	TOTAL NOTES PRINTED	BLOCKS	ESTIMATED VALUE VG/F	CU	LOW OFFICIAL SERIAL NUMBER	HIGH OFFICIAL SERIAL NUMBER
7	G CHICAGO		G--A	55.00	70.00	G00 141 106A	G08 899 035A
			G--*	60.00	90.00		
8	H ST. LOUIS		H--A	57.50	75.00	H00 157 167A	H00 194 410A
			H--*	62.50	100.00		
9	I MINNEAPOLIS		I--A	65.00	90.00	I00 009 898A	I00 036 852A
			I--*	75.00	125.00		
10	J KANSAS CITY		J--A	57.50	75.00		J00 920 118A
			J--*	62.50	100.00		
11	K DALLAS		K--A	57.50	75.00	K00 128 553A	K00 162 643A
			K--*	62.50	100.00		
12	L SAN FRANCISCO		L--A	55.00	70.00	L00 042 643A	L07 099 501A
			L--*	60.00	90.00		

TOTAL BLOCKS: Twenty four.
Collectors are requested to supply serial numbers that improve on above information.

CAT. NO. LF34
$50.00 FEDERAL RESERVE NOTE MULE (LIGHT GREEN SEAL) (12 Subject)
SERIES 1934

PLATE SERIALS: Back check number 163 and higher.

	DISTRICT	TOTAL NOTES PRINTED	BLOCKS	ESTIMATED VALUE VG/F	CU	LOW OBSERVED SERIAL NUMBER	HIGH OBSERVED SERIAL NUMBER
1	A BOSTON		A--A	55.00	70.00		A00 821 285A
			A--*				
2	B NEW YORK		B--A	55.00	70.00		B08 310 552A
			B--*				
3	C PHILADELPHIA		C--A	55.00	70.00		C01 407 354A
			C--*				
4	D CLEVELAND		D--A				
			D--*				
5	E RICHMOND		E--A				
			E--*				
6	F ATLANTA		F--A				
			F--*				
7	G CHICAGO		G--A				
			G--*				
8	H ST. LOUIS		H--A				
			H--*				
9	I MINNEAPOLIS		I--A				
			I--*				
10	J KANSAS CITY		J--A				
			J--*				
11	K DALLAS		K--A				
			K--*				
12	L SAN FRANCISCO		L--A				
			L--*				

TOTAL BLOCKS: Twenty four.
Collectors are requested to supply serial numbers that improve on above information.

CAT. NO. LF34A
$50.00 FEDERAL RESERVE NOTE (GREEN SEAL) 12 Subject
SERIES 1934A

SIGNATURES: W.A. Julian, Treasurer of the United States.
   Henry Morgenthau, Jr. Secretary of the Treasury.
PLATE SERIALS: Back check numbers begin with 163.
SERIAL NUMBERS: All districts continue from previous series.
IMPORTANT: All observations and reported information indicate that all $50.00 Federal Reserve notes from 1934A through 1950 are MULES. We would appreciate the assistance of collectors and dealers in providing any serial numbers on $50.00 note Series 1934A through Series 1950 with a back check number of 163 or higher (large size back check number).

CAT. NO. LF34A MULE
$50.00 FEDERAL RESERVE NOTE (DARK GREEN SEAL) MULE 12 Subject
SERIES 1934A MULE

SIGNATURES: W.A. Julian, Treasurer of the United States.
  Henry Morgenthau, Jr. Secretary of the Treasury.
PLATE SERIALS: Back check number 162 and lower (micro size)
SERIAL NUMBERS: All districts continue from previous series.

	DISTRICT	TOTAL NOTES PRINTED (1)	BLOCKS	ESTIMATED VALUE VG/F	CU	LOW OBSERVED SERIAL NUMBER	HIGH OBSERVED SERIAL NUMBER
1	A BOSTON	406,200	A--A A--*	55.00	85.00	A02 197 478A	
2	B NEW YORK	4,710,648	B--A B--*	55.00	80.00	B04 672 222A	B17 173 989A
3	C PHILADELPHIA	none					
4	D CLEVELAND	864,168	D--A D--*	55.00	85.00	D00 703 136A	D07 950 056A
5	E RICHMOND	2,235,372	E--A E--*	55.00	80.00	E03 219 261A	
6	F ATLANTA	416,100	F--A F--*	55.00	85.00	F01 393 635A	F03 201 653A
7	G CHICAGO	1,014,600	G--A G--*	55.00	80.00	G04 411 186A	G07 966 649A
8	H ST. LOUIS	361,944	H--A H--*	55.00	85.00	H37 124 135A	
9	I MINNEAPOLIS	93,300	I--A I--*	65.00	100.00		
10	J KANSAS CITY	189,300	J--A J--*	55.00	85.00	J00 595 835A	
11	K DALLAS	266,700	K--A	55.00	85.00	K00 394 159A	K01 653 036A
12	L SAN FRANCISCO	162,000	L--A L--*	55.00	85.00	L00 414 384A	L02 871 431A

TOTAL BLOCKS: Twenty Four.

(1) Totals printed for all varieties. Would particularly appreciate a report of any star notes of any variety of Series 1934A.

CAT. NO. LF34A MULE
$50.00 FEDERAL RESERVE NOTE (LIGHT GREEN SEAL) MULE 12 Subject
SERIES 1934A MULE

PLATE SERIALS: Back check number 162 and lower.

	DISTRICT	TOTAL NOTES PRINTED	BLOCKS	ESTIMATED VALUE VG/F	CU	LOW OBSERVED SERIAL NUMBER	HIGH OBSERVED SERIAL NUMBER
2	B NEW YORK		B--A B--*	55.00 65.00	75.00 125.00	B12 060 695A B00 113 592*	B16 338 861A
4	D CLEVELAND		D--A	55.00	75.00	D07 015 187A	
7	G CHICAGO		G--*	100.00	350.00	G00 045 058*	
8	H ST. LOUIS		H--A	60.00	100.00	H01 791 902A	
10	J KANSAS CITY		J--A	75.00	125.00	J00 920 112A	J00 920 119A

TOTAL BLOCKS KNOWN: Six.

| 12 | L SAN FRANCISCO | 162,000 | L--A
L--* | 55.00 | 85.00 | L00 414 384A | L02 871 431A |

CAT. NO. LF34B
$50.00 FEDERAL RESERVE NOTE (GREEN SEAL) 12 Subject
SERIES 1934B

SIGNATURES: W.A. Julian, Treasurer of the United States.
  Fred M. Vinson, Secretary of the Treasury.
PLATE SERIALS: Back check number 163 and higher.
SERIAL NUMBERS: All districts continue from previous series.
IMPORTANT: Please see reference under $50.00 Series 1934A. No NON-MULE notes have been observed or reported for Series 1934B. Collectors and dealers are kindly requested to report any $50.00 notes of this series with back check number 163 and higher (large size back check number).

CAT. NO. LF34B MULE
$50.00 FEDERAL RESERVE NOTE (GREEN SEAL) MULE 12 Subject
SERIES 1934B MULE

SIGNATURES: W.A. Julian, Treasurer of the United States.
Fred M. Vinson, Secretary of the Treasury.
PLATE SERIALS: Back check number 162 and lower.
SERIAL NUMBERS: All districts continued from previous series.

	DISTRICT	TOTAL NOTES PRINTED	BLOCKS	ESTIMATED VALUE VG/F	CU	LOW OBSERVED SERIAL NUMBER	HIGH OBSERVED SERIAL NUMBER
1	A BOSTON	none					
2	B NEW YORK	none					
3	C PHILADELPHIA	509,100	C--A	65.00	100.00	C05 604 319A	C06 351 435A
4	D CLEVELAND	359,100	D--A	65.00	100.00	D09 552 910A	D10 146 571A
			D--*	150.00	500.00	D00 116 564*	
5	E RICHMOND	596,700	E--A	65.00	100.00	E07 284 378A	
6	F ATLANTA	416,720	F--A	65.00	100.00	F03 352 864A	F03 604 187A
7	G CHICAGO	306,000	G--A	65.00	100.00	G09 399 017A	
8	H ST. LOUIS	306,000	H--A	65.00	100.00	H01 745 970A	H01 844 335A
9	I MINNEAPOLIS	120,000	I--A	75.00	125.00	I00 590 563A	I00 692 511A
10	J KANSAS CITY	221,340	J--A	65.00	100.00	J01 276 118A	J01 495 360A
11	K DALLAS	120,108	K--A	75.00	125.00	K01 446 697A	K01 455 543A
12	L SAN FRANCISCO	441,000	L--A	65.00	100.00	L07 831 530A	L08 019 470A

TOTAL BLOCKS KNOWN: Eleven.

CAT. NO. LF34C
$50.00 FEDERAL RESERVE NOTE (GREEN SEAL) 12 Subject
SERIES 1934C

SIGNATURES: W.A. Julian, Treasurer of the United States.
John W. Snyder, Secretary of the Treasury.
PLATE SERIALS: Back check numbers begin with 163.
SERIAL NUMBERS: All districts continue from previous series.
IMPORTANT: Please see reference under $50.00 Series 1934A. No NON-MULE notes have been observed or reported for Series 1934B. Collectors and dealers are kindly requested to report any $50.00 notes of this series with back check number 163 or higher (large size check number).

CAT. NO. LF34C MULE
$50.00 FEDERAL RESERVE NOTE (GREEN SEAL) MULE 12 Subject
SERIES 1934C MULE

SIGNATURES: W.A. Julian, Treasurer of the United States.
John W. Snyder, Secretary of the Treasury.
PLATE SERIALS: Back check number 162 and lower.
SERIAL NUMBERS: All districts continue from previous series.

	DISTRICT	TOTAL NOTES PRINTED	BLOCKS	ESTIMATED VALUE VG/F	CU	LOW OBSERVED SERIAL NUMBER	HIGH OBSERVED SERIAL NUMBER
1	A BOSTON	117,600	A--A	75.00	125.00	A03 048 570A	
2	B NEW YORK	1,556,400	B--A	55.00	75.00	B16 487 892A	B19 095 949A
			B--*	100.00	250.00	B00 153 289*	
3	C PHILADELPHIA	107,283	C--A	75.00	125.00	C05 888 759A	C07 683 555A
4	D CLEVELAND	374,400	D--A	65.00	85.00	D09 466 522A	D11 740 142A
			D--*	100.00	250.00	D00 117 789*	D00 145 476*
5	E RICHMOND	1,821,960	E--A	55.00	75.00	E07 599 689A	E08 786 836A
6	F ATLANTA	107,640	F--A	75.00	125.00		
7	G CHICAGO	294,432	G--A	65.00	85.00	G09 419 965A	G09 623 069A
8	H ST. LOUIS	535,200	H--A	65.00	75.00	H02 296 901A	H02 570 405A
9	I MINNEAPOLIS	118,800	I--A	75.00	125.00		
10	J KANSAS CITY	303,600	J--A	65.00	85.00	J01 558 727A	J01 805 454A
11	K DALLAS	429,900	K--A	65.00	85.00		
			K--*	100.00	250.00	K00 025 502*	

TOTAL BLOCKS KNOWN: Eleven.

CAT. NO. LF34D
$50.00 FEDERAL RESERVE NOTE (GREEN SEAL) 12 Subject
SERIES 1934D

SIGNATURES: Georgia Neese Clark, Treasurer of the United States.
   John W. Snyder, Secretary of the Treasury.
PLATE SERIALS: Back check numbers begin with 163.
SERIAL NUMBERS: All districts continue from previous series.
IMPORTANT: Please see reference under $50.00 Series 1934A. No NON-MULE notes have been observed or reported for Series 1934D. Collectors and dealers are kindly requested to report any $50.00 notes of this series with back check number 163 and higher (large size back check number).

CAT. NO. LF34D MULE
$50.00 FEDERAL RESERVE NOTE (GREEN SEAL) MULE 12 Subject
SERIES 1934D MULE

SIGNATURES: Georgia Neese Clark, Treasurer of the United States.
   John W. Snyder, Secretary of the Treasury.
PLATE SERIALS: Back check number 162 and lower.
SERIAL NUMBERS: All districts continue from previous series.

	DISTRICT	TOTAL NOTES PRINTED	BLOCKS	EST. VG/F	EST. CU	LOW OBSERVED SERIAL NUMBER	HIGH OBSERVED SERIAL NUMBER
1	A BOSTON	279,600	A--A	55.00	75.00	A03 129 512A	A03 468 000A
			A--*	100.00	250.00	A00 032 419*	
2	B NEW YORK	898,776	B--A	55.00	75.00	B18 748 105A	B19 248 000A
3	C PHILADELPHIA	699,000	C--A	55.00	75.00	C07 422 017A	C08 004 000A
4	D CLEVELAND	none					
5	E RICHMOND	156,000	E--A				E09 216 000A
6	F ATLANTA	216,000	F--A				F04 020 000A
			F--*	100.00	250.00	F00 036 681*	
7	G CHICAGO	494,016	G--A	55.00	75.00	G07 479 216A	G10 188 000A
			G--*	100.00	250.00	G00 100 066*	
8	H ST. LOUIS	none					
9	I MINNEAPOLIS	none(1)	I--A	250.00		I00 750 686A	
10	J KANSAS CITY	none					
11	K DALLAS	103,200	K--A	65.00	100.00	K01 856 747A	K01 984 000A
12	L SAN FRANCISCO	none					

TOTAL BLOCKS KNOWN: Nine. (Although reported printed, no EA or FA are known, (1) Although records indicate no $50.00 1934D were printed for Minneapolis, one piece is known.

CAT. NO. LF50
$50.00 FEDERAL RESERVE NOTE (GREEN SEAL) 12 Subject
SERIES 1950

SIGNATURES: Georgia Neese Clark, Treasurer of the United States.
   John W. Snyder, Secretary of the Treasury.
PLATE SERIALS: Back check numbers begin with 163.
SERIAL NUMBERS: All districts begin with 00 000 001 for star and regular notes.
IMPORTANT: Please see reference under $50.00 Series 1934A. No NON-MULE notes have been observed or reported for Series 1950. Collectors and dealers are kindly requested to report any $50.00 notes of this series with back check number 163 or higher (large size check number).

CAT. NO. LF50 MULE
$50.00 FEDERAL RESERVE NOTE (GREEN SEAL) MULE 12 Subject
SERIES 1950 MULE

SIGNATURES: Georgia Neese Clark, Treasurer of the United States.
  John W. Snyder, Secretary of the Treasury.
PLATE SERIALS: Back check number 162 and lower (micro size).
SERIAL NUMBERS: All districts begin with 00 000 001 both star and regular notes.

	DISTRICT	TOTAL NOTES PRINTED	BLOCKS	ESTIMATED VALUE VG/F	CU	LOW OFFICIAL SERIAL NUMBER	HIGH OFFICIAL SERIAL NUMBER	
1	A BOSTON	1,248,000	A--A		75.00		A01 248 000A	
			A--*		85.00			
2	B NEW YORK	10,236,000	B--A		75.00		B10 236 000A	
			B--*		85.00			
3	C PHILADELPHIA	2,352,000	C--A		75.00		C02 352 000A	
			C--*		85.00			
4	D CLEVELAND	6,180,000	D--A		75.00		D06 180 000A	
			D--*		85.00			
5	E RICHMOND	5,064,000	E--A		75.00		E05 064 000A	
			E--*		85.00			
6	F ATLANTA	1,812,000	F--A		75.00		F01 812 000A	
			F--*		85.00			
7	G CHICAGO	4,212,000	G--A		75.00		G04 212 000A	
			G--*		85.00			
8	H ST. LOUIS	892,000	H--A		75.00		H00 892 000A	
			H--*		85.00			
9	I MINNEAPOLIS	384,000	I--A		80.00		I00 384 000A	
			I--*		90.00			
10	J KANSAS CITY	696,000	J--A		75.00		J00 696 000A	
			J--*		85.00			
11	K DALLAS	1,100,000	K--A		75.00		K01 100 000A	
			K--*		85.00		K00 004 300*	(2)
12	L SAN FRANCISCO	3,996,000	L--A		75.00		L03 996 000A	
			L--*		85.00			

TOTAL BLOCKS: Twenty four. Higher serial numbers were assigned to this series but were not used.

(2) High Observed.

CAT. NO. LF50A
$50.00 FEDERAL RESERVE NOTE (GREEN SEAL) (18 Subject)
SERIES 1950A

SERIAL NUMBERS: Continued sequence from previous series.
SIGNATURES: Ivy Baker Priest, Treasurer of the United States.
  George M. Humphrey, Secretary of the Treasury.

	DISTRICT	TOTAL NOTES PRINTED	BLOCKS	ESTIMATED VALUE VG/F	CU	LOW OFFICIAL SERIAL NUMBER	HIGH OFFICIAL SERIAL NUMBER
1	A BOSTON	720,000	A--A		75.00	A01 296 001A	A02 016 000A
			A--*		85.00		
2	B NEW YORK	6,480,000	B--A		75.00	B10 368 001B	B16 848 00A
			B--*		85.00		
3	C PHILADELPHIA	1,728,000	C--A		75.00	C02 448 001A	C04 176 000A
			C--*		85.00		
4	D CLEVELAND	1,872,000	D--A		75.00	D06 192 001A	D08 064 000A
			D--*		85.00		
5	E RICHMOND	2,016,000	E--A		75.00	E05 184 001A	E07 200 000A
			E--*		85.00		
6	F ATLANTA	288,000	F--A		85.00	F01 872 000A	F02 160 000A
			F--*		100.00		
7	G CHICAGO	2,016,000	G--A		75.00	G04 320 001A	G06 336 000A
			G--*		85.00	G00 208 571*	
8	H ST. LOUIS	576,000	H--A		75.00	H01 008 001A	H01 584 000A
			H--*		85.00		
9	I MINNEAPOLIS	none					
10	J KANSAS CITY	144,000	J--A		85.00	J00 720 001A	J00 864 000A
			J--*		100.00		

	DISTRICT	TOTAL NOTES PRINTED	BLOCKS	ESTIMATED VALUE VG/F	CU	LOW OFFICIAL SERIAL NUMBER	HIGH OFFICIAL SERIAL NUMBER
11	K DALLAS	864,000	K--A		75.00	K01 152 001A	K02 016 000A
			K--*		85.00		
12	L SAN FRANCISCO	576,000	L--A		75.00	L04 032 001A	L04 608 000A
			L--*		85.00		

TOTAL BLOCKS: Twenty two.

CAT. NO. LF50B
$50.00 FEDERAL RESERVE NOTE (GREEN SEAL) (18 Subject)
SERIES 1950B

SERIAL NUMBERS: Continued sequence from previous series.
SIGNATURES: Ivy Baker Priest, Treasurer of the United States.
  Robert B. Anderson, Secretary of the Treasury.

	DISTRICT	TOTAL NOTES PRINTED	BLOCKS	ESTIMATED VALUE VG/F	CU	LOW OFFICIAL SERIAL NUMBER	HIGH OFFICIAL SERIAL NUMBER
1	A BOSTON	864,000	A--A		75.00	A02 016 001A	A02 880 000A
			A--*		85.00		
2	B NEW YORK	8,352,000	B--A		75.00	B16 848 001A	B25 200 000A
			B--*		85.00		
3	C PHILADELPHIA	2,592,000	C--A		75.00	C04 176 001A	C06 768 000A
			C--*		85.00		
4	D CLEVELAND	1,728,000	D--A		75.00	D08 064 001A	D09 792 000A
			D--*		85.00		
5	E RICHMOND	1,584,000	E--A		75.00		
			E--*		85.00	E07 200 001A	E08 784 000A
6	F ATLANTA	none					
7	G CHICAGO	4,320,000	G--A		75.00	G06 336 001A	G10 656 000A
			G--*		85.00		
8	H ST. LOUIS	576,000	H--A		75.00	H01 584 001A	H02 160 000A
			H--*		85.00		
9	I MINNEAPOLIS	none					
10	J KANSAS CITY	1,008,000	J--A		75.00	J00 864 001A	J01 872 000A
			J--*		85.00		J00 362 687*
11	K DALLAS	1,008,000	K--A		75.00	K02 016 001A	K03 024 000A
			K--*		85.00		K00 445 855*
12	L SAN FRANCISCO	1,872,000	L--A		75.00	L04 608 001A	L06 480 000A
			L--*		85.00		

TOTAL BLOCKS: Twenty.

CAT. NO. LF50C
$50.00 FEDERAL RESERVE NOTE (GREEN SEAL) (18 Subject)
SERIES 1950C

SERIAL NUMBERS: Contined sequence from previous series.
SIGNATURES: Elizabeth Rudel Smith, Treasurer of the United States.
  C. Douglas Dillon, Secretary of the Treasury.

	DISTRICT	TOTAL NOTES PRINTED	BLOCKS	ESTIMATED VALUE VG/F	CU	LOW OFFICIAL SERIAL NUMBER	HIGH OFFICIAL SERIAL NUMBER	
1	A BOSTON	720,000	A--A		75.00	A02 880 001A	A03 600 000A	
			A--*		85.00			
2	B NEW YORK	5,328,000	B--A		75.00	B25 200 001A	B30 528 000A	
			B--*		85.00		B02 120 622*	(1)
3	C PHILADELPHIA	1,296,000	C--A		75.00	C06 768 001A	C08 064 000A	
			C--*		85.00			
4	D CLEVELAND	1,296,000	D--A		75.00	D09 792 001A	D11 088 000A	
			D--*		85.00			
5	E RICHMOND	1,296,000	E--A		75.00	E08 784 001A	E10 080 000A	
			E--*		85.00			
6	F ATLANTA	none						
7	G CHICAGO	1,728,000	G--A		75.00	G10 656 001A	G12 384 000A	
			G--*		85.00			
8	H ST. LOUIS	576,000	H--A		75.00	H02 160 001A	H02 736 000A	
			H--*		85.00		H00 664 170*	(1)
9	I MINNEAPOLIS	144,000	I--A		75.00	I00 432 001A	I00 576 000A	
			I--*		85.00	I00 217 587*	I00 248 473*	(2)

	DISTRICT	TOTAL NOTES PRINTED	BLOCKS	ESTIMATED VALUE VG/F	CU	LOW OFFICIAL SERIAL NUMBER	HIGH OFFICIAL SERIAL NUMBER	
10	J KANSAS CITY	432,000	J--A		75.00	J01 872 001A	J02 304 000A	
			J--*		85.00	J00 488 285*	J00 489 436*	(1)
11	K DALLAS	720,000	K--A		75.00	K03 024 001A	K03 744 000A	
			K--*		85.00			
12	L SAN FRANCISCO	1,152,000	L--A		75.00	L06 480 001A	L07 632 000A	
			L--*		85.00			

TOTAL BLOCKS: Twenty two.
(1) High Observed
(2) Low Observed

CAT. NO. LF50D
$50.00 FEDERAL RESERVE NOTE (GREEN SEAL) (18 Subject)
SERIES 1950D

SERIAL NUMBERS: Continued sequence from previous series.
SIGNATURES: Kathryn O'Hay Granahan, Treasurer of the United States.
C. Douglas Dillon, Secretary of the Treasury.

	DISTRICT	TOTAL NOTES PRINTED	BLOCKS	ESTIMATED VALUE VG/F	CU	LOW OFFICIAL SERIAL NUMBER	HIGH OFFICIAL SERIAL NUMBER
1	A BOSTON	1,728,000	A--A		75.00	A03 600 001A	A05 328 000A
			A--*		85.00		
2	B NEW YORK	7,200,000	B--A		75.00	B30 538 001A	B37 728 000A
			B--*		85.00	B02 413 559*	
3	C PHILADELPHIA	2,736,000	C--A		75.00	C08 064 000A	C10 800 000A
			C--*		85.00		
4	D CLEVELAND	2,880,000	D--A		75.00	D11 088 001A	D13 968 000A
			D--*		85.00	D01 057 317*	
5	E RICHMOND	2,016,000	E--A		75.00	E10 080 001A	E12 096 000A
			E--*		85.00		
6	F ATLANTA	576,000	F--A		75.00	F02 160 001A	F02 736 000A
			F--*		85.00		
7	G CHICAGO	4,176,000	G--A		75.00	G12 384 001A	G16 560 000A
			G--*		85.00		
8	H ST. LOUIS	1,440,000	H--A		75.00	H02 736 001A	H04 176 000A
			H--*		85.00	H00 787 337*	H00 848 570*
9	I MINNEAPOLIS	288,000	I--A		80.00	I00 576 001A	I00 864 000A
			I--*		90.00		
10	J KANSAS CITY	720,000	J--A		75.00	J02 304 001A	J03 024 000A
			J--*		85.00		
11	K DALLAS	1,296,000	K--A		75.00	K03 744 001A	K05 040 000A
			K--*		85.00		
12	L SAN FRANCISCO	2,150,000	L--A		75.00	L07 632 001A	L09 792 000A
			L--*		85.00		

TOTAL BLOCKS: Twenty four.

CAT. NO. LF50E
$50.00 FEDERAL RESERVE NOTE (GREEN SEAL) (18 Subject)
SERIES 1950E

SERIAL NUMBERS: Districts printed continued sequence from previous series.
SIGNATURES: Kathryn O'Hay Granahan, Treasurer of the United States.
Henry H. Fowler, Secretary of the Treasurer.

	DISTRICT	TOTAL NOTES PRINTED	BLOCKS	ESTIMATED VALUE VG/F	CU	LOW OFFICIAL SERIAL NUMBER	HIGH OFFICIAL SERIAL NUMBER
2	B NEW YORK	3,024,000	B--A		80.00	B37 728 001A	B40 752 000A
			B--*		90.00	B02 847 457*	
7	G CHICAGO	1,008,000	G--A		80.00	G16 560 001A	G17 568 000A
			G--*		90.00		
12	L SAN FRANCISCO	1,306,000	L--A		80.00	L09 792 001A	L11 088 000A
			L--*		90.00		

TOTAL BLOCKS: Six.

No $50.00 note Series 1963 were printed.

CAT. NO. LF63A
$50.00 FEDERAL RESERVE NOTE (GREEN SEAL) (32 Subject)
SERIES 1963A

SERIAL NUMBERS: All serial numbers both regular and star notes begin with 00 000 001.
PLATE SERIALS: Face and back check begin with 1. Motto IN GOD WE TRUST added on back.
SIGNATURES: Kathryn O'Hay Granahan, Treasurer of the United States.
   Henry H. Fowler, Secretary of the Treasury.

	DISTRICT	TOTAL NOTES PRINTED	BLOCKS	VG/F	CU	LOW OFFICIAL SERIAL NUMBER	HIGH OFFICIAL SERIAL NUMBER
1	A BOSTON	1,536,000	A--A		75.00		A01 536 000A
		320,000	A--*		85.00		A00 320 000*
2	B NEW YORK	11,008,000	B--A		75.00		B11 008 000A
		1,408,000	B--*		85.00		B01 408 000*
3	C PHILADELPHIA	3,328,000	C--A		75.00		C03 328 000A
		704,000	C--*		85.00		C00 704 000*
4	D CLEVELAND	3,584,000	D--A		75.00		D03 584 000A
		256,000	D--*		85.00		D00 256 000*
5	E RICHMOND	3,072,000	E--A		75.00		E03 072 000A
		704,000	E--*		85.00		E00 704 000*
6	F ATLANTA	768,000	F--A		75.00		F00 768 000A
		384,000	F--*		85.00		F00 384 000*
7	G CHICAGO	6,912,000	G--A		75.00		G06 912 000A
		768,000	G--*		85.00		G00 768 000*
8	H ST. LOUIS	512,000	H--A		75.00		H00 512 000A
		128,000	H--*		90.00		H00 128 000*
9	I MINNEAPOLIS	512,000	I--A		75.00		I00 512 000A
		128,000	I--*		90.00		I00 128 000*
10	J KANSAS CITY	512,000	J--A		75.00		J00 512 000A
		64,000	J--*		100.00		J00 064 000*
11	K DALLAS	1,536,000	K--A		75.00		K01 536 000A
		128,000	K--*		90.00		K00 128 000*
12	L SAN FRANCISCO	4,352,000	L--A		75.00		L04 352 000A
		704,000	L--*		85.00		L00 704 000*

TOTAL BLOCKS: Twenty four.

CAT. NO. LF69
$50.00 FEDERAL RESERVE NOTE (GREEN SEAL) (32 Subject)
SERIES 1969

SERIAL NUMBERS: All serial numbers both regular and star notes begin with 00 000 001.
SIGNATURES: Dorothy Andrews Elston, Treasurer of the United States.
   David M. Kennedy, Secretary of the Treasury.

	DISTRICT	TOTAL NOTES PRINTED	BLOCKS	VG/F	CU	LOW OFFICIAL SERIAL NUMBER	HIGH OFFICIAL SERIAL NUMBER
1	A BOSTON	2,048,000	A--A		65.00		A02 048 000A
		none	A--*				
2	B NEW YORK	12,032,000	B--A		65.00		B12 032 000A
		384,000	B--*		75.00		B00 384 000*
3	C PHILADELPHIA	3,584,000	C--A		65.00		C03 584 000A
		128,000	C--*		80.00		C00 128 000*
4	D CLEVELAND	3,584,000	D--A		65.00		D03 584 000A
		192,000	D--*		75.00		D00 192 000*
5	E RICHMOND	2,560,000	E--A		65.00		E02 560 000A
		64,000	E--*		90.00		E00 064 000*
6	F ATLANTA	256,000	F--A		65.00		F00 256 000A
		none	F--*				

	DISTRICT	TOTAL NOTES PRINTED	BLOCKS	ESTIMATED VALUE VG/F	ESTIMATED VALUE CU	LOW OFFICIAL SERIAL NUMBER	HIGH OFFICIAL SERIAL NUMBER
7	G CHICAGO	9,728,000	G--A		65.00		G09 728 000A
		256,000	G--*		75.00		G00 256 000*
8	H ST. LOUIS	256,000	H--A		65.00		H00 256 000A
		none	H--*				
9	I MINNEAPOLIS	512,000	I--A		65.00		I00 512 000A
		none	I--*				
10	J KANSAS CITY	1,280,000	J--A		65.00		J01 280 000A
		64,000	J--*		90.00		J00 064 000*
11	K DALLAS	1,536,000	K--A		65.00		K01 536 000A
		64,000	K--*		90.00		K00 064 000*
12	L SAN FRANCISCO	6,912,000	L--A		65.00		L06 912 000A
		256,000	L--*		75.00		L00 256 000*

TOTAL BLOCKS: Twenty.

CAT. NO. LF69A
$50.00 FEDERAL RESERVE NOTE (GREEN SEAL) (32 Subject)
SERIES 1969A

SERIAL NUMBERS: Continued sequence from previous series.
SIGNATURES: Dorothy Andrews Kabis, Treasurer of the United States
   John B. Connally, Secretary of the Treasury
ESTIMATED VALUES: All regular notes $65.00 each CU, Stars $75.00 each CU.

	DISTRICT	TOTAL NOTES PRINTED	BLOCKS	ESTIMATED VALUE VG/F	ESTIMATED VALUE CU	LOW OFFICIAL SERIAL NUMBER	HIGH OFFICIAL SERIAL NUMBER
1	A BOSTON	1,536,000	A--A			A02 048 001A	A03 584 000A
		128,000	A--*			A00 000 001*	A00 128 000*
2	B NEW YORK	9,728,000	B--A			B12 032 001A	B21 760 000A
		704,000	B--*			B00 384 001*	B01 088 000*
3	C PHILADELPHIA	2,560,000	C--A			C03 584 001A	C06 144 000A
		none					
4	D CLEVELAND	2,816,000	D--A			D03 548 001A	D06 400 000A
		none					
5	E RICHMOND	2,304,000	E--A			E02 560 001A	E04 864 000A
		64,000	E--*			E00 064 001*	E00 128 000*
6	F ATLANTA	256,000	F--A			F00 256 001A	F00 512 000A
		64,000	F--*			F00 000 001*	F00 064 000*
7	G CHICAGO	3,584,000	G--A			G09 728 001A	G13 312 000A
		192,000	G--*			G00 256 001*	G00 448 000*
8	H ST. LOUIS	256,000	H--A			H00 256 001A	H00 512 000A
		none	H--*				
9	I MINNEAPOLIS	512,000	I--A			I00 512 001A	I01 024 000A
		none	I--*				
10	J KANSAS CITY	256,000	J--A			J01 280 001A	J01 536 000A
		none	J--*				
11	K DALLAS	1,024,000	K--A			K01 536 001A	K02 560 000A
		64,000	K--*			K00 064 001*	K00 128 000*
12	L SAN FRANCISCO	5,120,000	L--A			L06 912 001A	L12 032 000A
		256,000	L--*			L00 256 001*	L00 512 000*

TOTAL BLOCKS: Nineteen.

CAT. NO. LF69B
$50.00 FEDERAL RESERVE NOTE (GREEN SEAL) (32 Subject)
SERIES 1969B

SERIAL NUMBERS: Continued sequence from previous series.
ESTIMATED VALUES: All regular notes $65.00 each CU, Stars $75.00 each CU.
SIGNATURES: Romana Acosta Banuelos, Treasurer of the United States
   John B. Connally, Secretary of the Treasury

	DISTRICT	TOTAL NOTES PRINTED	BLOCKS	ESTIMATED VALUE VG/F	ESTIMATED VALUE CU	LOW OFFICIAL SERIAL NUMBER	HIGH OFFICIAL SERIAL NUMBER
1	A BOSTON	1,024,000	A--A			A03 584 001A	A04 6008 000A
		none	A--*				
2	B NEW YORK	2,560,000	B--A			B21 760 001A	B24 320 000A
		none	B--*				
3	C PHILADELPHIA	none	C--A				
		none	C--*				

	DISTRICT	TOTAL NOTES PRINTED	BLOCKS	ESTIMATED VALUE VG/F CU	LOW OFFICIAL SERIAL NUMBER	HIGH OFFICIAL SERIAL NUMBER
4	D CLEVELAND	none	D--A			
		none	D--*			
5	E RICHMOND	1,536,000	E--A		E04 864 001A	E06 400 000A
		none	E--*			
6	F ATLANTA	512,000	F--A		F00 512 001A	F01 024 000A
		none	F--*			
7	G CHICAGO	1,124,000	G--A		G13 312 001A	G14 336 000A
		none	G--*			
8	H ST. LOUIS	none	H--A			
		none	H--*			
9	I MINNEAPOLIS	none	I--A			
		none	I--*			
10	J KANSAS CITY	none	J--A			
		none	J--*			
11	K DALLAS	1,024,000	K--A		K02 560 001A	K03 584 000A
		128,000	K--*		K00 128 001*	K00 256 000*
12	SAN FRANCISCO	none	L--A			
		none	L--*			

TOTAL BLOCKS: Seven.

CAT. NO. LF69C
$50.00 FEDERAL RESERVE NOTE (GREEN SEAL) (32 Subject)
SERIES 1969C

SIGNATURES: Romano Acosta Banuelos, Treasurer of the United States
George P. Shultz, Secretary of the Treasury
ESTIMATED VALUES: All regular notes $55.00, stars $60.00 CU.

	DISTRICT	TOTAL NOTES PRINTED	BLOCKS	ESTIMATED VALUE VG/F CU	LOW OFFICIAL SERIAL NUMBER	HIGH OFFICIAL SERIAL NUMBER
1	A BOSTON #	1,792,000	A--A		A04 608 001A	A06 400 000A
		64,000	A--*		A00 128 001*	A00 192 000*
2	B NEW YORK #	7,040,000	B--A		B24 320 001A	B31 360 000A
		192,000	B--*		B01 088 001*	B01 280 000*
3	C PHILADELPHIA		C--A		C06 144 001A	C09 728 000A
		256,000	C--*		C00 128 001*	C00 384 000*
4	D CLEVELAND #	5,120,000	D--A		D06 400 001A	D11 520 000A
		192,000	D--*		D00 192 001*	D00 384 000*
5	E RICHMOND	2,304,000	E--A		E06 400 001A	E08 704 000A
		64,000	E--*		E00 128 001*	E00 192 000*
6	F ATLANTA	256,000	F--A		F01 024 001A	F01 280 000A
		64,000	F--*		F00 064 001*	F00 128 000*
7	G CHICAGO #	6,784,000	G--A		G14 336 001A	G21 120 000A
		576,000	G--*		G00 448 001*	G01 024 000*
8	H ST. LOUIS #	2,688,000	H--A		H00 512 001A	H03 200 000A
		64,000	H--*		H00 000 001*	H00 064 000*
9	I MINNEAPOLIS	256,000	I--A		I01 024 001A	H01 280 000A
		64,000	I--*		I00 000 001*	I00 064 000*
10	J KANSAS CITY	1,280,000	J--A		J01 536 001A	J02 816 000A
		128,000	J--*		J00 064 001*	J00 192 000*
11	K DALLAS #	3,456,000	K--A		K03 584 001A	K07 040 000A
		64,000	K--*		K00 256 001*	K00 320 000*
12	L SAN FRANCISCO #	4,608,000	L--A		L12 032 001A	L16 640 000A
		256,000	L--*		L00 512 001*	L00 768 000*

TOTAL BLOCKS: Twenty-four.
The production unit was changed from 8,000 sheets to 20,000 sheets for:

BANK	STARTING WITH SERIAL NUMBER	BANK	STARTING WITH SERIAL NUMBER
Boston	A05 760 001A	St. Louis	H01 920 001A
New York	B24 320 001A	Dallas	K03 840 001A
Cleveland	D10 240 001A	San Francisco	L15 360 001A
Chicago	G17 920 001A		

The formula to relate the position and check letter for serials later than above would be the same as used on the lower denominations.

CAT. NO. LF74
$50.00 FEDERAL RESERVE NOTE (GREEN SEAL) 32 Subject
SERIES 1974

SIGNATURES: Francine I. Neff, Treasurer of the United States.
   William E. Simon, Secretary of the Treasury.
PLATE SERIALS: Face and back check numbers continue from previous series.
SERIAL NUMBERS: All districts continue from previous series.

	DISTRICT	TOTAL NOTES PRINTED	BLOCKS	ESTIMATED VALUE VG/F	CU	LOW OFFICIAL SERIAL NUMBER	HIGH OFFICIAL SERIAL NUMBER	
1	A BOSTON		A--A		60.00	A06 400 001A	A07 680 000A	cv
					60.00	A07 080 001A	A10 240 000A	cp
			A--*		65.00	A00 192 001A	A00 448 000A	cv
2	B NEW YORK		B--A		60.00	B31 360 001A	B48 000 000A	cv
					60.00	B48 000 001A	B69 760 000A	cp
			B--*		65.00	B01 280 001*	B02 048 000*	cv
3	C PHILADELPHIA		C--A		60.00	C09 728 001A	C12 160 000A	cv
					60.00	C12 160 001A	C17 280 000A	cp
			C--*		65.00	C00 384 001*	C00 576 000*	cv
4	D CLEVELAND		D--A		60.00	D11 520 001A	D20 480 000A	cv
					60.00	D20 480 001A	D32 640 000A	cp
			D--*		65.00	D00 384 001*	D01 024 000*	cv
5	E RICHMOND		E--A		60.00	E08 704 001A	E14 720 000A	cv
					60.00	E14 720 001A	E23 040 000A	cp
			E--*		65.00	E00 192 001*	E00 768 000*	cv
6	F ATLANTA		F--A		60.00	F01 280 001A	F01 920 000A	cv
					60.00	F01 920 001A	F02 560 000A	cp
			F--*			none printed		
7	G CHICAGO		G--A		60.00	G21 120 001A	G36 480 000A	cv
					60.00	G36 480 001A	G51 840 000A	cp
			G--*		65.00	G01 024 001*	G02 560 000*	cv
8	H ST. LOUIS		H--A		60.00	H03 200 001A	H05 120 000A	cp
			H--*		65.00	H00 064 001*	H00 192 000*	cv
9	I MINNEAPOLIS		I--A		60.00	I01 280 001A	I02 560 000A	cv
					60.00	I02 560 001A	I03 840 000A	cp
			I--*		65.00	I00 064 001*	I00 256 000*	cv
10	J KANSAS CITY		J--A		60.00	J02 816 001A	J05 120 000A	cv
					60.00	J05 120 001A	J07 680 000A	cp
			J--*		65.00	J00 192 001*	J00 384 000*	cv
11	K DALLAS		K--A		60.00	K07 040 001A	K07 680 000A	cv
					60.00	K07 680 000A	K15 360 000A	cp
			K--*		65.00	K00 320 001*	K00 448 000*	cv
12	L SAN FRANCISCO		L--A		60.00	L16 640 001A	L23 680 000A	cv
					60.00	L23 680 001A	L24 320 000A	cv
			L--*		65.00	L00 768 001*	L00 832 000A	cv

TOTAL BLOCKS KNOWN: Twenty three.

\# The production unit was changed from 8,000 sheets to 20,000 sheets for:

BANK	STARTING WITH SERIAL NUMBER
Philadelphia	C10 240 001A
Richmond	E08 960 001A
Atlanta	F01 280 001A
Minneapolis	I01 280 001A
Kansas City	J04 480 001A

CAT. NO. LF77
$50.00 FEDERAL RESERVE NOTE (GREEN SEAL) 32 Subject
SERIES 1977

SIGNATURES: Azie Taylor Morton, Treasurer of the United States.
   W. Michael Blumenthal, Secretary of the Treasury.
PLATE SERIALS: Both face and back check numbers continue from previous series.
SERIAL NUMBERS: All districts begin with 00 000 001.

	DISTRICT	TOTAL NOTES PRINTED	BLOCKS	ESTIMATED VALUE VG/F	CU	LOW OFFICIAL SERIAL NUMBER	HIGH OFFICIAL SERIAL NUMBER
1	A BOSTON		A--A		55.00	A00 000 001A	A16 640 000A
			A--*		65.00	A00 000 001*	A00 192 001*
					100.00	A01 936 001*	A01 940 000*

DISTRICT	TOTAL NOTES PRINTED	BLOCKS	ESTIMATED VALUE VG/F	VALUE CU	LOW OFFICIAL SERIAL NUMBER	HIGH OFFICIAL SERIAL NUMBER
				100.00	A01 956 001*	A01 960 000*
				100.00	A01 976 001*	A01 980 000*
				100.00	A01 996 001*	A02 000 000*
				100.00	A02 016 001*	A02 020 000*
				100.00	A02 036 001*	A02 040 000*
				100.00	A02 056 001*	A02 060 000*
				100.00	A02 076 001*	A02 080 000*
				100.00	A02 096 001*	A02 100 000*
				100.00	A02 116 001*	A02 120 000*
				100.00	A02 136 001*	A02 140 000*
				100.00	A02 156 001*	A02 160 000*
				100.00	A02 176 001*	A02 180 000*
				100.00	A02 196 001*	A02 200 000*
				100.00	A02 216 001*	A02 220 000*
				100.00	A02 236 001*	A02 240 000*
				100.00	A02 256 001*	A02 260 000*
				100.00	A02 276 001*	A02 280 000*
				100.00	A02 296 001*	A02 300 000*
				100.00	A02 316 001*	A02 320 000*
				100.00	A02 336 001*	A02 340 000*
				100.00	A02 356 001*	A02 360 000*
				100.00	A02 376 001*	A02 380 000*
				100.00	A02 396 001*	A02 400 000*
				100.00	A02 416 001*	A02 420 000*
				100.00	A02 436 001*	A02 440 000*
				100.00	A02 456 001*	A02 460 000*
				100.00	A02 476 001*	A02 480 000*
				100.00	A02 496 001*	A02 500 000*
				100.00	A02 516 001*	A02 520 000*
				100.00	A02 536 001*	A02 540 000*
				100.00	A02 556 001*	A02 560 000*
				100.00	A02 576 001*	A02 580 000*
				100.00	A02 596 001*	A02 600 000*
				100.00	A02 616 001*	A02 620 000*
				100.00	A02 636 001*	A02 640 000*
				100.00	A02 656 001*	A02 660 000*
				100.00	A02 676 001*	A02 680 000*
				100.00	A02 696 001*	A02 700 000*
				100.00	A02 716 001*	A02 720 000*
				100.00	A02 736 001*	A02 740 000*
				100.00	A02 756 001*	A02 760 000*
				100.00	A02 776 001*	A02 780 000*
				100.00	A02 796 001*	A02 800 000*
				100.00	A02 816 001*	A02 820 000*
				100.00	A02 836 001*	A02 840 000*
				100.00	A02 856 001*	A02 860 000*
				100.00	A02 876 001*	A02 880 000*
				100.00	A02 896 001*	A02 900 000*
				100.00	A02 916 001*	A02 920 000*
				100.00	A02 936 001*	A02 940 000*
				100.00	A02 956 001*	A02 960 000*
				100.00	A02 976 001*	A02 980 000*
				100.00	A02 996 001*	A03 000 000*
				100.00	A03 016 001*	A03 020 000*
				100.00	A03 036 001*	A03 040 000*
				100.00	A03 056 001*	A03 060 000*
				100.00	A03 076 001*	A03 080 000*
				100.00	A03 096 001*	A03 100 000*
				100.00	A03 116 001*	A03 120 000*
				100.00	A03 136 001*	A03 140 000*
				100.00	A03 156 001*	A03 160 000*
				100.00	A03 176 001*	A03 180 000*
				100.00	A03 196 001*	A03 200 000*
				100.00	A03 216 001*	A03 220 000*
				100.00	A03 236 001*	A03 240 000*
				100.00	A03 256 001*	A03 260 000*
				100.00	A03 276 001*	A02 280 000*
				100.00	A03 296 001*	A03 300 000*
				100.00	A03 316 001*	A03 320 000*

DISTRICT	TOTAL NOTES PRINTED	BLOCKS	ESTIMATED VALUE VG/F CU	LOW OFFICIAL SERIAL NUMBER	HIGH OFFICIAL SERIAL NUMBER
			100.00	A03 336 001*	A03 340 000*
			100.00	A03 356 001*	A03 360 000*
			100.00	A03 376 001*	A03 380 000*
			100.00	A03 396 001*	A03 400 000*
			100.00	A03 416 001*	A03 420 000*
			100.00	A03 436 001*	A03 440 000*
			100.00	A03 456 001*	A03 460 000*
			100.00	A03 476 001*	A03 480 000*
			100.00	A03 496 001*	A03 500 000*
			100.00	A03 516 001*	A03 520 000*
			100.00	A03 536 001*	A03 540 000*
			100.00	A03 556 001*	A03 560 000*
			100.00	A03 576 001*	A03 580 000*
			100.00	A03 596 001*	A03 600 000*
			100.00	A03 616 001*	A03 620 000*
			100.00	A03 636 001*	A03 640 000*
			100.00	A03 656 001*	A03 660 000*
			100.00	A03 676 001*	A03 680 000*
			100.00	A03 696 001*	A03 700 000*
			100.00	A03 716 001*	A03 720 000*
			100.00	A03 736 001*	A03 740 000*
			100.00	A03 756 001*	A03 760 000*
			100.00	A03 776 001*	A03 780 000*
			100.00	A03 796 001*	A03 800 000*
			100.00	A03 816 001*	A03 820 000*
			100.00	A03 836 001*	A03 840 000*
			100.00	A03 844 001*	A03 860 000*
			100.00	A03 864 001*	A03 880 000*
			100.00	A03 884 001*	A03 900 000*
			100.00	A03 904 001*	A03 920 000*
			100.00	A03 924 001*	A03 940 000*
			100.00	A03 944 001*	A03 960 000*
			100.00	A03 964 001*	A03 980 000*
			100.00	A03 984 001*	A04 000 000*
			100.00	A04 004 001*	A04 020 000*
			100.00	A04 024 001*	A04 040 000*
			100.00	A04 044 001*	A04 060 000*
			100.00	A04 064 001*	A04 080 000*
			100.00	A04 084 001*	A04 100 000*
			100.00	A04 104 001*	A04 120 000*
			100.00	A04 124 001*	A04 140 000*
			100.00	A04 144 001*	A04 160 000*
			100.00	A04 164 001*	A04 180 000*
			100.00	A04 184 001*	A04 200 000*
			100.00	A04 204 001*	A04 220 000*
			100.00	A04 224 001*	A04 240 000*
			100.00	A04 244 001*	A04 260 000*
			100.00	A04 264 001*	A04 280 000*
			100.00	A04 284 001*	A04 300 000*
			100.00	A04 304 001*	A04 320 000*
			100.00	A04 324 001*	A04 340 000*
			100.00	A04 344 001*	A04 360 000*
			100.00	A04 364 001*	A04 380 000*
			100.00	A04 384 001*	A04 400 000*
			100.00	A04 404 001*	A04 420 000*
			100.00	A04 424 001*	A04 440 000*
			100.00	A04 444 001*	A04 460 000*
			100.00	A04 464 001*	A04 480 000*
2 B NEW YORK		B--A	55.00	B00 000 001A	B49 920 000A
		B--*	65.00	B00 000 001*	B00 960 000*
			100.00	B09 614 001*	B09 620 000*
			100.00	B09 634 001*	B09 640 000*
			100.00	B09 654 001*	B09 660 000*
			100.00	B09 674 001*	B09 680 000*
			100.00	B09 694 001*	B09 700 000*
			100.00	B09 714 001*	G09 720 000*
			100.00	B09 734 001*	B09 740 000*
			100.00	B09 754 001*	B09 760 000*
			100.00	B09 774 001*	B09 780 000*

VALUE CU	LOW OFFICIAL SERIAL NUMBER	HIGH OFFICIAL SERIAL NUMBER	VALUE CU	LOW OFFICIAL SERIAL NUMBER	HIGH OFFICIAL SERIAL NUMBER
100.00	B09 794 001*	B09 800 000*	100.00	B11 174 001*	B11 180 000*
100.00	B09 814 001*	B09 820 000*	100.00	B11 194 001*	B11 200 000*
100.00	B09 834 001*	B09 840 000*	100.00	B11 214 001*	B11 220 000*
100.00	B09 854 001*	B09 860 000*	100.00	B11 234 001*	B11 240 000*
100.00	B09 874 001*	B09 880 000*	100.00	B11 254 001*	B11 260 000*
100.00	B09 894 001*	B09 900 000*	100.00	B11 274 001*	B11 280 000*
100.00	B09 914 001*	B09 920 000*	100.00	B11 294 001*	B11 300 000*
100.00	B09 934 001*	B09 940 000*	100.00	B11 314 001*	B11 320 000*
100.00	B09 954 001*	B09 960 000*	100.00	B11 334 001*	B11 340 000*
100.00	B09 974 001*	B09 980 000*	100.00	B11 354 001*	B11 360 000*
100.00	B09 994 001*	B10 000 000*	100.00	B11 374 001*	B11 380 000*
100.00	B10 014 001*	B10 020 000*	100.00	B11 394 001*	B11 400 000*
100.00	B10 034 001*	B10 040 000*	100.00	B11 414 001*	B11 420 000*
100.00	B10 054 001*	B10 060 000*	100.00	B11 434 001*	B11 440 000*
100.00	B10 074 001*	B10 080 000*	100.00	B11 454 001*	B11 460 000*
100.00	B10 094 001*	B10 100 000*	100.00	B11 474 001*	B11 480 000*
100.00	B10 114 001*	B10 120 000*	100.00	B11 494 001*	B11 500 000*
100.00	B10 134 001*	B10 140 000*	100.00	B11 514 001*	B11 520 000*
100.00	B10 154 001*	B10 160 000*	100.00	B11 532 001*	B11 540 000*
100.00	B10 174 001*	B10 180 000*	100.00	B11 552 001*	B11 560 000*
100.00	B10 194 001*	B10 200 000*	100.00	B11 572 001*	B11 580 000*
100.00	B10 214 001*	B10 220 000*	100.00	B11 592 001*	B11 600 000*
100.00	B10 234 001*	B10 240 000*	100.00	B11 612 001*	B11 620 000*
100.00	B10 252 001*	B10 260 000*	100.00	B11 632 001*	B11 640 000*
100.00	B10 272 001*	B10 280 000*	100.00	B11 652 001*	B11 660 000*
100.00	B10 292 001*	B10 300 000*	100.00	B11 672 001*	B11 680 000*
100.00	B10 312 001*	B10 320 000*	100.00	B11 692 001*	B11 700 000*
100.00	B10 332 001*	B10 340 000*	100.00	B11 712 001*	B11 720 000*
100.00	B10 352 001*	B10 360 000*	100.00	B11 732 001*	B11 740 000*
100.00	B10 372 001*	B10 380 000*	100.00	B11 752 001*	G11 760 000*
100.00	B10 392 001*	B10 400 000*	100.00	B11 772 001*	B11 780 000*
100.00	B10 412 001*	B10 420 000*	100.00	B11 792 001*	B11 800 000*
100.00	B10 432 001*	B10 440 000*	100.00	B11 812 001*	B11 820 000*
100.00	B10 452 001*	B10 460 000*	100.00	B11 832 001*	B11 840 000*
100.00	B10 472 001*	B10 480 000*	100.00	B11 852 001*	B11 860 000*
100.00	B10 492 001*	B10 500 000*	100.00	B11 872 001*	B11 880 000*
100.00	B10 512 001*	B10 520 000*	100.00	B11 892 001*	B11 900 000*
100.00	B10 532 001*	B10 540 000*	100.00	B11 912 001*	B11 920 000*
100.00	B10 552 001*	B10 560 000*	100.00	B11 932 001*	B11 940 000*
100.00	B10 572 001*	B10 580 000*	100.00	B11 952 001*	B11 960 000*
100.00	B10 592 001*	B10 600 000*	100.00	B11 972 001*	B11 980 000*
100.00	B10 612 001*	B10 620 000*	100.00	B11 992 001*	B12 000 000*
100.00	B10 632 001*	B10 640 000*	100.00	B12 012 001*	B12 020 000*
100.00	B10 652 001*	B10 660 000*	100.00	B12 032 001*	B12 040 000*
100.00	B10 672 001*	B10 680 000*	100.00	B12 052 001*	B12 060 000*
100.00	B10 692 001*	B10 700 000*	100.00	B12 072 001*	B12 080 000*
100.00	B10 712 001*	B10 720 000*	100.00	B12 092 001*	B12 100 000*
100.00	B10 732 001*	B10 740 000*	100.00	B12 112 001*	B12 120 000*
100.00	B10 752 001*	B10 760 000*	100.00	B12 132 001*	B12 140 000*
100.00	B10 772 001*	B10 780 000*	100.00	B12 152 001*	B12 160 000*
100.00	B10 792 001*	B10 800 000*	100.00	B12 172 001*	B12 180 000*
100.00	B10 812 001*	B10 820 000*	100.00	B12 192 001*	B12 200 000*
100.00	B10 832 001*	B10 840 000*	100.00	B12 212 001*	B12 220 000*
100.00	B10 852 001*	B10 860 000*	100.00	B12 232 001*	B12 240 000*
100.00	B10 872 001*	B10 880 000*	100.00	B12 252 001*	B12 260 000*
100.00	B10 894 001*	B10 900 000*	100.00	B12 272 001*	B12 280 000*
100.00	B10 914 001*	B10 920 000*	100.00	B12 292 001*	B12 300 000*
100.00	B10 934 001*	B10 940 000*	100.00	B12 312 001*	B12 320 000*
100.00	B10 954 001*	B10 960 000*	100.00	B12 332 001*	B12 340 000*
100.00	B10 974 001*	B10 980 000*	100.00	B12 352 001*	B12 360 000*
100.00	B10 994 001*	B11 000 000*	100.00	B12 372 001*	B12 380 000*
100.00	B11 014 001*	B11 020 000*	100.00	B12 392 001*	B12 400 000*
100.00	B11 034 001*	B11 040 000*	100.00	B12 412 001*	B12 420 000*
100.00	B11 054 001*	B11 060 000*	100.00	B12 432 001*	B12 440 000*
100.00	B11 074 001*	B11 080 000*	100.00	B12 452 001*	B12 460 000*
100.00	B11 094 001*	B11 100 000*	100.00	B12 472 001*	B12 480 000*
100.00	B11 114 001*	B11 120 000*	100.00	B12 492 001*	B12 500 000*
100.00	B11 134 001*	B11 140 000*	100.00	B12 512 001*	B12 520 000*
100.00	B11 154 001*	B11 160 000*	100.00	B12 532 001*	B12 540 000*

DISTRICT	TOTAL NOTES PRINTED	BLOCKS	ESTIMATED VALUE VG/F	CU	LOW OFFICIAL SERIAL NUMBER	HIGH OFFICIAL SERIAL NUMBER
				100.00	B12 552 001*	B12 560 000*
				100.00	B12 572 001*	B12 580 000*
				100.00	B12 592 001*	B12 600 000*
				100.00	B12 612 001*	B12 620 000*
				100.00	B12 632 001*	B12 640 000*
				100.00	B12 652 001*	B12 660 000*
				100.00	B12 672 001*	B12 680 000*
				100.00	B12 692 001*	B12 700 000*
				100.00	B12 712 001*	B12 720 000*
				100.00	B12 732 001*	B12 740 000*
				100.00	B12 752 001*	B12 760 000*
				100.00	B12 772 001*	B12 780 000*
				100.00	B12 792 001*	B12 800 000*
3 C PHILADELPHIA		C--A		55.00	C00 000 001A	C05 120 000A
		C--*		100.00	C00 016 001*	C00 020 000*
				100.00	C00 036 001*	C00 040 000*
				100.00	C00 056 001*	C00 060 000*
				100.00	C00 076 001*	C00 080 000*
				100.00	C00 096 001*	C00 100 000*
				100.00	C00 116 001*	C00 120 000*
				100.00	C00 136 001*	C00 140 000*
				100.00	C00 156 001*	C00 160 000*
				100.00	C00 176 001*	C00 180 000*
				100.00	C00 196 001*	C00 200 000*
				100.00	C00 216 001*	C00 220 000*
				100.00	C00 236 001*	C00 240 000*
				100.00	C00 256 001*	C00 260 000*
				100.00	C00 276 001*	C00 280 000*
				100.00	C00 296 001*	C00 300 000*
				100.00	C00 316 001*	C00 320 000*
				100.00	C00 336 001*	C00 340 000*
				100.00	C00 356 001*	C00 360 000*
				100.00	C00 376 001*	C00 380 000*
				100.00	C00 396 001*	C00 400 000*
				100.00	C00 416 001*	C00 420 000*
				100.00	C00 436 001*	C00 440 000*
				100.00	C00 456 001*	C00 460 000*
				100.00	C00 476 001*	C00 480 000*
				100.00	C00 496 001*	C00 500 000*
				100.00	C00 516 001*	C00 520 000*
				100.00	C00 536 001*	C00 540 000*
				100.00	C00 556 001*	C00 560 000*
				100.00	C00 576 001*	C00 580 000*
				100.00	C00 596 001*	C00 600 000*
				100.00	C00 616 001*	C00 620 000*
				100.00	C00 636 001*	C00 640 000*
4 D CLEVELAND		D--A		55.00	D00 000 001A	D23 040 000A
		D--*		65.00	D00 000 001*	D00 832 000*
				100.00	D08 338 001*	D08 340 000*
				100.00	D08 358 001*	D08 360 000*
				100.00	D08 378 001*	D08 380 000*
				100.00	D08 398 001*	D08 400 000*
				100.00	D08 418 001*	D08 420 000*
				100.00	D08 438 001*	D08 440 000*
				100.00	D08 458 001*	D08 460 000*
				100.00	D08 478 001*	D08 480 000*
				100.00	D08 498 001A	D08 500 000*
				100.00	D08 518 001*	D08 520 000*
				100.00	D08 538 001*	D08 540 000*
				100.00	D08 558 001*	D08 560 000*
				100.00	D08 578 001*	D08 580 000*
				100.00	D08 598 001*	D08 600 000*
				100.00	D08 618 001*	D08 620 000*
				100.00	D08 638 001*	D08 640 000*
				100.00	D08 658 001*	D08 660 000*
				100.00	D08 678 001*	D08 680 000*
				100.00	D08 698 001*	D08 700 000*
				100.00	D08 718 001*	D08 720 000*
				100.00	D08 738 001*	D08 740 000*

DISTRICT	TOTAL NOTES PRINTED	BLOCKS	ESTIMATED VALUE VG/F	CU	LOW OFFICIAL SERIAL NUMBER	HIGH OFFICIAL SERIAL NUMBER
				100.00	D08 758 001*	D08 760 000*
				100.00	D08 778 001*	D08 780 000*
				100.00	D08 798 001*	D08 800 000*
				100.00	D08 818 001*	D08 820 000*
				100.00	D08 838 001*	D08 840 000*
				100.00	D08 858 001*	D08 860 000*
				100.00	D08 878 001*	D08 880 000*
				100.00	D08 898 001*	D08 900 000*
				100.00	D08 918 001*	D08 920 000*
				100.00	D08 938 001*	D08 940 000*
				100.00	D08 958 001*	D08 960 000*
				100.00	D08 976 001*	D08 980 000*
				100.00	D08 996 001*	D09 000 000*
				100.00	D09 016 001*	D09 020 000*
				100.00	D09 036 001*	D09 040 000*
				100.00	D09 056 001*	D09 060 000*
				100.00	D09 076 001*	D09 080 000*
				100.00	D09 096 001*	D09 100 000*
				100.00	D09 116 001*	D09 120 000*
				100.00	D09 136 001*	D09 140 000*
				100.00	D09 156 001*	D09 160 000*
				100.00	D09 176 001*	D09 180 000*
				100.00	D09 196 001*	D09 200 000*
				100.00	D09 216 001*	D09 220 000*
				100.00	D09 236 001*	D09 240 000*
				100.00	D09 256 001*	D09 260 000*
				100.00	D09 276 001*	D09 280 000*
				100.00	D09 296 001*	D09 300 000*
				100.00	D09 316 001*	D09 320 000*
				100.00	D09 336 001*	D09 340 000*
				100.00	D09 356 001*	D09 360 000*
				100.00	D09 376 001*	D09 380 000*
				100.00	D09 396 001*	D09 400 000*
				100.00	D09 416 001*	D09 420 000*
				100.00	D09 436 001*	D09 440 000*
				100.00	D09 456 001*	D09 460 000*
				100.00	D09 476 001*	D09 480 000*
				100.00	D09 496 001*	D09 500 000*
				100.00	D09 516 001*	D09 520 000*
				100.00	D09 536 001*	D09 540 000*
				100.00	D09 556 001*	D09 560 000*
				100.00	D09 576 001*	D09 580 000*
				100.00	D09 596 001*	D09 600 000*
5	E RICHMOND		E--A	55.00	E00 000 001A	E19 200 000A
			E--*	65.00	E00 000 001*	E00 256 000*
				100.00	E02 572 001*	E02 580 000*
				100.00	E02 592 001*	E02 600 000*
				100.00	E02 612 001*	E02 620 000*
				100.00	E02 632 001*	E02 640 000*
				100.00	E02 652 001*	E02 660 000*
				100.00	E02 672 001*	E02 680 000*
				100.00	E02 692 001*	E02 700 000*
				100.00	E02 712 001*	E02 720 000*
				100.00	E02 732 001*	E02 740 000*
				100.00	E02 752 001*	E02 760 000*
				100.00	E02 772 001*	E02 780 000*
				100.00	E02 792 001*	E02 800 000*
				100.00	E02 812 001*	E02 820 000*
				100.00	E02 832 001*	E02 840 000*
				100.00	E02 852 001*	E02 860 000*
				100.00	E02 872 001*	E02 880 000*
				100.00	E02 892 001*	E02 900 000*
				100.00	E02 912 001*	E02 920 000*
				100.00	E02 932 001*	E02 940 000*
				100.00	E02 952 001*	E02 960 000*
				100.00	E02 972 001*	E02 980 000*
				100.00	E02 992 001*	E03 000 000*
				100.00	E03 012 001*	E03 020 000*
				100.00	E03 032 001*	E03 040 000*

DISTRICT	TOTAL NOTES PRINTED	BLOCKS	ESTIMATED VALUE VG/F	VALUE CU	LOW OFFICIAL SERIAL NUMBER	HIGH OFFICIAL SERIAL NUMBER
				100.00	E03 052 001*	E03 060 000*
				100.00	E03 072 001*	E03 080 000*
				100.00	E03 092 001*	E03 100 000*
				100.00	E03 112 001*	E03 120 000*
				100.00	E03 132 001*	E03 140 000*
				100.00	E03 152 001*	E03 160 000*
				100.00	E03 172 001*	E03 180 000*
				100.00	E03 192 001*	E03 200 000*
				100.00	E03 216 001*	E03 220 000*
				100.00	E03 236 001*	E03 240 000*
				100.00	E03 256 001*	E03 260 000*
				100.00	E03 276 001*	E03 280 000*
				100.00	E03 296 001*	E03 300 000*
				100.00	E03 316 001*	E03 320 000*
				100.00	E03 336 001*	E03 340 000*
				100.00	E03 356 001*	E03 360 000*
				100.00	E03 376 001*	E03 380 000*
				100.00	E03 396 001*	E03 400 000*
				100.00	E03 416 001*	E03 420 000*
				100.00	E03 436 001*	E03 440 000*
				100.00	E03 456 001*	E03 460 000*
				100.00	E03 476 001*	E03 480 000*
				100.00	E03 496 001*	E03 500 000*
				100.00	E03 516 001*	E03 520 000*
				100.00	E03 536 001*	E03 540 000*
				100.00	E03 556 001*	E03 560 000*
				100.00	E03 576 001*	E03 580 000*
				100.00	E03 596 001*	E03 600 000*
				100.00	E03 616 001*	E03 620 000*
				100.00	E03 636 001*	E03 640 000*
				100.00	E03 656 001*	E03 660 000*
				100.00	E03 676 001*	E03 680 000*
				100.00	E03 696 001*	E03 700 000*
				100.00	E03 716 001*	E03 720 000*
				100.00	E03 736 001*	E03 740 000*
				100.00	E03 756 001*	E03 760 000*
				100.00	E03 776 001*	E03 780 000*
				100.00	E03 796 001*	E03 800 000*
				100.00	E03 816 001*	E03 820 000*
				100.00	E03 836 001*	E03 840 000*
6	F ATLANTA	F--A		55.00	F00 000 001A	F02 560 000A
		F--*		65.00	F00 000 001*	F00 640 000*
7	G CHICAGO	G--A		55.00	G00 000 001A	G47 360 000A
		G--*		65.00	G00 000 001*	G00 768 000*
				100.00	G11 532 001*	G11 540 000*
				100.00	G11 552 001*	G11 560 000*
				100.00	G11 572 001*	G11 580 000*
				100.00	G11 592 001*	G11 600 000*
				100.00	G11 612 001*	G11 620 000*
				100.00	G11 632 001*	G11 640 000*
				100.00	G11 652 001*	G11 660 000*
				100.00	G11 672 001*	G11 680 000*
				100.00	G11 692 001*	G11 700 000*
				100.00	G11 712 001*	G11 720 000*
				100.00	G11 732 001*	G11 740 000*
				100.00	G11 752 001*	G11 760 000*
				100.00	G11 772 001*	G11 780 000*
				100.00	G11 792 001*	G11 800 000*
				100.00	G11 812 001*	G11 820 000*
				100.00	G11 832 001*	G11 840 000*
				100.00	G11 852 001*	G11 860 000*
				100.00	G11 872 001*	G11 880 000*
				100.00	G11 892 001*	G11 900 000*
				100.00	G11 912 001*	G11 920 000*
				100.00	G11 932 001*	G11 940 000*
				100.00	G11 952 001*	G11 960 000*
				100.00	G11 972 001*	G11 980 000*
				100.00	G11 992 001*	G12 000 000*
				100.00	G12 012 001*	G12 020 000*

DISTRICT	TOTAL NOTES PRINTED	BLOCKS	ESTIMATED VALUE VG/F	CU	LOW OFFICIAL SERIAL NUMBER	HIGH OFFICIAL SERIAL NUMBER
				100.00	G12 032 001*	G12 040 000*
				100.00	G12 052 001*	G12 060 000*
				100.00	G12 072 001*	G12 080 000*
				100.00	G12 092 001*	G12 100 000*
				100.00	G12 112 001*	G12 120 000*
				100.00	G12 132 001*	G12 140 000*
				100.00	G12 152 001*	G12 160 000*
				100.00	G13 456 001*	G13 460 000*
				100.00	G13 476 001*	G13 480 000*
				100.00	G13 496 001*	G13 500 000*
				100.00	G13 516 001*	G13 520 000*
				100.00	G13 536 001*	G13 540 000*
				100.00	G13 556 001*	G13 560 000*
				100.00	G13 576 001*	G13 580 000*
				100.00	G13 596 001*	G13 600 000*
				100.00	G13 616 001*	G13 620 000*
				100.00	G13 636 001*	G13 640 000*
				100.00	G13 656 001*	G13 660 000*
				100.00	G13 676 001*	G13 680 000*
				100.00	G13 696 001*	G13 700 000*
				100.00	G13 716 001*	G13 720 000*
				100.00	G13 736 001*	G13 740 000*
				100.00	G13 756 001*	G13 760 000*
				100.00	G13 776 001*	G13 780 000*
				100.00	G13 796 001*	G13 800 000*
				100.00	G13 816 000*	G13 820 000*
				100.00	G13 836 001*	G13 840 000*
				100.00	G13 856 001*	G13 860 000*
				100.00	G13 876 001*	G13 880 000*
				100.00	G13 896 001*	G13 900 000*
				100.00	G13 916 001*	G13 920 000*
				100.00	G13 936 001*	G13 940 000*
				100.00	G13 956 001*	G13 960 000*
				100.00	G13 976 001*	G13 980 000*
				100.00	G13 996 001*	G14 000 000*
				100.00	G14 016 001*	G14 020 000*
				100.00	G14 036 001*	G14 040 000*
				100.00	G14 056 001*	G14 060 000*
				100.00	G14 076 001*	G14 080 000*
8	H ST. LOUIS	H--A		55.00	H00 000 001A	H03 840 000A
		H--*		100.00	H00 016 001*	H00 020 000*
				100.00	H00 036 001*	H00 040 000*
				100.00	H00 056 001*	H00 060 000*
				100.00	H00 076 001*	H00 080 000*
				100.00	H00 096 001*	H00 100 000*
				100.00	H00 116 001*	H00 120 000*
				100.00	H00 136 001*	H00 140 000*
				100.00	H00 156 001*	H00 160 000*
				100.00	H00 176 001*	H00 180 000*
				100.00	H00 196 001*	H00 200 000*
				100.00	H00 196 001*	H00 200 000*
				100.00	H00 216 001*	H00 220 000*
				100.00	H00 236 001*	H00 240 000*
				100.00	H00 256 001*	H00 260 000*
				100.00	H00 276 001*	H00 280 000*
				100.00	H00 296 001*	H00 300 000*
				100.00	H00 316 001*	H00 320 000*
				100.00	H00 336 001*	H00 340 000*
				100.00	H00 356 001*	H00 360 000*
				100.00	H00 376 001*	H00 380 000*
				100.00	H00 396 001*	H00 400 000*
				100.00	H00 416 001*	H00 420 000*
				100.00	H00 436 001*	H00 440 000*
				100.00	H00 456 001*	H00 460 000*
				100.00	H00 476 001*	H00 480 000*
				100.00	H00 496 001*	H00 500 000*
				100.00	H00 516 001*	H00 520 000*
				100.00	H00 536 001*	H00 540 000*
				100.00	SH00 556 001*	H00 560 000*

DISTRICT	TOTAL NOTES PRINTED	BLOCKS	ESTIMATED VALUE VG/F	VALUE CU	LOW OFFICIAL SERIAL NUMBER	HIGH OFFICIAL SERIAL NUMBER
				100.00	H00 576 001*	H00 580 000*
				100.00	H00 596 001*	H00 600 000*
				100.00	H00 616 001*	H00 620 000*
				100.00	H00 636 001*	H00 640 000*
				100.00	H00 656 001*	H00 660 000*
				100.00	H00 676 001*	H00 680 000*
				100.00	H00 696 001*	H00 700 000*
				100.00	H00 716 001*	H00 720 000*
				100.00	H00 736 001*	H00 740 000*
				100.00	H00 756 001*	H00 760 000*
				100.00	H00 776 001*	H00 780 000*
				100.00	H00 796 001*	H00 800 000*
				100.00	H00 816 001*	H00 820 000*
				100.00	H00 836 001*	H00 840 000*
				100.00	H00 856 001*	H00 860 000*
				100.00	H00 876 001*	H00 880 000*
				100.00	H00 896 001*	H00 900 000*
				100.00	H00 916 001*	H00 920 000*
				100.00	H00 936 001*	H00 940 000*
				100.00	H00 956 001*	H00 960 000*
				100.00	H00 976 001*	H00 980 000*
				100.00	H00 996 001*	H01 000 000*
				100.00	H01 016 001*	H01 020 000*
				100.00	H01 036 001*	H01 040 000*
				100.00	H01 056 001*	H01 060 000*
				100.00	H01 076 001*	H01 080 000*
				100.00	H01 096 001*	H01 100 000*
				100.00	H01 116 001*	H01 120 000*
				100.00	H01 136 001*	H01 140 000*
				100.00	H01 156 001*	H01 160 000*
				100.00	H01 176 001*	H01 180 000*
				100.00	H01 196 001*	H01 200 000*
				100.00	H01 216 001*	H01 220 000*
				100.00	H01 236 001*	H01 240 000*
				100.00	H01 256 001*	H01 260 000*
				100.00	H01 276 001*	H01 280 000*
				100.00	H01 292 001*	H01 300 000*
				100.00	H01 312 001*	H01 320 000*
				100.00	H01 332 001*	H01 340 000*
				100.00	H01 352 001*	H01 360 000*
				100.00	H01 372 001*	H01 380 000*
				100.00	H01 392 001*	H01 400 000*
				100.00	H01 412 001*	H01 420 000*
				100.00	H01 432 001*	H01 440 000*
				100.00	H01 452 001*	H01 460 000*
				100.00	H01 472 001*	H01 480 000*
				100.00	H01 492 001*	H01 500 000*
				100.00	H01 512 001*	H01 520 000*
				100.00	H01 532 001*	H01 540 000*
				100.00	H01 552 001*	H01 560 000*
				100.00	H01 572 001*	H01 580 000*
				100.00	H01 592 001*	H01 600 000*
				100.00	H01 612 001*	H01 620 000*
				100.00	H01 632 001*	H01 640 000*
				100.00	H01 652 001*	H01 660 000*
				100.00	H01 672 001*	H01 680 000*
				100.00	H01 692 001*	H01 700 000*
				100.00	H01 712 001*	H01 720 000*
				100.00	H01 732 001*	H01 740 000*
				100.00	H01 752 001*	H01 760 000*
				100.00	H01 772 001*	H01 780 000*
				100.00	H01 792 001*	H01 800 000*
				100.00	H01 812 001*	H01 820 000*
				100.00	H01 832 001*	H01 840 000*
				100.00	H01 852 001*	H01 860 000*
				100.00	H01 872 001*	H01 880 000*
				100.00	H01 892 001*	H01 900 000*
				100.00	H01 912 001*	H01 920 000*
9	I MINNEAPOLIS	I--A		55.00	I00 000 001A	I03 840 000A

DISTRICT	TOTAL NOTES PRINTED	BLOCKS	ESTIMATED VALUE VG/F	CU	LOW OFFICIAL SERIAL NUMBER	HIGH OFFICIAL SERIAL NUMBER
		I--*		100.00	I00 016 001*	I00 020 000*
				100.00	I00 036 001*	I00 040 000*
				100.00	I00 056 001*	I00 060 000*
				100.00	I00 076 001*	I00 080 000*
				100.00	I00 096 001*	I00 100 000*
				100.00	I00 116 001*	I00 120 000*
				100.00	I00 136 001*	I00 140 000*
				100.00	I00 156 001*	I00 160 000*
				100.00	I00 176 001*	I00 180 000*
				100.00	I00 196 001*	I00 200 000*
				100.00	I00 216 001*	I00 220 000*
				100.00	I00 236 001*	I00 240 000*
				100.00	I00 256 001*	I00 260 000*
				100.00	I00 276 001*	I00 280 000*
				100.00	I00 296 001*	I00 300 000*
				100.00	I00 316 001*	I00 320 000*
				100.00	I00 336 001*	I00 340 000*
				100.00	I00 356 001*	I00 360 000*
				100.00	I00 376 001*	I00 380 000*
				100.00	I00 396 001*	I00 400 000*
				100.00	I00 416 001*	I00 420 000*
				100.00	I00 436 001*	I00 440 000*
				100.00	I00 456 001*	I00 460 000*
				100.00	I00 476 001*	I00 480 000*
				100.00	I00 496 001*	I00 500 000*
				100.00	I00 516 001*	I00 520 000*
				100.00	I00 536 001*	I00 540 000*
				100.00	I00 556 001*	I00 560 000*
				100.00	I00 576 001*	I00 580 000*
				100.00	I00 596 001*	I00 600 000*
				100.00	I00 616 001*	I00 620 000*
				100.00	I00 636 001*	I00 640 000*
10 J KANSAS CITY		J--A		55.00	J00 000 001A	J07 680 000A
		J--*		65.00	J00 000 001*	J00 064 000*
				100.00	J00 658 001*	J00 660 000*
				100.00	J00 678 001*	J00 680 000*
				100.00	J00 698 001*	J00 700 000*
				100.00	J00 718 001*	J00 720 000*
				100.00	J00 738 001*	J00 740 000*
				100.00	J00 758 001*	J00 760 000*
				100.00	J00 778 001*	J00 780 000*
				100.00	J00 798 001*	J00 800 000*
				100.00	J00 818 001*	J00 820 000*
				100.00	J00 838 001*	J00 840 000*
				100.00	J00 858 001*	J00 860 000*
				100.00	J00 878 001*	J00 880 000*
				100.00	J00 898 001*	J00 900 000*
				100.00	J00 918 001*	J00 920 000*
				100.00	J00 938 001*	J00 940 000*
				100.00	J00 958 001*	J00 960 000*
				100.00	J00 978 001*	J00 980 000*
				100.00	J00 998 001*	J01 000 000*
				100.00	J01 018 001*	J01 020 000*
				100.00	J01 038 001*	J01 040 000*
				100.00	J01 058 001*	J01 060 000*
				100.00	J01 078 001*	J01 080 000*
				100.00	J01 098 001*	J01 100 000*
				100.00	J01 118 001*	J01 120 000*
				100.00	J01 138 001*	J01 140 000*
				100.00	J01 158 001*	J01 160 000*
				100.00	J01 178 001*	J01 180 000*
				100.00	J01 198 001*	J01 200 000*
				100.00	J01 218 001*	J01 220 000*
				100.00	J01 238 001*	J01 240 000*
				100.00	J01 258 001*	J01 260 000*
				100.00	J01 278 001*	J01 280 000*
				100.00	J01 296 001*	J01 300 000*
				100.00	J01 316 001*	J01 320 000*
				100.00	J01 336 001*	J01 340 000*

DISTRICT	TOTAL NOTES PRINTED	BLOCKS	ESTIMATED VALUE VG/F	VALUE CU	LOW OFFICIAL SERIAL NUMBER	HIGH OFFICIAL SERIAL NUMBER
				100.00	J01 356 001*	J01 360 000*
				100.00	J01 376 001*	J01 380 000*
				100.00	J01 396 001*	J01 400 000*
				100.00	J01 416 001*	J01 420 000*
				100.00	J01 436 001*	J01 440 000*
				100.00	J01 456 001*	J01 460 000*
				100.00	J01 476 001*	J01 480 000*
				100.00	J01 496 001*	J01 500 000*
				100.00	J01 516 001*	J01 520 000*
				100.00	J01 536 001*	J01 540 000*
				100.00	J01 556 001*	J01 560 000*
				100.00	J01 576 001*	J01 580 000*
				100.00	J01 596 001*	J01 600 000*
				100.00	J01 616 001*	J01 620 000*
				100.00	J01 636 001*	J01 640 000*
				100.00	J01 656 001*	J01 660 000*
				100.00	J01 676 001*	J01 680 000*
				100.00	J01 696 001*	J01 700 000*
				100.00	J01 716 001*	J01 720 000*
				100.00	J01 736 001*	J01 740 000*
				100.00	J01 756 001*	J01 760 000*
				100.00	J01 776 001*	J01 780 000*
				100.00	J01 796 001*	J01 800 000*
				100.00	J01 816 001*	J01 820 000*
				100.00	J01 836 001*	J01 840 000*
				100.00	J01 856 001*	J01 860 000*
				100.00	J01 876 001*	J01 880 000*
				100.00	J01 896 001*	J01 900 000*
				100.00	J01 916 001*	J01 920 000*
11 K DALLAS		K--A		55.00	K00 000 001A	K14 080 000A
		K--*		65.00	K00 000 001*	K00 192 000*
				100.00	K01 936 001*	K01 940 000*
				100.00	K01 956 001*	K01 960 000*
				100.00	K01 976 001*	K01 980 000*
				100.00	K01 996 001*	K02 000 000*
				100.00	K02 016 001*	K02 020 000*
				100.00	K02 036 001*	K02 040 000*
				100.00	K02 056 001*	K02 060 000*
				100.00	K02 076 001*	K02 080 000*
				100.00	K02 096 001*	K02 100 000*
				100.00	K02 116 001*	K02 120 000*
				100.00	K02 136 001*	K02 140 000*
				100.00	K02 156 001*	K02 160 000*
				100.00	K02 176 001*	K02 180 000*
				100.00	K02 196 001*	K02 200 000*
				100.00	K02 216 001*	K02 220 000*
				100.00	K02 236 001*	K02 240 000*
				100.00	K02 256 001*	K02 260 000*
				100.00	K02 276 001*	K02 280 000*
				100.00	K02 296 001*	K02 300 000*
				100.00	K02 316 001*	K02 320 000*
				100.00	K02 336 001*	K02 340 000*
				100.00	K02 356 001*	K02 360 000*
				100.00	K02 376 001*	K02 380 000*
				100.00	K02 396 001*	K02 400 000*
				100.00	K02 416 001*	K02 420 000*
				100.00	K02 436 001*	K02 440 000*
				100.00	K02 456 001*	K02 460 000*
				100.00	K02 476 001*	K02 480 000*
				100.00	K02 496 001*	K02 500 000*
				100.00	K02 516 001*	K02 520 000*
				100.00	K02 536 001*	K02 540 000*
				100.00	K02 556 001*	K02 560 000*
				100.00	K02 576 001*	K02 580 000*
				100.00	K02 596 001*	K02 600 000*
				100.00	K02 616 001*	K02 620 000*
				100.00	K02 636 001*	K02 640 000*
				100.00	K02 656 001*	K02 660 000*
				100.00	K02 676 001*	K02 680 000*

DISTRICT	TOTAL NOTES PRINTED	BLOCKS	ESTIMATED VALUE VG/F	CU	LOW OFFICIAL SERIAL NUMBER	HIGH OFFICIAL SERIAL NUMBER
				100.00	K02 696 001*	K02 700 000*
				100.00	K02 716 001*	K02 720 000*
				100.00	K02 736 001*	K02 740 000*
				100.00	K02 756 001*	K02 760 000*
				100.00	K02 776 001*	K02 780 000*
				100.00	K02 796 001*	K02 800 000*
				100.00	K02 816 001*	K02 820 000*
				100.00	K02 836 001*	K02 840 000*
				100.00	K02 856 001*	K02 860 000*
				100.00	K02 876 001*	K02 880 000*
				100.00	K02 896 001*	K02 900 000*
				100.00	K02 916 001*	K02 920 000*
				100.00	K02 936 001*	K02 940 000*
				100.00	K02 956 001*	K02 960 000*
				100.00	K02 976 001*	K02 980 000*
				100.00	K02 996 001*	K03 000 000*
				100.00	K03 016 001*	K03 020 000*
				100.00	K03 036 001*	K03 040 000*
				100.00	K03 056 001*	K03 060 000*
				100.00	K03 076 001*	K03 080 000*
				100.00	K03 096 001*	K03 100 000*
				100.00	K03 116 001*	K03 120 000*
				100.00	K03 136 001*	K03 140 000*
				100.00	K03 156 001*	K03 160 000*
				100.00	K03 176 001*	K03 180 000*
				100.00	K03 196 001*	K03 200 000*
12 L SAN FRANCISCO		L--A		55.00	L00 000 001A	L19 200 000A
		L--*		65.00	L00 000 001*	L00 256 000*
				100.00	L02 576 001*	L02 580 000*
				100.00	L02 596 001*	L02 600 000*
				100.00	L02 616 001*	L02 620 000*
				100.00	L02 636 001*	L02 640 000*
				100.00	L02 656 001*	L02 660 000*
				100.00	L02 676 001*	L02 680 000*
				100.00	L02 696 001*	L02 700 000*
				100.00	L02 716 001*	L02 720 000*
				100.00	L02 736 001*	L02 740 000*
				100.00	L02 756 001*	L02 760 000*
				100.00	L02 776 001*	L02 780 000*
				100.00	L02 796 001*	L02 800 000*
				100.00	L02 816 001*	L02 820 000*
				100.00	L02 836 001*	L02 840 000*
				100.00	L02 856 001*	L02 860 000*
				100.00	L02 876 001*	L02 880 000*
				100.00	L02 896 001*	L02 900 000*
				100.00	L02 916 001*	L02 920 000*
				100.00	L02 936 001*	L02 940 000*
				100.00	L02 956 001*	L02 960 000*
				100.00	L02 976 001*	L02 980 000*
				100.00	L02 996 001*	L03 000 000*
				100.00	L03 016 001*	L03 020 000*
				100.00	L03 036 001*	L03 040 000*
				100.00	L03 056 001*	L03 060 000*
				100.00	L03 076 001*	L03 080 000*
				100.00	L03 096 001*	L03 100 000*
				100.00	L03 116 001*	L03 120 000*
				100.00	L03 136 001*	L03 140 000*
				100.00	L03 156 001*	L03 160 000*
				100.00	L03 176 001*	L03 180 000*
				100.00	L03 196 001*	L03 200 000*
				100.00	L03 216 001*	L03 220 000*
				100.00	L03 236 001*	L03 240 000*
				100.00	L03 256 001*	L03 260 000*
				100.00	L03 276 001*	L03 280 000*
				100.00	L03 296 001*	L03 300 000*
				100.00	L03 316 001*	L03 320 000*
				100.00	L03 336 001*	L03 340 000*
				100.00	L03 356 001*	L03 360 000*
				100.00	L03 376 001*	L03 380 000*

DISTRICT	TOTAL NOTES PRINTED	BLOCKS	ESTIMATED VALUE VG/F	CU	LOW OFFICIAL SERIAL NUMBER	HIGH OFFICIAL SERIAL NUMBER
				100.00	L03 396 001*	L03 400 000*
				100.00	L03 416 001*	L03 420 000*
				100.00	L03 436 001*	L03 440 000*
				100.00	L03 456 001*	L03 460 000*
				100.00	L03 476 001*	L03 480 000*
				100.00	L03 496 001*	L03 500 000*
				100.00	L03 516 001*	L03 520 000*
				100.00	L03 536 001*	L03 540 000*
				100.00	L03 556 001*	L03 560 000*
				100.00	L03 576 001*	L03 580 000*
				100.00	L03 596 001*	L03 600 000*
				100.00	L03 616 001*	L03 620 000*
				100.00	L03 636 001*	L03 640 000*
				100.00	L03 656 001*	L03 660 000*
				100.00	L03 676 001*	L03 680 000*
				100.00	L03 696 001*	L03 700 000*
				100.00	L03 716 001*	L03 720 000*
				100.00	L03 736 001*	L03 740 000*
				100.00	L03 756 001*	L03 760 000*
				100.00	L03 776 001*	L03 780 000*
				100.00	L03 796 001*	L03 800 000*
				100.00	L03 816 001*	L03 820 000*
				100.00	L03 836 001*	L03 840 000*
				100.00	L03 852 001*	L03 860 000*
				100.00	L03 872 001*	L03 880 000*
				100.00	L03 892 001*	L03 900 000*
				100.00	L03 912 001*	L03 920 000*
				100.00	L03 932 001*	L03 940 000*
				100.00	L03 952 001*	L03 960 000*
				100.00	L03 972 001*	L03 980 000*
				100.00	L03 992 001*	L04 000 000*
				100.00	L04 012 001*	L04 020 000*
				100.00	L04 032 001*	L04 040 000*
				100.00	L04 052 001*	L04 060 000*
				100.00	L04 072 001*	L04 080 000*
				100.00	L04 092 001*	L04 100 000*
				100.00	L04 112 001*	L04 120 000*
				100.00	L04 132 001*	L04 140 000*
				100.00	L04 152 001*	L04 160 000*
				100.00	L04 172 001*	L04 180 000*
				100.00	L04 192 001*	L04 200 000*
				100.00	L04 212 001*	L04 220 000*
				100.00	L04 232 001*	L04 240 000*
				100.00	L04 252 001*	L04 260 000*
				100.00	L04 272 001*	L04 280 000*
				100.00	L04 292 001*	L04 300 000*
				100.00	L04 312 001*	L04 320 000*
				100.00	L04 332 001*	L04 340 000*
				100.00	L04 352 001*	L04 360 000*
				100.00	L04 372 001*	L04 380 000*
				100.00	L04 392 001*	L04 400 000*
				100.00	L04 412 001*	L04 420 000*
				100.00	L04 432 001*	L04 440 000*
				100.00	L04 452 001*	L04 460 000*
				100.00	L04 472 001*	L04 480 000*

TOTAL BLOCKS: Twenty four.
(1) Printings through November 1981.
The production unit was changed from 20,000 to 40,000 sheets for:

BANK	STARTING AT SERIAL NUMBER	BANK	STARTING AT SERIAL NUMBER
Boston	A07 680 001A	Chicago	G32 000 001A
New York	B30 720 001A	St. Louis	H01 280 001A
Philadelphia	C03 840 001A	Minneapolis	I02 560 001A
Cleveland	D15 360 001A	Kansas City	J03 840 001A
Richmond	E11 520 001A	Dallas	K05 120 001A
Atlanta	F01 280 001A	San Francisco	L10 240 001A

NO $50.00 FEDERAL RESERVE NOTES SERIES 1977A WERE PRINTED

CAT. NO. CL66
$100.00 UNITED STATES NOTE (LEGAL TENDER) (RED SEAL) (32 Subject)
SERIES 1966

SERIAL NUMBERS:
   (Official) A00 000 001A through A00 768 000A
   Star Serials:
   (Official) *00 000 001A through *00 128 000A
PLATE SERIALS: Face check numbers begin with 1.
SIGNATURES: Kathryn O'Hay Granahan, Treasurer of the United States
   Henry H. Fowler, Secretary of the Treasury
DESIGN: 100 to left of portrait of Franklin. To right One Hundred with red   Treasury seal imposed.
   Back design has INDEPENDENCE HALL, Philadelphia, Pa. Has motto.

ESTIMATED VALUES:	BLOCK	VG/F	CU
	A--A		150.00
	*--A		200.00

TOTAL BLOCKS KNOWN: Two.

CAT. NO. CL66A
$100.00 UNITED STATES NOTE (LEGAL TENDER — RED SEAL) (32 Subject)
SERIES 1966A

SERIAL NUMBERS:
   (Official) A00 768 001A through A01 280 000A
   Star Notes: No star notes printed for this series.
SIGNATURES: Dorothy Andrews Elston, Treasurer of the United States
   David M. Kennedy, Secretary of the Treasury

ESTIMATED VALUES:	BLOCK	VG/F	CU
	A--A		175.00

TOTAL BLOCKS KNOWN: One.

CAT. NO. CG28
$100.00 GOLD CERTIFICATE
SERIES 1928

SERIAL NUMBERS:
   (Official Range) A00 000 001A through A03 240 000A
   Star Notes:
   (Low Official) *00 000 001A *00 011 566A (High Observed)
PLATE SERIALS: Face check #1 through #24.
SIGNATURES: Walter O. Woods, Treasurer of the United States.
   Andrew W. Mellon, Secretary of the Treasury.

ESTIMATED VALUES:	BLOCK	VG/F	CU
	A--A	175.00	500.00
	*--A	225.00	850.00

TOTAL BLOCKS KNOWN: Two.

CAT. NO. CN29
$100.00 FEDERAL RESERVE BANK NOTE (BROWN SEAL) (12 Subject)
SERIES 1929

SERIAL NUMBERS: Both regular and star notes begin with 00 000 001.
PLATE SERIALS: Face check numbers begin with #1.
SIGNATURES: Same as $5.00 FRBN.

	DISTRICT	TOTAL NOTES PRINTED	BLOCKS	VG/F	CU	LOW OBSERVED SERIAL NUMBER	HIGH OFFICIAL SERIAL NUMBER
1	A BOSTON		Unknown				
2	B NEW YORK	12,000	B--A	125.00	200.00	B00 144 204A	B00 480 000A
			B--*	135.00	275.00		
3	C PHILADELPHIA		Unknown				
4	D CLEVELAND	12,000	D--A	135.00	225.00	D00 092 982A	D00 570 082A
			D--*	150.00	300.00	D00 003 918*	
5	E RICHMOND	36,000	E--A	125.00	225.00	E00 015 341A	E00 192 000A
			E--*	150.00	350.00	E00 006 700*	

	DISTRICT	TOTAL NOTES PRINTED	BLOCKS	ESTIMATED VALUE VG/F	CU	LOW OFFICIAL SERIAL NUMBER	HIGH OFFICIAL SERIAL NUMBER
6	F ATLANTA	Unknown					
7	G CHICAGO	12,000	G--A	125.00	200.00	G00 181 939A	G00 384 000A
			G--*	135.00	275.00		
8	H ST. LOUIS	Unknown					
9	I MINNEAPOLIS	12,000	I--A	125.00	225.00	I00 002 489A	I00 144 000
			I--*	150.00	350.00		
10	J KANSAS CITY	12,000	J--A	125.00	250.00	J00 027 566A	J00 096 000A
			J--*	200.00	400.00	J00 008 506*	J00 011 891*
11	K DALLAS	12,000	K--A	150.00	350.00	K00 004 288A	K00 036 000A
			K--*	250.00	500.00		
12	L SAN FRANCISCO	Unknown					

TOTAL BLOCKS: Fourteen.
Collectors are requested to supply any information that will improve on above data.

CAT. NO. CF28
$100.00 FEDERAL RESERVE NOTE (GREEN SEAL) (12 Subject)
SERIES 1928

SERIAL NUMBERS: All serial numbers both regular and star notes begin with 00 000 001.
PLATE SERIALS: Face and check begin with 1.
SIGNATURES: Walter O. Woods, Treasurer of the United States.
    A.W. Mellon, Secretary of the Treasury.

	DISTRICT	TOTAL NOTES PRINTED	BLOCKS	ESTIMATED VALUE VG/F	CU	LOW OBSERVED SERIAL NUMBER	HIGH OBSERVED SERIAL NUMBER
1	A BOSTON	376,000	A--A	125.00	175.00		
			A--*	150.00	225.00		
2	B NEW YORK	755,400	B--A	125.00	175.00	B00 292 351A	B00 306 676A
			B--*	150.00	225.00	B00 001 414*	
3	C PHILADELPHIA	389,100	C--A	125.00	175.00	C00 191 030A	C00 418 732A
			C--*	150.00	225.00		
4	D CLEVELAND	542,400	D--A	125.00	175.00	D00 060 067A	D00 383 761A
			D--*	150.00	225.00		
5	E RICHMOND	364,416	E--A	125.00	175.00	E00 041 310A	E00 198 174A
			E--*	150.00	225.00		
6	F ATLANTA	357,000	F--A	125.00	175.00	F00 314 340A	
			F--*	150.00	225.00		
7	G CHICAGO	783,300	G--A	125.00	175.00	G00 048 733A	G01 285 266A
			G--*	150.00	225.00	G00 000 059*	G00 022 719*
8	H ST. LOUIS	187,200	H--A	135.00	200.00	H00 049 870A	H00 187 252A
			H--*	160.00	250.00		
9	I MINNEAPOLIS	102,000	I--A	135.00	200.00		
			I--*	160.00	250.00		
10	J KANSAS CITY	234,612	J--A	125.00	175.00		
			J--*	150.00	225.00		
11	K DALLAS	80,140	K--A	160.00	250.00	K00 048 748A	K00 067 002A
			K--*	200.00	350.00		
12	L SAN FRANCISCO	486,000	L--A	125.00	175.00		
			L--*	150.00	225.00	L00 000 494*	

TOTAL BLOCKS: Twenty four.
Collectors are requested to supply any serial numbers.

CAT. NO. CF28A
$100.00 FEDERAL RESERVE NOTE (GREEN SEAL) (12 Subject)
SERIES 1928A

SERIAL NUMBERS: All districts continued sequence from previous series.
DESIGN CHANGE: District letter in seal replaced by numeral. Face check begins with 1.
SIGNATURES: Walter O. Woods, Treasurer of the United States
   A.W. Mellon, Secretary of the Treasury

	DISTRICT	TOTAL NOTES PRINTED	BLOCKS	ESTIMATED VALUE VG/F	CU	LOW OBSERVED SERIAL NUMBER	HIGH OBSERVED SERIAL NUMBER
1	A BOSTON	980,400	A--A	125.00	175.00	A00 726 436A	
			A--*	150.00	225.00		
2	B NEW YORK	2,938,176	B--A	125.00	175.00	B01 117 228A	B02 342 430A
			B--*	150.00	225.00		
3	C PHILADELPHIA	1,496,844	C--A	125.00	175.00	C00 378 456A	C00 522 572A
			C--*	150.00	225.00		
4	D CLEVELAND	992,436	D--A	125.00	175.00	D00 555 962A	
			D--*	150.00	225.00		
5	E RICHMOND	621,364	E--A	125.00	175.00	E0 477 467A	
			E--*	150.00	225.00		
6	F ATLANTA	371,400	F--A	125.00	175.00	F00 377 479A	
			F--*	150.00	225.00		
7	G CHICAGO	4,010,424	G--A	125.00	175.00	G00 693 813A	G02 470 635A
			G--*	150.00	225.00		
8	H ST. LOUIS	749,544	H--A	125.00	175.00	H00 172 058A	H00 558 585A
			H--*	150.00	225.00	H00 009 994*	
9	I MINNEAPOLIS	503,040	I--A	125.00	175.00	I00 124 640A	
			I--*	150.00	225.00		
10	J KANSAS CITY	681,804	J--A	125.00	175.00	J00 197 764A	
			J--*	150.00	225.00		
11	K DALLAS	594,456	K--A	125.00	175.00	K00 081 337A	
			K--*	150.00	225.00		
12	L SAN FRANCISCO	1,228,032	L--A	125.00	175.00	L00 590 772A	L00 947 243A
			L--*	150.00	225.00		

TOTAL BLOCKS: Twenty-four.
Collectors are requested to supply any serial numbers.

CAT. NO. CF34
$100.00 FEDERAL RESERVE NOTE (GREEN SEAL) (12 Subject)
SERIES 1934

SERIAL NUMBERS: All serial numbers both regular and star notes begin with 00 000 001.
PLATE SERIALS: Back check number up to 112.
SIGNATURES: W.A. Julian, Treasurer of the United States
   Henry Morgenthau, Jr., Secretary of the Treasury

	DISTRICT	TOTAL NOTES PRINTED (1)	BLOCKS	ESTIMATED VALUE VG/F	CU	LOW OBSERVED SERIAL NUMBER	HIGH OBSERVED SERIAL NUMBER
1	A BOSTON	3,710,000	A--A	120.00	165.00	A00 850 539A	A03 458 035A
			A--*	135.00	200.00	A00 038 278*	
2	B NEW YORK	3,086,000	B--A	120.00	165.00	B00 216 498A	B03 962 686A
			B--*	135.00	200.00		
3	C PHILADELPHIA	2,776,800	C--A	120.00	165.00	C00 646 932A	C03 565 041A
			C--*	135.00	200.00	C00 012 798*	C00 018 053*
4	D CLEVELAND	3,447,108	D--A	120.00	165.00		
			D--*	135.00	200.00		
5	E RICHMOND	4,317,600	E--A	120.00	165.00	E00 460 483A	E04 194 652A
			E--*	135.00	200.00		
6	F ATLANTA	3,264,420	F--A	120.00	165.00	F00 069 074A	F03 158 929A
			F--*	135.00	200.00		

	DISTRICT	TOTAL NOTES PRINTED	BLOCKS	ESTIMATED VALUE VG/F	CU	LOW OFFICIAL SERIAL NUMBER	HIGH OFFICIAL SERIAL NUMBER
7	G CHICAGO	7,075,000	G--A	120.00	165.00	G00 076 989A	G09 717 675A
			G--*	135.00	200.00	G00 013 795*	G00 020 584*
8	H ST. LOUIS	2,106,192	H--A	120.00	165.00	H00 634 881A	H02 133 175A
			H--*	135.00	200.00	H00 014 404*	H00 021 836*
9	I MINNEAPOLIS	852,600	I--A	125.00	175.00	I00 126 341A	I00 899 072A
			I--*	150.00	225.00		
10	J KANSAS CITY	1,932,900	J--A	120.00	165.00	J00 596 082A	
			J--*	135.00	200.00	J00 012 942*	J00 035 525*
11	K DALLAS	1,506,516	K--A	120.00	165.00	K00 159 585A	K01 021 819A
			K--*	135.00	200.00	K00 005 732*	
12	L SAN FRANCISCO	6,521,940	L--A	120.00	165.00	L00 986 517A	L06 816 724A
			L--*	135.00	200.00	L00 025 535*	L00 081 420*

TOTAL BLOCKS: Twenty-four.
Collectors are requested to supply serial numbers that improve on above information.
Face and back check numbers with seal color are required to properly catalog.
(1) Total for both seal colors.

CAT. NO. CF34
$100.00 FEDERAL RESERVE NOTE (DARK GREEN) 12 Subject MULE
SERIES 1934 MULE

PLATE SERIALS: Back check 113 and higher.

	DISTRICT	TOTAL NOTES PRINTED	BLOCKS	ESTIMATED VALUE VG/F	CU	LOW OBSERVED SERIAL NUMBER	HIGH OBSERVED SERIAL NUMBER
1	A BOSTON		A--A	150.00	250.00	A02 876 991A	
3	C PHILADELPHIA		C--A	150.00	250.00	C02 973 508A	
10	J KANSAS CITY		J--A	150.00	250.00	J01 880 175A	
12	L SAN FRANCISCO		L--A	150.00	250.00	L05 938 350A	L06 593 880A

TOTAL BLOCK KNOWN: Four.

CAT. NO. CF34
$100.00 FEDERAL RESERVE NOTE (LIGHT GREEN SEAL) (12 Subject)
SERIES 1934

PLATE SERIALS: Back check number up to 112. (Mules would be back check 113 and higher.)

	DISTRICT	TOTAL NOTES PRINTED	BLOCKS	ESTIMATED VALUE VG/F	CU	LOW OBSERVED SERIAL NUMBER	HIGH OBSERVED SERIAL NUMBER
1	A BOSTON		A--A	120.00	165.00	A00 171 113A	A00 953 008A
			A--*	135.00	200.00		
2	B NEW YORK		B--A	120.00	165.00	B00 636 922A	B03 355 227A
			B--*	135.00	200.00		
3	C PHILADELPHIA		C--A	120.00	165.00	C00 022 498A	C00 753 965A
			C--*	135.00	200.00	C00 002 010*	
4	D CLEVELAND		D--A	120.00	165.00	D00 047 045A	D02 957 552A
			D--*	135.00	200.00	D00 000 001*	
5	E RICHMOND		E--A	120.00	165.00	E00 093 889A	E00 321 871A
			E--*	135.00	200.00		
6	F ATLANTA		F--A	120.00	165.00	F00 108 864A	F03 216 128A
			F--*	135.00	200.00		
7	G CHICAGO		G--A	120.00	165.00	G00 002 194A	G06 375 531A
			G--*	135.00	200.00	G00 009 410*	
8	H ST. LOUIS		H--A	120.00	165.00	H00 000 518A	H00 400 007A
			H--*	135.00	200.00		
9	I MINNEAPOLIS		I--A	125.00	175.00	I00 069 410A	I00 119 453A
			I--*	150.00	225.00	I00 006 697*	
10	J KANSAS CITY		J--A	120.00	165.00	J00 006 043A	J00 035 525A
			J--*	135.00	200.00		
11	K DALLAS		K--A	120.00	165.00	K00 017 478A	K01 267 294A
			K--*	135.00	200.00		
12	L SAN FRANCISCO		L--A	120.00	165.00	L00 384 679A	L05 536 476A
			L--*	135.00	200.00		L00 025 535*

TOTAL BLOCKS KNOWN: Fifteen.
Collectors are requested to supply serial numbers that improve on above information.
Face and back check numbers with seal color are required to properly catalog.

CAT. NO. CF34A
$100.00 FEDERAL RESERVE NOTE (DARK GREEN SEAL) (12 Subject)
SERIES 1934A

SERIAL NUMBERS: Continued sequence from previous series.
PLATE SERIALS: Back check number 113 and higher. (MULES would be back check 112 and lower.)
SIGNATURES: W.A. Julian, Treasurer of the United States.
 Henry Morgenthau, Jr., Secretary of the Treasury.

	DISTRICT	TOTAL NOTES PRINTED	BLOCKS	ESTIMATED VALUE VG/F	CU	LOW OBSERVED SERIAL NUMBER	HIGH OBSERVED SERIAL NUMBER
1	A BOSTON	102,000	A--A	125.00	175.00		
			A--*	135.00	200.00		
2	B NEW YORK	15,278,892	B--A	115.00	150.00	B05 525 202A	B17 131 507A
			B--*	125.00	175.00	B00 155 943*	B00 149 863*
3	C PHILADELPHIA	588,000	C--A	115.00	150.00	C01 325 038A	C02 586 618A
			C--*	125.00	175.00		
4	D CLEVELAND	645,300	D--A	115.00	150.00		
			D--*	125.00	175.00		
5	E RICHMOND	770,100	E--A	115.00	150.00		
			E--*	125.00	175.00		
6	F ATLANTA	589,896	F--A	115.00	150.00		
			F--*	125.00	175.00		
7	G CHICAGO	3,328,800	G--A	115.00	150.00	G00 226 618A	G00 273 627A
			G--*	125.00	175.00		
8	H ST. LOUIS	434,208	H--A	115.00	150.00		
			H--*	125.00	175.00		
9	I MINNEAPOLIS	153,000	I--A	125.00	175.00	I00 816 356A	
			I--*	135.00	200.00		
10	J KANSAS CITY	455,100	J--A	115.00	150.00	J00 078 918A	
			J--*	125.00	175.00		
11	K DALLAS	226,164	K--A	115.00	150.00	K00 534 394A	K00 800 499A
			K--*	125.00	175.00		
12	L SAN FRANCISCO	1,130,400	L--A	115.00	150.00		
			L--*	125.00	175.00		

TOTAL BLOCKS; Twenty four.
Collectors are requested to supply serial numbers.

CAT. NO. CF34A
$100.00 FEDERAL RESERVE NOTE (DARK SEAL MULE) (12 Subject)
SERIES 1934A

PLATE SERIALS: Back check up to 112.

	DISTRICT	TOTAL NOTES PRINTED	BLOCKS	ESTIMATED VALUE VG/F	CU	LOW OBSERVED SERIAL NUMBER	HIGH OBSERVED SERIAL NUMBER
2	B NEW YORK		B--A	115.00	150.00	B04 343 434A	B18 050 566A
			B--*	125.00	175.00	B00 063 693*	B00 108 827*
3	C PHILADELPHIA		C--A	115.00	150.00	C01 647 445A	C02 842 098A
4	D CLEVELAND		D--A	115.00	150.00	D01 861 704A	D02 782 124A
5	E RICHMOND		E--A	115.00	150.00	E00 998 410A	E06 298 291A
6	F ATLANTA		F--A	115.00	150.00	F04 009 312A	
7	G CHICAGO		G--A	115.00	150.00	G02 367 535A	G09 136 129A
			G--*	125.00	175.00	G00 050 063*	G00 061 287*
8	H ST. LOUIS		H--A	115.00	150.00	H00 931 248A	H01 629 146A
10	J KANSAS CITY		J--A	115.00	150.00	J02 476 621A	
11	K DALLAS		K--A	115.00	150.00	K00 510 577A	
12	L SAN FRANCISCO		L--A	115.00	150.00	L05 350 891A	

TOTAL BLOCKS KNOWN: Twelve.

CAT. NO. CF34B
$100.00 FEDERAL RESERVE NOTE (GREEN SEAL) (12 Subject)
SERIES 1934B

SERIAL NUMBERS: Contined sequence from previous series.
PLATE SERIALS: Back check number 113 and higher.
SIGNATURES: W.A. Julian of the United States.
 Fred M. Vinson, Secretary of the Treasury.

	DISTRICT	TOTAL NOTES PRINTED	BLOCKS	ESTIMATED VALUE VG/F	CU	LOW OBSERVED SERIAL NUMBER	HIGH OBSERVED SERIAL NUMBER
1	A BOSTON	41,400	A--A	160.00	250.00		
			A--*	175.00	300.00		

	DISTRICT	TOTAL NOTES PRINTED	BLOCKS	ESTIMATED VALUE VG/F	CU	LOW OFFICIAL SERIAL NUMBER	HIGH OFFICIAL SERIAL NUMBER
2	B NEW YORK	none	B--A				
		none	B--*				
3	C PHILADELPHIA	39,600	C--A	160.00	250.00	C03 758 953A	C03 769 891A
			C--*	175.00	300.00		
4	D CLEVELAND	61,200	D--A	160.00	250.00		
			D--*	175.00	300.00		
5	E RICHMOND	977,400	E--A	135.00	175.00		
			E--*	150.00	225.00		
6	F ATLANTA	645,000	F--A	135.00	175.00	F04 109 312A	
			F--*	150.00	225.00		
7	G CHICAGO	396,000	G--A	125.00	175.00	G10 663 300A	
			G--*	150.00	225.00		
8	H ST. LOUIS	676,200	H--A	125.00	175.00	H02 518 355A	H02 916 928A
			H--*	150.00	225.00		
9	I MINNEAPOLIS	377,000	I--A	125.00	175.00		
			I--*	150.00	225.00		
10	J KANSAS CITY	364,500	J--A	125.00	175.00	J02 476 621A	J02 644 307A
			J--*	150.00	225.00		
11	K DALLAS	392,700	K--A	125.00	175.00		
			K--*	150.00	225.00		
12	L SAN FRANCISCO	none	L--A				
		none	L--*				

TOTAL BLOCKS: Twenty.
Collectors requested to supply any serial numbers.

CAT. NO. CF34B
$100.00 FEDERAL RESERVE NOTE (GREEN SEAL) MULE 12 Subject
SERIES 1934B MULE

PLATE SERIALS: Back check number up to 112.

	DISTRICT	TOTAL NOTES PRINTED	BLOCKS	ESTIMATED VALUE VG/F	CU	LOW OBSERVED SERIAL NUMBER	HIGH OBSERVED SERIAL NUMBER
1	A BOSTON		A--A	150.00	225.00	A03 685 891A	
2	B NEW YORK		B--A	150.00	225.00	B13 971 535A	
3	C PHILADELPHIA		C--A	150.00	225.00	C03 691 382A	C03 773 271A
5	E RICHMOND		E--A	150.00	225.00	E04 960 680A	
6	F ATLANTA		F--A	150.00	225.00	F03 905 459A	
7	G CHICAGO		G--A	150.00	225.00	G10 260 001A	G10 700 618A
8	H ST. LOUIS		H--A	150.00	225.00	H02 994 191A	H03 098 683A
9	I MINNEAPOLIS		I--A	150.00	225.00	I01 011 740A	I01 238 696A
10	J KANSAS CITY		J--A	150.00	225.00	J02 378 551A	J02 886 755A
11	K DALLAS		K--A	150.00	225.00	K01 636 156A	K02 075 431A
			K--*	350.00	500.00	K00 028 713*	

TOTAL BLOCKS KNOWN: Eleven.

CAT. NO. CF34C
$100.00 FEDERAL RESERVE NOTE (GREEN SEAL) (12 Subject)
SERIES 1934C

SERIAL NUMBERS: Continued sequence from previous series.
PLATE SERIALS: Back check 113 and higher.
SIGNATURES: W.A. Julian, Treasurer of the United States
  John W. Snyder, Secretary of the Treasury

	DISTRICT	TOTAL NOTES PRINTED	BLOCKS	ESTIMATED VALUE VG/F	CU	LOW OBSERVED SERIAL NUMBER	HIGH OBSERVED SERIAL NUMBER
1	A BOSTON	13,800	A--A	200.00	300.00		
			A--*			possibly none printed	
2	B NEW YORK	1,556,400	B--A	115.00	135.00		
			B--*	125.00	175.00		
3	C PHILADELPHIA	13,200	C--A	200.00	300.00		
			C--*			possibly none printed	
4	D CLEVELAND	1,473,200	D--A	115.00	135.00		
				D--*	125.00	175.00	

	DISTRICT	TOTAL NOTES PRINTED	BLOCKS	ESTIMATED VALUE VG/F	CU	LOW OFFICIAL SERIAL NUMBER	HIGH OFFICIAL SERIAL NUMBER
5	E RICHMOND (1)	none	E--A				
		none	E--*				
6	F ATLANTA	493,900	F--A	125.00	165.00		
			F--*	135.00	175.00		
7	G CHICAGO	612,000	G-AS	115.00	135.00		
			G--*	125.00	175.00		
8	H ST. LOUIS	957,000	H--A	115.00	135.00		H03 791 599A
			H--*	125.00	175.00		
9	I MINNEAPOLIS	392,904	I--A	115.00	135.00		
			I--*	125.00	175.00		
10	J KANSAS CITY	401,100	J--A	115.00	135.00		
			J--*	125.00	175.00		
11	K DALLAS	280,700	K--A	115.00	135.00	K02 179 536A	
			K--*	125.00	175.00		
12	L SAN FRANCISCO	432,600	L--A	115.00	135.00		
			L--*	125.00	175.00		

TOTAL BLOCKS: Twenty-two.
Collectors are requested to supply any serial numbers.
(1) Although Bureau records indicate no Series 1934C, $100.00 FRN were printed for Richmond, a MULE note for this series for Richmond has been reported.

CAT. NO. CF34C
$100.00 FEDERAL RESERVE NOTE (GREEN SEAL) MULE 12 subject
SERIES 1934C MULE

	DISTRICT	TOTAL NOTES PRINTED	BLOCKS	ESTIMATED VALUE VG/F	CU	LOW OBSERVED SERIAL NUMBER	HIGH OBSERVED SERIAL NUMBER
3	C PHILADELPHIA		C--A	150.00	200.00	C03 719 564A	C03 777 657 A
4	D CLEVELAND		D--A	150.00	200.00	D03 867 222A	D03 941 112A
5	E RICHMOND		E--A	150.00	200.00	E04 574 908A	E06 724 336A
6	F ATLANTA		F--A	150.00	200.00	F03 814 818A	F04 303 994A
			F--*	250.00	500.00	F00 057 872*	
7	G CHICAGO		G--A	150.00	200.00	G10 906 938A	G11 118 036A
8	H ST. LOUIS		H--A	150.00	200.00	H02 938 155A	H04 089 439A
			H--*	250.00	500.00	H00 049 795*	
9	I MINNEAPOLIS		I--A	150.00	200.00	I01 355 348A	
10	J KANSAS CITY		J--A	150.00	200.00	J02 435 400A	J03 004 263A
11	K DALLAS		K--A	150.00	200.00	K02 075 428A	
12	L SAN FRANCISCO		L--A	150.00	200.00	L07 717 988A	

TOTAL BLOCKS KNOWN: Twelve.
NOTE: BEP records show that no 1934C $100.00 notes were printed for Richmond.

CAT. NO. CF34D
$100.00 FEDERAL RESERVE NOTE (GREEN SEAL) (12 Subject)
SERIES 1934D

SERIAL NUMBERS: Continued sequence from previous series.
PLATE SERIALS: Back check 113 and higher.
SIGNATURES: Georgia Neese Clark, Treasurer of the United States
  John W. Snyder, Secretary of the Treasury

	DISTRICT	TOTAL NOTES PRINTED	BLOCKS	ESTIMATED VALUE VG/F	CU	LOW OBSERVED SERIAL NUMBER	HIGH OBSERVED SERIAL NUMBER
2	B NEW YORK	156	B--A	1,000.	2,500.		
3	C PHILADELPHIA	308,400	C--A	125.00	200.00		
6	F ATLANTA	260,400	F--A	125.00	200.00		
7	G CHICAGO	78,000	G--A	150.00	250.00		
8	H ST. LOUIS	166,800	H--A	125.00	200.00		
11	K DALLAS	66,000	K--A	150.00	250.00	K02 334 983A	

TOTAL BLOCKS: Six.
Collectors are requested to supply any serial numbers. No star notes have been observed or reported for this series although they do possibly exist.

CAT. NO. CF34D
$100.00 FEDERAL RESERVE NOTE (GREEN SEAL) MULE 12 Subject
SERIES 1934D MULE

PLATE SERIALS: Back check number 112 or lower.

	DISTRICT	TOTAL NOTES PRINTED	BLOCKS	ESTIMATED VALUE VG/F	CU	LOW OBSERVED SERIAL NUMBER	HIGH OBSERVED SERIAL NUMBER
3	C PHILADELPHIA		C--A	125.00	200.00	C03 486 749A	C03 680 845A
7	G CHICAGO		G--A	125.00	200.00	G08 504 434A	G11 238 414A
8	H ST. LOUIS		H--A	125.00	200.00	H03 910 708A	H04 076 543A
11	K DALLAS		K--A	125.00	200.00	K02 346 085A	

TOTAL BLOCKS KNOWN: Four.

CAT. NO. CF50
$100.00 FEDERAL RESERVE NOTE (GREEN SEAL) (12 Subject)
SERIES 1950

SERIAL NUMBERS: All serial numbers both regular and star notes begin with 00 000 001.
PLATE SERIALS: Back check number 113 and higher.
SIGNATURES: Georgia Neese Clark, Treasurer of the United States
John W. Snyder, Secretary of the Treasury

	DISTRICT	TOTAL NOTES PRINTED	BLOCKS	ESTIMATED VALUE VG/F	CU	LOW OFFICIAL SERIAL NUMBER	HIGH OFFICIAL SERIAL NUMBER
1	A BOSTON	768,000	A--A		135.00		A00 768 000A
			A--*		150.00		
2	B NEW YORK	3,908,000	B--A		135.00		B03 908 000A
			B--*		150.00		
3	C PHILADELPHIA	1,332,000	C--A		135.00		C01 332 000A
			C--*		150.00		C00 012 034*(1)
4	D CLEVELAND	1,632,000	D--A		135.00		D01 632 000A
			D--*		150.00		
5	E RICHMOND	4,076,000	E--A		135.00		E04 076 000A
			E--*		150.00		
6	F ATLANTA	1,824,000	F--A		135.00		F01 824 000A
			F--*		150.00		
7	G CHICAGO	4,428,000	G--A		135.00		G04 428 000A
			G--*		150.00		
8	H ST. LOUIS	1,284,000	H--A		135.00		H01 284 000A
			H--*		150.00		
9	I MINNEAPOLIS	564,000	I--A		135.00		I00 564 000A
			I--*		150.00		
10	J KANSAS CITY	864,000	J--A		135.00		J00 864 000A
			J--*		150.00		
11	K DALLAS	1,216,000	K--A		135.00		K01 216 000A
			K--*		150.00		
12	L SAN FRANCISCO	2,524,000	L--A		135.00		L02 524 000A
			L--*		150.00		

TOTAL BLOCKS: Twenty-four.
(1) Low observed.

CAT. NO. CF50
$100.00 FEDERAL RESERVE NOTE (GREEN SEAL) MULE 12 Subject
SERIES 1950 MULE

PLATE SERIALS: Back check number up to 112.

	DISTRICT	TOTAL NOTES PRINTED	BLOCKS	ESTIMATED VALUE VG/F	CU	LOW OBSERVED SERIAL NUMBER	HIGH OBSERVED SERIAL NUMBER
2	B NEW YORK		B--A		150.00	B01 321 953A	B06 795 081A
3	C PHILADELPHIA		C--A		150.00	C00 053 387A	C01 084 365A
4	D CLEVELAND		D--A		150.00	D00 855 975A	D01 414 048A
5	E RICHMOND		E--A		150.00	E02 541 614A	
7	G CHICAGO		G--A		150.00	G00 014 163A	G04 256 957A
10	J KANSAS CITY		J--A		150.00	J00 121 019A	J00 810 832A
11	K DALLAS		K--A		150.00	K00 959 412A	
12	L SAN FRANCISCO		L--A		150.00	L00 516 976A	L01 509 796A
			L--*		350.00	L00 009 491*	

TOTAL BLOCKS KNOWN: Nine.

CAT. NO. CF50A
$100.00 FEDERAL RESERVE NOTE (GREEN SEAL) (18 Subject)
SERIES 1950A

SERIAL NUMBERS: Continued sequence from previous series. Numbers between high serial number of last series and low serial number of this series were not used.
SIGNATURES: Ivy Baker Priest, Treasurer of the United States.
George M. Humphrey, Secretary of the Treasury.

	DISTRICT	TOTAL NOTES PRINTED	BLOCKS	ESTIMATED VALUE VG/F	CU	LOW OFFICIAL SERIAL NUMBER	HIGH OFFICIAL SERIAL NUMBER	
1	A BOSTON	1,008,000	A--A		120.00	A00 864 001A	A01 872 000A	
			A--*		135.00			
2	B NEW YORK	2,880,000	B--A		120.00	B04 032 001A	B06 912 000A	
			B--*		135.00	B00 180 750*(1)		
3	C PHILADELPHIA	576,000	C--A		120.00	C01 440 001A	C02 016 000A	
			C--*		135.00			
4	D CLEVELAND	288,000	D--A		120.00	D01 728 001A	D02 016 000A	
			D--*		135.00			
5	E RICHMOND	2,160,000	E--A		120.00	E04 176 001A	E06 336 000A	
			E--*		135.00			
6	F ATLANTA	288,000	F--A		120.00	F01 872 001A	F02 160 000A	
			F--*		135.00			
7	G CHICAGO	864,000	G--A		120.00	G04 464 001A	G05 328 000A	
			G--*		135.00			
8	H ST. LOUIS	432,000	H--A		120.00	H01 296 001A	H01 728 000A	
			H--*		135.00			
9	I MINNEAPOLIS	144,000	I--A		125.00	I00 576 001A	I00 720 000A	
			I--*		150.00			
10	J KANSAS CITY	288,000	J--A		120.00	J00 864 001A	J01 152 000A	(1)
			J--*		135.00			
11	K DALLAS	432,000	K--A		120.00	K01 296 001A	K01 728 000A	(1)
			K--*		135.00			
12	L SAN FRANCISCO	720,000	L--A		120.00	L02 592 001A	L03 312 000A	
			L--*		135.00			

TOTAL BLOCKS: Twenty four.
(1) Low Observed

CAT. NO. CF50B
$100.00 FEDERAL RESERVE NOTE (GREEN SEAL) (18 Subject)
SERIES 1950B

SERIAL NUMBERS: Continued sequence from previous series.
SIGNATURES: Ivy Baker Priest, Treasurer of the United States.
Robert B. Anderson, Secretary of the Treasury.

	DISTRICT	TOTAL NOTES PRINTED	BLOCKS	ESTIMATED VALUE VG/F	CU	LOW OFFICIAL SERIAL NUMBER	HIGH OFFICIAL SERIAL NUMBER
1	A BOSTON	720,000	A-A		120.00	A01 872 001A	A02 592 000A
			A--*		135.00		
2	B NEW YORK	6,636,000	B--A		120.00	B06 912 001A	B13 248 000A
			B--*		135.00		
3	C PHILADELPHIA	720,000	C--A		120.00	C02 016 001A	C02 736 000A
			C--*		135.00		
4	D CLEVELAND	432,000	D--A		120.00	D02 016 001A	D02 448 000A
			D--*		135.00		
5	E RICHMOND	1,008,000	E--A		120.00	E06 336 001A	E07 344 000A
			E--*		135.00		
6	F ATLANTA	576,000	F--A		120.00	F02 160 001A	F02 736 000A
			F--*		135.00		
7	G CHICAGO	2,592,000	G--A		120.00	G05 328 001A	G07 920 000A
			G--*		135.00	G00401 346*(1)	
8	H ST. LOUIS	1,152,000	H--A		120.00	H01 728 001A	H02 880 000A
			H--*		135.00		
9	I MINNEAPOLIS	288,000	I--A		120.00	I00 720 001A	I01 008 000A
			I--*		135.00		
10	J KANSAS CITY	720,000	J--A		120.00	J01 152 001A	J01 872 000A
			J--*		135.00		

	DISTRICT	TOTAL NOTES PRINTED	BLOCKS	ESTIMATED VALUE VG/F	CU	LOW OFFICIAL SERIAL NUMBER	HIGH OFFICIAL SERIAL NUMBER
11	K DALLAS	1,728,000	K--A		120.00	K01 728 001A	K03 456 000A
			K--*		135.00	K00 345 060* (1)	
12	L SAN FRANCISCO	2,880,000	L--A		120.00	L03 312 001A	L06 192 000A
			L--*		135.00		

TOTAL BLOCKS: Twenty four.

CAT. NO. CF50C
$100.00 FEDERAL RESERVE NOTE (GREEN SEAL) (18 Subject)
SERIES 1950C

SERIAL NUMBERS: Continued sequence from previous series.
SIGNATURES: Elizabeth Rudel Smith, Treasurer of the United States.
  C. Douglas Dillon, Secretary of the Treasury.

	DISTRICT	TOTAL NOTES PRINTED	BLOCKS	ESTIMATED VALUE VG/F	CU	LOW OFFICIAL SERIAL NUMBER	HIGH OFFICIAL SERIAL NUMBER
1	A BOSTON	864,000	A--A		120.00	A02 592 001A	A03 456 000A
			A--*		135.00		
2	B NEW YORK	2,448,000	B--A		120.00	B13 248 001A	B15 696 000A
			B--*		135.00		
3	C PHILADELPHIA	576,000	C--A		120.00	C02 736 001A	C03 312 000A
			C--*		135.00		
4	D CLEVELAND	576,000	D--A		120.00	D02 448 001A	D03 024 000A
			D--*		135.00		
5	E RICHMOND	1,440,000	E--A		120.00	E07 344 001A	E08 784 000A
			E--*		135.00		
6	F ATLANTA	1,296,000	F--A		120.00	F02 736 001A	F04 032 000A
			F--*		135.00		
7	G CHICAGO	1,584,000	G--A		120.00	G07 920 001A	G09 504 000A
			G--*		135.00		
8	H ST. LOUIS	720,000	H--A		120.00	H02 880 001A	H03 600 000A
			H--*		135.00	H00 456 335* (1)	
9	I MINNEAPOLIS	288,000	I--A		120.00	I01 008 001A	I01 296 000A
			I--*		135.00		
10	J KANSAS CITY	432,000	J--A		120.00	J01 872 001A	J02 304 000A
			J--*		135.00		
11	K DALLAS	720,000	K--A		120.00	K03 456 001A	K04 176 000A
			K--*		135.00		
12	L SAN FRANCISCO	2,160,000	L--A		120.00	L06 192 001A	L08 352 000A
			L--*		135.00		

TOTAL BLOCKS: Twenty four.

CAT. NO. CF50D
$100.00 FEDERAL RESERVE NOTE (GREEN SEAL) (18 Subject)
SERIES 1950D

SERIAL NUMBERS: Continued sequence from previous series.
SIGNATURES: Kathryn O'Hay Granahan, Treasurer of the United States.
  C. Douglas Dillon, Secretary of the Treasury.

	DISTRICT	TOTAL NOTES PRINTED	BLOCKS	ESTIMATED VALUE VG/F	CU	LOW OFFICIAL SERIAL NUMBER	HIGH OFFICIAL SERIAL NUMBER
1	A BOSTON	1,872,000	A--A		120.00	A03 456 001A	A05 328 000A
			A--*		135.00		
2	B NEW YORK	7,632,000	B--A		120.00	B15 696 001A	B23 328 000A
			B--*		135.00		
3	C PHILADELPHIA	1,872,000	C--A		120.00	C03 312 001A	C05 184 000A
			C--*		135.00		
4	D CLEVELAND	1,584,000	D--A		120.00	D03 024 001A	D04 608 000A
			D--*		135.00		
5	E RICHMOND	2,880,000	E--A		120.00	E08 784 001A	E11 664 000A
			E--*		135.00	E00 492 556* (1)	E00 558 910* (2)
6	F ATLANTA	1,872,000	F--A		120.00	F04 032 001A	F05 904 000A
			F--*		135.00		
7	G CHICAGO	4,608,000	G--A		120.00	G09 504 001A	G14 112 000A
			G--*		135.00		

	DISTRICT	TOTAL NOTES PRINTED	BLOCKS	ESTIMATED VALUE VG/F	CU	LOW OFFICIAL SERIAL NUMBER	HIGH OFFICIAL SERIAL NUMBER
8	H ST. LOUIS	1,440,000	H--A		135.00	H03 600 001A	H05 040 000A
			H--*		135.00		
9	I MINNEAPOLIS	432,000	I--A		120.00	I01 296 001A	I07 728 000A
			I--*		135.00		
10	J KANSAS CITY	864,000	J--A		120.00	J02 304 001A	J03 168 000A
			J--*		135.00		
11	K DALLAS	1,728,000	K--A		120.00	K04 176 001A	K05 904 000A
			K--*		135.00		
12	L SAN FRANCISCO	3,312,000	L--A		120.00	L08 352 001A	L11 664 000A
			L--*		135.00		

TOTAL BLOCKS: Twenty four.
(1) Low Observed
(2) High Observed

CAT. NO. CF50E
$100.00 FEDERAL RESERVE NOTE (GREEN SEAL) (18 Subject)
SERIES 1950E

SERIAL NUMBERS: Districts printed continued sequence from previous series.
SIGNATURES: Kathryn O'Hay Granahan, Treasurer of the United States.
   Henry H. Fowler, Secretary of the Treasury.

	DISTRICT	TOTAL NOTES PRINTED	BLOCKS	ESTIMATED VALUE VG/F	CU	LOW OFFICIAL SERIAL NUMBER	HIGH OFFICIAL SERIAL NUMBER
2	B NEW YORK	3,024,000	B--A		115.00	B23 328 001A	B26 352 000A
			B--*		135.00	B01 301 125*(1)	
7	G CHICAGO	576,000	G--A		125.00	G14 112 001A	G14 688 000A
			G--*		160.00		
12	L SAN FRANCISCO	2,736,000	L--A		115.00	L11 664 001A	L14 400 000A
			L--*		135.00	L01 020 680*	

TOTAL BLOCKS: Six. (1) Low Observed.

No $100.00 notes for Series 1963 were printed.

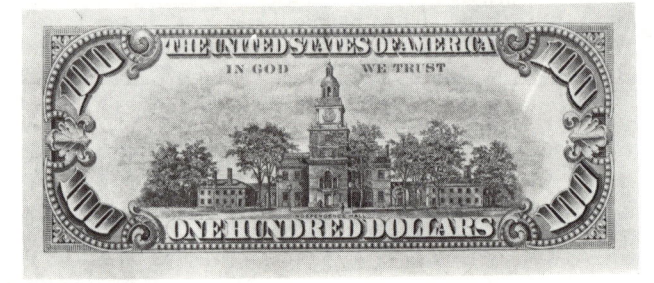

CAT. NO. CF63A
$100.00 FEDERAL RESERVE NOTE (GREEN SEAL) (32 Subject)
SERIES 1963A

SERIAL NUMBERS: All serial numbers both regular and star notes begin with 00 000 001.
PLATE SERIALS: Both face and back check numbers begin with 1. Motto IN GOD WE TRUST added to back.
SIGNATURES: Kathryn O'Hay Granahan, Treasurer of the United States.
   Henry H. Fowler, Secretary of the Treasury.

	DISTRICT	TOTAL NOTES PRINTED	BLOCKS	ESTIMATED VALUE VG/F	CU	LOW OFFICIAL SERIAL NUMBER	HIGH OFFICIAL SERIAL NUMBER
1	A BOSTON	1,536,000	A--A		115.00		A01 536 000A
		128,000	A--*		125.00		A00 128 000*
2	B NEW YORK	12,544,000	B--A		115.00		B12 544 000A
		1,536,000	B--*		125.00		B01 536 000*
3	C PHILADELPHIA	1,792,000	C--A		115.00		C01 792 000A
		192,000	C--*		125.00		C00 192 000*
4	D CLEVELAND	2,304,000	D--A		115.00		D02 304 000A
		192,000	D--*		125.00		D00 192 000*
5	E RICHMOND	2,816,000	E--A		115.00		E02 816 000A
		192,000	E--*		125.00		E00 192 000*

	DISTRICT	TOTAL NOTES PRINTED	BLOCKS	ESTIMATED VALUE VG/F	CU	LOW OFFICIAL SERIAL NUMBER	HIGH OFFICIAL SERIAL NUMBER
6	F ATLANTA	1,280,000	F--A		115.00		F01 280 000A
		128,000	F--*		125.00		F00 128 000*
7	G CHICAGO	4,352,000	G--A		115.00		G04 352 000A
		512,000	G--*		125.00		G00 512 000*
8	H ST. LOUIS	1,536,000	H--A		115.00		H01 536 000A
		256,000	H--*		125.00		H00 256 000*
9	I MINNEAPOLIS	512,000	I--A		115.00		I00 512 000A
		128,000	I--*		125.00		I00 128 000*
10	J KANSAS CITY	1,024,000	J--A		115.00		J01 024 000A
		128,000	J--*		125.00		J00 128 000*
11	K DALLAS	1,536,000	K--A		115.00		K01 536 000A
		192,000	K--*		125.00		K00 192 000*
12	L SAN FRANCISCO	6,400,000	L--A		115.00		L06 400 000A
		832,000	L--*		125.00		L00 832 000*

TOTAL BLOCKS: Twenty four.

CAT. NO. CF69
$100.00 FEDERAL RESERVE NOTE (GREEN SEAL) (32 Subject)
SERIES 1969

SERIAL NUMBERS: All serial numbers both regular and star notes begin with 00 000 001.
SIGNATURES: Dorothy Andrews Elston, Treasurer of the United States.
David M. Kennedy, Secretary of the Treasury.

	DISTRICT	TOTAL NOTES PRINTED	BLOCKS	ESTIMATED VALUE VG/F	CU	LOW OFFICIAL SERIAL NUMBER	HIGH OFFICIAL SERIAL NUMBER
1	A BOSTON	2,048,000	A--A		115.00		A02 048 000A
		128,000	A--*		125.00		A00 128 000*
2	B NEW YORK	11,520,000	B--A		115.00		B11 520 000A
		128,000	B--*		125.00		B00 128 000*
3	C PHILADELPHIA	2,560,000	C--A		115.00		C02 560 000A
		128,000	C--*		115.00		C00 128 000*
4	D CLEVELAND	768,000	D--A		115.00		D00 768 000A
		64,000	D--*		135.00		D00 064 000*
5	E RICHMOND	2,560,000	E--A		115.00		E02 560 000A
		192,000	E--*		125.00		E00 192 000*
6	F ATLANTA	2,304,000	F--A		115.00		F02 304 000A
		128,000	F--*		125.00		F00 128 000*
7	G CHICAGO	5,888,000	G--A		115.00		G05 888 000A
		256,000	G--*		125.00		G00 256 000*
8	H ST. LOUIS	1,280,000	H--A		115.00		H01 280 000A
		64,000	H--*		135.00		H00 064 000*
9	I MINNEAPOLIS	512,000	I--A		115.00		I00 512 000A
		64,000	I--*		135.00		I00 064 000*
10	J KANSAS CITY	1,792,000	J--A		115.00		J01 792 000A
		384,000	J--*		125.00		J00 384 000*
11	K DALLAS	2,048,000	K--A		115.00		K02 048 000A
		128,000	K--*		125.00		K00 128 000*
12	L SAN FRANCISCO	7,168,000	L--A		115.00		L07 168 000A
		320,000	L--*		125.00		L00 320 000*

TOTAL BLOCKS: Twenty four.

CAT. NO. CF69A
$100.00 FEDERAL RESERVE NOTE (GREEN SEAL) (32 Subject)
SERIES 1969A

SERIAL NUMBERS: Continued sequence from previous series.
SIGNATURES: Dorothy Andrews Kabis, Treasurer of the United States.
John B. Connally, Secretary of the Treasurer.

	DISTRICT	TOTAL NOTES PRINTED	BLOCKS	ESTIMATED VALUE VG/F	CU	LOW OFFICIAL SERIAL NUMBER	HIGH OFFICIAL SERIAL NUMBER
1	A BOSTON	1,280,000	A--A		110.00	A02 048 001A	A03 328 000A
		320,000	A--*		125.00	A00 128 001*	A00 448 000*
2	B NEW YORK	11,264,000	B--A		110.00	B11 520 001A	B22 782 000A
		640,000	B--*		125.00	B00 128 001*	B00 768 000*

	DISTRICT	TOTAL NOTES PRINTED	BLOCKS	ESTIMATED VALUE VG/F CU	LOW OFFICIAL SERIAL NUMBER	HIGH OFFICIAL SERIAL NUMBER
3	C PHILADELPHIA	2,048,000	C--A	110.00	C02 560 001A	C05 120 000A
		448,000	C--*	125.00	C00 128 001*	C00 576 000*
4	D CLEVELAND	1,280,000	D--A	110.00	D00 768 001A	D03 584 000A
		192,000	D--*	125.00	D00 064 001*	D00 256 000*
5	E RICHMOND	2,304,000	E--A	110.00	E02 560 001A	E04 864 000A
		192,000	E--*	125.00	E00 192 001*	E00 384 000*
6	F ATLANTA	2,304,000	F--A	110.00	F02 304 001A	F04 608 000A
		640,000	F--*	125.00	F00 128 001*	F00 192 000*
7	G CHICAGO	5,376,000	G--A	110.00	G05 888 001A	G11 264 000A
		320,000	G--*	125.00	G00 256 001*	G00 576 000*
8	H ST. LOUIS	1,024,000	H--A	110.00	H01 280 001A	H02 304 000A
		664,000	H--*	135.00	H00 064 001*	H00 128 000*
9	I MINNEAPOLIS	1,024,000	I--A	110.00	I00 512 001A	I01 536 000A
		none	I--*		none printed	
10	J KANSAS CITY	512,000	J--A	110.00	J01 792 001A	J02 304 000A
		none	J--*		none printed	
11	K DALLAS	3,328,000	K--A	110.00	K02 048 001A	K05 376 000A
		128,000	K--*	125.00	K00 128 001*	K00 256 000*
12	L SAN FRANCISCO	4,352,000	L--A	110.00	L07 168 001A	L11 520 000A
		576,000	L--*	125.00	L00 320 001*	L00 959 000*

TOTAL BLOCKS: Twenty two.

$100.00 FEDERAL RESERVE NOTE
SERIES 1969B
No notes for this denomination were printed for this series.

CAT. NO. CF69C
$100.00 FEDERAL RESERVE NOTE (GREEN SEAL) (32 Subject)
SERIES 1969C

SIGNATURES: Romano Acosta Banuelos, Treasurer of the United States.
    George P. Schultz, Secretary of the Treasury.

ESTIMATED VALUES: All regular notes $110.00, stars $125.00 CU.

	DISTRICT	TOTAL NOTES PRINTED	BLOCKS	ESTIMATED VALUE VG/F CU	LOW OFFICIAL SERIAL NUMBER	HIGH OFFICIAL SERIAL NUMBER
1	A BOSTON	2,048,000	A--A		A03 328 001A	A05 376 000A
		64,000	A--*		A00 448 001*	A00 512 000*
2	B NEW YORK#	15,616,000	B--A		B22 784 001A	B38 400 000A
		256,000	B--*		B00 768 001*	B01 024 000*
3	C PHILADELPHIA#	2,816,000	C--A		C05 120 001A	C07 936 000A
		64,000	C--*		C00 576 001*	C00 640 000*
4	D CLEVELAND#	3,456,000	D--A		D03 584 001A	D07 040 000A
		64,000	D--*		D00 256 001*	D00 320 000*
5	E RICHMOND#	7,296,000	E--A		E04 864 001A	E12 160 000A
		128,000	E--*		E00 384 001*	E00 512 000*
6	F ATLANTA#	2,432,000	F--A		F04 608 001A	F07 040 000A
		64,000	F--*		F00 192 001*	F00 256 000
7	G CHICAGO#	6,016,000	G--A		G11 264 001A	G17 280 000A
		320,000	G--*		G00 576 001*	G00 896 000*
8	H ST. LOUIS#	5,376,000	H--A		H02 304 001A	H07 680 000A
		64,000	H--*		H00 128 001*	H00 192 000*
9	I MINNEAPOLIS	512,000	I--A		I01 536 001A	I02 048 000A
		64,000	I--*		I00 064 001*	I00 128 000*
10	J KANSAS CITY#	4,736,000	J--A		J02 304 001A	J07 040 000A
		192,000	J--*		J00 384 001*	J00 576 000*
11	K DALLAS#	2,944,000	K--A		K05 376 001A	K08 320 000A
		64,000	K--*		K00 256 001*	K00 320 000*
12	L SAN FRANCISCO#	10,240,000	L--A		L11 520 001A	L21 760 000A
		512,000	L--*		L00 896 001*	L01 408 000*

TOTAL BLOCKS: Twenty-four.
  #The production unit was changed from 8,000 sheets to 20,000 sheets for:

BANK	STARTING WITH SERIAL NUMBER
New York	B26 880 001A
Philadelphia	C08 320 001A
Cleveland	D03 840 001A
Richmond	E08 960 001A
Atlanta	F06 400 001A
Chicago	G14 080 001A
St. Louis	H05 120 001A
Kansas City	J05 120 001A
Dallas	K06 400 001A
San Francisco	L16 640 001A

The formula to relate the position and check letter for serials later than above would be the same as used on the lower denominations.

CAT. NO. CF74
$100.00 FEDERAL RESERVE NOTE (GREEN SEAL) (32 Subject)
SERIES 1974

SIGNATURES: Francine I. Neff, Treasurer of the United States.
William E. Simon, Secretary of the Treasury.
PLATE SERIALS: Both face and back check numbers continue from previous series.
SERIAL NUMBERS: All districts continue from previous series.

	DISTRICT	TOTAL NOTES PRINTED	BLOCKS	ESTIMATED VALUE VG/F	CU	LOW OFFICIAL SERIAL NUMBER	HIGH OFFICIAL SERIAL NUMBER	
1	A BOSTON		A--A		110.00	A05 376 001A	A08 320 000A	cv
					110.00	A08 320 001A	A17 280 000A	cp
			A--*		115.00	A00 512 001*	A00 768 000*	cv
2	B NEW YORK		B--A		110.00	B32 400 001A	B53 760 000A	cv
					110.00	B53 760 001A	B99 840 000A	cp
					110.00	B00 000 001A	B01 280 000B	cp
			B--*		115.00	B01 024 001*	B02 752 000*	cv
3	C PHILADELPHIA		C--A		110.00	C07 936 001A	C11 520 000A	cv
					110.00	C11 520 001A	C16 000 000A	cp
			C--*		115.00	C00 640 001*	C00 768 000*	cv
4	D CLEVELAND		D--A		110.00	D07 040 001A	D09 600 000A	cv
					110.00	D09 600 001A	D33 920 000A	cp
			D--*		115.00	D00 320 001*	D00 512 000*	cv
5	E RICHMOND		E--A		110.00	E12 160 001A	E16 640 000A	cv
					110.00	E16 640 001A	E23 680 000A	cp
			E--*		115.00	E00 512 001*	E00 640 000*	cv
6	F ATLANTA		F--A		110.00	F07 040 001A	F09 600 000A	cv
					110.00	F09 600 001A	F11 520 000A	cp
			F--*		115.00	F00 256 0018	F00 384 000*	cv
7	G CHICAGO		G--A		110.00	G17 280 001A	G33 920 000A	cv
					110.00	G33 920 001A	G44 160 000A	cp
			G--*		115.00	G00 896 001*	G02 112 000*	cv
8	H ST. LOUIS		H--A		110.00	H07 680 001A	H08 960 000A	cv
					110.00	H08 960 001A	H13 440 000A	cp
			H--*		115.00	H00 192 001*	H00 384 000*	cv
9	I MINNEAPOLIS		I--A		110.00	I02 048 001A	I04 480 000A	cv
					110.00	I04 480 001A	I07 040 000A	cp
			I--*		115.00	I00 128 001*	I00 384 000*	cv
10	J KANSAS CITY		J--A		110.00	J07 040 001A	J08 320 000A	cv
					110.00	J08 320 001A	J12 800 000A	cp
			J--*		115.00	J00 576 001*	J01 024 000*	cv
11	K DALLAS		K--A		110.00	K08 320 001A	K09 600 000A	cv
					110.00	K09 600 001A	K18 560 000A	cp
			K--*		115.00	K00 320 001*	K00 512 000*	cv
12	L SAN FRANCISCO		L--A		110.00	L21 760 001A	L39 040 000A	cv
					110.00	L39 040 001A	L51 200 000A	cp
			L--*		115.00	L01 408 001*	L02 176 000*	cv
					115.00	L02 240 001*	L02 304 000*	cv

TOTAL BLOCKS: Twenty four.

The production unit was changed from 8,000 sheets to 20,000 sheets for:

BANK	STARTING WITH SERIAL NUMBER
Boston	A05 760 001A
Minneapolis	I02 560 001A

CAT. NO. CF77
$100.00 FEDERAL RESERVE NOTE (GREEN SEAL) (32 Subject)
SERIES 1977

SIGNATURES: Azie Taylor Morton, Treasurer of the United States.
W. Michael Blumenthal, Secretary of the Treasury.
PLATE SERIALS: Both face and back check continue from previous series.
SERIAL NUMBERS: All districts revert to 00 000 001.

	DISTRICT	TOTAL NOTES PRINTED	BLOCKS	ESTIMATED VALUE VG/F	CU	LOW OFFICIAL SERIAL NUMBER	HIGH OFFICIAL SERIAL NUMBER(1)
1	A BOSTON		A--A		110.00	A00 000 001A	A19 200 000A
			A--*		125.00	A00 014 001*	A00 020 000*
					125.00	A00 034 001*	A00 040 000*
					125.00	A00 054 001*	A00 060 000*
					125.00	A00 074 001*	A00 080 000*
					125.00	A00 094 001*	A00 100 000*
					125.00	A00 114 001*	A00 120 000*
					125.00	A00 134 001*	A00 140 000*
					125.00	A00 154 001*	A00 160 000*
					125.00	A00 174 001*	A00 180 000*
					125.00	A00 194 001*	A00 200 000*
					125.00	A00 214 001*	A00 220 000*
					125.00	A00 234 001*	A00 240 000*
					125.00	A00 254 001*	A00 260 000*
					125.00	A00 274 001*	A00 280 000*
					125.00	A00 294 001*	A00 300 000*
					125.00	A00 314 001*	A00 320 000*
					125.00	A00 334 001*	A00 340 000*
					125.00	A00 354 001*	A00 360 000*
					125.00	A00 374 001*	A00 380 000*
					125.00	A00 394 001*	A00 400 000*
					125.00	A00 414 001*	A00 420 000*
					125.00	A00 434 001*	A00 440 000*
					125.00	A00 454 001*	A00 460 000*
					125.00	A00 474 001*	A00 480 000*
					125.00	A00 494 001*	A00 500 000*
					125.00	A00 514 001*	A00 520 000*
					125.00	A00 534 001*	A00 540 000*
					125.00	A00 554 001*	A00 560 000*
					125.00	A00 574 001*	A00 580 000*
					125.00	A00 594 001*	A00 600 000*
					125.00	A00 614 001*	A00 620 000*
					125.00	A00 634 001*	A00 640 000*
					125.00	A00 656 001*	A00 660 000*
					125.00	A00 676 001*	A00 680 000*
					125.00	A00 696 001*	A00 700 000*
					125.00	A00 716 001*	A00 720 000*
					125.00	A00 736 001*	A00 740 000*
					125.00	A00 756 001*	A00 760 000*
					125.00	A00 776 001*	A00 780 000*
					125.00	A00 796 001*	A00 800 000*
					125.00	A00 816 001*	A00 820 000*
					125.00	A00 836 001*	A00 840 000*
					125.00	A00 856 001*	A00 860 000*
					125.00	A00 876 001*	A00 880 000*
					125.00	A00 896 001*	A00 900 000*
					125.00	A00 916 001*	A00 920 000*
					125.00	A00 936 001*	A00 940 000*
					125.00	A00 956 001*	A00 960 000*
					125.00	A00 976 001*	A00 980 000*
					125.00	A00 996 001*	A01 000 000*
					125.00	A01 016 001*	A01 020 000*
					125.00	A01 036 001*	A01 040 000*
					125.00	A01 056 001*	A01 060 000*
					125.00	A01 076 001*	A01 080 000*
					125.00	A01 096 001*	A01 100 000*
					125.00	A01 116 001*	A01 120 000*
					125.00	A01 136 001*	A01 140 000*
					125.00	A01 156 001*	A01 160 000*
					125.00	A01 176 001*	A01 180 000*

DISTRICT	TOTAL NOTES PRINTED	BLOCKS	ESTIMATED VALUE VG/F CU	LOW OFFICIAL SERIAL NUMBER	HIGH OFFICIAL SERIAL NUMBER
			125.00	A01 196 001*	A01 200 000*
			125.00	A01 216 001*	A01 220 000*
			125.00	A01 236 001*	A01 240 000*
			125.00	A01 256 001*	A01 260 000*
2 B NEW YORK			125.00	A01 276 001*	A01 280 000*
		B--A	110.00	B00 000 001A	B99 840 000A
		B--B	110.00	B00 000 001B	B53 760 000B
		B--*	115.00	B00 000 001*	B00 704 000*
			125.00	B07 054 001*	B07 060 000*
			125.00	B07 074 001*	B07 080 000*
			125.00	B07 094 001*	B07 100 000*
			125.00	B07 114 001*	B07 120 000*
			125.00	B07 134 001*	B07 140 000*
			125.00	B07 154 001*	B07 160 000*
			125.00	B07 174 001*	B07 180 000*
			125.00	B07 194 001*	B07 200 000*
			125.00	B07 124 001*	B07 220 000*
			125.00	B07 234 001*	B07 240 000*
			125.00	B07 254 001*	B07 260 000*
			125.00	B07 274 001*	B07 280 000*
			125.00	B07 294 001*	B07 300 000*
			125.00	B07 314 001*	B07 320 000*
			125.00	B07 334 001*	B07 340 000*
			125.00	B07 354 001*	B07 360 000*
			125.00	B07 374 001*	B07 380 000*
			125.00	B07 394 001*	B07 400 000*
			125.00	B07 414 001*	B07 420 000*
			125.00	B07 434 001*	B07 440 000*
			125.00	B07 454 001*	B07 460 000*
			125.00	B07 474 001*	B07 480 000*
			125.00	B07 494 001*	B07 500 000*
			125.00	B07 514 001*	B07 520 000*
			125.00	B07 534 001*	B07 540 000*
			125.00	B07 554 001*	B07 560 000*
			125.00	B07 574 001*	B07 580 000*
			125.00	B07 594 001*	B07 600 000*
			125.00	B07 614 001*	B07 620 000*
			125.00	B07 634 001*	B07 640 000*
			125.00	B07 654 001*	B07 660 000*
			125.00	B07 674 001*	B07 680 000*
			115.00	B07 680 001*	B08 320 000*
			125.00	B08 336 001*	B08 340 000*
			125.00	B08 356 001*	B08 360 000*
			125.00	B08 376 001*	B08 380 000*
			125.00	B08 396 001*	B08 400 000*
			125.00	B08 416 001*	B08 420 000*
			125.00	B08 436 001*	B08 440 000*
			125.00	B08 456 001*	B08 460 000*
			125.00	B08 476 001*	B08 480 000*
			125.00	B08 496 001*	B08 500 000*
			125.00	B08 516 001*	B08 520 000*
			125.00	B08 536 001*	B08 540 000*
			125.00	B08 556 001*	B08 560 000*
			125.00	B08 576 001*	B08 580 000*
			125.00	B08 596 001*	B08 600 000*
			125.00	B08 616 001*	B08 620 000*
			125.00	B08 636 001*	B08 640 000*
			125.00	B08 656 001*	B08 660 000*
			125.00	B08 676 001*	B08 680 000*
			125.00	B08 696 001*	B08 700 000*
			125.00	B08 716 001*	B08 720 000*
			125.00	B08 736 001*	B08 740 000*
			125.00	B08 756 001*	B08 760 000*
			125.00	B08 776 001*	B08 780 000*
			125.00	B08 796 001*	B08 800 000*
			125.00	B08 816 001*	B08 820 000*
			125.00	B08 836 001*	B08 840 000*
			125.00	B08 856 001*	B08 860 000*
			125.00	B08 876 001*	B08 880 000*

DISTRICT	TOTAL NOTES PRINTED	BLOCKS	ESTIMATED VALUE VG/F	VALUE CU	LOW OFFICIAL SERIAL NUMBER	HIGH OFFICIAL SERIAL NUMBER
				125.00	B08 896 001*	B08 900 000*
				125.00	B08 916 001*	B08 920 000*
				125.00	B08 936 001*	B08 940 000*
				125.00	B08 956 001*	B08 960 000*
3 C PHILADELPHIA		C--A		110.00	C00 000 001A	C05 120 000A
		C--*		125.00	C00 016 001*	C00 020 000*
				125.00	C00 036 001*	C00 040 000*
				125.00	C00 056 001*	C00 060 000*
				125.00	C00 076 001*	C00 080 000*
				125.00	C00 096 001*	C00 100 000*
				125.00	C00 116 001*	C00 120 000*
				125.00	C00 136 001*	C00 140 000*
				125.00	C00 156 001*	C00 160 000*
				125.00	C00 176 001*	C00 180 000*
				125.00	C00 196 001*	C00 200 000*
				125.00	C00 216 001*	C00 220 000*
				125.00	C00 236 001*	C00 240 000*
				125.00	C00 256 001*	C00 260 000*
				125.00	C00 276 001*	C00 280 000*
				125.00	C00 296 001*	C00 300 000*
				125.00	C00 316 001*	C00 320 000*
				125.00	C00 336 001*	C00 340 000*
				125.00	C00 356 001*	C00 360 000*
				125.00	C00 376 001*	C00 380 000*
				125.00	C00 396 001*	C00 400 000*
				125.00	C00 416 001*	C00 420 000*
				125.00	C00 436 001*	C00 440 000*
				125.00	C00 456 001*	C00 460 000*
				125.00	C00 476 001*	C00 480 000*
				125.00	C00 496 001*	C00 500 000*
				125.00	C00 516 001*	C00 520 000*
				125.00	C00 536 001*	C00 540 000*
				125.00	C00 556 001*	C00 560 000*
				125.00	C00 576 001*	C00 580 000*
				125.00	C00 596 001*	C00 600 000*
				125.00	C00 616 001*	C00 620 000*
				125.00	C00 636 001*	C00 640 000*
4 D CLEVELAND		D--A		110.00	D00 000 001A	D14 080 000A
		D--*		115.00	D00 000 001*	D00 064 000*
				125.00	D00 656 001*	D00 660 000*
				125.00	D00 676 001*	D00 680 000*
				125.00	D00 696 001*	D00 700 000*
				125.00	D00 716 001*	D00 720 000*
				125.00	D00 736 001*	D00 740 000*
				125.00	D00 756 001*	D00 760 000*
				125.00	D00 776 001*	D00 780 000*
				125.00	D00 796 001*	D00 800 000*
				125.00	D00 816 001*	D00 820 000*
				125.00	D00 836 001*	D00 840 000*
				125.00	D00 856 001*	D00 860 000*
				125.00	D00 876 001*	D00 880 000*
				125.00	D00 896 001*	D00 900 000*
				125.00	D00 916 001*	D00 920 000*
				125.00	D00 936 001*	D00 940 000*
				125.00	D00 956 001*	D00 960 000*
				125.00	D00 976 001*	D00 980 000*
				125.00	D00 996 001*	D01 000 000*
				125.00	D01 016 001*	D01 020 000*
				125.00	D01 036 001*	D01 040 000*
				125.00	D01 056 001*	D01 060 000*
				125.00	D01 076 001*	D01 080 000*
				125.00	D01 096 001*	D01 100 000*
				125.00	D01 116 001*	D01 120 000*
				125.00	D01 136 001*	D01 140 000*
				125.00	D01 156 001*	D01 160 000*
				125.00	D01 176 001*	D01 180 000*
				125.00	D01 196 001*	D01 200 000*
				125.00	D01 216 001*	D01 220 000*
				125.00	D01 236 001*	D01 240 000*

DISTRICT	TOTAL NOTES PRINTED	BLOCKS	ESTIMATED VALUE VG/F	VALUE CU	LOW OFFICIAL SERIAL NUMBER	HIGH OFFICIAL SERIAL NUMBER
				125.00	D01 256 001*	D01 260 000*
				125.00	D01 276 001*	D01 280 000*
5 E RICHMOND		E--A		110.00	E00 000 001A	E17 920 000A
		D--*		115.00	E00 000 001*	E00 128 000*
				125.00	E01 296 001*	E01 300 000*
				125.00	E01 316 001*	E01 320 000*
				125.00	E01 336 001*	E01 340 000*
				125.00	E01 356 001*	E01 360 000*
				125.00	E01 376 001*	E01 380 000*
				125.00	E01 396 001*	E01 400 000*
				125.00	E01 416 001*	E01 420 000*
				125.00	E01 436 001*	E01 440 000*
				125.00	E01 456 001*	E01 460 000*
				125.00	E01 476 001*	E01 480 000*
				125.00	E01 496 001*	E01 500 000*
				125.00	E01 516 001*	E01 520 000*
				125.00	E01 536 001*	E01 540 000*
				125.00	E01 556 001*	E01 560 000*
				125.00	E01 576 001*	E01 580 000*
				125.00	E01 596 001*	E01 600 000*
				125.00	E01 616 001*	E01 620 000*
				125.00	E01 636 001*	E01 640 000*
				125.00	E01 656 001*	E01 660 000*
				125.00	E01 676 001*	E01 680 000*
				125.00	E01 696 001*	E01 700 000*
				125.00	E01 716 001*	E01 720 000*
				125.00	E01 736 001*	E01 740 000*
				125.00	E01 756 001*	E01 760 000*
				125.00	E01 776 001*	E01 780 000*
				125.00	E01 796 001*	E01 800 000*
				125.00	E01 816 001*	E01 820 000*
				125.00	E01 836 001*	E01 840 000*
				125.00	E01 856 001*	E01 860 000*
				125.00	E01 876 001*	E01 880 000*
				125.00	E01 896 001*	E01 900 000*
				125.00	E01 916 001*	E01 920 000*
6 F ATLANTA		F--A		110.00	F00 000 001A	F03 840 000A
		F--*		115.00	F00 000 001*	F00 064 000*
7 G CHICAGO		G--A		110.00	G00 000 001A	G33 280 000A
		G--*		115.00	G00 000 001*	G00 192 000*
				115.00	G00 320 001*	G00 384 000*
				125.00	G03 858 001*	G03 860 000*
				125.00	G03 878 001*	G03 880 000*
				125.00	G03 898 001*	G03 900 000*
				125.00	G03 918 001*	G03 920 000*
				125.00	G03 938 001*	G03 940 000*
				125.00	G03 958 001*	G03 960 000*
				125.00	G03 978 001*	G03 980 000*
				125.00	G03 998 001*	G04 000 000*
				125.00	G04 018 001*	G04 020 000*
				125.00	G04 038 001*	G04 040 000*
				125.00	G04 058 001*	G04 060 000*
				125.00	G04 078 001*	G04 080 000*
				125.00	G04 098 001*	G04 100 000*
				125.00	G04 118 001*	G04 120 000*
				125.00	G04 138 001*	G04 140 000*
				125.00	G04 158 001*	G04 160 000*
				125.00	G04 178 001*	G04 180 000*
				125.00	G04 198 001*	G04 200 000*
				125.00	G04 218 001*	G04 220 000*
				125.00	G04 238 001*	G04 240 000*
				125.00	G04 258 001*	G04 260 000*
				125.00	G04 278 001*	G04 280 000*
				125.00	G04 298 001*	G04 300 000*
				125.00	G04 318 001*	G04 320 000*
				125.00	G04 338 001*	G04 340 000*
				125.00	G04 358 001*	G04 360 000*
				125.00	G04 378 001*	G04 380 000*
				125.00	G04 398 001*	G04 400 000*

DISTRICT	TOTAL NOTES PRINTED	BLOCKS	ESTIMATED VALUE VG/F	CU	LOW OFFICIAL SERIAL NUMBER	HIGH OFFICIAL SERIAL NUMBER
				125.00	G04 418 001*	G04 420 000*
				125.00	G04 438 001*	G04 440 000*
				125.00	G04 458 001*	G04 460 000*
				125.00	G04 478 001*	G04 480 000*
				125.00	G04 492 001*	G04 500 000*
				125.00	G04 512 001*	G04 520 000*
				125.00	G04 532 001*	G04 540 000*
				125.00	G04 552 001*	G04 560 000*
				125.00	G04 572 001*	G04 580 000*
				125.00	G04 592 001*	G04 600 000*
				125.00	G04 612 001*	G04 620 000*
				125.00	G04 632 001*	G04 640 000*
				125.00	G04 652 001*	G04 660 000*
				125.00	G04 672 001*	G04 680 000*
				125.00	G04 692 001*	G04 700 000*
				125.00	G04 712 001*	G04 720 000*
				125.00	G04 732 001*	G04 740 000*
				125.00	G04 752 001*	G04 760 000*
				125.00	G04 772 001*	G04 780 000*
				125.00	G04 792 001*	G04 800 000*
				125.00	G04 812 001*	G04 820 000*
				125.00	G04 832 001*	G04 840 000*
				125.00	G04 852 001*	G04 860 000*
				125.00	G04 872 001*	G04 880 000*
				125.00	G04 892 001*	G04 900 000*
				125.00	G04 912 001*	G04 920 000*
				125.00	G04 932 001*	G04 940 000*
				125.00	G04 952 001*	G04 960 000*
				125.00	G04 972 001*	G04 980 000*
				125.00	G04 992 001*	G05 000 000*
				125.00	G05 012 001*	G05 020 000*
				125.00	G05 032 001*	G05 040 000*
				125.00	G05 052 001*	G05 060 000*
				125.00	G05 072 001*	G05 080 000*
				125.00	G05 092 001*	G05 100 000*
				125.00	G05 112 001*	G05 120 000*
8	H ST. LOUIS	H--A		110.00	H00 000 001A	H15 360 000A
		H--*		115.00	H00 000 001*	H00 192 000*
				125.00	H01 936 001*	H01 940 000*
				125.00	H01 956 001*	H01 960 000*
				125.00	H01 976 001*	H01 980 000*
				125.00	H01 996 001*	H02 000 000*
				125.00	H02 016 001*	H02 020 000*
				125.00	H02 036 001*	H02 040 000*
				125.00	H02 056 001*	H02 060 000*
				125.00	H02 076 001*	H02 080 000*
				125.00	H02 096 001*	H02 100 000*
				125.00	H02 116 001*	H02 120 000*
				125.00	H02 136 001*	H02 140 000*
				125.00	H02 156 001*	H02 160 000*
				125.00	H02 176 001*	H02 180 000*
				125.00	H02 196 001*	H02 200 000*
				125.00	H02 216 001*	H02 220 000*
				125.00	H02 236 001*	H02 240 000*
				125.00	H02 256 001*	H02 260 000*
				125.00	H02 276 001*	H02 280 000*
				125.00	H02 296 001*	H02 300 000*
				125.00	H02 316 001*	H02 320 000*
				125.00	H02 336 001*	H02 340 000*
				125.00	H02 356 001*	H02 360 000*
				125.00	H02 376 001*	H02 380 000*
				125.00	H02 396 001*	H02 400 000*
				125.00	H02 416 001*	H02 420 000*
				125.00	H02 436 001*	H02 440 000*
				125.00	H02 456 001*	H02 460 000*
				125.00	H02 476 001*	H02 480 000*
				125.00	H02 496 001*	H02 500 000*
				125.00	H02 516 001*	H02 520 000*
				125.00	H02 536 001*	H02 540 000*

VALUE CU	LOW OFFICIAL SERIAL NUMBER	HIGH OFFICIAL SERIAL NUMBER		ESTIMATED VALUE VG/F	VALUE CU	LOW OFFICIAL SERIAL NUMBER	HIGH OFFICIAL SERIAL NUMBER
125.00	H02 556 001*	H02 560 000*			125.00	H02 856 001*	H02 860 000*
125.00	H02 576 001*	H02 580 000*			125.00	H02 876 001*	H02 880 000*
125.00	H02 596 001*	H02 600 000*			125.00	H02 896 001*	H02 900 000*
125.00	H02 616 001*	H02 620 000*			125.00	H02 916 001*	H02 920 000*
125.00	H02 636 001*	H02 640 000*			125.00	H02 936 001*	H02 940 000*
125.00	H02 656 001*	H02 660 000*			125.00	H02 956 001*	H02 960 000*
125.00	H02 676 001*	H02 680 000*			125.00	H02 976 001*	H02 980 000*
125.00	H02 696 001*	H02 700 000*			125.00	H02 996 001*	H03 000 000*
125.00	H02 716 001*	H02 720 000*			125.00	H03 016 001*	H03 020 000*
125.00	H02 736 001*	H02 740 000*			125.00	H03 036 001*	H03 040 000*
125.00	H02 756 001*	H02 760 000*			125.00	H03 056 001*	H03 060 000*
125.00	H02 776 001*	H02 780 000*			125.00	H03 076 001*	H03 080 000*
125.00	H02 796 001*	H02 800 000*			125.00	H03 096 001*	H03 100 000*
125.00	H02 816 001*	H02 820 000*			125.00	H03 116 001*	H03 120 000*
125.00	H02 836 001*	H02 840 000*			125.00	H03 136 001*	H03 140 000*
					125.00	H03 156 001*	H03 160 000*
	DISTRICT	TOTAL NOTES PRINTED	BLOCKS		125.00	H03 176 001*	H03 180 000*
					125.00	H03 196 001*	H03 200 000*
9	I MINNEAPOLIS		I--A		110.00	I00 000 001A	I05 120 000A
			I--*		115.00	I00 000 001*	I00 064 000*
					125.00	I00 656 001*	I00 660 000*
					125.00	I00 676 001*	I00 680 000*
					125.00	I00 696 001*	I00 700 000*
					125.00	I00 716 001*	I00 720 000*
					125.00	I00 736 001*	I00 740 000*
					125.00	I00 756 001*	I00 760 000*
					125.00	I00 776 001*	I00 780 000*
					125.00	I00 796 001*	I00 800 000*
					125.00	I00 816 001*	I00 820 000*
					125.00	I00 836 001*	I00 840 000*
					125.00	I00 856 001*	I00 860 000*
					125.00	I00 876 001*	I00 880 000*
					125.00	I00 896 001*	I00 900 000*
					125.00	I00 916 001*	I00 920 000*
					125.00	I00 936 001*	I00 940 000*
					125.00	I00 956 001*	I00 960 000*
					125.00	I00 976 001*	I00 980 000*
					125.00	I00 996 001*	I01 000 000*
					125.00	I01 016 001*	I01 020 000*
					125.00	I01 036 001*	I01 040 000*
					125.00	I01 056 001*	I01 060 000*
					125.00	I01 076 001*	I01 080 000*
					125.00	I01 096 001*	I01 100 000*
					125.00	I01 116 001*	I01 120 000*
					125.00	I01 136 001*	I01 140 000*
					125.00	I01 156 001*	I01 160 000*
					125.00	I01 176 001*	I01 180 000*
					125.00	I01 196 001*	I01 200 000*
					125.00	I01 216 001*	I01 220 000*
					125.00	I01 236 001*	I01 240 000*
					125.00	I01 256 001*	I01 260 000*
					125.00	I01 276 001*	I01 280 000*
10	J KANSAS CITY		J--A		110.00	J00 000 001A	J14 080 000A
			J--*		115.00	J00 000 001*	J00 256 000*
					125.00	J02 576 001*	J02 580 000*
					125.00	J02 596 001*	J02 600 000*
					125.00	J02 616 001*	J02 620 000*
					125.00	J02 636 001*	J02 640 000*
					125.00	J02 656 001*	J02 660 000*
					125.00	J02 676 001*	J02 680 000*
					125.00	J02 696 001*	J02 700 000*
					125.00	J02 716 001*	J02 720 000*
					125.00	J02 736 001*	J02 740 000*
					125.00	J02 756 001*	J02 760 000*
					125.00	J02 776 001*	J02 780 000*
					125.00	J02 796 001*	J02 800 000*
					125.00	J02 816 001*	J02 820 000*
					125.00	J02 836 001*	J02 840 000*
					125.00	J02 856 001*	J02 860 000*

DISTRICT	TOTAL NOTES PRINTED	BLOCKS	ESTIMATED VALUE VG/F	VALUE CU	LOW OFFICIAL SERIAL NUMBER	HIGH OFFICIAL SERIAL NUMBER
				125.00	J02 876 001*	J02 880 000*
				125.00	J02 896 001*	J02 900 000*
				125.00	J02 916 001*	J02 920 000*
				125.00	J02 936 001*	J02 940 000*
				125.00	J02 956 001*	J02 960 000*
				125.00	J02 976 001*	J02 980 000*
				125.00	J02 996 001*	J03 000 000*
				125.00	J03 016 001*	J03 020 000*
				125.00	J03 036 001*	J03 040 000*
				125.00	J03 056 001*	J03 060 000*
				125.00	J03 076 001*	J03 080 000*
				125.00	J03 096 001*	J03 100 000*
				125.00	J03 116 001*	J03 120 000*
				125.00	J03 136 001*	J03 140 000*
				125.00	J03 156 001*	J03 160 000*
				125.00	J03 176 001*	J03 180 000*
				125.00	J03 196 001*	J03 200 000*
				125.00	J02 216 001*	J03 220 000*
				125.00	J03 236 001*	J03 240 000*
				125.00	J03 256 001*	J03 260 000*
				125.00	J03 276 001*	J03 280 000*
				125.00	J03 296 001*	J03 300 000*
				125.00	J03 316 001*	J03 320 000*
				125.00	J03 336 001*	J03 340 000*
				125.00	J03 356 001*	J03 360 000*
				125.00	J03 376 001*	J03 380 000*
				125.00	J03 396 001*	J03 400 000*
				125.00	J03 416 001*	J03 420 000*
				125.00	J03 436 001*	J03 440 000*
				125.00	J03 456 001*	J03 460 000*
				125.00	J03 476 001*	J03 480 000*
				125.00	J03 496 001*	J03 500 000*
				125.00	J03 516 001*	J03 520 000*
				125.00	J03 536 001*	J03 540 000*
				125.00	J03 556 001*	J03 560 000*
				125.00	J03 576 001*	J03 580 000*
				125.00	J03 596 001*	J03 600 000*
				125.00	J03 616 001*	J03 620 000*
				125.00	J03 636 001*	J03 640 000*
				125.00	J03 656 001*	J03 660 000*
				125.00	J03 676 001*	J03 680 000*
				125.00	J03 696 001*	J03 700 000*
				125.00	J03 716 001*	J03 720 000*
				125.00	J03 736 001*	J03 740 000*
				125.00	J03 756 001*	J04 760 000*
				125.00	J03 776 001*	J03 780 000*
				125.00	J03 796 001*	J03 800 000*
				125.00	J03 816 001*	J03 820 000*
				125.00	J03 836 001*	J03 840 000*
11	K DALLAS		K--A	110.00	K00 000 001A	K29 440 000*
			K--*	115.00	K00 000 001*	K00 128 000*
				125.00	K01 296 001*	K01 300 000*
				125.00	K01 316 001*	K01 320 000*
				125.00	K01 336 001*	K01 340 000*
				125.00	K01 356 001*	K01 360 000*
				125.00	K01 376 001*	K01 380 000*
				125.00	K01 396 001*	K01 400 000*
				125.00	K01 416 001*	K01 420 000*
				125.00	K01 436 001*	K01 440 000*
				125.00	K01 456 001*	K01 460 000*
				125.00	K01 476 001*	K01 480 000*
				125.00	K01 496 001*	K01 500 000*
				125.00	K01 516 001*	K01 520 000*
				125.00	K01 536 001*	K01 540 000*
				125.00	K01 556 001*	K01 560 000*
				125.00	K01 576 001*	K01 580 000*
				125.00	K01 596 001*	K01 600 000*
				125.00	K01 616 001*	K01 620 000*
				125.00	K01 636 001*	K01 640 000*

VALUE CU	LOW OFFICIAL SERIAL NUMBER	HIGH OFFICIAL SERIAL NUMBER		ESTIMATED VALUE VG/F	VALUE CU	LOW OFFICIAL SERIAL NUMBER	HIGH OFFICIAL SERIAL NUMBER
125.00	K01 656 001*	K01 660 000*			125.00	K02 092 001*	K02 100 000*
125.00	K01 676 001*	K01 680 000*			125.00	K02 112 001*	K02 120 000*
125.00	K01 696 001*	K01 700 000*			125.00	K02 132 001*	K02 140 000*
125.00	K01 716 001*	K01 720 000*			125.00	K02 152 001*	K02 160 000*
125.00	K01 736 001*	K01 740 000*			125.00	K02 172 001*	K02 180 000*
125.00	K01 756 001*	K01 760 000*			125.00	K02 192 001*	K02 200 000*
125.00	K01 776 001*	K01 780 000*			125.00	K02 212 001*	K02 220 000*
125.00	K01 796 001*	K01 800 000*			125.00	K02 232 001*	K02 240 000*
125.00	K01 816 001*	K01 820 000*			125.00	K02 252 001*	K02 260 000*
125.00	K01 836 001*	K01 840 000*			125.00	K02 272 001*	K02 280 000*
125.00	K01 856 001*	K01 860 000*			125.00	K02 292 001*	K02 300 000*
125.00	K01 876 001*	K01 880 000*			125.00	K02 312 001*	K02 320 000*
125.00	K01 896 001*	K01 900 000*			125.00	K02 332 001*	K02 340 000*
125.00	K01 916 001*	K01 920 000*			125.00	K02 352 001*	K02 360 000*
125.00	K01 932 001*	K01 940 000*			125.00	K02 372 001*	K02 380 000*
125.00	K01 952 001*	K01 960 000*			125.00	K02 392 001*	K02 400 000*
125.00	K01 972 001*	K01 980 000*			125.00	K02 412 001*	K02 420 000*
125.00	K01 992 001*	K02 000 000*			125.00	K02 432 001*	K02 440 000*
125.00	K02 012 001*	K02 020 000*			125.00	K02 452 001*	K02 460 000*
125.00	K02 032 001*	K02 040 000*			125.00	K02 472 001*	K02 480 000*
125.00	K02 052 001*	K02 060 000*			125.00	K02 492 001*	K02 500 000*
125.00	K02 072 001*	K02 080 000*			125.00	K02 512 001*	K02 520 000*

	DISTRICT	TOTAL NOTES PRINTED	BLOCKS
12	L SAN FRANCISCO		L--A
			L--*

VALUE CU	LOW OFFICIAL SERIAL NUMBER	HIGH OFFICIAL SERIAL NUMBER
125.00	K02 532 001*	K02 540 000*
125.00	K02 552 001*	K02 560 000*
110.00	L00 000 001A	L39 680 000A
115.00	L00 000 001*	L00 192 000*
125.00	L01 928 001*	L01 940 000*
125.00	L01 948 001*	L01 960 000*
125.00	L01 968 001*	L01 980 000*
125.00	L01 988 001*	L02 000 000*
125.00	L02 008 001*	L02 020 000*
125.00	L02 028 001*	L02 040 000*
125.00	L02 048 001*	L02 060 000*
125.00	L02 068 001*	L02 080 000*
125.00	L02 088 001*	L02 100 000*
125.00	L02 108 001*	L02 120 000*
125.00	L02 128 001*	L02 140 000*
125.00	L02 148 001*	L02 160 000*
125.00	L02 168 001*	L02 180 000*
125.00	L02 188 001*	L02 200 000*
125.00	L02 208 001*	L02 220 000*
125.00	L02 228 001*	L02 240 000*
125.00	L02 248 001*	L02 260 000*
125.00	L02 268 001*	L02 280 000*
125.00	L02 288 001*	L02 300 000*
125.00	L02 308 001*	L02 320 000*
125.00	L02 328 001*	L02 340 000*
125.00	L02 348 001*	L02 360 000*
125.00	L02 368 001*	L02 380 000*
125.00	L02 388 001*	L02 400 000*
125.00	L02 408 001*	L02 420 000*
125.00	L02 428 001*	L02 440 000*
125.00	L02 448 001*	L02 460 000*
125.00	L02 468 001*	L02 480 000*
125.00	L02 488 001*	L02 500 000*
125.00	L02 508 001*	L02 520 000*
125.00	L02 528 001*	L02 540 000*
125.00	L02 548 001*	L02 560 000*

The production unit was changed from 20,000 sheets to 40,000 sheets for:

BANK	WITH SERIAL STARTING	BANK	WITH SERIAL STARTING
Boston	A08 960 001A	Chicago	G26 880 001A
New York	B88 320 001A	St. Louis	H07 680 001A
Philadelphia	will start with first 1981 run	Minneapolis	I03 840 001A
Cleveland	D10 240 001A	Kansas City	J07 680 001A
Richmond	E12 800 001A	Dallas	K16 640 001A
Atlanta	F02 560 001A	San Francisco	L33 280 001A

TREASURY DEPARTMENT	WASHINGTON, D.C.
FOR IMMEDIATE RELEASE	July 14, 1969

(THIS IS A SIMULTANEOUS RELEASE BY TREASURY AND FEDERAL RESERVE SYSTEM)

LARGE DENOMINATIONS OF CURRENCY TO BE DISCONTINUED

The Treasury Department and the Federal Reserve System announced today that the issuance of currency in denominations of $500, $1,000, $5,000 and $10,000 will be discontinued immediately. Use of these large denominations has declined sharply over the last two decades and the need for them appears insufficient to warrant the added cost of production and custody of new supplies.

The large denomination notes were first authorized primarily for interbank transactions by an amendment to the Federal Reserve Act in 1918. With demand for them shrinking, printings of new notes of these denominations were discontinued in 1946, and the supply that was on hand at that time has now diminished to the point where continued issuance of such notes would require additional printings. Surveys have indicated that transactions for which the large denomination notes have been used could be met by other means, such as checks or $100 notes.

Under the decision announced today all existing supplies of large denomination bills at the Federal Reserve Banks will be turned over to the Treasury for destruction as will circulating notes that find their way back to the Federal Banks in the normal course of business.

The Federal Reserve will continue to issue notes in denominations of $1, $5, $10, $20, $50 and $100. Currency comprises only about 25 percent of the nation's money supply, the vast bulk of which is made up of demand deposits (checking accounts).

K-140

The sharp decline since World War II in the number of large denomination notes in circulation is shown in the following end-of-year figures:

	1945	1968
$500	903,404	488,295
$1,000	797,852	291,894
$5,000	1,405	634
$10,000	2,327	383

Because of the infrequency of sale or purchase of notes of $500.00 denomination and the higher denominations, we believe any effort to place a price estimate on such notes would be fictious. While many of the higher denomination notes are exceedingly rare, the number of collectors is even rarer so that price becomes a matter of what the buyer is willing to pay and what the seller is willing to take.

This section is the result of intensive research among old official Bureau records and much of it is recorded for the first time in published form.

Undoubtedly MULES exist in the higher denominations, however no attempt has been made to catalog this variety at this time.

In July 1969, the Federal Reserve system announced that the $500.00, $1,000.00, $5,000.00 and $10,000.00 notes would be discontinued and directed member banks to return to Fed for destruction such notes as came in.

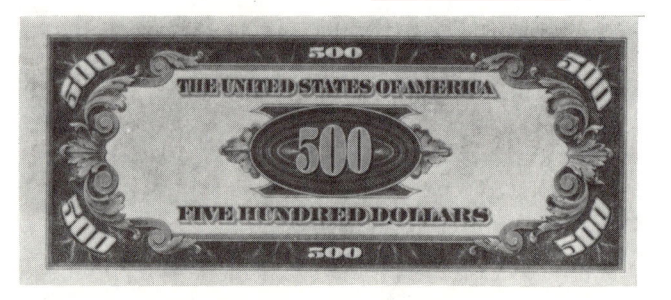

CAT. NO. DG28
$500.00 GOLD CERTIFICATE (YELLOW SEAL) (12 Subject)
SERIES 1928

SERIAL NUMBERS: A00 000 001A through A00 240 000A
Low Observed: A00 013 089A A00 048 806 High Observed.

PLATE SERIALS: Begin with 1.
SIGNATURES: Walter O. Woods, Treasurer of the United States.
   A.W. Mellon, Secretary of the Treasury.
TOTAL QUANTITY PRINTED: 420,000.
TOTAL BLOCKS: Two. A--A and A--*.

CAT. NO. DF28
$500.00 FEDERAL RESERVE NOTE (GREEN SEAL) (12 Subject)
SERIES 1928

SERIAL NUMBERS: All serial numbers both regular and star notes begin with 00 000 001.
PLATE SERIALS: Face and back check begin with 1.
SIGNATURES: Walter O. Woods, Treasurer of the United States.
   A.W. Mellon, Secretary of the Treasury.

	DISTRICT	TOTAL NOTES PRINTED	BLOCKS	ESTIMATED VALUE VG/F	CU	LOW OBSERVED SERIAL NUMBER	HIGH OBSERVED SERIAL NUMBER
1	A BOSTON	69,120	A--A / A--*			A00 026 924A	
2	B NEW YORK	299,400	B--A / B--*			B00 005 902A	B00 137 067A
3	C PHILADELPHIA	135,120	C--A / C--*			C00 003 745A	C00 008 701A
4	D CLEVELAND	166,440	D--A / D--*			D00 022 636A	D00 030 771A
5	E RICHMOND	84,720	E--A / E--*			E00 017 036A	E00 017 152A
6	F ATLANTA	69,360	F--A / F--*			F00 000 085A	F00 010 070A
7	G CHICAGO	573,600	G--A / G--*			G00 163 638A	
8	H ST. LOUIS	66,180	H--A / H--*			H00 002 195A	H00 027 310A
9	I MINNEAPOLIS	34,680	I--A / I--*				
10	J KANSAS CITY	510,720	J--A / J--*			J00 011 191A	J00 011 631A
11	K DALLAS	70,560	K--A / K--*			K00 001 336A	K00 009 711A
12	L SAN FRANCISCO	64,080	L--A / L--*			L00 013 036A	

TOTAL BLOCKS: Twenty four.
Collectors are requested to supply serial numbers.

CAT. NO. DF34
$500.00 FEDERAL RESERVE NOTE (GREEN SEAL) (12 Subject)
SERIES 1934

SERIAL NUMBERS: All serial numbers both regular and star notes begin with 00 000 001.
PLATE SERIALS: Face and back check begin with 1.
SIGNATURES: W.A. Julian, Treasurer of the United States.
   Henry Morgenthau, Jr., Secretary of the Treasury.

	DISTRICT	TOTAL NOTES PRINTED	BLOCKS	ESTIMATED VALUE VG/F	CU	LOW OBSERVED SERIAL NUMBER	HIGH OBSERVED SERIAL NUMBER
1	A BOSTON	56,628	A--A / A--*			A00 008 154A	A00 041 132A

	DISTRICT	TOTAL NOTES PRINTED	BLOCKS	ESTIMATED VALUE VG/F　CU	LOW OFFICIAL SERIAL NUMBER	HIGH OFFICIAL SERIAL NUMBER
2	B NEW YORK	288,000	B--A B--*		B00 002 193A	B00 254 373A
3	C PHILADELPHIA	31,200	C--A C--*		C00 015 557A	C00 023 541A
4	D CLEVELAND	39,000	D--A D--*		D00 003 665A	D00 025 647A
5	E RICHMOND	40,800	E--A E--*			E00 061 089A
6	F ATLANTA	46,200	F--A F--*		F00 009 481A F00 000 204*	F00 063 770A F00 002 799*
7	G CHICAGO	212,400	G--A G--*		G00 120 252A G00 003 703*	G00 264 376A G00 094 810*
8	H ST. LOUIS	24,000	G--A H--*		H00 006 614A	H00 067 144A
9	I MINNEAPOLIS	24,000	I--A I--*		I00 001 036A	
10	J KANSAS CITY	40,800	J--A J--*		J00 006 930A J00 000 001*	J00 067 164A
11	K DALLAS	31,200	K--A K--*		K00 000 063A	K00 028 863A
12	L SAN FRANCISCO	83,400	L--A L--*		L00 007 326A L00 000 208*	L00 153 444A

TOTAL BLOCKS: Twenty four.
Collectors are requested to supply serial numbers.

CAT. NO. DF34A
$500.00 FEDERAL RESERVE NOTE (GREEN SEAL) (12 Subject)
SERIES 1934A

SERIAL NUMBERS: Continue sequence from previous series.
SIGNATURES: W.A. Julian, Treasurer of the United States.
 Henry Morgenthau, Jr., Secretary of the Treasury.

	DISTRICT	TOTAL NOTES PRINTED	BLOCKS	ESTIMATED VALUE VG/F　CU	LOW OBSERVED SERIAL NUMBER	HIGH OBSERVED SERIAL NUMBER
2	B NEW YORK	276,000	B--A		B00 268 014A	B00 426 371A
3	C PHILADELPHIA	45,300	C--A		C00 025 038A	C00 310 675A
4	D CLEVELAND	28,800	D--A		D00 047 894A	D00 050 263A
5	E RICHMOND	36,000	E--A		E00 020 284A F00 037 292A	E00 035 390A F00 095 149A
7	G CHICAGO	214,800	G--A		G00 177 659A	G00 380 363A
8	H ST. LOUIS	57,600	H--A		H00 003 397A	H00 063 398A
9	I MINNEAPOLIS	14,400	I--A			
10	J KANSAS CITY	55,200	J--A		J00 026 293A	J00 078 168A
11	K DALLAS	34,800	K--A		K00 019 595A	K00 038 793A
12	L SAN FRANCISCO	93,000	L--A		L00 066 726A	L00 153 446A

TOTAL BLOCKS: Ten. IMPORTANT: No star notes have been seen or reported for this series. Collectors are requested to supply serials, especially for star notes.

CAT. NO. DF34B
$500.00 FEDERAL RESERVE NOTE (GREEN SEAL) (12 Subject)
SERIES 1934B

SERIAL NUMBERS: Continued sequence from previous series.
SIGNATURES: W.A. Julian, Treasurer of the United States.
 Fred M. Vinson, Secretary of the Treasury.

	DISTRICT	TOTAL NOTES PRINTED	BLOCKS	ESTIMATED VALUE VG/F　CU	LOW OBSERVED SERIAL NUMBER	HIGH OBSERVED SERIAL NUMBER
6	F ATLANTA	2,472	F--A			

CAT. NO. DF34C
$500.00 FEDERAL RESERVE NOTE (GREEN SEAL) (12 Subject)
SERIES 1934C

SERIAL NUMBERS: Continue sequence from previous series.
SIGNATURES: W.A. Julian, Treasurer of the United States.
　John W. Snyder, Secretary of the Treasury.

	DISTRICT	TOTAL NOTES PRINTED	BLOCKS	ESTIMATED VALUE VG/F	CU	LOW OBSERVED SERIAL NUMBER	HIGH OBSERVED SERIAL NUMBER
1	A BOSTON	1,440	A--A				
2	B NEW YORK	204	B--A				

TOTAL BLOCKS: Two.

CAT. NO. MG28
$1,000.00 GOLD CERTIFICATE (YELLOW SEAL) (12 Subject)
SERIES 1928

SERIAL NUMBERS: A 00 000 001 A through A 00 288 000 A.
　Low Observed: A 00 010 675 A　High Observed: A 00 085 976 A
PLATE SERIALS: Begin with 1.
SIGNATURES: Walter O. Woods, Treasurer of the United States.
　A. W. Mellon, Secretary of the Treasury.
TOTAL QUANTITY PRINTED: 288,000.
TOTAL BLOCKS: Two. A--A and A--*.

CAT. NO. MG34
$1,000.00 GOLD CERTIFICATE (YELLOW SEAL) (12 Subject)
SERIES 1934

SERIAL NUMBERS: A 00 000 001 A through A 00 084 000 A.
PLATE SERIALS: Begin with 1.
SIGNATURES: W.A. Julian, Treasurer of the United States.
　Henry Morgenthau, Jr. Secretary of the Treasury.
TOTAL QUANTITY PRINTED: 84,000.
TOTAL BLOCKS: Two. A--A and A-*.

CAT NO. MF28
$1,000.00 FEDERAL RESERVE NOTE (GREEN SEAL) (12 Subject)
SERIES 1928

SERIAL NUMBERS: All serial numbers both regular and star notes begin with 00 000 001.

PLATE SERIALS: Face and back check begin with 1.
SIGNATURES: Walter O. Woods, Treasurer of the United States.
   A.W. Mellon, Secretary of the Treasury.

	DISTRICT	TOTAL NOTES PRINTED	BLOCKS	ESTIMATED VALUE VG/F	CU	LOW OBSERVED SERIAL NUMBER	HIGH OBSERVED SERIAL NUMBER
1	A BOSTON	58,320	A--A A--*				
2	B NEW YORK	139,200	B--A B--*			B00 056 916A	B00 089 961A
3	C PHILADELPHIA	96,708	C--A C--*				
4	D CLEVELAND	79,680	D--A D--*			D00 014 869A	D00 019 879A
5	E RICHMOND	66,840	E--A E--*			E00 010 484A	E00 018 183A
6	F ATLANTA	47,400	F--A F--*				
7	G CHICAGO	355,800	G--A G--*			G00 046 861A	G00 141 890A
8	H ST. LOUIS	60,000	H--A H--*			H00 002 806A	H00 035 826A
9	I MINNEAPOLIS	26,640	I--A I--*				
10	J KANSAS CITY	62,172	J--A J--*			J00 003 914A	J00 004 024A
11	K DALLAS	42,960	K--A K--*			K00 001 472A	K00 008 415A
12	L SAN FRANCISCO	67,920	L--A L--*			L00 010 713A	

TOTAL BLOCKS: Twenty four.
Collectors are requested to supply serial numbers.

CAT NO. MF34
$1,000.00 FEDERAL RESERVE NOTE (GREEN SEAL) (12 Subject)
SERIES 1934

SERIAL NUMBERS: All serial numbers both regular and star notes begin with 00 000 001.
PLATE SERIALS: Face and back check begin with 1.
SIGNATURES: W.A. Julian, Treasurer of the United States.
   Henry Morgenthau, Jr., Secretary of the Treasury.

	DISTRICT	TOTAL NOTES PRINTED	BLOCKS	ESTIMATED VALUE VG/F	CU	LOW OBSERVED SERIAL NUMBER	HIGH OBSERVED SERIAL NUMBER
1	A BOSTON	46,200	A--A A--*			A00 001 971A	A00 020 887A
2	B NEW YORK	332,784	B--A B--*			B00 026 895A	B00 290 594A
3	C PHILADELPHIA	33,000	C--A C--*			C00 009 681A	
4	D CLEVELAND	35,400	D--A D--*			D00 008 278A D00 000 497*	D00 026 980A D00 001 202*
5	E RICHMOND	19,560	E--A E--*			E00 000 124A	E00 008 414A
6	F ATLANTA	67,800	F--A F--*			F00 013 438A	F00 079 571A
7	G CHICAGO	167,040	G--A G--*			G00 006 722A G00 001 234*	G00 268 451A G00 003 509*
8	H. ST. LOUIS	22,440	H--A H--*			H00 006 530A H00 001 094*	H00 011 605A
9	I MINNEAPOLIS	12,000	I--A I--*			I00 005 286A	I00 014 116A
10	J KANSAS CITY	51,840	J--A J--*			J00 006 687A	J00 057 596A
11	K DALLAS	46,800	K--A K--*			K00 004 584A	K00 026 595A
12	L SAN FRANCISCO	90,600	L--A L--*			L00 010 643A L00 003 651*	L00 066 320A

TOTAL BLOCKS: Twenty four.
Collectors are requested to supply serials.

CAT. NO. MF34A
$1,000.00 FEDERAL RESERVE NOTE (GREEN SEAL) (12 Subject)
SERIES 1934A

SERIAL NUMBERS: Continue sequence from previous series.
SIGNATURES: W.A. Julian, Treasurer of the United States
   Henry Morgenthau, Jr., Secretary of the Treasury

	DISTRICT	TOTAL NOTES PRINTED	BLOCKS	ESTIMATED VALUE VG/F	CU	LOW OBSERVED SERIAL NUMBER	HIGH OBSERVED SERIAL NUMBER
1	A BOSTON	30,000	A--A A--*			A00 023 154A	A00 048 409A
2	B NEW YORK	174,348	B--A B--*			B00 336 581A	B00 382 334A
3	C PHILADELPHIA	78,000	C--A C--*			C00 026 784A	C00 040 941A
4	D CLEVELAND	28,800	D--A D--*			D00 037 884A	
5	E RICHMOND	16,800	E--A E--*			E00 028 252A	
6	F ATLANTA	80,964	F--A F--*			F00 048 331A	F00 125 483A
7	G CHICAGO	134,400	G--A G--*			G00 029 644A G00 004 094*	G00 268 666A
8	H ST. LOUIS	39,600	H--A H--*			H00 003 996A	H00 048 484A
9	I MINNEAPOLIS	4,800	I--A I--*			I00 012 547A	
10	J KANSAS CITY	21,600	J--A J--*			J00 039 330A	J00 056 646A
12	L SAN FRANCISCO	36,600	L--A L--*			L00 082 141A L00 003 651*	L00 088 864A

TOTAL BLOCKS: Twenty-two.
Collectors are requested to supply serial numbers.

CAT. NO. MF34C
$1,000.00 FEDERAL RESERVE NOTE (GREEN SEAL) (12 Subject)
SERIES 1934C

SERIAL NUMBERS: Continued sequence from previous series.
SIGNATURES: W.A. Julian, Treasurer of the United States
   John W. Snyder, Secretary of the Treasury

	DISTRICT	TOTAL NOTES PRINTED	BLOCKS	ESTIMATED VALUE VG/F	CU	LOW OBSERVED SERIAL NUMBER	HIGH OBSERVED SERIAL NUMBER
1	A BOSTON	1,200	A--A				
2	B NEW YORK	168	B--A				

TOTAL BLOCKS: Two.
Collectors are requested to supply serial numbers.

CAT. NO. $\overline{VF}$28
$5,000.00 GOLD CERTIFICATE (YELLOW SEAL) (12 Subject)
SERIES 1928

SERIAL NUMBERS: A00 000 001A through A 00 024 000A.
PLATE SERIALS: Begin with 1.
SIGNATURES: Walter O. Woods, Treasurer of the United States.
   A.W. Mellon, Secretary of the Treasury.
TOTAL QUANTITY PRINTED: 24,000.
TOTAL BLOCKS: Two. A--A and A--*.

CAT. NO. $\overline{VF}$28
$5,000.00 FEDERAL RESERVE NOTE (GREEN SEAL) (12 Subject)
SERIES 1928

SERIAL NUMBERS: All serial numbers both regular and star notes begin with 00 000 001.

PLATE SERIALS: Face and back begin with 1.
SIGNATURES: Walter O. Woods, Treasurer of the United States
   A.W. Mellon, Secretary of the Treasury

	DISTRICT	TOTAL NOTES PRINTED	BLOCKS	ESTIMATED VALUE VG/F	CU	LOW OBSERVED SERIAL NUMBER	HIGH OBSERVED SERIAL NUMBER
1	A BOSTON	1,320	A--A A--*				
2	B NEW YORK	2,640	B--A B--*				
3	C PHILADELPHIA	none					
4	D CLEVELAND	3,000	D--A D--*				
5	E RICHMOND	3,984	E--A E--*				
6	F ATLANTA	1,440	F--A F--*				
7	G CHICAGO	3,480	G--A G--*				
8	H ST. LOUIS	none					
9	I MINNEAPOLIS	none					
10	J KANSAS CITY	720	J--A J--*				
11	K DALLAS	360	K--A K--*				
12	L SAN FRANCISCO	51,300	L--A L--*				

TOTAL BLOCKS: Eighteen.
Collectors are requested to supply serial numbers.

CAT. NO. V̄F34
$5,000.00 FEDERAL RESERVE NOTE (GREEN SEAL) (12 Subject)
SERIES 1934

SERIAL NUMBERS: All serial numbers both regular and star notes begin with 00 000 001.
PLATE SERIALS: Face and back check begin with 1.
SIGNATURES: W.A. Julian, Treasurer of the United States.
   Henry Morgenthau, Jr., Secretary of the Treasury.

	DISTRICT	TOTAL NOTES PRINTED	BLOCKS	ESTIMATED VALUE VG/F	CU	LOW OBSERVED SERIAL NUMBER	HIGH OBSERVED SERIAL NUMBER
1	A BOSTON	9,480	A--A A--*				
2	B NEW YORK	11,520	B--A B--*			B00 000 691A	B00 002 403A
3	C PHILADELPHIA	3,000	C--A C--*				
4	D CLEVELAND	1,680	D--A D--*				
5	E RICHMOND	2,400	E--A E--*				
6	F ATLANTA	3,600	F--A F--*				
7	G CHICAGO	6,600	G--A G--*				
8	H ST. LOUIS	2,400	H--A H--*			H00 000 340A	H00 000 425A
9	I MINNEAPOLIS	none					

DISTRICT	TOTAL NOTES PRINTED	BLOCKS	ESTIMATED VALUE VG/F	CU	LOW OFFICIAL SERIAL NUMBER	HIGH OFFICIAL SERIAL NUMBER
10 J KANSAS CITY	2,400	J--A J--*				J00 000 073A
11 K DALLAS	2,400	K--A K--*			K00 000 042A	K00 000 125A
12 L SAN FRANCISCO	6,000	L--A L--*				

TOTAL BLOCKS: Twenty Two.
Collectors are requested to supply serial numbers.

CAT. NO. V̄F34A
$5,000.00 FEDERAL RESERVE NOTE (GREEN SEAL) (12 Subject)
SERIES 1934A

SERIAL NUMBERS: Continued sequence from previous series.
SIGNATURES: W.A. Julian, Treasurer of the United States.
   Henry Morgenthau, Jr., Secretary of the Treasury.

DISTRICT	TOTAL NOTES PRINTED	BLOCKS	ESTIMATED VALUE VG/F	CU	LOW OBSERVED SERIAL NUMBER	HIGH OBSERVED SERIAL NUMBER
8 H ST. LOUIS	1,440	H--A				

TOTAL BLOCKS: One.

CAT. NO. V̄F34B
$5,000.00 FEDERAL RESERVE NOTES (GREEN SEAL) (12 Subject)
SERIES 1934B

SERIAL NUMBERS: Continued sequence from previous series.
SIGNATURES: W.A. Julian, Treasurer of the United States.
   Fred M. Vinson, Secretary of the Treasury.

DISTRICT	TOTAL NOTES PRINTED	BLOCKS	ESTIMATED VALUE VG/F	CU	LOW OBSERVED SERIAL NUMBER	HIGH OBSERVED SERIAL NUMBER
1 A BOSTON	1,200	A--A				
2 B NEW YORK	12	B--A				

TOTAL BLOCKS: Two.

CAT. NO. X̄G28
$10,000.00 GOLD CERTIFICATE (YELLOW SEAL) (12 Subject)
SERIES 1928

SERIAL NUMBERS: A00 000 001A through A00 048 000A.
PLATE SERIALS: Begin with 1.
SIGNATURES: Walter O. Woods, Treasurer of the United States.
   A.W. Mellon, Secretary of the Treasury.
TOTAL QUANTITY PRINTED: 48,000.
TOTAL BLOCKS: Two. A--A and A--*.

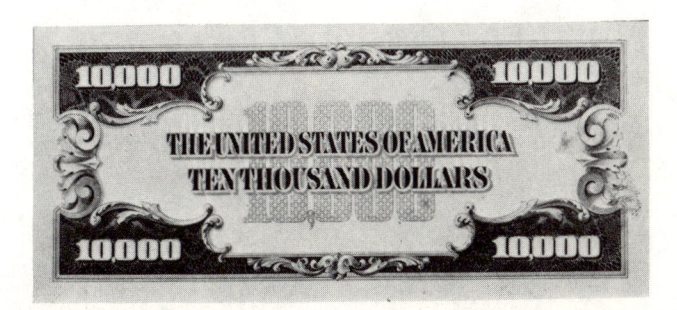

CAT. NO. X̄G34
$10,000.00 GOLD CERTIFICATE (YELLOW SEAL) (12 Subject)
SERIES 1934

SERIAL NUMBERS: A00 000 001A through A00 036 000A.
PLATE SERIALS: Begin with 1.
SIGNATURES: W.A. Julian, Treasurer of the United States.
   Henry Morgenthau, Jr., Secretary of the Treasury.
TOTAL QUANTITY PRINTED: 36,000.
TOTAL BLOCKS: Two. A--A and A--*.

CAT. NO. XF28
$10,000.00 FEDERAL RESERVE NOTE (GREEN SEAL) (12 Subject)
SERIES 1928

SERIAL NUMBERS: All serial numbers both regular and star notes begin with 00 000 001.
PLATE SERIALS: Face and back check numbers start with 1.
SIGNATURES: Walter O. Woods, Treasurer of the United States.
   A.W. Mellon, Secretary of the Treasury.

	DISTRICT	TOTAL NOTES PRINTED	BLOCKS	ESTIMATED VALUE VG/F	CU	LOW OBSERVED SERIAL NUMBER	HIGH OBSERVED SERIAL NUMBER
1	A BOSTON	1,320	A--A, A--*				
2	B NEW YORK	4,680	B--A, B--*				
3	C PHILADELPHIA	none					
4	D CLEVELAND	960	D--A, D--*				
5	E RICHMOND	3,024	E--A, E--*				
6	F ATLANTA	1,440	F--A, F--*				
7	G CHICAGO	1,800	G--A, G--*				
8	H ST. LOUIS	480	H--A, H--*				
9	I MINNEAPOLIS	480	I--A, I--*				
10	J KANSAS CITY	480	J--A, J--*				
11	K DALLAS	360	K--A, K--*				
12	L SAN FRANCISCO	1,824	L--A, L--*				

TOTAL BLOCKS: Twenty two.
Collectors are requested to supply serial numbers.

CAT. NO. XF34
$10,000 FEDERAL RESERVE NOTE (GREEN SEAL) (12 Subject)
SERIES 1934

SERIAL NUMBERS: All serial numbers both regular and star notes begin with 00 000 001.
PLATE SERIALS: Face and back check numbers start with 1.
SIGNATURES: W.A. Julian, Treasurer of the United States.
   Henry Morgenthau, Jr., Secretary of the Treasury.

	DISTRICT	TOTAL NOTES PRINTED	BLOCKS	ESTIMATED VALUE VG/F	CU	LOW OBSERVED SERIAL NUMBER	HIGH OBSERVED SERIAL NUMBER
1	A BOSTON	9,720	A--A, A--*				
2	B NEW YORK	11,520	B--A, B--*			B00 000 366A	B00 004 692A
3	C PHILADELPHIA	6,000	C--A, C--*				
4	D CLEVELAND	1,480	D--A, D--*				
5	E RICHMOND	1,200	E--A, E--*				
6	F ATLANTA	2,400	F--A, F--*				
7	G CHICAGO	3,840	G--A, G--*				
8	H ST. LOUIS	2,040	H--A, H--*				
9	I MINNEAPOLIS	none					
10	J KANSAS CITY	1,200	J--A				J00 000 556A
11	K DALLAS	1,200	K--A, K--*			K00 000 042A	K00 000 127A
12	L SAN FRANCISCO	3,600	L--A, L--*				

Note: 100 of these notes comprise the million dollar display in the lobby of Bennie Binion's Horseshoe Club in Las Vegas. All notes are Series 1934 Block B--A.

TOTAL BLOCKS: Twenty two. Collectors are requested to supply serial numbers.

CAT. NO. XF34A
$10,000.00 FEDERAL RESERVE NOTE (12 Subject)
SERIES 1934A

SIGNATURES: W.A. Julian, Treasurer of the United States.
   Henry Morgenthau, Jr., Secretary of the Treasury.

DISTRICT	TOTAL NOTES PRINTED	BLOCKS	ESTIMATED VALUE VG/F	CU	LOW OBSERVED SERIAL NUMBER	HIGH OBSERVED SERIAL NUMBER
7 G CHICAGO	1,560	G--A				

TOTAL BLOCKS: One.

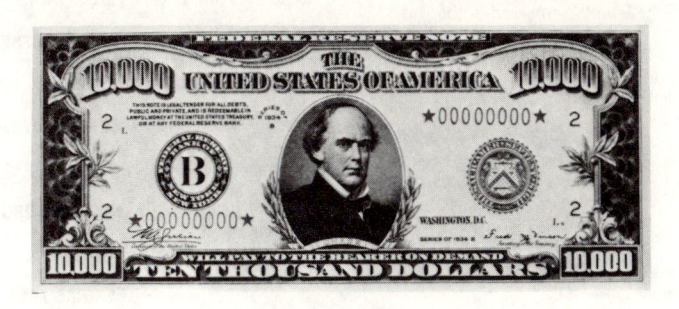

CAT. NO. XF34B
$10,000.00 FEDERAL RESERVE NOTE
SERIES 1934B

SERIAL NUMBERS: Continued sequence from previous series.
SIGNATURES: W.A. Julian, Treasurer of the United States.
   Fred M. Vinson, Secretary of the Treasury.

DISTRICT	TOTAL NOTES PRINTED	BLOCKS	ESTIMATED VALUE VG/F	CU	LOW OBSERVED SERIAL NUMBER	HIGH OBSERVED SERIAL NUMBER
2 B NEW YORK	24	B--A				

TOTAL BLOCKS: One.

$100,000.00 GOLD CERTIFICATE (12 Subject)
SERIES 1934

SERIAL NUMBERS: A00 000 001A through A00 042 000A.
PLATE SERIALS: Begin with 1.
SIGNATURES: W.A. Julian, Treasurer of the United States.
   Henry Morgenthau, Jr., Secretary of the Treasury.
TOTAL QUANTITY PRINTED: 42,000.
TOTAL BLOCKS: Two. A--A and A--*.

UNCUT SHEETS

Perhaps the most prized and certainly the rarest item in any modern size paper money collection is an uncut sheet. Despite intensive research throughout the Treasury Department including the records of the Bureau of Engraving and Printing we find neither validity or completeness in the meagre records that were examined. Information presented, which is the best available is contradicted many times by the census of known uncut sheets that follows the list of uncut sheets printed (?) or issued (?). We cannot learn for sure exactly HOW the uncut sheets reached the private collector. We do know that uncut sheets were available to collectors AT FACE value in the CASH DIVISION, Main Treasury Bldg. Washington, D.C. from the start of current size notes until Secretary Humphrey stopped the sale of uncut sheets during his tenure. Some scant records examined indicate the purchaser signed a "ledger" when making his purchase. Apparently there was no limit since some signatures appear several times on the same ledger sheet for purchase of separately serial number identified sheets of the same denomination and series. What we have not been able to learn is who requested (or ordered) the uncut sheets from the Bureau and how many were ordered. We have been unable to locate any delivery records of sheets from the Bureau to the Cash Division. We have fairly reliable HEARSAY evidence that IF the sheets remained in the Cash Division unsold, they were eventually cut up and passed over the teller counter as single notes.

Any information relative to either the printing, the issue, or the existence of uncut sheets is most cordially welcome.

Listed below is the best information available on the number of uncut sheets printed, followed by a census of uncut sheets known to exist in recent years.

$1.00 UNITED STATES NOTE — LEGAL TENDER (RED SEAL)
SERIES 1928 (12 Subject Sheets)

SIGNATURES	SERIAL NUMBER RANGE	NUMBER OF SHEETS
W.O. Woods, Treasurer of the United States	A00 000 001A - A00 000 120A	10
W.H. Woodin, Secretary of the Treasury	A01 872 001A - A01 872 012A	1

$1.00 SILVER CERTIFICATE (BLUE SEAL)
SERIES 1928 (12 Subject Sheets)

| H.T. Tate, Treasurer of the United States | A00 000 001A - A00 004 000A | No Record |
| A.W. Mellon, Secretary of the Treasury | | |

SERIES 1928 B (12 Subject Sheets)

| Walter O. Woods, Treasurer of the United States | Unknown | 6 |
| Ogden L. Mills, Secretary of the Treasury | | |

SERIES 1928 C (12 Subject Sheets)

| Walter O. Woods, Treasurer of the United States | B29 448 001B - B29 448 120B | 1 |
| W.H. Woodin, Secretary of the Treasury | D23 328 001B - D23 328 012B | 10 |

SERIES 1928 D (12 Subject Sheets)

| W.A. Julian, Treasurer of the United States | D82 596 001B - D82 596 720B | 60 |
| W.H. Woodin, Secretary of the Treasury | | |

SERIES 1928 E (12 Subject Sheets)

| W.A. Julian, Treasurer of the United States | F72 000 001B - F72 000 300B | 25 |
| Henry Morgenthau, Jr., Secretary of the Treasury | | |

SERIES 1934 (12 Subject Sheets)

| W.A. Julian, Treasurer of the United States | A00 000 001A - A00 000 300A | 25 |
| Henry Morgenthau, Jr., Secretary of the Treasury | | |

$1.00 SILVER CERTIFICATE (BLUE SEAL)
SERIES 1934B (12 Subject Sheets)

SIGNATURES	SERIAL NUMBER RANGE	NUMBER OF SHEETS
W.A. Julian, Treasurer of the United States		No Record
Fred M. Vinson, Secretary of the Treasury		

No record of any issues however sheets known to exist indicate an issue of 25 sheets.

SERIES 1935 (12 Subject Sheets)

| W.A. Julian, Treasurer of the United States | A00 000 001A - A00 001 200A | 100 |
| Henry Morgenthau, Jr., Secretary of the Treasury | | |

SERIES 1935 A (12 Subject Sheets)

W.A. Julian, Treasurer of the United States	V43 128 001A - V43 129 200A	100
Henry Morgenthau, Jr., Secretary of the Treasury	F41 952 001C - F41 954 148C N. Africa	25
	F41 964 001C - F41 966 148C Hawaii	25

SERIES 1935 B (12 Subject Sheets)

| W.A. Julian, Treasurer of the United States | C93 348 001D - C93 385 200D | 100 |
| Fred M. Vinson, Secretary of the Treasury | | |

SERIES 1935 C

| W.A. Julian, Treasurer of the United States | K99 996 001D - K99 997 200D | 100 |
| John W. Snyder, Secretary of the Treasury | | |

SERIES 1935 D (12 Subject Sheets)

Georgia Neese Clark, Treasurer of the U.S.	R88 104 001E - R88 105 200E	100
John W. Snyder, Secretary of the Treasury	Z33 324 001E - Z33 325 200E	100
	B05 520 001G - B05 521 200G	100

SERIES 1935 D (18 Subject Sheets)

| | G00 000 001G - G00 136 100G | 100 |
| | N46 807 999G - N46 944 000G | 2 |

SERIES 1935 E (18 Subject Sheets)

Ivy Baker Priest, Treasurer of the United States	N46 944 001G - N47 080 100G	100
George M. Humphrey, Secretary of the Treasury	R95 040 001G - R95 176 100G	100
	U75 168 001G - U75 304 100G	100
	X31 680 001G - X31 816 100G	100

$2.00 UNITED STATES NOTE — LEGAL TENDER (RED SEAL)
SERIES 1928C (12 Subject Sheets)

SIGNATURES	SERIAL NUMBER RANGE	NUMBER OF SHEETS
W.A. Julian, Treasurer of the United States	B09 012 001A - B09 012 300A	25
Henry Morgenthau, Jr., Secretary of the Treasury	B83 988 001A - B83 988 600A	50

SERIES 1928D (12 Subject Sheets)

W.A. Julian, Treasurer of the United States.
Henry Morgenthau, Jr. Secretary of the Treasury.
Records indicate 50 sheets Serials B83 988 001A through B83 988 600A were printed for this series however we know the records here are wrong simply because sheets known with these serials are all Series 1928C. No sheets of this series are known.

SERIES 1928E (12 Subject Sheets)

| W.A. Julian, Treasurer of the United States | D35 532 001A - D35 532 600A | 50 |
| Fred M. Vinson, Secretary of the Treasury | | |

SERIES 1928F (12 Subject Sheets)

| W.A. Julian, Treasurer of the United States | D39 552 001A - D39 553 200A | 100 |
| John W. Snyder, Secretary of the Treasury | | |

SERIES 1928G (12 Subject Sheets)

| Georgia Neese Clark, Treasurer of the U.S. | E07 074 001A - E07 705 200A | 100 |
| John W. Snyder, Secretary of the United States | | |

SERIES 1953 (18 Subject Sheets)

| Ivy Baker Priest, Treasurer of the United States | A00 000 001A - A00 136 100A | 100 |
| George M. Humphrey, Secretary of the Treasury | | |

$5.00 UNITED STATES NOTES — LEGAL TENDER (RED SEAL)
SERIES 1928E (12 Subject Sheets)

| W.A. Julian, Treasurer of the United States | (One sheet offered as Item 1111, in A. Kosoff sale of October 26, 1971.) | |
| Fred M. Vinson, Secretary of the Treasury | | |

SERIES 1928E (12 Subject Sheets)

| W.A. Julian, Treasurer of the United States | G68 352 001A - G68 353 200A | 100 |
| John W. Snyder, Secretary of the Treasury | | |

SERIES 1953 (18 Subject Sheets)

| Ivy Baker Priest, Treasurer of the United States | A00 000 001A - A00 136 100A | 100 |
| George M. Humphrey, Secretary of the Treasury | | |

$5.00 SILVER CERTIFICATE (BLUE SEAL)

SIGNATURES	SERIAL NUMBER RANGE	NUMBER OF SHEETS

SERIES 1934 (12 Subject Sheets)

| W.A. Julian, Treasurer of the United States | A00 000 001A - A00 000 300A | 25 |
| Henry Morgenthau, Jr., Secretary of the Treasury | | |

SERIES 1934C (12 Subject Sheets)

| W.A. Julian, Treasurer of the United States | L50 808 001A - L50 809 200A | 100 |
| John W. Snyder, Secretary of the Treasury | | |

SERIES 1934D (12 Subject Sheets)

| Georgia Neese Clark, Treasurer of the United States | Q71 628 001A - Q71 629 200A | 100 |
| John W. Snyder, Secretary of the United States | | |

SERIES 1953 (18 Subject Sheets)

| Ivy Baker Priest, Treasurer of the United States | A00 000 001A - A00 136 100A | 100 |
| George M. Humphrey, Secretary of the Treasury | | |

$10.00 SILVER CERTIFICATE (BLUE SEAL)
SERIES 1933 (12 Subject Sheets)

| W.A. Julian, Treasurer of the United States | A00 372 001A - A00 372 012A | 1 |
| W.H. Woodin, Secretary of the Treasury | | |

SERIES 1933A (12 Subject Sheets)

| W.A. Julian, Treasurer of the United States | A00 372 013A - A00 372 024A | 1 |
| Henry Morgenthau, Jr., Secretary of the Treasury | | |

SERIES 1934 (12 Subject Sheets)

| W.A. Julian, Treasurer of the United States | A00 000 001A - A00 000 120A | 10 |
| Henry Morgenthau, Jr., Secretary of the Treasury | | |

SERIES 1953 (18 Subject Sheets)

| Ivy Baker Priest, Treasurer of the United States | A00 000 001A - A00 136 100A | 100 |
| George M. Humphrey, Secretary of the Treasury | | |

CENSUS OF UNCUT SHEETS RECENTLY KNOWN TO EXIST IN UNCUT CONDITION

We believe that the collector is entitled to more than a fictional list of uncut sheets with price estimates for some sheets that don't even exist, and as far as we can learn, never existed. In our efforts to provide as much valid, accurate information as possible we are undertaking to complete a census by serial number of sheets that have been recently seen in uncut state. We are fully aware of the incompleteness of this census and sincerely hope that anyone seeing an uncut sheet not listed here will provide the description and serial numbers so that future census can be improved. As with all information submitted, your reports will be held is strict confidence.

We are deeply indebted and very grateful to Mr. Aubrey E. Bebee (Omaha, Nebraska) for his kind assistance and wonderful cooperation in supplying much of the sheet information and estimates of price. Mr. Bebee is internationally recognized as the top authority in this field. Much thanks are also due Mr. John Morris and Mr. Robert H. Lloyd for their considerable help in this area.

UNCUT SHEETS

$1.00 UNITED STATES NOTES (LEGAL TENDER) RED SEAL (12 Subject)
SERIES 1928
Estimated Value $20,000.00

A00 000 013A through A00 000 024A
A00 000 025A through A00 000 036A
A00 000 037A through A00 000 048A
A00 000 049A through A00 000 060A
A00 000 061A through A00 000 072A
A00 000 085A through A00 000 096A
A00 000 097A through A00 000 108A
A00 000 109A through A00 000 120A

$1.00 SILVER CERTIFICATE BLUE SEAL (12 Subject)

SERIES 1928
Estimated Value $3,000.00

A00 000 061A through A00 000 072A
A00 000 121A through A00 000 132A
A00 000 193A through A00 000 204A
A00 000 205A through A00 000 216A
A00 000 277a through A00 000 288A
A00 000 433A through A00 000 444A
A00 000 589A through A00 000 600A
A00 000 601A through A00 000 612A
A00 000 637A through A00 000 648A
A00 000 661A through A00 000 672A
A00 000 673A through A00 000 684A
A00 000 697A through A00 000 708A
A00 000 709A through A00 000 720A
A00 000 733A through A00 000 744A

SERIES 1928A
None Known

SERIES 1928B
None Known

SERIES 1928C
Estimated Value $15,000.00

B29 448 001B through B29 448 012B
B29 448 037B through B29 448 048B
B29 448 049B through B29 448 060B
B29 448 061B through B29 448 072B
B29 448 073B through B29 448 084B

SERIES 1928D
Estimated Value $5,500.00

D82 596 037B through D82 596 048B
D82 596 049B through D82 596 060B
D82 596 061B through D82 596 072B
D82 596 085B through D82 596 096B
D82 596 109B through D82 596 120B
D82 596 121B through D82 596 132B
D82 596 133B through D82 596 144B
D82 596 205B through D82 596 216B
D82 596 217B through D82 596 228B
D82 596 265B through D82 596 276B
D82 596 277B through D82 596 288B
D82 596 313B through D82 596 324B
D82 596 337B through D82 596 348B
D82 596 349B through D82 596 360B
D82 596 361B through D82 596 372B
D82 596 433B through D82 596 444B
D82 596 445B through D82 596 456B
D82 596 481B through D82 596 492B
D82 596 517B through D82 596 528B
D82 596 529B through D82 596 540B
D82 596 577B through D82 596 588B
D82 596 661B through D82 596 672B
D82 596 673B through D82 596 684B

SERIES 1928E
Estimated Value $19,000.00

F72 000 049B through F72 000 060B
F72 000 097B through F72 000 108B
F72 000 133B through F72 000 144B
F72 000 145B through F72 000 156B
F72 000 217B through F72 000 228B
F72 000 241B through F72 000 252B
F72 000 277B through F72 000 300B
F72 000 289B through F72 000 300B

SERIES 1934
Estimated Value $3,500.00

A00 000 037A through A00 000 048A
A00 000 073A through A00 000 084A
A00 000 085A through A00 000 096A
A00 000 097A through A00 000 108A
A00 000 109A through A00 000 120A
A00 000 121A through A00 000 132A
A00 000 145A through A00 000 156A
A00 000 157A through A00 000 168A
A00 000 181A through A00 000 192A
A00 000 217A through A00 000 228A

SERIES 1935
Estimated Value $3,000.00

A00 000 061A through A00 000 072A
A00 000 157A through A00 000 168A
A00 000 169A through A00 000 180A
A00 000 205A through A00 000 216A
A00 000 217A through A00 000 228A
A00 000 313A through A00 000 324A
A00 000 325A through A00 000 336A
A00 000 361A through A00 000 372A
A00 000 397A through A00 000 408A
A00 000 445A through A00 000 456A
A00 000 457A through A00 000 468A
A00 000 565A through A00 000 576A
A00 000 601A through A00 000 612A
A00 000 613A through A00 000 624A
A00 000 625A through A00 000 636A
A00 000 637A through A00 000 648A
A00 000 661A through A00 000 672A
A00 000 733A through A00 000 744A
A00 000 769A through A00 000 780A
A00 000 781A through A00 000 792A
A00 000 793A through A00 000 804A
A00 000 805A through A00 000 816A
A00 000 829A through A00 000 840A
A00 000 841A through A00 000 852A
A00 000 853A through A00 000 864A
A00 000 973A through A00 000 984A
A00 001 057A through A00 001 068A
A00 001 177A through A00 001 188A

SERIES 1935A
Estimated Value $2,000.00

V43 128 025A through V43 128 036A
V43 129 045A through V43 129 056A
V43 129 069A through V43 129 080A
V43 129 081A through V43 129 092A
V43 129 093A through V43 129 104A
V43 128 109A through V43 128 120A
V43 128 313A through V43 128 324A
V43 128 325A through V43 128 336A
V43 128 373A through V43 128 384A
V43 128 505A through V43 128 516A
V43 128 529A through V43 128 540A
V43 128 565A through V43 128 576A
V43 128 589A through V43 128 600A
V43 128 601A through V43 128 612A
V43 128 613A through V43 128 624A
V43 128 661A through V43 128 672A
V43 128 817A through V43 128 828A
V43 128 901A through V43 128 912A
V43 129 153A through V43 128 164A

SERIES 1935 A MULE

V43 128 037A through V43 128 048A

SERIES 1935A NORTH AFRICA (YELLOW SEAL)
Estimated Value $7,000.00

F41 952 007C through F41 952 012C left half
F41 954 005C through F41 954 010C right half
F41 952 019C through F41 952 024C left half
F41 954 017C through F41 954 022C right half
F41 952 031C through F41 952 036C left half
F41 954 029C through F41 954 034C right half
F41 952 049C through F41 952 054C left half
F41 954 047C through F41 954 052C right half
F41 952 067C through F41 952 072C left half
F41 954 065C through F41 954 070C right half
F41 952 085C through F41 952 090C left half
F41 954 083C through F41 954 088C right half
F41 952 091C through F41 952 096C left half
F41 954 089C through F41 954 094 C right half
F41 952 211C through F41 952 216C left half
F41 954 209C through F41 954 214C right half
F41 952 217C through F41 952 222C left half
F41 954 215C through F41 954 220C right half
F41 952 223C through F41 952 228C left half
F41 954 221C through F41 954 226C right half
F41 952 229C through F41 952 234C left half
F41 954 227C through F41 954 232C right half
F41 952 253C through F41 952 258C left half
F41 954 251C through F41 954 256C right half
F41 952 265C through F41 952 270C left half
F41 954 263C through F41 954 268C right half
F41 952 271C through F41 952 276C left half
F41 954 269C through F41 954 274C right half

$1.00 SILVER CERTIFICATE (BROWN SEAL) (12 Subject)
SERIES 1935A HAWAII BROWN SEAL

Estimated Value $6,000.00
F41 964 077C through F41 964 012C left half
F41 966 005C through F41 966 010C right half
F41 964 013C through F41 964 018C left half
F41 966 011C through F41 966 016C right half
F41 964 019C through F41 964 024C left half
F41 966 017C through F41 966 022C right half
F41 964 025C through F41 964 030C left half
F41 966 023C through F41 966 028C right half
F41 964 037C through F41 964 042C left half
F41 966 035C through F41 966 040C right half
F41 964 043C through F41 964 048C left half
F41 966 041C through F41 966 046C right half
F41 964 055C through F41 964 060C left half
F41 966 053C through F41 966 058C right half
F41 964 061C through F41 964 066C left half
F41 966 059C through F41 966 064C right half
F41 964 067C through F41 964 072C left half
F41 966 065C through F41 966 070C right half
F41 964 079C through F41 964 084C left half
F41 966 077C through F41 966 082C right half
F41 964 103C through F41 964 108C left half

F41 966 101C through F41 966 106C right half
F41 964 127C through F41 964 132C left half
F41 966 125C through F41 966 130C right half
F41 964 151C through F41 964 156C left half
F41 966 149C through F41 966 154C right half
F41 964 211C through F41 964 216C left half
F41 966 209C through F41 966 214C right half
F41 964 229C through F41 964 234C left half
F41 966 227C through F41 966 232C right half
F41 964 235C through F41 964 240C left half
F51 966 233C through F41 966 238C right half
F41 964 283C through F41 964 288C left half
F41 966 281C through F41 966 286C right half
F41 964 301C through F41 964 306C left half
F41 966 299C through F41 966 304C right half
F41 964 313C through F41 964 318C left half
F41 966 311C through F41 966 316C right half
F41 964 325C through F41 964 330C left half
F41 966 323C through F41 966 328C right half

$1.00 SILVER CERTIFICATE (BLUE SEAL) 12 SUBJECT
SERIES 1935B

Estimated Value $2,500.00
C93 384 073D through C93 384 084D
C93 384 097D through C93 384 108D
C93 384 157D through C93 384 168D
C93 384 301D through C93 384 312D
C93 384 313D through C93 384 324D
C93 384 325D through C93 384 336D
C93 384 337D through C93 384 348D
C93 384 349D through C93 384 360D
C93 384 361D through C93 384 372D
C93 384 433D through C93 384 444D
C93 384 493D through C93 384 504D
C93 384 517D through C93 384 528D
C93 384 541D through C93 384 552D
C93 384 553D through C93 384 564D
C93 384 589D through C93 384 600D
C93 384 625D through C93 384 636D
C93 384 637D through C93 384 648D
C93 384 697D through C93 384 708D
C93 384 709D through C93 384 720D
C93 384 817D through C93 384 828D
C93 384 841D through C93 384 852D
C93 384 877D through C93 384 888D
C93 384 961D through C93 384 972D
C93 385 009D through C93 385 020D
C93 385 021D through C93 385 032D
C93 385 069D through C93 385 080D
C93 385 141D through C93 385 152D
C93 385 177D through C93 385 188D

SERIES 1935C

Estimated Value $2,300.00
K99 996 265D through K99 996 276D
K99 996 289D through K99 996 300D
K99 996 313D through K99 996 324D
K99 996 325D through K99 996 336D
K99 996 349D through K99 996 360D
K99 996 361D through K99 996 372D
K99 996 373D through K99 996 384D
K99 996 385D through K99 996 396D
K99 996 409D through K99 996 420D
K99 996 433D through K99 996 444D
K99 996 457D through K99 996 468D
K99 996 529D through K99 996 540D
K99 996 541D through K99 996 552D
K99 996 565D through K99 996 576D
K99 996 577D through K99 996 588D
K99 996 589D through K99 996 600D
K99 996 613D through K99 996 624D
K99 996 637D through K99 996 648D
K99 996 661D through K99 996 672D
K99 996 685D through K99 996 696D
K99 996 757D through K99 996 768D
K99 996 781D through K99 996 792D
K99 996 817D through K99 996 828D
K99 996 853D through K99 996 864D
K99 996 865D through K99 996 876D
K99 996 889D through K99 996 900D
K99 996 925D through K99 996 936D
K99 996 973D through K99 996 984D

SERIES 1935D (12 Subject)

Estimated Value $2,500.00
R88 104 637E through R88 104 648E
R88 104 673E through R88 104 684E
R88 104 697E through R88 104 708E
R88 104 733E through R88 104 744E
R88 104 769E through R88 104 780E
R88 104 793E through R88 104 804E
R88 104 841E through R88 104 852E
R88 104 865E through R88 104 876E
R88 104 961E through R88 104 972E
R88 105 081E through R88 105 092E
R88 105 129E through R88 105 140E
R88 105 177E through R88 105 188E
R88 105 189E through R88 105 200E
Z33 324 073E through R33 324 084E
Z33 324 085E through R33 324 096E
Z33 324 325E through R33 324 336E
Z33 324 373E through R33 324 384E
Z33 324 493E through Z33 324 504E
Z33 324 505E through Z33 324 516E
Z33 324 697E through Z33 324 708E
Z33 324 769E through Z33 324 780E
Z33 324 781E through Z33 324 792E
Z33 324 829E through Z33 324 840E
Z33 324 985E through Z33 324 996E
Z33 324 853E through Z33 324 864E
Z33 325 021E through Z33 325 032E
Z33 325 045E through Z33 325 956E
Z33 325 153E through Z33 325 164E
Z33 325 325E through Z33 325 336E
B05 520 049G through B05 520 060G
B05 520 337G through B05 520 348G
B05 520 361G through B05 520 372G
B05 520 505G through B05 520 516G
B05 520 601G through B05 520 612G
B05 520 709G through B05 520 720G
B05 520 733G through B05 520 744G
B05 520 745G through B05 520 756G
B05 520 757G through B05 520 768G
B05 520 769G through B05 520 780G
B05 520 793G through B05 520 804G
B05 520 817G through B05 520 828G
B05 520 889G through B05 520 900G
B05 520 997G through B05 520 008G
B05 521 033G through B05 521 044G
B05 521 105G through B05 521 116G
B05 521 117G through B05 521 128G
B05 521 129G through B05 521 140G
B05 521 141G through B05 521 152G
B05 521 153G through B05 521 164G
B05 521 165G through B05 521 176G

$1.00 SILVER CERTIFICATE (BLUE SEAL) (12 Subject)
SERIES 1935D (18 Subject)

Estimated Value $3,500.00
G00 000 011G through G00 136 011G
G00 000 012G through G00 136 012G
G00 000 013G through G00 136 013G
G00 000 014G through G00 136 014G
G00 000 015G through G00 136 015G
G00 000 016G through G00 136 016G
G00 000 017G through G00 136 017G
G00 000 018G through G00 136 018G
G00 000 019G through G00 136 019G
G00 000 020G through G00 136 020G
G00 000 021G through G00 136 021G
G00 000 025G through G00 136 025G
G00 000 053G through G00 136 053G
G00 000 055G through G00 136 055G
G00 000 056G through G00 136 056G
G00 000 057G through G00 136 057G
G00 000 058G through G00 136 058G
G00 000 059G through G00 136 059G
G00 000 060G through G00 136 060G
G00 000 070G through G00 136 070G
G00 000 072G through G00 136 072G
G00 000 073G through G00 136 073G
G00 000 078G through G00 136 078G
G00 000 085G through G00 136 085G
G00 000 086G through G00 136 086G
G00 000 087G through G00 136 087G
G00 000 088G through G00 136 088G
G00 000 089G through G00 136 089G
G00 000 090G through G00 136 090G
G00 000 092G through G00 136 092G
G00 000 097G through G00 136 097G
G00 000 099G through G00 136 099G
G00 000 100G through G00 136 100G

SERIES 1935E (18 Subject)

Estimated Value $3,000.00
N46 944 006G through N47 080 006G
N46 944 013G through N47 080 013G
N46 944 018G through N47 080 018G
N46 944 026G through N47 080 026G
N46 944 027G through N47 080 027G
N46 944 031G through N47 080 031G
N46 944 032G through N47 080 032G
N46 944 033G through N47 080 033G
N46 944 037G through N47 080 037G
N46 944 044G through N47 080 044G
N46 944 045G through N47 080 045G
N46 944 046G through N47 080 046G
N46 944 057G through N47 080 057G
N46 944 058G through N47 080 058G
N46 944 059G through N47 080 059G
N46 944 064G through N47 080 064G
N46 944 079G through N47 080 079G
R95 040 003G through R95 176 003G
R95 040 010G through R95 176 010G
R95 040 019G through R95 176 019G
R95 040 044G through R95 176 044G
R95 040 079G through R95 176 079G
N46 944 085G through N47 080 085G
N46 944 793G through N47 080 793G
R95 040 018G through R95 176 018G
R95 040 034G through R95 176 034G
R95 040 035G through R95 176 035G
R95 040 036G through R95 176 036G
R95 040 037G through R95 176 037G
R95 040 048G through R95 176 048G
R95 040 063G through R95 176 063G
R95 040 072G through R95 176 072G
R95 040 076G through R95 176 076G
R95 040 083G through R95 176 083G
R95 040 093G through R95 176 093G
R95 040 096G through R95 176 096G
R95 040 097G through R95 176 097G
U75 168 010G through U75 304 010G
U75 168 012G through U75 304 012G
U75 168 018G through U75 304 018G
U75 168 029G through U75 304 029G
U75 168 030G through U75 304 030G
U75 168 043G through U75 304 043G
U75 168 055G through U75 304 055G
U75 168 056G through U75 304 056G
U75 168 062G through U75 304 062G
U75 168 067G through U75 304 067G
U75 168 069G through U75 304 069G
U75 168 089G through U75 304 089G
U75 208 090G through U75 344 090G
X31 680 002G through X31 816 001G
X31 680 013G through X31 816 013G
X31 680 038G through X31 816 038G

$1.00 FEDERAL RESERVE NOTE (GREEN SEAL) (32 Subject)
SERIES 1981

A99 840 001A through A99 999 999A
A99 840 001B through A99 999 999B
A99 840 001C through A99 999 999C
A99 840 001D through A99 999 999D
A99 840 001E through A99 999 999E
A99 840 001F through A99 999 999F
A99 840 001G through A99 999 999G
A99 840 001H through A99 999 999H

UNCUT HALF SHEETS
$1.00 FEDERAL RESERVE NOTE (GREEN SEAL) (16 Subject)
SERIES 1981

B99 840 001A through B99 999 999A
B99 840 001B through B99 999 999B
B99 840 001C through B99 999 999C
B99 840 001D through B99 999 999D

Although there had been rumors for months about the possible sale of uncut sheets, it was at the American Numismatic Association banquet in New Orleans, La. on Aug. 1, 1981 that Mr. Harry C. Clements officially announced that the Bureau of Engraving and Printing would resume the sale of uncut sheets to the general public. The earlier sale of uncut sheets had been stopped by Secretary of the Treasury Humphrey in 1953.

At a ceremony held in the Visitor Center, Bureau of Engraving and Printing Washington, D.C., the Director of the Bureau Mr. Harry C. Clements presented the first sheet (A99 840 001A) to Governor Chuck O'Donnell of the American Numismatic Association. The sheet is on permanent display at ANA Headquarters in Colorado Springs, Colorado.

Bureau of Engraving & Printing Prices over the counter (Washington D.C.)

Half Sheets (16 Subject)	Full Sheets (32 Subject)
$20.25	$38.00
By Mail	
$26.00	$45.00

UNCUT SHEETS
$2.00 UNITED STATES NOTES (LEGAL TENDER) RED SEAL (12 Subject)
SERIES 1928

Estimated Value $5,000.00
A00 000 037A through A00 000 048A
A00 000 049A through A00 000 060A

SERIES 1928A

none known

SERIES 1928B

none known

SERIES 1928C

Estimated Value $4,000.00
B09 012 001A through B09 012 012A
B09 012 013A through B09 012 024A
B09 012 037A through B09 012 048A
B09 012 049A through B09 012 060A
B09 012 073A through B09 012 084A
B09 012 097A through B09 012 103A
B09 012 157A through B09 012 168A
B09 012 181A through B09 012 192A
B09 012 217A through B09 012 228A
B09 012 229A through B09 012 240A
B09 012 253A through B09 012 264A
B09 012 277A through B09 012 288A
B83 988 013A through B83 988 024A
B83 988 085A through B83 988 096A
B83 988 108A through B83 988 120A
B83 988 121A through B83 988 132A
B83 988 145A through B83 988 156A
B83 988 157A through B83 988 168A
B83 988 181A through B83 988 192A
B83 988 253A through B83 988 264A
B83 988 373A through B83 988 384A
B83 988 397A through B83 988 408A
B83 988 409A through B83 988 420A
B83 988 457A through B83 988 468A
B83 988 469A through B83 988 480A
B83 988 481A through B83 988 492A
B83 988 493A through B83 988 504A

SERIES 1928D

none known

SERIES 1928E

Estimated Value $2,900.00
D35 532 001A through D35 532 012A
D35 532 013A through D35 532 024A
D35 532 037A through D35 532 048A
D35 532 061A through D35 532 072A
D35 532 073A through D35 532 084A
D35 532 085A through D35 532 096A
D35 532 133A through D35 532 144A
D35 532 145A through D35 532 156A
D35 532 157A through D35 532 168A
D35 532 169A through D35 532 180A
D35 532 193A through D35 532 204A
D35 532 205A through D35 532 216A
D35 532 229A through D35 532 240A
D35 532 289A through D35 532 300A
D35 532 301A through D35 532 312A
D35 532 349A through D35 532 360A
D35 532 361A through D35 532 372A
D35 532 385A through D35 532 396A
D35 532 397A through D35 532 408A
D35 532 409A through D35 532 420A
D35 532 433A through D35 532 444A
D35 532 445A through D35 532 456A
D35 532 469A through D35 532 480A
D35 532 481A through D35 532 492A
D35 532 493A through D35 532 504A
D35 532 541A through D35 532 552A

SERIES 1928F

Estimated Value $2,400.00
D39 552 001A through D39 552 012A
D39 552 013A through D39 552 024A
D39 552 025A through D39 552 036A
D39 552 037A through D39 552 048A
D39 552 073A through D39 552 084A
D39 552 061A through D39 552 072A
D39 552 097A through D39 552 108A
D39 552 145A through D39 552 156A
D39 552 169A through D39 552 180A
D39 552 181A through D39 552 192A
D39 552 241A through D39 552 252A
D39 552 265A through D39 552 276A
D39 552 277A through D39 552 288A
D39 552 313A through D39 552 324A
D39 552 337A through D39 552 348A
D39 552 373A through D39 552 384A
D39 522 397A through D39 552 408A
D39 522 553A through D39 552 564A
D39 552 721A through D39 552 732A
D39 552 937A through D39 552 948A
D39 552 961A through D39 552 972A
D39 553 003A through D39 553 044A
D39 553 069A through D39 553 080A

SERIES 1928G (12 Subject)

Estimated Value $2,400.00
E07 704 037A through E07 704 048A
E07 704 073A through E07 704 084A
E07 704 097A through E07 704 108A
E07 704 145A through E07 704 156A
E07 704 169A through E07 704 180A
E07 704 181A through E07 704 192A
E07 704 193A through E07 704 204A
E07 704 229A through E07 704 240A
E07 704 325A through E07 704 336A
E07 704 481A through E07 704 492A
E07 704 493A through E07 704 504A
E07 704 541A through E07 704 552A
E07 704 649A through E07 704 660A
E07 704 661A through E07 704 672A
E07 704 709A through E07 704 720A
E07 704 781A through E07 704 792A
E07 704 829A through E07 704 840A
E07 704 841A through E07 704 852A
E07 704 853A through E07 704 864A
E07 704 877A through E07 704 888A
E07 704 961A through E07 704 972A
E04 704 973A through E04 704 984A
E07 704 985A through E07 705 996A
E07 705 021A through E07 705 032A
E07 705 057A through E07 705 068A
E07 705 177A through E07 705 128A
E07 705 177A through E07 705 188A
E07 705 189A through E07 705 200A

SERIES 1953 (18 Subject)

Estimated Value $3,250.00
A00 000 028A through A00 135 028A
A00 000 032A through A00 136 032A
A00 000 034A through A00 136 034A
A00 000 039A through A00 136 039A
A00 000 040A through A00 136 040A
A00 000 041A through A00 136 041A

A00 000 043A through A00 136 043A
A00 000 045A through A00 136 045A
A00 000 048A through A00 136 048A
A00 000 051A through A00 136 051A
A00 000 052A through A00 136 052A
A00 000 053A through A00 136 053A
A00 000 055A through A00 136 055A
A00 000 058A through A00 136 058A
A00 000 062A through A00 136 062A
A00 000 063A through A00 136 063A
A00 000 066A through A00 136 066A
A00 000 067A through A00 136 067A
A00 000 071A through A00 136 071A
A00 000 073A through A00 136 073A
A00 000 074A through A00 136 074A
A00 000 078A through A00 136 078A
A00 000 079A through A00 136 079A
A00 000 080A through A00 136 080A
A00 000 084A through A00 136 084A
A00 000 087A through A00 136 087A

$5.00 SILVER CERTIFICATE BLUE SEAL (12 Subject)
SERIES 1934A

Estimated Value $4,500.00
A00 000 013A through A00 000 024A
A00 000 025A through A00 000 036A
A00 000 049A through A00 000 060A
A00 000 061A through A00 000 072A
A00 000 073A through A00 000 084A
A00 000 084A through A00 000 096A
A00 000 097A through A00 000 108A
A00 000 157A through A00 000 168A
A00 000 169A through A00 000 180A
A00 000 217A through A00 000 228A
A00 000 229A through A00 000 240A
A00 000 265A through A00 000 276A

SERIES 1934A

none known

SERIES 1934B

Estimated Value $5,000.00
L27 456 001A through L27 456 012A
L27 456 013A through L27 456 024A
L27 456 049A through L27 456 060A
L27 456 097A through L27 456 108A
L27 456 121A through L27 456 132A
L27 456 157A through L27 456 168A
L27 456 169A through L27 456 180A
L27 456 193A through L27 456 204A
L27 456 217A through L27 456 228A
L27 456 229A through L27 456 240A

SERIES 1934C

Estimated Value $4,000.00
L50 808 001A through L50 808 012A
L50 808 013A through L50 808 024A
L50 808 037A through L50 808 048A
L50 808 049A through L50 808 060A
L50 808 061A through L50 808 072A
L50 808 073A through L50 808 084A
L50 808 085A through L50 808 096A
L50 808 097A through L50 808 108A
L50 808 133A through L50 808 144A
L50 808 157A through L50 808 168A

SERIES 1934D

Estimated Value $3,500.00
Q71 628 001A through Q71 628 012A
Q71 628 013A through Q71 628 024A
Q71 628 025A through Q71 628 036A
Q71 628 037A through Q71 628 048A
Q71 628 085A through Q71 628 096A
Q71 628 193A through Q71 628 204A
Q71 628 205A through Q71 628 216A
Q71 628 373A through Q71 628 384A
Q71 628 397A through Q71 628 408A
Q71 628 409A through Q71 628 420A
Q71 628 445A through Q71 628 456A
Q71 628 457A through Q71 628 468A
Q71 628 469A through Q71 628 480A
Q71 628 541A through Q71 628 552A
Q71 628 601A through Q71 628 612A
Q71 628 649A through Q71 628 660A
Q71 628 721A through Q71 628 732A

Q71 628 829A through Q71 628 840A
Q71 628 961A through Q71 628 972A
Q71 628 973A through Q71 628 984A
Q71 628 997A through Q71 628 008A
Q71 629 021A through Q71 629 032A
Q71 629 033A through Q71 629 044A
Q71 629 045A through Q71 629 056A
Q71 629 057A through Q71 629 068A
Q71 629 177A through Q71 629 188A

SERIES 1953 (18 Subject)

Estimated Value $4,000.00
A00 000 027A through A00 136 027A
A00 000 029A through A00 136 029A
A00 000 030A through A00 136 030A
A00 000 031A through A00 136 031A
A00 000 032A through A00 136 032A
A00 000 036A through A00 136 036A
A00 000 037A through A00 136 037A
A00 000 039A through A00 136 039A
A00 000 050A through A00 136 050A
A00 000 052A through A00 136 052A
A00 000 055A through A00 136 055A
A00 000 057A through A00 136 057A
A00 000 058A through A00 136 058A
A00 000 059A through A00 136 059A
A00 000 060A through A00 136 060A
A00 000 063A through A00 136 063A
A00 000 067A through A00 136 076A
A00 000 069A through A00 136 069A
A00 000 070A through A00 136 070A
A00 000 075A through A00 136 075A
A00 000 079A through A00 136 079A

$5.00 UNITED STATES NOTES (LEGAL TENDER) RED SEAL (12 Subject)
SERIES 1928

Estimated Value $7,500.00
A00 000 049A through A00 000 060A

SERIES 1928A

none known

SERIES 1928B

none known

SERIES 1928C

none known

SERIES 1928D

Estimated Value $6,000.00
G58 956 001A through G58 956 012A
G58 956 013A through G58 956 024A
G58 956 037A through G58 956 048A
G58 956 061A through G58 956 072A
G58 956 073A through G58 956 084A
G58 956 109A through G58 956 120A
G58 956 121A through G58 956 132A
G58 956 145A through G58 956 156A
G58 956 169A through G58 956 180A
G58 956 205A through G58 956 216A
G58 956 217A through G58 956 228A
G58 956 241A through G58 956 252A
G58 956 253A through G58 956 264A
G58 956 277A through G58 956 288A

SERIES 1928E

Estimated Value $3,500.00
G68 352 001A through G68 352 012A
G68 352 013A through G68 352 024A
G68 352 025A through G68 352 036A
G68 352 037A through G68 352 048A
G68 352 049A through G68 352 060A
G68 352 073A through G68 352 084A
G68 352 085A through G68 352 096A
G68 352 097A through G68 352 108A
G68 352 109A through G68 352 120A
G68 352 145A through G68 352 156A
G68 352 181A through G68 352 192A
G68 352 193A through G68 352 204A
G68 352 217A through G68 352 228A
G68 352 241A through G68 352 252A
G68 352 313A through G68 352 324A
G68 352 325A through G68 352 336A
G68 352 337A through G68 352 348A
G68 352 421A through G68 352 432A

$5.00 UNITED STATES NOTES (LEGAL TENDER) RED SEAL SERIES 1953 (18 Subject)

Estimated Value $5,000.00
A00 000 031A through A00 136 031A
A00 000 032A through A00 136 032A
A00 000 033A through A00 136 033A
A00 000 035A through A00 136 035A
A00 000 040A through A00 136 040A
A00 000 044A through A00 136 044A
A00 000 046A through A00 136 046A
A00 000 053A through A00 136 053A
A00 000 055A through A00 136 055A
A00 000 056A through A00 136 056A
A00 000 057A through A00 136 057A
A00 000 058A through A00 136 058A
A00 000 059A through A00 136 059A
A00 000 060A through A00 136 060A

$5.00 FEDERAL RESERVE NOTE GREEN SEAL (12 Subject) SERIES 1928

Estimated Value $7,500.00
C00 000 025A through C00 000 036A
G00 000 037A through G00 000 048A
K00 000 013A through K00 000 024A
K00 000 025A through K00 000 036A

SERIES 1928B

Estimated Value $10,000.00
I04 692 049A through I04 692 060A

SERIES 1934C

Estimated Value $10,000.00
L50 808 133A through L50 808 144A

$10.00 FEDERAL RESERVE BANK NOTE SERIES 1929 (BROWN SEAL)

Estimated Value $20,000.00
B00 000 085A through B00 000 096A
B00 000 097A through B00 000 108A

$10.00 FEDERAL RESERVE NOTE GREEN SEAL (12 Subject) SERIES 1928

Estimated Value $20,000.00
C00 000 013A through C00 000 024A
C00 000 037A through C00 000 048A
G00 000 037A through G00 000 048A
I02 760 049A through I02 760 060A
K00 000 013A through K00 000 024A

$10.00 SILVER CERTIFICATE BLUE SEAL (12 Subject) SERIES 1934

Estimated Value $5,000.00
A00 000 013A through A00 000 024A
A00 000 025A through A00 000 036A
A00 000 037A through A00 000 048A
A00 000 061A through A00 000 072A
A00 000 073A through A00 000 084A
A00 000 085A through A00 000 096A
A00 000 108A through A00 000 120A

SERIES 1953

Estimated Value $6,000.00
A00 000 030A through A00 136 030A
A00 000 033A through A00 136 033A
A00 000 034A through A00 136 034A
A00 000 038A through A00 136 038A
A00 000 043A through A00 136 043A
A00 000 047A through A00 136 047A
A00 000 049A through A00 136 049A
A00 000 050A through A00 136 050A
A00 000 051A through A00 136 051A
A00 000 055A through A00 136 055A

$20.00 FEDERAL RESERVE NOTE GREEN SEAL (12 Subject) SERIES 1928

Estimated Value $25,000.00
C00 000 001A through C00 000 012A
C00 000 037A through C00 000 048A
G00 000 037A through G00 000 048A
I01 800 037A through I01 800 048A

$100.00 UNITED STATES NOTE SERIES 1966 RED SEAL (12 Subject)

*00 000 161A through *00 002 161A
This sheet is on permanent loan to the American Numismatic Association and is on display at the Headquarters in Colorado Springs, Colorado.

CHANGEOVER PAIRS

Technically speaking, changeover pairs, sometimes called hold-over or cross-over pairs should be the highest serial number of one series and the lowest serial number of the following series OF THE SAME DENOMINATION AND CLASS of note. Hence a $1.00 legal tender note Series 1928 could not be coupled with the next higher serial number of a 1928A $1.00 silver certificate and qualify as a changeover note. Also the $5. FRN could not be coupled with the $5. legal tender and fit the criteria of a changeover pair. Pairs of notes where the serial number is higher on the earlier series have been marginally accepted by collectors as so-called changeover pairs — but are referred to as REVERSE CHANGEOVERS.

During the early years (1928-1935) of printing the current size notes, because of the high cost of the engraved plates, and because the signatures were engraved IN the plates, it was customary for the Bureau of Engraving and Printing to use the plates long after the official whose signature appeared in the plate had left office. The result of this practice was that several series were being face printed simultaneously. When a stack of one series was placed on top of another series and sent to the third (serial number) printing, then consecutive numbered notes of different series were produced. An examination of the plate record card usage in BEP indicates quite a number of cases where several series were being printed on the same day. This is substantiated by the existence of known pairs of notes with consecutive serial numbers in various series combinations. For the $1.00 silver certificate for example, we know that both the 1928 and 1928A series were face printed on the same day. When these stacks were mixed and sent to the third printing, changeover pairs were produced — sometimes in proper sequence — sometimes in reverse sequence. We know also that 28A/28B, 28A/28C, 28A/28D, 28A/28E, 28B/28C, 28B/28D, 28B/28E, 28C/28D, 28C/28E and 28D/28E are run simultaneously, hence we know of or suspect changeover pairs in all of these combinations. For the $2.00 legal tender we know that Series 1928C/D/E/F were being printed simultaneously and again, we know of or suspect all of these combinations. The $5.00 FRN series 1934 through 1934D and the $5.00 silver certificate Series 1934 through 1934D were printed simultaneously, and finally we know that the $5.00 legal tender Series 1928D, E, and F were face printed simultaneously. Higher denominations too numerous to mention were also printed as is confirmed by the existence of one or more changeover pairs presently known.

Because the wide and narrow backs of the $1.00 silver certificate Series 1935D are found intermingled in packs, changeover pairs of the variety are known in practically all blocks. Because of the relatively high number of changeover pairs in this series no census is attempted.

And finally, in the current $1.00 FRN (and higher denominations as well), while NOT being printed concurrently, some of the more astute collectors have managed to get the same serial number packs for consecutive series, and by matching the serial number of the earlier series with the next higher serial number of the later series, have created valid changeover pairs. This of course can be done with any series and any denomination if one worked hard enough at it — or was lucky enough to stumble up on the right combination of packs of notes.

While collectors have accepted as changeovers "skip" series, that is consecutive serial numbers on the 28A — 28E or 28B — 28D despite the fact other series were printed in between, we doubt that collectors would accept a skip in series for current FRN's EXCEPT where NO notes were printed in the intervening series. NO notes were printed for the $1.00 FRN Boston for Series 1969C — hence consecutive serial numbered notes for Boston Series 1969B/1969D would qualify as so-called changeover pairs.

Census of known changeover pairs follows, the author earnestly solicits your assistance in reporting any changeover pairs (except the 1935D) not listed.

$1.00 SILVER CERTIFICATES

1928	H24 067 110A	1928A	H24 067 111A	250.00
	H31 865 568A		H31 865 569A	250.00
1928A	F98 281 830A	1928	F98 281 831A	125.00
	G36 363 636A		G36 363 637A	150.00
	G52 576 944A		G52 576 945A	150.00
	G87 380 634A		G87 380 635A	150.00
	G99 279 258A		G99 279 259A	150.00
	H98 173 746A		H98 173 747A	250.00
1928A	H62 614 692A	1928B	H62 614 693A	125.00
	Y22 437 608A		Y22 437 609A	125.00
	Y22 726 056A		Y22 726 057A	125.00

							I40 540 452B		I40 504 453B	250.00
	Y32 068 044A		Y32 068 045A	125.00			I40 504 470B		I40 504 471B	250.00
	Y77 437 620A		Y77 437 621A	125.00			I40 504 494B		I40 504 495B	250.00
	Y77 437 710A		Y77 437 711A	125.00			I40 504 992B		I40 504 993B	250.00
	Y83 044 722A		Y83 044 723A	125.00		1928B	I92 908 290B	1928E	I92 908 291B	1,000.00
	Y83 044 758A		Y83 044 759A	125.00		1928C	H99 610 002B	1928B	H99 610 003B	350.00
	Y91 160 196A		Y91 160 197A	125.00			H99 610 020B		H99 610 021B	350.00
	Y91 160 436A		Y91 160 437A	125.00			H99 610 068B		H99 610 069B	350.00
	A11 118 390B		A11 118 391B	125.00			H99 610 068B		H99 610 069B	350.00
	B40 149 366B		B40 149 367B	125.00		1928D	H69 717 360B	1928B	H69 717 361B	275.00
	D33 000 702B		D33 000 703B	125.00			H69 717 372B		H69 717 373B	275.00
	E14 561 478B		E14 561 479B	125.00			I45 994 416B		I45 994 417B	275.00
	F17 863 118B		F17 863 119B	125.00			I64 933 206B		I64 933 207B	275.00
	F17 863 506B		F17 863 507B	125.00		1928D	H90 945 102B	1928C	H90 945 103B	500.00
	F17 863 554B		F17 863 555B	125.00		1928D	I52 499 060B	1928E	I52 488 061B	1,500.00
	F18 533 022B		F18 533 023B	125.00		1928E	I92 908 296B	1928B	I92 908 297B	1,300.00
	F22 934 106B		F22 934 107B	125.00		1928E	I52 488 054B	1928D	I52 488 055B	1,400.00
	F22 934 118B		F22 934 119B	125.00
	F22 934 130B		F22 934 131B	125.00
	F22 934 142B		F22 934 143B	125.00
	F22 934 154B		F22 934 155B	125.00
	F86 995 698B		F86 995 699B	125.00
	G03 965 052B		G03 965 053B	125.00
	G08 974 296B		G08 974 297B	125.00
	G09 087 486B		G09 087 487B	125.00
	G10 848 366B		G10 848 367B	125.00
	G29 341 914B		G29 341 915B	125.00
	G30 587 748B		G30 587 749B	125.00
	G52 576 944B		G52 576 945B	125.00
	G65 105 172B		G65 105 173B	125.00
	G72 518 850B		G72 518 851B	125.00
	G84 450 114B		G84 450 115B	125.00
	G90 273 552B		G90 273 553B	125.00
	H14 303 748B		H14 303 749B	150.00
	H23 495 970B		H23 495 971B	150.00
	H27 275 438B		H27 275 439B	150.00
	H38 698 602B		H38 698 603B	150.00
	H38 698 608B		H38 698 609B	150.00
	H55 163 196B		H55 163 197B	150.00
	H59 559 198B		H59 559 199B	150.00
	H66 614 687B		H66 614 688B	150.00
	I04 750 386B		I04 750 387B	250.00
	I33 500 436B		I33 500 437B	250.00
	*35 790 882A		*35 790 883A	250.00
1928A	*35 168 274A	1928C	*35 168 275A	500.00
1928B	Y88 301 814A	1928A	Y88 301 815A	175.00
	A10 358 598B		A10 358 599B	150.00
	A53 342 832B		A53 342 833B	150.00
	B55 757 382B		H55 757 383B	150.00
	C37 209 018B		C37 209 019B	150.00
	C85 181 274B		C85 181 275B	150.00
	F22 934 112B		F22 934 113B	150.00
	F22 934 124B		F22 934 125B	150.00
	F22 934 148B		F22 934 149B	150.00
	F86 995 680B		F86 995 681B	150.00
	F86 995 692B		F86 995 693B	150.00
	F87 881 970B		F87 881 971B	150.00
	G03 152 376B		G03 152 377B	150.00
	G30 587 742B		G30 587 743B	150.00
	G85 181 274B		G85 181 275B	150.00
	H27 375 480B		H27 375 481B	150.00
	H53 342 832B		H53 342 833B	150.00
	H66 205 332B		H66 205 333B	150.00
	H66 205 356B		H66 205 357B	150.00
	H66 205 476B		H66 205 477B	150.00
	*34 169 982A		*34 169 983A	200.00
1928B	F03 430 794B	1928C	F03 430 795B	400.00
	F41 758 236B		F41 758 237B	400.00
	H10 183 452B		H10 183 453B	400.00
	H10 183 902B		H10 183 903B	400.00
	H45 843 084B		H45 843 085B	400.00
	H45 843 270B		H45 843 271B	400.00
	H45 843 288B		H45 843 289B	400.00
1928B	F48 461 562B	1928D	F48 461 563B	300.00
	H23 667 810B		H23 667 811B	250.00
	H30 383 910B		H30 383 911B	250.00
	H30 383 958B		H30 383 959B	250.00
	H69 719 366B		H69 719 367B	250.00
	H98 188 212B		H98 188 213B	250.00
	I13 277 676B		I13 277 677B	250.00
	I39 766 404B		I39 766 405B	250.00
	I40 504 050B		I40 504 051B	250.00
	I40 504 110B		I40 504 111B	250.00
	I40 504 170B		I40 504 171B	250.00
	I40 504 308B		I40 504 309B	250.00
	I40 504 326B		I40 504 327B	250.00
	I40 504 440B		I40 504 441B	250.00

| 1935 | (with 1935 back) | 1935 | (with 1935A back) MULE |

Pairs of this variety are known in several block combinations. Estimated price would be approximately the sum of the individual blocks doubled.

| 1935A | (with 1935A back) | 1935A | (with 1935 back) MULE |

Same as above.

| 1935D | wide | 1935D | narrow |
| 1935D | narrow | 1935D | wide |

Same as above. Pairs are known in all block combinations except U-E, G-G, and N-G.

$2.00 UNITED STATES NOTES

1928B	B05 689 638A	1928A	B05 689 639A	300.00
1928D	D30 112 536A	1928E	D30 112 537A	150.00
	D30 112 896A		D30 112 897A	150.00
	D31 420 986A		D31 420 987A	150.00
	D32 341 014A		D32 341 105A	150.00
	D32 341 062A		D32 341 063A	150.00
	D32 341 132A		D32 341 133A	150.00
	D32 342 574A		D32 342 575A	150.00
	D32 343 096A		D32 343 097A	150.00
	D32 343 132A		D32 343 133A	150.00
	D32 343 168A		D32 343 169A	150.00
	D32 343 192A		D32 343 193A	150.00
	D32 343 354A		D32 343 355A	150.00
	D32 343 378A		D32 343 379A	150.00
	D32 343 468A		D32 343 469A	150.00
	D32 343 480A		D32 343 481A	150.00
	D32 885 508A		D32 885 509A	150.00
1928E	D30 112 260A	1928D	D30 112 261A	150.00
	D30 112 464A		D30 112 465A	150.00
	D30 112 548A		D30 112 549A	150.00
	D32 341 020A		D32 241 021A	150.00
	D32 342 778A		D32 342 779A	150.00
	D32 343 114A		D32 343 115A	150.00
	D32 343 162A		D32 343 163A	150.00
1928E	D39 591 132A	1928F	D39 591 133A	175.00
	D39 591 186A		D39 591 187A	175.00
1928F	D80 445 084A	1928G	D80 445 085A	200.00

$5.00 UNITED STATES NOTES

1928A	D01 359 498A	1928	D01 359 499A	300.00
1928B	E56 022 618A	1928C mule	E56 022 619A	250.00
1928B mule	E58 751 094A	1928C	E58 751 095A	250.00
	E65 171 952A		E65 171 953A	250.00
1928C	E65 171 958A	1928B mule	E65 171 959A	250.00
1928C	E81 416 388A	1928C mule	E81 416 389A	350.00
1928C mule	E65 171 946A	1928B mule	E65 171 947A	350.00
1928C mule	E81 416 328A	1928C	E81 416 329A	350.00
	E81 416 358A		E81 416 359A	
1928C	G54 848 322A	1928D	G54 848 323A	250.00

331

1928D	G55 758 072A	1928C	G55 758 073A	250.00
1928D	G56 058 504A	1928E	G56 058 505A	250.00
1928E		1928F		250.00

(Reportedly one pair known, serials not reported.)

$5.00 SILVER CERTIFICATES

1934	D95 883 696A	1934A	D95 883 697A	200.00
1934	D72 791 016A	1934A mule	D72 791 017A	250.00
	D82 075 890A		D82 075 891A	250.00
	D95 883 624A		D95 883 625A	250.00
1934		1934 mule		
1934A		1934A mule		

Pairs of these varieties are known. Estimated price would be double the sum of the individual blocks

1934A	L06 718 356A	1934B	L06 718 357A	200.00
	L11 507 076A		L00 507 077A	200.00
	L12 976 266A		L12 976 267A	200.00
1934A mule	F11 487 672A	1934A	F11 487 673A	150.00
1934B	L50 330 556A	1934C	L50 330 557A	150.00
	L50 330 568A		L50 330 569A	150.00
	L51 477 228A		L51 477 229A	150.00
	L74 667 702A		L74 667 703A	150.00
	L80 808 066A		L80 808 067A	150.00
1934C	L80 808 060A	1934B	L80 808 061A	200.00
	L86 524 098A		L86 524 099A	200.00
	M30 229 668A		M30 229 669A	200.00
	Q47 622 414A		Q47 622 415A	150.00
1934C	Q47 482 254A	1934D	Q47 482 255A	150.00
	Q48 088 626A		Q48 088 627A	150.00
	Q48 088 674A		Q48 088 675A	150.00
	Q55 331 346A		Q55 331 347A	150.00
	Q55 331 958A		Q55 331 959A	150.00
	Q56 907 930A		Q56 907 931A	150.00
	Q57 972 972A		Q57 972 973A	150.00
	Q60 674 436A		Q60 674 437A	150.00
	Q60 674 460A		Q60 674 461A	150.00
	*17 397 810A		*17 397 811A	200.00
	*17 459 160A		*17 459 161A	200.00
	*17 687 718A		*17 687 719A	200.00
	*17 700 966A		*17 700 967A	200.00
1934D	Q48 175 314A	1934C	Q48 175 315A	200.00
	Q48 808 680A		Q48 808 681A	200.00
	Q55 331 940A		Q55 331 941A	200.00
	Q57 972 942A		Q57 972 943A	200.00
	Q57 972 966A		Q57 972 967A	200.00
	*17 448 270A		*17 448 271A	250.00
	*17 448 282A		*17 448 283A	250.00
	*17 459 178A		*17 459 179A	250.00
	*17 459 448A		*17 459 449A	250.00
	*17 459 514A		*17 459 515A	250.00
	*17 687 712A		*17 687 713A	250.00

$5.00 FEDERAL RESERVE NOTES

1928	J04 822 494A	1928A	J04 822 495A	500.00
1934	B33 072 168A	1934A	B33 072 169A	200.00
	G23 511 570A		G23 511 571A	200.00
	G24 537 156A		G24 537 157A	200.00
1934 mule	B29 015 562B	1934A	B29 015 563B	200.00
	B96 471 204A		B96 471 205A	200.00
	C52 611 672A		C52 611 673A	200.00
1934	D57 994 350A	1934B	D57 994 351A	300.00
1934A	C30 365 118A	1934	C30 365 119A	175.00
	G24 537 150A		G24 537 151A	175.00
	L24 794 934A		L24 794 935A	175.00
	C72 036 156A	1934B	C72 036 157A	200.00
	C72 036 185A		C72 036 186A	200.00
	C72 036 204A		C72 036 205A	200.00
	B76 314 420B		B76 314 421B	200.00
	B78 089 004B		B78 089 005B	200.00
	B78 604 392B		B78 604 393B	200.00
	B83 602 866B		B83 602 867B	200.00
	C72 036 120A		C72 036 121A	200.00
	C72 036 168A		C72 036 169A	200.00
	C72 036 372A		C72 036 373A	200.00
	C72 036 504A		C72 036 505A	200.00
	C72 036 552A		C72 036 553A	200.00
	D63 026 892A		D63 026 893A	200.00
1934B	B80 562 372B	1934A	B80 562 373B	150.00
	B81 038 868B		B81 038 869B	150.00
	B83 602 824B		B83 602 825B	150.00
	C72 036 126A		C72 036 127A	150.00
	C72 036 150A		C72 036 151A	150.00
	C72 036 186A(1)		C72 036 187A	

(1)See this serial under 34B above. Actually this is a run of three notes — 34A-34B-34A. If sold as a trio estimated value is $350.00

	C72 036 462A		C72 036 463A	150.00
	D60 932 532A		D60 932 533A	150.00
	D62 128 722A		D62 128 723A	150.00
	G13 872 054B		G13 872 055B	150.00
	G13 872 066B		G13 872 067B	150.00
1934B	L74 667 702A	1934C	L74 667 703A	150.00
1934C	D69 301 788A	1934B	D69 301 789A	150.00
1934C	B64 863 882C	1934D	B64 863 883C	100.00
	B64 863 948C		B64 863 949C	100.00
	B64 863 966C		B64 863 967C	100.00
	B64 863 996C		B64 863 997C	100.00

$10.00 SILVER CERTIFICATE

1934	A44 023 045A	1934 mule	A44 023 046A	50.00
1934A	B18 525 576A	1934B	B18 525 577A	1,000.00
1934B	B18 432 102A	1934A	B18 432 103A	900.00

$10.00 FEDERAL RESERVE NOTES

1928	F06 645 486A	1928A	F06 645 487A	350.00
1934	J20 907 474A	1934A	J20 907 475A	250.00
1934A	F33 075 792A	1934 mule	F33 075 793A	250.00
	G65 813 328A		G65 813 329A	250.00
	J00 623 940*		J00 623 941*	350.00
1934A	B79 076 856D	1934B	B79 076 857D	200.00
	B80 851 308D		B80 851 309D	200.00
	B80 864 112D		B80 864 113D	200.00
	C23 630 227B		C23 630 227B	200.00
	C23 630 274B		C23 630 275B	200.00
	C26 942 310B		C26 942 311B	200.00
	C26 942 430B		C26 942 431B	200.00
	C26 942 526B		C26 942 527B	200.00
	C26 942 580B		C26 942 581B	200.00
	L55 944 379B		L55 944 380B	200.00
1934A mule	G66 224 412A	1934B	G66 224 413A	250.00
1934B	B77 069 424D	1934A	B77 069 425D	175.00
	C23 630 220B		C23 630 221B	175.00
	C26 942 304B		C26 942 305B	175.00
	C26 942 376B		C26 942 377B	175.00
	C26 942 448B		C26 942 449B	175.00
	C26 942 520B		C26 942 521B	175.00
	C26 942 532B		C26 942 533B	175.00
	C26 942 586B		C26 942 587B	175.00
	C26 942 928B		C26 942 929B	175.00
	G37 051 704B		G37 051 705B	175.00
1934C	C02 424 420*	1934D	C02 424 421*	400.00
	C02 424 468*		C02 424 469*	400.00
	C02 424 492*		C02 424 493*	400.00
	C02 469 720*		C02 469 721*	400.00
1934D	C02 424 498*	1934C	C02 424 499*	350.00
	C02 424 648*		C02 424 649*	350.00
	C02 425 314*		C02 425 315*	350.00
	C02 425 368*		C02 425 369*	350.00
	C02 469 096*		C02 469 097*	350.00
	C02 469 972*		C02 469 973*	350.00
	C02 475 090*		C02 475 091*	350.00
	C02 475 102*		C02 475 103*	350.00

$20.00 FEDERAL RESERVE NOTES

1934	D53 144 562A	1934A	D53 144 563A	350.00
1934	L19 857 588A	1934A mule	L19 857 589A	350.00
1934 mule	D53 144 562A	1934A	D53 144 563A	350.00

1934 mule	D59 844 186A	1934A	D59 844 187A	450.00	
1934A	D52 931 742A	1934	D52 931 743A	300.00	
	E48 966 960A		E48 966 961A	300.00	
	H12 146 910A		H12 146 911A	300.00	
1934A mule	B30 870 654A	1934	B30 870 655A	300.00	
	D53 171 052A		D53 171 053A	300.00	
1934A	C34 623 084A	1934 mule	C34 623 085A	300.00	
1934A	B18 265 104B	1934B	B18 265 105B	350.00	
	B18 265 134B		B18 265 135B	350.00	
	B18 265 662B		B18 265 663B	350.00	
	B18 265 674B		B18 265 675B	350.00	
	B18 265 686B		B18 265 687B	350.00	
	B18 265 698B		B18 265 699B	350.00	
	B18 417 342B		B18 417 343B	350.00	
	B34 669 086B		B34 669 087B	350.00	
	B34 669 098B		B34 669 099B	350.00	
	G06 978 396B		G06 978 397B	350.00	
	G07 854 756B		G07 854 757B	350.00	
	G07 854 780B		G07 854 781B	350.00	
1934B	B18 265 128B	1934A	B18 265 129B	300.00	
	B18 265 140B		B18 265 141B	300.00	
	B18 265 656B		B18 265 657B	300.00	
	B18 265 668B		B18 265 669B	300.00	
	B18 265 680B		B18 265 681B	300.00	
	B18 265 692B		B18 265 693B	300.00	
	B24 785 304B		B24 785 305B	300.00	
	B34 669 056B		B34 669 057B	300.00	
	B34 669 080B		B34 669 081B	300.00	
	B34 669 092B		B34 669 093B	300.00	
	G07 854 744B		G07 854 745B	300.00	
	G07 854 762B		G07 854 763B	300.00	

$50.00 FEDERAL RESERVE NOTES

1934	D06 698 418A	1934A	D06 698 419A	750.00
	J00 920 964A		J00 920 965A	750.00
1934B	C06 150 792A	1934C	C06 150 793A	500.00

$100.00 FEDERAL RESERVE NOTES

1934C	G10 966 228A	1934B	G10 966 229A	750.00
	J02 520 786A		J02 520 787A	750.00
1934C	G11 364 348A	1934D	G11 364 349A	750.00

$500.00 FEDERAL RESERVE NOTES

1934	L00 153 444A	1934A	L00 153 445A	1,500.00

PRICE ESTIMATES FOR NOVEL SERIAL NUMBERS

PALINDROMES (radars) are notes whose serial number reads the same backward as forward. Generally prefix and suffix letters are not important however when present such as AA, BB, CC, etc. add slightly to value.

	$1.00	$2.00	$5.00 lt	$5.00 sc	$10.00	$20.00
ONE DIGIT	125.00	150.00	135.00	125.00	135.00	150.00
TWO DIGIT	25.00	35.00	35.00	25.00	32.50	40.00
THREE DIGIT	10.00	15.00	17.50	15.00	17.50	27.50
FOUR DIGIT	5.00	10.00	15.00	10.00	15.00	27.50

SEQUENCE NOTES

	$1.00	$2.00	$5.00 lt	$5.00 sc	$10.00	$20.00
SINGLE DIGIT (00 000 001)	125.00	200.00	150.00	150.00	135.00	145.00
TWO DIGIT (00 000 012)	90.00	135.00	115.00	115.00	115.00	125.00
23	40.00	85.00	50.00	50.00	60.00	60.00
34	25.00	60.00	30.00	30.00	35.00	40.00
45	25.00	60.00	30.00	30.00	35.00	40.00
56	17.50	35.00	20.00	20.00	25.00	35.00
67	17.50	35.00	20.00	20.00	25.00	35.00
78	17.50	27.50	22.50	22.50	30.00	35.00
89	17.50	27.50	22.50	22.50	27.50	35.00
THREE DIGIT (00 000 123)						
234, 456, etc.	22.50	40.00	27.50	27.50	32.50	40.00
FOUR DIGIT	25.00	50.00	30.00	30.00	37.50	50.00
FIVE DIGIT	30.00	40.00	35.00	35.00	40.00	50.00
SIX DIGIT	50.00	75.00	50.00	50.00	50.00	60.00
SEVEN DIGIT	75.00	100.00	75.00	75.00	75.00	85.00
EIGHT DIGIT	125.00	200.00	125.00	125.00	130.00	145.00

REVERSE SEQUENCE (consecutive in descending order) 20% less than ascending sequence.
REPEATERS: (Premium generally limited to $1.00 notes.)
TWO DIGIT (Example 27 27 27 27) $25.00
FOUR DIGIT (Example 4345 4345) $15.00

MULTIPLE ENDINGS: (premium applies to $1.00 notes only)

Triple (Example 111, 222, 333, etc.) 3.00
Quadruple (Example 3333, 4444, 5555, etc) 5.00
Quintuple (Example 66666, 88888, etc) 10.00
Sextuple (Example 777777, 999999, etc) 15.00
Septuple (Example 4444444, 6666666, etc) 25.00

MULTIPLE DIGITS MATCHED (so called poker notes) Other digits may be any number and similar digits may be arranged in any way.
Five digits the same 5.00
Six digits the same 7.50
Seven digits the same 10.00

EVEN NOTES (zeros precede and end)
Even hundreds (Example 00 000 400) 25.00
Even thousands (Example 00 002 000) 15.00
Even ten thousand (Example 00 010 000) 10.00
Even hundred thousand (Example 00 300 000) 10.00
Even millions (Example 21 000 000) 15.00

MATCHED BEGINNING AND END (Example 43 000 043)
Two digit match 8.00
Three digit match 10.00
Four digit match 15.00

ODD NUMBER NOTES - Any note that has a catch serial number - far too many number arrangements to categorize - but some examples offered such as 00 46 46 00, 00 37 38 39, 00 454 545, 401 402 03 etc.
Price estimate $5.00 to $100.00 depending on appeal.
NOTE: Consideration must be given when novel serial number is on an otherwise scarce or rare note. Premium for novel number is in addition to any other premium.

PRICE ESTIMATES FOR LOW SERIAL NUMBER NOTES

As with any pioneering effort, we expect to be bombarded with yells of too "high" or too "low" - high yells of course will come from buyers, the low yells from sellers. We welcome them all. The infrequency with which any appreciable quantity come on the market has created widespread differences in pricing by the various dealers throughout the country so that we are hopeful WITH YOUR comments future editions can provide price estimates that are fair to both buyer and seller. We do not mean that this first effort is a casual one. Thousands of price lists, hundreds of examinations of notes and prices and countless hours correlating available data form the basis of prices shown. We believe we are close - but of course we hope for perfection - YOUR comments will help!

All price estimates are for CU notes, prices for circulated notes would be corresponding lower. PRICES are IN ADDITION to any other premiums that would apply - for example the 1963 $1.00 FRN Block D--B is currently selling for $75.00. Serial number 00 000 001 in this note would certainly sell for $200.00 or better.

DENOMINATION

SERIAL NUMBER (0's precede)		1.00	2.00	5.00	10.00	20.00	50.00	100.00
	1	125.00	200.00	150.00	135.00	145.00	150.00	175.00
	2	100.00	150.00	125.00	125.00	135.00	135.00	150.00
3 thru	9	85.00	125.00	100.00	100.00	110.00	125.00	135.00
	10	90.00	135.00	115.00	115.00	125.00	130.00	140.00
	11	90.00	135.00	115.00	115.00	125.00	130.00	140.00
	12	90.00	135.00	115.00	115.00	125.00	130.00	140.00
13 thru	19	35.00	75.00	40.00	50.00	50.00	100.00	125.00
	20	40.00	85.00	50.00	60.00	60.00	115.00	135.00
	21	40.00	85.00	50.00	60.00	60.00	115.00	135.00
	22	50.00	100.00	60.00	70.00	70.00	125.00	135.00
	23	40.00	85.00	50.00	60.00	60.00	115.00	135.00
24 thru	29	30.00	60.00	35.00	40.00	45.00	70.00	125.00
	30	35.00	75.00	40.00	50.00	50.00	100.00	135.00
	31	25.00	60.00	30.00	35.00	40.00	75.00	125.00
	32	27.50	65.00	32.50	37.50	42.50	75.00	135.00
	33	40.00	85.00	50.00	60.00	65.00	100.00	150.00
	34	25.00	60.00	30.00	35.00	40.00	75.00	125.00
35 thru	39	20.00	50.00	25.00	30.00	35.00	65.00	125.00
	40	25.00	60.00	30.00	35.00	40.00		see footnote
41 and	42	20.00	50.00	25.00	30.00	35.00		
	43	22.50	55.00	27.50	32.50	37.50		
44 and	45	35.00	75.00	40.00	50.00	60.00		
46 thru	49	17.50	35.00	20.00	25.00	35.00		
	50	22.50	50.00	27.50	32.50	37.50		
51 thru	53	15.00	25.00	20.00	25.00	35.00		
	54	17.50	35.00	20.00	25.00	35.00		
	55	25.00	60.00	30.00	35.00	40.00		
	56	17.50	35.00	20.00	25.00	35.00		
57 thru	59	15.00	25.00	20.00	25.00	35.00		
	60	22.50	40.00	25.00	35.00	42.50		
61 thru	64	15.00	25.00	20.00	25.00	35.00		
	65	17.50	35.00	20.00	25.00	35.00		
	66	25.00	60.00	30.00	35.00	40.00		
	67	17.50	35.00	20.00	25.00	35.00		
68 and	69	15.00	25.00	20.00	25.00	35.00		
	70	22.50	40.00	25.00	35.00	42.50		
71 thru	75	15.00	25.00	20.00	25.00	35.00		
	76	17.50	27.50	22.50	30.00	37.50		
	77	25.00	60.00	30.00	35.00	40.00		
	78	17.50	27.50	22.50	30.00	35.00		
	79	15.00	25.00	20.00	25.00	35.00		
	80	22.50	40.00	25.00	35.00	42.50		
81 thru	86	15.00	25.00	20.00	25.00	35.00		
	87	17.50	27.50	22.50	27.50	37.50		
	88	25.00	50.00	30.00	35.00	42.50		
	89	17.50	27.50	22.50	27.50	35.00		
	90	22.50	40.00	25.00	30.00	40.00		
91 thru	97	15.00	25.00	20.00	25.00	35.00		
	98	17.50	27.50	22.50	27.50	35.00		
	99	25.00	50.00	30.00	35.00	42.50		

EVEN HUNDREDS					
100-900	25.00	35.00	30.00	35.00	42.50
TRIPLES					
111-999	25.00	35.00	30.00	35.00	42.50
SEQUENCE NOTES (includes reverse sequence)					
123, 456, 345, etc.	22.50	40.00	27.50	32.50	40.00
ALL OTHER NUMBERS					
101-998	12.50	15.00	15.00	17.50	30.00
EVEN THOUSANDS					
1000-9000	15.00	25.00	20.00	25.00	32.50
QUADRUPLES					
1111-9999	15.00	25.00	20.00	25.00	32.50
SEQUENCE NOTES (includes reverse sequence)					
3456, 4567, etc.	25.00	50.00	30.00	37.50	50.00
ALL OTHER NUMBERS					
1001-9998	5.00	10.00	7.50	12.50	22.50

FOOTNOTE: Because of the high face value the $50.00 and $100.00 notes command only a nominal premium.

POTENTIAL NEW DISCOVERIES

A long list of notes that SHOULD EXIST but have never been reported await some industrious and LUCKY collector who will undertake the search. GOOK LUCK to you all!

$1.00 silver certificates
    Series 1928A Block D--A
    Series 1935C NARROW Block U--E (possibly Block T--E and V--E)
    Series 1935D NARROW Block U--E (one known - other probably exist)

$2.00 United States Notes
    Series 1928C MULE Block *--A
    Series 1928D MULE Block D--A

$5.00 United States Notes
    Series 1928B MULE Block D--A
    Series 1928D MULE Block *--A
    Series 1928E MULE Block *--A
    Series 1928F NARROW Block H--A
    Series 1928F WIDE II Block H--A

$5.00 silver certificates
    Series 1934 MULE Blocks A--A, B--A, C--A, D--A and *--A
    Series 1934A Block D--A
    Series 1934A MULE Blocks I--A and J--A
    Series 1934B MULE Block M--A
    Series 1934C MULE Block Q--A
    Series 1934D NARROW Blocks Q--A, R--A and S--A
    Series 1934D WIDE II Blocks Q--A, R--A, S--A and T--A

$10.00 silver certificates
    Series 1934 Block B--A
    Series 1934A MULE Blocks B--A and *--A

$5.00 Federal Reserve Notes and higher Denomination Federal Reserve Notes.

Consult main body of this text. ANY note for which no serial number is shown is a new discovery and a potential rarity. Such discoveries, if reported, will be listed in the next edition of this HANDBOOK and proper credit will be accorded the individual making the first report.

NOTES